EXCLUSIVE ECONOMIC ZONE CLAIMS: AN ANALYSIS AND PRIMARY DOCUMENTS

ROBERT W. SMITH

Exclusive Economic Zone Claims

An Analysis and Primary Documents

1986 **MARTINUS NIJHOFF PUBLISHERS**
a member of the KLUWER ACADEMIC PUBLISHERS GROUP
DORDRECHT / BOSTON / LANCASTER

Distributors

for the United States and Canada: Kluwer Academic Publishers, 190 Old Derby Street, Hingham, MA 02043, USA
for the UK and Ireland: Kluwer Academic Publishers, MTP Press Limited, Falcon House, Queen Square, Lancaster LA1 1RN, UK
for all other countries: Kluwer Academic Publishers Group, Distribution Center, P.O. Box 322, 3300 AH Dordrecht, The Netherlands

Library of Congress Cataloging in Publication Data

Smith, Robert W.
Exclusive economic zone claims.

Includes bibliographies and index.
1. Economic zones (Maritime law) I. Title.
JX4144.5.S65 1986 341.4'48 85-21726
ISBN 90-247-3250-6

ISBN 90-247-3250-6

PRINTED IN THE NETHERLANDS

To Sandra, Laura and Tesia

Contents

Acknowledgments

This present study represents over 10 years of interest in studying national maritime claims, including the collection and analysis of marine legislations, while employed in the Office of The Geographer, U.S. Department of State. I have found that one of the most difficult aspects of this endeavor has been in obtaining primary documents from which to base my analyses. Knowing that others have experienced similar frustrations, I pursued this project with the goal of compiling a reference book from which other professionals could base their analyses.

My first expression of gratitude, therefore, is extended to those people who have assisted me over the years in collecting the laws and decrees which appear in this book. First, there are the unkown U.S. foreign service officers who, in the course of following their host country's activities, have sent in the foreign national marine laws. Second, I would like to thank several of my foreign colleagues who also have tried to stay abreast of maritime developments, including Cmdr. Robert Halliday, U.K. Territorial Waters Officer; Cmdr. Peter Beazley, who formerly held that position; Cmdr. E. John Cooper, former Canadian Territorial Waters Officer; Peter Shannon and Jaque Grinberg of the Australian Foreign Ministry. Third, a thank you is extended to Ambassador Satya Nandan, Special Representative of the UN Secretary-General for the Law of the Sea, and his staff for their continuing efforts to publicize these maritime claims.

In the U.S. Government there are several people who have been extremely helpful at various stages of this book. My colleagues in the Office of The Geographer have been a continuing source of professional guidance and assistance; in particular, Daniel Dzurek for his help on the manuscript, William Hezlep and Sandra Shaw for their cartographic expertise in producing the map and graphics. For their assistance in reading and commenting on various drafts I thank David Colson of the Legal Adviser's Office, Peter Bernhardt and Anne Hamilton of the Office of Law and Policy, both offices in the State Department; and to Cmdr. Geoffrey Greiveldinger, U.S. Navy.

Words of appreciation for this product should be given to all those people listed above, and to the many people I probably have regretfully failed to cite. This book reflects my own ideas and conclusions, however, and not necessarily those of the U.S. Government, or any other government. Any errors to be found in the following pages are the sole responsibility of the author who, for professional reasons only, will be receptive to all comments and complaints.

Washington, D.C.
September 1985

Robert W. Smith

List of Tables, Figures, and Maps

Tables

Figures

Map

PART I

Analysis

CHAPTER 1

Trends in National Maritime Claims

Introduction[1]

The area of the world's oceans totals approximately 105.3 million square nautical miles (sq.nm), which represents 71 percent of the earth's surface. As of March 1986, 105 states claimed a 200 mile maritime zone of some nature; of these 103, 15 claimed a territorial sea, 69 an economic zone, and 21 a fishing zone[2]. As a result, about 28.5 million sq.nm of ocean space were placed under these coastal states' jurisdictions. This is an area exceeding the combined land area of five continents: North and South America, Africa, Europe and Australia. Thus, 27 percent of the oceans is now under some form of jurisdiction of states constituting only about 62 percent of the world's independent countries. If all coastal states were to claim 200 nm limits, the extent of ocean area under national jurisdiction would reach approximately 31.9 million sq.nm, or about 30 percent of the world's marine surface.

In 1951 S. Whittemore Boggs, the U.S. State Department Geographer, wrote that 'never have national claims in adjacent seas been so numerous, so varied, or so inconsistent'[3]. Thirty-four years later this comment may still be valid, although there is a trend towards states establishing similar, but not in all cases identical, maritime zones. The Third United Nations Conference on the Law of the Sea (UNCLOS III) was convened in 1973, in part, to establish a comprehensive law of the sea that would create acceptable parameters within which states could assert jurisdiction to offshore areas. The Conference produced the 1982 United Nations Convention on the Law of the Sea (LOS Convention).

The 1982 LOS Convention has not yet entered into force, therefore it may still be too early to judge its effect on the law of the sea and the utilization of the oceans. There are many national claims that exceed the limits reflected in the 1982 LOS Convention text. The 26 states claiming territorial seas greater than 12 nm, for example, exceed the limits established in LOS Convention Article 3.

This chapter will present an overview of the unilateral national claims made by coastal states to the territorial sea, fishing zone, and continental shelf from 1958, the year of the first United Nations Conference on the Law of the Sea, to May 1985.

In Chapter 2, national claims to exclusive economic zones are analyzed to compare these claims to the 1982 LOS Convention. Part II of this book contains copies of national claims made to the exclusive economic zone.

National Maritime Claims

From the early 17th century to the 1950's, the major maritime states maintained the doctrine of freedom of the seas as the basic premise of international sea law. Except for narrow belts of territorial seas, primarily claimed for security purposes, the high seas beyond were regarded as free to the ships and commerce of all states.

Over the past three decades a new significance has been given to diverse uses, in addition to navigation, of the marine environment. Navigation today continues to affect the trade and national security of virtually every country. Navigational uses range from warships, submarines, and nuclear-powered vessels, to super-tankers, fishing vessels, and other commercial merchant ships. Fishing operations have become quite significant and efficient for many states, with other countries receiving important revenue from selling fishing licenses for their national zones. As of 1983, about 26 percent of the world's oil was produced from offshore areas[4], and it is likely that this percentage will rise in the future. In recent years a number of mining companies have developed the technology to recover valuable minerals from the deep seabed. Certain offshore areas are used as sites for waste disposal. Scientific research and recreational activities also have become important throughout the world.

Accompanying these technological advances and increased uses of the oceans has been the trend of coastal states to assert further control over the activities off their shores. National claims to the oceans can take two forms: (a) geographical, that is, claims to increased areas; and (b) functional, that is, claims to greater regulatory powers within the same geographic area. Actual claims are of many different types. They range from a short, general proclamation or decree asserting a type of jurisdictional claim without giving many specifics, to a comprehensive marine law that provides details on how different maritime activities will be regulated by the coastal state. The effect of most national marine claims has been to create, or to alter the limits of, territorial seas and resource zones.

Since 1958, the year of the first United Nations Conference on the Law of the Sea, more than 500 claims have been made establishing or altering limits of territorial seas, fishing zones, continental shelves, and exclusive economic zones. Table 1 categorizes these claims chronologically, and Figure 1 illustrates the total maritime claims made each year from 1958 to May 1985. In any given marine law or decree, claims may be made to more than one type of zone: thus, the numbers in Table 1 reflect the claims made to the various zones and not to the number of laws and decrees.

Table 1. National Maritime Claims.

Claim	1958–64	1965–71	1972–78	1979–85 May	TOTAL
Territorial Sea	35	57	78	42	212
Fishing Zone	12	36	61	9	119
Continental Shelf	18	53	37	8	116
Excl. Economic Zone	0	0	55	30	84
Newly Independent State	23	14	16	8	61

Source: Office of The Geographer, U.S. Department of State, based on *Limits in the Seas* No. 36 (Rev. 5), 'National Claims to Maritime Jurisdiction', March 6, 1985.

There is a hierarchy to these different maritime zones. When a state claims a territorial sea, it claims complete sovereignty over that particular band of ocean space. Under international law this sovereignty is limited only by the duty of the coastal state to allow for innocent passage of foreign vessels and for transit passage in straits used for international navigation[5]. Thus, when a state asserts a territorial sea limit, all marine jurisdiction, including jurisdiction over fishing and seabed activities, for that state extends to that limit. Similarly, if a state creates an exclusive economic zone, then it is assumed that jurisdiction over fishing and the resources of the seabed, at least to the seaward limit of the economic zone, is incorporated in that claim.

Certain general trends can be discerned in maritime claims from the perspective of the numbers made in any given year. Between 1958 and 1962 the annual number of marine claims ranged from 2 (in 1961) to 8 (in 1962) with the total for this time period being 29. Of this total 16, or 55 percent, were for the territorial sea. The first significant rise in the number of claims made in a single year came in 1963 when 21 claims were made, 11 for a territorial sea. Of these claims, 43 percent were made by states that had gained independence since 1958.

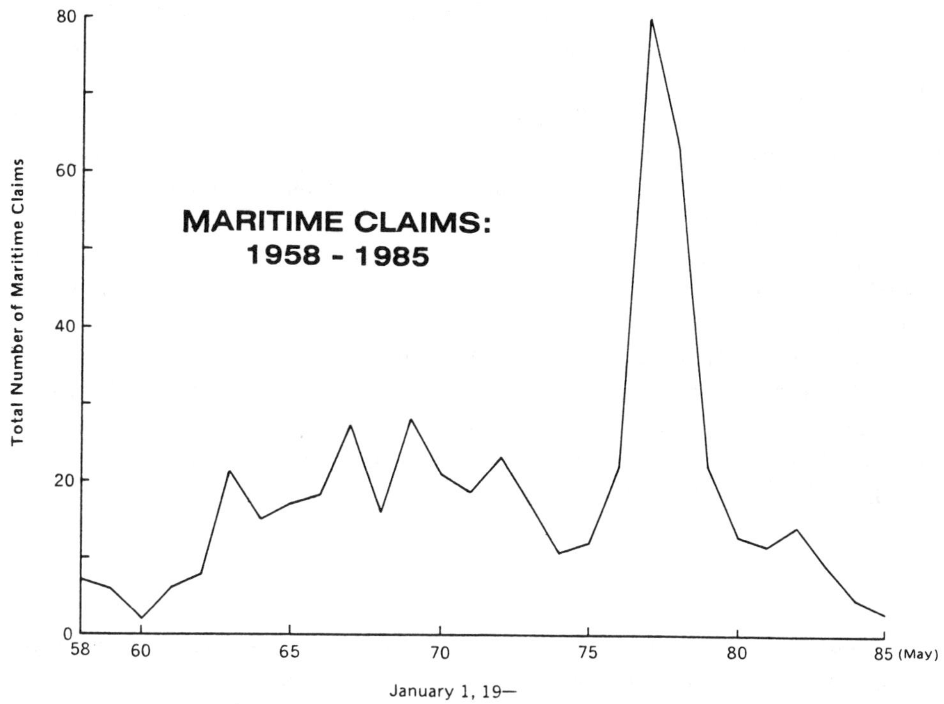

Source: Office of The Geographer, U.S. Department of State, based on Office of The Geographer, *Limits in the Seas* No. 36 (Rev. 5) "National Claims to Maritime Jurisdiction," March 6, 1985.

Figure 1

The impact of newly independent states upon the arrangement of ocean regimes is significant. As Table 1 shows, 61 coastal states achieved independence between 1958 and May 1985[6]. In 1960 alone, 13 littoral states gained independence. This means that only 78 coastal states, or slightly over half of the present 139 independent coastal states, had the opportunity to participate at the First United Nations Law of the Sea Conference in 1958. It is therefore not surprising that following independence, a state would act to assert jurisdiction over offshore areas. Between 1958 and May 1985, newly independent states accounted for approximately 41 percent of the maritime claims. As might be expected, this group of states was most active in implementing new territorial sea claims, accounting for about half of all claims made by the group and 48 percent of all territorial sea claims made during this time period. For the resource zones (fishing, continental shelf, and EEZ), the overall percentage is slightly lower, with the newly independent states responsible for about 36 percent of all claims made. This figure probably would have been higher had not the concept of the exclusive economic zone developed at UNCLOS III during the 1970s. Claims to an exclusive economic zone (EEZ), in many instances, make separate claims to a fishing zone and to the continental shelf unnecessary.

A dramatic increase in maritime claims by newly independent states and other states occurred in the period 1976–1979 (Figure 1). This phenomenon can best be explained by noting that the first negotiating text of UNCLOS III was produced in May 1975, following the second substantive session[7]. This text reflects a general consensus of the international community on, *inter alia,* 12 miles as the maximum territorial sea breadth, and the acceptance, in principle, of a 200-mile exclusive economic zone. Of the 187 maritime claims made during this 4 year period, 60 were claims to the territorial sea (32 percent) and 59 were claims creating EEZs (31 percent). The EEZs established during these years account for almost three-fourths of all such claims made to date.

Assertions to offshore jurisdiction slowed considerably in the 1980s. By the end of 1982, when the Law of the Sea Convention was first opened for signature, all but 12 of the current EEZ claims had been made. Of the 105 200-mile claims presently in force, 95 had entered into force by the end of 1982 (see fold-out map for 200-mile claims)[8].

As noted earlier, approximately 31.9 million sq.nm would be encompassed if all coastal states were to extend their national jurisdiction to 200 miles, or to the maximum limit possible, given potential boundaries with neighbors. Of this area, less than 11 percent (about 3.4 million sq.nm) remains to be placed under the jurisdiction of those 34 countries that have not yet asserted their maximum claims. Due to coastal geography (i.e, coastline length and configurations, with respect to neighbours) several of these states are zone-locked and have little to gain in any maritime extension, such as Singapore, Bahrain, and Jordan. Other states, such as Libya, Malta, Greece, and Turkey, have bilateral considerations that perhaps have caused them to delay claiming extended zones.

Present claims to national maritime jurisdictions are listed in Annex 1 of this chapter. Also in this listing are estimated areas of claimed or potential 200-mile zones. Before focusing on the various elements of the exclusive economic zone and the type of national claims made to it, in Chapter 2, a brief review will be made of the other type of maritime claims cited above.

The Territorial Sea

Prior to the consensus reached at UNCLOS III, a major failure in the attempt to codify the law of the sea had been the inability of the international community to agree on a uniform maximum breadth of the territorial sea. At the beginning of 1958, eight different territorial-sea limits were being claimed, ranging from 3 to 200 miles (Table 2). More than half the states (45) claimed a breadth of 3 miles; four others, the Nordic states, claimed 4 miles. At that time 15 coastal states asserted territorial seas between 5 and 10 miles, and 9 others had 12-mile limits. Only three states, Ecuador, El Salvador, and Peru, had 200-mile claims.

Table 2. Territorial Sea Claims as of January 1, 1958.

Breadth (Nautical miles)	Number of States
3	42
4	4
5	1
6	6
9	1
10	1
12	17
200	3
No legislation	4

Source: Office of The Geographer, *Limits in the Sea* No. 36 (Rev. 5), 'National Claims to Maritime Jurisdiction', March 6, 1985.

The 1958 Convention on the Territorial Sea and the Contiguous Zone states that the coastal state's sovereignty 'extends beyond its land territory and its internal waters, to a belt of sea adjacent to its coast described as the territorial sea [and that] the sovereignty of a coastal state extends to the air space over the territorial sea as well as to its bed and subsoil'[9]. As noted earlier, within the territorial sea the coastal state must allow for 'innocent passage' and special transit rights in international straits. This conference failed, however, to reach agreement on the maximum breadth a state could claim.

During the next two years, between Law of the Sea Conferences, very few national marine laws were established. In 1959, for example, only two states (Libya and Iran) passed 12-mile territorial-sea laws. At the second UN Law of the Sea Conference in 1960, Canada and the United States proposed a 6 + 6 formula whereby each coastal state could claim a 6-mile territorial sea and an additional 6-mile contiguous fisheries zone. The Conference failed by one vote to approve this proposal.

Whereas at the beginning of 1960 only 24 states (30 percent of all territorial sea claims) claimed 12-mile territorial seas, a decade later the number had more than doubled (46 percent of all claims). By January 1, 1980, 80 states (59 percent of territorial sea claims) had 12-mile territorial sea limits, and as of March 1986 the total is 90 states (67 percent of the total claims). Figure 2 depicts the trend of four major territorial-sea categories: less than 12 miles, 12 miles, 13 to 199 miles, and 200 miles.

There has been a steady increase in the number of states claiming 12 miles as their territorial sea limit. Most of the conversion to the 12-mile limit has come from newly-independent states or from those states previously claiming limits of less than 12 miles. In June 1985, for example, the Netherlands extended its territorial sea from 3 to 12 miles. There has not been much change in numbers in the latter two categories in the last 10 years. In 1964 Guinea made the first claim in the 13–199 mile category when it implemented a 130-mile territorial sea. Guinea, in fact, has been quite active in altering its claim over the past two decades. In 1965 it increased its 130-mile claim to 200 miles. Then, in 1980, it rolled the limit back to 12

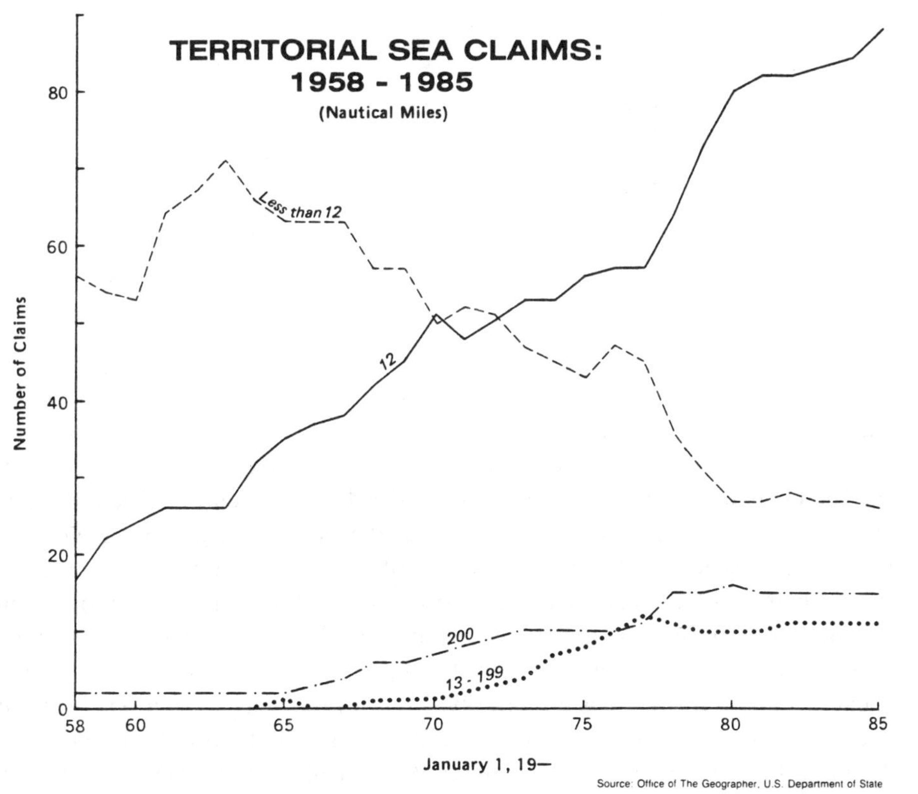

Figure 2

miles. Since 1975 between 8 and 11 states have made claims to territorial seas with breadths ranging between 13 and 199 miles. Most recently, in February 1985, Senegal passed new legislation rolling back its 150-mile claim to 12 miles. And, in June 1985, the Netherlands passed a law increasing its territorial sea from 3 to 12 miles.

Since 1978 the number of states claiming 200-mile territorial seas has remained relatively constant at 15, with the number reaching 16 at one point, on January 1, 1980. Of the 15 states claiming 200-mile limits as of May 1985, all are developing countries with 7 in Africa and 8 in Central and South America (see fold-out map). It should be noted that in the laws of three of the Latin American states (Argentina, El Salvador, and Uruguay) overflight and navigation are permitted beyond 12 miles.

In addition to Guinea's, and Senegal's actions in 1980 and 1985, respectively Guinea-Bissau brought its 150-mile claim back to 12 miles in 1978 and, in 1977, Cape Verde reduced its 100-mile territorial sea claim 12 miles. During the same time period, however, several states increased territorial sea limits beyond 12 miles. As shown in Table 3, 11 states made new territorial sea claims between 1976 and 1981 in excess of 12 miles. Of these claims, 8 were made by African states, 1 Latin American state (Nicaragua), 1 European country (Albania) and 1 state from the Middle East (Syria).

Table 3. States making Territorial Sea Claims in excess of 12 miles: 1976–1985.

Year	State	New territorial sea claim (n.miles)
1976	Albania	15
	Benin	200
	Senegal*	150
1977	Liberia	200
	Ghana	200
	Togo	30
	The Gambia	200
	Congo	200
1978	Mauritania	70
1979	Nicaragua	200
1981	Syria	35

* Changed to 12 miles in 1985.

As states adopt the 1982 Law of the Sea Convention, the trend will be towards bringing national legislation in line with the 12-mile maximum in Article 3 of that Convention. Of the 26 states presently having territorial sea claims exceeding 12 miles, all but 4 have signed the Law of the Sea Convention, and four (Cameroon, The Gambia, Ghana, and Togo) have ratified the Convention. The four that have not signed the Convention are Albania, Syria, Ecuador and Peru. Ecuador and Peru did not sign the Convention because their respective 200-mile claims are written into their constitutions; they stated that they had to change their domestic legal documents prior to accepting the international convention. Although the 200-mile exclusive economic zone was created, in part, to satisfy the needs and desires of countries claiming 200-mile territorial seas, it is likely that the 15 states that presently claim 200-mile limits may not implement 12-mile territorial seas until the 1982 Law of the Sea Convention enters into force.

One territorial sea caveat which concerns several maritime states pertains to requirements placed on certain types of ships prior to entering the territorial sea. In particular, requirements are written into the laws of approximately 38 states, for the passage through the territorial sea of foreign warships, nuclear-powered ships, or vessels carrying nuclear materials (Table 4). Twenty-nine states require that warships receive permission prior to entering the territorial sea, while another 9 states require prior notification. Five countries demand similar prerequisites for the transit of the territorial sea by nuclear-powered ships, or those vessels carrying nuclear materials. On June 1, 1985, Libya implemented unique regulations which, *inter alia,* allow for *commercial ship* innocent passage through Libyan territorial sea in daylight hours only, provided prior information (at least 12 hours in advance of the proposed transit) is given to Libyan authorities.

There is no provision either in the 1958 Convention on the Territorial Sea and the Contiguous Zone or in the 1982 Law of the Sea Convention for imposing these types of restrictions on territorial sea transit. In fact, unsuccessful attempts were made at each conference to place such coastal state rights in the conventions. This issue is not limited to one or two maverick claims, but rather a fundamental global issue that may create future discord in the international community.

The Continental Shelf

The first wave of post-World War II national claims to expanded ocean areas began with President Truman's 1945 Proclamation on the Continental Shelf[10]. At this time, the United States asserted exclusive jurisdiction over the resources of the continental shelf off its coasts. The Truman Proclamation specifically stated that the waters above the shelf were to remain high seas and that freedom of navigation and overflight were not to be affected.

Numerous, and similar, national claims soon followed the Truman Proclamation. By the time the First UN Law of the Sea Conference convened the idea of national jurisdiction over the continental shelf had gained wide acceptance. The Conference reached a consensus on a definition of the continental shelf for two reasons. First, the definition was, to a large degree, vague and flexible. Article 1 (a) of the Convention on the Continental Shelf states that the continental shelf refers 'to the seabed and subsoil of the submarine areas adjacent to the coast but outside the area of the territorial sea, to a depth of 200 meters or, beyond that limit, to where the depth of the superjacent waters admits of the exploitation of the natural resources of the said areas'[11]. Second, no country at that time had the technology to exploit economically the seabed beyond 200 meters. In 1958, it was said in Geneva that 'exploitability' would not be tested for a generation. Within the next decade, however, the technological advances of a limited number of states had already begun to make the continental shelf definition unsatisfactory.

With respect to absolute numbers of claims made to the continental shelf, applying varying definitions, 116 claims were made between 1958 and May 1985 (Table 1). Of these claims 53, or 46 percent of the total number of shelf claims made, were implemented between 1965 and 1971. In the 1980s specific claims to the continental shelf have been made only 5 times. It should be noted, however, that the 1958 Convention on the Continental Shelf, (as well as the 1982 LOS Convention) provides that a coastal state's continental shelf rights do not depend on proclamation or occupation.

Table 4. Requirements for entry into the territorial sea.

	By warships		By nuclear-powered ships/ships carrying nuclear materials:	
STATE	Permission	Prior notification	Permission	Prior notification
Albania	*			
Algeria	*			
Antigua and Barbuda	*			
Bangladesh	*			
Barbados	*			
Brazil	*			
Bulgaria	*			
Burma	*			
China	*			
Denmark	*	*		
Djibouti				*
Egypt		*	*	
Finland		*		
German Dem.Rep.	*			
Grenada	*			
Guyana	*			
India		*		
Indonesia		*		
Iran	*			
Korea, North	*		*	
Korea, South		* (except in international straits)		
Maldives	*			
Mauritius		*		
Nicaragua	*			
Nigeria		*		
Pakistan	*			*
Poland	*			
Romania	*			
Seychelles		*		
Somalia	*			
Soviet Union	*			
Sri Lanka	*			
Sudan	*			
Sweden	* (except in Ore Sund)			
Syria	*			
Vietnam	*			
Yemen (Aden)	*			*
Yugoslavia	*			

At the Third UN Conference on the Law of the Sea, the 1958 definition was discarded, and an attempt was made to develop a logical and satisfactory definition of the continental margin that included not only the continental shelf but also the continental slope and rise. Article 76 of the 1982 LOS Convention defines the continental shelf. Paragraph 1 of this article states.

> The continental shelf of a coastal State comprises the sea-bed and subsoil of the submarine areas that extend beyond its territorial sea throughout the natural prolongation of its land territory to the outer

> edge of the continental margin, or to a distance of 200 nautical miles from the baselines from which the breadth of the territorial sea is measured where the outer edge of the continental margin does not extend up to that distance.

This paragraph remained the same from its first appearance (in the *Informal Single Negotiating Text* (ISNT) produced in May 1975) to the final text. Although a full analysis of the continental shelf article will not be given here, a few observations will be made. First, the actual use of the term 'continental shelf' will continue to cause confusion, as legal concepts are mixed with physical definitions. As noted at the time the ISNT was produced,

> As much as physical scientists may object to the misuses of scientific terminology by legal scholars or diplomats, we assume that as a consequence of the 1958 Convention on the Continental Shelf and the use of 'Continental shelf' in national legislation, no other expression would be an acceptable substitute for continental shelf in the present negotiations. However, the use of 'continental shelf' will invariably lead to confusion in meanings[12].

The part of this continental shelf definition that affects the vast majority of the world's states, however, is not the criterion related to nature ('natural prolongation'), but rather to the distance factor of 200 nautical miles. Regardless of the offshore seafloor features, a state may claim, *at a minimum,* a 200-nautical-mile continental shelf. However, under the exclusive economic zone provisions of the 1982 LOS Convention, a state may claim jurisdiction to 200 nautical miles including jurisdictional rights over living and non-living resources of the seafloor and seabed. Thus, for those states whose physical continental margin does not extend further than 200 nautical miles from the baseline from which the territorial sea is measured, the whole concept of a continental shelf is of less importance than in previous years. Even the continental shelf article on boundary delimitation between states having opposite or adjacent coasts (Article 83), is identical (except that the term 'continental shelf' is substituted for 'exclusive economic zone') to Article 74 in the section on the exclusive economic zone.

Paragraphs 3–7 of Article 76, which provide a rather complex formula for defining the 'continental shelf' only apply to states that have physical continental margins extending beyond 200 miles from the coast. At this time it is unclear exactly how many states will apply the Article 76 formula when defining the outer limits of their continental shelves.

Fishing

Under the 1958 Convention on Fishing and Conservation of the Living Resources of the High Seas[13], the right to fish was a guaranteed freedom of the high seas, subject only to vague conservation requirements. In 1958 the fishing limits of 57 of the 79 independent coastal states coincided with their territorial sea; 22 states, however, claimed fishing jurisdiction beyond the limits of their territorial seas. In the almost three decades since 1958, 117 claims specifying fishing limits have been made (Table 1). The peak of fishing zone claims came in 1977 and 1978 when 24 and 16 claims were made, respectively. It was at this time that the new exclusive economic zone concept was gaining acceptance within the international community. During these same two years 22 and 23 EEZ claims were made.

As noted earlier, when a state asserts a territorial sea claim, it asserts (subject to the right of innocent passage and passage rights in international straits), sovereignty over the area for all purposes, including fisheries matters. Thus, often a state has not needed to pass particular fishery legislation if its fishery limits correspond with those of the territorial sea. And since the exclusive economic zone includes all fishing jurisdiction, claims to the EEZ also make fishery limits unnecessary. As of May 1985, 88 states claim 200-mile resource zones. Of these claims 64 are EEZ claims and 24 are limited to fisheries. Another 4 states have fishery claims exceeding 12 miles, but less than 200; and 15 states claim 200-mile territorial seas (see fold-out map for all 200-mile claims).

Notes

1. Parts of this chapter update and expand the author's article: 'Trends in National Maritime Claims', *Professional Geographer* 32(2), 1980, pp. 216–223.
2. All miles in this study are international nautical miles; one international nautical mile = 6,076 feet = 1852 meters.
3. S. Whittemore Boggs, 'National Claims in Adjacent Seas', *The Geographical Review* XLI (1951), p. 105.
4. Elisabeth Mann Borgese and Norton Ginsburg (eds). *Ocean Yearbook 5.* Appendix 1D, p. 492. Chicago: University of Chicago Press, 1982.
5. Section III (Articles 14 to 23) of the 1958 Convention on the Territorial Sea and the Contiguous Zone provides for the rights of innocent passage through the territorial sea.
6. During this same time period 14 land-locked countries became independent.
7. *Informal Single Negotiating Text, A/CONF.62/WP.8/Part I,* Third United Nations Conference on the Law of the Sea, May 7, 1975.
8. Primary documents pertaining to the exclusive economic zones of the following countries were received after May 1985, and therefore the fold-out map does not depict 200-mile EEZs for these countries: Equatorial Guinea, Gabon, Kiribati, Madagascar, and Saint Vincent and the Grenadines.
9. United Nations. 'Convention on the Territorial Sea and the Contiguous Zone, Articles 1(1) and 2'. UN *Doc. A/Conf.13/L.52.*
10. U.S. Department of State. 'Policy of the United States with Respect to the Natural Resources of the Subsoil and Seabed of the Continental Shelf'. Proclamation No. 2667. Reprinted in XIII *Bulletin, Department of State,* No. 327, September 30, 1945.
11. United Nations. 'Convention on the Continental Shelf'. UN *Doc. A/Conf.13/L.55.*
12. Robert D. Hodgson and Robert W. Smith, 'The Informal Single Negotiating Text (Committee II): A Geographical Perspective', in *Ocean Development and International Law Journal,* Vol. 3, No. 3, p. 254.
13. United Nations. *Doc. A/Conf.13/L.54.*

ANNEX 1

Summary of Ocean Claims of the World's Nations (September 1985)
(distances in nautical miles)

	Territorial sea	Exclusive fisheries	Continental shelf	Economic zone	Area (sq.nm- '000s)*	Third UN Convention on the Law of the Sea Signed (X = 10 Dec. 82)	Ratified
Albania	15	–	–	–	3.6	–	–
Algeria	12	–	–	–	40.0	X[+]	–
Angola	20	200	–	–	176.6	X[+]	–
Antigua and Barbuda	12	–	–	200	32.1[1]	2-7-83	–
Argentina	200	–	200 m/E	–	339.5	10-5-84	–
Australia	3	200	200 m/E	–	1854.0[2]	X	–
The Bahamas	3	200	200 m/E	–	221.4	X	7-29-83
Bahrain	3	–	CS	–	1.5	X	5-30-85
Bangladesh	12	–	CM	200	22.4	X	–
Barbados	12	–	–	200	48.8	X	–
Belgium	3	200 (B)	CS	–	.8	12-05-84	–
Belize	3	–	–	–	8.1	X	8-13-83
Benin	200	–	–	–	7.9	8-30-83	–
Brazil	200	–	200 m/E	–	924.0	X[+]	–
Brunei	12	200 (B)	–	–	7.1	12-05-84	–
Bulgaria	12	–	–	–	9.6	X	–
Burma	12	–	CM/200	200	148.6	X	–
Cambodia	12	–	200	200	16.2	7-01-83	–
Cameroon	50	–	CS	–	4.5	X	7-17-85
Canada	12	200	200 m/E	–	857.0[3]	X	–
Cape Verde	12	–	–	200	230.2	X[+]	–
Chile	3	200	200	–	667.3	X[+]	–
China	12	–	–	–	395.0	X	–
Colombia	12	–	200 m/E	200	175.9	X	–
Comoros	12	–	–	200	72.6	12-06-84	–
Congo	200	–	–	–	7.2	X	–
Costa Rica	12	–	200	200	75.5	X[+]	–
Cuba	12	–	200 m	200	105.8	X[+]	8-15-84
Cyprus	12	–	200 m/E	–	29.0	X	–
Denmark	3	200	200 m/E	–	426.9[3,4]	X	–
Djibouti	12	–	–	200	1.8	X	–
Dominica	12	–	–	200	4.4[1]	3-28-83	–
Dominican Republic	6	–	CM/200	200	78.4	X	–
Ecuador	200	–	200 m	–	338.0	–	–
Egypt	12	–	200 m/E	200	50.6	X	8-26-83[+] +
El Salvador	200	–	–	–	26.8	12-05-84	–
Equatorial Guinea	12	–	–	200	82.6	1-30-84	–
Ethiopia	12	–	–	–	22.1	X	–
Fiji	12	–	200 m/E	200	334.0[1]	X	12-10-82
Finland	4	12	200 m/E	–	28.6	X[+]	–
France	12	–	200 m/E	200	2100.0[1,2,4]	X[+]	–
Gabon	12	–	–	200	62.3	X	–
The Gambia	200	–	CS	–	5.7	X	5-22-84
Germany (GDR)	12	200 (B)	200 m/E	–	2.8	X[+]	–

Notes and abbreviations at end of table.

	Territorial sea	Exclusive fisheries	Continental shelf	Economic zone	Area (sq.nm-'000s)*	Third UN Convention on the Law of the Sea Signed (X = 10 Dec. 82)	Ratified
Germany (FRG)	3	200	200 m/E	–	11.9	–	–
Ghana	200	–	100 f/E	–	63.6	X	6-07-83
Greece	6	–	200 m/E	–	147.3	X+	–
Grenada	12	–	–	200	8.0[1]	X	–
Guatemala	12	–	CS	200	28.9	7-08-83	–
Guinea	12	–	–	200	20.7	–	–
Guinea-Bissau	12	–	–	200	43.9	X	–
Guyana	12	200	CM/200	–	38.0	X	–
Haiti	12	–	E	200	46.8	X	–
Honduras	12	–	200 m/E	200	63.8[1]	X	–
Iceland	12	–	CM/200	200	252.8	X	6-15-85
India	12	–	CM/200	200	587.6	X	–
Indonesia	12	–	E	200	1577.3	X	–
Iran	12	50 (B)	CS	–	45.4	X+	–
Iraq	12	–	CS	–	–	X+	7-30-85
Ireland	3	200	–	–	110.9	X	–
Israel	6	–	E	–	6.8	–	–
Italy	12	–	200 m/E	–	161.0	12-07-84+	–
Ivory Coast	12	–	200 m	200	30.5	X	3-26-84
Jamaica	12	–	–	–	86.8	X	3-21-83
Japan	12/3	200	–	–	1126.0	2-07-83	–
Jordan	3	–	–	–	–	–	–
Kenya	12	–	–	200	34.5	X	–
Kiribati	12	–	–	200	770.0[1]	–	–
Korea (North)	12	–	–	200	37.8	X	–
Korea (South)	12/3	12	–	–	101.6	3-14-83	–
Kuwait	12	–	CS	–	3.5	X	–
Lebanon	12	–	–	–	6.6	12-07-84	–
Liberia	200	–	200 m/E	–	67.0	X	–
Libya	12	–	–	–	98.6	12-03-84	–
Madagascar	12	–	150	200	376.8	2-25-83	–
Malaysia	12	200	200 m/E	–	138.7	X	–
Maldives	S	S	S	S	279.7	X	–
Malta	12	25	200 m/E	–	19.3	X	–
Mauritania	70	–	CM/200	200	45.0	X	–
Mauritius	12	–	CM/200	200	344.5	X	–
Mexico	12	–	–	200	831.5	X	3-18-83
Monaco	12	–	–	–	–	X	–
Morocco	12	–	200 m/E	200	81.1	X	–
Mozambique	12	–	–	200	163.9	X	–
Nauru	12	–	–	200	92.8[2]	X	–
Netherlands	12	200	–	–	49.0[1,4]	X	–
New Zealand	12	–	CM/200	200	1792.8[2,4]	X	–
Nicaragua	200	–	200 m	–	46.6	12-09-84	–
Nigeria	30	–	200 m/E	200	61.5	X	–
Norway	4	–	200 m/E	200	590.5	X	–
Oman	12	–	200 m/E	200	163.8	7-01-83+	–
Pakistan	12	–	CM/200	200	92.9	X	–

Notes and abbreviations at end of table.

	Territorial sea	Exclusive fisheries	Continental shelf	Economic zone	Area (sq.nm-'000s)*	Third UN Convention on the Law of the Sea Signed (X = 10 Dec. 82)	Ratified
Panama	200	–	–	–	89.4	X	–
Papua New Guinea	12	–	200 m/E	200	504.0[1]	X	–
Peru	200	–	200	–	229.4	–	–
Philippines	S	–	E	200	551.4	X+	5-08-84++
Poland	12	200	–	–	8.3	X	–
Portugal	12	–	200 m/E	200	517.4	X	–
Qatar	3	–	CS	B	7.0	11-27-84	–
Romania	12	–	200 m/E	–	9.3	X+	–
Saint Christopher and Nevis	12	–	–	200	3.3[1]	12-07-84	–
Saint Lucia	12	–	–	200	4.7[1]	X	3-27-85
Saint Vincent and the Grenadines	12	–	–	200	9.5	X	–
Sao Tome and Principe	12	–	–	200	37.4	7-12-83	–
Saudi Arabia	12	–	CS	–	54.3	12-07-84	–
Senegal	12	200	CM/200	–	60.0	X	10-25-84
Seychelles	12	–	CM/200	200	393.4[3]	X	–
Sierra Leone	200	–	–	–	45.4	X	–
Singapore	3	B	–	–	.1	X	–
Solomon Islands	12	–	–	200	445.0[1]	X	–
Somalia	200	–	–	–	228.0	X	–
South Africa	12	200	200 m/E	–	452.9	12-05-84	–
Soviet Union	12	–	200 m/E	200	1309.5[5]	X+	–
Spain	12	–	–	200	355.6	12-04-84	–
Sri Lanka	12	–	CM/200	200	150.6	X	–
Sudan	12	–	200 m/E	–	26.7	X+	1-23-85
Suriname	12	–	–	200	29.5	X	–
Sweden	12	200	200 m/E	–	45.3	X+	–
Syria	35	–	200 m/E	–	3.0	–	–
Tanzania	50	–	–	–	65.1	X	–
Thailand	12	–	200 m/E	200	27.6	X	–
Togo	30	–	–	200	.6[3]	X	4-16-85
Tonga	12	–	200 m/E	200	158.4[2]	–	–
Trinidad and Tobago	12	200	200 m/E	–	22.4	X	–
Tunisia	12	–	–	–	25.0	X	4-24-85
Turkey	6/12	–	–	–	69.0[1]	–	–
Tuvalu	12	–	–	200	225.0[1]	X	–
(Ukrainian SSR)	12	–	200 m/E	200	[5]	X+	–
United Arab Emirates	3/12	–	B	B	17.3	X	–
United Kingdom	3	200	200 m/E	–	520.4[4]	–	–
United States	3	–	200 m	200	3107.0[4]	–	–
Uruguay	200	–	200 m/E	–	34.8	X+	–
Vanuatu	12	–	CM/200	200	186.0[1]	X	–
Venezuela	12	–	200 m/E	200	106.1	–	–
Vietnam	12	–	CM/200	200	210.6	X	–
Western Samoa	12	–	–	200	38.1[2]	9-28-84	–
Yemen (Aden)	12	–	CM/200	200	160.5	X	–

Notes and abbreviations at end of table.

	Territorial sea	Exclusive fisheries	Continental shelf	Economic zone	Area (sq.nm-'000s)*	Third UN Convention on the Law of the Sea Signed (X = 10 Dec. 82)	Ratified
Yemen (Sanaa)	12	–	200 m	–	9.9	X+	–
Yugoslavia	12	–	200 m/E	–	15.3	X	11-27-85
Zaire	12	200	–	–	–	8-22-83	–

Notes

* Unless otherwise noted, data is from Office of The Geographer, U.S. Department of State, *Limits in the Seas* No. 46, 'Theoretical Areal Allocations of Seabed to Coastal States', August 12, 1972.

1. Calculations by the author.
2. J.R.V. Prescott, 'Existing and Potential Maritime Claims in the Southwest Pacific Ocean', in *Ocean Yearbook 2,* Elisabeth Mann Borgese and Norton Ginsburg (eds.), p. 334. The University of Chicago Press, Chicago, 1980.
3. Calculations made by Cmdr. E. John Cooper, former Canadian Territorial Waters Officer.
4. Includes overseas dependencies and possessions.
5. Area of Ukrainian SSR exclusive economic zone included in USSR figure.

Abbreviations

CS – Continental shelf, not specific.
CM – Continental margin.
E – Depth of exploitation.
S – Special claim.
B – Defined by its bilateral maritime boundaries or by an equidistant line.
m – Meters (depth).
f – Fathoms (depth).
\+ – Declaration made at the time of signature of the Convention.
\+ + – Declaration made at the time of ratification of the Convention.

ANNEX 2

Chronology of Territorial Sea and Fishing Zone Claims: 1958 to Sept. 1985

Date	State	Maritime claim[1] Territorial sea	Fishing zone	Date of next claim	
1958					
Feb. 16	Saudi Arabia	12			
Feb. 17	Egypt	12 (6)			
Sept. 1	Iceland		12 (4)	Sept. 1,	1972
Sept. 4	China	12 (3)			
Oct. 2	GUINEA[2]	(3)		June 6,	1964
Nov. 4	Iraq	12 (3)			
Dec. 18	Panama	12		Feb. 2,	1967
1959					
Feb. 18	Libya	12			
April 12	Iran	12 (6)		Oct. 30,	1973
Oct. 1	Ireland	3	3		1964
1960					
Jan. 1	CAMEROON	(3)		June 25,	1962
Feb. 18	Indonesia	12 (3)			
April 27	TOGO	(3)		July 2,	1964
June 27	MADAGASCAR	(3)		Feb. 27,	1963
June 30	ZAIRE	(3)		July 10,	1974
July 1	SOMALIA	(6)		Sept. 10,	1972
Aug. 1	BENIN	(3)		March 7,	1968
Aug. 2	Sudan	12 (3)			
Aug. 7	IVORY COAST	(3)		Aug. 1,	1967
Aug. 15	CONGO	(3)		July 4,	1963
Aug. 16	CYPRUS	(3)		Aug. 3,	1964
Aug. 17	GABON	(3)		Jan. 12,	1963
Aug. 20	SENEGAL	(3)		June 21,	1961
Oct. 1	NIGERIA	(3)		April 8,	1967
Nov. 28	MAURITANIA	(3)		May 3,	1962
1961					
March 24	Norway		12		
April 27	SIERRA LEONE	(3)		Jan. 1,	1965
June 17	Philippines	[3]			
June 19	KUWAIT	(3)		Dec. 24,	1967
June 21	Senegal	6 (3)	12	April 10,	1972
Dec. 9	TANZANIA	(3)		Aug. 9,	1963
1962					
Jan. 1	WESTERN SAMOA	(3)		July 15,	1971
May 3	Mauritania	6 (3)		Jan. 21,	1967
June 3	Morocco		12	March 2,	1973
June 25	Cameroon	6 (3)		Nov. 13,	1967
July 25	ALGERIA	(3)		Oct. 12,	1963
Aug. 6	JAMAICA	(3)		July 19,	1971
Aug. 31	TRINIDAD AND TOBAGO	(3)		Dec. 6,	1969
Oct. 12	Tunisia		12 (3)	Dec. 30,	1963

Notes at end of table.

Date	State	Maritime claim[1] Territorial sea	Fishing zone	Date of next claim
Dec. 24	Spain		6	April 8, 1967
1963				
Jan. 12	Gabon	12 (3)		Oct. 5, 1970
Feb. 21	Uruguay	6 (3)	12	May, 11, 1969
Feb. 27	Madagascar	12 (3)		Sept. 28, 1973
April 19	Ghana	12 (3)	112	March 16, 1973
June 29	South Africa	6 (3)	12	Nov. 1, 1977
July 4	Congo	3		Dec. 20, 1977
Aug. 9	Tanzania	12 (3)		Aug. 24, 1973
Oct. 12	Algeria	12 (3)	12	
Dec. 12	KENYA	(3)		June 13, 1969
Dec. 28	Syria	12 (3)		Aug. 16, 1981
Dec. 30	Tunisia	6 (3)		Aug. 2, 1973
1964				
–	Ireland		12	Jan. 1, 1977
–	U.K.		12	Jan. 1, 1977
May 15	Turkey	6[4]		May 20, 1982
June 6	Guinea	30 (3)		Dec. 31, 1965
July 2	Togo	12 (3)		Aug. 16, 1977
July 16	Canada		12 (3)	Dec. 26, 1970
Aug. 3	Cyprus	12 (3)		
Sept. 1	Vietnam	12 (3)		
Sept. 21	MALTA	(3)		Dec. 10, 1971
1965				
–	Honduras	12 (3)		
Jan. 1	Sierra Leone		12	Jan. 14, 1965
Jan. 14	Sierra Leone	12 (3)		April 19, 1971
Feb. 18	THE GAMBIA	(3)		April 19, 1968
April 5	Nicaragua		200 (12)	Dec. 19, 1979
April 24	Yugoslavia	10 (6)	12	April 7, 1979
May 26	Denmark		12	Dec. 21, 1966
July 26	MALDIVES	[5]		Feb. 24, 1969
Aug. 9	SINGAPORE	(3)		April 29, 1966
Dec. 18	Korea, Rep. of		12	April 30, 1978
Dec. 31	Guinea	200 (130)		July 30, 1980
1966				
Jan. 1	New Zealand	3	12	April 1, 1978
April 29	Singapore		[6]	
May 26	GUYANA	(3)		Oct. 4, 1977
Aug. 22	Portugal		12	May 28, 1977
Oct. 6	Thailand	12 (3)		
Oct. 14	U.S.A.		12	March 1, 1977
Nov. 10	Ecuador	200 (12)		
Nov. 18	Brazil	6 (3)		April 25, 1969
Nov. 30	BARBADOS	(3)		Jan. 1, 1979
Dec. 13	Mexico		12 (9)	Dec. 10, 1969
Dec. 26	Pakistan	12 (3)		March 21, 1973

Notes at end of table.

Date	State	Maritime claim[1] Territorial sea	Fishing zone	Date of next claim
1967				
Jan. 19	Argentina	200 (3)		
Jan. 21	Mauritania	12 (6)		July 31, 1972
Feb. 2	Panama	200 (12)		
April 8	Nigeria	12 (3)		Aug. 26, 1971
April 20	Monaco	3	12	Feb. 14, 1973
April 30	Yemen (Sanaa)	12		
June 7	France		12	Dec. 24, 1971
Aug. 1	Ivory Coast	6 (3)	12	Nov. 17, 1977
Sept. 13	Dominican Republic	6	12 (15)	
Sept. 30	India	12 (6)		
Nov. 13	Cameroon	18 (6)		Dec. 5, 1974
Nov. 17	Australia		12	Sept. 26, 1979
Nov. 30	YEMEN (ADEN)	(3)		Feb. 9, 1970
Dec. 24	Kuwait	12 (3)		
1968				
Jan. 31	NAURU	(3)		Feb. 11, 1972
March 7	Benin	12 (3)	12	April 2, 1976
March 12	MAURITIUS	(3)		April 16, 1970
April 19	The Gambia	6 (3)		July 10, 1969
June 24	Liberia	12 (3)		May 10, 1977
Sept. 5	Sweden		12	Jan. 1, 1978
Oct. 12	EQUATORIAL GUINEA	(6)		Sept. 24, 1970
Nov. 15	Burma	12 (3)		
1969				
Feb. 24	Maldives	[5]	100[7]	
April 25	Brazil	12 (6)		March 27, 1970
May 11	Uruguay	12 (6)		Dec. 3, 1969
June 13	Kenya	12 (3)		
July 10	The Gambia		24 (12)	June, 1971
Aug. 2	Malaysia	12 (3)		April 25, 1980
Sept. 27	Cambodia	12 (5)		Jan. 15, 1978
Dec. 3	Uruguay	200 (12)		
Dec. 6	Trinidad and Tobago	12 (3)		
Dec. 10	Mexico	12 (9)		
1970				
Feb. 9	Yemen (Aden)	12 (3)		
Feb. 12	Poland		12 (3)	Jan. 1, 1978
March 15	Albania	12 (10)		Feb. 23, 1976
March 27	Brazil	200 (12)		
April 5	UAE (Sharjah)	12		
April 16	Mauritius	12 (3)		
June 4	TONGA	[8]		June 15, 1972
Sept. 24	Equatorial Guinea	12 (6)		
Oct. 5	Gabon	25 (12)		Jan. 5, 1972
Oct. 10	FIJI	(3)		Dec. 3, 1976
Dec. 26	Canada	12 (3)		Jan. 1, 1977

Notes at end of table.

Date	State	Maritime claim[1] Territorial sea	Fishing zone	Date of next claim
1971				
Jan. 7	Sri Lanka	12 (6)		
April 19	Sierra Leone	200 (12)		
June	The Gambia		50 (24)	Aug. 27, 1977
July 15	Western Samoa	12 (3)		
July 19	Jamaica	12 (3)		
Aug. 14	BAHRAIN	(3)		
Aug. 26	Nigeria	30 (12)		
Sept. 3	QATAR	(3)		June 1974
Dec. 2	UAE	3[9]		
Dec. 24	France	12 (3)		
1972				
Jan. 5	Gabon	30 (25)		July 16, 1972
Feb. 11	Nauru	12 (3)		Sept. 15, 1978
Feb. 15	Costa Rica	12 (3)		
April 4	BANGLADESH	(3)		April 13, 1974
April 6	Haiti	12 (6)	15	
April 10	Senegal		116 (12)	April 2, 1976
June 15	Tonga	12[10]		June 25, 1979
July 16	Gabon	100 (30)		Nov. 3, 1972
July 20	Oman	12 (3)	50	
July 31	Mauritius	30 (12)		Feb. 28, 1978
Sept. 1	Iceland		50 (12)	Oct. 15, 1975
Sept. 10	Somalia	200 (6)		
Nov. 3	Gabon		150	July 12, 1984
1973				
Feb. 14	Monaco	12 (3)		
March 2	Morocco	12 (3)	70 (12)	
March 16	Ghana	30 (12)	130 (112)	July 22, 1977
March 21	Pakistan		50 (12)	
July 10	THE BAHAMAS	(3)		June 16, 1977
Aug. 2	Tunisia	12 (6)		
Aug. 24	Tanzania	50 (12)		
Sept. 28	Madagascar	50 (12)	150	Sept. 21, 1985
Oct. 30	Iran		50[11]	
1974				
Feb. 7	GRENADA	(3)		
April 13	Bangladesh	12 (3)		
July 10	Zaire	12 (3)		
Aug. 14	Italy	12 (6)		
Sept. 10	GUINEA-BISSAU	(6)		Dec. 31, 1974
Dec. 5	Cameroon	50 (18)		
Dec. 31	Guinea-Bissau	150 (6)		May 19, 1978
1975				
Jan. 1	Finland		12	
June 25	MOZAMBIQUE	(6)		Aug. 19, 1976
July 5	CAPE VERDE	(6)		Dec. 13, 1975
July 12	SAO TOME AND PRINCIPE	(6)		June 16, 1978

Notes at end of table.

Date	State	Maritime claim[1]		Date of next claim
		Territorial sea	Fishing zone	
Sept. 16	PAPUA NEW GUINEA	(3)		March 17, 1978
Oct. 15	Iceland		200 (50)	
Oct. 25	Malta		20 (12)	July 21, 1978
Nov. 6	Angola	20 (6)	200 (12)	Nov. 11, 1975
Nov. 11	ANGOLA	20	200	
Nov. 25	SURINAME	(3)		June 11, 1978
Dec. 13	Cape Verde	100 (6)		Dec. 31, 1977
Dec. 31	COMOROS	(12)		
1976				
Feb. 23	Albania	15 (12)		
April 2	Benin	200 (12)		
April 2	Senegal		200 (116)	April 9, 1976
April 9	Senegal	150 (6)		Feb. 25, 1985
June 28	SEYCHELLES	(3)		Aug. 1, 1977
Aug. 19	Mozambique	12 (6)		
Dec. 3	Fiji	12 (3)		
1977				
Jan. 1	Canada		200 (12)	
Jan. 1	Denmark		200 (12)	
Jan. 1	Germany, Fed. Rep.		200 (3)	
Jan. 1	Ireland		200 (12)	
Jan. 1	United Kingdom		200 (12)	
Jan. 4	Spain	12 (3)		
Feb. 26	Cuba	12 (3)		
March 1	U.S.S.R.		200 (12)	
March 1	U.S.A.		200 (12)	
May 10	Liberia	200 (12)		
May 28	Portugal	12 (6)		
June 16	The Bahamas		200 (12)	
June 27	DJIBOUTI	(12)		Jan. 9, 1979
July 1	Japan	12 (3)	200	
July 22	Ghana	200 (30)		
Aug. 1	Seychelles 12 (3)			
Aug. 16	Togo	30 (12)		
Aug. 27	The Gambia	200 (12)		
Oct. 4	Guyana	12 (3)		
Nov. 1	South Africa	12 (6)	200 (12)	
Nov. 17	Ivory Coast	12 (6)		
Dec. 20	Congo	200 (3)		
Dec. 21	Kiribati	3		April 1, 1978
Dec. 25	Netherlands		200 (12)	
Dec. 31	Cape Verde	12 (100)		
1978				
Jan. 1	German Dem. Rep.		[12]	
Jan. 1	Poland	12 (3)	[13]	
Jan. 1	Sweden		200 (12)	
Jan. 10	Solomon Islands (UK)		200	July 7, 1978
Feb. 28	Mauritania	70 (30)		
March 17	Papua New Guinea		200 (12)	March 31, 1978

Notes at end of table.

Date	State	Maritime claim[1] Territorial sea	Fishing zone	Date of next claim
March 31	Papau New Guinea	12 (3)		
April 1	Kiribati (UK)		200	July 12, 1979
April 1	New Zealand	12 (3)		
April 30	Korea, Rep. of	12 (3)		
May 11	Tuvalu (UK)	3		Oct. 1, 1978
May 19	Guinea-Bissau	12 (150)		
June 11	Suriname	12 (3)		
June 16	Sao Tome and Principe	12 (6)		
July 7	SOLOMON ISLANDS	(3)	(200)	Aug. 14, 1979
July 21	Malta	12 (6)	25 (20)	
Aug. 4	Colombia	12 (3)		
Aug. 8	Vanuatu (Fr./UK)	12	200	
Sept. 15	Nauru		200	
Oct. 1	TUVALU	(3)		Jan. 1, 1979
Oct. 10	Belgium		12 (3)	
Nov. 3	DOMINICA	(3)		Aug. 25, 1981
1979				
Jan. 1	Barbados	12 (3)		
Jan. 1	Tuvalu		200	Jan. 1, 1984
Jan. 9	Djibouti	12 (3)		
Feb. 22	SAINT LUCIA	(3)		July 18, 1984
April 7	Yugoslavia	12 (10)		
June 1	Iceland	12 (4)		
June 25	Tonga	12		
July 1	Sweden	12 (4)		
July 12	KIRIBATI	(3)	(200)	May 16, 1983
Aug. 14	Solomon Islands	12 (3)		
Sept. 26	Australia		200 (12)	
Oct. 27	SAINT VINCENT AND THE GRENADINES	(3)	(12)	June 8, 1983
Dec. 19	Nicaragua	200 (3)		
1980				
April 25	Malaysia		200 (12)	
July 30	Guinea	12 (200)		
July 30	VANUATU	(12)	(200)	
1981				
Aug. 16	Syria	35 (12)		
Aug. 25	Dominica	12 (3)	200	
Sept. 21	BELIZE	(3)		
Nov. 1	ANTIGUA AND BARBUDA	(3)		Aug. 17, 1982
1982				
May 20	Turkey	12[14]		
Aug. 17	Antigua and Barbuda	12 (3)		
1983				
Jan. 1	Brunei (UK)		200[12]	July 1, 1984
May 16	Kiribati	12 (3)		
June 8	Saint Vincent and the Grenadines	12 (3)		

Notes at end of table.

Date	State	Maritime claim[1] Territorial sea	Fishing zone	Date of next claim
Sept. 16	Lebanon	12 (6)		
Sept. 19	SAINT CHRISTOPHER AND NEVIS	(3)		Aug. 1984
1984				
Jan. 1	Tuvalu	12 (3)		
July 1	BRUNEI	(12)	(200)	
July 18	Saint Lucia	12 (3)		
July 24	Gabon	12 (100)		
Aug.	Saint Christopher and Nevis	12 (3)		
1985				
Jan. 1	German Dem. Rep.	12 (3)		
Feb. 25	Senegal	12 (150)		
March 16	Germany, Fed. Rep.	[15]		
Sept. 21	Madagascar	12 (50)		

Notes

1. Unless otherwise specified, a state's fishing limit is assumed to coincide with the territorial sea limit. Citations are made only when the breadth of the zone has been altered. Numbers in parentheses () indicate a previous claim or, if on date of independence, claim of former mother country. Many of the fishing claims are also economic zone claims and will be discussed in Chapter 2.
2. Country names in capital letters indicates date of independence.
3. Claim based on Treaty of Paris (1898) and subsequent treaties, breadth varies, up to 285 nautical miles from the coast.
4. Twelve nautical miles in the Black Sea and Mediterranean Sea.
5. The Maldives 1964 Constitution defines the Republic using by geographical coordinates, which extend the country' limits from 3 to 55 nautical miles from the coast.
6. Limits defined as within and beyond the territorial sea, as defined in treaties and practice.
7. The Maldives fishing zone parallels the limits defined in the 1964 Constitution, at a distance of approximately 100 miles.
8. Rectangular limits established by a Royal Proclamation of June 11, 1887.
9. Sharjah claims a 12-mile territorial sea.
10. Applies to Minerva Reef only.
11. In the Gulf of Oman; in the Persian Gulf limits are the continental shelf, continental shelf boundaries, or median line.
12. As delimited with neighbors, or to the median line.
13. Lines connecting extreme points of specified lateral limits.
14. Remains 6 miles in the Aegean Sea.
15. Creates a box in Helgolander Bucht which, at one point, extends the territorial sea to 16 miles.

CHAPTER 2

Exclusive Economic Zone Claims

Introduction

Claims by countries to jurisdiction over various offshore resources, over living resources in particular, have been made for centuries. But it has been only since the second World War that the concept of making a comprehensive assertion to all marine resources in a specified area off one's coast beyond the territorial sea first developed. On September 28, 1945, President Truman issued two proclamations asserting US jurisdiction to marine resources beyond the US 3-mile territorial sea. Although taken together the proclamations address US rights to both living and non-living resources, the rights claimed for fishing are not for exclusive jurisdiction. With respect to the continental shelf adjacent to US coasts President Truman stated[1],

> 'Having concern for the urgency of conserving and prudently utilizing its natural resources, the Government of the United States regards the natural resources of the subsoil and sea bed of the continental shelf beneath the high seas but contiguous to the coasts of the United States as appertaining to the United States, subject to its jurisdiction and control. In cases where the continental shelf extends to the shores of another state, or is shared with an adjacent state, the boundary shall be determined by the United States and the state concerned in accordance with equitable principles. The character as high seas of the waters above the continental shelf and the right to their free and unimpeded navigation are in no way thus affected.'

There are four important aspects to this proclamation: first, a recognition of the need to conserve and prudently use the natural resources; second, the actual jurisdictional claim to the continental shelf; third, the recognition that the US shelf may abut a neighbor's shelf, requiring a boundary to be determined in accordance with equitable principles; and, fourth, the preservation of the traditional high seas freedom of navigation.

Concurrently, in his 'Fisheries Proclamation', President Truman made the following assertion for the United States[2],

> 'In view of the pressing need for conservation and protection of fishery resources, the Government of the United States regards it as proper to establish conservation zones in those areas of the high seas contiguous to the coasts of the United States wherein fishing activities have been or in the future may be developed and maintained on a substantial scale. Where such activities have been or shall hereafter be developed and maintained by its nationals alone, the United States regards it as proper to establish explicitly bounded conservation zones in which fishing activities shall be subject to the regulation and control of the United States.'

The proclamation continues on to make two other points. First, where fishing activities are pursued off the US coasts by US nationals and by foreign nationals, these activities would be developed and maintained by agreement between the US and the respective foreign state. And, as in the continental shelf proclamation, freedom of navigation through these waters was recognized. Thus, in both proclamations the United States limited its claims to specified jurisdictional rights, and acknowledged its obligations to negotiate boundaries with neighboring states, to reach fishing agreements with foreign states that traditionally fish in areas off US coasts, and to permit traditional high seas navigation freedoms.

Following the Truman Proclamations other countries made claims to offshore areas for the purpose of asserting exclusive rights to the natural resources. The Mexican (1945) and Argentine (1946) claims, for example, emphasized the continental shelf, although Argentina employed the term 'epicontinental sea'. With respect to asserting exclusive jurisdiction to all aspects of offshore resources- i.e., the conservation, preservation, utilization, and management of all marine resources- and setting the conceptual framework of what is now known as the exclusive economic zone, Chile, Ecuador, and Peru can be identified as the forerunners. Although all three states made unilateral claims to 200 miles prior to their First Conference on the Exploitation and Conservation of the Maritime Resources of the South Pacific in 1952, the declaration which was issued at the conclusion of this conference best reflects the attitudes and desires of these countries[3]. In the preamble to this 1952 Declaration on the Maritime Zone (also known as the Santiago Declaration of 1952) the three states justified their maritime claims[4]:

> '. . . it is the duty of each Government to prevent the said resources from being used outside the area of its jurisdiction so as to endanger their existence, integrity and conservation to the prejudice of peoples so situated geographically that their seas are irreplaceable sources of essential food and economic materials.'

After stating, in Article I, that the 'territorial sea and contiguous zone is insufficient to permit the conservation, development and use of those resources, to which the coastal countries are entitled' the three South American states reassert the first 200-mile resources claim in Article II,

> 'The Governments of Chile, Ecuador and Peru therefore proclaim as a principle of their international maritime policy that each of them possesses sole sovereignty and jurisdiction over the area of sea adjacent to the coast of its own country and extending not less than 200 nautical miles from the said coast.'

These three states pursued different paths with regard to implementing national maritime legislation over offshore resources. In 1953 Chile passed a resolution claiming a 200-mile maritime zone with an emphasis on the seabed, and allowing for other high seas freedoms, such as the freedom of navigation, beyond 3 miles. Ecuador, which in 1951 had claimed a 200-mile fishery zone, in 1966 claimed a 200-mile territorial sea. In 1947 Peru declared a 200-mile territorial sea which it reasserted in 1965. To date, both Ecuador and Peru maintain their excessive territorial sea claims, a factor which led both states to refrain from signing the 1982 LOS Convention. Thus, it is ironic that of the three states which began the exclusive economic zone concept, none has implemented national legislation for an economic zone which has evolved since the early 1950s, an economic zone which finally found written expression in the 1982 LOS Convention.

The Exclusive Economic Zone in the 1982 Law of the Sea Convention

The exclusive economic zone concept gained general acceptance early in the UNCLOS III negotiations. Yet, a balance between coastal state interests, particularly developing states, and the interests of maritime, landlocked, and geographically disadvantaged states was required before final acceptance of an EEZ text could be achieved. The underlying purpose for creating this new legal maritime regime was to curtail the trend of national claims to broader territorial seas, to preserve as many high seas freedoms as possible, while at the same time giving to coastal states increased rights over the resources off their coasts.

As noted early in the negotiations by Stevenson and Oxman 'the problem of coastal state resource jurisdiction beyond the territorial sea involves more interests of more states than any other problem in the law of the sea negotiations.'[5] In 1976, Oxman cited the following economic zone issues that, following the third substantive session, remained unresolved:

> '. . . the juridical status of the zone, the access of landlocked and geographically disadvantaged states to fisheries in the zones of their neighbors, related problems of the continental margin where it extends beyond 200 miles, scientific research in the zone, delimitation between opposite and adjacent states, and the application of third-party procedures to disputes regarding the zone.'[6]

Fundamental among these issues was the legal status of the waters of the exclusive economic zone. Intense debates arose regarding the characterization of the legal nature of coastal state rights in the EEZ and their relationship to rights of other states in the zone. Some states strongly advocated a 200-mile territorial sea. Somalia, for example, stated,

> '. . . the most logical regime for the national maritime zone was that of the territorial sea rather than that of the exclusive economic zone. The interests of developing countries would be best served by a territorial sea of not more than 200 miles . . . It was not the exclusive economic zone idea but only the territorial sea doctrine that could effectively meet the serious challenge of distant-water fleets . . .'[7]

The above statement asserts that only a territorial sea claim would meet the coastal state's needs in protecting its living resources. At another meeting, the Somalian delegation made a statement that can be viewed as extreme, but probably expressed an unspoken concern that many developing states may have had during the early stages of the UNCLOS III negotiations:

> '[T]he concept of the exclusive economic zone implied the existence of restrictions on the sovereignty of the coastal State since it limited its jurisdiction to the economic sphere. Furthermore, in the event of its adoption, there were no guarantees that under the pretext of freedom of navigation the technologically advanced maritime Powers would not persist in completely disregarding the territorial integrity of developing States by fishing in their territorial waters, and in endangering their essential security through sea-based espionage activities for instance.'[8]

It is interesting to note that while Somalia signed the LOS Convention on December 10, 1982, it continues to maintain the 200-mile territorial sea that it implemented in 1972. And, included in this law is the requirement for foreign warships to obtain permission prior to innocent passage through the territorial sea.

At UNCLOS III, however, the consensus clearly was that non-resource related high seas freedoms would be preserved in the exclusive economic zone, including for example, the freedoms of navigation and overflight and the freedom to lay pipelines and submarine cables. Yet, even the exercise of these freedoms may be affected by the exercise of EEZ rights by the coastal state. Article 58 recognizes the enjoyment of high seas freedoms by all states, 'subject to the relevant provisions of this Convention . . .,' and with 'due regard to the rights and duties of the coastal state . . .'. In principle at least, the LOS Convention strikes a balance between the rights and duties of the coastal state, on the one hand, and of all other states, on the other hand.

While there was a concerted attempt to anticipate all situations that may arise in the EEZ, it was undoubtedly known that unforeseen uses and activities would arise that would not be specifically addressed in the LOS Convention text. Thus, as Oxman discussed in 1975 the issue of 'residual rights' concerned many states,

> 'The problem centered on the 'residual rights' which the Convention does not attribute either to the coastal state or to all states. This is linked to the question whether the status of the economic zone is high seas (without prejudice, of course, to the specified rights of the coastal state in the zone).'[9]

Thus, the debate focused on whether the waters beyond the territorial sea limit and within the economic zone were high seas, with certain rights and jurisdiction allowed the coastal state, via the LOS Convention, or if these waters comprised a zone 'sui generis', being neither territorial sea nor high seas, but having a unique legal status. This debate has not ended, although attempts were certainly made by the time the final LOS Convention was drafted to accommodate both approaches.

The purpose of this book is neither to present a negotiating history of the Convention, nor to provide a full legal analysis of the terms and implications of the EEZ articles. The main intent of this study is to provide an overview of how states have thus far implemented the exclusive economic zone concept in national laws. Most of the effort for this book has been given to compiling the laws and decrees that states have written for establishing economic zones. While it is quite important to understand the genesis and development of this legal regime, the true test of the degree to which the international community agrees on the meaning of the EEZ will come by state practice. It is perhaps too early to form conclusions on this state practice, but national legislations will be the bases for national marine enforcement policies. And, they also will likely be the key to understanding future disputes over the interpretation of the LOS Convention.

However, before discussing the economic zone from the perspective of state practice, it is worth noting a number of elements contained in Part V of the LOS Convention; articles 55 through 75 pertain to the exclusive economic zone. To gain a full appreciation and understanding of the EEZ articles one must also look to Part VII, on the high seas. Both Parts are reproduced in Annex 2 of this chapter.

Article 55, distinguishes the EEZ geographically from the territorial sea:

> 'The exclusive economic zone is an area beyond and adjacent to the territorial sea, subject to the specific legal regime established in this Part, under which the rights and jurisdiction of the coastal State and the rights and freedoms of other States are governed by the relevant provisions of this Convention.'

Article 56 deals with the rights, jurisdiction and duties of the coastal state in the EEZ. Paragraph 1 distinguishes sovereign rights from jurisdictional rights:

1. In the exclusive economic zone, the coastal State has:

   (a) sovereign rights for the purpose of exploring and exploiting, conserving and managing the natural resources, whether living or non-living, of the waters superjacent to the sea-bed and of the sea-bed and its subsoil, and with regard to other activities for the economic exploitation and exploration of the zone, such as the production of energy from the water, currents and winds;

   (b) jurisdiction as provided for in the relevant provisions of this Convention with regard to:
      (i) the establishment and use of artificial islands, intallations and structures;
      (ii) marine scientific research;
      (iii) the protection and preservation of the marine environment

   (c) other rights and duties provided for in this Convention.

Those coastal state rights set forth in Article 56 1(a) are 'sovereign' and clearly economic. The phrase relating to 'other activities . . .' first was placed under the Article 56(b) jurisdiction category, but was later switched to the 'sovereign rights' paragraph to emphasize the economic nature of this zone.[10]

Sub-paragraph (b) lists those rights over which the coastal state has jurisdiction and which are linked to other provisions of the Convention. And sub-paragraph (c) incorporates all other rights and duties provided for in the Convention.

Article 57 defines the breadth of the economic zone to be no more than 200 miles from the baseline from which the territorial sea is measured. Due to the proximity of neighboring states no country is able to extend its EEZ to a full 200 miles in all directions. Assuming that every coastal state decides to claim a maximum allowable EEZ, then every coastal state in the world will have to negotiate at least one boundary with at least one neighboring state. In semi-enclosed seas, such as the Mediterranean, Caribbean, Persian Gulf, Baltic Sea, and South China Sea, for example, there are no areas in which any one bordering state can claim a full 200-mile zone. Thus, Article 74, on the delimitation of EEZs between states with opposite or adjacent coasts, becomes relevant to all coastal states.

Article 58 pertains to the rights and duties of other states in the exclusive economic zone, with paragraph 2 specifically referencing the high seas articles (88 to 115). Whereas Article 56 (2) states that coastal states 'shall have due regard to the rights and duties of other States . . .' in the EEZ, Article 58 (3) places similar requirements on the other states,

> 'In exercising their rights and performing their duties under this Convention in the exclusive economic zone, States shall have due regard to the rights and duties of the coastal State and shall comply with the laws and regulations adopted by the coastal State in accordance with the provisions of this Convention and other rules of international law in so far as they are not incompatible with this Part.'

While not specific, Article 59 provides a basis for resolving disputes over rights and duties not addressed in the Convention. The conflict 'should be resolved on the basis of equity and in the light of all the relevant circumstances, taking into account the respective importance of the interests involved to the parties as well as to the international community as a whole'. Some day there will a case taken to the International Court of Justice, or some other form of international adjudication, where the judges will be faced with volumes of evidence provided by two or more states in attempting to prove the 'interests involved'. Until such a case develops, it is difficult to place much practical significance on this article.

Article 60 sets out, in a fair amount of detail, the provisions for the coastal state to construct and to authorize and regulate the construction, operation, and use of artificial islands, installations and structures in the EEZ. Of the remaining 15 articles on the EEZ, 13 specifically relate to jurisdiction over living resources in the zone. Of particular importance to foreign fishermen is Article 73 on the enforcement of laws and regulations of the coastal state. Nowhere in this Article is there a provision explicitly recognizing the coastal state's right to imprison violators, and paragraph 3 specifically states that coastal state penalties for violations of fisheries legislation in the EEZ 'may not include imprisonment'. It will be shown later in this chapter that several countries, in their national laws creating EEZs, have included imprisonment clauses and, thereby violating the LOS provisions.

Finally Article 75 requires coastal states either to depict their exclusive economic zones on appropriate-scaled charts, or to provide a listing of the zone's geographical coordinates, including the geodetic datum. And, the coastal state must give due publicity to such charts or geographical listings and deposit them with the Secretary-General of the United Nations. Only with a clearly defined economic zone can a coastal state properly enforce its sovereign rights and jurisdictions. Only with appropriate charts or geographical points can users definitely know their location with respect to claimed national waters.

Chronology of National Claims

The first use of the term 'exclusive economic zone' in national legislation dates only to Madagascar's 1973 law. In this law, however, the term is not used in the same sense as in UNCLOS III. The title of the ordinance, 'Fixing the limits of the territorial sea and the continental shelf of the Malagasy Republic' indicates that the creation of an EEZ was not the intent of the drafters of this law. In fact, the term 'exclusive economic zone' here meant 'continental shelf'. The law asserts the continental shelf as extending 100 miles beyond the claimed 50-mile territorial sea. Article 2 of the law states,

> 'The 'continental shelf' of the Malagasy Republic (exclusive economic zone) shall extend to a limit fixed

at one hundred (100) nautical miles beyond its territorial sea.'[11]

Madagascar's law entered into force two months prior to the commencement of the 1st session of UNCLOS III in New York (see Table 5). In September 1985 Madagascar implemented a new law rolling back its 50-mile territorial sea claim to 12 miles and created a 200-mile EEZ. In April 1974 Bangladesh was the first country specifically to assert a claim using the term 'exclusive economic zone'. While there are certain aspects of this law that do not conform strictly with the eventual 1982 LOS Convention, the economic zone claim appears to have been made in the context of UNCLOS III. This assertion occurred between the first two sessions of the Conference.

The first UN negotiating text appeared in May 1975, at the conclusion of the 3rd UNCLOS III session (*Single Negotiating Text*). Subsequently, Costa Rica amended its Constitution to assert an exclusive-economic-zone type jurisdiction to 200 miles, although it did not use that term. The *Revised Single Negotiating Text* was produced at the Conference's 4th session. By this time the concept of the exclusive economic zone had been generally accepted by the international community. In 1976, between the 4th and 5th UNCLOS III sessions, three more EEZ claims were made (Comoros, Guatemala, and Mexico). After the 5th session ended, in September 1976, the claims to this new legal zone increased dramatically (see Table 5 and Figure 3).

In 1977 and 1978, 55 national claims were implemented. France, alone, accounted for 13 claims as it implemented legislation for metropolitan France, as well as issuing decrees for its overseas departments and dependencies. One French decree, issued February 3, 1978, applies to four of its overseas dependencies in the Indian Ocean- Tromelin, Glorious Archipelago, Juan-de-Nova, and the Europa and Bassas-da-India. It should be noted that sovereignty over these islands, as well as over Mayotte, is disputed between France and several states in the Indian Ocean.

In terms of absolute numbers, the EEZ claims did taper off slightly after 1978. Seven claims were made in 1979, 4 in 1980, 5 in 1981, and 3 in 1982, 5 in 1983, 6 in 1984, and 1 in 1985. It can be seen from Table 5 that beginning in mid-1978, and the 7th session of UNCLOS III, countries were spending considerable time at the negotiating table. Beginning at the 7th session there were two sessions a year until the December 10, 1982 signing.

By May 1985, approximately 65 independent states had implemented exclusive economic zones, and another 18 claims had been asserted for overseas departments, dependencies, or territories[12]. As noted in Chapter 1, 104 200-mile claims have been made by independent coastal states by May 1985 encompassing approximately 28.5 million sq.nautical miles (n.miles). Of this area, about 19.4 million sq.n.miles pertain to the 68 national EEZ claims (2.5 sq.million n.miles are enclosed by the 15 200-mile territorial sea assertions; 6.6 sq.million n.miles are incorporated in the 21 200-mile fishing zone claims- see Annex 1 to Chapter 1). The United States, France, and New Zealand, three states that have overseas territories, dependencies, or departments possess the largest economic zones (see Table 6).

Table 5. Chronology of Exclusive Economic Zone Claims and Important UNCLOS III dates.

1970	
Dec. 17	UN Resolution 2750: Decision to Convene UNCLOS III
1973	
Sept. 28	Madagascar
Dec. 3–15	1st Session of UNCLOS III (New York)
1974	
April 13	Bangladesh
June 2	Qatar
June 20–Aug. 29	2nd Session of UNCLOS III (Caracas-Main Trends Papers)
1975	
Mar. 17–May 9	3rd Session of UNCLOS III (Geneva-Single Negotiating Text)
May 20	Costa Rica
1976	
Mar. 15–May 7	4th Session of UNCLOS III (New York-Revised Single Negotiating Text)
June 15	Comoros
July 1	Guatemala

Table 5. Chronology of Exclusive Economic Zone Claims and Important UNCLOS III dates

31	Mexico
Aug. 2– Sept. 17	5th Session of UNCLOS III (New York)
Aug. 19	Mozambique
Dec. 5	Maldives
31	Pakistan
1977	
Jan. 1	Norway
15	India
15	Sri Lanka
Feb. 11	France
22	French Guiana (Fr.)
25	St. Pierre & Miquelon (Fr.)
26	Cuba
Apr. 1	Dominican Republic
8	Haiti
9	Burma
May 12	Vietnam
May 23– July 15	6th Session of UNCLOS III (New York-Informal Composite Negotiating Text)
May 28	Portugal
June 30	Guyana
Aug. 1	Korea, North
1	Mauritius
1	Seychelles
16	Togo
25	Western Samoa
Nov. 14	Cook Islands (N.Z.)
17	Ivory Coast
Dec. 23	Tokelau (N.Z.)
31	Cape Verde
1978	
Jan. 15	Yemen (Aden)
Feb. 3	Clipperton I. (Fr.)
3	French Polynesia (Fr.)
3	Mayotte (Fr.)
3	New Caledonia (Fr.)
3	Reunion (Fr.)
3	Islands of Tromelin, Glorious Archipelago, Juan-de-Nova, and the Europa and Bassas-da-India (Fr.)
3	French Southern and Antarctic Lands (Fr.)
3	Wallis and Futuna Islands (Fr.)
20	Spain
28	Mauritania
March 6	Guadeloupe (Fr.)
6	Martinique (Fr.)
March 28– July 15	7th Session of UNCLOS III (Geneva)
March 31	Papua New Guinea
April 1	New Zealand
1	Niue (N.Z.)
May 19	Guinea-Bissau
June 11	Suriname
16	Sao Tome & Principe
July 26	Venezuela
Aug. 1– Sept. 15	7th Session-Resumed (New York)
Aug. 4	Colombia
Oct. 5	Nigeria
Nov. 1	Grenada
1979	
Jan. 1	Barbados
9	Djibouti
Feb. 28	Kenya
March 19– April 27	8th Session of UNCLOS III (Geneva-Informal Composite Negotiating Text, Rev. 1)
June 1	Iceland
25	Tonga
July 11	Philippines
14	Solomon Islands
July 19– Aug. 24	8th Session-Resumed (New York)
1980	
March 3– April 4	9th Session of UNCLOS III (New York-Informal Composite Negotiating Text, Rev. 2)
March 21	Indonesia
June 13	Honduras
July 28	9th Session-Resumed (Geneva-Draft Convention on the Law of the Sea, Informal Text)
30	Guinea
Aug. 25	United Arab Emirates
1981	
Feb. 20	Oman
23	Thailand
March 9– April 24	10th Session of UNCLOS III (New York)
April 8	Morocco
Aug. 1–28	10th Session-Resumed (Geneva-Draft Convention on the Law of the Sea)
25	Dominica
Dec. 1	Fiji
1982	
March 8– April 30	11th Session of UNCLOS III (New York-Convention on the Law of the Sea Adopted)
July 31	Cambodia
Sept. 1	Antigua and Barbuda
Sept. 22–24	11th Session-Resumed (New York)
Oct. 6	Vanuatu
Dec. 10	Convention on the Law of the Sea signed by 119 states (Kingston)
1983	
March 10	United States
May 16	Kiribati
May 27	Trinidad and Tobago
June 8	St. Vincent and the Grenadines
Aug. 26	Egypt
1984	
Jan. 1	Tuvalu
March 1	USSR
July 12	Gabon
July 18	St. Lucia
Aug. 31	Saint Christopher and Nevis
Nov. 24	Equatorial Guinea
1985	
Sept. 21	Madagascar

Table 6. Largest 15 Exclusive Economic Zones[1]

State	Area (sq.n.miles-'000s)
1. United States	3,107.0[2]
2. France	2,100.0[2]
3. New Zealand	1,792.8[2]
4. Indonesia	1,577.3
5. USSR	1,309.5
6. Mexico	831.5
7. Norway	590.5
8. India	587.6
9. Philippines	551.4
10. Portugal	517.4
11. Papua New Guinea	504.0
12. Solomon Islands	445.0
13. Seychelles	393.4
14. Madagascar	376.8[3]
15. Spain	355.6[2]

[1] For sources, see Annex 1, Chapter 1.
[2] Includes overseas dependencies and possessions.
[3] Calculated for its 150-mile claim.

The Exclusive Economic Zone in State Practice

Regarding state practice of exclusive economic zone claims, it is incorrect, and often misleading, arbitrarily to lump all claims into one large grouping. Stating that 68 independent coastal states and 16 or more dependencies claimed EEZs by May 1985 merely quantifies the number of laws, decrees, or proclamations that have been issued. Several aspects of EEZ claims are diverse. Table 5 and Figure 3, for example, illustrate the chronology of EEZ claims. This range in timing, as well as the fact that about half of the independent coastal countries have yet to declare an economic zone, may indicate differing views of the relationship of the exclusive economic zone concept to national ocean policies. For example, intense debates are occurring in several countries that presently claim 200-mile territorial seas on whether or not to alter the status of these waters to an exclusive economic zone. Although many of these states have signed the LOS Convention, this particular issue may make the decision to ratify the Convention a difficult one.

The means by which states have asserted their EEZs have differed as well. The legal documents have ranged from single-page proclamations or decrees, to lengthy maritime laws in which the EEZ is but one of several maritime zones addressed by the coastal state. An attempt has been made in Part II of this book to reproduce those primary documents which create the EEZs. For completeness, and for the sake of producing source material for further analysis by others, entire laws have been reproduced, although the establishment of the economic zone is but one part of the law. As noted earlier, it is quite possible that other claims exist that do not appear in Part II.

To consider that all exclusive economic zone claims are substantively homogeneous would be an error. Similarly, to equate a country's EEZ claim to the LOS Convention provisions without carefully examining the actual legal documents would also be a serious mistake. While many of the laws generally conform to LOS Convention EEZ articles, there are usually some differences to be found in most legislation. Some differences may be insignificant, while some minor word alteration could create interpretative disputes.

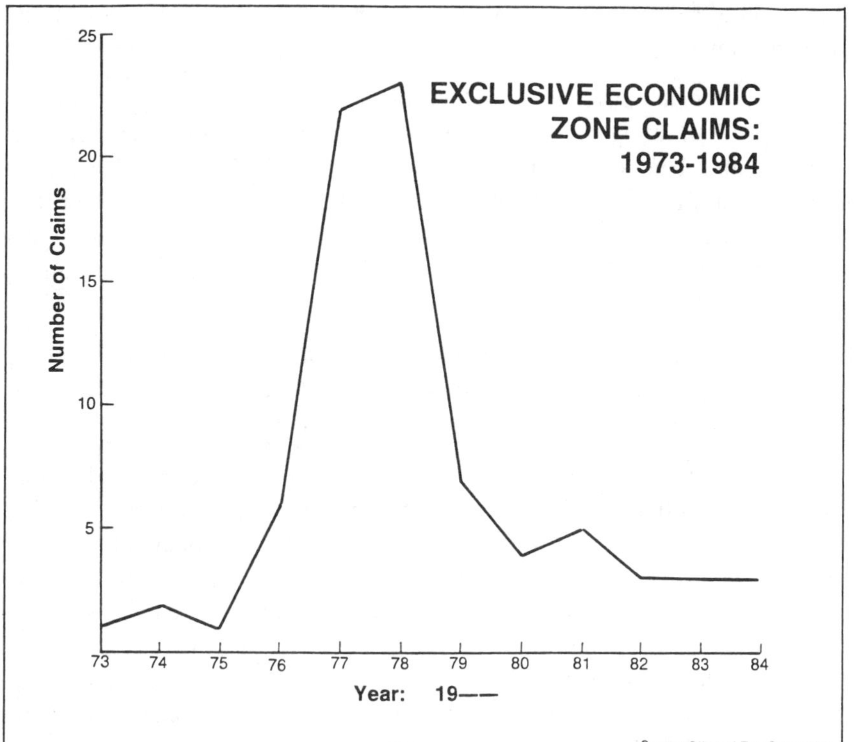

Figure 3

It will be many years before a comprehensive analysis can be made on the impact of the EEZ on the law of the sea, in general, and on marine resource utilization, in particular. State practice is still in its infancy, barely a decade old. Internationally accepted legal provisions for this newly created zone first appeared in the 1982 Law of the Sea Convention, a legal document that has yet to enter into force. For the following analysis of the major contents in state EEZ claims, the exclusive economic zone articles in the 1982 LOS Convention provide the basis from which to compare the different claims (see Table 7).

Table 7 lists those independent countries and dependencies claiming an EEZ and a categorization of major contents in the respective national laws. The first five columns refer to sovereign or jurisdictional rights cited in Article 56 of the LOS Convention:

Column 1: *Natural Resources* refers to Article 56 (1)(a)- '. . . sovereign rights for the purpose of exploring and exploiting, conserving and managing the natural resources, whether living or non-living, of the waters superjacent to the sea-bed and of the sea-bed and its subsoil . . .';

Column 2: *Production of Energy, etc.* refers to Article 56 (1)(a)- '. . . and with regard to other activities for the economic exploitation and exploration of the zone, such as the production of energy from the water, currents, and winds . . .';

Column 3: *Artificial Islands, etc.* refers to Article 56 (1)(b)(ii)- '. . . the establishment and use of artificial islands, installations and structures . . .' and to Article 60 which gives more details on artificial islands, installations and structures in the EEZ;

Column 4: *Scientific Research* refers to Article 56 (1)(b)(ii)- '. . . marine scientific research . . .';

Column 5: *Protection of Environment* refers to Article 56 (1)(b)(iii)- '... the protection and preservation of the marine environment ...'

Column 6 pertains to special areas that might be claimed in the EEZ. The LOS Convention provides for only two such zones. First, safety zones, not to exceed a breadth of 500 meters, are allowed for artificial islands, installations and structures (Article 60). According to Article 60 (5), such safety zones must be designed to 'ensure that they are reasonably related to the nature and function of the artificial islands, installations or structures ...' Second, with respect to pollution control, a country may, under special circumstances and after meeting certain obligations, adopt special mandatory requirements in a 'clearly defined area', Article 211 (6a).

An 'X' is placed in the column when a national law specifically contains the respective LOS Convention provision. If a country asserts a claim that exceeds, or potentially could exceed, the rights and authority allowed under the LOS Convention, an 'E' is placed in the column.

Sovereign rights over living and non-living resources of the water, seabed, and subsoil, are claimed in some manner by all states that claim an EEZ. However, in many instances it is difficult to determine whether a country, through the respective law, *now* intends to implement and enforce the various exclusive economic zone rights, or is merely expressing the authority it has, under international law, to assert these rights in the future. Western Samoa, for example, has enacted its Exclusive Economic Zone Act 1977 in which it claims a 200-mile EEZ. The essence of the law is to provide detailed fishery regulations. In almost the last article of the law, an enabling article appears stating, '[W]here no other provision is for the time being made by any other enactment for any such purposes, the Head of State, acting on the advice of Cabinet, may from time to time, make regulations not inconsistent with any other enactment for all or any of the following purposes: ...' What follows in this law, in part, are the substantive sections of Article 56 of the LOS Convention.

While Western Samoa may not now enforce many of the EEZ provisions, it has claimed the right, and it has empowered certain national authorities to enforce such provisions in the future. For the purpose of classifying EEZ claimants and rights claimed, enabling articles, similar to the Western Samoan article quoted above, have been considered actual claims.

Papua New Guinea's 1977 law is unclear as to the type of jurisdiction being claimed. A careful reading of the law suggests only a living resource regime, but several reports indicate that Papua New Guinea may be claiming an EEZ based on this law.

For all the other political entities that are listed in Part II, rights are claimed to the living and non-living resources of the EEZ. Of the 87 claims listed in Part II, 57 (66%) include a specific claim to jurisdiction with regard to other economic activities in the zone, including the production of energy from the water, currents, and winds- column 2, Table 7.

Sixty-two laws (71%) include authority to govern the establishment and use of artificial islands, installations and structures (column 3, Table 7). The following 13 states have phrased their legislation in such a way as to potentially exceed the rights given to coastal states under the LOS Convention:

Burma
Guyana
Honduras
India
Indonesia
Maldives
Mauritius
Pakistan
Philippines
Seychelles
Sri Lanka
Vanuatu
Yemen (Aden)

Table 7. Costal State Exclusive Economic Zone Claims Compared with 1982 Law of the Sea Convention Limits[1].

	LOS Convention Claims[2]					EEZ and Other Claims[3]			
State	Natural resources	Production of Energy, etc.	Artificial Islands, etc.	Scientific Research	Protection of Environment	Security Claim in Contiguous Zone	Special Areas	Possible imprisonment	Comments
Antigua and Barbuda	X	X	X	X	X	–	–	Y	
Bangladesh	X	–	X	X	E	–	Y	Y	Claims to artificial islands and scientific research made within continental shelf limits.
Barbados	X	X	X	X	X	–	–	Y	
Burma	X	X	E	X	X	–	Y	Y	
Cambodia	X	X	X	X	X	–	Y	–	
Cape Verde	X	–	X	X	X	–	–	Y	
Colombia	X	–	–	X	X	–	–	–	
Comoros	X	X	–	X	X	–	–	–	
Costa Rica	X	–	–	–	X	–	–	–	
Cuba	X	X	X	X	X	–	–	–	
Djibouti	X	X	X	X	X	–	–	–	
Dominica	X	X	X	X	X	–	–	–	
Dominican Republic	X	X	X	X	X	–	–	–	
Egypt	X	X	X	X	X	–	–	–	
Equatorial Guinea	X	–	X	X	X	–	–	–	
Fiji	X	X	X	X	X	–	–	–	
France	X	–	–	–	X	–	–	–	
Clipperton	X	–	–	–	X	–	–	–	
French Guiana	X	–	–	–	X	–	–	–	
French Polynesia	X	–	–	–	X	–	–	–	
French Southern and Antarctic Lands	X	–	–	–	X	–	–	–	
Guadeloupe	X	–	–	–	X	–	–	–	
Martinique	X	–	–	–	X	–	–	–	
Mayotte	X	–	–	–	X	–	–	–	
New Caledonia	X	–	–	–	X	–	–	–	
Reunion	X	–	–	–	X	–	–	–	
Saint Pierre and Miquelon	X	–	–	–	X	–	–	–	
Tromelin, *et al.*	X	–	–	–	X	–	–	–	
Wallis and Futuna	X	–	–	–	X	–	–	–	
Gabon	X	X	X	X	X	–	–	–	
Grenada	X	X	X	X	X	–	–	Y	
Guatemala	X	X	X	X	X	–	–	–	Claims right to participate in certain navigation and communication activities in EEZ.
Guinea	X	–	–	–	–	–	–	–	
Guinea-Bissau	X	–	–	–	–	–	–	Y	
Guyana	X	X	E	X	E	E	–	Y	Unclear whether EEZ has been implemented
Haiti	X	X	X	X	X	–	Y	–	
Honduras	X	X	E	X	X	–	–	–	
Iceland	X	X	X	X	X	–	–	–	

Footnotes at end of table.

State	LOS Convention claims[2]					EEZ and Other Claims[3]			Comments
	Natural resources	Production of Energy, etc.	Artificial Islands, etc.	Scientific Research	Protection of Environment	Security Claim in Contiguous Zone	Special Areas	Possible imprisonment	
India	X	X	E	X	E	E	Y	Y	
Indonesia	X	X	E	X	X	–	–	–	
Ivory Coast	X	X	X	X	E	–	–	–	
Kenya	X	X	X	X	X	–	–	–	
Kiribati	X	X	X	X	X	–	–	–	
Korea, Dem. People's Rep. of	X	–	X	X	–	–	–	–	Based on a report of a decree
Madagascar	X	X	X	X	X	–	–	–	
Malaysia	X	X	X	X	E	–	–	–	
Maldives	X	X	E	X	–	–	–	Y	Foreign fishing vessels require consent prior to entering EEZ
Mauritania	X	X	X	X	X	–	–	–	
Mauritius	X	X	E	X	E	E	–	Y	
Mexico	X	X	X	X	X	–	–	–	
Morocco	X	X	X	X	X	–	–	–	
Mozambique	X	–	–	–	–	–	–	–	
New Zealand	X	X	X	X	X	–	–	–	Detailed fishing regulations.
Cook Islands	X	X	X	X	X	–	–	–	Detailed fishing regulations.
Niue	X	X	X	X	X	–	–	Y	Detailed fishing regulations.
Tokelau	X	X	X	X	X	–	–	–	Detailed fishing regulations.
Nigeria	X	–	X	X	–	E	–	Y	
Norway	X	X	X	X	X	–	–	–	
Oman	X	–	–	–	–	–	–	–	
Pakistan	X	X	E	X	E	E	Y	Y	Possible added restrictions may include consent to lay cables and pipelines.
Papua New Guinea									Unclear whether *National Seas Act 1977* establishes exclusive economic zone.
Philippines	X	X	E	X	X	–	–	Y	
Portugal	X	X	X	X	X	–	–	Y	May establish regulations with regard to pipelines and submarine cables.
Qatar	X	–	–	–	–	–	–	–	
Saint Christopher and Nevis	X	–	–	–	–	–	–	–	
Saint Lucia	X	X	X	X	X	–	–	–	
Saint Vincent and the Grenadines	X	X	X	X	X	–	–	–	
Sao Tome and Principe	X	X	X	X	X	–	–	–	Laying of pipeline or submarine cables subject to agreement.
Seychelles	X	X	E	X	E	E	–	Y	
Solomon Islands	X	X	X	X	X	X	–	–	
Spain	X	–	–	–	X	–	–	–	Possible restrictions to navigation of fishing vessels.
Sri Lanka	X	X	E	X	E	E	Y	–	Pollution prevention zone extends to EEZ limits.
Suriname	X	X	X	X	X	–	–	Y	
Thailand	X	X	X	X	X	–	–	–	

Footnotes at end of table.

State	Natural resources	Production of Energy, etc.	Artificial Islands, etc.	Scientific Research	Protection of Environment	Security Claim in Contiguous Zone	Special Areas	Possible imprisonment	Comments
	LOS Convention claims[2]					EEZ and Other Claims[3]			
Togo	X	–	–	–	–	–	–	–	
Tonga	X	X	X	X	X	–	–	–	
Trinidad and Tobago	X	X	X	X	X	–	–	–	
Tuvalu	X	X	X	X	X	–	–	–	
UAE	X	–	X	X	X	–	–	–	
US	X	X	X	–	X	–	–	–	
USSR	X	X	X	X	E	E	–	–	
Vanuatu	X	–	E	X	X	–	–	Y	
Venezuela	X	X	X	X	X	–	–	–	
Vietnam	X	X	X	X	X	–	Y	–	
Western Samoa	X	X	X	X	X	–	–	–	Detailed fishing regulations.
Yemen, People's Dem. Rep. of	X	X	E	X	X	–	Y	Y	

1. The first five columns refer to sovereign or jurisdictional rights cited in Article 56 of the Law of the Sea Convention, as follows: *Natural resources,* 1(a), '... sovereign rights for the purpose of exploring and exploiting, conserving and managing the natural resources, whether living or non-living, of the waters superjacent to the sea-bed and of the sea-bed and its subsoil ...';
Production of Energy, etc., 1(a), '... and with regard to other activities for the economic exploitation and exploration of the zone, such as the production of energy from the water, currents, and winds ...';
Artificial Islands, etc., 1(b)(i), '... the establishment and use of artificial islands, installations and structures ...';
Scientific Research, 1(b)(ii), '... marine scientific research ...';
Protection of Environment, 1(b)(iii), '... the protection and preservation of the marine environment ...'
2. X = Claims that generally follow the LOS Convention; E = Claims that exceed the LOS Convention.
3. Y = Claims made that are not provided for in the LOS Convention.

Article 60 of the LOS Convention addresses the issue of artificial islands, installations and structures in the EEZ giving the coastal state the exclusive right to authorize and regulate the construction, operation, and use of artificial islands with no qualifications (Article 60 (1)(a)). With respect to installations and structures Article 60 (1)(b) grants coastal states exclusive rights over only those 'for purposes provided for in Article 56 and other economic purposes.' or those which '... may interfere with the exercise of the rights of the coastal State in the zone.'

Within this jurisdiction the coastal states have the authority with regard '... to customs, fiscal, health, safety and immigration laws and regulations.' (Article 60 (2)). Due notice must be given by the coastal state of any artificial island installation or structure (Article 60 (3)), and provisions are made for safety zones around such features (Article 60 (4–7)).

The jurisdiction over installations and structures, as written in the LOS Convention, is clearly related to the economic activities of the zone. The states listed above have included in their respective national legislation phrases which, while short, could be meaningful depending on the manner by which they are interpreted and applied. Burma, for example, in its 1977 law, states in Article 18 (b) that in the EEZ it has:

> 'exclusive rights and jurisdiction for the construction, maintenance or operation of artificial islands, offshore terminals, installations and other structures and *devices* necessary for the exploration and exploitation of its natural resources, both living and non-living, or for the convenience of shipping or *for any other purpose.'* (Emphasis added).

On this matter Guyana, India, Maldives, Mauritius, Pakistan, Seychelles, Sri Lanka, and Vanuatu all have identical language in their laws. Honduras, Indonesia, Philippines, and Yemen (Aden) have slight variations. The addition of the word device or the phrase 'for any other purpose' may have significant implication.

Most states specifically citing jurisdiction over scientific research (63 states-column 4, Table 7) and the protection of the environment (76 states-column 5, Table 7) appear to do so in conformity with the LOS Convention. The legislation of a number of states contains a claim to 'exclusive jurisdiction' regarding the protection of the marine environment (as opposed to 'jurisdiction'). This is because an earlier draft of the LOS Convention, on which these states' legislation are likely based, provided for 'exclusive jurisdiction' in this matter. The language was later modified to reflect the fact that both coastal states and vessel flag states share responsibility for enforcing international standards for the reduction and control of certain types of marine pollution in the EEZ.

Environmental claims that exceed the LOS Convention provisions are made by Bangladesh and the Ivory Coast. In Article 6 of the Ivory Coast's 1977 law, it reserves the right to 'take *any measures* and undertake *any action* to prevent, reduce, or control pollution of the marine environment, irrespective of the source.' (Emphasis added). Bangladesh asserts the right to 'take such measures as it may deem appropriate' to prevent and control marine pollution. Article 194 (1) of the LOS Convention allows states to '. . . take, individually or jointly as appropriate, all measures *consistent with this Convention* that are necessary to prevent, reduce and control pollution of the marine environment from any source . . .' (Emphasis added). There could be a significant difference between the LOS Convention and the application of their claims by Bangladesh or Ivory Coast.

Malaysia's exclusive economic zone bill (which has not yet entered into force) also contains certain provisions which exceed those of the LOS Convention. For example, the bill states that, '[I]f *any* oil, mixture containing oil or pollutant is discharged or escapes into the exclusive economic zone from any vessel, land-based source, installation, device or aircraft, from or through the atmosphere or by dumping'. (Emphasis added). The definition of oil and pollutants is broader than that provided for in generally accepted international standards, as are the enforcement powers granted to officers with respect to vessels transiting the EEZ. These provisions, if strictly enforced, could result in undue interference with the freedoms of navigation and overflight. But, Article 194 (4) of the LOS Convention specifically states that states 'shall refrain from unjustifiable interference with activities carried out by other states in the exercise of their rights and in pursuance of their duties in conformity with this Convention'.

The sixth column in Table 7 pertains to claims made to create special or designated areas within the EEZ. The following 9 states have provisions in their EEZ laws allowing the establishment of such areas:

Bangladesh	Pakistan
Guyana	Seychelles
India	Sri Lanka
Mauritius	U.S.S.R.
Nigeria	

The Seychelles, for example, in Article 9 of its 1977 EEZ law authorized its President to '. . . declare any area of the continental shelf or the exclusive economic zone to be a designated area.' Within this designated area the President may claim jurisdiction to many of the items listed in Article 56 of the LOS Convention and, in addition:

'(v) customs and other fiscal matters in relation to the designated area;
(vi) the regulation of entry into and passage of foreign ships through the designated area;
(vii) the establishment of fairways, sealanes, traffic separation schemes or any mode of ensuring freedom of navigation which is not prejudicial to the interest of Seychelles.'

These claims exceed rights allowed in the LOS Convention. As stated earlier, the designation of special areas in the EEZ is restricted to safety zones or areas pertaining to pollution regulations under special circumstances. If Seychelles-type laws were acceptable, then the potential is great for the EEZ to become a very restrictive zone; perhaps even more than the traditional territorial sea. Navigation rights may be severely threatened. Guyana, India, Mauritius, Nigeria, Pakistan, and Sri Lanka all have identical provisions.

The last two columns in Table 7, 'other claims', represent types of sovereign or jurisdictional claims not sanctioned by the LOS Convention. The presence of these items in national legislations automatically render an 'Y' placed in the column indicating that the claim violates the LOS Convention. There may be other categories that have not been listed, but these claims reflect potentially major departures from the LOS Convention.

Column 7 of Table 7 lists those states making security claims within their contiguous zones. Under the LOS Convention a state may claim a maximum contiguous zone (Article 33) of 24 miles from the baseline from which the territorial sea is measured. In this zone a coastal state may exercise the control necessary to:

> '(a) prevent infringement of its customs, fiscal, immigration or sanitary laws and regulations with its territory or territorial sea;
> (b) punish infringement of the above laws and regulations committed within its territory or territorial sea.'

There is *no* provision allowing a state to claim jurisdiction over security in this zone. The following 9 states have included security jurisdiction in their laws:

Bangladesh	Pakistan
Burma	Sri Lanka
Cambodia	Vietnam
Haiti	Yemen (Aden)
India	

With the exception of Haiti and Yemen (Aden) there appears to be a distinct South and Southeast Asia locational factor of countries making the security claim.

Finally, the last column in Table 7 lists those states that include in their EEZ laws provision for possible imprisonment of offenders of the law. The imprisonment articles are aimed at fishermen who violate national fishery regulations. Article 73 (3) of the LOS Convention expressly prohibits the coastal state from placing such offenders in prison unless agreed to between the concerned states:

> 'Coastal state penalties for violations of fisheries laws and regulations in the exclusive economic zone may not include imprisonment, in the absence of agreements to the contrary by the States concerned, or any form of corporal punishment.'

States which include an imprisonment provision, or potential imprisonment penalties, in their EEZ laws include:

Antigua and Barbuda	Mauritius
Bangladesh	Niue
Barbados	Nigeria
Burma	Pakistan
Cape Verde	Philippines
Grenada	Portugal

Guinea-Bissau	Seychelles
Guyana	Suriname
India	Vanuatu
Maldives	Yemen (Aden)

Although not indicated in Table 7, several states have general enabling language in their laws which could give national officials broader regulatory powers, and thereby add further restrictions in the EEZ. Barbados, for example, makes the following sweeping statement in Article 8 of its 1978 law:

> '(1) The Governor-General may, by order, with such exceptions and modifications as may be specified in the order, extend the application of any enactment to the Zone or any part thereof, and an enactment so extended shall have effect in relation to the Zone as if it had been enacted by this Act.'

There are at least 10 other states which have similar, if not identical, provisions. Although it is unlikely that states geographically will broaden their EEZs (i.e., beyond 200 miles from the coast), there is potential for additional jurisdictional, or regulatory claims to be made within the limits of existing zones. Since the Second World War, an enclosure movement over ocean space has been occurring adding coastal states rights to ever broadening offshore limits. To accommodate these rights while, at the same time, preserving traditional high sea freedoms, the international community struck a delicate balance in formulating the exclusive economic zone articles in the LOS Convention. Unless EEZ state practice conforms to the provisions of this Convention, the exclusive economic zone could become the vehicle even further restrictions on offshore activities.

Notes

1. Proclamation No. 2667, 'Policy of the United States With Respect to the Natural Resources of the Subsoil and Sea Bed of the Continental Shelf', Sept. 28, 1945, 10 *Fed.Reg. 12303*; XIII *Bulletin*, Department of State, No. 327, Sept. 30, 1945, p. 485.
2. Proclamation No. 2668, 'Policy of the United States With Respect to Coastal Fisheries in Certain Areas of the High Seas', Sept. 28, 1945, 10 *Fed.Reg. 12304.*
3. For a discussion of the Latin American claims see, Francisco Orrego Vicuna (ed.), *The Exclusive Economic Zone*. Westview Press, Boulder, Colo., 1984, and F.V. Garcia-Amador, 'The Latin American Contribution to the Development of the Law of the Sea', 68 *American Journal of International Law* 33 (1974).
4. Conference on the Exploitation and Conservation of the Maritime Resources of the South Pacific. *Agreements and Other Documents 1952–1966 (English Version)*. Lima, Peru: General Secretariat, 1967.
5. John Stevenson and Bernard Oxman, 'The Preparations for the Law of the Sea Conference', 68 *American Journal of International Law* 1 (1974), p. 13.
6. Bernard Oxman, 'The Third United Nations Conference on the Law of the Sea: The 1976 New York Sessions', 71 *American Journal of International Law* (1977), p. 250.
7. UNCLOS III, *Official Records*, vol. II, 26th Meeting, p. 209. Found in, Nasila S. Rembe, *Africa and the International Law of the Sea*. Sijthoff & Noordhoff (The Netherlands, 1980), p. 125.
8. UNCLOS III, *Official Records*, vol. I, *Plenary Session*. 42nd Meeting, p. 186. Found in Rembe (1980), p. 126.
9. Bernard Oxman, 'The Third United Nations Conference on the Law of the Sea: The 1975 Geneva Session', 69 *American Journal of International Law* (1975), pp. 777–778.
10. Bernard Oxman, 'The Third United Nations Conference on the Law of the Sea: The 1977 New York Session', 72 *American Journal of Internation Law* (1978), p. 68.
11. Ordinance No. 73-060. *Journal Officiel*, September 28, 1973. For text of ordinance, see Part II.
12. The term 'approximate' is used since it is possible that other laws and decrees exist that have not come to the attention of the author by September 1985.

ANNEX 1

1982 United Nations Convention on the Law of the Sea

PART V

EXCLUSIVE ECONOMIC ZONE

Article 55
Specific legal regime of the exclusive economic zone

The exclusive economic zone is an area beyond and adjacent to the territorial sea, subject to the specific legal régime established in this Part, under which the rights and jurisdiction of the coastal State and the rights and freedoms of other States are governed by the relevant provisions of this Convention.

Article 56
Rights, jurisdiction and duties of the coastal State in the exclusive economic zone

1. In the exclusive economic zone, the coastal State has:

(a) sovereign rights for the purpose of exploring and exploiting, conserving and managing the natural resources, whether living or non-living, of the waters superjacent to the sea-bed and of the sea-bed and its subsoil, and with regard to other activities for the economic exploitation and exploration of the zone, such as the production of energy from the water, currents and winds;
(b) jurisdiction as provided for in the relevant provisions of this Convention with regard to:
  (i) the establishment and use of artificial islands, installations and structures;
  (ii) marine scientific research;
  (iii) the protection and preservation of the marine environment;
(c) other rights and duties provided for in this Convention.

2. In exercising its rights and performing its duties under this Convention in the exclusive economic zone, the coastal State shall have due regard to the rights and duties of other States and shall act in a manner compatible with the provisions of this Convention.

3. The rights set out in this article with respect to the sea-bed and subsoil shall be exercised in accordance with Part VI.

Article 57
Breadth of the exclusive economic zone

The exclusive economic zone shall not extend beyond 200 nautical miles from the baselines from which the breadth of the territorial sea is measured.

Article 58
Rights and duties of other States in the exclusive economic zone

1. In the exclusive economic zone, all States, whether coastal or land-locked, enjoy, subject to the relevant provisions of this Convention, the freedoms referred to in article 87 of navigation and overflight and of the laying of sub-marine cables and pipelines, and other internationally lawful uses of the sea related to these freedoms, such as those associated with the operation of ships, aircraft and submarine

cables and pipelines, and compatible with the other provisions of this Convention.

2. Articles 88 to 115 and other pertinent rules of international law apply to the exclusive economic zone in so far as they are not incompatible with this Part.

3. In exercising their rights and performing their duties under this Convention in the exclusive economic zone, States shall have due regard to the rights and duties of the coastal State and shall comply with the laws and regulations adopted by the coastal State in accordance with the provisions of this Convention and other rules of international law in so far as they are not incompatible with this Part.

Article 59
Basis for the resolution of conflicts regarding the attribution of rights and jurisdiction in the exclusive economic zone

In cases where this Convention does not attribute rights or jurisdiction to the coastal State or to other States within the exclusive economic zone, and a conflict arises between the interests of the coastal State and any other State or States the conflict should be resolved on the basis of equity and in the light of all the relevant circumstances, taking into account the respective importance of the interests involved to the parties as well as to the international community as a whole.

Article 60
Artificial islands, installations and structures in the exclusive economic zone

1. In the exclusive economic zone, the coastal State shall have the exclusive right to construct and to authorize and regulate the construction, operation and use of:
   (a) artificial islands;
   (b) installations and structures for the purposes provided for in article 56 and other economic purposes;
   (c) installations and structures which may interfere with the exercise of the rights of the coastal State in the zone.

2. The coastal State shall have exclusive jurisdiction over such artificial islands, installations and structures, including jurisdiction with regard to customs, fiscal, health, safety and immigration laws and regulations.

3. Due notice must be given of the construction of such artificial islands, installations or structure, and permanent means for giving warning of their presence must be maintained. Any installations or structure which are abandoned or disused shall be removed to ensure safety of navigation, taking into account any generally accepted international standards established in this regard by the competent international organization. Such removal shall also have due regard to fishing, the protection of the marine environment and the rights and duties of other States. Appropriate publicity shall be given to the depth, position and dimensions of any installations or structures not entirely removed.

4. The coastal State may, where necessary, establish reasonable safety zones around such artificial islands, installations and structures in which it may take appropriate measures to ensure the safety both of navigation and of the artificial islands, installations and structures.

5. The breadth of the safety zones shall be determined by the coastal State, taking into account applicable international standards. Such zones shall be designed to ensure that they are reasonably related to the nature and function of the artificial islands, installations or structures, and shall not exceed a distance of 500 metres around them, measured from each point of their outer edge, except as authorized by generally accepted international standards or as recommended by the competent international

organization. Due notice shall be given of the extent of safety zones.

6. All ships must respect these safety zones and shall comply with generally accepted international standards regarding navigation in the vicinity of artificial islands installations, structures and safety zones.

7. Artificial islands, installations and structures and the safety zones around them may not be established where interference may be caused to the use of recognized sea lanes essential to international navigation.

8. Artificial islands, installations and structures do not possess the status of islands. They have no territorial sea of their own, and their presence does not affect the delimitation of the territorial sea, the exclusive economic zone or the continental shelf.

Article 61
Conservation of the living resources

1. The coastal State shall determine the allowable catch of the living resources in its exclusive economic zone.

2. The coastal State, taking into account the best scientific evidence available to it, shall ensure through proper conservation and management measures that the maintenance of the living resources in the exclusive economic zone is not endangered by over-exploitation. As appropriate, the coastal State and competent international organizations, whether subregional, regional or global, shall co-operate to this end.

3. Such measures shall also be designed to maintain or restore populations of harvested species at levels which can produce the maximum sustainable yield, as qualified by relevant environmental and economic factors, including the economic needs of coastal fishing communities and the special requirements of developing States, and taking into account fishing patterns, the interdependence of stocks and any generally recommended international minimum standards, whether subregional, regional or global.

4. In taking such measures the coastal State shall take into consideration the effects on species associated with or dependent upon harvested species with a view to maintaining or restoring populations of such associated or dependent species above levels at which their reproduction may become seriously threatened.

5. Available scientific information, catch and fishing effort statistics, and other data relevant to the conservation of fish stocks shall be contributed and exchanged on a regular basis through competent international organizations, whether subregional, regional or global, where appropriate and with participation by all States concerned, including States whose nationals are allowed to fish in the exclusive economic zone.

Article 62
Utilization of the living resources

1. The coastal State shall promote the objective of optimum utilization of the living resources in the exclusive economic zone without prejudice to article 61.

2. The coastal State shall determine its capacity to harvest the living resources of the exclusive economic zone. Where the coastal State does not have the capacity to harvest the entire allowable catch, it shall, through agreements or other arrangements and pursuant to the terms, conditions, laws and regulations referred to in paragraph 4, give other States access to the surplus of the allowable catch, having particular regard to the provisions of articles 69 and 70, especially in relation to the developing States mentioned therein.

3. In giving access to other States to its exclusive economic zone under this article, the coastal State shall take into account all relevant factors, including, *inter alia,* the significance of the living resources of the area to the economy of the coastal State concerned and its other national interests, the provisions of articles 69 and 70, the requirements of developing States in the subregion or region in harvesting part of the surplus and the need to minimize economic dislocation in States whose nationals have habitually fished in the zone or which have made substantial efforts in research and identification of stocks.

4. Nationals of other States fishing in the exclusive economic zone shall comply with the conservation measures and with the other terms and conditions established in the laws and regulations of the coastal State. These laws and regulations shall be consistent with this Convention and may relate, *inter alia,* to the following:

(a) licensing of fishermen, fishing vessels and equipment, including payment of fees and other forms of remuneration, which, in the case of developing coastal States, may consist of adequate compensation in the field of financing, equipment and technology relating to the fishing industry;
(b) determining the species which may be caught, and fixing quotas of catch, whether in relation to particular stocks or groups of stocks or catch per vessel over a period of time or to the catch by nationals of any State during a specified period;
(c) regulating seasons and areas of fishing, the types, sizes and amount of gear, and the types, sizes and number of fishing vessels that may be used;
(d) fixing the age and size of fish and other species that may be caught;
(e) specifying information required of fishing vessels, including catch and effort statistics and vessel position reports;
(f) requiring, under the authorization and control of the coastal State, the conduct of specified fisheries research programmes and regulating the conduct of such research, including the sampling of catches, disposition of samples and reporting of associated scientific data;
(g) the placing of observers or trainees on board such vessels by the coastal State;
(h) the landing of all or any part of the catch by such vessels in the ports of the coastal State;
(i) terms and conditions relating to joint ventures or other co-operative arrangements;
(j) requirements for the training of personnel and the transfer of fisheries technology, including enhancement of the coastal State's capability of undertaking fisheries research;
(k) enforcement procedures.

5. Coastal States shall give due notice of conservation and management laws and regulations.

Article 63

Stocks occurring within the exclusive economic zones of two or more coastal States or both within the exclusive economic zone and in an area beyond and adjacent to it

1. Where the same stock or stocks of associated species occur within the exclusive economic zones of two or more coastal States, these States shall seek, either directly or through appropriate subregional or regional organizations, to agree upon the measures necessary to co-ordinate and ensure the conservation and development of such stocks without prejudice to the other provisions of this Part.

2. Where the same stock or stocks of associated species occur both within the exclusive economic zone and in an area beyond and adjacent to the zone, the coastal State and the States fishing for such stocks in the adjacent area shall seek, either directly or through appropriate subregional or regional organizations, to agree upon the measures necessary for the conservation of these stocks in the adjacent area.

Article 64
Highly migratory species

1. The coastal State and other States whose nationals fish in the region for the highly migratory species listed in Annex I shall co-operate directly or through appropriate international organizations with a view to ensuring conservation and promoting the objective of optimum utilization of such species throughout the region, both within and beyond the exclusive economic zone. In regions for which no appropriate international organization exists, the coastal State and other States whose nationals harvest these species in the region shall co-operate to establish such an organization and participate in its work.

2. The provisions of paragraph 1 apply in addition to the other provisions of this Part.

Article 65
Marine mammals

Nothing in this Part restricts the right of a coastal State or the competence of an international organization, as appropriate, to prohibit, limit or regulate the exploitation of marine mammals more strictly than provided for in this Part. States shall co-operate with a view to the conservation of marine mammals and in the case of cetaceans shall in particular work through the appropriate international organizations for their conservation, management and study.

Article 66
Anadromous stocks

1. States in whose rivers anadromous stocks originate shall have the primary interest in and responsibility for such stocks.

2. The State of origin of anadromous stocks shall ensure their conservation by the establishment of appropriate regulatory measures for fishing in all waters landward of the outer limits of its exclusive economic zone and for fishing provided for in paragraph 3(b). The State of origin may, after consultations with the other States referred to in paragraphs 3 and 4 fishing these stocks, establish total allowable catches for stocks originating in its rivers.

3. (a) Fisheries for anadromous stocks shall be conducted only in waters landward of the outer limits of exclusive economic zones, except in cases where this provision would result in economic dislocation for a State other than the State of origin. With respect to such fishing beyond the outer limits of the exclusive economic zone, States concerned shall maintain consultations with a view to achieving agreement on terms and conditions of such fishing giving due regard to the conservation requirements and the needs of the State of origin in respect of these stocks.
   (b) The State of origin shall co-operate in minimizing economic dislocation in such other States fishing these stocks, taking into account the normal catch and the mode of operations of such States, and all the areas in which such fishing has occurred.
   (c) States referred to in subparagraph (b), participating by agreement with the State of origin in measures to renew anadromous stocks, particularly by expenditures for that purpose, shall be given special consideration by the State of origin in the harvesting of stocks originating in its rivers.
   (d) Enforcement of regulations regarding anadromous stocks beyond the exclusive economic zone shall be by agreement between the State of origin and the other States concerned.

4. In cases where anadromous stocks migrate into or through the waters landward of the outer limits of the exclusive economic zone of a State other than the State of origin, such State shall co-operate with the State of origin with regard to the conservation and management of such stocks.

5. The State of origin of anadromous stocks and other States fishing these stocks shall make arrangements for the implementation of the provisions of this article, where appropriate, through regional organizations.

Article 67
Catadromous species

1. A coastal State in whose waters catadromous species spend the greater part of their life cycle shall have responsibility for the management of these species and shall ensure the ingress and egress of migrating fish.

2. Harvesting of catadromous species shall be conducted only in waters landward of the outer limits of exclusive economic zones. When conducted in exclusive economic zones, harvesting shall be subject to this article and the other provisions of this Convention concerning fishing in these zones.

3. In cases where catadromous fish migrate through the exclusive economic zone of another State, whether as juvenile or maturing fish, the management, including harvesting, of such fish shall be regulated by agreement between the State mentioned in paragraph 1 and the other State concerned. Such agreement shall ensure the rational management of the species and take into account the responsibilities of the State mentioned in paragraph 1 for the maintenance of these species.

Article 68
Sedentary species

This Part does not apply to sedentary species as defined in article 77, paragraph 4.

Article 69
Right of land-locked States

1. Land-locked States shall have the right to participate, on an equitable basis, in the exploitation of an appropriate part of the surplus of the living resources of the exclusive economic zones of coastal States of the same subregion or region, taking into account the relevant economic and geographical circumstances of all the States concerned and in conformity with the provisions of this article and of articles 61 and 62.

2. The terms and modalities of such participation shall be established by the States concerned through bilateral, subregional or regional agreements taking into account, *inter alia*:

(a) the need to avoid effects detrimental to fishing communities or fishing industries of the coastal State;
(b) the extent to which the land-locked State, in accordance with the provisions of this article, is participating or is entitled to participate under existing bilateral, subregional or regional agreements in the exploitation of living resources of the exclusive economic zones of other coastal States;
(c) the extent to which other land-locked States and geographically disadvantaged States are participating in the exploitation of the living resources of the exclusive economic zone of the coastal State and the consequent need to avoid a particular burden for any single coastal State or a part of it;
(d) the nutritional needs of the populations of the respective States.

3. When the harvesting capacity of a coastal State approaches a point which would enable it to harvest the entire allowable catch of the living resources in its exclusive economic zone, the coastal State and other States concerned shall co-operate in the establishment of equitable arrangements on a bilateral,

subregional or regional basis to allow for participation of developing land-locked States of the same subregion or region in the exploitation of the living resources of the exclusive economic zones of coastal States of the subregion or region, as may be appropriate in the circumstances and on terms satisfactory to all parties. In the implementation of this provision the factors mentioned in paragraph 2 shall also be taken into account.

4. Developed land-locked States shall, under the provisions of this article, be entitled to participate in the exploitation of living resources only in the exclusive economic zones of developed coastal States of the same subregion or region having regard to the extent to which the coastal State, in giving access to other States to the living resources of its exclusive economic zone, has taken into account the need to minimize detrimental effects on fishing communities and economic dislocation in States whose nationals have habitually fished in the zone.

5. The above provisions are without prejudice to arrangements agreed upon in subregions or regions where the coastal States may grant to land-locked States of the same subregion or region equal or preferential rights for the exploitation of the living resources in the exclusive economic zones.

Article 70
Right of geographically disadvantaged States

1. Geographically disadvantaged States shall have the right to participate, on an equitable basis, in the exploitation of an appropriate part of the surplus of the living resources of the exclusive economic zones of coastal States of the same subregion or region, taking into account the relevant economic and geographical circumstances of all the States concerned and in conformity with the provisions of this article and of articles 61 and 62.

2. For the purposes of this Part, 'geographically disadvantaged States' means coastal States, including States bordering enclosed or semi-enclosed seas, whose geographical situation makes them dependent upon the exploitation of the living resources of the exclusive economic zones of other States in the subregion or region for adequate supplies of fish for the nutritional purposes of their populations or parts thereof, and coastal States which can claim no exclusive economic zones of their own.

3. The terms and modalities of such participation shall be established by the States concerned through bilateral, subregional or regional agreements taking into account, *inter alia*:

(a) the need to avoid effects detrimental to fishing communities or fishing industries of the coastal State;
(b) the extent to which the geographically disadvantaged State, in accordance with the provisions of this article, is participating or is entitled to participate under existing bilateral, subregional or regional agreements in the exploitation of living resources of the exclusive economic zones of other coastal States;
(c) the extent to which other geographically disadvantaged States and landlocked States are participating in the exploitation of the living resources of the exclusive economic zone of the coastal State and the consequent need to avoid a particular burden for any single coastal State or a part of it;
(d) the nutritional needs of the populations of the respective States.

4. When the harvesting capacity of a coastal State approaches a point which would enable it to harvest the entire allowable catch of the living resources in its exclusive economic zone, the coastal State and other States concerned shall co-operate in the establishment of equitable arrangements on a bilateral, subregional or regional basis to allow for participation of developing geographically disadvantaged States

of the same subregion or region in the exploitation of the living resources of the exclusive economic zones of coastal States of the subregion or region, as may be appropriate in the circumstances and on terms satisfactory to all parties. In the implementation of this provision the factors mentioned in paragraph 3 shall also be taken into account.

5. Developed geographically disadvantaged States shall, under the provisions of this article, be entitled to participate in the exploitation of living resources only in the exclusive economic zones of developed coastal States of the same subregion or region having regard to the extent to which the coastal State, in giving access to other States to the living resources of its exclusive economic zone, has taken into account the need to minimize detrimental effects on fishing communities and economic dislocation in States whose nationals have habitually fished in the zone.

6. The above provisions are without prejudice to arrangements agreed upon in subregions or regions where the coastal States may grant to geographically disadvantaged States of the same subregion or region equal or preferential rights for the exploitation of the living resources in the exclusive economic zones.

Article 71
Non-applicability of articles 69 and 70

The provisions of articles 69 and 70 do not apply in the case of a coastal State whose economy is overwhelmingly dependent on the exploitation of the living resources of its exclusive economic zone.

Article 72
Restrictions on transfer of rights

1. Rights provided under articles 69 and 70 to exploit living resources shall not be directly or indirectly transferred to third States or their nationals by lease or licence, by establishing joint ventures or in any other manner which has the effect of such transfer unless otherwise agreed by the States concerned.

2. The foregoing provision does not preclude the States concerned from obtaining technical or financial assistance from third States or international organizations in order to facilitate the exercise of the rights pursuant to articles 69 and 70, provided that it does not have the effect referred to in paragraph 1.

Article 73
Enforcement of laws and regulations of the coastal State

1. The coastal State may, in the exercise of its sovereign rights to explore, exploit, conserve and manage the living resources in the exclusive economic zone, take such measures, including boarding, inspection, arrest and judicial proceedings, as may be necessary to ensure compliance with the laws and regulations adopted by it in conformity with this Convention.

2. Arrested vessels and their crews shall be promptly released upon the posting of reasonable bond or other security.

3. Coastal State penalties for violations of fisheries laws and regulations in the exclusive economic zone may not include imprisonment, in the absence of agreements to the contrary by the States concerned, or any other form of corporal punishment.

4. In cases of arrest or detention of foreign vessels the coastal State shall promptly notify the flag State, through appropriate channels, of the action taken and of any penalties subsequently imposed.

Article 74
Delimitation of the exclusive economic zone between States with opposite or adjacent coasts

1. The delimitation of the exclusive economic zone between States with opposite or adjacent coasts shall be effected by agreement on the basis of international law, as referred to in Article 38 of the Statute of the International Court of Justice, in order to achieve an equitable solution.

2. If no agreement can be reached within a reasonable period of time, the States concerned shall resort to the procedures provided for in Part XV.

3. Pending agreement as provided for in paragraph 1, the States concerned, in a spirit of understanding and co-operation, shall make every effort to enter into provisional arrangements of a practical nature and, during this transitional period, not to jeopardize or hamper the reaching of the final agreement. Such arrangements shall be without prejudice to the final delimitation.

4. Where there is an agreement in force between the States concerned, questions relating to the delimitation of the exclusive economic zone shall be determined in accordance with the provisions of that agreement.

Article 75
Charts and lists of geographical co-ordinates

1. Subject to this Part, the outer limit lines of the exclusive economic zone and the lines of delimitation drawn in accordance with article 74 shall be shown on charts of a scale or scales adequate for ascertaining their position. Where appropriate, lists of geographical co-ordinates of points, specifying the geodetic datum, may be substituted for such outer limit lines or lines of delimitation.

2. The coastal State shall give due publicity to such charts or lists of geographical co-ordinates and shall deposit a copy of each such chart or list with the Secretary-General of the United Nations.

ANNEX 2

1982 United Nations Convention on the Law of the Sea

PART VII

HIGH SEAS

SECTION 1. GENERAL PROVISIONS

Article 86
Application of the provisions of this Part

The provisions of this Part apply to all parts of the sea that are not included in the exclusive economic zone, in the territorial sea or in the internal waters of a State, or in the archipelagic waters of an archipelagic State. This article does not entail any abridgement of the freedoms enjoyed by all States in the exclusive economic zone in accordance with article 58.

Article 87
Freedom of the high seas

1. The high seas are open to all States, whether coastal or land-locked. Freedom of the high seas is exercised under the conditions laid down by this Convention and by other rules of international law. It comprises, *inter alia,* both for coastal and land-locked States:

(a) freedom of navigation;
(b) freedom of overflight;
(c) freedom to lay submarine cables and pipelines, subject to Part VI;
(d) freedom to construct artificial islands and other installations permitted under international law, subject to Part VI;
(e) freedom of fishing, subject to the conditions laid down in section 2;
(f) freedom of scientific research, subject to Parts VI and XIII.

2. These freedoms shall be exercised by all States with due regard for the interests of other States in their exercise of the freedom of the high seas, and also with due regard for the rights under this Convention with respect to activities in the Area.

Article 88
Reservation of the high seas for peaceful purposes

The high seas shall be reserved for peaceful purposes.

Article 89
Invalidity of claims of sovereignty over the high seas

No State may validly purport to subject any part of the high seas to its sovereignty.

Article 90
Right of navigation

Every State, whether coastal or land-locked, has the right to sail ships flying its flag on the high seas.

Article 91
Nationality of ships

1. Every State shall fix the conditions for the grant of its nationality to ships, for the registration of ships in its territory, and for the right to fly its flag. Ships have the nationality of the State whose flag they are entitled to fly. There must exist a genuine link between the State and the ship.

2. Every State shall issue to ships to which it has granted the right to fly its flag documents to that effect.

Article 92
Status of ships

1. Ships shall sail under the flag of one State only and, save in exceptional cases expressly provided for in international treaties or in this Convention, shall be subject to its exclusive jurisdiction on the high seas. A ship may not change its flag during a voyage or while in a port of call, save in the case of a real transfer of ownership or change of registry.

2. A ship which sails under the flags of two or more States, using them according to convenience, may not claim any of the nationalities in question with respect to any other State, and may be assimilated to a ship without nationality.

Article 93
Ships flying the flag of the United Nations, its specialized agencies and the International Atomic Energy Agency

The preceding articles do not prejudice the question of ships employed on the official service of the United Nations, its specialized agencies or the International Atomic Energy Agency, flying the flag of the organization.

Article 94
Duties of the flag State

1. Every State shall effectively exercise its jurisdiction and control in administrative, technical and social matters over ships flying its flag.

2. In particular every State shall:

(a) maintain a register of ships containing the names and particulars of ships, flying its flag, except those which are excluded from generally accepted international regulations on account of their small size; and
(b) assume jurisdiction under its internal law over each ship flying its flag and its master, officers and crew in respect of administrative, technical and social matters concerning the ship.

3. Every State shall take such measures for ships flying its flag as are necessary to ensure safety at sea with regard, *inter alia,* to:

(a) the construction, equipment and seaworthiness of ships;
(b) the manning of ships, labour conditions and the training of crews, taking into account the

applicable international instruments;
(c) the use of signals, the maintenance of communications and the prevention of collisions.

4. Such measures shall include those necessary to ensure:

(a) that each ship, before registration and thereafter at appropriate intervals, is surveyed by a qualified surveyor of ships, and has on board such charts, nautical publications and navigational equipment and instruments as are appropriate for the safe navigation of the ship;
(b) that each ship is in the charge of a master and officers who possess appropriate qualifications, in particular in seamanship, navigation, communications and marine engineering, and that the crew is appropriate in qualification and numbers for the type, size, machinery and equipment of the ship;
(c) that the master, officers and, to the extent appropriate, the crew are fully conversant with and required to observe the applicable international regulations concerning the safety of life at sea, the prevention of collisions, the prevention, reduction and control of marine pollution, and the maintenance of communications by radio.

5. In taking the measures called for in paragraphs 3 and 4 each State is required to conform to generally accepted international regulations, procedures and practices and to take any steps which may be necessary to secure their observance.

6. A State which has clear grounds to believe that proper jurisdiction and control with respect to a ship have not been exercised may report the facts to the flag State. Upon receiving such a report, the flag State shall investigate the matter and, if appropriate, take any action necessary to remedy the situation.

7. Each State shall cause an inquiry to be held by or before a suitably qualified person or persons into every marine casualty or incident of navigation on the high seas involving a ship flying its flag and causing loss of life or serious injury to nationals of another State or serious damage to ships or installations of another State or to the marine environment. The flag State and the other State shall co-operate in the conduct of any inquiry held by that other State into any such marine casualty or incident of navigation.

Article 95
Immunity of warships on the high seas

Warships on the high seas have complete immunity from the jurisdiction of any State other than the flag State.

Article 96
Immunity of ships used only on government non-commercial service

Ships owned or operated by a State and used only on government non-commercial service shall, on the high seas, have complete immunity from the jurisdiction of any State other than the flag State.

Article 97
Penal jurisdiction in matters of collision or any other incident of navigation

1. In the event of a collision or any other incident of navigation concerning a ship on the high seas, involving the penal or disciplinary responsibility of the master or of any other person in the service of the ship, no penal or disciplinary proceedings may be instituted against such person except before the judicical or administrative authorities either of the flag State or of the State of which such person is a national.

2. In disciplinary matters, the State which has issued a master's certificate or a certificate of

competence or licence shall alone be competent, after due legal process, to pronounce the withdrawal of such certificates, even if the holder is not a national of the State which issued them.

3. No arrest or detention of the ship, even as a measure of investigation, shall be ordered by any authorities other than those of the flag State.

Article 98
Duty to render assistance

1. Every State shall require the master of a ship flying its flag, in so far as he can do so without serious danger to the ship, the crew or the passengers:

(a) to render assistance to any person found at sea in danger of being lost;
(b) to proceed with all possible speed to the rescue of persons in distress, if informed of their need of assistance, in so far as such action may reasonably be expected of him;
(c) after a collision, to render assistance to the other ship, its crew and its passengers and, where possible, to inform the other ship of the name of his own ship, its port of registry and the nearest port at which it will call.

2. Every coastal State shall promote the establishment, operation and maintenance of an adequate and effective search and rescue service regarding safety on and over the sea and, where circumstances so require, by way of mutual regional arrangements co-operate with neighbouring States for this purpose.

Article 99
Prohibition of the transport of slaves

Every State shall take effective measures to prevent and punish the transport of slaves in ships authorized to fly its flag and to prevent the unlawful use of its flag for that purpose. Any slave taking refuge on board any ship, whatever its flag, shall *ipso facto* be free.

Article 100
Duty to co-operate in the repression of piracy

All States shall co-operate to the fullest possible extent in the repression of piracy on the high seas or in any other place outside the jurisdiction of any State.

Article 101
Definition of piracy

Piracy consists of any of the following acts:

(a) any illegal acts of violence or detention, or any act of depredation, committed for private ends by the crew or the passengers of a private ship or a private aircraft, and directed:
   (i) on the high seas, against another ship or aircraft, or against persons or property on board such ship or aircraft;
   (ii) against a ship, aircraft, persons or property in a place outside the jurisdiction of any State;
(b) any act of voluntary participation in the operation of a ship or of an aircraft with knowledge of facts making it a pirate ship or aircraft;
(c) any act of inciting or of intentionally facilitating an act described in subparagraph (a) or (b).

Article 102
Piracy by a warship, government ship or government aircraft whose crew has mutinied

The acts of piracy, as defined in article 101, committed by a warship, government ship or government aircraft whose crew has mutinied and taken control of the ship or aircraft are assimilated to acts committed by a private ship or aircraft.

Article 103
Definition of a pirate ship or aircraft

A ship or aircraft is considered a pirate ship or aircraft if it is intended by the persons in dominant control to be used for the purpose of committing one of the acts referred to in article 101. The same applies if the ship or aircraft has been used to commit any such act, so long as it remains under the control of the persons guilty of that act.

Article 104
Retention or loss of the nationality of a pirate ship or aircraft

A ship or aircraft may retain its nationality although it has become a pirate ship or aircraft. The retention or loss of nationality is determined by the law of the State from which such nationality was derived.

Article 105
Seizure of a pirate ship or aircraft

On the high seas, or in any other place outside the jurisdiction of any State, every State may seize a pirate ship or aircraft, or a ship or aircraft taken by piracy and under the control of pirates, and arrest the persons and seize the property on board. The courts of the State which carried out the seizure may decide upon the penalties to be imposed, and may also determine the action to be taken with regard to the ships, aircraft or property, subject to the rights of third parties acting in good faith.

Article 106
Liability for seizure without adequate grounds

Where the seizure of a ship or aircraft on suspicion of piracy has been effected without adequate grounds, the State making the seizure shall be liable to the State the nationality of which is possessed by the ship or aircraft for any loss or damage caused by the seizure.

Article 107
Ships and aircraft which are entitled to seize on account of piracy

A seizure on account of piracy may be carried out only by warships or military aircraft, or other ships or aircraft clearly marked and identifiable as being on government service and authorized to that effect.

Article 108
Illicit traffic in narcotic drugs or psychotropic substances

1. All States shall co-operate in the suppression of illicit traffic in narcotic drugs and psychotropic substances engaged in by ships on the high seas contrary to international conventions.

2. Any State which has reasonable grounds for believing that a ship flying its flag is engaged in illicit traffic in narcotic drugs or psychotropic substances may request the co-operation of other States to suppress such traffic.

Article 109
Unauthorized broadcasting from the high seas

1. All States shall co-operate in the suppression of unauthorized broadcasting from the high seas.

2. For the purposes of this Convention, 'unauthorized broadcasting' means the transmission of sound

radio or television broadcasts from a ship or installation on the high seas intended for reception by the general public contrary to international regulations, but excluding the transmission of distress calls.

3. Any person engaged in unauthorized broadcasting may be prosecuted before the court of:

(a) the flag State of the ship;
(b) the State of registry of the installation;
(c) the State of which the person is a national;
(d) any State where the transmissions can be received; or
(e) any State where authorized radio communication is suffering interference.

4. On the high seas, a State having jurisdiction in accordance with paragraph 3 may, in conformity with article 110, arrest any person or ship engaged in unauthorized broadcasting and seize the broadcasting apparatus.

Article 110
Right of visit

1. Except where acts of interference derive from powers conferred by treaty, a warship which encounters on the high seas a foreign ship, other than a ship entitled to complete immunity in accordance with articles 95 and 96, is not justified in boarding it unless there is reasonable ground for suspecting that:

(a) the ship is engaged in piracy;
(b) the ship is engaged in the slave trade;
(c) the ship is engaged in unauthorized broadcasting and the flag State of the warship has jurisdiction under article 109;
(d) the ship is without nationality; or
(e) though flying a foreign flag or refusing to show its flag, the ship is, in reality, of the same nationality as the warship.

2. In the cases provided for in paragraph 1, the warship may proceed to verify the ship's right to fly its flag. To this end, it may send a boat under the command of an officer to the suspected ship. If suspicion remains after the documents have been checked, it may proceed to a further examination on board the ship, which must be carried out with all possible consideration.

3. If the suspicions prove to be unfounded, and provided that the ship boarded has not committed any act justifying them, it shall be compensated for any loss or damage that may have been sustained.

4. These provisions apply *mutatis mutandis* to military aircraft.

5. These provisions also apply to any other duly authorized ships or aircraft clearly marked and identifiable as being on government service.

Article 111
Right of hot pursuit

1. The hot pursuit of a foreign ship may be undertaken when the competent authorities of the coastal State have good reason to believe that the ship has violated the laws and regulations of that State. Such pursuit must be commenced when the foreign ship or one of its boats is within the internal waters, the archipelagic waters, the territorial sea or the contiguous zone of the pursuing State, and may only be continued outside the territorial sea or the contiguous zone if the pursuit has not been interrupted. It is not necessary that, at the time when the foreign ship within the territorial sea or the contiguous zone receives the order to stop, the ship giving the order should likewise be within the territorial sea or the contiguous

zone. If the foreign ship is within a contiguous zone, as defined in article 33, the pursuit may only be undertaken if there has been a violation of the rights for the protection of which the zone was established.

2. The right of hot pursuit shall apply *mutatis mutandis* to violations in the exclusive economic zone or on the continental shelf, including safety zones around continental shelf installations, of the laws and regulations of the coastal State applicable in accordance with this Convention to the exclusive economic zone or the continental shelf, including such safety zones.

3. The right of hot pursuit ceases as soon as the ship pursued enters the territorial sea of its own State or of a third State.

4. Hot pursuit is not deemed to have begun unless the pursuing ship has satisfied itself by such practicable means as may be available that the ship pursued or one of its boats or othr craft working as a team and using the ship pursued as a mother ship is within the limits of the territorial sea, or, as the case may be, within the contiguous zone or the exclusive economic zone or above the continental shelf. The pursuit may only be commenced after a visual or auditory signal to stop has been given at a distance which enables it to be seen or heard by the foreign ship.

5. The right of hot pursuit may be exercised only by warships or military aircraft, or other ships or aircraft clearly marked and identifiable as being on government service and authorized to that effect.

6. Where hot pursuit is effected by an aircraft;

(a) the provisions of paragraphs 1 to 4 shall apply *mutatis mutandis*;
(b) the aircraft giving the order to stop must itself actively pursue the ship until a ship or another aircraft of the coastal State, summoned by the aircraft, arrives to take over the pursuit, unless the aircraft is itself able to arrest the ship. It does not suffice to justify an arrest outside the territorial sea that the ship was merely sighted by the aircraft as an offender or suspected offender, if it was not both ordered to stop and pursued by the aircraft itself or other aircraft or ships which continue the pursuit without interruption.

7. The release of a ship arrested within the jurisdiction of a State and escorted to a port of that State for the purposes of an inquiry before the competent authorities may not be claimed solely on the ground that the ship, in the course of its voyage, was escorted across a portion of the exclusive economic zone or the high seas, if the circumstances rendered this necessary.

8. Where a ship has been stopped or arrested outside the territorial sea in circumstances which do not justify the exercise of the right of hot pursuit, it shall be compensated for any loss or damage that may have been thereby sustained.

Article 112
Right to lay submarine cables and pipelines

1. All States are entitled to lay submarine cables and pipelines on the bed of the high seas beyond the continental shelf.

2. Article 79, paragraph 5, applies to such cables and pipelines.

Article 113
Breaking or injury of a submarine cable or pipeline

Every State shall adopt the laws and regulations necessary to provide that the breaking or injury by a ship flying its flag or by a person subject to its jurisdiction of a submarine cable beneath the high seas done wilfully or through culpable negligence, in such a manner as to be liable to interrupt or obstruct telegraphic or telephonic communications, and similarly the breaking or injury of a submarine pipeline or high-voltage power cable, shall be a punishable offence. This provision shall apply also to conduct calculated or likely to result in such breaking or injury. However, it shall not apply to any break or injury caused by persons who acted merely with the legitimate object of saving their lives or their ships, after having taken all necessary precautions to avoid such break or injury.

Article 114
Breaking or injury by owners of a submarine cable or pipeline of another submarine cable or pipeline

Every State shall adopt the laws and regulations necessary to provide that, if persons subject to its jurisdiction who are the owners of a submarine cable or pipeline beneath the high seas, in laying or repairing that cable or pipeline, cause a break in or injury to another cable or pipeline, they shall bear the cost of the repairs.

Article 115
Indemnity for loss incurred in avoiding injury to a submarine cable or pipeline

Every State shall adopt the laws and regulations necessary to ensure that the owners of ships who can prove that they have sacrificed an anchor, a net or any other fishing gear, in order to avoid injuring a submarine cable or pipeline, shall be indemnified by the owner of the cable or pipeline, provided that the owner of the ship has taken all reasonable precautionary measures beforehand.

SECTION 2. CONSERVATION AND MANAGEMENT OF THE LIVING RESOURCES OF THE HIGH SEAS

Article 116
Right to fish on the high seas

All States have the right for their nationals to engage in fishing on the high seas subject to:

(a) their treaty obligations;
(b) the rights and duties as well as the interests of coastal States provided for, *inter alia,* in article 63, paragraph 2, and articles 64 to 67; and
(c) the provisions of this section.

Article 117
Duty of States to adopt with respect to their nationals measures for the conservation of the living resources of the high seas

All States have the duty to take, or to co-operate with other States in taking, such measures for their respective nationals as may be necessary for the conservation of the living resources of the high seas.

Article 118
Co-operation of States in the conservation and management of living resources

States shall co-operate with each other in the conservation and management of living resources in the areas of the high seas. States whose nationals exploit identical living resources, or different living resources in the same area, shall enter into negotiations with a view to taking the measures necessary for the conservation of the living resources concerned. They shall, as appropriate, co-operate to establish subregional or regional fisheries organizations to this end.

Article 119
Conservation of the living resources of the high seas

1. In determining the allowable catch and establishing other conservation measures for the living resources in the high seas, States shall:

(a) take measures which are designed, on the best scientific evidence available to the States concerned, to maintain or restore populations of harvested species at levels which can produce the maximum sustainable yield, as qualified by relevant environmental and economic factors, including the special requirements of developing States, and taking into account fishing patterns, the interdependence of stocks and any generally recommended international minimum standards, whether subregional, regional or global;

(b) take into consideration the effects on species associated with or dependent upon harvested species with a view to maintaining or restoring populations of such associated or dependent species above levels at which their reproduction may become seriously threatened.

2. Available scientific information, catch and fishing effort statistics, and other data relevant to the conservation of fish stocks shall be contributed and exchanged on a regular basis through competent international organizations, whether subregional, regional or global, where appropriate and with participation by all States concerned.

3. States concerned shall ensure that conservation measures and their implementation do not discriminate in form or in fact against the fishermen of any State.

Article 120
Marine mammals

Article 65 also applies to the conservation and management of marine mammals in the high seas.

PART II

Primary documents

1. Antigua and Barbuda

A. Proclamation No. 20, August 30, 1982
Source: Government Printing Office, Antigua and Barbuda

B. The Territorial Waters Act, 1982 (No. 18 of 1982)
Entered into force: September 1, 1982
Source: Government Printing Office, Antigua and Barbuda

STATUTORY INSTRUMENTS
1982, No. 20

Proclamation dated the 30th day of August, 1982, bringing into operation the Territorial Waters Act, 1982, (No. 18 of 1982).

BY THE GOVERNOR-GENERAL

A PROCLAMATION

Wilfred Jacobs,
Governor-General.

WHEREAS by section 24 of the Territorial Waters Act, 1982 (No. 18 of 1982) it is provided that the said Act shall come into operation on such day as the *Governor-General* may by proclamation appoint.

NOW THEREFORE, I Wilfred Jacobs, Knight Grand Cross of the Most Distinguished Order of St. Michael and St. George, Knight Commander of the Royal Victorian Order, Officer of the Most Excellent Order of the British Empire, One of Her Majesty's Counsel, Governor-General of Antigua and Barbuda, do by this my proclamation appoint the 1st day of September, 1982 as the date on which the said Act shall come into operation.

Given at the *Governor-General's Office St. John's* this 30th day of August, 1982 in the thirty-first year of Her Majesty's reign.

GOD SAVE THE QUEEN!

I Assent,

Wilfred Jacobs,
Governor-General

17th August, 1982

ANTIGUA AND BARBUDA
No. 18 of 1982

An Act to provide for the extension of the limits of the territorial waters of Antigua and Barbuda and Redonda, to make provisions for contiguous, exclusive economic and fishery zones and for matters connected therewith or incidental thereto.

ON PROCLAMATION

ENACTED by the Parliament of Antigua and Burbuda as follows—

Short title

1. This Act may be cited as the Territorial Waters Act, 1982.

Interpretation

2. In this Act—

'baselines' means the baselines of the territorial waters specified in or prescribed under section 4;
'Competent Authority' means the Minister or any person designated by him as the Competent Authority for the purposes of this Act;
'exclusive economic zone' means the exclusive economic zone of Antigua and Barbuda and Redonda as defined in section 7;
'fishery zone' means the fishery zone of Antigua and Barbuda and Redonda as defined in section 8;
'foreign ship' means the ship of a foreign state;
'foreign state' means a state other than Antigua and Barbuda;
'innocent passage' means passage which is not deemed to be prejudicial to the peace, good order or security of Antigua and Barbuda;
'Internal waters' means the internal waters of Antigua and Barbuda and Redonda as defined in section 5;
'low-water line' means the low-water line of the coasts of Antigua and Barbuda and Redonda at mean low-water spring tide;
'Minister' means the Minister responsible for External Affairs;
'nautical mile' means the international nautical mile;
'passage' means the navigation of a ship in territorial waters without stopping or hovering, but includes stopping, hovering and anchoring in so far as the same are rendered necessary by force majeure or by reason of distress or for the purpose of affording assistance to persons, ships or aircraft in danger or distress;

'ship' includes vessel, boat or sea-craft of any kind;

'submarine areas' includes the sea-bed and subsoil thereof;

'territorial waters' means the territorial waters of Antigua and Barbuda and Redonda as defined in section 3.

Limits of Territorial Waters

3. (1) Subject to the provisions of subsections (2), (3), (4), (5) and (6), of this section, the territorial waters of Antigua and Barbuda and Redonda comprise those areas of the sea, having as their landward limit the baseline specified by section 4 or prescribed under that section, as the case may be, and as their seaward limit a boundary line which at every point is a distance of twelve nautical miles or such other distance from the nearest point of those baselines as the Minister by order prescribes.

(2) The Minister may by order prescribe that by reason of historical, geographical or other special circumstances as respects Antigua and Barbuda and any foreign state, the territorial waters shall not be deemed to extend beyond the median line, that is to say, a line every point of which is equidistant from the nearest points of the baselines and the corresponding baselines of the foreign state concerned.

(3) No order may be made under subsection (2) unless, before that order is made, agreement has been reached in terms of the provisions of subsection (2), between Antigua and Barbuda and the foreign state concerned.

(4) Notwithstanding the provisions of any other law, there shall be provision in every order made under subsection (2) that, pursuant to agreement as in subsection (3), a law in terms similar to the provisions of the order—

(i) forms part of the law of the foreign state concerned at the date upon which the order is made; or

(ii) will form part of the law of that foreign state upon such date as is specified in the order being a date subsequent to the date upon which the order is made.

(5) Where an order under subsection (2) makes provision as in subsection (4) (i), that order shall come into operation as law in Antigua and Barbuda on the date upon which it is published in the *Gazette*; and where such an order makes provision as in subsection (4) (ii), it shall come into operation as law in Antigua and Barbuda on the date specified in the order as being the date upon which a law of the foreign state concerned in terms similar to the provisions of the order will form part of the law of that foreign state.

(6) An order made under and by virtue of subsection (2) shall, unless previously revoked, cease to have effect as law in Antigua and Barbuda at the same time as any similar law as above in this section of any foreign state concerned ceases to have effect as law in that foreign state.

(7) The territorial waters including the submarine areas thereof, form part of the territory of Antigua and Barbuda.

(8) An order made under this section shall be subject to affirmative resolution of the Legislature and shall be judicially noticed.

Baselines of Territorial Waters

4. (1) Subject to subsection (2), the low water line along the coasts of Antigua and Barbuda and Redonda shall be the baselines of the territorial waters.

(2) The Minister may, in the place of the baselines referred to in subsection (1), by order prescribe other baselines making use of a mixture of straight lines drawn from points on the coasts of Antigua and Barbuda and Redonda and the low water line.

(3) Where baselines are prescribed under subsection (2) the Minister shall cause the baselines together with the seaward boundary of the territorial waters to be marked on a scaled map or chart and such map or chart shall be judicially noticed for all purposes of the law as indicating the baselines from which the

territorial waters shall be measured and the boundaries breadth and limit of the territorial waters.

(4) The Minister shall make provision for the safe custody of the map or chart referred to in subsection (3) and shall by notice specify the place where it may be open to inspection by the public and the place where certified copies thereof may be obtained.

(5) For the purposes of this Act, permanent harbour works which form a part of the harbour, dock or port system of Antigua and Barbuda shall be treated as forming part of the coasts of Antigua and Barbuda and Redonda.

Internal waters

5. The areas of the sea which are on the landward side of the baselines specified in section 4 or prescribed under that section, as the case may be, are the internal waters and, together with the submarine areas thereof, form part of the territory of Antigua and Barbuda.

Contiguous zone

6. (1) The contiguous zone to the territorial waters comprises those areas of the sea that are contiguous to the territorial waters, having as their seaward limit a boundary line which at every point is a distance of twenty-four nautical miles or such other distance from the nearest point of the baselines as the Minister by order prescribes.

(2) It shall be lawful for Government to exercise within the contiguous zone such sovereign rights as Government may, from time to time, deem necessary to prevent the infringement of any customs, fiscal, immigration, or sanitary law both within Antigua and Barbuda and the territorial waters.

Exclusive economic zone

7. The exclusive economic zone comprises those areas of the sea and of the submarine area that are beyond and adjacent to the territorial waters, having as their seaward limit a boundary line which at every point is a distance of two hundred nautical miles or such other distance from the nearest point of the baselines as the Minister by order prescribes.

Fishery zone

8. The fishery zone comprises those areas of the sea that are beyond and adjacent to the territorial waters, having as their seaward limit a boundary line which at every point is a distance of two hundred nautical miles or such other distance from the nearest point of the baselines as the Minister by order prescribes.

Jurisdiction in territorial waters

9. Antigua and Barbuda shall exercise sovereignty in and over the territorial waters and the internal waters and such sovereignty shall extend to the submarine areas thereof.

Jurisdiction in exclusive economic zone

10. In the exclusive economic zone Antigua and Barbuda shall, subject to international law, exercise:—

- *(a)* sovereign rights for the purpose of exploration, exploitation, conservation and management of the natural resources, both living and nonliving, of the exclusive economic zone as well as sovereign rights with regard to producing energy from tides, winds and currents in the exclusive economic zone;
- *(b)* jurisdiction with regard to
  - (i) the establishment and use of artificial islands, installations and structures;
  - (ii) marine scientific research, and
  - (iii) the protection and preservation of the marine environment; and
- *(c)* such other rights and duties for which provision is made by international law.

Jurisdiction in fishery zone

11. In the fishery zone Antigua and Barbuda shall exercise the sovereign right and exclusive authority to explore and exploit, conserve and manage the fishery resources of the fishery zone and the submarine areas thereof in accordance with international law.

International activities in exclusive economic zone

12. Antigua and Barbuda recognises the freedoms of navigation and of the laying of submarine cables and pipelines and other related activities within the exclusive economic zone in accordance with the principles, practice and provisions of international law.

Negotiating maritime boundaries

13. Where the sea or waters of any foreign state are adjacent or opposite to the territorial waters or the exclusive economic zone and there is any dispute, difference or disagreement between that foreign state and Government concerning any matter or thing relating to the seaward limits of the territorial waters or the exclusive economic zone, it shall be lawful for Government to enter into negotiations with that foreign state with a view to resolving or otherwise settling such dispute, difference or disagreement.

Entitlement to right of innocent passage

14. (1) Subject to subsection (2) and section 15 (1), a foreign ship shall be entitled to enjoy the right of innocent passage in territorial waters.

(2) A foreign ship of war shall not navigate in territorial waters without the prior permission of the Competent Authority obtained by the State to which the ship belongs.

Non-innocent passage

15. (1) Subject to subsection (2), the passage of a foreign ship shall be deemed to be prejudicial to the peace, good order or security of Antigua and Barbuda if, without the prior permission of the Competent Authority obtained by the captain or person in charge of the ship, the ship while in territorial waters, engages in any of the following activities:—

(a) exercises or practises with weaponry of any kind;
(b) any act aimed at collecting information relating to the defence, security or economic or social conditions and circumstances of Antigua and Barbuda;
(c) the taking on board or off-loading of any person, commodity or currency in breach of any law relating to exchange control, customs, immigration, health or drugs and therapeutic substances;
(d) any Act of pollution calculated to or likely to cause damage or harm to Antigua and Barbuda, its resources or its marine environment;
(e) fishing or extracting living or non-living resources;
(f) the carrying out of research of whatever kind or survey activities;
(g) any act aimed at interfering with any system of communication or telecommunication whether such system is on land, on the sea or under it;
(h) being a submarine or other underwater ship, underwater navigation;
(i) any other activity not having a direct bearing on passage.

(2) The passage of a foreign ship of war in territorial waters shall be deemed to be prejudicial to the peace, good order or security of Antigua and Barbuda if the ship navigates in territorial waters without the permission required by section 14 (2).

Power of police and authorised persons

16. (1) Where a foreign ship engages in any of the activities specified in section 15 (1) or where a member of the Police Force or person authorised by the Minister in writing suspects upon reasonable grounds that a foreign ship is engaged in any such activity, such member of the Police Force or authorised person may—

(*a*) stop and board the offending ship for the purpose of carrying out enquiries and investigations;
(*b*) without a warrant arrest the offending ship and bring it to a port in Antigua and Barbuda;
(*c*) without a warrant arrest the captain and any person on board the ship participating in the activity of the ship which is deemed to be prejudicial to the peace, good order or security of Antigua and Barbuda.

(2) Where the passage of a foreign ship is deemed to be prejudicial to the peace, good order or security of Antigua and Barbuda, the captain or other person in charge of such ship and any person participating in the activities of the ship which is deemed to be so prejudicial, is guilty of an offence under this Act.

Immunity

17. (1) Where the passage of a foreign ship is deemed to be prejudicial to the peace, good order or security of Antigua and Barbuda and the ship or any person on board thereof who participates in the activity which is deemed to be prejudicial is entitled to state or other immunity recognised by law, the flag state of such ship and the state of nationality of such person shall be deemed to bear international responsibility for the activity of the ship.

(2) Where the flag state of a ship or the state of nationality of a person is deemed to bear international responsibility under this section, the Minister shall take all steps possible to obtain redress under international law.

Jurisdiction

18. (1) For the purposes of the exercise of the jurisdiction of the courts of Antigua and Barbuda, the territory of Antigua and Barbuda shall include the internal waters and the territorial waters.

(2) Where any offence punishable on summary conviction is committed or suspected to have been committed within or in relation to the internal waters or the territorial waters, the offence may be dealt with and determined by a magistrate appointed to any magisterial District, and such magistrate shall have and exercise all the powers, privileges, rights and jurisdiction as are conferred on him by the Magistrate's Code of Procedure Act.

Cap. 48

(3) The quasi-criminal and the civil jurisdiction conferred on a magistrate by the Magistrate's Code of Procedure Act shall in relation to the internal waters and the territorial waters be exercised by a magistrate appointed to any magisterial District.

(4) The jurisdiction conferred on any court under this Act shall be without prejudice to any jurisdiction conferred on or exercisable by such court apart from this Act.

Regulations

19. (1) The Minister may make regulations—

(*a*) for the safety of navigation and the regulation of marine traffic;
(*b*) for the conservation of the living resources of the sea;
(*c*) for the preservation of the marine environment of Antigua and Barbuda and the prevention and control of pollution thereto;
(*d*) for the regulation of fishing;
(*e*) relating to the grant of permits and the conditions to be attached thereto for fishing by nationals of foreign states and by means of foreign ships;
(*f*) for the inspection and admission in evidence before the courts of the chart or map to which

section 4 refers or any part thereof;

(g) prescribing the fees to be paid for permits granted in accordance with regulations made under paragraph *(e)*;

(h) generally, for regulating the use of the internal waters and the territorial waters including prescribing the fees to be paid for any activity in relation thereto;

(i) providing for the forfeiture to the Crown of any ship engaged, or any equipment used, in any of the activities specified in section 15; and

(j) annexing to the contravention of any regulation made under this section a punishment on summary conviction of a fine of $5,000 or of imprisonment for a term of 2 years or both.

(2) Regulations made under this section shall be subject to affirmative resolution of the Legislature and shall be judicially noticed.

Offence

20. (1) A person who assaults or obstructs a person acting under the authority of this Act or the regulations is guilty of an offence under this Act.

(2) A person who is guilty of an offence under subsection (1) or section 16 (2) is liable.—

(a) a conviction on indictment to a fine of $10,000 or imprisonment for a term of 5 years or both; or

(b) on summary conviction to a fine of $5,000 or imprisonment for a term of 2 years or both.

(3) The court may in addition to any penalty which it may impose under this section for an offence under section 16 (2), order the forfeiture to the Crown of any ship engaged, or equipment used, in any activity which is the subject of the offence.

Binding of the Crown

21. This Act binds the Crown.

Application of laws

22. (1) Any reference in an enactment or law having effect as a part of the law of Antigua and Barbuda prior to the commencement of this Act, to coastal waters, territorial waters, waters of Antigua and Barbuda and Redonda or any analagous expression in whatever terms used, shall be construed as a reference to internal waters and territorial waters.

(2) Any reference in any enactment or law having effect as a part of the law of Antigua and Barbuda prior to the commencement of this Act to a distance of three miles or a longer or shorter distance in relation to coastal waters, territorial waters, waters of Antigua and Barbuda and Redonda or any analagous expression in whatever terms used, shall be construed as a reference to a distance of twelve nautical miles or such other distance as may be prescribed under section 3.

Repeal and amendments, 41 & 42 Vict. c. 73

23. (1) The Territorial Waters Jurisdiction Act, 1878 of the United Kingdom Parliament and any Act of the United Kingdom Parliament altering that Act, in so far as they form part of the law of Antigua and Barbuda, are repealed.

Schedule

(2) The enactments specified in the first column of the Schedule are amended in the respects specified in the second column thereof.

Commencement

24. This Act shall come into operation on such day as the Governor-General may by proclamation appoint.

Passed the House of Representatives the 30th day of June, 1982.

C.L. Murray,
Speaker.
L.A. Dowe,
Clerk to the House of Representatives.

Passed the Senate this 19th day of July, 1982.

B.T. Carrott,
President.
L.A. Dowe,
Clerk to the Senate.

SCHEDULE (Section 23(2)

First Column	Second Column
The Magistrate's Code of Procedure Act–Cap. 48	In section 38, insert 'the Government of Antigua and Barbuda or' immediately after 'in which'.
The Interpretation Act, 1982.	Insert in the appropriate alphabetical order in section 57 the following definition— 'internal waters' means the internal waters of Antigua and Barbuda and Redonda as defined in section 5 of the Territorial Waters Act, 1982.

2. Bangladesh

A. Territorial Waters and Maritime Zones Act, 1974
Entered into force: April 13, 1974.
Source: *The Bangladesh Gazette, Extra,* Feb. 14, 1974
(Part V, pp. 2334–2337).
B. Ministry of Foreign Affairs Declaration No. LT-I/3/74, April 13, 1974

ACT No. XXVI of 1974

An Act to provide for the declaration of the territorial waters and maritime zones

WHEREAS clause (2) of Article 143 of the Constitution provides that Parliament may, from time to time, by law provide for the determination of the territorial waters and the continental shelf of Bangladesh;

AND WHEREAS it is necessary to provide for the declaration of the territorial waters, continental shelf and other maritime zones and for matter ancillary thereto;

It is hereby enacted as follows:—

Short title

1. This Act may be called the Territorial Waters and Maritime Zones Act, 1974.

Definitions

2. In this Act, unless there is anything repugnant to the subject or context,—

(a) 'conservation zone' means a conservation zone established under section 6;
(b) 'contiguous zone' means the zone of the high seas declared by section 4 to be the contiguous zone of Bangladesh;
(c) 'continental shelf' means the continental shelf of Bangladesh referred to in section 7;
(d) 'economic zone' means the zone of the high seas declared under section 5 to be the economic zone of Bangladesh;
(e) 'territorial waters' means the limits of sea declared under section 3 to be the territorial waters of Bangladesh.

Territorial waters

3. (1) The Government may, by notification in the official Gazette, declare the limits of the sea beyond the land territory and internal waters of Bangladesh which shall be the territorial waters of Bangladesh specifying in the notification the baseline—

(a) from which such limits shall be measured; and
(b) the waters on the landward side of which shall form part of the internal waters of Bangladesh.

(2) Where a single island, rock or a composite group thereof constituting the part of the territory of Bangladesh is situated seawards from the main coast or baseline, territorial waters shall extend to the limits declared by notification under sub-section (1) measured from the low waterline along the coast of such island, rock or composite group.

(3) The Sovereignty of the Republic extends to the territorial waters as well as to the air space over and the bed and subsoil of, such waters.

(4) No foreign ship shall, unless it enjoys the right of innocent passage, pass through the territorial waters.

(5) Foreign ship having the right of innocent passage through the territorial waters shall, while exercising such right, observe the laws and rules in force in Bangladesh.

(6) The Government may, by notification in the official Gazette, suspend, in the specified areas of the territorial waters, the innocent passage of any ship if it is of opinion that such suspension is necessary for the security of the Republic.

(7) No foreign warship shall pass through the territorial waters except with the previous permission of the Government.

(8) The Government may take such steps as may be necessary—

(a) to prevent the passage through the territorial waters of any foreign ship having no right of innocent passage;
(b) to prevent and punish the contravention of any law or rule in force in Bangladesh by any foreign ship exercising the right of innocent passage;
(c) to prevent the passage of any foreign warship without previous permission of Government; and
(d) to prevent and punish any activity which is prejudicial to the security or interest of the Republic.

Explanation

In this section 'warship' includes any surface or sub-surface vessel or craft which is or may be used for the purpose of naval warfare.

Contiguous zone

4. (1) The zone of the high seas contiguous to the territorial waters and extending seawards to a line six nautical miles measured from the outer limits of the territorial waters is hereby declared to be the contiguous zone of Bangladesh.

(2) The Government may exercise such powers and take such measures in or in respect of the contiguous zone as it may consider necessary to prevent and punish the contravening of, and attempt to contravene, any law or regulation in force in Bangladesh relating to—

(a) the security of the Republic;
(b) the immigration and sanitation; and
(c) customs and other fiscal matters.

Economic zone

5. (1) The Government may, by notification in the official Gazette, declare any zone of the high seas adjacent to the territorial waters to be the economic zone of Bangladesh specifying therein the limits of such zone.

(2) All natural resources within the economic zone, both living and non-living, on or under the seabed and subsoil or on the water surface or within the water column shall vest exclusively in the Republic.

(3) Nothing in sub-section (2) shall be deemed to affect fishing within the economic zone by a citizen of Bangladesh who uses for the purpose vessels which are not mechanically propelled.

Conservation zone

6. The Government may, with a view to the maintenance of the productivity of the living resources of the sea, by notification in the official Gazette, establish conservation zones in such areas of the sea adjacent to the territorial waters as may be specified in the notification and may take such conservation measures in any zone so established as it may deem appropriate for the purpose including measures to protect the living resources of the sea from indiscriminate exploitation, depletion or destruction.

Continental shelf

7. (1) The continental shelf of Bangladesh comprises—

(a) the seabed and subsoil of the submarine area adjacent to the coast of Bangladesh but beyond the limits of the territorial waters up to the outer limits of the continental margin bordering on the ocean basin or abyssal floor; and

(b) the seabed and subsoil of the analogous submarine areas adjacent to the coasts of any island, rock or any composite group thereof constituting part of the territory of Bangladesh.

(2) Subject to sub-section (1), the Government may, by notification in the official Gazette, specify the limits thereof.

(3) No person shall, except under and in accordance with the terms of, a licence or permission granted by Government explore or exploit any resources of the continental shelf or carry out any search or excavation or conduct any research within the limits of the continental shelf:

Provided that no such licence or permission shall be necessary for fishing by a citizen of Bangladesh who uses for the purpose vessels which are not mechanically propelled.

Explanation

Resources of the continental shelf include mineral and other non-living resources together with living organisms belonging to sedentary species, that is to say, organisms which at the harvestable stage, either are immobile on or under the seabed or are unable to move except in constant physical contact with the seabed or the subsoil.

(4) The Government may construct, maintain or operate within the continental shelf installations and other devices necessary for the exploration and exploitation of its resouces.

Control of pollution

8. The Government may, with a view to preventing and controlling marine pollution and preserving the quality and ecological balance in the marine environment in the high seas adjacent to the territorial waters, take such measures as it may deem appropriate for the purpose.

Power to make rules

9. (1) The Government may make rules for carrying out the purposes of this Act.

(2) In particular and without prejudice to the generality of the foregoing power, such rules may provide—

(a) for the regulation of the conduct of any person in or upon the territorial waters, contiguous zone, economic zone, conservation zone and continental shelf;

(b) for measures to protect, use and exploit the resources of the economic zone;

(c) for conservation measures to protect the living resources of the sea;

(d) for measures regulating the exploration and exploitation of resources within the continental shelf;

(e) for measures designed to prevent and control of marine pollution of the high seas.

(3) In making any rule under this section the Government may provide that a contravention of the rule shall be punishable with imprisonment which may extend to one year or with fine which may extend to five thousand takas.

MINISTRY OF FOREIGN AFFAIRS
Dacca, April 13, 1974

No. LT-I/3/74

In exercise of the powers conferred by sub-section (1) of section 3 of the Territorial Waters and Maritime Zones Act, 1974 (Act No. XXVI of 1974), and in supersession of any previous declaration on the subject, the Government is pleased to declare that the limits of the sea specified in paragraph 2 beyond the land territory and internal waters of Bangladesh shall be the territorial waters of Bangladesh.

2. The limits of the sea referred to in paragraph 1 shall be twelve nautical miles measured seaward and the baselines set out in paragraph 3 so that each point of the outer limit of the sea to the nearest point inward on the baselines is twelve nautical miles.

3. The baselines from which territorial waters shall be measured seaward are the straight lines linking sucesssively the baseline points set out below:

Baseline point	Geographical Co-ordinates baseline point	
	Latitude	Longitude
No. 1	21°12′ 00″ N.	89°06′ 45″ E.
No. 2	21°15′ 00″ N.	89°16′ 00″ E.
No. 3	21°29′ 00″ N.	89°36′ 00″ E.
No. 4	21°21′ 00″ N.	89°55′ 00″ E.
No. 5	21°11′ 00″ N.	90°33′ 00″ E.
No. 6	21°07′ 30″ N.	91°06′ 00″ E.
No. 7	21°10′ 00″ N.	91°56′ 00″ E.
No. 8	20°21′ 45″ N.	92°17′ 30″ E.

No. LT-1/3/74. – In exercise of the powers conferred by sub-section (1) of section 5 of the Territorial Waters and Maritime Zones Act, 1974 (Act No. XXVI of 1974), the Government is pleased to declare that the Zone of the high seas extending to 200 nautical miles measured from the baselines shall be the economic zone of Bangladesh.

By order of the President

FAKHRUDDIN AHMED

Additional Foreign Secretary.

3. Barbados

A. Marine Boundaries and Jurisdiction Act, 1978–3.
Entered into force: January 1, 1979
Source: *Supplement to Official Gazette,* March 2, 1978
B. Proclamation of December 29, 1978.
Source: *Supplement to Official Gazette,* No. 2, January 4, 1979

MARINE BOUNDARIES AND JURISDICTION ACT. 1978–3

Arrangement of Sections

Section

PART V
General

SCHEDULE

I assent
D.H.L. WARD
Governor-General
25th February, 1978.

1978–3

An Act to provide for the establishment of Marine Boundaries and Jurisdiction.

(By Proclamation) Commencement.

ENACTED by the Parliament of Barbados as follows—

PART I
Preliminary

Short title

1. This Act may be cited as the Marine Boundaries and Jurisdiction Act, 1978.

Interpretation

2. For the purposes of this Act—

'Barbadian vessel' or 'Barbadian structure' means a vessel or structure, as the case may be—

(a) wholly owned by a citizen of Barbados or by a body corporate whose members or, if that body corporate is a company, whose shareholders, as the case may be, are all citizens of Barbados, or

(b) certified in writing by the Cabinet as having such substantial economic connections with Barbados in relation to its ownership as to be deemed, for the purposes of this Act, to be a Barbadian vessel or Barbadian structure, as the case may be;

Act 1977–26

'baselines' has the meaning assigned to it by section 4 of the Barbados Territorial Waters Act, 1977;

'Exclusive Economic Zone' or 'Zone' means the marine zone established by section 3 (1);

'fish' includes marine fishes, *Crustacea,* sea-eggs, whales, porpoises, *Mollusca* or other marine animals and includes marine plant life;

'fishing' means—

(*a*) the catching, taking or harvesting of fish;

(*b*) any activity reasonably expected to result in the catching, taking or harvesting of fish; or

(*c*) any operation at sea in connection with, or in preparation for, the catching, taking or harvesting of fish or an activity referred to in paragraph (b);

'fishing vessel' means any ship, vessel, boat or other craft used for, or of a type normally used for, fishing or aiding or assisting another vessel at sea in the performance of any activity relating to fishing;
'foreign fishing vessel', 'foreign vessel', or 'foreign structure' means a fishing vessel, vessel or structure, as the case may be, of a foreign State;
'foreign State' means a State other than Barbados;

'internal waters' has the meaning assigned to it by section 5 of the Barbados Territorial Waters Act, 1977;
'marine conservation officer' means a person designated a marine conservation officer under section 14;
'mile' means the international nautical mile;
'ship' includes vessel, boat or other sea-going or ocean-going craft;
'structure' includes any artificial island, off-shore terminal or off-shore installation;
'territorial waters', in relation to Barbados, has the meaning assigned to it by section 3 of the Barbados Territorial Waters Act, 1977, and includes internal waters.

PART II
Economic Zone

Exclusive Economic Zone

3. (1) There is established, contiguous to the territorial waters, a marine zone to be known as the Exclusive Economic Zone having as its inner limit the boundary line of the seaward limit of the territorial waters and as its outer limit a boundary line which, subject to subsection (3), at every point is a distance of 200 miles from the nearest point of the baselines of the territorial waters or such other distance from the nearest point of those baselines as the Minister responsible for External Affairs, by order, prescribes.

(2) An order made under subsection (1) is subject to affirmative resolution, and shall be judicially noticed.

(3) Notwithstanding subsection (1), where the median line as defined by subsection (4) between Barbados and any adjacent or opposite State is less than 200 miles from the baselines of the territorial waters, the outer boundary limit of the Zone shall be that fixed by agreement between Barbados and that other State, but where there is no such agreement, the outer boundary limit shall be the median line.

(4) The median line is a line every point of which is equidistant from the nearest points of the baselines of the territorial waters, on the one hand, and the corresponding baselines of the territorial waters of any adjacent or opposite State as recognised by the Minister, on the other hand.

(5) An agreement entered into pursuant to subsection (3) shall be laid before Parliament, and shall be judicially noticed.

Marking of boundary lines of Zone on charts or maps

4. (1) The Minister responsible for External Affairs shall cause the boundary lines of the Zone to be marked on a scaled map or chart, and that map or chart shall be judicially noticed.

(2) The Minister responsible for External Affairs shall make provision for the safe custody of the map or chart referred to in subsection (1), and shall, by notice, specify the place where any person may inspect that map or chart or purchase a certified copy thereof.

Rights in, and jurisdiction over, Zone

5. There is vested in the Government of Barbados—

(a) all rights in, and jurisdiction over, the Zone in respect of—

(i) the exploration, exploitation, conservation, protection or management of the natural living and non-living resources of the sea-bed, subsoil and superjacent waters,

(ii) the construction, maintenance or use of structures or devices relating to the exploration or exploitation of the resources of the Zone, the regulation and safety of shipping, or any other economic purpose,

(iii) the authorisation, regulation or control of scientific research,

(iv) the preservation and protection of the marine environment and the prevention and control of marine pollution,

(v) all other activities relating to the economic exploration and exploitation of the Zone; and

(b) all other rights in, and jurisdiction over, the Zone recognised by international law.

Exploitation of resources of Zone

6. (1) Subject to this Act, no person shall within the Zone, except under or in accordance with an agreement with the Government of Barbados or a permit granted by the Cabinet—

(a) explore or exploit any resources thereof;
(b) carry out any search or excavation;
(c) conduct any research;
(d) drill in or construct, maintain or operate any structure or device; or
(e) carry out any economic activity.

(2) This section does not apply to fishing by a citizen of Barbados in or from a Barbadian vessel.

(3) Any person who contravenes this section is guilty of an offence and liable—

(a) on conviction on indictment, to a fine of $ 50,000 or imprisonment for a term of 5 years or both; or

(b) on summary conviction, to a fine of $ 20,000 or imprisonment for a term of 2 years or both,

and, in addition, the court may order the forfeiture of any vessel, structure, equipment, device or thing in connection with which the offence was committed.

Freedom of navigation, overflight, and laying of cables etc.

7. Subject to sections 8 and 11, ships and aircraft of all states are not, in or over the Zone, as the case may be, restricted in or prohibited from the enjoyment of the freedom of navigation, overflight, the laying of cables and pipelines and the other lawful use, of the sea related to navigation and communication recognised by international law.

Application of certain enactments of Zone

8. (1) The Governor-General may, by order, with such exceptions and modifications as may be specified in the order, extend the application of any enactment to the Zone or any part thereof, and an enactment so extended shall have effect in relation to the Zone as if it had been enacted by this Act.

(2) An order made under this section is subject to affirmative resolution, and shall be judicially noticed.

Jurisdiction of courts

9. (1) The jurisdiction and powers of the courts extend to the Zone for the purpose of giving effect to the provisions of this Act and any other enactment extended to the Zone under section 8 as if the Zone were a part of the territory of Barbados.

(2) Where an offence is, by virtue of this Act or any enactment extended to the Zone under section 8, punishable on summary conviction or indictment, it may be enquired into or determined, as the case may be, by a magistrate assigned to any magistrial district, and that magistrate has, in respect of the offence, all the powers, privileges, rights and jurisdiction, conferred on him by the Magistrates Jurisdiction and Procedure Act.

(3) The quasi-criminal and the civil jurisdiction conferred on a magistrate by the Magistrates Jurisdiction and Procedure Act is, in relation to the Zone, exercisable by a magistrate assigned to any magisterial district.

(4) The jurisdiction and power conferred on the courts under this Act do not affect any jurisdiction or powers conferred on, or exercisable by, those courts under any other law.

Locus of offence etc.

10. (1) In any proceedings in a court in relation to the Zone, the averment that an offence was committed or that an act was done within the limits of the Zone shall, until the contrary is proved, be deemed to be *prima facie* evidence that the *locus in quo* was within the Zone.

(2) An incident shall, for the purposes of any law conferring jurisdiction on a court in Barbados, be deemed to have occurred in Barbados if—

(a) that incident occurs in, on, under above or in relation to any vessel, structure or device or any waters within 500 yards of that structure or device, in the Zone; or
(b) that incident, if having occurred in Barbados, would be an offence or give rise to quasi-criminal proceedings or a civil cause of action.

PART III
Fishing in the Zone

Permission to fish in the Zone or territorial waters

11. (1) No person shall engage in fishing within the Zone or the territorial waters unless—

(a) he is a citizen of Barbados;
(b) he is the holder of a valid permit granted under subsection (4); or
(c) there is in existence in relation to him an agreement with the Government of Barbados.

(2) The master or other person in charge of a foreign vessel shall not permit that vessel to be used for the purpose of fishing in the Zone or the territorial waters unless there is on board that vessel a valid permit granted under subsection (4).

(3) The master or other person in charge of a foreign fishing vessel on board of which there is not a valid permit granted under this section in respect of that vessel shall not, except for the purpose of exercising the freedom of navigation referred to in section 7 or granted pursuant to an agreement under section 6, permit or cause that vessel to enter the Zone; and where a vessel enters the Zone in accordance with the terms of that permit or agreement, that master or other person shall not cause or permit the vessel to remain in the Zone after the purpose for which it entered the Zone has been fulfilled or the agreement has expired.

(4) The Cabinet may—

(a) grant to a person, who is not a citizen of Barbados; or
(b) grant in respect of a foreign fishing vessel,

a permit to engage in fishing within the Zone, the territorial waters, or any designated part thereof.

(5) Any person who contravenes this section or a term or condition of a permit granted under this Act is guilty of an offence and liable on summary conviction to a fine of $ 20,000 or imprisonment for a term of 2 years or both, and, in addition, the court may order the forfeiture of any vessel, fish, fishing gear, equipment, device or thing in connection with which the offence was committed.

Form, content of permit

12. (1) A permit granted under section 11 in respect of a foreign vessel may contain—

(a) the name of the owner or charterer;
(b) the name of the vessel;
(c) a description of the vessel;
(d) a description of the area designated for fishing;
(e) the periods or times allowed for fishing and the number of voyages authorised;
(f) the descriptions and quantities of fish permitted to be taken;
(g) the method of fishing;
(h) conditions respecting the landing of fish or parts of fish;
(i) the name of the port of place for the landing of fish caught;
(j) the permitted use of any fish caught;
(k) any other term or condition, including fees and charges payable, approved by Cabinet.

Variation, revocation or suspension of permit

13. A permit granted under section 11 may be varied, suspended or revoked, if it appears necessary or expedient to the Cabinet.

PART IV

Marine Conservation Officers

14. For the purposes of this Act, the following persons are designated marine conservation officers—

(a) fisheries officers of the Ministry responsible for Fisheries;
(b) members of the Defence Force of Barbados;
(c) members of the Police Force;
(d) officers of Customs;
(e) officers of the Coast Guard; and
(f) any other person approved by Cabinet.

15. (1) A marine conservation officer may, in performing his duties, exercise all the powers conferred on him by this Act in respect of—

(a) a Barbadian vessel or Barbadian structure that is at sea or in port; or
(b) a foreign vessel or foreign structure that he reasonably suspects of being used in connection with fishing or any other activity carried on in contravention of this Act or the regulations.

(2) In the performance of his duties under this section, a marine conservation officer may—

(a) reasonably call on any person to assist him;
(b) use such force as is reasonably necessary;
(c) require any person to do anything that appears reasonably necessary for the purpose of facilitating the performance of those duties;
(d) order that any vessel or structure be stopped;
(e) board any vessel or structure;

(f) search or examine any vessel or structure or any fish, equipment or thing on board thereof;
(g) require any person on board a vessel or structure to produce any document or thing relating to that vessel or structure or the persons on board thereof.

(3) A marine conservation officer who has reasonable grounds to suspect that an offence has been committed under this Act or the regulations by any person, including any person on board a vessel or structure, may, without warrant or other process—

(a) seize the vessel or structure together with any fish, fishing gear or other equipment suspected of being used in the commission of the offence; and
(b) detain the person he suspects.

(4) Where a vessel, structure or thing is seized or a person is detained under subsection (3), a marine conservation officer shall, where possible, take the vessel, structure, thing or person as soon as practicable to a Barbadian port, and within a reasonable time cause the person detained to be brought before a magistrate's court to answer a charge in connection with the offence that gave rise to the seizure or detention.

(5) A court may order that any vessel, structure, fishing gear or other equipment, device or thing seized under subsection (3) be forfeited where the owner thereof is unknown and no claim thereto is made within 1 month of the seizure under that subsection.

Sale of fish likely to spoil

16. (1) A marine conservation officer may, to avoid spoilage or decay of any fish he seizes under section 15, sell that fish in such manner as a fisheries officer of the Ministry responsible for Fisheries directs.

(2) All moneys resulting from a sale of fish under subsection (1) shall be paid into the Consolidated Fund.

(3) A marine conservation officer who makes a sale of fish under subsection (1) shall give to the person from whom he seized the fish a receipt containing—

(a) the date of the sale;
(b) the quantity of fish;
(c) the amount realised by the sale,

and the receipt shall be signed by the officer.

(4) Where a court dismisses a charge against a person brought before it under section 15, it shall, in any case where the fish in the possession of that person was sold, order compensation not exceeding the net amount realised by the sale to be paid to that person.

(5) Compensation payable under subsection (4) shall be charged on, and paid out of, the Consolidated Fund.

Exemption from liability

17. No liability attaches to the Crown, a marine conservation officer or fisheries officer in respect of acts done by that officer in good faith in the performance of his duties under this Act.

PART V
General

General offences

18. Any person who—

(*a*) assaults, resists, obstructs or intimidates a marine conservation officer or any person assisting him, in the execution of his duty;

(*b*) uses indecent, abusive or insulting language to a marine conservation officer in the execution of his duty;

(*c*) interferes with or hinders a marine conservation officer in the execution of his duty;

(*d*) by any gratuity, bribe, promise or other inducement, prevents a marine conservation officer from carrying out his duty;

(*e*) without the authority of a marine conservation officer, removes, alters or interferes with any articles seized under section 15;

(*f*) contravenes any provision of this Act for which no penalty is provided or the regulations,

is guilty of an offence and liable on summary conviction to a fine of $ 5,000 or imprisonment for a term of 2 years or both and, in addition, the court may order the forfeiture of any vessel, structure, equipment, device or thing in connection with which the offence was committed.

Return of property seized

19. Subject to section 16, a court may order that property seized under subsection (3) of section 15 be returned to the person from whom it was taken or to a person named by that person where—

(*a*) the court dismisses a charge brought against that person under his Act or the regulations, and it is of the opinion that the property can be returned consistently with the interests of justice; or

(*b*) no charge has been brought against any person within a reasonable time after a seizure has been effected under that subsection.

Regulations

20. (1) The Cabinet may make regulations generally for carrying into effect the provisions of this Act, and in particular respecting—

(*a*) any activity relating to the exploration, exploitation and protection of the resources of the Zone;

(*b*) any activity relating to the economic exploration or exploitation of the Zone;

(*c*) the safety and protection of structures or devices in the Zone;

(*d*) the authorisation, control and regulation of scientific research in the Zone;

(*e*) the customs and other fiscal matters relating to the Zone;

(*f*) the duties, powers, functions and conditions of service of marine conservation officers; and

(*g*) the fees to be paid under this Act.

(2) Regulations made under this section are subject to affirmative resolution, and shall be judicially noticed.

Directions

21. The Minister responsible for External Affairs may give directions respecting the disposal or release of any vessel, structure, equipment, device or thing that is ordered by a court to be forfeited under this Act or the regulations.

Amendments to enactments. Schedule.

22. The enactments specified in the first column of the Schedule are amended in the respects specified in the second column thereof.

Commencement

23. This Act shall come into operation on such day as the Governor-General appoints by proclamation.

SCHEDULE (Section 22)

First column — Second column

Magistrate's Jurisdiction and Procedure Act, Cap. 116

Insert immediately after section 18 the following as section 19—

'Summary offences committed on the high seas etc.

19. (1) Where a person residing or being, or suspected of residing or being, within the limits of the jurisdiction of any magistrate has committed on the high seas an offence punishable on summary conviction, the magistrate of the district within which any vessel or boat on which that offence was committed first arrives after the commission of the offence may enquire into, try and adjudicate that offence in the same manner as if the offence had been committed on shore within the limits of his jurisdictions.

Act 1977–26

(2) For the purposes of this section 'high seas' does not include the territorial waters established by the Barbados Territorial Waters Act, 1977 or the Exclusive Economic Zone established by the Marine Boundaries and Jurisdiction Act, 1978.'.

Fishing Industry Act Cap. 262

Insert, in their appropriate alphabetical order, in section 2 the following definitions—

'Barbadian fishing boat' means a fishing boat—

(a) wholly owned by a citizen of Barbados or by a body corporate whose members, or if that body corporate is a company, whose shareholders, as the case may be, are all citizens of Barbados; or

(b) certified in writing by the Cabinet as having such substantial economic connections with Barbados in relation to its ownership as to be deemed for the purposes of this Act to be Barbadian;

'fishing' means—

(a) the catching, taking or harvesting of fish;

(b) any activity reasonably expected to result in the catching, taking or harvesting of fish; or

(c) any operation at sea in connection with, or in preparation for, the catching, taking or harvesting of fish or an activity referred to in paragraph (b).

'foreign vessel' means a vessel of a foreign state;
'vessel' includes ship, boat or other sea-going or ocean-going craft;

Act 1978

'Zone' has the meaning assigned to it by section 2 of the Marine Boundaries and Jurisdiction Act, 1978'.

Insert immediately after the word, 'a' appearing in the first line of section 3 (1) thereof the word, 'Barbadian'.

Insert in section 4 immediately after the word, 'every' appearing in the first line of subsection (1) thereof the word, 'Barbadian'.

Insert in section 5 immediately after the word, 'a' appearing in the first line of subsection (1) thereof the word, 'Barbadian'.

Insert in section 6 immediately after the word, 'No' appearing in the first line thereof the word, 'Barbadian'.

Insert in section 7 immediately after the word, 'any' appearing in the second line of subsection (1) thereof the word, 'Barbadian'.

Insert in section 8 immediately after the words, 'sea any' appearing in the first line thereof the word, 'Barbadian'.

Insert immediately after section 8 the following new section as section 8A—

Foreign vessels

8A. (1) The master or other person in charge of a foreign vessel shall not cause or permit that vessel to be engaged in fishing within the Zone or territorial waters unless—

Act 1978

(a) there is on board that vessel a valid permit granted in respect of that vessel under the Marine Boundaries and Jurisdiction Act, 1978; or

(b) there is in force in relation to that vessel an agreement made under section 6 of that Act.

Act 1977–26

(2) Notwithstanding section 7 of the Barbados Territorial Waters Act, 1977, the engagement of a foreign vessel in fishing in the Zone or territorial waters under authority granted pursuant to subsection (1) of that Act shall not constitute passage prejudicial to the peace, good order or security of Barbados within the meaning of that section.'.

Barbados Territorial Waters Act, 1977. (Act 1977–26)

Delete the words 'Magistrates Jurisdiction and Procedure Act, Cap. 116', appearing in the first column of the Schedule and all the words appearing opposite thereto in the second column.

Statutory Instrument Supplement No. 1
Supplement to Official Gazette No. 2 dated 4th january, 1979.

S.I. 1979 No. 1

By His Excellency Sir Deighton Harcourt Lisle Ward, Knight Grand Cross of the Most Distinguished Order of Saint Michael and Saint George and Knight Grand Cross of the Royal Victorian Order, Governor-General of Barbados.

D.H.L. WARD
Governor-General

A PROCLAMATION

Whereas by Section 23 of the Marine Boundaries and Jurisdiction Act, 1978 it is provided that the said Act shall come into operation on such day as the Governor-General appoints by proclamation;

And Whereas it is expedient that the said Act shall come into operation on the 1st day of January, 1979:

Now Therefore by virtue of the power and authority in me vested, I do hereby appoint the 1st day of January, 1979 as the day on which the said Act shall come into operation.

Given under my hand and the Public Seal of Barbados this 29th day of December, 1978 and in the twenty-seventh year of Her Majesty's Reign.

4. Burma

Territorial Sea and Maritime Zones Law, 1977 (No. 3 of 1977).
Entered into force: April 9, 1977.
Source: *The Working People's Daily* (in English), April 10, 1977, p. 1–4.

TERRITORIAL SEA AND MARITIME ZONES LAW

(Pyithu Hluttaw Law No 3 of 1977)

PREAMBLE

Whereas the territorial sea of Burma has been declared to extend into the sea to a distance of twelve nautical miles;

Whereas it is necessary for the purpose of safeguarding the national interests of Burma to declare the extent of the contiguous zone, the continental shelf and the exclusive economic zone of Burma;

And whereas it is necessary to provide for matters ancillary thereto;

The Pyithu Hluttaw makes the following Law:

Chapter (1)
Title and Definitions

1. This Law may be called the Territorial Sea and Maritime Zones Law.

2. The following expressions contained in this Law shall have the following meanings:

(a) 'Burma' means the Socialist Republic of the Union of Burma;
(b) 'Council of Ministers' means the Council of Ministers of Burma;
(c) 'Baselines' means the baselines specified in the Annex to this Law.

Chapter (2)

Territorial Sea

3. The territorial sea of Burma extends seawards to a distance of twelve nautical miles from the baselines.

4. The sovereignty of Burma extends to the territorial sea, to its bed and subsoil and to the air space over the territorial sea.

5. Subject to the provisions of this Law, ships of all States other than warships shall enjoy the right of innocent passage through the territorial sea. Passage shall be deemed to be innocent so long as it is not prejudicial to the peace, good order or security of Burma.

6. During passage through the territorial sea:

(a) a foreign ship shall observe the existing laws and rules of Burma;
(b) a foreign fishing vessel shall keep its fishing gear and equipment in a secured position for sea. Such a vessel shall traverse the territorial sea by the shortest way without stopping or anchoring, except by reason of force majeure;
(c) no foreign research ship shall undertake any research activity without the prior express permission of the Council of Ministers.

7. Proof of innocence of passage shall be furnished by the foreign ship exercising the right of innocent passage when called for by the competent authorities of Burma.

8. The Council of Ministers may suspend temporarily, in specified areas of the territorial sea, the innocent passage of foreign ships if it considers that such suspension is necessary to safeguard the peace, good order or security of Burma.

9. *(a)* No foreign warship shall pass through the territorial sea without the prior express permission of the Council of Ministers.

(b) A foreign warship entering the territorial sea without the prior express permission of the Council of Ministers shall be required to leave the area immediately.

(c) During passage through the territorial sea, foreign submarines and other underwater vehicles shall navigate on the surface of the sea and show their flag.

Chapter (3)
Contiguous Zone

10. The contiguous zone of Burma is an area beyond and adjacent to the territorial sea and extends to a distance of twenty-four nautical miles from the baselines.

11. In the contiguous zone Burma exercises such control as it may consider necessary to:

(a) safeguard the security of Burma;
(b) prevent and punish infringement of its customs, fiscal, immigration or sanitary regulations within its territory or territorial sea.

Chapter (4)
Continental Shelf

12. The continental shelf of Burma comprises the seabed and subsoil of the submarine areas that extend beyond the territorial sea throughout the natural prolongation of its land territory to the outer edge of the continental margin, or to a distance of two hundred nautical miles from the baselines where the outer edge of the continental margin does not extend up to that distance.

13. Burma exercises exclusive sovereign rights in respect of its continental shelf.

14. Without prejudice to the generality of the provisions of section 13, Burma has in the continental shelf:

(a) sovereign rights for the purposes of exploration, exploitation, conservation and management of its natural resources, both living and non-living;
(b) exclusive rights and jurisdiction for the construction, maintenance or operation of artificial islands, offshore terminals, installations and other structures and devices necessary for the

exploration and exploitation of its natural resources, both living and non-living, or for the convenience of shipping or for any other purpose;

(c) exclusive jurisdiction to authorize, regulate and control scientific research;

(d) exclusive jurisdiction to preserve and protect the marine environment and to prevent and control marine pollution; and

(e) such other rights as are recognized from time to time by international law.

15. *(a)* The natural resources of the continental shelf include vegetable organisms and living organisms belonging to sedentary species, that is to say, organisms which, at the harvestable stage, either are immobile on or under the seabed or are unable to move except in constant physical contact with the seabed or the subsoil;

(b) Where the Council of Ministers considers that a marine organism of any kind is part of the living natural resources of the continental shelf, it may, by notification in the official Gazette, declare that organism to be part of the living natural resources of the continental shelf.

16. No one shall, without the prior express permission of the Council of Ministers, carry out in the continental shelf, any of the following:

(a) exploration;

(b) exploitation of the natural resources, both living and non-living;

(c) research;

(d) search, excavation, drilling; or

(e) construction, maintenance or operation of any artificial island, offshore terminal, installation or other structure or device.

Chapter (5)

Exclusive Economic Zone

17. The exclusive economic zone of Burma is an area beyond and adjacent to the territorial sea and extends to a distance of two hundred nautical miles from the baselines.

18. Burma has in the exclusive economic zone:

(a) sovereign rights for the purposes of exploration, exploitation, conservation and management of its natural resources, both living and non-living, as well as for producing energy from water and winds;

(b) exclusive rights and jurisdiction for the construction, maintenance or operation of artificial islands, offshore terminals, installations and other structures and devices necessary for the exploration and exploitation of its natural resources, both living and non-living, or for the convenience of shipping or for any other purpose;

(c) exclusive jurisdiction to authorize, regulate and control scientific research;

(d) exclusive jurisdiction to preserve and protect the marine environment and to prevent and control marine pollution; and

(c) such other rights as are recognized from time to time by international law.

19. Subject to the exercise by Burma of its rights:

(a) ships of all States shall enjoy the right of freedom of navigation within the exclusive economic zone;

(b) aircraft of all States shall enjoy freedom of overflight within the air space over the zone.

20. No one shall conduct any activity in the exclusive economic zone in relation to exploration, exploitation or research, without the prior express permission of the Council of Ministers:

Provided that, nothing in this section shall apply to fishing in accordance with law by a citizen of Burma.

Chapter (6)

Offences and Penalties

21. Whoever contravenes or attempts to contravene or abets the contravention of any provision of this Law or of any rule made thereunder shall be punishable with imprisonment which may extend to ten years, or with fine, or with both:

Provided that, the provisions of this section shall not preclude the right to take action under any other existing law.

22. Any ship other than a warship which is involved in the contravention of any provision of this Law punishable under section 21 shall be liable to confiscation together with its equipment and instruments as well as everything aboard that ship.

23. There shall be no prosecution under this Law without the prior sanction of the Council of Ministers.

Chapter (7)

Miscellaneous

24. For the purpose of successfully implementing the provisions of this Law, the Council of Ministers may promulgate such regulations, bye-laws, orders, directives and procedures as may be necessary.

25. Nothing in this Law shall affect the right of hot pursuit that may be exercised by Burma against any offender for any offence committed in the territorial sea, the contiguous zone, the continental shelf or the exclusive economic zone.

ANNEX

For the purpose of this Law, the low-water lines as marked on large-scale charts officially recognized by Burma shall be the baselines for measuring the breadth of the territorial sea, the contiguous zone, the continental shelf and the exclusive economic zone of Burma:

Provided that, where by reason of the geographical conditions prevailing on the coasts of Burma or of the economic requirements of the coastal regions straight baselines have been drawn between fixed points on the mainland, on islands or rocks, measurement shall be made from such baselines. The fixed points between which such straight baselines shall be drawn are indicated in detail in the following schedule:

SCHEDULE

1. *Arakan Coast*				
(a)	Southern Point of	....	Lat	20° 11′ 49″ N
	MAYU ISLAND	....	Long	92° 32′ 19″ E
(b)	BORONGA POINT	....	Lat	19° 48′ 30″ N
			Long	93° 01′ 42″ E
(c)	SOUTH TERRIBLES	....	Lat	19° 22′ 56″ N
			Long	93° 16′ 20″ E
(d)	Western Point of	....	Lat	18° 51′ 48″ N
	HENRY ROCKS	....	Long	93° 26′ 15″ E
(e)	Western Point of	....	Lat	18° 20′ 50″ N
	NERBUDDA ISLAND		Long	93° 56′ 25″ E
(f)	ST. JOHN'S or	....	Lat	17° 27′ 39″ N
	CHURCH ROCKS		Long	94° 19′ 46″ E
(g)	NORTH WEST GROUP	....	Lat	16° 55′ 28″ N
			Long	94° 12′ 45″ E
(h)	KORONGE ISLAND	....	Lat	16° 31′ 20″ N
			Long	94° 14′ 21″ E
(i)	SOUTH ROCK	....	Lat	16° 18′ 55″ N
			Long	94° 11′ 20″ E
(j)	BLACK ROCK	....	Lat	16° 11′ 50″ N
			Long	94° 10′ 50″ E
(k)	ALGUADA REEF	....	Lat	15° 42′ 13″ N
	(PATHEIN LIGHT)		Long	94° 12′ 06″ E
2. *Gulf of Martaban*				
(a)	ALGUADA REEF	....	Lat	15° 42′ 13″ N
	(PATHEIN LIGHT)		Long	94° 12′ 06″ E
(b)	Western Point of	....	Lat	14° 24′ 15″ N
	LONG ISLAND		Long	97° 46′ 02″ E
3. *Tenasserim Coast*				
(a)	Western Point of	....	Lat	14° 24′ 15″ N
	LONG ISLAND		Long	97° 46′ 02″ E
(b)	NORTH ISLAND	....	Lat	14° 09′ 00″ N
			Long	97° 46′ 54″ E
(c)	WEST CANISTER	....	Lat	12° 41′ 30″ N
	ISLAND		Long	97° 43′ 40″ E
(d)	Northern Point of	....	Lat	12° 30′ 30″ N
	SAURIM ISLAND		Long	97° 47′ 42″ E
(c)	Western Point of	....	Lat	12° 03′ 03″ N
	H. PRINCEP ISLAND		Long	97° 38′ 00″ E
(f)	GREAT WESTERN	....	Lat	11° 47′ 15″ N
	TORRES		Long	97° 26′ 15″ E
(g)	North Western Point of	....	Lat	10° 38′ 15″ N
	NORTH TWIN		Long	97° 41′ 45″ E
(h)	Western Point of	....	Lat	10° 28′ 12″ N
	SOUTH TWIN		Long	97° 40′ 45″ E
(i)	WESTERN ROCKY	....	Lat	09° 51′ 24″ N
	ISLAND		Long	97° 52′ 18″ E
(j)	HAYCOCK ISLAND	....	Lat	09° 40′ 45″ N
			Long	97° 54′ 30″ E
(k)	Western Point of	....	Lat	09° 35′ 54″ N
	MURRAY ISLAND		Long	97° 58′ 12″ E

5. Cambodia

Ministry of Foreign Affairs Statement.
Entered into force: July 31, 1982.
Source: Cambodian Ministry of Foreign Affairs.

COUNCIL OF STATE ISSUES DECREE ON TERRITORIAL WATERS

[Text] Phom Penh, 8 Aug (SPK) — The Council of State of the PRK has just promulgated a decree on the limits of the PRK's maritime zones and continental shelf

The full text of the decree, signed on 31 July by Chairman of the Council of State Heng Samrin, reads:

The chairman of the Council of State, considering that the PRK has full sovereignty and inviolable rights over its territorial waters and its continental shelf;
Considering that the PRK must watch over its sovereignty, security and national defense toward the sea and ensure the best exploitation of natural resources in its territorial waters and continental shelf in order to serve the national defense and reconstruction efforts and the improvement of the people's living standards;
Considering the Constitution of the PRK;
And the Council of Ministers having been informed;
Has decreed the following:

Article 1

The full and entire sovereignty of the PRK extends beyond its territory and internal waters to a maritime zone adjacent to its coasts and its internal waters, designated by the name of the territorial waters of the PRK.

This sovereignty also extends to the airspace above the territorial waters of the PRK as well as to the seabed and subsoil of these waters.

Article 2

The width of the territorial waters of the PRK is 12 nautical miles (1 nautical mile equaling 1,852 meters) measured from straight baselines, linking the points of the coast and the furtherest points of Kampuchea's [Cambodia's] furtherest islands; these baselines are traced along the low-water mark.

These straight baselines are concretely defined in Annex 1 of this decree.

The internal waters of the PRK are the waters located between the baseline of the territorial waters and the coasts of Kampuchea [Cambodia].

Article 3

The outer limit of the territorial waters of the PRK is a line each point of which is at a distance equal to the width of the territorial waters from the closest point of the baseline.

In the maritime zone between Kach Kut Island and the terminus of the land border between Kampuchea [Cambodia] and Thailand, the limit of the territorial water of the PRK follows the dividing line of the maritime waters determined by the historic border stipulated in the Franco-Siamese treaty of 23 March 1907.

Article 4

The contiguous zone of the PRK is a maritime zone located beyond and adjacent to its territorial waters, with a width of 12 nautical miles measured from the outer limit of the territorial waters of the PRK.

In its contiguous zone, the PRK exercises necessary control in order to oversee its security and to prevent and check violations of its customs, fiscal, health and emigration and immigration laws.

Article 5

The exclusive economic zone of the PRK is a maritime zone located beyond its territorial waters and adjacent to the latter. This zone extends to 200 nautical miles measured from the baseline used to measure the width of the territorial waters of the PRK.

The PRK has sovereign rights over the exploration and exploitation and the preservation and management of all organic or inorganic natural resources of the seabed, of its subsoil and of the waters above it and over other activities leading to the exploration and exploitation of its exclusive economic zone.

In its exclusive economic zone, the PRK has exclusive jurisdiction regarding the setting up and use of installations, devices and artificial islands and marine research; and has jurisdiction over the preservation of the marine environment and the control of pollution.

Without prior authorization or agreement by the PRK, foreign ships are forbidden to fish or exploit any natural resources in any form, or to undertake scientific research in the exclusive economic zone of the PRK. When they have obtained prior authorization or agreement, they must conform with the laws and regulations of the PRK concerning fishing, the exploitation of other natural resources and scientific research, and with other regulations relating to them decreed by the PRK, and must strictly carry out all obligations provided in the licenses or the contracts.

Article 6

The continental shelf of the PRK comprises the seabed and the subsoil of the submarine areas that extend beyond the territorial waters throughout the natural prolongation of its land territory to a distance of 200 nautical miles from the baseline used to measure the width of the territorial waters of the PRK.

The PRK exercises sovereign rights over its continental shelf for the purposes of exploration, exploitation, preservation and management of its natural resources comprising mineral resources and other inorganic or organic resources belonging to sedentary species living on the continental shelf.

The PRK has the exclusive right to regulate the setting up and use of installations, devices and articifical islands or drilling on its continental shelf for the purposes of exploration, exploitation or any other purpose.

All activities carried out by foreigners on the continental shelf of Kampuchea [Cambodia], for whatever end, must be the object of an authorization or an agreement by the PRK Government and conform with the laws and regulations of the PRK.

Article 7

The PRK will settle, by means of negotiations with interested states, all problems concerning the maritime zones and continental shelf in a fair and logical manner on the basis of mutual respect for sovereignty, independence and territorial integrity.

Article 8

The PRK will negotiate and agree with the SRV [Vietnam] on the maritime border in the historic waters zone of the two countries fixed in the agreement on the historic waters of the two countries signed on 7 July 1982 in line with the spirit and letter of the Treaty of Peace, Friendship and Cooperation between the two states signed on 18 February 1979.

Article 9

All provisions contrary to this decres are purely and simply abrogated.

Article 10

The minister of national defense, the minister of interior and the ministers concerned are charged, each in his proper field, with the implementation of this decree.

ANNEX 1

The Baseline Retained for the Limitation of the Territorial Waters of the PRK

The baseline retained for the limitation of the territorial waters of the PRK is made up of segments of a line passing successively through the following points, the coordinates of which are expressed in degrees, minutes and tenths of a minute, the longitude being counted from the meridian of Greenwich.

Number	Geographical Place	Latitude (North)	Longitude (East)
1	Border point on low-water mark between Thailand and the PRK according to treaty of 23 March 1907	11° 38′ 8″	102° 54′ 3″
2	Kack Kusrovie	11° 06′ 8″	102° 47′ 3″
3	Kack Voar	10° 14′ 0″	102° 52′ 5″
4	Poulo Wai	09° 55′ 5″	102° 53′ 2″
5	Point 0 out at sea on the southwest limit of the historic waters of the PRK	According to the agreement of 7 July 1982	

6. Cape Verde

Decree Law No. 126/77
Entered into force: December 31, 1977
Source: *Boletim Oficial,* December 31, 1977, No. 53 (Translated from Portuguese by the Department of State).

Saturday, December 31, 1977 No. 53

REPUBLIC OF CAPE VERDE

Boletim Oficial [Official Gazette]

Decree Law No. 126/77 of December 31

Considering the need to safeguard the fundamental interests of the Nation with regard to the living and nonliving resources of the maritime space of the Republic of Cape Verde;

Considering the importance of fisheries for the national economy, particularly with regard to the revitalization of ports and small-scale local fishing;

Considering changes in the Law of the Sea;

In View Of the provisions of the National Popular Assembly resolution of December 31, 1977;

By Virtue Of the powers conferred by Article 15 (4) of the Law of July 5, 1975 on the Political Organization of the State, the Government decrees and I promulgate the following law:

Article 1

The territorial sea of the Republic of Cape Verde has a breadth of 12 nautical miles, measured from the baselines defined in this decree law. The outer limit of the territorial sea is located at a distance of 12 nautical miles from the nearest point of the given baseline.

Article 2

The baseline from which the breadth of the territorial sea of the Republic of Cape Verde is measured consists of the straight lines that join the outermost points of the coast and islands, as determined by the following principal geographic coordinates:

Latitude	Longitude		
1 — 14° 53′ 8″ N	23° 31′ W	/W —	Ponta Temerosa — Santiago
2 — 14° 49′ N	24° 22′ 5″ W		Ponta do Pescadeiro — Fogo
3 — 14° 48′ 4″ N	24° 42′ 2″ W		Ponta Nho Martinho — Brava
4 — 14° 50′ 1″ N	24° 45′ 4″ W		Ponta Prainha — Brava
5 — 17° 02′ 5″ N	25° 22′ W		Ponta Preta — Santo Antão
6 — 17° 12′ 2″ N	25° 05′ 9″ W		Ponta do Sol — Santo Antão
7 — 16° 51′ 2″ N	22° 55′ 5″ W		Ponta Norte — Sal
8 — 16° 50′ N	22° 53′ 7″ W		Ponta da Casaca — Sal
9 — 16° 09′ 1″ N	22° 39′ 8″ W		Ilhéu Baluarte — Boa Vista
10 — 16° 02′ 9″ N	22° 41′ 2″ W		Pé do Branco — Boa Vista
11 — 15° 10′ 1″ N	23° 05′ 6″ W		Ponta Flamengos — Maio
12 — 15° 07′ N	23° 09′ 2″ W		Ponta Poça Grande — Maio
13 — 14° 54′ 2″ N	23° 29′ 3″ W	/W —	Ponta das Bicudas — Santiago
14 — 14° 53′ 9″ N	23° 30′ 7″ W	/E —	Ponta Temerosa

Article 3

The waters enclosed by the baselines constitute the archipelagic waters of the Republic of Cape Verde.

Article 4

The sovereignty which the State of Cape Verde exercises over all the territory composed of the emerged surface, the archipelagic waters, and the territorial sea, as defined in the foregoing articles, also extends to the air space above that territory, to the bed and subsoil of the aquatic territory formed by the archipelagic waters and the territorial sea, and all living and nonliving natural resources found in the aforementioned areas.

Article 5

Without prejudice to the provisions of the preceding articles and in accordance with the principles of international law, the Republic of Cape Verde respects the freedom of innocent passage and overflight along established navigation routes.

Article 6

The outer limit of the exclusive economic zone of the State of Cape Verde is a line every point of which is at a distance of 200 nautical miles from the nearest point of the baseline from which the breadth of the territorial sea is measured.

Article 7

1. Within the zone defined in the previous article, the State of Cape Verde exercises exclusive jurisdiction in matters of conservation and exploitation of living and nonliving natural resources.

2. Except as otherwise specified in this decree-law, foreign vessels are prohibited from fishing in the exclusive economic zone.

Article 8

1. In order to ensure rational exploitation of the living resources of the exclusive economic zone, the State of Cape Verde may, by means of bilateral agreements, authorize access by other States to the surplus of the allowable catch.

2. Fishing in the archipelagic waters and the territorial sea of the Republic of Cape Verde is reserved for nationals.

3. Harvesting of crustaceans in the exclusive economic zone is also reserved for nationals.

Article 9

For purposes of this decree-law, the terms 'fisheries' and 'fishing' are understood to mean the pursuit, catching, harvesting, or utilization of the living resources of the sea.

Article 10

The Government will publish and enforce fisheries regulations for the archipelagic waters, the territorial sea, and the exclusive economic zone.

Article 11

The State of Cape Verde will cooperate with the competent international, regional, and subregional organizations with respect to conservation of the living resources of the sea.

Article 12

Taking into account the applicable rules of international law, the Government may establish special regulations for the exclusive economic zone, specifically with regard to:

(a) Protection of the environment;
(b) Scientific research;
(c) Artificial installations, both permanent and temporary;
(d) Submarine cables and pipelines;
(e) Exploration and exploitation.

Article 13

1. Violation of the provisions of Article 7 (2) shall be punishable by a fine of up to 20,000 escudos per ton of gross tonnage of the violating vessel.

Violation of the provisions of Article 8 (2, 3) shall be punishable by a fine of up to 35,000 escudos per ton of gross tonnage of the violating vessel.

3. The court which tries the violation may, in accordance with the seriousness of the case, order the seizure and forfeiture to the State of the vessel and its equipment, accessories, nets, gear, tackle, and fish.

4. In cases of repeated violation, the penalty shall be increased from a fine to imprisonment.

Article 14

The State of Cape Verde will respect the right of States adjoining economic zones and declares its willingness to establish bilateral negotiations concerning such conflicts of law as may arise from the application of the principles contained in this decree-law.

Article 15

All legal provisions contrary to this decree-law are hereby revoked.

Article 16

This decree-law enters into force immediately.

Seen and approved in the Council of Ministers Pedro Pires, Abílio Duarte, Silvino da Luz, Osvaldo Lopes da Silva, Carlos Reis, Herculano Vieira, João Pereira Silva, David Almada.

Promulgated on December 5, 1977.

Let these presents be published.

Aristides Maria Pereira, President of the Republic.

To be presented to the National Popular Assembly.

7. Colombia

Law No. 10.
Entered into force: August 4, 1978.
Source: *Diario Oficiel,* August 1978.

Law No. 10 of August 4, 1978 Establishing Regulations on the Territorial Sea, Exclusive Economic Zone, and Continental Shelf, and Other Provisions

The Congress of Colombia Hereby Decrees

Article 1

The territorial sea of the Colombian nation, over which it excercises full sovereignty, extends beyond its continental and insular territory and its internal waters up to a breadth of 12 nautical miles or 22 km 224 m.

National sovereignty also extends to the space above the territorial sea and to the seabed and subsoil of that sea.

Article 2

Vessels of any State shall enjoy the right of innocent passage through the territorial sea in accordance with the rules of international law.

Article 3

The outer limit of the territorial sea shall be determined by a line all points of which are at a distance of 12 nautical miles from the nearest points of the baselines referred to in the following article.

Article 4

The normal baseline used to measure the breadth of the territorial sea shall be the low-water line off the coast. In localities where the coastline has deep inlets or indentations, or where there is a fringe of islands along the coast in their immediate vicinity, measurement shall be by means of straight baselines joining appropriate points. Waters lying between the baselines and the coast shall be considered internal waters.

Article 5

In gulfs and bays whose natural entrance points are no more than 24 miles apart, the territorial sea shall be measured from a line of demarcation joining the said points. The waters enclosed by that line shall be considered internal waters.

If the mouth of the gulf or bay exceeds 24 miles, a straight baseline of that length may be drawn within it enclosing the maximum area of water possible.

Article 6

If a river flows directly into the sea, the baseline shall be a straight line across the mouth of the river between points on the low-tide line of its banks.

Article 7

There is hereby established, adjacent to the territorial sea, an exclusive economic zone whose outer limit shall extend 200 nautical miles measured from the baselines from which the breadth of the territorial sea is measured.

Article 8

In the zone established by the preceding article the Colombian nation shall exercise sovereign rights for the purpose of exploring, exploiting, conserving, and managing the natural resources, both living and nonliving, of the seabed, subsoil, and superjacent waters; it shall also exercise exclusive jurisdiction for scientific research and the preservation of the marine environment.

Article 9

In implementing the present Law, the Government shall mark out in its continental territory, in the archipelago of San Andrés y Providencia, and other insular territories the lines referred to in the preceding articles, which shall be published on official maritime charts in accordance with pertinent international regulations.

Article 10

Colombian sovereignty shall extend to the continental shelf for the purpose of exploring and exploiting natural resources.

Article 11

The Government shall be granted 12 months following approval of the present Law to establish provisions and reorganize or create national administrative agencies and departments needed to supervise and defend Colombian maritime areas and to make proper use of living and nonliving natural resources in such areas to meet the needs of the Colombian people and the economic development of the country.

By virtue of this authority the National Government may make any loans, appropriations, and budget transfers that it considers necessary.

Article 12

All provisions contrary to the present Law are hereby repealed.

Article 13

This Law shall enter into force upon its promulgation.

Done at Bogotá, D.E., on July 25, 1978.

(Signed) Guillermo Plazas Alcid
(President of the Senate of the Republic)

(Signed) Jorge Mario Eastman
(President of the House of Representatives)

(Signed) Amaury Guerrero
(Secretary General of the Senate)

(Signed) Jairo Morera Lizcano
(Secretary General of the House of Representatives)

Republic of Colombia, National Government

Bogotá, D.E., August 4, 1978

To be published and enforced.

(Signed) Alfonso López Michelsen

(Signed) Indalecio Liévano Aguirre
(Minister of Foreign Affairs)

(Signed) Alvaro Aleán Gómez
(Chief Archivist)

8. Comoros

Ordinance No. 76–038/CE.
Entered into force: June 15, 1976.
Source: *United Nations ST/LEG/SER.B/19,* pp. 15–16.

THE ISLAMIC FEDERAL REPUBLIC OF THE COMOROS

Unity-Justice-Progress

FEDERAL ASSEMBLY

LAW No. 82–005 relating to the delimitation of the maritime zones of the Islamic Federal Republic of the Comoros

The Federal Assembly of the Comoros

Deliberating in accordance with the Constitution, adopted at its meeting of 6 May 1982 the following Law:

SECTION I:
THE LEGAL STATUS OF THE ARCHIPELAGIC WATERS OF THE COMOROS, OF THE AIRSPACE OVER THE ARCHIPELAGIC WATERS AND OF THEIR BED AND SUBSOIL

Article 1

The sovereignty of the 'Comorian' State extends to the waters enclosed by the baselines, described as archipelagic waters, regardless of their depth or distance from the coast.

The 'Comorian' State extends its sovereignty to the airspace over the archipelagic waters, as well as to their bed and subsoil, and the resources contained therein.

Article 2

The right of innocent passage through the archipelagic waters of the Comoros must be respected. The Comoros may, however, suspend temporarily in its waters the right of innocent passage if such suspension is essential for the protection of its security.

SECTION II:
THE LEGAL STATUS OF THE TERRITORIAL SEA OF THE COMOROS

Article 3

Limit of the territorial sea of the Comoros

The Comoros limits its territorial sea to 12 nautical miles measured from baselines. The inner limit of the territorial sea is a line every point of which is at a distance from the nearest point of the baseline equal to the breadth of the territorial sea.

Article 4

Rights, jurisdiction and duties of the Comoros in the territorial sea

The sovereignty of the Comoros extends, beyond its land territory and internal or archipelagic waters, to an adjacent belt of sea, described as the territorial sea.

This sovereignty extends to the airspace over the territorial sea as well as to its bed and subsoil.

Article 5

Right of innocent passage in the territorial sea

Ships of all States, whether coastal or land-locked, shall enjoy the right of innocent passage through the territorial sea of the Comoros, which means that passage shall be continuous and expeditious and not prejudicial to the peace and good order or the security of the Comoros. The right of innocent passage may be regulated or suspended by decree in accordance with international law. In the territorial waters of the Comoros, submarines must remain on the surface and show their flag.

SECTION III:
LEGAL REGIME OF THE EXCLUSIVE ECONOMIC ZONE OF THE COMOROS

Article 6

Limit of the exclusive economic zone of the Comoros

The exclusive economic zone is delimited on one side, by the outer limit of the territorial sea and, on the other side, by a line every point of which is at a distance of 200 miles from the nearest point on the baseline or equidistant from the baselines of the Comorian coast and those of the coasts of the foreign countries opposite it, save as otherwise specifically agreed.

Article 7

Rights, jurisdiction and duties of the Comoros in the exclusive economic zone

In its exclusive economic zone:

(*a*) The Comoros shall have sovereign rights for the purpose of exploring and exploiting, conserving and managing the natural resources, whether living or non-living, of the sea-bed and its subsoil and of the waters superjacent to the sea-bed, and with regard to other activities for the economic exploitation and exploration of the zone, such as the production of energy from the water, currents and winds:

(*b*) The Comoros shall have jurisdiction with regard to:
Marine scientific research;
Preservation of the marine environment;
Prevention of marine pollution.

The conduct of scientific or technical research shall be subject to licensing by the Comorian State.

(*c*) All Comorians may fish freely in the exclusive economic zone of the Comoros.

Article 8

Rights and duties of other States in the exclusive economic zone of the Comoros

(*a*) In the exclusive economic zone of the Comoros, all States shall enjoy the freedom of navigation and overflight and of the laying of submarine cables and pipelines, provided that such freedoms are compatible with the provisions of the Convention on the Law of the Sea (no threat to the peace).

(*b*) Third States shall have regard to the rights and duties of the Comoros and comply with the laws and regulations enacted by it in accordance with the rules of international law.

(c) Conflict resolution: where a conflict arises between the interests of the Comoros and any other State or States, the conflict shall be resolved on the basis of equity, taking into account the respective importance of the interests involved to the parties as well as to the international community as a whole.

Article 9

Conservation of living resources in the exclusive economic zone of the Comoros

(a) The allowable level of exploitation of living and mineral resources in the exclusive economic zone shall be determined by decree.

(b) The Comoros shall ensure through proper conservation and management measures that the maintenance of the living resources in the exclusive economic zone is not endangered by over-exploitation.

As appropriate, the Comoros and the subregional, regional and global organizations concerned [. . .] is not endangered by over-exploitation.

(c) The Comoros shall determine its capacity to exploit the living and mineral resources of the zone. Where it does not have the capacity to attain the allowable level of exploitation, it shall, through agreements, give other States access.

Article 10

Violations of the provisions of this Law and of the provisions of regulations adopted to give it effect shall be punishable by a fine of between 10 million and 80 million CFA Francs and/or temporary seizure of the vessel.

Article 11

Law No. 71–1060 of 24 December 1971 relating to the delimitation of French territorial waters is hereby repealed in the Comoros.

Order No. 78–003/DPM of 20 July 1978 specifying the limits of Comorian territorial waters is hereby repealed.

This Law shall be applied as the Law of the State.

Moroni, 6 May 1982

Secretaries

(Signed) Mohamed Ali Mroivili

(Signed) Attoumani Said

President of the Federal Assembly

(Signed) Abdourahman Ben Cheikh Achiraf

9. Costa Rica

Decree No. 5699.
Entered into force: May 20, 1975.
Source: *Costa Rican Constitution* (Translated from Spanish by the Department of State).

THE LEGISLATIVE ASSEMBLY OF THE REPUBLIC OF COSTA RICA

Decrees

Sole article

Article 6 of the Constitution is hereby amended to read as follows:

Article 6

The State exercises complete and exclusive sovereignty over the air space above its territory, its territorial waters for a distance of 12 miles from the low-water line along its coasts, its continental shelf, and its insular sill, in accordance with the principles of international law.

Furthermore, it exercises special jurisdiction over the seas adjacent to its territory for an extent of 200 miles from the aforesaid line, in order to protect, conserve, and utilize on an exclusive basis all natural resources and riches existing in the waters, soil, and subsoil of those zones, in conformity with the aforesaid principles.

To be communicated to the Executive Branch.

Legislative Assembly, San José, May 20, 1975.

Alfonso Carro Zúñiga
President

Carlos Luis Rodriguez Hernández
Second Secretary

Rafael Angel Rojas Jiménez
First Secretary

10. Cuba

Decree Law No. 2 of February 24, 1977.
Entered into force: February 26, 1977.
Source: *Gaceta Oficial,* February 26, 1977 (Translated from Spanish by the Department of State).

Decree-Law 2 of February 24, 1977

Article 1

The economic zone of the Republic of Cuba is hereby established as the zone, adjacent to its territorial sea, which extends for 200 nautical miles measured from the baseline from which the breadth of its territorial sea is measured. The outer limit of this economic zone shall de delineated by geographic coordinates.

The Cuban State will respect the equal rights of all contiguous States to their respective economic zones and it hereby expresses it readiness to undertake bilateral negotiations on any legal disputes arising from the application of these principles.

Article 2

The Republic will exercise the following rights in the economic zone established herein:

I. Sovereign rights for the purposes of exploration, exploitation, conservation, and management of the living non-living natural resources of the seabeds, including the subsoil and superjacent waters;

II. Exclusive rights and jurisdiction with regard to the emplacement and utilization of man-made islands, installations, and structures; and

III. Exclusive jurisdiction with regard to other activities for the economic exploration and exploitation of the zone, including the use of sea currents and any other rendered possible by scientific and technological development;

IV. Jurisdiction with regard to:
(A) The preservation of the marine environment, including pollution control and elimination; and
(B) Scientific research.

Article 3

In the economic zone, foreign states will enjoy the freedoms of navigation and overflight and the freedom to lay submarine cables and pipelines, as well as any other legitimate international use of the sea related to navigation and communications.

Article 4

To promote optimum use of the living resources of the economic zone, the Republic of Cuba will, by concluding the corresponding agreements, give other States access to the surplus of the allowable catch of species, in accordance with the terms, conditions, and regulations in force.

Article 5

All legal and regulatory provisions running counter to the provisions of this decree-law, which shall enter into force on the date of its publication in the Official Gazette of the Republic, are hereby repealed.

Done in the Palace of the Revolution, Havana, on February 24, 1977.

Fidel Castro Ruz

11. Djibouti

Law 52/AN/78.
Entered into force: January 9, 1979.
Source: *Journal Officiel,* January 9, 1979 (Translated from French by the Department of State).

Republic of Djibouti
Office of the President of the Republic

LAW No. 52/AN/78 concerning the territorial sea, the contiguous zone, the exclusive economic zone, the maritime boundaries, and fishing

THE NATIONAL ASSEMBLY HAS ADOPTED.
THE PRESIDENT OF THE REPUBLIC PROMULGATES
THE FOLLOWING LAW:

ON THE BASIS OF constitutional laws Nos. 77–001 and 77–002 of June 27, 1977.

ON THE BASIS OF decree No. 78–092 of October 2, 1978 concerning the appointment of members of the government.

Section I
Terms and Definition

Article one

This law pertains to the delimitation of territorial waters, the contiguous zone, the exclusive economic zone, the maritime boundaries, and fishing.

Article two

For the purposes of this law, the following expressions and terms used herein correspond to the following definitions, unless these definitions are out of context:

Republic	The Republic of Djibouti
Ministry of Agricultures	The Ministry of Agriculture of the Republic of Djibouti
Coast	The continental and insular coastline of the Republic of Djibouti bounded by the Gulf of Tadjoura, the Red Sea, and the Indian Ocean.
Contiguous zone	Stretch of water beyond the territorial sea of the Republic and adjacent to it, as defined in Article 10 of this Law.
Pollution of the Marine Environment	The introduction by man, directly or indirectly, of substances or energy into the marine environment which results in such deleterious effects as harm to marine flora and fauna, hazards to human health, hindrance to marine activities, including fishing and other legitimate uses of the sea; impairment of quality for use of sea water and reduction of amenities.
Bay	Any bay, indentation, cove, arm, or neck of the sea.
Nautical mile	1,852 meters (international nautical mile).

Section II
Territorial Sea and Contiguous Zone

Article three

The Republic shall exercise its sovereignty over the territorial sea and also over the subjacent sea-beds, their subsoils, and the superjacent air space.

Article four

The territorial sea extends over a breadth of 12 nautical miles starting from the baselines. The baselines used to measure the breadth of the territorial sea are the low-water mark and also the straight baselines and the closing lines of bays.

The closing lines of bays used to determine the baselines from which the breadth of the territorial waters adjacent to the territory of the Republic is measured are, for the Gulf of Tadjoura, the lines connecting points A and B, and points B and C, defined as follows:

POINT A:	North point of the mouth of Dalley Wadi (latitude 11° 50′. 40 N; longitude 43° 05′. 10 E);
POINT B:	Musha Island lighthouse (latitude 11° 43′. 90 N; longitude 43° 12′. 80 E);
POINT C:	South point of the mouth of Aatar Wadi (latitude 11° 30′. 20 N; longitude 43° 15′. 50 E).

Article five

Foreign vessels entitled to the right of innocent passage in the waters of the territorial sea of the Republic; the passage shall be considered innocent provided it is not prejudicial to the security of the Republic, its territorial integrity, or its independence. The passage must be continuous and rapid.

Article six

In the territorial sea, submarine and other submersible vessels shall be required to navigate on the surface and to hoist their flag. Aircraft movements from vessels shall be prohibited as well as exercises that involve firing weapons.

Article seven

Foreign vessels that are nuclear-propelled or are transporting nuclear materials or other radioactive substances must notify the competent authorities of the Republic prior to their entry and passage in the territorial sea.

Article eight

Foreign vessels exercising the right of innocent passage in the territorial sea must comply with the laws and regulations in force in the Republic, as well as with all international regulations pertaining to maritime transport and navigation.

Article nine

The Republic reserves the possibility of suspending the right of innocent passage in the territorial sea in certain circumstances and under certain conditions.

Article ten

The outer limit of the contiguous zone is determined by the points located 24 nautical miles from the point closest to the baselines listed in Article Four of this law.

Article eleven

The authorities of the Republic shall have the right to exercise within the contiguous zone the control necessary in order to:

(a) Prevent violations of fiscal, health, and immigration laws and regulations within the territory of the Republic or the territorial sea;

(b) Punish violations of the same laws or regulations committed within the territory of the Republic or its territorial sea.

Section III
Exclusive Economic Zone

Article twelve

The Republic shall possess an exclusive economic zone extending over a breadth of 200 nautical miles from the baselines of the territorial sea.

Article thirteen

In the economic zone, including the sea-beds, their subsoil, and the superjacent waters, the Republic shall have:

(a) Sovereign and exclusive right for the purpose of conserving, exploring, exploiting, and managing the natural resources, renewable and non-renewable, as well as for the purpose of producing energy from the water, currents, and winds;

(b) The sovereign and exclusive right, to construct, repair, exploit, and utilize artificial islands, installations, and other structures necessary for exploring and exploiting the resources of the exclusive economic zone of the Republic;

(c) Exclusive jurisdiction over the marine environment for the purpose of conserving and protecting it and for combatting marine pollution; the Republic shall also possess sovereign rights for the purpose of authorizing, organizing, and supervising scientific research;

(d) Other rights and obligations provided for by international law.

Article fourteen

Without prejudice to the aforementioned rights, the Republic guarantees to all States the freedoms of navigation and overflight and the freedom of laying submarine cables and pipelines in its exclusive economic zone.

Section IV
Maritime Boundaries

Article fifteen

The maritime boundaries of the territorial sea, the contiguous zone, and the economic zone between the Republic and a neighboring State whose coastlines are adjacent to or opposite those of the Republic shall be determined by an agreement with that State.

Pending the conclusion of an agreement for determining the maritime boundaries, those boundaries shall not extend beyond a median line between the two States or beyond a line all points of which are equidistant from the points closest to the baselines used to measure the breadth of the territorial seas of the Republic and of the State concerned.

The provisions of this law shall not have the effect of modifying the international rules of navigation in the Strait of Bab el Mandeb.

Section V
Fishing

Article sixteen

Fishing for commercial purposes in the territorial waters, the contiguous zone, and the economic zone shall be subject to prior authorization by the Ministry of Agriculture.

Article seventeen

To the extent that they do not resell the product of their fishing, the citizens of the Republic, foreign residents, and tourists in transit shall be exempt from the ministerial authorization mentioned in Article Sixteen.

Article eighteen

Any person fishing for commercial or non-commercial purposes must respect the fishing regulations of the Republic and particularly the prohibitions pertaining to these zones for the protection of submarine fauna.

Article nineteen

Violators of the provisions of Articles Sixteen and Seventeen shall be subject to fines the amounts of which shall be established by decree.

Article twenty

This law shall be enforced as a law of the State and published in the *Journal Officiel* of the Republic.

Done at Djibouti, Januari 9, 1979

12. Dominica

Territorial Sea, Contiguous Zone, Exclusive Economic Zone and Fishery Zones Act, 1981 (No. 26 of 1981).
Entered into force: August 25, 1981.
Source: *United Nations LE 113 (3–3),* December 30, 1981.

25th August, 1981

AN ACT TO ESTABLISH THE LIMITS OF THE TERRITORIAL SEA, THE CONTIGUOUS ZONE, THE EXCLUSIVE ECONOMIC AND FISHERY ZONES OF THE COMMONWEALTH OF DOMINICA

(Gazetted 10th September, 1981)

BE IT ENACTED by the Parliament of the Commonwealth of Dominica as follows:—

Short title

1. This Act may be cited as the

TERRITORIAL SEA, CONTIGUOUS ZONE, EXCLUSIVE ECONOMIC AND FISHERY ZONES ACT. 1981

Interpretation

2. In this Act
'baseline' means the line from which the breadth of the territorial sea is drawn as determined in accordance with the straight baseline system;
'contiguous zone' means that area of sea contiguous to the territorial sea over which the Commonwealth of Dominica may exercise sovereign rights necessary to prevent infringement of its customs, fiscal, immigration or sanitary regulations within its territory or territorial sea;
'exclusive economic zone' means an area beyond and adjacent to the territorial sea, over which the Commonwealth of Dominica may exercise sovereign rights, and jurisdiction subject to the provisions of international law;
'fishery zone' means the areas of superjacent waters which extend to a distance of two hundred nautical miles from the baseline from which the breadth of the territorial sea is drawn;
'innocent passage' means passage of a ship or aircraft which is not prejudicial to the peace, good order and security of the Commonwealth of Dominica;
'internal waters' means the areas of waters lying on the landward side of the baseline;
'passage' means navigation through the territorial sea and the airspace thereof for purposes provided in international law;
'territorial sea' means that area of sea over which the Commonwealth of Dominica exercises sovereignty.

Establishment of the territorial sea

3. The territorial sea of the Commonwealth of Dominica comprises those areas of sea having as their inner limits, the baseline as defined and as their outer limits, a line measured seaward from the baseline, every point of which line extends to a distance of twelve (12) nautical miles from the nearest point of the baseline.

Establishment of the contiguous zone

4. The contiguous zone to the territorial sea of the Commonwealth of Dominica comprises that area of sea which is contiguous to its territorial sea and shall extend twenty-four miles from the baseline from which the breadth of the territorial sea is measured.

Establishment of Exclusive Economic zone

5. The exclusive economic zone of the Commonwealth of Dominica comprises those areas of the sea, sea-bed and sub-soil that are beyond and adjacent to the territorial sea of the Commonwealth of Dominica, having as their outer limits a line measured seaward from the aforesaid baseline, every point of which line is distant two hundred nautical miles from the nearest point of the aforesaid baseline.

Establishment of Fishery zone

6. The fishery zone of the Commonwealth of Dominica comprises that area of sea, that is beyond and adjacent to the territorial sea of the Commonwealth of Dominica and having as its seaward boundary a line so drawn that each point upon it is distant two hundred (200) nautical miles from the nearest point of the baseline from which the breadth of the territorial sea is measured.

Jurisdiction in territorial sea

7. In the territorial sea and internal waters the Commonwealth of Dominica shall exercise sovereignty and such sovereignty shall extend to the sea-bed and sub-soil thereof and to the airspace over such sea.

Jurisdiction in Exclusive Economic Zone

8. In the exclusive economic zone the Commonwealth of Dominica shall exercise:—

(a) sovereign rights for the purpose of exploration, exploitation, conservation and management, of the natural resources, both living and non-living, of the sea-bed, sub-soil and superjacent waters and other sovereign rights with regard to producing energy from tides, winds and currents therein;

(b) jurisdiction with regard to:—

(i) the establishment and use of artificial islands, installations and structures;

(ii) marine scientific research; and

(iii) the protection and preservation of the marine environment;

(c) other rights and duties provided for in international law.

Jurisdiction in Fishery Zone

9. In the fishery zone the Commonwealth of Dominica shall exercise the sovereign right and exclusive authority to explore and exploit, conserve and manage the fishery resources of the superjacent waters, the seabed and subsoil therein, in accordance with International Law.

Recognition of innocent passage

10. (1) The Commonwealth of Dominica recognises the right of innocent passage of foreign ships and warships in the territorial sea and the overflight of aircraft in the airspace thereof subject to the principles and provisions of International Law.

Acknowledgement of international activities in the Exclusive Economic Zone

(2) The Commonwealth of Dominica shall recognise the freedoms of navigation and overflight of aircraft and of the laying of submarine cables and pipelines and other related activities in the exclusive economic zone, in accordance with the principles and provisions of International Law.

Intention to negotiate maritime boundaries

11. Where the boundary lines of the territorial sea and of the exclusive economic zone of the Commonwealth of Dominica poses of delimitation with the territories and States adjacent or opposite, the Government of the Commonwealth of Dominica shall be ready, able and willing, at appropriate times, to enter into negotiations on equitable principles, with the States concerned with a view to reaching amicable agreements.

Future legislation

12. The Government of the Commonwealth of Dominica will pass further legislation in respect of the foregoing provisions and matters related thereto from time to time as it deems expedient.

Passed in the House of Assembly on the 10th day of August, 1981.

M. Albertha Jno. Baptiste
Acting Clerk of the House of Assembly

13. Dominican Republic

Law No. 573
Entered into force: April 1, 1977.
Source: Organization of American States (OAS), June 10, 1977 (Translated from Spanish by OAS).

THE NATIONAL CONGRESS IN THE NAME OF THE REPUBLIC

Law No. 573

Considering

The present evident trend on the part of several countries to claim for themselves the resources of the sea and to extend the limits of their jurisdictional waters; and that the United Nations is promoting harmonious regulation of these trends, which will constitute the standards for definitive codification of the Law of the Sea;

Considering

That it is necessary for the Dominican State to encourage utilization of the marine resources found beyond its territorial waters;

Considering

That, in the light of the progress achieved by science and technology in this field and the duty that we have to conserve these valuable resources for use by present and future generations, we cannot defer updating our legislation, to promote full and effective exercise by this state of the riparian rights to which it is entitled; and

Having seen

Article 5 of the Constitution of the Dominican Republic; and

Having seen

The Declaration of Santo Domingo, issued by the Especialized Conference of the Caribbean countries on the Problems of the Sea, dated July 9, 1972,

HAS ENACTED THE FOLLOWING LAW

Article 1

The title of Law No. 186 of September 13, 1967 and articles 3, 4, 5, 6, 7, and 8 are amended as follows:

Title

'On the Territorial Sea, Contiguous Zone, Exclusive Economic Zone, and Continental Shelf.

Article 2

This law nulifies any provision that may be contrary to it.

Article 3

A contiguous zone, suplementary to the territorial sea, called 'Contiguous Zone' is hereby established. It consists of a band of water, beginning on the outer limit of the territorial sea and shall extend 24 nautical miles, counted from the base lines from which the width of the territorial sea is measured.

Paragraph 1

The Dominican state shall take the necessary supervisory measures in the contiguous zone to:

a. Avoid any violations of its customs, tax, migration, and health laws that might be committed in its territory or on its territorial sea;

b. Punish violations of these laws committed in its territory or on its territorial sea.

Article 4

A zone outside of and adjacent to the territorial sea is hereby established, which shall be called 'exclusive economic zone'.

Paragraph 1

The exclusive economic zone shall extend in the direction of the high sea to a distance of 200 nautical miles beginning, at the base lines from which the width of the territorial sea is measured. The limits of the zone shall be set by a polygon, which measured from the first longitudinal point of our boundary with the neighbouring Republic of Haiti, at the mouth of the Massacre River or Dajabo, passes through the points whose geographic positions are as follows:

a)	Border Point — Massacre River	
b)	Lat. 19° 50′ 30″ N.	Long. 72° 02′ W.
c)	Lat. 20° 33′ 30″ N.	Long. 72° 08′ 20″ W.
d)	Lat. 20° 36′ N.	Long. 71° 38′ W.
e)	Lat. 20° 33′ N.	Long. 71° 27′ W.
f)	Lat. 20° 34′ 30″ N.	Long. 71° 08′ 30″ W.
g)	Lat. 20° 44′ 30″ N.	Long. 70° 23′ 30″ W.
h)	Lat. 21° 11′ 30″ N.	Long. 69° 29′ W.
i)	Lat. 22° 23′ 30″ N.	Long. 67° 45′ W.
j)	Lat. 21° 49′ N.	Long. 67° 24′ W.
k)	Lat. 18° 33′ 20″ N.	Long. 67° 44′ W.
l)	Lat. 18° 29′ 30″ N.	Long. 67° 47′ 30″ W.
m)	Lat. 18° 21′ 40″ N.	Long. 68° 07′ W.
n)	Lat. 18° 06′ N.	Long. 68° 15′ 30″ W.
ñ)	Lat. 16° 08′ 30″ N.	Long. 68° 21′ 30″ W.
o)	Lat. 15° 18′ N.	Long. 69° 29′ 30″ W.
p)	Lat. 15° 02′ N.	Long. 73° 27′ 30″ W.
q)	Lat. 16° 50′ N.	Long. 72° 49′ W.
r)	Lat. 17° 49′ N.	Long. 72° 05′ 30″ W.
s)	Last longitudinal border point with Haiti, in Pedernales.	

Up to joining with the last longitudinal border point on the border with Haiti at the mouth of the Pedernales River.

Article 5

In this zone the Dominica state shall exercise sovereign rights to explore, use, conserve, and manage both living and nonliving natural resources of the depths of the subsoil and the overlying waters.

Paragraph 1

Similarly, it shall exercise exclusive rights and jurisdiction with regard to establishment and utilization of artificial islands, installations, and structures within the zone.

Paragraph 2

The Dominican state shall exercise exclusive jurisdiction with respect to other activities, with a view to exploring and making economic use of the zone, such as production of power from water, currents, and wind.

Paragraph 3

The Dominican state shall exercise jurisdiction with respect to the conservation of the marine environment, including control and reduction of pollution.

Paragraph 4

The Dominican state shall regulate investigation, exploration, and use of the resources within this zone.

Article 6

Establishment of this exclusive economic zone shall not affect the right of freedom of navigation and flight over this zone and the suspension of cables and laying of submarine pipelines; neither shall it affect other legitimate and reasonable international uses of the sea, without prejudice to adherence to the laws and regulations inacted by the Dominican state in accordance with the present law and with the standards of international law.

Article 7

The Dominican state shall exercise sovereign rights over the continental shelf for purposes of its exploration and use of its natural resources.

Paragraph 1

For the purposes of this article, the term 'Continental shelf' includes the seabed and subsoil of the submarine zones extending beyond the territorial sea and the entire length of the natural prolongation of Dominican territory on land, up to the outer border of the continental margin, that is, up to a distance of 200 nautical miles from the base lines from which the territorial sea is measured, in cases in which the outer border of the continental margin does not extend to that distance.

Paragraph 2

The rights referred to in this article are exclusive, in the sense that if the state does not explore the continental shelf or does not use its continental resources, no one may undertake such activities without its express consent.

Paragraph 3

The natural resources referred to in these provisions are mineral resources and other nonliving resources of the seabed and of the subsoil, and also living organism of sedentary species; that is, those that during the period of farming are immobile in the seabed or in its subsoil, and can only move when in constant physical contact with that seabed or subsoil.

Article 8

The provisions of this law shall be applied in harmony with the relevant standards of international law and conventions in force on the matter, which shall be applied to the exclusive economic zone insofar as they are not incompatible.

DONE in the Meeting Room of the Chamber of Deputies, Palace of the National Congress, Santo

Domingo de Guzma, National District, capital of the Dominican Republic, on the second day of March of the year one thousand nine hundred and seventy seven; one hundred and thirty fourth year of the Independence and one hundred and fourteenth year of the Restoration.

Atilio A. Guzmán Fernández,
President
Miriam Marte de Sibilia,
Secretary
José Eligio Bautista Ramos,
Secretary

DONE in the Meeting Room of the Senate, Palace of the National Congress, Santo Domingo de Guzma, National District, capital of the Dominican Republic, on the twenty second day of March of the year one thousand nine hundred and seventy seven; one hundred and thirty fourth year of the Independence and one hundred and fourteenth year of the Restoration.

Adriano A. Uribe Silva,
President of the Senate
Josefina Portes de Valenzuela,
Secretary
Elías Sarraff Eder,
Ad-Hoc Secretary

JOAQUIN BALAGUER
President of the Dominican Republic

In exercise of the powers conferred upon me by Article 55 of the Constitution of the Republic;

I PROMULGATE this law and order that it be published in the Gaceta Oficial, so that it may be known and obeyed.

DONE in Santo Domingo, National Distric, Capital of the Dominican Republic, on the first day of April of the year one thousand nine hundred and seventy seven, one hundred and thirty fourth year of the Independence and one hundred and fourteenth year of the Restoration.

Joaquín Balaguer

14. Egypt

Declarations (upon ratification of the United Nations Convention on the Law of the Sea, of December 10, 1982).
Entered into force: August 26, 1983.
Source: *United Nations — C.N. 272. 1983. Treaties — 16* (Depositary Notification — Translated from Arabic by the United Nations).

On 26 August 1983, the instrument of ratification by the Government of Egypt of the above-mentioned Convention was deposited with the Secretary-General.

Upon ratification, the Government of Egypt, with reference to article 310 of the Convention, made the following declarations:

(Translation) (Original: Arabic)

Declaration concerning the territorial sea

1. The Arab Republic of Egypt establishes the breadth of its territorial sea at 12 nautical miles, pursuant to article 5 of the Ordinance of 18 January 1951 as amended by the Decree of 17 Februay 1958, in line with the provisions of article 3 of the Convention;

2. The Arab Republic of Egypt will publish, at the earliest opportunity, charts showing the baselines from which the breadth of its territorial sea in the Mediterranean Sea and in the Red Sea is measured, as well as the lines marking the outer limit of the territorial sea, in accordance with usual practice.

Declaration concerning the contiguous zone

The Arab Republic of Egypt has decided that its contiguous zone (as defined in the Ordinance of 18 January 1951 as amended by the Presidential Decree of 17 February 1958) extends to 24 nautical miles from the baselines from which the breadth of the territorial sea is measured, as provided for in article 33 of the Convention.

Declaration concerning the passage of nuclear-powered and similar ships through the territorial sea of Egypt

Pursuant to the provisions of the Convention relating to the right of the coastal State to regulate the passage of ships through its territorial sea and whereas the passage of foreign nuclear-powered ships and ships carrying nuclear or other inherently dangerous and noxious substances poses a number of hazards,

Whereas article 23 of the Convention stipulates that the ships in question shall, when exercising the right of innocent passage through the territorial sea, carry documents and observe special precautionary measures established for such ships by international agreements,

The Government of the Arab Republic of Egypt declares that it will require the aforementioned ships to obtain authorization before entering the territorial sea of Egypt, until such international agreements are concluded and Egypt becomes a party to them.

Declaration concerning the passage of warships through the territorial sea of Egypt

[With reference to the provisions of the Convention relating to the right of the coastal State to regulate the passage of ships through its territorial sea:] Warships shall be ensured innocent passage through the territorial sea of Egypt, subject to prior notification.

Declaration concerning passage through the Strait of Tiran and the Gulf of Aqaba

The provisions of the 1979 Peace Treaty between Egypt and Israel concerning passage through the Strait of Tiran and the Gulf of Aqaba come within the framework of the general régime of waters forming straits referred to in part III of the Convention, wherein it is stipulated that the general régime not affect the legal status of waters forming straits and shall include certain obligations with regard to security and the maintenance of order in the State bordering the strait.

Declaration concerning the exercise by Egypt of its rights in the exclusive economic zone

The Arab Republic of Egypt will exercise as from this day the rights attributed to it by the provisions of parts V and VI of the United Nations Convention on the Law of the Sea in the exclusive economic zone situated beyond and adjacent to its territorial sea in the Mediterranean Sea and in the Red Sea.

The Arab Republic of Egypt will also exercise its sovereign rights in this zone for the purpose of exploring and exploiting, conserving and managing the natural resources, whether living or non-living, of the sea-bed and subsoil and the superjacent waters, and with regard to all other activities for the economic exploration and exploitation of the zone, such as the production of energy from the water, currents and winds.

The Arab Republic of Egypt will exercise its jurisdiction over the exclusive economic zone according to the modalities laid down in the Convention with regard to the establishment and use of artificial islands, installations and structures, marine scientific research, the protection and preservation of the marine environment and the other rights and duties provided for in the Convention.

The Arab Republic of Egypt proclaims that, in exercising its rights and performing its duties under the Convention in the exclusive economic zone, it will have due regard for the rights and duties of other States and will act in a manner compatible with the provisions of the Convention.

The Arab Republic of Egypt undertakes to establish the outer limits of its exclusive economic zone in accordance with the rules, criteria and modalities laid down in the Convention.

[The Arab Republic of] Egypt declares that it will take the necessary action and make the necessary arrangements to regulate all matters relating to its exclusive economic zones.

Declaration concerning the procedure chosen for the settlement of disputes in conformity with the United Nations

[With reference to the provisions of article 287 of the Convention:] The Arab Republic of Egypt declares that it accepts the arbitral procedure, the modalities of which are defined in annex VII to the Convention, as the procedure for the settlement of any dispute which might arise between Egypt and any other State relating to the interpretation or application of the Convention.

The Arab Republic of Egypt further declares that it excludes from the scope of application of this procedure those disputes contemplated in article 297 of the Convention.

Statement concerning the Arabic version of the text of the Convention

The Government of the Arab Republic of Egypt is gratified that the Third United Nations Conference on the Law of the Sea adopted the new Convention in six languages, including Arabic, with all the texts being equally authentic, thus establishing absolute equality between all the versions and preventing any one from prevailing over another.

However, when the official Arabic version of the Convention is compared with the other official versions, it becomes clear that, in some cases, the official Arabic text does not exactly correspond to the other versions, in that it fails to reflect precisely the content of certain provisions of the Convention which were found acceptable and adopted by States in establishing a legal régime governing the seas.

For these reasons . . ., the Government of the Arab Republic of Egypt takes the opportunity afforded by the deposit of the instruments of ratification of the United Nations Convention on the Law of the Sea to declare that it will adopt the interpretation which is best corroborated by the various official texts of the Convention.

15. Equatorial Guinea

Act No. 15/1984 of 12 November 1984 on the Territorial Sea and Exclusive Economic Zone of the Republic of Equatorial Guinea
Entered into Force: November 12, 1984
Source: United Nations. *Law of the Sea Bulletin* No. 6, October 1985, pp. 19–22.

PART I

THE TERRITORIAL SEA

Article 1

The sovereignty of the Republic of Equatorial Guinea extends to the entire national territory consisting, in accordance with the boundaries inherited from the colonial era, of the mainland area of Río Muni and the islands of Bioko, Annobón, Corisco, Elobey Grande, Elobey Chico and adjacent islets, internal waters and the adjacent belt of sea described as the territorial sea.

This sovereignty is exercised, in accordance with international law, over the water column, the sea-bed and subsoil, the resources of this sea and the superjacent airspace.

Article 2

The breadth of the territorial sea shall be 12 nautical miles measured from the baselines.

Article 3

The baseline for measuring the breadth of the territorial sea is the low-water line along the coast.

Where there are river mouths, bays, ports, islands and other indentations, however, the baselines for measuring the territorial sea shall be the straight baselines set, in accordance with international law, by the Technical Commission established by this Act.

Article 4

Except where otherwise provided, waters on the landward side of the baseline of the territorial sea form part of the internal waters of the Republic of Equatorial Guines.

Article 5

With regard to coastal States the coastline of which is adjacent to or opposite the coastline of the Republic of Equatorial Guinea, the territorial sea shall not extend beyond a median line every point of which is equidistant from the nearest points on the baselines from which the breadth of the territorial sea of each of the two States, drawn in accordance with international law, is measured.

Article 6

Ships of all States, whether coastal or land-locked, enjoy the right of innocent passage through the territorial sea of the Republic of Equatorial Guinea.

Article 7

Passage is innocent so long as it is not prejudicial to the peace, good order or security of Equatorial Guinea.

Passage of a foreign ship shall be considered to be prejudicial to the peace, good order or security of

Equatorial Guinea if in the territorial sea it engages in any of the following activities:

(a) Any threat or use of force against the sovereignty, territorial integrity or political independence of Equatorial Guinea, or in any other manner in violation of the principles of international law embodied in the Charter of the United Nations;
(b) Any exercise or practice with weapons of any kind;
(c) Any act of propaganda or any act aimed at collecting information to the prejudice of the defence or security of Equatorial Guinea;
(d) The launching, landing or taking on board of any aircraft or military device;
(e) The loading or unloading of any commodity, currency or person contrary to the customs, fiscal, immigration or sanitary laws and regulations of Equatorial Guinea;
(f) Any act of serious international pollution contrary to international law;
(g) The carrying out of any fishing activities, research activities or hydrographic surveys without the corresponding authorization or licence;
(h) Any act aimed at interfering with any systems of communication or any other facilities or installations of Equatorial Guinea;
(i) Any other activity not having a direct bearing on passage.

Article 8

In the territorial sea, submarines and any other foreign underwater vehicles are required to navigate on the surface and to show their flag.

Article 9

Notwithstanding the provisions of article 6 of this Act, foreign ships, by the mere fact of exercising the right of innocent passage through the territorial sea, shall have to comply with any laws and regulations relating to innocent passage enacted by Equatorial Guinea in respect of all or any of the following:

(a) The safety of navigation and the regulation of maritime traffic;
(b) The protection of navigational aids and other facilities or installations;
(c) The protection of cables and pipelines;
(d) The conservation of the living resources of the sea;
(e) The prevention of infringement of fisheries laws and regulations;
(f) The preservation of the environment and the prevention, reduction and control of pollution thereof;
(g) Marine scientific research and hydrographic surveys;
(h) The prevention of infringement of customs, fiscal, immigration and sanitary laws and regulations.

PART II

THE EXCLUSIVE ECONOMIC ZONE

Article 10

The exclusive economic zone is an area beyond and adjacent to the territorial sea.

The exclusive economic zone of the Republic of Equatorial Guinea extends from the outer limit of the territorial sea of the Republic of Equatorial Guinea up to a distance of 200 nautical miles from the baselines from which the breadth of the territorial sea is measured.

Article 11

1. Except where otherwise provided in international treaties concluded with States whose coastlines are opposite or adjacent to those of Equatorial Guinea, the outer limit of the exclusive economic zone of Equatorial Guinea shall not extend beyond the equidistant median line.

2. Equidistant line means that line every point of which is at an equal distance from the nearest points on the line of passage drawn from each State in accordance with international law.

Article 12

In the exclusive economic zone, the Republic of Equatorial Guinea has sovereign rights for the purpose of exploiting, exploring, conserving and managing the natural resources, whether living or non-living, of the sea-bed and subsoil and the superjacent waters, and with regard to other activities for the economic exploitation of the zone.

Article 13

In the exclusive economic zone, the Republic of Equatorial Guinea has exclusive jurisdiction with regard to:

(a) Marine scientific research;
(b) The establishment and use of artificial islands, installations and structures;
(c) The protection and preservation of the environment;
(d) Any other matters which the Government of the Republic of Equatorial Guinea may establish, in accordance with international law.

Article 14

In the exclusive economic zone, fishing shall be reserved for nationals of Equatorial Guinea.

Foreign fishermen shall be able to fish in the exclusive economic zone only when a provision to this effect exists in international treaties concluded by the Republic of Equatorial Guinea with the corresponding States or when the competent authority of Equatorial Guinea grants a special licence outside the framework of an international agreement.

Additional provisions

1. There is hereby established a Technical Commission consisting of representatives of the Ministries of Foreign Affairs and Co-operation; Water, Woods and Reforestation; National Defence; Justice and Worship; Mines and Hydrocarbons; and Public Works, Housing and Urban Development, which shall be responsible for preparing, for submission to the Council of Ministers, charts of an adequate scale showing the baselines used to measure the breadth of the territorial sea, and the limits derived therefrom, in accordance with the provisions of this Act.

2. Such charts shall be accompanied by lists of geographical co-ordinates of points, each of which shall specify the geodetic datum. These charts shall form part of this Act.

3. The above-mentioned Ministries shall designate their respective representatives to the Technical Commission within one month from the date of publication of this Act in the official information media.

4. Any matter not covered by this Act shall be covered by the provisions of the United Nations Convention on the Law of the Sea of 30 April 1982.

Final provisions

1. All legislation conflicting with this Act, in particular Decree-Law No. 17/1970 of 24 September 1970 and Decree-Law No. 28/1976 of 17 October 1976, is hereby revoked.

2. This Act shall enter into force on the date of its publication in the official information media.

16. Fiji

Marine Spaces Act, 1977 and Marine Spaces Order, 1981.
Entered into force: December 1, 1981.
Sources: *Laws of Fiji, Chapter 158A, Marine Spaces and Fiji Royal Gazette, Supplement No. 41,* November 27, 1981.

Acts Nos. 18 of 1977, 15 of 1978

AN ACT TO MAKE PROVISION FOR THE DEMARCATION OF THE MARINE SPACES APPERTAINING TO FIJI, DECLARING THE RIGHTS OF FIJI IN RELATION THERETO: TO REGULATE THE EXPLOITATION OF THE RESOURCES THEREOF AND OTHER ACTIVITIES THEREIN AND TO MAKE FURTHER PROVISION FOR THE REGULATION OF FISHING

[21st April, 1978]

Part 1 — Preliminary

Short title

1. This Act may be cited as the Marine Spaces Act.

Interpretation

2. (1) In this Act, unless the context otherwise requires—
'archipelagic waters' means the archipelagic water of Fiji, as defined in section 4;
'baseline' means the line from which the width of the territorial sea is measured;
'conservation and management' includes all rules, regulations, methods and measures, which are—

- *(a)* required to rebuild, restore or maintain, or which are useful in rebuilding, restoring or maintaining, any fishery resource or the marine environment; and
- *(b)* designed to assure that—
  - (i) a supply of food and other products may be taken, and that recreational benefits may be obtained, on a continuing basis;
  - (ii) irreversible or long-term adverse effects on fishery resources or the marine environment are avoided; and
  - (iii) there will be a multiplicity of options available with respect to future uses of these resources;

'exclusive economic zone' means the exclusive zone of Fiji as defined in section 6;
'Fiji archipelago' means all islands forming part of Fiji, other than the Island of Rotuma and its Dependencies and the island of Ceva-i-Ra;
'Fiji fisheries waters' means all waters appertaining to Fiji and includes all internal waters, archipelagic waters, territorial seas and all waters within the exclusive economic zone;
'Fiji fishing vessel' means any fishing vessel which is registered in Fiji or the operations of which are based on a place in Fiji and which is wholly owned by, or is under exclusive charter to, a natural person who is a resident of, or a company incorporated in, Fiji;
'fish' includes all forms of aquatic animal life except sedentary species as described in paragraph *(b)* of the

definition of 'natural resources' in section 2 of the Continental Shelf Act; *(Cap. 149.)*
'fishery' means any one or more stocks of fish and plant which can be treated as a unit for the purposes of conservation and management and which are identified on the basis of geographical, scientific, technical, recreational and economic characteristics, and includes any fishing for any such stocks; *(Amended by 15 of 1978, s. 2)*
'fishery resource' means any fishery, any stock of fish, any species of fish and any habitat of fish;
'fishing' means the catching, taking or harvesting of fish, including any operations at sea in support of, or in preparation for, any such activity;
'fishing vessel' means any boat, craft, ship or other vessel which is used for, equipped to be used for, or of a type normally used for—

(a) fishing; or
(b) aiding or assisting any other boat, craft, ship or vessel at sea in the performance of any activity relating to fishing, including, but not limited to, preparation, processing, refrigeration, storage, supply or transportation;

'foreign fishing vessel' means any fishing vessel other than a Fiji fishing vessel;
'internal waters' means the internal waters of Fiji, as defined in section 3;
'island' means a naturally formed area of land which is surrounded by and above water at mean high-water spring tides;
'licensee' means the holder of a licence issued under the provisions of section 14;
'low-water line' means the line of low water at mean low-water spring tides as depicted on the largest scale nautical chart of the area produced by any authority and for the time being held and used by the Minister responsible for marine affairs;
'master', in the case of any fishing vessel, means the person for the time being having charge of that vessel;
'mile' means the international nautical mile of one thousand eight hundred and fifty-two metres as depicted on official charts; *(Amended by 15 of 1978, s. 2)*
'Minister' means the Minister responsible for fisheries matters;
'owner', in relation to a fishing vessel, means any person or body of persons whether incorporated or not by whom the vessel is owned and includes any charterer, sub-charterer, lessee or sub-lessee of the vessel;
'Rotuma archipelago' means the island of Rotuma and its dependencies;
'stock of fish' means a species, sub-species, geographical grouping or other category of fish which can be treated as a unit;
'territorial seas' means the territorial seas of Fiji as defined in section 5;
'total allowable catch', with respect to the yield from any fishery, means the amount of fish that will produce from the fishery the maximum sustainable yield, as qualified by any relevant economic or environmental factors and taking into account fishing patterns, the Interdependence of stocks of fish, and any generally recommended subregional, regional, or global standards.

(2) For the purposes of this Act, permanent harbour works that form an integral part of a harbour system shall be treated as forming part of the coast.

Part II — Marine spaces

Internal waters

3. (1) Except where closing lines are drawn under the provisions of subsection (2) the outer limits of the internal waters of Fiji shall be a line drawn along the low-water line of the coast of each island, provided nevertheless that in the case of islands situated on atolls or islands having fringing reefs the line shall be drawn along the seaward low-water line of the reef.

(2) The Minister responsible for Foreign Affairs may, in accordance with the rules of international law,

declare, by reference to physical features marked on official charts or to lists of geographical co-ordinates specifying the geodetic datum, the points between which closing lines are to be drawn for the purpose of determining the outer limits of the internal waters of Fiji in the case of mouths of rivers, bays and permanent harbour works.

(3) Where closing lines are drawn under the provisions of subsection (2) the internal waters of Fiji shall include all waters on the landward side of those closing lines.

Archipelagic waters

4. (1) The archipelagic waters of Fiji comprise all areas of sea contained within the baselines established under the provisions of this section.

(2) The Minister responsible for Foreign Affairs, in accordance with the rules of international law may by order declare, by reference to physical features marked on official charts or to lists of geographical co-ordinates specifying the geodetic datum, the points between which straight baselines are to be drawn for the purpose of determining the outermost limits of the archipelagic waters of Fiji and the innermost limits of the territorial sea of the Fiji archipelago and the Rotuma archipelago.

(Amended by 15 of 1978, s. 3)

Territorial seas

5. (1) The territorial seas of Fiji comprise all areas of sea having as their innermost limits the baselines established under the provisions of this section and as their outermost limits a line measured seaward from those baselines every point of which is at a distance of twelve miles from the nearest point of the baselines.

(2) Where archipelagic baselines are drawn under the provisions of section 4, those baselines shall be the baselines from which the breadth of the territorial sea of the Fiji archipelago and the Rotuma archipelago shall be measured.

(Amended by 15 of 1978, s. 5)

(3) In all other cases the baseline from which the breadth of the territorial sea is measured is the line determining the outer limits of the internal waters of Fiji drawn under the provisions of section 3.

Exclusive economic zone

6. (1)Subject to the following provisions of this section, the exclusive economic zone of Fiji comprises all areas of sea having, as their innermost limits the outermost limits of the territorial seas, and, as their outermost limits, a line drawn seaward from the baselines every point of which is at a distance of 200 miles from the nearest point of the appropriate baseline.

(2) The Minister responsible for Foreign Affairs may by order, for the purpose of implementing any international agreement or the award of any international body, or otherwise, declare that the outer limits of the exclusive economic zone of Fiji extend to such line, any point of which may be at a distance of less than 200 miles from the nearest point of the appropriate baseline, as may be specified in such order.

(3) Where the median line, as defined in subsection (4), is less than 200 miles from the nearest baseline, and no other line is for the time being specified under the provisions of subsection (2), the outer limits of the exclusive economic zone of Fiji extend to the median line.

(4) The median line is a line every point of which is equidistant from the nearest points of the baselines from which the breadth of the territorial seas of Fiji and of any opposite or adjacent State or territory are measured.

Continental Shelf Act to apply

7. All areas of seabed and the subsoil thereof contained within the exclusive economic zone of Fiji are deemed to form part of the continental shelf of Fiji for the purposes of the Continental Shelf Act, and to be subject to the provisions of that Act as if they were areas designated under the provisions of subsection (2) of section 3 of that Act. *(Cap. 149.)*

Charts and publicity

8. (1) The Minister responsible for Foreign Affairs shall cause all closing lines, baselines and other lines drawn under the provisions of this Act for the purpose of determining the limits of the internal waters, territorial seas and exclusive economic zone of Fiji to be clearly indicated on charts of a scale or scales adequate for them to be readily determined and shall give due publicity to such charts by notice in the Gazette and shall cause a copy of each such chart to be deposited with the Secretary-General of the United Nations.

(2) In any proceedings in any court, a certificate purporting to be signed by the Director of Marine that any specified nautical chart of any area is the largest scale nautical chart of that area produced by any authority and for the time being held by the Minister responsible for marine affairs shall be admissible in evidence of the matters stated in the certificate.

Legal character of marine spaces

9. (1) The sovereignty of Fiji extends beyond its land territory and internal waters over its archipelagic waters and territorial seas and to the airspace thereover as well as to the seabed and subsoil thereunder.

(2) Within the exclusive economic zone Fiji has sovereign rights for the purpose of exploring and exploiting, conserving and managing the natural resources, whether living or non-living of the seabed and subsoil and the superjacent waters.

(3) The exercise by Fiji of its sovereignty and sovereign rights under the provisions of this section is subject to the rules of international law.

Rights of other States in marine spaces

10. (1) Subject to the provisions of subsections (2), (3), (4) and (5), ships and aircraft of all States shall, in accordance with the rules of international law, have the right of innocent passage through and over the territorial seas and archipelagic waters.

(2) The Minister responsible for Foreign Affairs may, in accordance with the rules of international law, by order, designate sealanes and air routes, suitable for the continuous and expeditious passage of foreign ships and aircraft, through and over the archipelagic waters and the adjacent territorial seas, and may also prescribe traffic separation schemes for the purpose of ensuring the safe passage of ships through narrow channels in such sealanes.

(3) In such sealanes and air routes all ships and aircraft may, in accordance with the rules of international law, enjoy the right of navigation and overflight, in their normal modes, for the purpose of continuous, expeditious and unobstructed transit through and over the archipelagic waters and the adjacent territorial seas, from one part of the exclusive economic zone to another part of the exclusive economic zone.

(4) Until such time as sealanes or air routes are designated under the provisions of subsection (2) the rights of navigation and overflight referred to in subsection (3) may be exercised through and over all routes normally used for international navigation and overflight.

(5) The rights of navigation and overflight referred to in subsection (3) are subject to all laws of Fiji made in accordance with the rule of international law.

(6) Subject to the provisions of this Act and of any other written law made in accordance with the relevant rules of international law, all States and their nationals shall enjoy, in the exclusive economic zone, the high seas freedoms of navigation and overflight and of the laying of submarine cables and pipelines, and all other internationally lawful uses of the sea related to those freedoms, compatible with the rules of international law.

General regulations in exclusive economic zone

11. Where no other provision is for the time being made in any other written law for any such purpose, the Minister responsible for Foreign Affairs may make regulations, in accordance with the rules of international law, for all or any of the following purposes:—

(a) regulating the conduct of scientific research within the exclusive economic zone;
(b) regulating the exploration and exploitation of the exclusive economic zone for the production of energy from the waters, currents and winds, and for other economic purposes;
(c) regulating the construction, operation and use of artificial islands, installations and structures within the exclusive economic zone, including, but not confined to, the establishment of safety zones around islands, installations and structures;
(d) prescribing measures for the protection and preservation of the marine environment of the exclusive economic zone; and
(e) providing for such other matters as are necessary or expedient to give effect to Fiji's rights and obligations in relation to the exclusive economic zone or are necessary to give full effect to the provisions of this Act, other than matters in respect of which regulations may be made under the provisions of section 22.

Part III — Management and conservation of fisheries

Application of Fisheries Act

12. (1) The archipelagic waters and the waters comprised in the exclusive economic zone shall be part of Fiji fisheries waters as defined in subsection (1) of section 2 of the Fisheries Act and, subject to the provisions of subsection (2), the provisions of that Act shall apply accordingly within the archipelagic waters and the exclusive economic zone. *(Cap. 158.)*

(2) Notwithstanding any other provision in this section or in the Fisheries Act the provisions of that Act relating to the obtaining of licences to take fish or to the registration of fishing vessels shall not apply to the fishing activities of foreign fishing vessels or their crews in the exclusive economic zone. *(Cap. 158.)*

Calculation and apportionment of allowable catch by foreign fishing vessels

13. (1) The Minister shall from time to time determine on the basis of the best avaliable information—

(a) the total allowable catch in respect of every fishery within the exclusive economic zone; and
(b) the portion of that catch which Fiji's fishing vessel have the capacity to harvest.

(2) Where the Minister has determined, in respect of the total allowable catch for a fishery within the exclusive economic zone, the portion that Fiji fishing vessels have the capacity to harvest, the remaining portion shall constitute the allowable catch for that fishery for foreign fishing vessels.

(3) The Minister may from time to time apportion, among countries other than Fiji, the allowable catch for foreign fishing vessles in respect of any fishery within the exclusive economic zone, as determined under subsection (2).

(4) In making an apportionment under subsection (3), the Minister may take into account the following considerations:—

(a) whether the fishing vessels of countries to which the apportionment applies have engaged habitually in fishing within the exclusive economic zone;
(b) whether such countries have co-operated with Fiji in fisheries research and in the identification of fish stocks within the exclusive economic zone;
(c) whether such countries have co-operated with Fiji in the conservation and management of fisheries resources within the exclusive economic zone, and in the enforcement of Fiji law relating to such resources;
(d) the terms of any relevant international agreement;
(e) such other matters as the Minister determines to be relevant.

Licensing of foreign fishing vessels

14. (1) Subject to the provisions of subsection (2) the Minister may grant and issue licences authorising foreign fishing vessels to fish in the exclusive economic zone.

(2) In the exercise of his powers under the provisions of this section the Minister shall ensure to the extent of the information available to him that—

(a) the catch that all foreign fishing vessels licensed under this section are for the time being authorised to harvest from any fishery within the exclusive economic zone does not exceed the allowable catch for foreign fishing vessels for that fishery calculated under subsection (2) of section 13;

(b) the catch that all foreign fishing vessels of a particular country licensed under this section are for the time being authorised to harvest from any fishery within the exclusive economic zone does not exceed the apportionment made under subsection (3) of section 13 for that fishery in respect of that country.

(3) A licence issued under the the provisions of this section shall on payment by the applicant of the prescribed fee, be issued to the owner in respect of a specific boat to be identified by name in the licence and may authorise fishing generally or may confer limited authority by reference to all or any of the following limitations and conditions, namely as to—

(a) the area within which fishing is authorised;
(b) the periods, times or particular voyages during which fishing is authorised;
(c) the descriptions and quantities of fish which may be taken;
(d) the methods by which fish may be taken;
(e) the type of fishing gear, which may be used and the stowage of that gear when not in use;
(f) the use, transfer, transhipment, landing and processing of fish taken;
(g) entry by the vessel into Fiji ports;
(h) the compensation payable in the event of any loss or damage caused by the vessel to other fishing boats, gear or catches or to any fish stocks or to other Fiji interests;
(i) statistical and other information required to be given relating to the operations of the vessel including catch and effort statistics and vessel position reports;
(j) the conduct of fisheries research programmes;
(k) the training of Fiji personnel in the methods of fishing employed by the vessel and the transfer to Fiji of fisheries technology;
(l) the production of the licence on demand by any fisheries officer;
(m) the markings and other means of identification of the vessel;
(n) the placing of Fiji observers on the vessel;
(o) the carrying on board the vessel of specified nautical charts;
(p) the installation and maintenance in working order on the vessel of position fixing or other identification equipment;
(q) compliance by the vessel with directions and instructions of Fiji ships or aircraft; and
(r) such other conditions as the Minister considers necessary or expedient for the regulation of fishing or the conservation and management of fisheries.

Suspension and cancellation of licences

15. (1) Where the Minister is satisfied that—

(a) any foreign fishing vessel in respect of which a licence has been granted under section 14 is being or has been used for fishing within the exclusive economic zone in contravention of any conditions of the licence or any Fiji law relating to fishing; or

(b) the master, licensee or any crew member of a foreign fishing vessel has been convicted of an offence against this Act, or against any regulations made under the provisions of this Act, or against any other Fiji law relating to fishing, he may suspend the licence for such period as he shall specify, or cancel the licence.

(2) Where the Minister determines that it is necessary or expedient for the proper regulation of fishing within the exclusive economic zone to do so, he may vary the conditions of or suspend any licence or licences for such period as he shall specify, or he may cancel any licence or licences.

(3) No determination, variation, suspension, cancellation, or other action of the Minister under subsection (2) shall be reviewable by any court of law.

(4) While a licence is suspended under this section, it shall have no effect.

Licensing offences

16. (1) If any foreign fishing vessel that is not licensed under the provisions of section 14 is used for the purpose of fishing within the exclusive economic zone, the owner and the master of the vessel are each guilty of an offence and liable on conviction to a fine not exceeding one hundred thousand dollars each.

(2) If any foreign fishing vessel is used for the purpose of fishing within the exclusive economic zone in contravention of any of the limitations on or conditions of a licence issued under the provisions of section 14, the master and licensee of the vessel are each guilty of an offence and liable on conviction to a fine not exceeding twenty-five thousand dollars each.

Fisheries officers

17. (1) The following persons shall be fisheries officers for the purpose of this Act, that is to say—

(a) any fisheries officer appointed under the provisions of the Fisheries Act; *(Cap. 158.)*
(b) any customs officer appointed under the provisions of the Customs Act; *(Cap. 196.)*
(c) any police officer;
(d) any commissioned officer of the Royal Fiji Military Forces;
(e) any person in command or charge of any vessel or aircraft operated by or on behalf of the Royal Fiji Military Forces; and
(f) any other person appointed as a fisheries officer by the Minister responsible for fisheries matters.

(2) For the purpose of enforcing the provisions of this Act a fisheries officer may exercise in relation to any foreign fishing vessel within the limits of Fiji fisheries waters and in relation to any Fiji fishing vessel outside those limits the following powers:—

(a) he may go on board that vessel, and for that purpose may require the vessel to stop and to do anything else which will facilitate the boarding of the vessel;
(b) he may require the attendance before him of the master and other persons on board and may make any examination or inquiry which appears to him to be necessary for the purpose of enforcing the provisions of this Act and, in particular—
   (i) may search the vessel and examine any fish found on board and the equipment of the vessel, including the fishing gear, and require persons on board the vessel to do anything which appears to him to be necessary to facilitate the examination; and
   (ii) may require any person on board the vessel to produce any documents relating to that vessel or the persons on board which are in his custody or possession and take copies of any such document.

(3) Where any fisheries officer has reasonable cause to believe that an offence against any of the provisions of section 16 or against any other Fiji law relating to fishing in the exclusive economic zone has

been committed in respect of any foreign fishing vessel, he may, without warrant—

(a) arrest any person who he has reason to believe has committed such offence; and

(b) where he has reason to believe that any such offence has been committed by the master or licensee of the vessel, seize and detain a vessel together with all fish found on board and may take the same and the crew of the vessel to the port which appears to him to be the nearest convenient port.

(4) Any fisheries officer may exercise the powers conferred on him by this section with the aid of such assistants as he considers necessary for the purpose.

(5) Where any fishing vessel is detained under the provisions of subsection (3), it shall be held in the custody of the Crown until a decision is made not to institute proceedings in respect of the alleged offence or, if such proceedings are commenced the security required by the provisions of section 19 is given in respect of the vessel.

(6) All fish detained under the provisions of this section shall be held in the custody of the Crown in respect of the alleged offences for which it was detained, or, if such proceedings are instituted, until the proceedings are determined:

Provided that if adequate facilities are not available for the preservation of such fish pending the completion of the proceedings the Minister may take all steps necessary for the sale of such fish at its reasonable market value, the net proceeds of such sale to be paid into a fund to be held by the court in which such proceedings are taken pending the making of a final order by the court in respect of the forfeiture or otherwise of that fish.

(7) The decision whether or not to institute proceedings in respect of an alleged offence for which a foreign fishing vessel is detained under subsection (3) shall be made as soon as reasonably practicable after the vessel is detained.

(8) The release of a foreign fishing vessel from detention shall not affect any subsequent forfeiture of the vessel in respect of the conviction of any person for an offence.

(9) Where a fisheries officer arrests any person under the provisions of subsection (3) he shall cause that person to be taken as soon as reasonably practicable before a court to be dealt with in accordance with law.

Forfeiture of vessels, etc.

18. On conviction of the owner, master or licensee of an offence under section 16, the court may also order the forfeiture to the Crown of the fishing vessel and any fish, fishing gear, apparatus, cargo and stores found therein or thereon.

Security for release of foreign fishing vessel

19. (1) Where any foreign fishing vessel is detained under section 17, and proceedings are instituted against the master or licensee of the vessel in respect of the offence for which the vessel has been detained, the master or licensee of the vessel or any other person having an interest in the vessel may at any time before the determination of the proceedings apply to the court by which proceedings will be determined for the release of the vessel on the provision of security in accordance with this section.

(2) On hearing the application, the court shall order the release of the foreign fishing vessel on the execution by any suitable person or persons approved by the court for the purpose, of a bond in favour of the Crown, in the prescribed form and conditioned in accordance with subsection (4), in an amount not less than the aggregate of the value of the vessel and the maximum fine to which the defendant will be liable if he is convicted of the offence.

(3) Notwithstanding subsection (2), the court may, where it is satisfied that there are special circumstances to justify it in doing so, order that the bond shall be in a specified amount that is less than the

amount required by that subsection.

(4) The condition of the bond shall be that if—

- *(a)* the defendant is found not guilty of the offence; or
- *(b)* the defendant on being convicted of the offence pays in full within fourteen days after he is convicted the amount of the fine imposed by the court and the foreign fishing vessel is within that time surrendered to the Crown for forfeiture if so ordered by the court, then the bond shall be of no effect, but that otherwise the bond shall remain in full force and effect.

(5) The amount specified in the bond shall be recoverable in full as a debt due to the Crown jointly and severally by the person or persons by whom the bond is given, unless the person or persons prove the due performance of the condition on which the bond is defeasible.

(6) In this section 'foreign fishing vessel' includes all equipment on board the vessel.

Obstruction, etc., of fisheries officer

20. (1) Any person who—

- *(a)* obstructs or hinders any fisheries officer or any person assisting him in the exercise of any of his powers under this Act; or
- *(b)* fails to comply with any lawful requirement imposed or to answer any lawful enquiry made by a fisheries officer under this Act; or
- *(c)* being on board any fishing vessel being pursued or about to be boarded by a fisheries officer, throws overboard or destroys any fish, fishing gear or any other thing whatsoever, shall be guilty of an offence and liable on conviction to a fine not exceeding five thousand dollars.

(2) If an offence under subsection (1) takes place on board or alongside a fishing vessel, the master of that fishing vessel shall be guilty of a like offence and liable to a like penalty.

Non-liability of fisheries officers

21. No fisheries officer shall be personally liable in respect of any act done or omitted to be done by him in good faith in the execution or purported execution of this powers and duties under this Act.

Regulations

22. (1) The Minister may make regulations for all or any of the following purposes:—

- *(a)* prescribing the procedure and forms for application for and granting and renewal of licences under the provisions of the Act;
- *(b)* prescribing the terms and duration of licences;
- *(c)* prescribing the forms of licence that may be issued;
- *(d)* prescribing the classes of licences that may be issued which may include different classes of licences, whether by reference to size of vessel, size of catch, method of fishing, species of catch or otherwise;
- *(e)* prescribing the fees payable for licences which may include different fees for different classes of licences;
- *(f)* providing for the production of licences for inspection when required by a fisheries inspector or other specified authorities;
- *(g)* prescribing conditions under which foreign fishing vessels may fish in the exclusive economic zone;
- *(h)* prescribing measures for the conservation and management of fisheries resources within the exclusive economic zone;
- *(i)* prescribing measures for ensuring that foreign fishing vessels comply with the limitations and conditions of their licences;

(j) prescribing the manner in which and times when fishing gear is to be stowed;
(k) prescribing the form of bonds for the purpose of section 19;
(l) prescribing measures, not inconsistent with the provisions of this Act, for the regulation of fishing for highly migratory species within Fiji fisheries waters and in the case of Fji fishing vessels, beyond the limits of those waters; and
(m) providing for such other matters as appear to him to be necessary for giving full effect to Fiji's sovereignty or sovereign rights over Fiji fisheries waters.

(2) For the purpose of this section the expression 'highly migratory species' means species that in the course of their life cycle, migrate over great distances of ocean.

Fishing for research and sporting purposes excluded

23. The provisions of this Part shall not apply to nor prohibit or restrict fishing by foreign fishing vessels for fisheries research or sporting purposes with the prior consent in writing of the Minister and in accordance with such conditions as the Minister may impose in giving his consent.

Part IV — Miscellaneous

Offences deemed committed in Fiji

24. Any offence against the provisions of this Act that is committed within the exclusive economic zone shall be deemed to have been committed in Fiji.

Interim measures

25. Pending the entry into force of other provisions of this Act, the Minister may by order prescribe interim or transitional measures for the conservation and management of fisheries resources beyond the territorial seas of Fiji and for the limitation of foreign fishing within an area of two hundred miles from the baselines.

Controlled by the Office of the Prime Minister

Sections 3 and 4 — Marine Spaces (Declaration) Order

Order 12th Apr., 1978

Short title

1. This Order may be cited as the Marine Spaces (Declaration) Order.

Internal waters

2. For the purposes of section 3 of the Act, the physical features by reference to which the points between which closing lines are to be drawn are those shown on British Admiralty Chart No. 2691 or, in the case of Rotuma, on British Admiralty Chart No. 2992, connected by those red lines surrounding areas marked with red hatching.

Archipelagic waters

3. (1) For the purposes of section 4 of the Act, the physical features by reference to which the points between which straight baselines are to be drawn are those features which are marked with black figures 1 to 12, inclusive on British Admiralty Chart No. 1291.

(2) The Archipelagic basepoints are thoe which are marked with the red figures 1 to 34, inclusive on the said Chart No. 1291.

Charts

4. The Charts referred to in this Order are the copies kept in the custody of the Solicitor-General with further copies with the Department of Foreign Affairs and the Ministry for Home Affairs.

Controlled by the Office of the Prime Minister

[Legal Notice No. 116]

MARINE SPACES ACT
(Chapter 158A)

DATE OF COMING INTO FORCE OF REMAINING PROVISIONS

In exercise of the powers conferred upon me by section 1 of the Marine Spaces Act, I notify that the remaining provisions of the said Act, that is to say section 6 and Part III, shall come into force on the 1st day of December 1981.

Dated this 19th day of November 1981.

K.K.T. MARA
Minister responsible for Foreign Affairs

[Legal Notice No. 117]

MARINE SPACES ACT
(Chapter 158A)

MARINE SPACES (ARCHIPELAGIC BASELINES AND EXCLUSIVE ECONOMIC ZONE) ORDER, 1981

In exercise of the powers conferred upon me by sections 4 and 6 of the Marine Spaces Act, I have made the following Order:—

Short title

1. This Order may be cited as the Marine Spaces (Archipelagic Baselines and Exclusive Economic Zone) Order, 1981, and shall come into force on the 1st day of December 1981.

Baselines for the Fiji Archipelago

2. The points between which straight baselines are to be drawn for the purpose of determining the outermost limits of the archipelagic waters of Fiji and the innermost limits of the territorial sea of the Fiji archipelago are declared to be the geographical co-ordinates, based on the World Geodetic System 1972 (WGS72) datum, specified in the First Schedule, minus 7 seconds of latitude and 14 seconds of longitude in each case.

3. The outer limits of the exclusive economic zone of Fiji are declared to extend to a line drawn between, and joining in numerical sequence, the geographical co-ordinates, based on the World Geodetic System 1972 (WGS72) datum, specified in the Second Schedule.

Baselines for the Exclusive Economic Zone

4. For the purposes of paragraph 3, the baselines from which the exclusive economic zone of Fiji has been determined are—

(a) in the case of the Fiji archipelago, the straight baselines established in terms of paragraph 2;
(b) in the case of the Island of Rotuma and its dependencies the straight baselines established by the Marine Spaces (Territorial Seas) (Rotuma and its Dependencies) Order, 1981; and

(c) in the case of Ceva-i-Ra Island, a line drawn along the seaward low-water line of the reef.

Dated this 19th day of November 1981.

K.K.T. MARA
Minister responsible for Foreign Affairs

FIRST SCHEDULE
Archipelagic waters

Geographical Co-ordinates
[WGS 72 Geodetic Datum]

No.		*Latitude*	*Longitude*
1.	....	16° 05′ 30″ S.	179° 08′ 36″ W
2.	....	16° 44′ 48″ S.	178° 55′ 54″ W.
3.	....	17° 05′ 06″ S.	178° 40′ 24″ W.
4.	....	17° 10′ 00″ S	178° 37′ 06″ W.
5.	....	17° 55′ 30″ S.	178° 14′ 00″ W.
6.	....	18° 18′ 30″ S.	178° 12′ 48″ W.
7.	....	18° 53′ 00″ S.	178° 21′ 00″ W.
8.	....	18° 57′ 30″ S.	178° 19′ 45″ W.
9.	....	19° 14′ 00″ S.	178° 18′ 36″ W.
10.	....	19° 48′ 00″ S.	178° 13′ 24″ W.
11.	....	19° 53′ 30″ S.	178° 16′ 18″ W.
12.	....	20° 39′ 48″ S.	178° 41′ 24″ W.
13.	....	20° 59′ 54″ S.	178° 44′ 30″ W.
14.	....	21° 01′ 42″ S.	178° 50′ 48″ W.
15.	....	20° 44′ 00″ S.	178° 53′ 30″ W.
16.	....	19° 12′ 18″ S.	179° 44′ 48″ E.
17.	....	19° 11′ 30″ S.	178° 06′ 00″ E.
18.	....	19° 10′ 42″ S.	178° 00′ 00″ E.
19.	....	19° 08′ 42″ S.	177° 57′ 18″ E.
20.	....	19° 07′ 48″ S.	177° 56′ 54″ E.
21.	....	18° 36′ 24″ S.	177° 39′ 36″ E.
22.	....	18° 07′ 00″ S.	177° 19′ 00″ E.
23.	....	17° 56′ 36″ S.	177° 12′ 24″ E.
24.	....	17° 38′ 54″ S.	176° 59′ 48″ E.
25.	....	17° 11′ 54″ S.	176° 52′ 42″ E.
26.	....	17° 09′ 24″ S.	176° 53′ 30″ E.
27.	....	17° 06′ 54″ S.	176° 54′ 36″ E.
28.	....	16° 47′ 00″ S.	177° 17′ 00″ E.
29.	....	16° 39′ 06″ S.	177° 34′ 24″ E.
30.	....	16° 26′ 24″ S.	178° 05′ 48″ E.
31.	....	16° 19′ 24″ S.	178° 27′ 12″ E.
32.	....	16° 10′ 30″ S.	179° 04′ 00″ E.
33.	....	15° 42′ 30″ S.	179° 58′ 30″ W.
34.	....	15° 56′ 54″ S.	179° 23′ 30″ W.

SECOND SCHEDULE

Consecutive No.		*Latitude*	*Longitude*
1.	....	25° 04′ 23″ S.	174° 16′ 32″ E.
2.	....	20° 01′ 21″ S.	172° 45′ 53″ E.
3.	....	18° 32′ 36″ S.	173° 33′ 36″ E.

Thence along an arc of 200 miles (370,400 metres) radius centred on 17° 11′ 47″ S, 176° 52′ 28″ E, passing through the following positions.

4.	18° 18′ 49″ S.	173° 34′ 55″ E.
5.	18° 02′ 02″ S.	173° 29′ 43″ E.
6.	17° 44′ 52″ S.	173° 26′ 05″ E.
7.	17° 27′ 29″ S.	173° 24′ 02″ E.
8.	17° 09′ 59″ S.	173° 23′ 34″ E.
9.	16° 52′ 30″ S.	173° 24′ 41″ E.
10.	16° 35′ 11″ S.	173° 27′ 22″ E.
11.	16° 18′ 10″ S.	173° 31′ 36″ E.
12.	16° 01′ 33″ S.	173° 37′ 20″ E.
13.	15° 45′ 29″ S.	173° 44′ 31″ E.
14.	15° 30′ 04″ S.	173° 53′ 06″ E.
15.	15° 15′ 26″ S.	174° 03′ 01″ E.
16.	15° 01′ 41″ S.	174° 14′ 11″ E.
17.	14° 48′ 28″ S.	174° 27′ 14″ E.

Thence along an arc of 200 miles (370,400 metres) radius centred on 12° 29′ 56″ S, 176° 56′ 01″ E, passing through the following positions.

18.	14° 40′ 56″ S.	174° 20′ 20″ E.
19.	14° 27′ 07″ S.	174° 09′ 17″ E.
20.	14° 12′ 24″ S.	173° 59′ 33″ E.
21.	13° 56′ 54″ S.	173° 51′ 11″ E.
22.	13° 40′ 45″ S.	173° 44′ 14″ E.
23.	13° 24′ 05″ S.	173° 38′ 47″ E.
24.	13° 07′ 00″ S.	173° 34′ 50″ E.
25.	12° 49′ 38″ S.	173° 32′ 25″ E.
26.	12° 32′ 09″ S.	173° 31′ 33″ E.

Thence a line joining 26 and 27. Thence a continued arc of 200 miles (370,400 metres) radius centred on 12° 29′ 56″ S, 176° 56′ 01″ E, passing through the following positions.

27.	11° 57′ 16″ S.	173° 34′ 29″ E.
28.	11° 40′ 09″ S.	173° 38′ 15″ E.
29.	11° 23′ 25″ S.	173° 43′ 30″ E.
30.	11° 07′ 11″ S.	173° 50′ 11″ E.
31.	10° 51′ 36″ S.	173° 58′ 16″ E.
32.	10° 36′ 45″ S.	174° 07′ 40″ E.
33.	10° 22′ 46″ S.	174° 18′ 20″ E.
34.	10° 09′ 45″ S.	174° 30′ 10″ E.
35.	09° 57′ 47″ S.	174° 43′ 05″ E.
36.	09° 46′ 59″ S.	174° 57′ 00″ E.

Thence a line joining.

37.	09° 49′ 09″ S.	175° 51′ 52″ E.
38.	09° 49′ 19″ S.	175° 56′ 40″ E.
39.	09° 49′ 36″ S.	176° 05′ 12″ E.

Consecutive No.	*Latitude*	*Longitude*
40.	09° 49′ 52″ S.	176° 13′ 48″ E.
41.	10° 05′ 17″ S.	177° 06′ 03″ E.
42.	10° 06′ 53″ S.	177° 11′ 10″ E.
43.	10° 16′ 05″ S.	177° 17′ 30″ E.
44.	10° 18′ 18″ S.	177° 19′ 01″ E.
45.	11° 33′ 50″ S.	178° 14′ 47″ E.
46.	11° 38′ 45″ S.	178° 18′ 29″ E.

47.	....	11° 58′ 58″ S.	178° 33′ 48″ E.
48.	....	12° 07′ 15″ S.	178° 40′ 08″ E.
49.	....	12° 12′ 25″ S.	178° 44′ 04″ E.
50.	....	12° 36′ 34″ S.	179° 02′ 40″ E.
51.	....	13° 14′ 05″ S.	179° 31′ 48″ E.
52.	....	13° 19′ 41″ S.	179° 29′ 39″ E.
53.	....	14° 48′ 18″ S.	179° 14′ 23″ W.
54.	....	15° 17′ 47″ S.	178° 31′ 00″ W.
55.	....	15° 56′ 12″ S.	177° 22′ 35″ W.
56.	....	15° 59′ 08″ S.	177° 22′ 31″ W.
57.	....	16° 49′ 39″ S.	176° 53′ 48″ W.
58.	....	16° 50′ 06″ S.	176° 53′ 23″ W.
59.	....	17° 28′ 28″ S.	176° 16′ 24″ W.
60.	....	17° 40′ 49″ S.	176° 16′ 40″ W.
61.	....	17° 59′ 05″ S.	176° 21′ 27″ W.
62.	....	18° 35′ 17″ S.	176° 27′ 02″ W.
63.	....	18° 51′ 23″ S.	176° 34′ 46″ W.
64.	....	18° 54′ 51″ S.	176° 36′ 05″ W.
65.	....	19° 00′ 45″ S.	176° 37′ 40″ W.
66.	....	19° 15′ 09″ S.	176° 40′ 10″ W.
67.	....	19° 20′ 31″ S.	176° 40′ 01″ W.
68.	....	20° 26′ 07″ S.	176° 53′ 00″ W.
69.	....	20° 54′ 36″ S.	177° 01′ 27″ W.
70.	....	20° 57′ 42″ S.	177° 01′ 55″ W.
71.	....	21° 05′ 34″ S.	177° 07′ 57″ W.
72.	....	21° 22′ 21″ S.	177° 18′ 03″ W.
73.	....	22° 21′ 27″ S.	177° 54′ 12″ W.
74.	....	24° 22′ 08″ S.	179° 04′ 16″ W.

Thence along an arc of 200 miles (370,400 meters) radius centred on 21° 01′ 35″ S, 178° 50′ 34″ W passing through the following positions.

75.	....	24° 21′ 29″ S.	179° 09′ 39″ W.
76.	....	24° 19′ 08″ S.	179° 28′ 35″ W.
77.	....	24° 15′ 16″ S.	179° 47′ 11″ W.
78.	....	24° 09′ 53″ S.	179° 54′ 12″ E.
79.	....	24° 03′ 02″ S.	179° 36′ 39″ E.
80.	....	23° 54′ 47″ S.	179° 19′ 52″ E.
81.	....	23° 45′ 12″ S.	179° 03′ 58″ E.
82.	....	23° 34′ 20″ S.	178° 49′ 04″ E.
83.	....	23° 22′ 19″ S.	178° 35′ 17″ E.
84.	....	23° 09′ 12″ S.	178° 22′ 44″ E.
85.	....	22° 55′ 08″ S.	178° 11′ 31″ E.
86.	....	22° 43′ 23″ S.	178° 03′ 46″ E.

Thence along an arc of 200 miles (370,400 metres) radius centred on CEVA-I-RA Island (21° 44′ 18″ S, 174° 38′ 24″ E) passing through the following positions.

Consecutive No.		*Latitude*	*Longitude*
87.	....	22° 50′ 50″ S.	178° 01′ 52″ E.
88.	....	23° 07′ 09″ S.	177° 55′ 01″ E.
89.	....	23° 22′ 50″ S.	177° 46′ 39″ E.
90.	....	23° 37′ 47″ S.	177° 36′ 47″ E.
91.	....	24° 04′ 58″ S.	177° 12′ 54″ E.
92.	....	24° 17′ 01″ S.	176° 59′ 04″ E.
93.	....	24° 27′ 52″ S.	176° 44′ 05″ E.
94.	....	24° 37′ 28″ S.	176° 28′ 06″ E.

95.	....	24° 45′ 44″ S.	176° 11′ 13″ E.
96.	....	24° 52′ 35″ S.	175° 53′ 35″ E.
97.	....	24° 57′ 58″ S.	175° 35′ 20″ E.
98.	....	25° 01′ 51″ S.	175° 16′ 37″ E.
99.	....	25° 04′ 11″ S.	174° 57′ 35″ E.
100.	....	25° 04′ 58″ S.	174° 38′ 24″ E.
101.	....	25° 04′ 11″ S.	174° 19′ 13″ E.

Thence a line to join position 1.

These positions have been based on, or approximated to the best WGS 72 data currently available.

NOTE

(This Note does not form part of the Order but is published for general information).

The above Order constitutes the formal declaration by Fiji of its archipelagic waters and of its 200 miles exclusive economic zone.

Information on the availability of charts illustrating the limits of the internal waters, archipelagic waters the territorial seas and the exclusive economic zone of Fiji is given in Legal Notice No. 119 of 1981.

[Legal Notice No. 118]

MARINE SPACES ACT
(Chapter 158A)

MARINE SPACES (TERRITORIAL SEAS) (ROTUMA AND ITS DEPENDENCIES) ORDER, 1981

In exercise of the powers conferred upon me by section 4 of the Marine Spaces Act, I have made the following Order:—

Short title

1. This Order may be cited as the Marine Spaces. (Territorial Seas) (Rotuma and Its Dependencies) Order, 1981, and shall come into force on the 1st day of December 1981.

Territorial seas baselines

2. The points between which straight baselines are to be drawn for the purpose of determining the innermost limits of the territorial seas of Rotuma and its dependencies are declared to be the geographical co-ordinates, based on the World Geodetic System 1972 (WGS72) datum, specified in the Schedule, plus 3 seconds of latitude and plus 2 seconds of longitude in each case.

Dated this 19th day of November 1981.

K.K.T. MARA
Minister responsible Foreing Affairs

(Paragraph 2)

SCHEDULE

Geographical Co-ordinates
[WGS72 Geodetic Datum]

No.		*Latitude*	*Longitude*
1.	....	12° 28′ 41″ S.	177° 07′ 29″ E.
2.	....	12° 29′ 42″ S.	177° 08′ 21″ E.

3.	....	12° 29′ 54″ S.	177° 08′ 30″ E.
4.	....	12° 30′ 18″ S.	177° 08′ 39″ E.
5.	....	12° 31′ 19″ S.	177° 08′ 51″ E.
6.	....	12° 31′ 39″ S.	177° 08′ 50″ E.
7.	....	12° 31′ 45″ S.	177° 08′ 48″ E.
8.	....	12° 31′ 54″ S.	177° 08′ 30″ E.
9.	....	12° 31′ 40″ S.	177° 06′ 54″ E.
10.	....	12° 31′ 43″ S.	177° 05′ 21″ E.
11.	....	12° 31′ 21″ S.	177° 01′ 54″ E.
12.	....	12° 29′ 58″ S.	176° 56′ 04″ E.
13.	....	12° 29′ 53″ S.	176° 55′ 59″ E.
14.	....	12° 29′ 50″ S.	176° 56′ 02″ E.
15.	....	12° 28′ 33″ S.	176° 57′ 41″ E.
16.	....	12° 28′ 10″ S.	176° 58′ 15″ E.
17.	....	12° 27′ 47″ S.	176° 59′ 11″ E.
18.	....	12° 27′ 44″ S.	176° 59′ 20″ E.
19.	....	12° 27′ 46″ S.	176° 59′ 35″ E.

NOTE

(This Note does not form part of the Order but is published for general information).

The above Order declares the straight baselines constituting the innermost limits of the territorial seas of the Island of Rotuma and its dependencies. Information on the availability of charts illustrating the limits of the territorial seas of the Rotuma group of Islands is given a Legal Notice No. 119 of 1981.

[Legal Notice No. 119]

MARINE SPACES ACT
(Chapter 158A)

Pursuant to section 8 of the Marine Spaces Act, I notify that the charts specified in the Schedule, illustrating all baselines and other lines drawn under the provisions of the said Act for the purpose of determining the limits of the internal waters, archipelagic waters, the territorial seas and the exclusive economic zone of Fiji are available for inspection during normal business hours at the offices of—

(a) the Secretary for Foreign Affairs; and
(b) the Permanent Secretary for Home Affairs.

Copies of the lists of co-ordinates specified on the charts may be purchased from the office of the Hydrographic Unit of the Royal Fiji Military Forces.

Copies of the said charts have been deposited with the Secretary-General of the United Nations.

Dated this 19th day of November 1981.

K.K.T. MARA
Minister responsible Foreign Affairs

SCHEDULE

Chart	*Illustrating*
1.Fiji Marine Spaces Chart 81/1 which is British Admiralty Chart No. 2992 (overprinted by the Government of Fiji with red hatching and with the inset showing Foviung Emua Anchorage deleted and bearing on its face in red letters the words; 'Chart Showing Basepoints and Straight Baselines Enclosing the Internal Waters of Rotuma'.)	The innermost limits of the territorial seas of Rotuma and its dependencies.
2.Fiji Marine Spaces Chart 81/2 which is British Admiralty Chart No. 2691 (overprinted y the Government of Fiji with red hatching and showing Ceva-i-ra Island — spelled Theva-I-Ra Island — as an inset).	The internal waters, archipelagic waters and territorial seas of the Fiji archipelago, and in the case of Ceva-i-ra Island, the baseline from which the exclusive economic zone is determined.
3.Fiji Marine Spaces Chart 81/3 which is British Admiralty Chart No. 780 (overprinted by the Government of Fiji).	The exclusive economic zone of Fiji. The archipelagic baselines for the Fiji Archipelago. The territorial seas of Rotuma and its dependencies and of Ceva-i-ra Island.

NOTE

The consent of the United Kingdom Hydrographer has been given for the reproduction of the Charts enumerated above for the purposes of Fiji's Marine Spaces Act. However all baselines and other lines shown on the charts are the sole responsibility of the Government of Fiji.

[Legal Notice No. 120]

MARINE SPACES ACT
(Chapter 158A)

MARINE SPACES (DECLARATION) (REVOCATION) ORDER, 1981

In exercise of the powers conferred upon me by sections 3 and 4 of the Marine Spaces Act, I have made the following Order:—

Short title

1. This Order may be cited as the Marine Spaces (Declaration) (Revocation) Order, 1981, and shall come into force on the 1st day of December 1981.

Revocation

2. The Marine Spaces (Declaration) Order (appearing at page 1 of the subsidiary legislation included with Chapter 158A of the 1978 Revised Edition of the Laws) is revoked.

Dated this 19th day of November 1981.

K.K.T. MARA
Minister responsible for Foreign Affairs

NOTE

(This Note does not form part of the Order but is published for general information).

The above Order revokes the Order originally published as Legal Notice No. 56 of 1978 which has been rendered superfluous by virtue of the Marine Spaces (Declaration of Archipelagic Waters and Exclusive Economic Zone) Order, 1981 (Legal Notice No. 117 of 1981).

[Legal Notice No. 121]

FISHERIES (AMENDMENT) ACT, 1977
(No. 22 of 1977)

DATE OF COMING INTO FORCE

In exercise of the powers conferred upon me by section 1 of the Fisheries (Amendment) Act, 1977, I notify that the said Act shall come into force on the 1st day of December 1981.

Dated this 20th day of November 1981.

J. MAVOA
Minister for Agriculture and Fisheries

NOTE

(This Note does not form part of the above Legal Notice bu is published for general information).

This Legal Notice brings into force the Fisheries (Amendment) Act, 1977. The amendments made by the Act have been incorporated into the text of the principal Act which appears as Chapter 158 of the 1978 Revised Edition of the Laws.

[Legal Notice No. 122]

MARINE SPACES ACT
(Chapter 158A)

MARINE SPACES (FOREIGN FISHING VESSELS) REGULATIONS, 1979

DATE OF COMING INTO FORCE

In exercise of the powers conferred upon me by regulation 1 of the Marine Spaces (Foreign Fishing Vessels) Regulations, 1979, I notify that the said Regulations shall come into force on the 1st day of December 1981.

Dated this 20th day of November 1981.

J. MAVOA
Minister for Agriculture and Fisheries

17. France

A. Law No. 76–655.
Entered into force: July 18, 1976.
Source: *Journal Officiel de la République Française,* pp. 4291—4300 (Translated from French by the Department of State).

B. Decree No. 77–130.
Entered into force: February 11, 1977.
Source: *Journal Officiel de la République Française,* pp. 864 (Translated from French by the Department of State).

Law No. 76–655 of July 16, 1976 regarding the Economic Zone off the Coasts of the Territory of the Republic

The National Assembly and the Senate have adopted, and
The President of the Republic hereby promulgates the law which reads as follows:

Article 1

The Republic shall exercise, within the economic zone that may extend from the limit of the territorial waters to 188 nautical miles beyond that limit, sovereign rights regarding the exploration and exploitation of the natural resources, biological or non-biological, of the seabed, its sub-soil, and the superjacent waters. Those rights shall be exercised under the conditions and according to the procedures contained in the following articles.

Article 2

The provisions of Law No. 68–1181 of December 30, 1968, regarding the exploration of the continental shelf and the exploitation of its natural resources are applicable, with the exception of Article 1, to the seabed and its subsoil in the economic zone defined in Article 1 above.

Article 3

The provisions of the decree of January 9, 1852, as amended, on marine fishing and those of the law of March 1, 1888, as amended, prohibiting fishing by foreigners in territorial waters are applicable in the economic zone defined in Article 1 above.

However, regarding infractions committed in this zone:

1. The penalties provided for in the first paragraph of Article 6 of the aforementioned decree of January 9, 1852, are replaced by a fine of from F 1,800 to F 36,000, and those provided in the second, third, and fifth paragraphs of the same article are replaced by a fine of from F 720 to 14,400.

2. The fines provided in the third paragraph of Article 2 of the above-mentioned law of March 1, 1888 are replaced by a fine of from F 8,000 to F 160,000.

Moreover, the penalties provided in Articles 4, 5, 6, 7, 8, and 9 of Law No. 66–400 of June 18, 1966 regarding marine fishing and the exploitation of sea products in French Southern and Antarctic Lands are replaced, with respect to infractions committed in the economic zone off this territory, by the following fines:

Article 4: F 4,000 to 20,000
Article 5: F 2,000 to 60,000
Article 6: F 20,000 to 60,000
Article 7: F 2,000 to 60,000
Article 8: F 2,000 to 10,000
Article 9: double the largest fine provided above for each of Articles 5 to 8.

Article 4

Within the economic zone defined in Article 1 above, the French authorities shall exercise the powers recognized by international law regarding the protection of the marine environment.

Article 5

Decrees issued in the Council of State shall establish the conditions and dates of entry into force for the provisions of this law with respect to the economic zone off the various coasts of the territory of the Republic.

This law shall be enforced as a law of the State.

Done at Paris on July 16, 1976.

Valéry Giscard d'Estaing

By the President of the Republic:

Jacques Chirac
Prime Minister

Jean Lecanuet
Minister of State,
Keeper of the Seals,
Minister of Justice

Jean Sauvagnargues
Minister of Foreign Affairs

Ivon Bourges
Minister of Defense

André Fosset
Minister of the Quality of Life

Michel d'Ornano
Minister of Industry and Research

Marcel Cavaillé
Secretary of State to the Minister of
Equipment in Charge of Transportation

Olivier Stirn
Secretary of State to the Minister of
Interior in Charge of Departments and
Overseas Territories

MINISTRY OF EQUIPMENT TRANSPORTATION

Decree No. 77–130 of February 11, 1977, regarding the creation, in application of the law of July 16, 1976, of an economic zone off the coasts of the Republic's territory bounding the North Sea, the English Channel, and the Atlantic Ocean, from the Franco-Belgian border to the Franco-Spanish border.

The Prime Minister

On the basis of the report of the Minister of State, Keeper of the Seals, and Minister of Justice, the Minister of State and Minister of Interior, the Minister of Foreign Affairs, the Minister Delegate to the Prime Minister in Charge of Economy and Finance, the Minister of Defense, the Minister of Equipment, the Minister of Industry and Research, and the Minister of Quality of Life.

In view of: The Decree of January 9, 1852, on marine fishing, amended by the law of February 12, 1930, Order No. 58–1297 of December 23, 1958, Decree No. 69–576 of June 12, 1969, and Law No. 70–1302 of December 31, 1970;

The law of March 1, 1888, regarding the prohibition of fishing by foreigners in French territorial waters, amended by the laws of March 30, 1928, April 16, 1933, No. 64–438 of May 25, 1964, No. 67–451 of June 7, 1967, and No. 67–1086 of December 15, 1967;

Law No. 71–1060 of December 24, 1971, regarding the delimitation of French territorial waters;

Law No. 76–655 of July 16, 1976, regarding the economic zone off the coasts of the Republic's territory, in particular Article 5;

The Mining Code, together with the texts for its application;

Article R.25 of the Penal Code;

Decree No. 63–766 of July 30, 1963, and in particular Article 21, the next to the last paragraph;

The Council of State (Public Works Section) concurring;

Hereby decrees:

Article 1

The economic zone defined in Article 1 of the Law of July 16, 1976 shall extend, off the coasts of the Republic's territory bounding the North Sea, the English Channel, and the Atlantic Ocean, from the Franco-Belgian border to the Franco-Spanish border, for 188 nautical miles beyond the outer limit of the territorial waters, subject to delimitation agreements with neighboring States.

Regarding this zone, the provisions of the aforementioned law shall enter into force on the date of publication of this Decree.

Article 2

Subject to the provisions of the Treaty establishing the European Economic Community and the texts used for its application, fishing is, in accordance with the law of March 1, 1888, as amended, prohibited to foreign vessels in the aforementioned economic zone.

However, notwithstanding those provisions, fishing permits may be granted to certain vessels under the conditions provided by the treaty establishing the European Economic Community and the texts used for its application, by international agreements, and by French domestic law.

Article 3

Regarding fishery infractions committed in the economic zone referred to in Article 1, the penalties provided for in the first paragraph of Article 5, in the sixth paragraph of Article 6, in the first paragraph of Article 7, and in Articles 8 and 9 of the aforementioned Decree of January 9, 1852, as well as the second paragraph of Article 11 of the aforementioned law of March 1, 1888, are replaced by a fine of from F 600 to F 1,000.

Article 4

The Minister of State, Keeper of the Seals and Minister of Justice, the Minister of State and Minister of Interior, the Minister of Foreign Affairs, the Minister Delegate to the Prime Minister in Charge of Economy and Finance, the Minister of Defense, the Minister of Equipment, the Minister of Industry and Research, the Minister of Quality of Life, and the Secretary of State to the Minister of Equipment in Charge of Transportation are charged, each in his own area, with enforcing this Decree, which shall be published in the *Journal Officiel* of the French Republic.

Done at Paris on February 11, 1977.

Raymond Barre

By the Prime Minister:

Jean-Pierre Fourcade
Minister of Equipment

Michel Poniatowski
Minister of State,
Minister of Interior

Michel Durafour
Minister Delegate to the Prime Minister in Charge of Economy and Finance

Michel d'Ornano
Minister of Industry and Research

Marcel Cavaillé
Secretary of State to the Minister of Equipment (Transportation)

Olivier Guichard
Minister of State, Keeper of the Seals, Minister of Justice

Louis de Guiringaud
Minister of Foreign Affairs

Yvon Bourges
Minister of Defense

Vincent Ansquer
Minister of Quality of Life

18. French overseas departments and dependencies

A. St. Pierre and Miquelon
Decree No. 77–169.
Entered into force: February 25, 1977.
Source: *Journal Officiel, de la Republique Francaise,* February 27, 1977, pp. 1102—1103 (Translated from French by the Department of State).

Decree No. 77–169 of February 25, 1977, regarding the creation, in application of the provisions of the law of July 16, 1976, of an economic zone off the coasts of the Department of Saint-Pierre-et-Miquelon

The Prime Minister.

On the basis of the report of the Minister of State, Keeper of the Seals and Minister of Justice, the Minister of State and Minister of Interior, the Minister of Foreign Affairs, the Minister Delegate to the Prime Minister in Charge of Economy and Finance, the Minister of Defense, the Minister of Equipment, the Minister of Industry and Research, and the Minister of Quality of Life;

In view of: The Decree of January 9, 1852, on marine fishing, amended by the law of February 12, 1930, Order No. 58–1297 of December 23, 1958, Decree No. 69–576 of June 12, 1969, and by law No. 70–1302 of December 31, 1970;

The law of March 1, 1888, regarding the prohibition of fishing by foreigners in French territorial waters, modified by the laws of March 30, 1928, April 16, 1933, No. 64–438 of May 25, 1964, No. 67–451 of June 7, 1967, and No. 67–1086 of December 15, 1967;

Law No. 71–1060 of December 24, 1971, regarding the delimitation of French territorial waters;

Law No. 76–655 of July 16, 1976, regarding the economic zone off the coast of the Republic's territory, in particular Article 5;

Law No. 76–664 of July 19, 1976, regarding the organization of Saint-Pierre-et-Miquelon;

The Mining Code, together with the texts used for its application;

Article 25 of the Penal Code;

Decree No. 63–766 of July 30, 1963, and in particular Article 21 (next to the last paragraph);

The Council of State (Public Works Section) concurring,

Hereby decrees:

Article 1

The economic zone, defined in Article 1 of the Law of July 16, 1976, shall extend, off the coast of the Department of Saint-Pierre-et-Miquelon, for 188 nautical miles beyond the outer limit of territorial waters, subject to delimitation agreements with Canada.

Regarding this zone, the provisions of the aforementioned law shall enter into force on the date of publication of this Decree.

Article 2

Subject to the provisions of the Treaty establishing the European Economic Community and the texts used for its application, fishing is, in accordance with the law of March 1, 1888, prohibited to foreign vessels in the aforementioned economic zone.

However, notwithstanding those provisions, fishing permits may be granted to certain foreign vessels under the conditions provided by the Treaty establishing the European Economic Community and the texts used for its application, by international agreements, and by French domestic law.

Article 3

Regarding fishery infractions committed in the economic zone referred to in Article 1, the penalties provided for in the first paragraph of Article 5, the sixth paragraph of Article 6, the first paragraph of Article 7, and in Articles 8 and 9 of the aforementioned Decree of January 9, 1852, as well as the second paragraph of Article 11 of the aforementioned law of March 1, 1888, are replaced by a fine of from F 600 to F 1,000.

Article 4

The Minister of State, Keeper of the Seals, Minister of Justice, the Minister of State, Minister of Interior, the Minister of Foreign Affairs, the Minister Delegate to the Prime Minister in Charge of Economy and Finance, the Minister of Defense, the Minister of Equipment, the Minister of Industry and Research, the Minister of Quality of Life, the Secretary of State to the Minister of Interior, (Departments and Overseas Territories), and the Secretary of State to the Minister of Equipment (Transportation) are charged, each in his own area, with enforcing this Decree, which shall be published in the *Journal Officiel* of the French Republic.

Done at Paris on February 25, 1977.

Raymond Barre

For the Prime Minister:

Jean-Pierre Fourcade
Minister of Equipment

Olivier Guichard
Minister of State, Keeper of the Seals, Minister of Justice

Michel Poniatowski
Minister of State,
Minister of Interior

Louis de Guiringaud
Minister of Foreign Affairs

Michel Durafour
Minister Delegate to the Prime Minister in Charge of Economy and Finance

Yvon Bourges
Minister of Defense

Michel d'Ornano
Minister of Industry and Research

Vincent Ansquer
Minister of Quality of Life

Olivier Stirn
Secretary of State to the Minister of Interior (Departments and Overseas Territories)

Marcel Cavaillé
Secretary of State to the Minister of Equipment (Transportation)

B. French Guiana

Decree No. 77–170.
Entered into force: February 25, 1977.
Source: *Journal Officiel de la Republique Francaise,* February 27, 1977, p. 1103 (Translated from French by the Department of State).

Decree No. 77–170 of February 25, 1977 regarding the creation, in application of the provisions of the law of July 16, 1976, of an economic zone off the coast of the Department of French Guiana.

The Prime Minister,

On the basis of the report of the Minister of State, Keeper of the Seals and Minister of Justice, the Minister of State and Minister of Interior, the Minister of Foreign Affairs, the Minister Delegate to the Prime Minister in Change of Economy and Finance, the Minister of Defense, the Minister of Equipment, the Minister of Industry and Research, and the Minister of Quality of Life,

In view of:

The Decree of January 9, 1852, on marine fishing, modified by the law of February 12, 1930, Order No. 58–1297 of December 23, 1958, Decree No. 69–576 of June 12, 1969, and by Law No. 70–1302 of December 31, 1970;

The law of March 1, 1888, regarding the prohibition of fishing by foreigners in French territorial waters, modified by the laws of March 30, 1928, April 16, 1933, No. 64–438 of May 25, 1964, No. 67–451 of June 7, 1967, and No. 67–1086 of December 15, 1967;

Law No. 71–1060 of December 24, 1971, regarding the delimitation of French territorial waters;

Law No. 76–655 of July 16, 1976 regarding the economic zone off the coast of the Republic's territory, in particular Article 5;

The Mining Code, together with the texts used for its application;

Article R.25 of the Penal Code;

Decree No. 63–766 of July 30, 1963, and in particular Article 21 (next to the last paragraph);

The Council of State (Public Works Section) concurring,

Hereby decrees:

Article 1

The economic zone, defined in Article 1 of the law of July 16, 1976, shall extend, off the coast of the Department of French Guiana, 188 nautical miles beyond the limit of territorial waters, subject to delimitation agreements with neighboring States.

Regarding this zone, the provisions of the aforementioned law shall enter into force on the date of publication of this Decree.

Article 2

Subject to the provisions of the Treaty establishing the European Economic Community and the texts used for its application, fishing is, in accordance with the law of March 1, 1888, prohibited to foreign vessels in the aforementioned economic zone.

However, notwithstanding those provisions, fishing permits may be granted to certain foreign vessels under the conditions provided by the Treaty establishing the European Economic Community and the texts used for its application, by international agreements, and by French domestic law.

Article 3

Regarding fishery infractions committed in the economic zone referred to in Article 1, the penalties provided for in the first paragraph of Article 5, in the sixth paragraph of Article 6, in the first paragraph of Article 7, and in Articles 8 and 9 of the aforementioned Decree of January 9, 1852, as well as in the second paragraph of Article 11 of the aforementioned law of March 1, 1888, are replaced by a fine of from F 600 to F 1,000.

Article 4

The Minister of State, Keeper of the Seals and Minister of Justice, the Minister of State and Minister of Interior, the Minister of Foreign Affairs, the Minister Delegate to the Prime Minister in Charge of Economy and Finance, the Minister of Defense, the Minister of Equipment, the Minister of Industry and Research, the Minister of Quality of Life, the Secretary of State to the Minister of Interior (Departments and Overseas Territories), and the Secretary of State to the Minister of Equipment (Transportation) are charged, each in his own area, with enforcing this Decree, which shall be published in the *Journal Officiel of the French Republic.*

Done at Paris on February 25, 1977.

Raymond Barre

By the Prime Minister:

Jean-Pierre Fourcade
Minister of Equipment

Olivier Guichard
Minister of State, Keeper of the Seals, Minister of Justice

Michel Poniatowski
Minister of State, Minister of Interior

Louis de Guiringaud
Minister of Foreign Affairs

Michel Durafour
Minister Delegate to the Prime Minister in Charge of Economy and Finance

Yvon Bourges
Minister of Defense

Michel d'Ornano
Minister of Industry and Research

Vincent Ansquer
Minister of Quality of Life

Olivier Stirn
Secretary of State to the Minister of Interior (Departments and Overseas Territories)

Marcel Cavaillé
Secretary of State to the Minister of Equipment (Transportation)

C. Clipperton Island

Decree No. 78–147.
Entered into force: February 3, 1978.
Source: *Journal Officiel de la Republique Francaise,* February 11, 1978, p. 683 (Translated from French by the Department of State).

Decree No. 78–147 of February 3, 1978, establishing, in implementation of the law of July 16, 1976, an economic zone along the coasts of Clipperton Island.

The Prime Minister, on the advice of the Keeper of the Seals, Minister of Justice, the Minister of Foreign Affairs, the Minister of the Interior, the Minister of Defense, the Minister of Culture and Environment, the Minister Delegate for Economy and Finance, the Minister of Territorial Development, and the Minister of Industry, Commerce, and Handicrafts,

Having regard to the Constitution, in particular Article 37;

Having regard to the decree of January 9, 1852, on maritime fisheries, as amended by the law of February 12, 1930, Order No. 58–1297 of December 23, 1958, Decree No. 69–576 of June 12, 1969, and Law No. 70–1302 of December 31, 1970;

Having regard to the law of March 1, 1888, which seeks to prohibit foreign vessels from fishing in French territorial waters, as amended by the laws of March 30, 1928, April 16, 1933, No. 64–438 of May 25, 1964, No. 67–1086 of December 15, 1967, and Decree No. 67–451 of June 7, 1967;

Having regard to Decree No. 71–360 of May 6, 1971, implementing Law No. 68–1181 of December 30, 1968, on the exploration of the continental shelf and the development of its natural resources;

Having regard to the mining code, and the texts used for its implementation;

Having regard to Law No. 71–1060 of December 24, 1971, on the delimitation of French territorial waters;

Having regard to Law No. 76–655 of July 16, 1976, on the economic zone along the coast of the territory of the Republic, in particular Article 5;

Having regard to Articles 1, 9, 464, and 466 of the penal code in effect in the overseas territories;

Having regard to the decree of June 12, 1936, re-attaching Clipperton Island to the Government of French Establishments in Oceania;

Having regard to Decree No. 63–766 of July 30, 1963, in particular Article 21 (penultimate paragraph);

The Council of State (public works section) having been consulted:

Hereby decrees:

Article 1

The economic zone defined in Article 1 of the law of July 16, 1976, extends along the coasts of Clipperton Island, from the outer limit of the territorial waters to 188 nautical miles beyond this limit.

With regard to this zone, the said law will enter into force on the date of publication of this decree.

Article 2

In the economic zone defined above and notwithstanding the provisions of the law of March 1, 1888, as amended by the instruments cited above, fishing permits may be issued to certain foreign vessels under the conditions provided for in international agreements and in French domestic law.

Article 3

With regard to fishing violations committed in the economic zone defined in Article 1, the following penalties shall be replaced with a fine of F 600 to F 1,000: those provided for in the first paragraph of Article 5, in the sixth paragraph of Article 6, in the first paragraph of Article 7, and in Articles 8 and 9 of the above-mentioned decree of January 9, 1852, as amended, as well as in the second paragraph of Article 11 of the above-mentioned law of March 1, 1888.

Article 4

In view of the administrative structure of Clipperton, the following adjustments shall be made in the texts cited above:

The minister with responsibility for the merchant marine may delegate to the State representative for this island the powers he holds by virtue of Article 2 and Article 3 (1) of the decree of January 9, 1852, as amended;

Should the representatives of the administrations referred to in Article 31 of Decree No. 71–360 of

May 6, 1971, fail to take their place on the program study commission, the appropriate minister shall appoint representatives of the administrations concerned or of scientific agencies with jurisdiction in the territory to replace them.

Article 5

The Keeper of the Seals, Minister of Justice, the Minister of Foreign Affairs, the Minister of the Interior, the Minister of Defense, the Minister of Culture and Environment, the Minister Delegate for Economy and Finance, the Minister of Territorial Development, the Minister of Industry, Commerce, and Handicrafts, the Secretary of State to the Minister of the Interior (Overseas Departments and Territories) and the Secretary of State to the Minister of Territorial Development (Transportation) are responsible, in their respective areas of competence, for the execution of this decree, which will be published in the *Official Gazette* of the French Republic.

Done at Paris, February 3, 1978.

[Signed by the Prime Minister and the ministers concerned.]

D. French Polynesia

Decree No. 78–143.
Entered into force: February 3, 1978.
Source: *Journal Officiel de la Republique Francaise,* February 11, 1978, pp. 683–684 (Translated from French by the Department of State).

Decree No. 78–143 of February 3, 1978, establishing, in implementation of the law of July 16, 1976, an economic zone along the coasts of the territory of French Polynesia

The Prime Minister, on the advice of the Keeper of the Seals, Minister of Justice, the Minister of Foreign Affairs, the Minister of the Interior, the Minister of Defense, the Minister of Culture and Environment, the Minister Delegate for Economy and Finance, the Minister of Territorial Development, and the Minister of Industry, Commerce, and Handicrafts,

Having regard to the decree of January 9, 1852, on maritime fisheries, as amended by the law of February 12, 1930, Order No. 58–1297 of December 23, 1958, Decree No. 69–576 of June 12, 1969, and Law No. 70–1302 of December 31, 1970;

Having regard to the law of March 1, 1888, which seeks to prohibit foreign vessels from fishing in French territorial waters, as amended by the laws of March 30, 1928, April 16, 1933, No. 64–438 of May 25, 1964, No. 67–451 of June 7, 1967, and No. 67–1086 of December 15, 1967;

Having regard to Law No. 71–1060 of December 24, 1971, on the delimitation of French territorial waters;

Having regard to Law No. 76–655 of July 16, 1976, on the economic zone along the coast of the territory of the Republic, in particular Article 5;

Having regard to the mining code, and the texts used for its implementation;

Having regard to Articles 1, 9, 464, and 466 of the penal code in effect in the overseas territories;

Having regard to Law No. 77–772 of July 12, 1977 on French Polynesia;

Having regard to Decree No. 63–766 of July 30, 1963, in particular Article 21 (penultimate paragraph);

The Council of State (public works section) having been consulted:

Hereby decrees:

Article 1

The economic zone defined in Article 1 of the law of July 16, 1976, extends along the coasts of the territory of French Polynesia, from the outer limit of the territorial waters to 188 nautical miles beyond this limit, subject to delimitation agreements with neighboring States.

With regard to this zone, the said law will enter into force on the date of publication of this decree.

Article 2

In the economic zone defined above and notwithstanding the provisions of the law of March 1, 1888, as amended by the instruments cited above, fishing permits may be issued to certain foreign vessels under the conditions provided for in international agreements and in French domestic law.

Article 3

With regard to fishing violations committed in the economic zone defined in Article 1, the penalties provided for in the second paragraph of the above-mentioned law of March 1888 shall be replaced with a fine of 600 to 1,000 francs.

Article 4

The Keeper of the Seals, Minister of Justice, the Minister of Foreign Affaire, the Minister of the Interior, the Minister of Defense, the Minister of Culture and Environment, the Minister Delegate for Economy and Finance, the Minister of Territorial Development, the Minister of Industry, Commerce, and Handicrafts, the Secretary of State to the Minister of the Interior (Overseas Departments and Territories) and the Secretary of State to the Minister of Territorial Development (Transportation) are responsible, in their respective areas of competence, for the execution of this decree, which will be published in the *Official Gazette* of the French Republic.

Done at Paris, February 3, 1978.

[Signed by the Prime Minister and the ministers concerned.]

E. Mayotte

Decree No. 78–149.
Entered into force: February 3, 1978.
Source: *Journal Officiel de la Republique Francaise,* February 11, 1978 (Translated from French by the Department of State).

Decree No. 78–149 of February 3, 1978, establishing, in implementation of the law of July 16, 1976, an economic zone along the coasts of the territorial community of Mayotte

The Prime Minister, on the advice of the Keeper of the Seals, Minister of Justice, the Minister of Foreign Affairs, the Minister of the Interior, the Minister of Defense, the Minister of Culture and Environment, the Minister Delegate for Economy and Finance, the Minister of Territorial Development, and the Minister of Industry, Commerce, and Handicrafts,

Having regard to the Constitution, in particular Article 37;

Having regard to the decree of January 9, 1852, on maritime fisheries, as amended by the law of February 12, 1930, Order No. 58–1297 of December 23, 1958, Decree No. 69–576 of June 12, 1969, and Law No. 70–1302 of December 31, 1970;

Having regard to the law of March 1, 1888, which seeks to prohibit foreign nationals from fishing in French territorial waters, as amended by the laws of March 30, 1928, April 16, 1933, No. 64–438 of May 25, 1964, No. 67–451 of June 7, 1967, and No. 67–1086 of December 15, 1967;

Having regard to Law No. 71–1060 of December 24, 1971, on the delimitation of French territorial waters;

Having regard to Law No. 76–655 of July 16, 1976, on the economic zone along the coast of the territory of the Republic, in particular Article 5;

Having regard to Decree No. 71–360 of May 6, 1971, implementing Law No. 68–1181 of December 30, 1968, on the exploration of the continental shelf and the development of its natural resources;

Having regard to the mining code, and the texts used for its implementation;

Having regard to Articles 1, 9, 464, and 466 of the penal code in effect in the overseas territories;

Having regard to Decree No. 63–766 of July 30, 1963, in particular Article 21 (penultimate paragraph);

The Council of State (public works section) having been consulted:

Hereby decrees:

Article 1

The economic zone defined in Article 1 of the law of July 16, 1976, extends along the coasts of the territorial community of Mayotte, from the outer limit of the territorial waters to 188 nautical miles beyond this limit, subject to delimitation agreements with neighboring States.

With regard to this zone, the said law will enter into force on the date of publication of this decree.

Article 2

In the economic zone defined above and notwithstanding the provisions of the law of March 1, 1888, as amended by the instruments cited above, fishing permits may be issued to certain foreign vessels under the conditions provided for in international agreements and in French domestic law.

Article 3

In view of the administratieve structure of the territorial community of Mayotte, the following modifications shall be made in the texts cited above:

To Article 2 of Decree No. 69–576 of June 12, 1969, amending the decree of January 9, 1852, on maritime fisheries, the following words shall be added:

'At Mayotte, such delegation shall be extended to the government representative if no such service has been organized in the territorial community.'

The following shall be added to Article 3 of said decree:

'At Mayotte, after consulting with the representative of ISTPM or any other scientific agency with jurisdiction in the territorial community, the government representative shall exercise the powers assigned in the previous paragraph to the director of maritime affairs, if no such service has been organized.'

Article 4

If no representatives of the administrations referred to in Article 8 of Decree No. 71–360 of May 6, 1971, are available to sit on the program study commission mentioned in that article, the appropriate minister shall appoint a representative from his administration to sit on said commission.

Article 5

With regard to fishing violations committed in the economic zone defined in Article 1, the following penalties shall be replaced with a fine of F 600 to F 1,000: Those provided for in the first paragraph of Article 5, in the sixth paragraph of Article 6, in the first paragraph of Article 7, and in Articles 8 and 9 of the above-mentioned decree of January 9, 1852, as amended, as well as in the second paragraph of Article 11 of the above-mentioned law of March 1, 1888.

Article 6

The Keeper of the Seals, Minister of Justice, the Minister of Foreign Affairs, the Minister of the Interior, the Minister of Defense, the Minister of Culture and Environment, the Minister Delegate for Economy and Finance, the Minister of Territorial Development, the Minister of Industry, Commerce, and Handicrafts, the Secretary of State to the Minister of the Interior (Overseas Departments and Territories) and the Secretary of State to the Minister of Territorial Development (Transportation) are responsible, in their respective areas of competence, for the execution of this decree, which will be published in the *Official Gazette* of the French Republic.

Done at Paris, February 3, 1978.

[Signed by the Prime Minister and the ministers concerned.]

F. New Caledonia

Decree 78–142.
Entered into force: February 3, 1978.
Source: *Journal Officiel de la Republique Francaise,* February 11, 1978 (Translated from French by the Department of State).

Ministry of the Interior

Decree No. 78–142 of February 3, 1978, establishing, in implementation of the law of July 16, 1976, an economic zone along the coasts of the territory of New Caledonia and dependencies.

The Prime Minister, on the advice of the Keeper of the Seals, Minister of Justice, the Minister of Foreign Affairs, the Minister of the Interior, the Minister of Defense, the Minister of Culture and Environment, the Minister Delegate for Economy and Finance, the Minister of Territorial Development, and the Minister of Industry, Commerce, and Handicrafts,

Having regard to the decree of January 9, 1852, on the exercise of maritime fishing, as amended by the law of February 12, 1930, Order No. 58–1297 of December 23, 1958, Decree No. 69–576 of June 12, 1969, and Law No. 70–1302 of December 31, 1970;

Having regard to the law of March 1, 1888, which seeks to prohibit foreign vessels from fishing in French territorial waters, as amended by the laws of March 30, 1928, April 16, 1933, No. 64–438 of May 25, 1964, No. 67–1086 of December 15, 1967, and by Decree No. 67–451 of June 7, 1967.

Having regard to Law No. 71–1060 of December 24, 1971, on the delimitation of French territorial waters;

Having regard to Law No. 76–655 of July 16, 1976, on the economic zone along the coasts of the territory of the Republic, in particular Article 5;

Having regard to the mining code, and the series of texts used for its implementation;

Having regard to Law No. 76–1222 of July 16, 1976, on the organization of the territory of New Caledonia and dependencies, in particular Article 7;

Having regard to Articles 1, 9, 464, and 466 of the penal code in effect in the overseas territories;

Having regard to decree No. 63–766 of July 30, 1963, in particular Article 21 (penultimate paragraph);

The Council of State (public works section), having been consulted:
Hereby decrees:

Article 1

The economic zone defined in Article 1 of the law of July 16, 1976, extends along the coasts of the territory of New Caledonia and dependencies, from the outer limit of the territorial waters to 188 nautical miles beyond this limit, subject to delimitation agreements with neighboring States.

With regard to this zone, the provisions of the abovementioned law will enter in effect on the date of publication of this decree.

Article 2

In the economic zone defined above and notwithstanding the provisions of the law of March 1, 1888, as amended by the instruments cited above, fishing authorizations may be issued to certain foreign vessels under the conditions provided for in international agreements and in French domestic law.

Article 3

With regard to fishing violations committed in the economic zone defined in Article 1, the penalties provided for in the second paragraph of Article 11 of the above-mentioned law of March 1, 1888, shall be replaced with a fine of F 600 to F 1,000.

Article 4

The Keeper of the Seals, Minister of Justice, Minister of Foreign Affairs, the Minister of the Interior, the Minister of Defense, the Minister of Culture and Environment, the Minister Delegate for Economy and Finance, the Minister of Territorial Development, the Minister of Industry, Commerce, and Handcrafts, the Secretary of State to the Minister of the Interior (Overseas Departments and Territories) and the Secretary of State to the Minister of Territorial Development (Transportation) are responsible, in their respective areas of competence, for the execution of this decree, which will be published in the *Official Gazette* of the French Republic.

Done at Paris February 3, 1978.

Raymond Barre

By the Prime Minister:

Christian Bonnet
Minister of the Interior
Louis de Guiringaud
Minister of Foreign Affairs
Michel d'Ornano
Minister of Culture and Environment
Fernand Icart
Minister of Territorial Development
Olivier Stirn
Secretary of State to the Minister of the Interior (Overseas Departments and Territories)

Alain Peyrefitte
Keeper of the Seals, Minister of Justice
Yvon Bourges
Minister of Defense
Robert Boulin
Minister Delegate for Economy and Finance
René Monory
Minister of Industry, Commerce, and Handicrafts
Marcel Cavaillé
Secretary of State to the Minister of Territorial Development (Transportation)

G. Reunion

Decree No. 78–148.
Entered into force: February 3, 1978.
Source: *Journal Officiel de la Republique Francaise,* February 11, 1978, p. 687 (Translated from French by the Department of State).

Decree No. 78–148 of February 3, 1978, establishing, in implementation of the law of July 16, 1976, an economic zone along the coasts of the department of Reunion

The Prime Minister, on the advice of the Keeper of the Seals, Minister of Justice, the Minister of Foreign Affairs, the Minister of the Interior, the Minister of Defense, the Minister of Culture and Environment, the Minister Delegate for Economy and Finance, the Minister of Territorial Development, and the Minister of Industry, Commerce, and Handicrafts,

Having regard to the decree of January 9, 1852, on maritime fisheries, as amended by the law of February 12, 1930, Order No. 58–1297 of December 23, 1958, Decree No. 69–576 of June 12, 1969, and Law No. 70–1302 of December 31, 1970;

Having regard to the law of March 1, 1888, which seeks to prohibit foreign nationals from fishing in French territorial waters, as amended by the laws of March 30, 1928, April 16, 1933, No. 64–438 of May 25, 1964, No. 67–451 of June 7, 1967, and No. 67–1086 of December 15, 1967;

Having regard to Law No. 71–1060 of December 24, 1971, on the delimitation of French territorial waters;

Having regard to Law No. 76–655 of July 16, 1976, on the economic zone along the coast of the territory of the Republic, in particular Article 5;

Having regard to the mining code, and the texts used for its implementation;

Having regard to Article R 25 of the penal code;

Having regard to Decree No. 63–766 of July 30, 1963, in particular Article 21 (penultimate paragraph);

The Council of State (public works section) having been consulted:

Hereby decrees:

Article 1

The economic zone defined in Article 1 of the law of July 16, 1976, extends along the coasts of the department of Reunion, from the outer limit of the territorial waters to 188 nautical miles beyond this limit, subject to delimitation agreements with neighboring States.

With regard to this zone, the said law will enter into force on the date of publication of this decree.

Article 2

Subject to the provisions of the Treaty establishing the European Economic Community and the texts used for its implementation, fishing shall be, in accordance with the law of March 1, 1888, as amended, prohibited to foreign vessels in the above–mentioned economic zone.

However, notwithstanding said provisions, fishing permits may be issued to certain foreign vessels under the conditions provided for in the Treaty establishing the European Economic Community and the texts used for its implementation, in international agreements, and in French domestic law.

Article 3

With regard to fishing violations committed in the economic zone defined in Article 1, the following penalties shall be replaced with a fine of F 600 to F 1,000: those provided for in the first paragraph of Article 5, in the sixth paragraph of Article 6, in the first paragraph of Article 7, and in Articles 8 and 9 of the above-mentioned decree of January 9, 1852, as amended, as well as in the second paragraph of Article 11 of the above-mentioned law of March 1, 1888.

Article 4

The Keeper of the Seals, Minister of Justice, the Minister of Foreign Affairs, the Minister of the Interior, the Minister of Defense, the Minister of Culture and Environment, the Minister Delegate for Economy and Finance, the Minister of Territorial Development, the Minister of Industry, Commerce, and Handicrafts, the Secretary of State to the Minister of the Interior (Overseas Departments and Territories) and the Secretary of State to the Minister of Territorial Development (Transportation) are responsible, in their respective areas of competence, for the execution of this decree, which will be published in the *Official Gazette* of the French Republic.

Done at Paris, February 3, 1978.

[Signed by the Prime Minister and the ministers concerned.]

H. Islands of Tromelin, Glorious Archipelago, Juan-de-Nova, and the Europa and Bassas-da-India

Decree No. 78–146.
Entered into force: February 3, 1978.
Source: *Journal Officiel de la Republique Francaise,* February 11, 1978, p. 686 (Translated from French by the Department of State).

Decree No. 78–146 of February 3, 1978, establishing, in implementation of the law of July 16, 1976, an economic zone along the coasts of Tromelin Island, the Glorieuses islands, Juan-de-Nova (St. Christophe) Island, Europa Island and the Bassas-da-India Islands

The Prime Minister, on the advice of the Keeper of the Seals, Minister of Justice, the Minister of Foreign Affairs, the Minister of the Interior, the Minister of Defense, the Minister of Culture and Environment, the Minister Delegate for Economy and Finance, the Minister of Territorial Development, and the Minister of Industry, Commerce, and Handicrafts,

Having regard to the Constitution, in particular Article 37;

Having regard to the decree of January 9, 1852, on maritime fisheries, as amended by the law of February 12, 1930, Order No. 58–1297 of December 23, 1958, Decree No. 69–576 of June 12, 1969, and Law No. 70–1302 of December 31, 1970;

Having regard to the law of March 1, 1888, which seeks to prohibit foreign vessels from fishing in French territorial waters, as amended by the laws of March 30, 1928, April 16, 1933, No. 64–438 of May 25, 1964, No. 67–1086 of December 15, 1967 and Decree No. 67–451 of June 7, 1967;

Having regard to Decree No. 71–360 of May 6, 1971, implementing Law No. 68–1181 of December 30, 1968, on the exploration of the continental shelf and the development of its natural resources;

Having regard to the mining code, and the texts used for its implementation;

Having regard to Law No. 71–1060 of December 24, 1971, on the delimitation of French territorial waters;

Having regard of Law No. 76–655 of July 16, 1976, on the economic zone along the coast of the territory of the Republic, in particular Article 5;

Having regard to Articles 1, 9, 464, and 466 of the penal code in effect in the overseas territories;

Having regard to Decree No. 60–559 of April 1, 1960, on the administrative status of certain islands under French sovereignty;

Having regard to Decree No. 63–766 of July 30, 1963, in particular Article 21 (penultimate paragraph);

The Council of State (public works section) having been consulted;

Hereby decrees:

Article 1

The economic zone defined in Article 1 of the law of July 16, 1976, extends along the coasts of Tromelin Island, the Glorieuses islands, Juan-de-Nova (St. Christophe) Island, Europa Island and the Bassas-da-India Islands, from the outer limit of the territorial waters to 188 nautical miles beyond this limit, subject to delimitation agreements with neighboring States.

With regard to this zone, the said law will enter into force on the date of publication of this decree.

Article 2

In the economic zone defined above and notwithstanding the provisions of the law of March 1, 1888, as amended by the instruments cited above, fishing permits may be issued to certain foreign vessels under the conditions provided for in international agreements and in French domestic law.

Article 3

With regard to fishing violations committed in the economic zone defined in Article 1, the following penalties shall be replaced with a fine of F 600 to F 1,000: those provided for in the first paragraph of Article 5, in the sixth paragraph of Article 6, in the first paragraph of Article 7, and in Articles 8 and 9 of the above-mentioned decree of January 9, 1852, as amended, as well as in the second paragraph of Article 11 of the above-mentioned law of March 1, 1888.

Article 4

Bearing in mind the special administrative structure of the islands referred to in Decree No. 60–555 of April 1, 1960, the following adjustments shall be made in the texts cited below:

The minister with responsibility for the merchant marine may delegate to the State representative for these islands the powers he holds by virtue of Article 2 and Article 3 (1) of the decree of January 9, 1852, as amended;

Should the representatives of the administrations referred to in Article 31 of Decree No. 71–360 of May 6, 1971, fail to take their place on the program study commission, the appropriate minister shall appoint representatives of the administrations concerned or of scientific agencies with jurisdiction in the territory to replace them.

Article 5

The Keeper of the Seals, Minister of Justice, the Minister of Foreign Affairs, the Minister of the Interior, the Minister of Defense, the Minister of Culture and Environment, the Minister Delegate for Economy and Finance, the Minister of Territorial Development, the Minister of Industry, Commerce, and Handicrafts, the Secretary of State to the Minister of the Interior (Overseas Departments and Territories) and the Secretary of State to the Minister of Territorial Development (Transportation) are responsible, in their respective areas of competence, for the execution of this decree, which will be published in the *Official Gazette* of the French Republic.

Done at Paris, February 3, 1978.

[Signed by the Prime Minister and the ministers concerned.]

I. French Southern and Antarctic Lands

Decree No. 78–144.
Entered into force: February 3, 1978.
Source: *Journal Officiel de la Republique Francaise,* February 11, 1978 (Translated from French by the Department of State).

Decree No. 78–144 of February 3, 1978, establishing, in implementation of the law of July 16, 1976, an economic zone along the coasts of the French southern lands (Territory of the French Southern and Antarctic Lands)

The Prime Minister, on the advice of the Keeper of the Seals, Minister of Justice, the Minister of Foreign Affairs, the Minister of the Interior, the Minister of Defense, the Minister of Culture and Environment, the Minister Delegate for Economy and Finance, the Minister of Territorial Development, and the Minister of Industry, Commerce, and Handicrafts,

Having regard to the law of March 1, 1888, which seeks to prohibit foreign vessels from fishing in French territorial waters, as amended by the laws of March 30, 1928, April 16, 1933, No. 64–438 of May 25, 1964, No. 67–1086 of December 15, 1967, and No. 67–451 of June 7, 1967;

Having regard to Law No. 66–400 of June 18, 1966, on maritme fisheries and marine resource development in the French Southern and Antarctic Lands together with Decree No. 69–408 of April 25, 1969, establishing the administrative regulations for the implementation of said law;

Having regard to Law No. 71–1060 of December 24, 1971, on the delimitation of French territorial waters;

Having regard to Law No. 76–655 of July 16, 1976, on the economic zone along the coast of the territory of the Republic, in particular Article 5;

Having regard to Law No. 55–1052 of August 6, 1955, granting the French Southern and Antarctic Lands administrative and financial autonomy, in particular Article 1;

Having regard to Decree No. 71–360 of May 6, 1971, implementing Law No. 68–1181 of December 30, 1968, on the exploration of the continental shelf and the development of its natural resources;

Having regard to the mining code, and the texts used for its implementation;

Having regard to Decree No. 63–766 of July 30, 1963, in particular Article 21 (penultimate paragraph);

The Council of State (public works section) having been consulted:

Hereby decrees:

Article 1

The economic zone defined in Article 1 of the law of July 16, 1976, extends along the coasts of the French southern lands (Territory of the French Southern and Antarctic Lands), from the outer limit of the territorial waters to 188 nautical miles beyond this limit, subject to delimitation agreements with neighborng States.

With regard to this zone, the said law will enter into force on the date of publication of this decree.

Article 2

In the economic zone defined above and notwithstanding the provisions of the law of March 1, 1888, as amended by the instruments cited above, fishing permits may be issued to certain foreign vessels under the conditions provided for in international agreements and in French domestic law.

Article 3

The following provisions apply to fishing, and, generally speaking, to the development of biological marine resources in the economic zone mentioned in Article 1: those of the law of June 18, 1966, on maritime fisheries and marine resource development in the Territory of the French Southern and Antarctic Lands and those of the decree of April 25, 1969, establishing administrative regulations for the implementation of said law.

Article 4

Should the representatives of the administrations referred to in Article 31 of Decree No. 71–360 of May 6, 1971, fail to take their place on the program study commission, the appropriate minister shall appoint representatives of the central administrations concerned or of the scientific agencies with jurisdiction in the territory to replace them.

Article 5

The Keeper of the Seals, Minister of Justice, the Minister of Foreign Affairs, the Minister of the Interior, the Minister of Defense, the Minister of Culture and Environment, the Minister Delegate for Economy and Finance, the Minister of Territorial Development, the Minister of Industry, Commerce, and Handicrafts, the Secretary of State to the Minister of the Interior (Overseas Departments and Territories) and the Secretary of State to the Minister of Territorial Development (Transportation) are responsible, in their respective areas of competence, for the execution of this decree, which will be published in the Official Gazette of the French Republic.

Done at Paris, February 3, 1978.

[Signed by the Prime Minister and the ministers concerned.]

J. Wallis and Futuna Islands

Decree No. 78–145.
Entered into force: February 3, 1978.
Source: *Journal Officiel de la Republique Francaise,* February 11, 1978 (Translated from French by the Department of State).

Decree No. 78–145 of February 3, 1978, establishing, in implementation of the law of July 16, 1976, an economic zone along the coasts of the territories of Wallis and Futuna Islands

The Prime Minister, on the advice of the Keeper of the Seals, Minister of Justice, the Minister of Foreign Affairs, the Minister of the Interior, the Minister of Defense, the Minister of Culture and Environment, the Minister Delegate for Economy and Finance, the Minister of Territorial Development, and the Minister of Industry, Commerce and Handicrafts,

Having regard to the Constitution, in particular Article 37;

Having regard to the decree of January 9, 1852, on the exercise of maritime fishing, as amended by the law of February 12, 1930, Order No. 58–1297 of December 23, 1958, Decree No. 69–576 of June 12, 1969, and Law No. 70–1302 of December 31, 1970;

Having regard to the law of March 1, 1888, which seeks to prohibit foreign vessels from fishing in French territorial waters, as amended by the laws of March 30, 1928, April 16, 1933, No. 64–438 of May 25, 1964, No. 67–1086 of December 15, 1967, and by Decree No. 67–451 of June 7, 1967;

Having regard to Decree No. 71–360 of May 6, 1971, implementing Law No. 68–1181 of December 30,

1968, on the exploration of the continental shelf and the development of its natural resources;

Having regard to the mining code, and the series of texts used for its implementation;

Having regard to Law No. 71–1060 of December 24, 1971, on the delimitation of French territorial waters;

Having regard to Law No. 76–655 of July 16, 1976, on the economic zone along the coast of the territory of the Republic, in particular Article 5;

Having regard to Articles 1, 9, 464, and 466 of the penal code in effect in the overseas territories;

Having regard to Law No. 61–814 of July 29, 1961, according Wallis and Futuna Islands the status of overseas territories, as amended by Law No. 73–549 of June 28, 1973;

Having regard to Decree No. 63–766 of July 30, 1963, in particular Article 21 (penultimate paragraph);

The Council of State (public works section) having been consulted:

Hereby decrees:

Article 1

The economic zone defined in Article 1 of the law of July 16, 1976, extends along the coasts of the territories of Wallis and Futuna Islands, from the outer limit of the territorial waters to 188 nautical miles beyond this limit, subject to delimitation agreements with neighboring States.

With regard to this zone, the said law will enter into force on the date of publication of this decree.

Article 2

In the economic zone defined above and notwithstanding the provisions of the law of March 1, 1888, as amended by the instruments cited above, fishing permits may be issued to certain foreign vessels under the conditions provided for in international agreements and in French domestic law.

Article 3

With regard to fishing violations committed in the economic defined in Article 1, the following penalties shall be replaced with a fine of F 600 to F 1,000:

Those provided for in the first paragraph of Article 5, in the sixth paragraph of Article 6, in the first paragraph of Article 7, and in Articles 8 and 9 of the above-mentioned decree of January 9, 1852, as amended, as well as in the second paragraph of Article 11 of the above-mentioned law of March 1, 1888.

Article 4

In view of the administrative structure of the territory of Wallis and Futuna islands, the following modifications shall be made in the texts cited above:

The minister with responsibility for the merchant marine may delegate to the State representatives for the territory the powers he holds by virtue of article 2 and Article 3(1) of the decree of January 9, 1852, as amended;

If no representatives from the administrations indicated in Article 31 of Decree No. 71–360 of May 6, 1971, are available to sit on the program study commission, the appropriate minister shall appoint representatives of the administrations concerned or of scientific agencies with jurisdiction in the territory to replace them.

Article 5

The Keeper of the Seals, Minister of Justice, Minister of Foreign Affairs, the Minister of the Interior, the Minister of Defense, the Minister of Culture and Environment, the Minister Delegate for Economy and Finance, the Minister of Industry, Commerce, and Handicrafts, the Secretary of State to the Minister of the Interior (Overseas Departments and Territories) and the Secretary of State to the Minister of Territorial Development (Transportation) are responsible, in their respective areas of competence, for the execution of this decree, which will be published in the Official Gazette of the French Rpublic.

Done at Paris February 3, 1978

Raymond Barre

By the Prime Minister:

Christian Bonnet
Minister of the Interior
Louis de Guiringaud
Minister of Foreign Affairs
Michel D'Ornano
Minister of Culture and Environment
Fernand Icart
Minister of Territorial Development
Olivier Stirn
Secretary of State to the Minister of the Interior (Overseas Departments and Territories)

Alain Peyrefitte
Keeper of the Seals, Minister of Justice
Yvon Bourges
Minister of Defense
Robert Boulin
Minister Delegate for Economy and Finance
René Monory
Minister of Industry, Commerce, and Handicrafts
Marcel Cavaillé
Secretary of State to the Minister of Territorial Development (Transportation)

K. Guadeloupe & Martinique

Decrees No. 78–276 (Guadeloupe) and 78–277 (Martinique).
Entered into force: March 6, 1978.
Source: *Journal Officiel de la Republique Francaise,* March 11, 1978, pp. 1048–1049 (Translated from French by the Department of State).

Decree No. 78–276 of March 6, 1978, establishing, in application of the Law of July 16, 1976, an economic zone off the coasts of the Department of Guadeloupe.

The Prime Minister,

Acting on the report of the Keeper of the Seals, Minister of Justice, the Minister of Foreign Affairs, the Minister of Interior, the Minister of Defense, the Minister of Culture and the Environment, the Deputy Minister of Economy and Finance, the Minister of Equipment and Territorial Development, and the Minister of Industry, Trade, and Crafts;

Considering the Decree of January 9, 1852 on maritime fishing, as amended by the Law of February 12, 1930, *Ordonnance* No. 58–1297 of December 23, 1958, Decree No. 69–576 of June 12, 1969, and Law No. 70–1302 of December 31, 1970;

Considering the Law of March 1, 1888, prohibiting foreigners from fishing in French territorial waters, as amended by the Laws of March 30, 1928, April 16, 1933, No. 64–438 of May 25, 1964, No. 67–451 of June 7, 1967, and No. 67–1086 of December 15, 1967;

Considering Law No. 71–1060 of December 24, 1971, concerning delimitation of French territorial waters;

Considering Law No. 76–655 of July 16, 1976, concerning the economic zone off the coasts of the territory of the Republic, in particular Article 5 of that Law;

Considering the Mining Code together with the texts govering its implementation;

Considering Article R. 25 of the Penal Code;

Considering Decree No. 63–766 of July 30, 1963, in particular the next to the last paragraph of Article 21;

After consultation with the Council of State (Division of Public Works),
Has decreed as follows:

Article 1

The economic zone defined in Article 1 of the Law of July 16, 1976, shall extend, off the coasts of the Department of Guadeloupe, from the outer limit of the territorial waters up to 188 nautical miles beyond this that limit, subject to delimitation agreements with neighboring States.

With regard to this zone, the provisions of the above-mentioned law shall enter into force on the date of publication of this decree.

Article 2

Subject to the provisions of the Treaty establishing the European Economic Community and the texts governing its implementation, in conformity with the Law of March 1, 1888, as amended, foreign vessels shall be prohibited from fishing in the above-mentioned economic zone.

Notwithstanding these provisions, fishing authorizations may be issued to certain foreign vessels under the conditions stipulated by the Treaty establishing the European Economic Community and the texts governing its implementation, by international agreements, and by French municipal law.

Article 3

With regard to fishing violations committed in the economic zone referred to in Article 1, thepenalties stipulated in Article 5 (1), Article 6 (6), Article 7 (1), and Articles 8 and 9 of the above-mentioned Decree of January 9, 1852, and in Article 11 (2) of the above-mentioned Law of March 1, 1888, shall be replaced by a fine of F 600 to F 1,000.

Article 4

The Keeper of the Seals, Minister of Justice, the Minister of Foreign Affairs, the Minister of Interior, the Minister of Defense, the Minister of Culture and the Environment, the Deputy Minister of Economy and Finance, the Minister of Equipment and Territorial Development, the Minister of Industry, Trade, and Crafts, the Secretary of State to the Minister of Interior (Overseas Departments and Territories), and the Secretary of State to the Minister of Equipment and Territorial Development (Transportation) shall be charged, insofar as each one is concerned, with enforcing this Decree which shall be published in the *Journal Officiel* of the French Republic.

Done at Paris, March 6, 1978.

Raymond Barre
Prime Minister

Fernand Icart
Minister of Equipment and Territorial Development
Louis de Guiringaud
Minister of Foreign Affairs
Yvon Bourges
Minister of Defense
Robert Boulin
Deputy Minister of Economy
Olivier Stirn
Secretary of State to the Minister of Interior (Overseas Departments and Territories)

Alain Peyrefitte
Keeper of the Seals, Minister of Justice
Christian Bonnet
Minister of Interior
Michel d'Ornano
Minister of Culture and the Environment
Rene Morony
Minister of Industry, Trade, and Crafts
Marcel Cavaillé
Secretary of State to the Minister of Equipment and Territorial Development (Transportation)

Martinique

[The wording of Decree No. 78–277 of March 6, 1978, establishing, in application of the Law of July 16, 1976, an economic zone off the coasts of the Department of Martinique is identical to the wording of the above decree, except that Department of Martinique is substituted for Department of Guadeloupe in Article 1.]

19. Gabon

Law No. 9/84
Entered into force: July 12, 1984.
Source: Government of Gabon (Translated from French by the US Department of State)

Office of the President of the Republic

Gabonese Republic

Law No. 9/84
Establishing an Exclusive Economic Zone of 200 Nautical Miles

The National Assembly has deliberated and adopted and the President of the Republic and Head of State hereby promulgates the following Law:

Article 1

A maritime zone shall be established, designated Exclusive Economic Zone, located beyond the Gabonese territorial waters and adjacent to them.

Article 2

The Exclusive Economic Zone shall extend over a distance of 200 nautical miles, calculated from the straight baselines and the normal baselines used for measuring the breadth of the territorial sea.

Article 3

In the Exclusive Economic Zone, the Gabonese State shall have sovereign rights for the purpose of exploring and exploiting, conserving and managing, the natural, biological, and non-biological resources of the seabed, subsoil, and superjacent waters.

The sovereignty of the Gabonese State shall assert itself by its right to undertake the economic exploration and the exploitation of the zone, such as the production of energy from the water, currents, and winds.

Article 4

In this zone, the Gabonese State shall have the exclusive right to undertake the construction, use, and exploitation of artificial islands, installations, and structures for the purposes provided for in Article 3 above, or for other economic purposes.

Article 6

All ships must respect these safety zones and shall comply with generally accepted standards regarding navigation within the vicinity of artificial islands, installations, structures, and safety zones.

Article 7

The Gabonese State shall have exclusive jurisdiction over such artificial islands, installations, and structures, including jurisdiction with regard to customs, fiscal, health, safety, and immigration laws and regulations.

Article 8

The Gabonese State shall have exclusive competence within its Exclusive Economic Zone with regard to marine scientific research and the preservation of the marine environment.

Article 9

In the Exclusive Economic Zone, the exercise of fishing rights shall be reserved by priority to ships flying the Gabonese flag or operated by Gabonese nationals, or by individual and legal entities under Gabonese law.

Article 10

The Gabonese State shall determine the allowable catch of the living resources in its Exclusive Zone and shall take the proper conservation and management measures to prevent the over-exploitation of those resources.

Article 11

When the outer boundaries of the Exclusive Economic Zone determined in accordance with the provisions of Article 2 above encroach upon the Exclusive Economic Zone of a bordering or neighboring State, the common boundaries shall be established by agreement with the State in question or in accordance with the generally recognized principles of international law on delimination.

Article 12

Beyond the outer limit of the territorial sea, the institution of the Exclusive Economic Zone shall not affect the freedom of navigation and overflight, and the freedom to lay submarine cables and pipelines, and internationally lawful uses of the sea related to these freedoms.

Article 13

In exercising the freedoms mentioned in Article 12 above, foreign States and their nationals shall take into account the sovereign rights of the Gabonese State and shall respect the laws and regulations adopted by it in accordance with international law.

Article 14

In exercising the freedoms mentioned in Article 12 above, it shall be forbidden for any foreign ship to engage in any fishing activity in the Exclusive Economic Zone, including the stowing of fishing and research equipment and tackle, or in any activity polluting or damaging the marine environment harmful to the resources of that zone or to the economic interests of the Gabonese State.

Article 15

In an area designated as a contiguous zone, located beyond the territorial sea and adjacent to it, up to a distance of 24 nautical miles calculated from the straight baselines and the normal baselines used to measure the breadth of the territorial sea, the Gabonese State exercises the control necessary to:

— prevent infringement of its customs, fiscal, sanitation or immigration laws and regulations;

— punish the infractions of the above laws and regulations committed within its territory or territorial sea.

Article 16

The provisions of this Law do not obstruct the principles of international cooperation to which the Gabonese State subscribes and which are formalized by agreements with other States, without prejudice to its rights of sovereignty and with respect for its legitimate interests.

Article 17

This Law, which abrogates all previous conflicting provisions, shall be recorded and published in accordance with emergency procedure and executed as Law of the State.

Done at Libreville, July 12, 1984

Signed by the President of the Republic and Head of State, El Hadj Omar Bongo; the Prime Minister and Head of Government, Léon Mebiame; and other Ministers concerned.

20. Grenada

Marine Boundaries Act, Act No. 20.
Entered into force: November 1, 1978.
Source: *The Government Printer,* at the Government Printing Office, St. George's, Grenada, 1978.

MARINE BOUNDARIES ACT, 1978
ARRANGEMENT OF SECTIONS

Section

Part V
General

GRENADA

ACT NO. 20 OF 1978

I assent,

L.S.

19th May, 1978.

L.V. De Gale
Governor-General

AN ACT to provide for the establishment of Marine Boundaries.

[*19th May, 1978*]

Be it enacted by the Queen's Most Excellent Majesty, by and with the advice and consent of the Senate and House of Representatives of Grenada, and by the authority of the same, as follows:—

Part I
Preliminary

Short title

1. This Act may be cited as the

MARINE BOUNDARIES ACT, 1978

Interpretation

2. For the purposes of this Act—

'Grenadian vessel' or 'Grenadian structure' means a vessel or structure, as the case may be—

(*a*) wholly owned by a citizen of Grenada or by a body corporate whose members or, if that body corporate is a company, whose shareholders, as the case may be, are all citizens of Grenada, or
(*b*) certified in writing by the Minister as having such substantial economic connections with Grenada in relation to its ownership as to be deemed, for the purposes of this Act, to be a Grenadian vessel or Grenadian structure, as the case may be;

Act No. 17 of 1978

'baselines' has the meaning assigned to it by section 4 of the Grenada Territorial Waters Act, 1978;
'Exclusive Economic Zone' or 'Zone' means the marine zone established by section 3 (1) of 3 (3) as the case may be;

'fish' includes marine fishes, crustacea, sea-eggs, whales, porpoises, Mollusca or other marine animals and includes marine plant life;
'fishing' means—

- *(a)* the catching, taking or harvesting of fish;
- *(b)* any activity reasonably expected to result in the catching, taking or harvesting of fish; or
- *(c)* any operation at sea in connection with, or in preparation for, the catching, taking or harvesting of fish or an activity referred to in paragraph (b);

'fishing vessel' means any ship, vessel, boat or other craft used for, or of a type normally used for, fishing or aiding or assisting another vessel at sea in the performance of any activity relating to fishing;
'foreign fishing vessel', 'foreign vessel', or 'foreign structure' means a fishing vessel, vessel or structure, as the case may be, of a foreign State;
'foreign State' means a State other than Grenada;

Act No. 17 of 1978

'internal waters' has the meaning assigned to it by section 5 of the Grenada Territorial Waters Act, 1978;
'marine conservation officer' means a person designated a marine conservation officer under section 14;
'Minister' means the Minister responsible for External Affairs;
'mile' means the international nautical mile;
'ship' includes vessel, boat or other sea-going or ocean-going craft;

Act No. 17 of 1978

'structure' includes any artificial island, offshore terminal or offshore installation;
'territorial waters', in relation to Grenada, has the meaning assigned to it by section 3 of the Grenada Territorial Waters Act, 1978, and includes internal waters.

Part II

Economic Zone

Exclusive Economic Zone

3. (1) There is established, contiguous to the territorial waters, a marine zone to be known as the Exclusive Economic Zone having as its inner limit the boundary line of the seaward limit of the territorial waters and as its outer limit a boundary line which, subject to subsection (3), at every point is a distance of 200 miles from the nearest point of the baselines of the territorial waters or such other distance from the nearest point of those baselines as the Minister may, by order, prescribe.

(2) An order made under subsection (1) is subject to affirmative resolutions of the Senate and the House of Representatives.

(3) Notwithstanding subsection (1), where the median line as defined by subsection (4) between Grenada and any adjacent or opposite State is less than 200 miles from the baselines of the territorial waters, the outer boundary limit of the Zone shall be that fixed by agreement between Grenada and that other State, but where there is no such agreement, the outer boundary limit shall be the median line.

(4) The median line is a line every point of which is equidistant from the nearest points of the baselines of the territorial waters, on the one hand, and the corresponding baselines of the territorial waters of any adjacent or opposite State as recognised by the Minister, on the other hand.

(5) An agreement entered into pursuant to subsection (3) shall be laid before Parliament, and shall be judicially noticed.

Marking of boundary lines of Zone on charts or maps

4. (1) The Minister shall cause the boundary lines of the Zone to be marked on a scaled map or chart, and that map or chart shall be judicially noticed.

(2) The Minister shall make provision for the safe custody of the map or chart referred to in subsection (1), and shall, by notice, specify the place where any person may inspect that map or chart or purchase a certified copy thereof.

Rights in, and jurisdiction over, Zone

5. There is vested in the Government of Grenada—

(a) all rights in, and jurisdiction over, the Zone in respect of—

(i) the exploration, exploitation, conservation, protection or management of the natural living and non-living resources of the sea-bed; subsoil and superjacent waters,

(ii) the construction maintenance or use of structures or devices relating to the exploration or exploitation of the resources of the Zone, the regulation and safety of shipping, or any other economic purpose,

(iii) the authorisation, regulation or control of scientific research,

(iv) the preservation and protection of the marine environment and the prevention and control of marine pollution,

(v) all other activities relating to the economic exploration and exploitation of the Zone; and

(b) all other rights in, and jurisdiction over, the Zone recognised by international law.

Exploitation of resources of Zone

6. (1) Subject to this Act, no person shall within the Zone, except under or in accordance with an agreement with the Government of Grenada or a permit granted by the Minister—

(a) explore or exploit any resources thereof;
(b) carry out any search or excavation;
(c) conduct any research;
(d) drill in or construct, maintain or operate any structure or device; or
(e) carry out any economic activity.

(2) This section does not apply to fishing by a citizen of Grenada, in or from a Grenadian vessel.

(3) Any person who contravenes this section is guilty of an offence and liable—

(a) on conviction on indictment, to a fine not exceeding $50,000 or imprisonment for a term not exceeding 5 years or both; or

(b) on summary conviction, to a fine not exceeding $20,000 or imprisonment for a term not exceeding 2 years or both, and in addition, the court may order the forfeiture of any vessel, structure, equipment, device or thing in connection with which the offence was committed.

Freedom of navigation, overflight, and laying of cables etc.

7. Subject to sections 8 and 11, ships and aircraft of all states are not, in or over the Zone, as the case may be, restricted in or prohibited from the enjoyment of the freedom of navigation, overflight, the laying of cables and pipelines and the other lawful use of the sea related to navigation and communication recognised by international law.

Application of certain enactments of Zone

8. (1) The Governor-General may, by order, with such exceptions and modifications as may be specified in the order, extend the application of any enactment to the Zone or any part thereof, and on enactment so extended shall have effect in relation to the Zone as if it had been enacted by this Act.

(2) An order made under this section is subject to affirmative resolutions of the Senate and House of Representatives.

Jurisdiction of Courts

9. (1) The jurisdiction and powers of the courts extend to the Zone for the purpose of giving effect to the provisions of this Act and any other enactment extended to the Zone under section 8 as if the Zone were a part of the territory of Grenada.

(2) Where an offence is, by virtue of this Act or any enactment extended to the Zone under section 8, punishable on summary conviction or indictment, it may be enquired into or determined, as the case may be, by a magistrate assigned to any magisterial district, and that magistrate has, in respect of the offence, all the powers, privileges, rights and jurisdiction conferred on him by the Magistrates Ordinance.

Cap. 177

(3) The quasi-criminal and the civil jurisdiction conferred on a magistrate by the Magistrates Ordinance is, in relation to the Zone, exercisable by a magistrate assigned to any magisterial district.

(4) The jurisdiction and power conferred on the courts under this Act do not affect any jurisdiction or powers conferred on, or exercisable by, those courts under any other law.

Locus of offence etc.

10. (1) In any proceedings in a court in relation to the Zone, the averment that an offence was committed or that an act was done within the limits of the Zone shall, until the contrary is proved, be deemed to be *prima facie* evidence that the *locus in quo* was within the Zone.

(2) An incident shall, for the purposes of any law conferring jurisdiction on a court in Grenada, be deemed to have occurred in Grenada if—

- *(a)* that incident occurs in, on, under above or in relation to any vessel, structure or device or any waters within 500 yards of that structure or device, in the Zone; or
- *(b)* that incident, if having occurred in Grenada, would be an offence or give rise to quasi-criminal proceedings or a civil cause of action.

Part III

Fishing in the Zone

Permission to fish in the Zone or territorial waters

11. (1) No person shall engage in fishing within the Zone or the territorial waters unless—

- *(a)* he is a citizen of Grenada;
- *(b)* he is the holder of a valid permit granted under subsection (4); or
- *(c)* there is in existence in relation to him an agreement with the Government of Grenada.

(2) The master or other person in charge of a foreign vessel shall not permit that vessel to be used for the purpose of fishing in the Zone or the territorial waters unless there is on board that vessel a valid permit granted under subsection (4).

(3) The master or other person in charge of a foreign fishing vessel on board of which there is not a valid permit granted under this section in respect of that vessel shall not, except for the purpose of exercising the freedom of navigation referred to in section 7 or granted pursuant to an agreement under section 6, permit or cause that vessel to enter the Zone; and where a vessel enters the Zone in accordance with the terms of that permit or agreement, that master or other person shall not cause or permit the vessel to remain in the Zone after the purpose for which it entered the Zone has been fulfilled or the agreement has expired.

(4) The Minister may—

(a) grant to a person, who is not a citizen of Grenada; or
(b) grant in respect of a foreign fishing vessel, a permit to engage in fishing within the Zone, the territorial waters, or any designated part thereof.

(5) Any person who contravenes this section or a term or condition of a permit granted under this Act is guilty of an offence and liable on summary conviction to a fine not exceeding $ 20,000 or imprisonment for a term not exceeding 2 years or both, and in addition, the court may order the forfeiture of any vessel, fish, fishing gear, equipment, device or thing in connection with which the offence was committed.

Content of permit

12. (1) A permit granted under section 11 in respect of a foreign vessel may contain—

(a) the name of the owner or charterer;
(b) the name of the vessel;
(c) a description of the vessel;
(d) a description of the area designated for fishing;
(e) the periods or times allowed for fishing and the number of voyages authorised;
(f) the descriptions and quantities of fish permitted to be taken;
(g) the method of fishing;
(h) conditions respecting the landing of fish or parts of fish;
(i) the name of the port or place for the landing of fish caught;
(j) the permitted use of any fish caught; and
(k) any other term or condition, including fees and charges payable, approved by the Minister.

Variation, revocation or suspension of permit

13. A permit granted under section 11 may be varied, suspended or revoked, if it appears necessary or expedient to the Minister.

Part IV

Marine Conservation Officers

Conservation officers

14. For the purposes of this Act, the following persons are designated marine conservation officers—

(a) fisheries officers of the Ministry responsible for Fisheries;
(b) members of the Military Force of Grenada;
(c) members of the Police Force;
(d) officers of Customs;
(e) officers of the Coast Guard; and
(f) any other person approved by the Minister.

Powers of conservation officers

15 (1) A marine conservation officer may, in performing his duties, exercise all the powers conferred on him by this Act in respect of—

(a) a Grenadian vessel or Grenadian structure that is at sea or in port; or
(b) a foreign vessel or foreign structure that he reasonably suspects of being used in connection with fishing or any other activity carried on in contravention of this Act or the regulations.

(2) In the performance of his duties under this section, a marine conservation officer may—

(*a*) reasonably call on any person to assist him;
(*b*) use such force as is reasonably necessary;
(*c*) require any person to do anything that appears reasonably necessary for the purpose of facilitating the performance of those duties;
(*d*) order that any vessel or structure be stopped;
(*e*) board any vessel or structure;
(*f*) search or examine any vessel or structure or any fish, equipment or thing on board thereof;
(*g*) require any person on board a vessel or structure to produce any document or thing relating to that vessel or structure or the persons on board thereof.

(3) A marine conservation officer who has reasonable grounds to suspect that an offence has been committed under this Act or the regulations by any person, including any person on board a vessel or structure, may, without warrant or other process—

(*a*) seize the vessel or structure together with any fish, fishing gear or other equipment suspected of being used in the commission of the offence; and
(*b*) detain the person he suspects.

(4) Where a vessel, structure or thing is seized or a person is detained under subsection (3), a marine conservation officer shall, where possible, take the vessel, structure, thing or person as soon as practicable to a port in Grenada and within a reasonable time cause the person detained to be brought before a magistrate's court to answer a charge in connection with the offence that gave rise to the seizure or detention.

(5) A court may order that any vessel, structure, fishing gear or other equipment, device or thing seized under subsection (3) be forfeited where the owner thereof is unknown and no claim thereto is made within 1 month of the seizure under that subsection.

Sale of fish likely to spoil

16. (1) A marine conservation officer may, to avoid spoilage or decay of any fish he seizes under section 15, sell that fish in such manner as a fisheries officer of the Ministry responsible for Fisheries directs.

(2) All moneys resulting from a sale of fish under subsection (1) shall be paid into the Consolidated Fund.

(3) A marine conservation officer who makes a sale of fish under subsection (1) shall give to the person from whom he seized the fish a receipt containing

(*a*) the date of the sale;
(*b*) the quantity of fish;
(*c*) the amount realised by the sale, and the receipt shall be signed by the officer.

(4) Where a court dismisses a charge against a person brought before it under section 15, it shall, in any case where the fish in the possession of that person was sold, order compensation not exceeding the net amount realised by the sale to be paid to that person.

(5) Compensation payable under subsection (4) shall be charged on, and paid out of, the Consolidated Fund.

Exemption from liability

17. No liability attaches to the Crown, a marine conservation officer or fisheries officer in respect of acts done by that officer in good faith in the performance of his duties under this Act.

Part V
General

General offences

18. Any person who—

(a) assaults, resists, obstructs or intimidates a marine conservation officer or any person assisting him, in the execution of his duty;
(b) uses indecent, abusive or insulting language to a marine conservation officer in the execution of his duty;
(c) interferes with or hinders a marine conservation officer in the execution of his duty;
(d) by any gratuity, bribe, promise or other inducement, prevents a marine conservation officer from carrying out his duty;
(e) without the authority of a marine conservation officer, removes, alters or interfers with any articles seized under section 15;
(f) contravenes any provision of this Act for which no penalty is provided or the regulations,

is guilty of an offence and liable on summary conviction to a fine not exceeding $ 5,000 or imprisonment for a term not exceeding 2 years or both and, in addition, the court may order the forfeiture of any vessel, structure, equipment, device or thing in connection with which the offence was committed.

Return of property seized

19. Subject to section 16, a court may order that property seized under subsection (3) of section 15 be returned to the person from whom it was taken or to a person named by that person where—

(a) the court dismisses a charge brought against that person under this Act or the regulations, and it is of the opinion that the property can be returned consistently with the interests of justice; or
(b) no charge has been brought against any person within a reasonable time after a seizure has been effected under that subsection.

Regulations

20. (1) The Minister may make regulations generally for carrying into effect the provisions of this Act, and in particular respecting—

(a) any activity relating to the exploration, exploitation and protection of the resources of the Zone;
(b) any activity relating to the economic exploration or exploitation of the Zone;
(c) the safety and protection of structures or devices in the Zone;
(d) the authorisation, control and regulation of scientific research in the Zone;
(e) the customs and other fiscal matters relating to the Zone;
(f) the duties, powers, functions and conditions of service of marine conservation officers; and
(g) the fees to be paid under this Act.

(2) Regulations made under this section are subject to affirmative resolutions of the Senate and the House of Representatives.

Directions

21. The Minister may give directions respecting the disposal or release of any vessel, structure, equipment, device or thing that is ordered by a court to be forfeited under this Act or the regulations.

Commencement

22. This Act shall come into operation on such day as the Minister may appoint by notice in the *Gazette.*

Passed in the House of Representatives this 7th day of April, 1978.

Curtis V. Strachan
Clerk of the House of Representatives.

Passed in the Senate this 10th day of April, 1978.

Curtis V. Strachan
Clerk of the Senate.

21. Guatemala

Decree No. 20–76.
Entered into force: July 1, 1976.
Source: *United Nations ST/LEG/SER.B/19,* pp. 30—32.

DECREE OF THE CONGRESS No. 20—76

The Congress of the Republic of Guatemala,

Considering that the marine resources off the coast of the Guatemalan nation constitute a heritage of its inhabitants which must be safeguarded for the benefit of present and future generations;

Considering that such resources have been the object of exploitation of every kind by foreign fishing fleets, to the detriment of the conservation thereof;

Considering that there is a majority consensus in the international community on the extent of the territorial sea and on the necessity of exploiting other sea areas to the benefit of the coastal State;

Considering that there also exists international agreement in principle on the exploration and exploitation of the submarine shelf and the sea-bed, likewise to the benefit of the coastal State, without prejudice to the rights of mankind;

Considering that, in accordance with article 3 of the Constitution of the Republic, Guatemala exercises full sovereignty and dominion over its territory, which includes the sea-bed and subsoil, continental shelf, territorial waters and superjacent airspace and extends to the natural resources and wealth existing therein, without prejudice to free maritime and aerial navigation in accordance with the law and with the provisions of international treaties and conventions;

Considering that since 1939, as confirmed by Legislative Decree of the Legislative Assembly No. 2535, of 21 April 1941, Guatemala has declared that its territorial sea extends 12 nautical miles from the low-water line;

Considering that the international community has succeeded in identifying principles of the law of the sea which harmonize the divergent views of States;

Considering that, in accordance with article 129, paragraph 4, of the Constitution of the Republic, the tidal zone, the continental shelf and the airspace, to such extent and in such form as shall be determined by the law or by duly ratified international agreements, are the property of the nation and that, consequently, it is for the Congress of the Republic to delimit the extention of the maritime space over which its rights, jurisdiction and sovereignty shall be exercised;

Acting in exercise of the powers assigned it by article 170, paragraph 1, of the Constitution of the Republic;

Decrees as follows:

Article 1

Guatemala reiterates its sovereignty, beyond its land territory and its internal waters, to a belt of sea adjacent to its coast, described as the territorial sea, which extends 12 nautical miles from the relevant baselines. Such sovereignty extends to the airspace over the territorial sea as well as to its bed and subsoil.

Article 2

Ships of all States, whether coastal or not, shall enjoy the right of innocent passage through the territorial sea in accordance with international law.

Article 3

The Republic of Guatemala establishes an exclusive economic zone which shall extend 200 nautical miles from the baseline from which the breadth of the territorial sea is measured. This zone shall include:

(a) Sovereign rights for the purpose of exploring and of exploiting, conserving and managing the natural resources, both renewable and non-renewable, of the continental shelf (bed and subsoil), the sea-bed and subsoil and the superjacent waters;
(b) Exclusive rights and jurisdiction with regard to the establishment and use of artificial islands, installations an similar structures, including the customs, fiscal, sanitary and immigration regulations pertaining thereto;
(c) Exclusive jurisdiction with regard to:
 (i) Other activities for the exploration and economic exploitation of the zone, such as the production of energy derived from the water of from tides or winds;
 (ii) Scientific research;
(d) Jurisdiction with regard to the preservation of the marine environment, including the control and elimination of pollution;
(e) Such other rights and obligations as may derive from jurisdiction over the zone.

Article 4

Guatemala recognizes within its exclusive economic zone the right of other States, whether coastal or land-locked, to freedom of navigation and overflight, the laying of cables and pipelines and, subject to the participation of a representative of the Government, other internationally lawful uses of the sea relating to navigation and communications.

Article 5

The appropriate organs shall enact the laws and regulations relating to fishing, conservation of species, marine pollution and other relevant activities in the territorial sea, in the exclusive economic zone, on the continental shelf (bed and subsoil) and on the sea-bed.

Until such time as the appropriate laws and regulations are enacted, the laws and regulations relating to the territorial sea shall apply in the exclusive economic zone, to the extent that they are applicable to the nature of the said zone.

Article 6

The Executive shall conclude the relevant agreements with adjoining coastal States; it shall issue licences for fishing or any other activity relating to the exploration and exploitation of the territorial sea and of the exclusive economic zone and shall enforce the legislation on the subject.

Article 7

A qualified officer of the Navy shall participate, as a delegate, in the delegations of Guatemala to conferences relating to maritime questions.

Article 8

The Guatemalan Army shall be responsible for ensuring respect for the rights of the Republic over its territorial sea and over the exclusive economic zone.

Article 9

This Decree shall enter into force on the date of its publication in the *Diario Oficial.*

This Decree shall be transmitted to the Executive for publication and implementation.

DONE at the Palace of the Legislature, Guatemala City, on 9 June 1976.

Donaldo Alvarez Ruiz
President

22. Guinea

Decree No. 336/PRG/80.
Entered into force: July 30, 1980.
Source: *Journal Officiel de la Republique,* July 30, 1980 (Translated from French by the Department of State).

Decree Relative to the Limits of the Territorial Waters of the People's Revolutionary Republic of Guinea

THE PRESIDENT OF THE REPUBLIC,

In consideration of the Constitutional Law No. 4/AN dated 10 November 1958, promulgated by Ordinance No. 15 dated 15 November 1958;
In consideration of Law No. 001/AL/75 dated 7 January 1975 relative to the election of the President of the Republic;
In consideration of Decree No. 215/PRG dated 1 June 1980 relative to the nomination of the members of the Cabinet of the President of the Republic;
In consideration of the Convention signed in Paris on 12 May 1886 between France and Portugal dealing with the limits of the French and Portuguese possessions in Western Africa; as approved by a Law on 22 July 1887 promulgated by a Decree dated 10 September 1887 which stipulates in its first Article that the Senate and the Chamber of Deputies approve the said Convention, executed in Mons-sous-Vaudry by Jules Grevy, President of the Republic and by the Foreign Minister Flourens;
In consideration of paragraph 3 of Article III of the Charter of the Organization of African Unity and the solemn declaration of the meeting of Heads of States held in Cairo from 17 to 21 July 1964, relative to the strict respect of the principles of the Organization and of the boundaries of the States as they were at the time of their national independence, stipulating: quote:
'Whereas boundaries problem is a grave and permanent factor of dissension,
'Aware of the presence of forces outside of Africa aimed at dividing the African States,
'*In consideration* that the boundaries of the African States at the time of their independence constitute a tangible fact,
'Recalling the establishment, during the Second Ordinary Meeting of the Council, of a Committee of Eleven charged with studying in depth measures tending to reinforce African Unity,
'Solemnly declare that all the member States make the commitment to respect the boundaries existing at the time of their national independence.' end quote.

DECREES:

Chapter I

General Provisions

Article 1
The width of the Territorial Waters of the People's Revolutionary Republic of Guinea is twelve (12) nautical miles measured from the low water mark.

Article 2
The width of the Exclusive Economic Zone is of two hundred (200) nautical miles measured from the low water mark.

Article 3

Within the Exclusive Economic Zone, the Guinean State reserves for itself the exclusive right to explore, exploit, conserve and manage the natural resources, biologic or not, at the bottom of the sea, under the sea bed or in the overlaying waters.

Article 4

The limits of the Territorial Waters and of the Exclusive Economic Zone are set as follows:
— to the North, by a line starting at 10° 56′ 42″ North Latitude and 15° 05′ West Longitude, which shall follow the Thalweg of the Cajet River and shall extend to the South-West through the Pilots' Pass to reach the parallel 10° 40′ 00 (at a point established by the coordinates 10° 40′ 00 North and 15° 20′ 30″ West) with which it shall coincide towards the open seas for a distance of 200 nautical miles, to the South, by parallel 9° 03′ 18″ North latitude over a distance towards the open seas of 200 nautical miles measured from the low water mark.

Chapter II

Of the Control of the Coasts

Article 5

The Agents of the Merchant Marine responsible for the surveillance of the territorial waters, the Agents of the Customs Office, those of the National Navy and in general, all the officers of the Judiciary Police, are habilitated to take note of infractions, to write an official statement of the facts and to escort the culprit or culprits as well as their vessels or ships to the nearest Guinean port.

Within 24 hours following the landing, they must give to the civil servants of the Merchant Marine or to the Governor of the Administrative Region involved, their statements, written reports and all data evidencing the infraction.

Article 6

The Officer or Agent who has escorted or caused the seized vessel to be escorted, surrenders the said vessel to the Service of the Merchant Marine which shall take over all fishing gear — the prizes are, as the case may be, also taken over and sold without delay at a public auction by the officer assigned by the Merchant Marine, and such auction shall be upon authorization of the Governor of the Region.

The proceeds of the auction of the fishing results are turned over to the Treasury.

Chapter III

Of Infractions

Article 7

Fishing within the Guinean Territorial waters and within the Exclusive Economic Zone is forbidden to all foreign vessels.

Article 8

The Violation of the territorial waters, by navigating, fishing, pollution of waters, taking photographs; establishing descriptions having a technical or strategic character with a view to commit an aggression or to spy, the transportation of poisonous or dangerous matters, constitutes a serious injury to the sovereignty of the Guinean National State and as a consequence is a criminal infraction punishable as provided for in the Guinean Code of penal justice.

Article 9

The organization and the general regulation of sea fishing within the territorial waters and the Exclusive

Economic Zone shall be determined by an Arrete of the Minister of Transportation.

Article 10

The provisions of the following decrees, anti-dating and conflicting with the present decree, are abrogated: No. 224/PRG–64 dated 3 June 1964; No. 226/PRG–72 dated 1 September 1972; No. 42/PRG–79 dated 1 February 1979; No. 128/PRG–80 dated 24 March 1980; No. 264/PRG–80 dated 9 June 1980.

Article 11

The Ministers of Transportation, of Justice, of Finances, of the People's Army, of Animal Husbandry and Fisheries, are charged, in their respective domains, with the execution of the present decree which shall be registered and published in the Official Gazette of the Republic.

Conakry, 30 July 1980

23. Guinea-Bissau

Law No. 3/78.
Entered into force: May 19, 1978.
Source: *The Boletim Officiel,* May 20, 1978 (Translated from Portuguese by the Department of State).

Law No. 3/78

Extension of the Territorial Sea and Exclusive Economic Zone
Preamble

Having verified that an increasingly large number of foreign vessels are illegally engaged in fishing inside our exclusive economic zone in abusive violation of the laws of our country, namely Decree No. 14/74;

Considering the need to protect, preserve, and take full advantage of our natural resources, to ensure rational fisheries, and to facilitate the reproduction of biological species, it is imperative that measures be taken to delimit our borders, the territorial sea, and the exclusive economic zone, taking into account the recommendations of the international organizations concerned.

The National Popular Assembly, in the exercise of the powers vested in it by Articles 28 and 29 of the Constitution, hereby decrees and I promulgate the following law:

Article 1

The breadth of the territorial sea and the exclusive economic zone of the Republic of Guinea-Bissau is measured from the baseline defined by the Luso-French Convention of 1886, which joins the following reference points:

Point 1 — Cabo Roxo	Latitude 12° 20′ 20″ N Longitude 16° 43′ 05″ W
Point 2	Latitude 10° 40′ 00″ N Longitude 16° 43′ 05″ W
Point 3	Latitude 10° 40′ 00″ N Longitude 15° 20′ 30″ W
Point 4 — Confluence of the Rio Cajet	Latitude 10° 53′ 40″ N Longitude 15° 06′ 20″ W

Article 2

The territorial sea extends, within the national maritime borders, to 12 miles beyond the baseline defined above.

Article 3

1. The exclusive economic zone extends, within the national maritime borders, to 200 miles beyond the baseline defined above.

2. The State of Guinea-Bisseau has exclusive rights over exploration and exploitation of living and natural resources of the sea, the continental platform and slopes, and the seabeds of the aforementioned exclusive economic zone.

Article 4

All foreign vessels not authorized by the Government of the Republic of Guinea-Bissau are prohibited from fishing in the exclusive economic zone.

Article 5

Violation of the provisions of Article 4 shall be punishable under the law.

Article 6

For purposes of the delimitation of maritime boundaries with neighboring countries, in the context of the traditional friendship between their people and ours, the Government is authorized to continue the negotiations in progress in accordance with the pertinent United Nations recommendations and to take the necessary legislative measures.

Article 7

All laws to the contrary are hereby revoked.

Article 8

This law shall enter into effect immediately.
Approved in the session of May 19, 1978.
Carmen Pereira, Acting Vice President of the National Popular Assembly.

Promulgated on May 19, 1978.

Luiz Cabral
President of the Council of State.

24. Guyana

Maritime Boundaries Act, 1977, Act No. 10.
Entered into force: June 30, 1977.
Source: *United Nations ST/LEG/SER.B/19,* p. 33.

MARITIME BOUNDARIES ACT, 1977[1]

2. In this Act—

'continental shelf' means the continental shelf of Guyana;
'exclusive economic zone' means the exclusive economic zone of Guyana as designated under section 15;
'fish' includes all or any of the varieties of marine, estuarine or fresh water fishes, crustacea, whales, porpoises, manatees, mollusca or other marine animal and plant life or fresh water animal and plant life;
'fishery zone' means the fishery zone of Guyana established by section 23;
'fishing' means—

(a) the catching, taking or harvesting of fish;
(b) the attempted catching, taking or harvesting of fish;
(c) any other activity which can reasonably be expected to result in the catching, taking or harvesting of fish;
(d) any operations at sea in support of, or in preparation for, any activity described in paragraphs (a), (b) and (c),

but does not include any scientific activity which is conducted by a scientific research vessel;
'fishing boat' means any vessel, boat, ship, or other craft which is used for, equipped to be used for, or of a type which is normally used for—

(a) fishing; or
(b) aiding or assisting one or more vessels at sea in the performance of any activity relating to fishing, including, but not limited to, preparation, supply, storage, refrigeration, transportation or processing;

'fishing boat of Guyana' means a fishing boat which is registered in Guyana;
'foreign fishing boat' means a fishing boat which is not registered in Guyana;
'miles' means international nautical miles of 1,852 metres each;
'territorial sea' means the territorial sea of Guyana.

[1] Act No. 10 of 1977, passed by the National Assembly on 3 June 1977, entered into force on 30 June 1977. Text provided by the Permanent Representative of Guyana to the United Nations in a note verbale dated 15 November 1977. Pursuant to Sect. 44 of this Act, the Territorial Waters Jurisdiction Act 1878 of the United Kingdom (partially reproduced in ST/LEG/SER.B/6, p. 355), in so far as it forms part of the law of Guyana ceased to have effect.

Part I
The territorial sea

3. (1) Subject to section 34, the territorial sea comprises those areas of the sea having as their inner limits the baseline referred to in section 7 and as their outer limits the line every point on which is 12 miles from the nearest point of the baseline.

(2) References to the territorial sea in any law shall, in relation to any period after the commencement of the Act, be construed in accordance with subsection (1).

4. The internal waters of Guyana include any areas of the sea that are on the landward side of the baseline of the territorial sea.

5. The sovereignty of Guyana extends and has always extended to the territorial sea and to the sea-bed and subsoil underlying, and the airspace over such sea.

6. (1) Without prejudice to any other written law for the time being in force, all foreign ships (other than warships including submarines and other underwater vehicles) shall enjoy the right of innocent passage.

(2) For the purposes of this section, passage is innocent so long as it is not prejudicial to the peace, good order or security of Guyana.

(3) Foreign warships including submarines and other underwater vehicles may enter or pass through the territorial sea after giving prior notice to the Government of Guyana;

Provided that submarines and other underwater vehicles shall navigate on the surface and show their flag while passing through such sea.

(4) The Minister may exercise such powers and take such measures in or in relation to the territorial sea as he may consider necessary in the interest of the peace, good order or security of Guyana or any part thereof, and such measures may include the suspension, whether absolutely or subject to such exceptions and qualifications as he thinks fit, of the entry of all or any class of foreign ships into such area of the territorial sea.

7. (1) The baseline from which the territorial sea shall be measured shall be the low-water line along the coast and, where the coast line is broken by a river, a straight line joining the two points where the low-water line on the coast ends on either side of the river.

(2) The Minister responsible for lands and surveys may by order prescribe geographical co-ordinates of points from which straight lines may be drawn for the purpose of subsection (1).

8. (1) For the purposes of section 7, the low-water line in any specified area shall be the line of the mean low-water springs as depicted on the largest scale Guyana Government nautical chart on record at the Ministry responsible for lands and surveys for the time being of that area or, where no such chart of that area exists, the largest scale British Admiralty chart for the time being of that area.

(2) In any proceedings in any court, a certificate purporting to be signed by the Minister responsible for lands and surveys or a person authorized by him that—

- *(a)* any specified Guyana Government nautical chart of any area is the largest scale chart for the time being of that area; or
- *(b)* no Guyana Government nautical chart for any area exists and that any specified British Admiralty chart of that area is the largest scale British Admiralty chart for the time being of that area,

shall be admissible as evidence of the matter stated in the certificate.

(3) Every person signing any such certificate shall, in the absence of proof to the contrary, be presumed to be duly authorized to sign it.

Part II

The continental shelf

9. Subject to section 34, the continental shelf (which by virtue of the applied law, that is to say, the British Guiana (Alteration of Boundaries) Order in Council, 1954, was included in the boundaries of Guyana) comprises the sea-bed and subsoil of the submarine areas that extend beyond the limit of the territorial sea throughout the natural prolongation of the land territory of Guyana to the outer edge of the continental margin or to a distance of 200 miles from the baseline referred to in section 7, where the outer edge of the continental margin does not extend up to that distance.

10. (1) Guyana has, and always had, full and exclusive sovereign rights in respect of the continental shelf.

(2) Without prejudice to the generality of the provisions of subsection (1) Guyana has in the continental shelf—

(a) sovereign rights for the purposes of exploration, exploitation, conservation and management of all resources;
(b) exclusive rights and jurisdiction for the construction, maintenance or operation of artificial islands, offshore terminals, installations and other structures and devices necessary for the exploration and exploitation of the resources of the continental shelf or for the convenience of shipping or for any other purpose;
(c) exclusive jurisdiction to authorize, regulate and control scientific research; and
(d) exclusive jurisdiction to preserve and protect the marine environment and to prevent and control marine pollution.

11. No person (including a foreign Government) shall, except under and in accordance with the terms of a licence or a letter of authority granted by the Minister responsible for natural resources, explore the continental shelf or exploit its resources or carry out any search or excavation or conduct any research within the continental shelf or drill therein or construct, maintain or operate any artificial island, offshore terminal, installation or other structure or device therein for any purpose whatsoever.

12. The President may by order—

(a) declare any area of the continental shelf and its superjacent waters to be a designated area; and
(b) make such provisions as he may deem necessary with respect to—
  (i) the exploration, exploitation and protection of the resources of the continental shelf within such designated area;
  (ii) the safety and protection of artificial islands, offshore terminals, installations, and other structures and devices in such designated area;
  (iii) the protection of the marine environment of such designated area;
  (iv) customs and other fiscal matters in relation to such designated area; or
  (v) the entry into and passage through the designated area of foreign ships by the establishment of fairways, sealanes, traffic separation schemes or any other mode of ensuring freedom of navigation which is not prejudicial to the interests of Guyana.

13. The President may by order—

(a) extend with such restrictions and modifications as he thinks fit any enactment for the time being in force in Guyana or any part thereof to the continental shelf or any part (including any area declared to be a designated area under sect. 12) thereof; and
(b) make such provisions as he may consider necessary for facilitating the enforcement of such an enactment,

and any enactment so extended shall have effect as if the continental shelf or the part (including, as the case may be, any area declared to be a designated area under sect. 12) thereof to which it has been extended is a part of the territory of Guyana.

14. Without prejudice to the provisions of section 10 (1) and subject to any measures that may be necessary for protecting the interests of Guyana, the Government of Guyana may not impede the laying or maintenance of submarine cables or pipelines on the continental shelf by other States; provided, however, that the consent of the Government shall be necessary for the delineation of the course for the laying of such cables or pipelines.

Part III

The exclusive economic zone

15. The President may, if he considers it necessary or expedient having regard to international law and State practice, by order designate an area beyond and adjacent to the territorial sea an exclusive economic zone.

16. In the exclusive economic zone, Guyana shall have—

(a) sovereign rights for the purpose of exploration, exploitation, conservation and management of the natural resources, both living and non-living, as well as for producing energy from tides, winds and currents;
(b) exclusive rights and jurisdiction for the construction, maintenance or operation of artificial islands, offshore terminals, installations and other structures and devices necessary for the exploration and exploitation of the resources of the zone or for the convenience of shipping or for any other purpose;
(c) exclusive jurisdiction to authorize, regulate and control scientific research;
(d) exclusive jurisdiction to preserve and protect the marine environment and to prevent and control marine pollution;
(e) such other rights as are recognized by international law.

17. No person (including a foreign Government) shall, except under and in accordance with the terms of any agreement with the Government of Guyana or of a licence or a letter of authority granted by the Minister responsible for natural resources, explore or exploit any resources of the exclusive economic zone or carry out any search or excavation or conduct any research within the exclusive economic zone or drill therein or construct, maintain or operate any artificial island, offshore terminal, installation or other structure or device therein for any purpose whatsoever:

Provided that nothing in this section shall apply in relation to fishing by a citizen of Guyana.

18. The President may by order—

(a) declare any area of the exclusive economic zone to be a designated area; and
(b) make such provisions as he may deem necessary with respect to—
  (i) the exploration, exploitation and protection of the resources of such designated area;
  (ii) other activities for the economic exploitation and exploration of such designated area such as the production of energy from tides, winds and currents;
  (iii) the safety and protection of artificial islands, offshore terminals, installations and other structures and devices in such designated area;
  (iv) the protection of the marine environment of such designated area;
  (v) customs and other fiscal matters in relation to such designated area; or
  (vi) entry into and passage through the designated area of foreign ships by the establishment of

fairways, sealanes, traffic separation schemes or any other mode of ensuring freedom of navigation which is not prejudicial to the interests of Guyana.

19. The President may by order—

(a) extend, with such restrictions and modifications as he thinks fit, any enactment for the time being in force in Guyana or any part thereof to the exclusive economic zone or any part thereof; and
(b) make such provisions as he may consider necessary for facilitating the enforcement of such enactment,

and any enactment so extended shall have effect as if the exclusive economic zone or the part thereof to which it has been extended is a part of the territory of Guyana.

20. The provisions of section 14 shall apply in relation to the laying or maintenance of submarine cables or pipelines on the sea-bed of the exclusive economic zone as they apply in relation to the laying or maintenance of submarine cables or pipelines on the sea-bed of the continental shelf.

21. In the exclusive economic zone and the air space over the zone, ships and aircraft of all States shall, subject to the exercise by Guyana of its rights within the zone, enjoy freedom of navigation and overflight.

22. Any order made under section 15 may provide for the exclusion or modification in relation to the exclusive economic zone of the provisions of part II and part IV.

Part IV
The fishery zone

23. There is hereby established a fishery zone beyond and adjacent to the territorial sea and bounded on its seaward side by the line every point on which is 200 miles from the nearest point of the baseline of the territorial sea.

24. (1) The Minister responsible for fisheries may wherever it appears to him necessary or convenient by order make provision for regulating the conduct of, and safeguarding, fishing operations and operations ancillary thereto, including provisions with respect to the identification and marking of fishing boats and fishing gear.

(2) An order made under subsection (1) applies—

(a) to all fishing boats of Guyana, and things done by such boats and their crews wherever they may be; and
(b) to all foreign fishing boats and things done by such boats and their crews, in waters within the fishery zone.

(3) Where an order made under this section is not complied with in the case of a fishing boat or its crew the master, the owner, and the charterer, if any, are liable on summary conviction in the case of a first conviction under this section to a fine of $1,000 and in the case of a second or subsequent conviction to a fine of $2,000.

25. (1) The Minister responsible for fisheries may by order designate any country outside Guyana, and in relation to it, areas within the fishery zone in which, and the descriptions and quantities of fish for which, fishing boats registered in that country may fish.

(2) A foreign fishing boat not registered in a country for the time being designated under subsection (1) shall not enter the fishery zone except for a purpose recognized by international law or by any convention for the time being in force between the Government of Guyana and the Government of the country to which the boat belongs and any such boat which enters the zone for such a purpose—

(a) shall return outside the zone as soon as the purpose has been fulfilled; and
(b) shall not fish while within the zone.

(3) A foreign fishing boat registered in a country designated under subsection (1) shall not fish within the fishery zone except in an area and for the descriptions and quantities of fish for the time being designated in relation to that country.

(4) If this section is contravened in the case of any fishing boat the master of the boat is liable on summary conviction to a fine of $200,000 and the court may, on convicting him for an offence under this section, order a forfeiture of any fishing gear found in the boat or taken or used by any person from the boat.

(5) This section shall extend to prohibit or restrict fishing by fishing boats registered in a country outside Guyana in any area except with respect to which special provision is made by any arrangement between the Government of Guyana and the Government of that country for fishing by such boats for the purpose of scientific research.

26. The persons appointed fishery officers under the Fisheries Act are fishery officers for the purposes of this Act.

27. (1) For the purpose of enforcing the provisions of this Part or of any orders or regulations made under it a fishery officer may exercise in relation to any fishing boat within the fishery zone and in relation to any fishing boat of Guyana anywhere outside the zone the powers conferred by subsections (2) to (4).

(2) A fishery officer may go on board the boat, with or without persons assigned to assist him in his duties, and for that purpose may require the boat to stop and do anything else which may facilitate the boarding of the boat.

(3) A fishery officer may require the attendance of the master and other persons on board the boat and may make any examination and inquiry which appears to him to be necessary for the purpose mentioned in subsection (2) and, in particular, may—

(a) examine any fish on the boat and the equipment of the boat, including the fishing gear, and require persons on board the boat to do anything which appears to him to be necessary for facilitating the examination; and
(b) require any person on board the boat to produce any documents relating to the boat or the persons on board which are in his custody or possession and may take copies of any such document.

(4) Where it appears to a fishery officer that an offence has been committed under this Act by any person on board any boat he may without any warrant or other process seize the boat together with any net, line, stake, instrument or appliance suspected to have been used in the commission of the offence and detain any person found on board.

(5) Where any vessel or thing is seized or any person is detained under this section the fishery officer shall take such vessel, thing or person as soon as may be to the port which appears to him to be the nearest convenient place, and as soon as practicable thereafter the fishery officer shall lay a complaint in respect of the alleged offence and cause any person detained to be brought before a court of summary jurisdiction.

32. (1) Any person who on any fishing boat within the fishery zone or on a fishing boat of Guyana anywhere outside the zone—

(a) fails to comply with any requirement imposed, or to answer any question asked, by a fishery officer under this Act;

(*b*) prevents, or attempts to prevent, any other person from complying with any such requirement or answering any such question; or

(*c*) assaults any fishery officer while exercising any of the functions conferred on him by virtue of this Act or obstructs any such officer in the exercise of any of those functions,

is guilty of an offence.

(2) A person guilty of an offence under this section is liable on summary conviction to a fine of $ 2,000.

33. Where a fine is imposed by a magistrate's court on the master, owner or charterer or a member of the crew of a fishing boat who is convicted by the court of an offence under this Act the court may—

(*a*) issue a warrant of distress against the boat and its gear and catch and any property of the person convicted for the purpose of levying the amount of the fine; and

(*b*) if the boat is a foreign fishing boat, order it to be detained for a period of three months from the date of the conviction or until the fine is paid or the amount of the fine is levied in pursuance of any such warrant whichever occurs first.

Part V
General

34. The President may, whenever he considers it necessary or expedient so to do having regard to international law and State practice, by order alter the seaward limit of the territorial sea, the continental shelf, the exclusive economic zone and the fishery zone.

35. (1) The maritime boundaries between Guyana and any State whose coast is adjacent to that of Guyana in regard to their respective territorial seas, continental shelves, exclusive economic zones, fishery and other maritime zones shall be determined by agreement between Guyana and such States and pending such agreement shall not extend beyond the line every point of which is equidistant from the nearest point on the baseline from which the breadth of the territorial sea of Guyana and such State is measured.

(2) Every agreement entered into pursuant to subsection (1) shall, as soon as may be after it is entered into, be published in the Gazette.

(3) The provisions of subsection (1) shall have effect notwithstanding anything contained in any other provision of this Act.

37. (1) In part II or part III, any act or omission which—

(*a*) takes place on, under or above an offshore terminal, installation or structure or upon an artificial island in a designated area or any waters within 500 yards of such terminal, installation, structure or island; and

(*b*) would if taking place in Guyana constitute an offence under the law in force in Guyana,

shall be treated for the purposes of that law as taking place in Guyana.

(2) The Minister responsible for justice may by order make provision for the determination, in accordance with the law in force in Guyana as may be specified in the order, of questions arising out of acts or omissions taking place in a designated area or in any part of such an area, in connexion with the exploration of the sea-bed or subsoil or the exploitation of the natural resources, and for conferring jurisdiction with respect to such questions on courts in any part of Guyana.

38. Any person who contravenes or fails to comply with any provision in part II or part III is liable on summary conviction to a fine of $ 5,000.

39. (1)Where an offence under this Act or any law made thereunder has been committed by a company, every person who at the time the offence was committed was in charge of, and was responsible to the company for, the conduct of the business of the company, as well as the company, shall be deemed to be guilty of the offence and shall be liable to be proceeded against and punished accordingly:

Provided that nothing contained in this subsection shall render any such person liable to any punishment provided in this Act if he proves that the offence was committed without his knowledge or that he exercised all due diligence to prevent the commission of such offence.

41. (1) The President may make regulations for carrying out the purposes of this Act.

(2) In particular and without prejudice to the generality of the foregoing power, such regulations may provide for all or any of the following matters namely—

(a) regulation of the conduct of any person in the territorial sea, the continental shelf, the exclusive economic zone or the fishery zone;

(b) regulation of the exploration and exploitation, conservation and management of the resources of the continental shelf;

(c) regulation of the exploration, exploitation, conservation and management of the resources of the exclusive economic zone;

(d) regulation of the construction, maintenance and operation of artificial islands, offshore terminals, installations and other structures and devices referred to in part II and part III;

(e) preservation and protection of the marine environment and prevention and control of marine pollution for the purposes of this Act;

(f) authorization, regulation and control of the conduct of scientific research for the purposes of this Act;

(g) fees in relation to licences and letters of authority referred to in part II and part III or for any other purposes; or

(h) any matter incidental to any of the matters specified in paragraphs *(a)* to *(g)*.

(3) In making any regulation under this section, the President may provide that a contravention thereof shall be punishable with a fine of $ 10,000 and imprisonment for six months.

42. (1) If any difficulty arises in giving effect to the provisions of this Act or of any of the enactments extended under this Act, the President may by order amend any law as appears to him to be necessary or expedient for removing the difficulty.

25. Haiti

Decree No. 38.
Entered into force: April 8, 1977.
Source: *Le Moniteur (The Official Journal of Haiti)* No. 38 of June 12, 1977 (Translated from French by the Department of State).

DECREE

Jean-Claude Duvalier, President for Life of the Republic,

Having considered:

Articles 90 and 93 of the Constitution;

The Conventions on the Territorial Sea and Contiguous Zone and the Continental Shelf, done at Geneva on April 29, 1958, and ratified by the Republic of Haiti on October 26, 1959;

The Declaration of Santo Domingo, signed at Santo Domingo, Dominican Republic, by the Republic of Haiti in 1972;

The Decree of April 6, 1972, setting the limits of Haitian territorial waters at 12 nautical miles;

Article 11 of the aforesaid decree;

The April 6, 1977, declaration of the Haitian Government setting the limits of the territorial waters at 200 nautical miles; and

The August 21, 1976, Decree of the Legislative Chamber, suspending the guarantees provided under Articles 17, 18, 19, 20, 25, 31, 34, 48, 70, 71, 72, 93 (last paragraph), 95, 112, 113, and 122 (second paragraph) and granting full powers to the Chief of the Executive Branch, so that he may issue, up to the second Monday of April 1977, decrees having the force of law and containing any measures deemed necessary by him to safeguard the integrity of the national territory and the sovereignty of the State, consolidate order and peace, maintain the political, economic, and financial stability of the nation, improve the well-being of rural and urban populations, and defend the general interests of the Republic;

Whereas:

It is advisable to determine the limits of the territorial waters of the Republic of Haiti and negotiate the necessary agreements with the States concerned whenever that would serve the interests of the Republic;

The borders of States establish the limits of the territory over which they exercise their sovereignty;

The territory of a State includes not only its dry land but also its airspace and territorial sea and the sea-bed and subsoil covered by its waters;

It is desirable to use all available resources of the Republic of Haiti within the framework of the Economic Revolution;

The sea, sea-bed, and subsoil covered by this sea constitute a considerable source of mineral, energy, and other resources; and

In exercising their sovereignty, States have the right to establish an economic zone in addition to their territorial sea;

On the basis of the report of the Secretary of State for Foreign Affairs and Worship and of the Secretary of State for the Interior and National Defense, and after deliberation of the Council of Secretaries of State;

Hereby Decrees:

Article 1

The limit of the territorial sea over which the Republic of Haiti has sovereignty shall be set at 12 nautical miles from the low-water line of adjacent islands or the corresponding straight baselines.

Article 2

The internal waters and coast of the Republic of Haiti shall remain as established under the provisions of Articles 2 and 3 of the Decree of April 6, 1972.

Article 3

The Haitian State will exercise full sovereignty over the sea-bed and subsoil corresponding to the limits of its territorial sea as well as over the superjacent airspace.

Article 4

The zone contiguous to the territorial sea shall be set at 12 nautical miles from the outer limit of the territorial sea in the direction of the high seas.

Over this zone the Haitian State has jurisdiction with regard to the protection of its fiscal and customs interests and its security, as provided by the pertinent international laws.

Article 5

An 'Exclusive Haitian Economic Maritime Zone' extending over a distance of 200 nautical miles from the baseline of the territorial sea shall be established.

In this zone the Republic of Haiti will exercise:

(1) Sovereign rights with regard to the exploration, exploitation, conservation, and management of natural resources, whether animal, vegetable, or mineral, of the sea-bed, subsoil, and superjacent waters;

(2) Exclusive rights of jurisdiction with regard to the establishment and utilization of artificial islands, facilities, and structures;

(3) Exclusive jurisdictional authority with regard to:

(a) Activities to explore or exploit the zone, such as the production of energy through the use of water, marine currents, and winds, and

(b) Scientific research;

(4) Jurisdictional authority with regard to the conservation of the marine environment, including the control and reduction of pollution;

(5) Any other rights and obligations that may be established under Haitian law.

Article 6

The Haitian State will regulate fisheries in the territorial sea, in the contiguous zone, and in the exclusive maritime economic zone, taking into account the rational use and the conservation of mineral and biological resources.

Article 7

The Haitian State will exercise, within the limits indicated above, any control which it deems necessary to:

(1) Ensure navigational safety and prevent violations of its health, fiscal, customs, and immigration laws; and

(2) Prevent pollution, contamination, and other hazards which could threaten the biological balance of the marine environment.

Article 8

The continental platform of Haiti consists of the sea-bed and subsoil of submarine regions adjacent to the coast but located outside the territorial sea. It shall extend to the point where the depth of the superjacent waters allows exploitation of the natural resources of such regions.

Article 9

The Haitian State will exercise sovereign rights over the continental platform with regard to the exploration and exploitation of its natural resources.

These rights shall be exclusive. No one may engage in exploration or exploitation of this platform as referred to above without the explicit consent of the Haitian State, even if no such activities are being carried out by the Haitian State itself.

The rights of the Republic of Haiti over the continental platform shall be independent of its effective or feigned occupation as well as of any statement made.

Article 10

This decree shall enter into force within 24 hours of its promulgation. It shall supersede all laws or legal provisions, decrees or provisions of decrees, and decree-laws or provisions of decree-laws which run counter to it. It shall be published and executed at the request and within the respective purviews of the Secretaries of State for Foreign Affairs and Worship, Interior and National Defense, Justice, Agriculture, National Resources and Rural Development, Commerce and Industry, and Finance and Economic Affairs.

Done at the National Palace, Port-au-Prince, on April 8, 1977, the 174th year of independence.

Jean-Claude Duvalier, President
Edner Brutus, Secretary of State for Foreign Affairs and Worship
Pierre Biamby, Secretary of State for Interior and National Defense
Aurélien C. Jeanty, Secretary of State for Justice
Wilner Pierre-Louis, Secretary of State for Commerce and Industry
Emmanuel Bros, Secretary of State for Finance and Economic Affairs
Achille Salvant, Secretary of State for Social Affairs
Pierre Gousse, Secretary of State for Coordination and Information
Raoul Pierre-Louis, Secretary of State for National Education
Willy Verrier, Secretary of State for Public Health and Population
Henri P. Bayard, Secretary of State Without Portfolio
Fernand Laurin, Secretary of State for Public Works, Transportation, and Communications

26. Honduras

Decree Law No. 921.
Entered into force: June 13, 1980.
Source: *La Gaceta No. 23, 127* of June 13, 1980 (Translated from Spanish by the Department of State).

DECREE NO. 921
LAW ON UTILIZATION OF OCEAN NATURAL RESOURCES
THE GOVERNING MILITARY JUNTA IN A COUNCIL OF MINISTERS

Whereas: The sovereignty of the State of Honduras over the natural resources in its continental shelf and its superjacent waters, in both oceans, is independent of their actual exploitation inasmuch as such activities concern only the State and no one may engage in such activities without its express consent; however, it is matter of public interest and need to use such resources in a technically sound, sensible and efficient manner;

Decree Law No. 25 of January 17, 1951, establishes zones for the control and protection of the ocean resources over which Honduras enjoys sovereignty;

During the III United Nations Conference on the Law of the Sea most of the member states of the international community reiterated their legal conviction that the coastal States have sovereign rights over the natural resources located in an exclusive economic zone covering 200 nautical miles;

The development of fishing and the exploitation of hydrocarbons and other ocean resources are necessary in order to meet the nutritional requirements of the Honduran people, produce higher levels of income and more employment, and contribute to the development of the national economy,

Therefore, the Governing Military Junta, meeting as a Council of Ministers, pursuant to Decree No. 1 of December 6, 1972, Articles 5 and 254 of the Constitution of the Republic, and Decree No. 25 of January 17, 1951

Decrees

The following law on the Utilization of Ocean Natural Resources

Article 1

Without prejudice to the Constitution and the laws of the Republic regarding the territorial sea and the continental shelf, the State of Honduras enjoys the following rights in the exclusive economic zone that extends for a distance of 200 nautical miles, measured from the baselines used to establish the breadth of the territorial sea:

(a) Sovereign rights for purposes of exploiting, exploring, conserving, and managing all natural resources, both living and non-living, in the sea-bed and subsoil and the superjacent waters and over all economic exploration and exploitation in the zone, such as the production of energy from the water, the currents, and winds;

(b) Exclusive rights and jurisdiction regarding the authorization and regulation of the Constitution, exploitation and use of artificial islands and all types of installations and structures, including jurisdiction over customs, fiscal, health, safety, and immigration regulations;

(c) Jurisdiction and control over all matters regarding the regulation, authorization, and performance of marine scientific research activities, which shall not be conducted without prior consent

from the State of Honduras and the presence of a representative of the Honduran Government, whenever the Government considers it advisable;

(ch) Jurisdiction and control in order to preserve the marine environment and prevent, reduce, and control pollution from any source.

(d) All other rights and obligations resulting from sovereign rights over the zone's resources.

Article 2

In this zone all States, both coastal or land-locked, without prejudice to the preceding article, shall enjoy the freedoms of navigation and overflight and of the laying of submarine cables and pipelines and to engage in other internationally lawful uses of the sea directly related to the operation of vessels, aircraft, and submarine cables and pipelines.

Article 3

The State of Honduras shall make a sovereign decision concerning the allowable catch of the living resources in this zone, taking into account the goal of their optimum and efficient use and giving priority to the satisfaction of the nutritional requirements of the Honduran people and the demands of the economy and other national interests.

Without prejudice to the limitations on behalf of the Honduran people, or associations created or incorporated according to Honduran laws, that were created by appropriate legislation regarding concessions, licenses, or fishing permits in the territorial sea or on the Honduran continental shelf, the State may issue to foreigners licenses or permits for exploration and exploitation of the other resources existing in the zone in accordance with legislation in force, whenever applicable, or any legislation that may be issued.

Any problem that may arise with the administrative authorities in relation to application of this article may be submitted to the courts of the Republic.

Article 4

The State of Honduras, in view of its economic development, shall issue any legislation that it considers appropriate and shall regulate the following activities, among others:

(a) Licensing of fishermen, fishing vessels, and fishing equipment, including, payment of fees and other forms of remuneration which may consist of adequate compensation with respect to financing, equipment, or technology relating to the fishing industry;

(b) Determining the species which may be caught and fixing quotas of catch whether in relation to specific populations, to catch per vessel over a period of time or to the catch by nationals of a State during a specified period;

(c) Regulating seasons and areas of fishing, the types, sizes and amount of gear, and the numbers, sizes, and types of fishing vessels that may be used;

(d) Fixing the age and size of fish and other species that may be caught;

(e) Specifying information required of fishing vessels, including catch and effort statistics and vessel position reports;

(f) Requiring, under the authorization and control of Honduras, the conduct of specified fisheries research programs and regulating the conduct of such research, including the sampling of catches, the disposition of the samples, and reporting of associated scientific data;

(g) The placing by the State of observers or trainees on board such vessels;

(h) The landing by such vessels of all or a part of their catches in Honduran ports;

(i) Terms and conditions relating to joint ventures or other cooperative arrangements;

(j) Requirements with respect to training personnel and the transfer of fisheries technology, including enhancement of the ability of the State of Honduras to undertake fisheries research;

(k) The rules and procedures for enforcing these regulations.

Article 5

The State of Honduras may, while exercising its sovereign rights to explore, exploit, conserve, and manage the living resources in the zone, take such measures as may be necessary, including examination, registration, inspection, and seizure, and initiation of judicial proceedings to ensure compliance with its laws and regulations enacted in conformity with this Decree.

Whenever arrest or detention of a foreign vessel occurs, the flag State shall be notified promptly through appropriate channels of the action taken and the penalties imposed.

Article 6

This Decree does not ignore similar rights of other States on the basis of reciprocity nor does it in any way obstruct any obligations that may arise from a future convention on the law of the sea or treaties to which Honduras is a party that have been concluded on the basis of respect for territorial sovereignty or sovereign rights over the resources, in this case, of the Republic of Honduras.

Article 7

The Executive Branch shall establish regulations for this Decree.

An interministerial commission shall be formed consisting of the Ministeries of Natural Resources, Economy, Finance, Public Health, Defense and Public Security, Foreign Relations, and the National Port Authority, through the Ministry of Economy.

This commission shall prepare the appropriate regulations and shall act as a standing committee for consultation and recommendation of specific actions aimed at optimum utilization of natural resources to the benefit of the Honduran people's nutrition and standard of living, and generally, the country's economic development.

Article 8

Enforcement of this law and the legislation derived from it shall be the direct responsibility of the Ministry of Natural Resources, with the support of the Republic's air and naval forces.

Article 9

This Decree shall enter into force on the day on which it is published in the official gazette *La Gaceta.*

Done at Tegucigalpa, Central District, on the twenty-eighth day of April 1980.

Signed by

Policarpo Paz Garcia

Domingo Alvarez Cruz

Amilcar Zelaya Rodriguez

Jose Cristobal Diaz Garcia
Minister of Government and Justice

Eliseo Perez Cadalso
Minister of Foreign Affairs

Diego Landa Celano
Minister of Defense and Public Security

Eugenio Matute Canizales
Minister of Public Education

Valentin Mendoza A.
Minister of Finance and Public Credit

Carlos Manuel Zeron
Minister of Economy

Mario Flores Theresin
Minister of Communications, Public Works, and Transport

Luis Cousin
Minister of Public Health and Social Service

Adalberto Discua Rodriguez
Minister of Labor and Social Security

Rafael Leonardo Callejas
Minister of Natural Resources

Armando Alvarez Martinez
Minister of Culture and Tourism

Virgilio Caceres Pineda
Executive Secretary of the Economic Planning Council

Manuel Enrique Suarez Benavides
Executive Director of the National Agrarian Institute

27. Iceland

Law No. 41.
Entered into force: June 1, 1979.
Source: *United Nations ST/LEG/SER.B/19* (English text provided by the Charge d'Affairs of the Permanent Mission of Iceland to the United Nations in a letter of 31 July 1979).

Law

No. 41 of 1 June 1979 concerning the Territorial Sea, the Economic Zone and the Continental Shelf

I

The territorial sea

Article 1

The territorial sea of Iceland shall be delimited by a line every point of which is 12 nautical miles from a baseline drawn between the following points:

1. Horn	66° 27′ 4 N	22° 24′ 3 W
2. Asbuōarrif	66° 08′ 1 N	22° 11′ 0 W
3. Siglunes	66° 11′ 9 N	18° 49′ 9 W
4. Flatey	66° 10′ 3 N	17° 50′ 3 W
5. Lágey	66° 17′ 8 N	17° 06′ 8 W
6. Rauōinúpur	66° 30′ 7 N	16° 32′ 4 W
7. Rifstangi	66° 32′ 3 N	16° 11′ 8 W
8. Hraunhafnartangi	66° 32′ 2 N	16° 01′ 5 W
9. Langanes	66° 22′ 7 N	14° 31′ 9 W
10. Glettinganes	65° 30′ 5 N	13° 36′ 3 W
11. Norōfjarōarhorn	65° 10′ 0 N	13° 30′ 8 W
12. Gerpir	65° 04′ 7 N	13° 29′ 6 W
13. Hólmur	64° 58′ 9 N	13° 30′ 6 W
14. Setusker	64° 57′ 7 N	13° 31′ 5 W
15. Pursasker	64° 54′ 1 N	13° 36′ 8 W
16. Ystiboōi	64° 35′ 2 N	14° 01′ 5 W
17. Selsker	64° 32′ 8 N	14° 07′ 0 W
18. Uvitingar	64° 23′ 9 N	14° 28′ 0 W
19. Stokksnes	64° 14′ 1 N	14° 58′ 4 W
20. Hrollaugseyjar	64° 01′ 7 N	15° 58′ 7 W
21. Tvisker	63° 55′ 7 N	16° 11′ 3 W
22. Ingólfshöfōi	63° 47′ 8 N	16° 38′ 5 W
23. Hvalsiki	63° 44′ 1 N	17° 33′ 5 W
24. Meōallandssandur I	63° 32′ 4 N	17° 55′ 6 W
25. Meōallandssandur II	63° 30′ 6 N	17° 59′ 9 W
26. Myrnatangi	63° 27′ 4 N	18° 11′ 8 W
27. Kötlutangi	63° 23′ 4 N	18° 42′ 8 W
28. Lundadrangur	63° 23′ 5 N	19° 07′ 5 W
29. Surtsey	63° 17′ 7 N	20° 36′ 2 W
30. Eldeyjardrangur	63° 43′ 8 N	22° 59′ 4 W
31. Geirfugladrangur	63° 40′ 7 N	23° 17′ 1 W
32. Skálasnagi	64° 51′ 3 N	24° 02′ 5 W
33. Bjargtangar	65° 30′ 2 N	24° 32′ 1 W

34. Kópanes	65° 48° 4 N	24° 06′ 0 W
35. Barōi	66° 03′ 7 N	23° 47′ 4 W
36. Straumnes	66° 25′ 7 N	23° 08′ 4 W
37. Kögur	66° 28′ 3 N	22° 55′ 5 W
38. Horn	66° 27′ 9 N	22° 28′ 2 W

The territorial sea shall moreover be delimited by a line every point of which is 12 nautical miles from the low-water line of Kolbeinsey (67° 08′ 9 N 18° 41′ 3 W), Hvalbakur (64° 35′ 8 N 13° 16′ 6 W) and the outermost points and rocks of Grimsey.

Each nautical mile shall be equal to 1852 meters.

Article 2

The sovereignty of Iceland extends to the territorial sea, the bed of the territorial sea and the superjacent air space.

This sovereignty is exercised in accordance with Icelandic law and the rules of international law.

II
The economic zone

Article 3

The economic zone of Iceland is an area beyond the territorial sea delimited by a line every point of which is 200 nautical miles from the baselines from which the breadth of the territorial sea is measured, subject, however, to the provisions of article 7.

Article 4

In the economic zone, Iceland has:

(a) sovereign rights for the purpose of exploring, exploiting, conserving and managing the resources, whether living or non-living, of the sea-bed and subsoil and the superjacent waters, and with regard to other activities for the economic exploitation and exploration of the zone, such as the production of energy from the water, currents and winds;

(b) jurisdiction with regard to:
- (i) the establishment and use of man-made structures;
- (ii) scientific research;
- (iii) the preservation of the marine environment;

(c) other rights and duties under international law.

The exercise of rights and the performance of duties in the economic zone shall be in accordance with special legislation and in conformity with international agreements to which Iceland is a party.

III
The continental shelf

Article 5

The continental shelf of Iceland comprises the sea-bed and subsoil of the sub-marine areas that extend beyond the territorial sea throughout the natural prolongation of the land territory to the outer edge of the continental margin, or to a distance of 200 nautical miles from the baselines from which the breadth of the territorial sea is measured where the outer edge of the continental margin does not extend up to that distance, subject, however, to the provisions of article 7.

Article 6

Iceland exercises over the continental shelf sovereign rights for the purpose of exploring and exploiting the non-living resources thereof, together with living organisms which, at the harvestable stage, either are immobile on or under the sea-bed or are unable to move except in physical contact with the sea-bed.

The authorities concerned shall issue regulations concerning the exploration and exploitation of the resources of the continental shelf.

IV
Delimitation of areas between States

Article 7

The delimitation of the economic zone and the continental shelf between Iceland and other States shall, where appropriate, be effected by agreement with the States concerned. Such agreements shall be subject to approval by the Althing.

Until otherwise decided, the economic zone and the continental shelf of Iceland shall be 200 nautical miles from the baselines from which the territorial sea is measured, provided, however, that where the distance is less than 400 nautical miles between the baselines of the Faroe Islands and Greenland on the one hand and of Iceland on the other hand, the economic zone and the continental shelf of Iceland shall be delimited by the equidistant line.

V
Measures to prevent pollution

Article 8

Any measures which might pollute or otherwise damage the marine environment shall be avoided.

The Icelandic authorities concerned shall, by special legislation and in conformity with international agreements to which Iceland is a party, take measures to protect the marine environment against pollution and other harmful effects.

VI
Scientific research

Article 9

Scientific research in the territorial sea, the economic zone and the continental shelf shall be subject to the consent of the Icelandic authorities concerned.

In normal circumstances such consent shall be granted for research projects within the economic zone or on the continental shelf if the application emanates from another State or a competent international organization and the research project is to be carried out for peaceful purposes and in order to increase knowledge of the marine environment. Consent may, *inter alia,* be withheld if the application:

(a) is of direct significance for the exploration and exploitation of resources, whether living or non-living;

*(b)*involves drilling into the continental shelf or the use of explosives or substances harmful to the environment;

(c) involves the construction, operation or use of man-made structures.

Article 10

An application for a research permit in accordance with article 9 shall be submitted not less than six months in advance of the expected starting date of the project and shall be accompanied by full particulars concerning:

(a) the nature and objectives of the research project;
(b) the method and means to be used, including name, tonnage, type and class of vessels and a description of scientific equipment;
(c) the precise geographical areas in which the activities are to be conducted;
(d) the commencement and termination of the research period;
(e) the name of the sponsoring institution, its director, and the person in charge of the research project;
(f) the anticipated participation of the Icelandic authorities in the research project.

The Icelandic authorities shall communicate their decision on an application within four months if consent is to be withheld.

VII
General provisions

Article 11

Violations of the provisions of this Law shall be subject to penalties prescribed in prevailing legislation.

Article 12

Law No. 17 of 1 April 1969 concerning the continental shelf of Iceland hereby ceases to be in force. Furthermore, such provisions of law as are incompatible with this Law also cease to be in force.

Article 13

This Law shall enter into force immediately.

28. India

A. Maritime Zones Act, 1976
Entered into force: May 28, 1976 (except for Sections 5- contiguous zone- and 7- exclusive economic zone).
Source: *The Gazette of India, Extraordinary Part II-Section 2, No. 49,* May 28, 1976.

B. Act No. 80
Entered into force: January 15, 1977 (Sections 5 and 7 of the Maritime Zones Act, 1976).
Source: Notification of Act No. 80 reported by Ministry of Foreign Affairs in *The Indian Journal of International Law,* Vol. 16, No. 4, 1976, pp. 557–562.

PUBLISHED BY AUTHORITY
New Delhi, Friday, May 28, 1976, Jyaistha 7, 1898, No. 49

Separate paging is given to this Part in order that it may be filed as a separate compilation.

Rajya Sabha

The following Bills were introduced in the Rajya Sabha on the 28th May, 1976:—

I

Bill No. XXVIII of 1976

A Bill to provide for certain matters relating to the territorial waters, continental shelf, exclusive economic zone and other maritime zones of India.

Be it enacted by Parliament in the Twenty-seventh Year of the Republic in India as follows:—

Short title and commencement

1. (1) This Act may be called the Territorial Waters, Continental Shelf, Exclusive Economic Zone and other Maritime Zones Act, 1976.

(2) Sections 5 and 7 shall come into force on such date or on such different dates as the Central Government may, by notification in the Official Gazette, appoint; and the remaining provisions of this Act shall come into force at once.

Definition

2. In this Act, 'limit', in relation to the territorial waters, the continental shelf, the exclusive economic zone or any other maritime zone of India, means the limit of such waters, shelf or zone with reference to the mainland of India as well as the individual or composite group or groups of islands constituting part of the territory of India.

Sovereignty over, and limits of territorial waters.

3. (1) The sovereignty of India extends and has always extended to the territorial waters of India (hereinafter referred to as the territorial waters) and to the seabed and subsoil underlying, and the air space over, such waters.

(2) The limit of the territorial waters is the line every point of which is at a distance of twelve nautical miles from the nearest point of the appropriate baseline.

(3) Notwithstanding anything contained in sub-section (2), the Central Government may, whenever it

considers necessary so to do having regard to International Law and State practice, alter, by notification in the Official Gazette, the limit of the territorial waters.

(4) No notification shall be issued under sub-section (3) unless resolutions approving the issue of such notification are passed by both Houses of Parliament.

Use of territorial waters by foreign ships

4. (1) Without prejudice to the provisions of any other law for the time being in force, all foreign ships (other than warships including submarines and other underwater vehicles) shall enjoy the right of innocent passage through the territorial waters.

Explanation.—For the purposes of this section, passage is innocent so long as it is not prejudicial to the peace, good order or security of India.

(2) Foreign warships including submarines and other underwater vehicles may enter or pass through the territorial waters after giving prior notice to the Central Government:

Provided that submarines and other underwater vehicles shall navigate on the surface and show their flag while passing through such waters.

(3) The Central Government may, if satisfied that it is necessary so to do in the interests of the peace, good order or security of India or any part thereof, suspend, by notification in the Official Gazette, whether absolutely or subject to such exceptions and qualifications as may be specified in the notification, the entry of all or any class of foreign ships into such area of the territorial waters as may be specified in the notification.

Contiguous zone of India

5. (1) The contiguous zone of India (hereinafter referred to as the contiguous zone) is an area beyond and adjacent to the territorial waters and the limit of the contiguous zone is the line every point of which is at a distance of twenty-four nautical miles from the nearest point of the baseline referred to in sub-section (2) of section 3.

(2) Notwithstanding anything contained in sub-section (1), the Central Government may, whenever it considers necessary so to do having regard to International Law and State practice, alter, by notification in the Official Gazette, the limit of the contiguous zone.

(3) No notification shall be issued under sub-section (2) unless resolutions approving the issue of such notification are passed by both Houses of Parliament.

(4) The Central Government may exercise such powers and take such measures in or in relation to the contiguous zone as in may consider necessary with respect to,—

(a) the security of India, and

(b) immigration, sanitation, customs and other fiscal matters.

(5) The Central Government may, by notification in the Official Gazette,—

(a) extend with such restrictions and modifications as it thinks fit, any enactment, relating to any matter referred to in clause (a) or clause (b) of sub-section (4), for the time being in force in India or any part thereof, to the contiguous zone, and

(b) make such provisions as it may consider necessary in such notification for facilitating the enforcement of such enactment, and any enactment so extended shall have effect as if the contiguous zone is a part of the territory of India.

Continental shelf.

6. (1) The continental shelf of India (hereinafter referred to as the continental shelf) comprises the seabed and subsoil of the submarine areas that extend beyond the limit of its territorial waters throughout the natural prolongation of its land territory to the outer edge of the continental margin or to a distance of two hundred nautical miles from the baseline referred to in sub-section (2) of section 3 where the outer

edge of the continental margin does not extend up to that distance.

(2) India has, and always had, full and exclusive sovereign rights in respect of its continental shelf.

(3) Without prejudice to the generality of the provisions of sub-section (2), the Union has in the continental shelf,—

(a) sovereign rights for the purposes of exploration, exploitation, conservation and management of all resources;

(b) exclusive rights and jurisdiction for the construction, maintenance or operation of artificial islands, off-shore terminals, installations and other structures and devices necessary for the exploration and exploitation of the resources of the continental shelf or for the convenience of shipping or for any other purpose;

(c) exclusive jurisdiction to authorise, regulate and control scientific research; and

(d) exclusive jurisdiction to preserve and protect the marine environment and to prevent and control marine pollution.

(4) No person (including a foreign Government) shall, except under, and in accordance with, the terms of a licence or a letter of authority granted by the Central Government, explore the continental shelf or exploit its resources or carry out any scarch or excavation or conduct and research within the continental shelf or drill therein or construct, maintain or operate any artificial island, off-shore terminal, installation or other structure or device therein for any purpose whatsoever.

(5) The Central Government may, by notification in the Official Gazette,–

(a) declare any area of the continental shelf and its superjacent waters to be a designated area; and

(b) make such provisions as it may deem necessary with respect to,—

(i) the exploration, exploitation and protection of the resources of the continental shelf within such designated area; or

(ii) the safety and protection of artificial islands, off-shore terminals, installations and other structures and devices in such designated area; or

(iii) the protection of marine environment of such designated area; or

(iv) customs and other fiscal matters in relation to such designated area.

Explanation.—A notification issued under this sub-section may provide for the regulation of entry into and passage through the designated area of foreign ships by the establishment of fairways, sealanes, traffic separation schemes or any other mode of ensuring freedom of navigation which is not prejudicial to the interests of India.

(6) The Central Government may, by notification in the Official Gazette,—

(a) extend with such restrictions and modifications as it thinks fit, any enactment for the time being in force in India or any part thereof to the continental shelf or any part [including any designated area under sub-section (5)] thereof; and

(b) make such provisions as it may consider necessary for facilitating the enforcement of such enactment, and any enactment so extended shall have effect as if the continental shelf or the part [including, as the case may be, any designated area under sub-section (5)] thereof to which it has been extended is a part of the territory of India.

(7) Without prejudice to the provisions of sub-section (2) and subject to any measures that may be necessary for protecting the interests of India, the Central Government may not impede the laving or maintenance of submarine cables or pipelines on the continental shelf by foreign States:

Provided that the consent of the Central Government shall be necessary for the delineation of the course for the laying of such cables or pipelines.

Exclusive economic zone

7. (1) The exclusive economic zone of India (hereinafter referred to as the exclusive economic zone) is an area beyond and adjacent to the territorial waters, and the limit of such zone is two hundred nautical miles from the baseline referred to in sub-section (2) of section 3.

(2) Notwithstanding anything contained in sub-section (1), the Central Government may, whenever it considers necessary so to do having regard to International Law and State practice, alter, by notification in the Official Gazette, the limit of the exclusive economic zone.

(3) No notification shall be issued under sub-section (2) unless resolutions approving the issue of such notification are passed by both Houses of Parliament.

(4) In the exclusive economic zone, the Union has,—

(a) sovereign rights for the purpose of exploration, exploitation, conservation and management of the natural resources, both living and non-living as well as for producing energy from tides, winds and currents;

(b) exclusive rights and jurisdiction for the construction, maintenance or operation of artificial islands, off-shore terminals, installations and other structures and devices necessary for the exploration and exploitation of the resources of the zone or for the convenience of shipping or for any other purpose;

(c) exclusive jurisdiction to authorise, regulate and control scientific research;

(d) exclusive jurisdiction to preserve and protect the marine environment and to prevent and control marine pollution; and

(e) such other rights as are recognised by International law.

(5) No person (including a foreign Government) shall, except under, and in accordance with, the terms of any agreement with the Central Government or of a licence or a letter of authority granted by the Central Government, explore or exploit any resources of the exclusive economic zone or carry out any search or excavation or conduct any research within the exclusive economic zone or drill therein or construct, maintain or operate any artificial island, off-shore terminal, installation or other structure or device therein for any purpose whatsoever:

Provided that nothing in this sub-section shall apply in relation to fishing by a citizen of India.

(6) The Central Government may, by notification in the Official Gazette,—

(a) declare any area of the exclusive economic zone to be a designated area; and

(b) make such provisions as it may deem necessary with respect to,—

(i) the exploration, exploitation and protection of the resources of such designated area; or

(ii) other activities for the economic exploitation and exploration of such designated area such as the production of energy from tides, winds and currents; or

(iii) the safety and protection of artificial islands, off-shore terminals, installations and other structures and devices in such designated area; or

(iv) the protection of marine environment of such designated area; or

(v) customs and other fiscal matters in relation to such designated area.

Explanation.—A notification issued under this sub-section may provide for the regulation of entry into and passage through the designated area of foreign ships by the establishment of fairways, sealanes, traffic separation schemes or any other mode of ensuring freedom of navigation which is not prejudicial to the interests of India.

(7) The Central Government may, by notification in the official Gazette,—

(a) extend, with such restrictions and modifications as it thinks fit, any enactment for the time being in force in India or any part thereof to the exclusive economic zone or any part thereof; and

(b) make such provisions as it may consider necessary for facilitating the enforcement of such

enactment, and any enactment so extended shall have effect as if the exclusive economic zone or the part thereof to which it has been extended is a part of the territory of India.

(8) The provisions of sub-section (7) of section 6 shall apply in relation to the laying or maintenance of submarine cables or pipelines on the seabed of the exclusive economic zone as they apply in relation to the laying or maintenance of submarine cables or pipelines on the seabed of the continental shelf.

(9) In the exclusive economic zone and the air space over the zone, ships and aircraft of all States shall, subject to the exercise by India of its rights within the zone, enjoy freedom of navigation and overflight.

Historic waters

8. (1) The Central Government may, by notification in the Official Gazette, specify the limits of such waters adjacent to its land territory as are the historic waters of India.

(2) The sovereignty of India extends, and has always extended, to the historic waters of India and to the seabed and subsoil underlying, and the air space over, such waters.

Maritime boundaries between India and States having coasts opposite or adjacent to those of India

9. (1) The maritime boundaries between India and any State whose coast is opposite or adjacent to that of India in regard to their respective territorial waters, contiguous zones, continental shelves, exclusive economic zones and other maritime zones shall be as determined by agreement (whether entered into before or after the commencement of this section) between India and such State and pending such agreement between India and any such State, and unless any other provisional arrangements are agreed to between them, the maritime boundaries between India and such State shall not extend beyond the line every point of which is equidistant from the nearest point from which the breadth of the territorial waters of India and of such State are measured.

(2) Every agreement referred to in sub-section (1) shall, as soon as may be after it is entered into, be published in the Official Gazette.

(3) The provisions of sub-section (1) shall have effect notwithstanding anything contained in any other provision of this Act.

Publication of charts

10. The Central Government may cause the baseline referred to in sub-section (2) of section 3, the limits of the territorial waters, the contiguous zone, the continental shelf, the exclusive economic zone and the historic waters of India and the maritime boundaries as settled by agreements referred to in section 9 to be published in charts.

Offences

11. Whoever contravenes any provision of this Act or of any notification thereunder shall (without prejudice to any other action which may be taken against such person under any other provision of this or of any other enactment) be punishable with imprisonment which may extend to three years, or with fine, or with both.

Offences by companies

12. (1) Where an offence under this Act or the rules made thereunder has been committed by a company, every person who at the time the offence was committed was in charge of, and was responsible to the company for the conduct of the business of the company, as well as the company shall be deemed to be guilty of the offence and shall be liable to be proceeded against and punished accordingly:

Provided that nothing contained in this sub-section shall render any such person liable to any punishment provided in this Act if he proves that the offence was committed without his knowledge or that he exercised all due diligence to prevent the commission of such offence.

(2) Notwithstanding anything contained in sub-section (1) where an offence under this Act or the rules

made thereunder has been committed by a company and it is proved that the offence has been committed with the consent or the connivance of, or is attributable to any neglect on the part of, any director, manager, secretary or other officer of the company, such director, manager, secretary or other officer shall also be deemed to be guilty of that offence and shall be liable to be proceeded against and punished accordingly.

Explanation.—For the purposes of this section,—

(a) 'company' means any body corporate and includes a firm or other association of individuals; and

(b) 'director', in relation to a firm, means a partner in the firm.

Place of trial

13. Any person committing an offence under this Act or any rules made thereunder or under any of the enactments extended under this Act or under the rules made thereunder may be tried for the offence in any place in which may be found or in such other place as the Central Government may, by general or special order, published in the Official Gazette, direct in this behalf.

Previous sanction of the Central Government for prosecution

14. No prosecution shall be instituted against any person in respect, of any offence under this Act or the rules made thereunder without the previous sanction of the Central Government or such officer or authority as may be authorised by that Government by order in writing in this behalf.

Power to make rules

15. (1) The Central Government may, by notification in the Official Gazette, make rules for carrying out the purposes of this Act.

(2) In particular and without prejudice to the generality of the foregoing power, such rules may provide for all or any of the following matters, namely:—

(a) regulation of the conduct of any person in the territorial waters, the contiguous zone, the continental shelf, the exclusive economic zone or any other maritime zone of India;

(b) regulation of the exploration and exploitation, conservation and management of the resources of the continental shelf;

(c) regulation of the exploration, exploitation, conservation and management of the resources of the exclusive economic zone;

(d) regulation of the construction, maintenance and operation of artificial islands, off-shore terminals, installations and other structures and devices referred to in sections 6 and 7;

(e) preservation and protection of the marine environment and prevention and control of marine pollution for the purposes of this Act;

(f) authorisation, regulation and control of the conduct of scientific research for the purposes of this Act;

(g) fees in relation to licences and letters of authority referred to in sub-section (4) of section 6 and sub-section (5) of section 7 or for any other purpose; or

(h) any matter incidental to any of the matters specified in clauses *(a)* to *(g)*.

(3) In making any rule under this section, the Central Government may provide that a contravention thereof shall be punishable with imprisonment which may extend to three years, or with fine which may extend to any amount, or with both.

(4) Every rule made under this Act and every notification issued under sub-section (5) of section 6 or sub-section (6) of section 7 shall be laid, as soon as may be after it is made or issued, before each House of Parliament while it is in session for a total period of thirty days which may be comprised in one session or in two or more successive sessions and if, before the expiry of the session immediately following the

session or the successive sessions aforesaid both Houses agree in making any modification in the rule or the notification or both Houses agree that the rule or notification should not be issued, the rule or notification shall, thereafter, have effect only in such modified form or be of no effect, as the case may be; so, however, that any such modification or annulment shall be without prejudice to the validity of anything previously done under that rule or notification.

Removal of difficulties

16. (1) If any difficulty arises in giving effect to the provisions of this Act or of any of the enactments extended under this Act, the Central Government may, by order published in the Official Gazette, make such provisions not inconsistent with the provisions of this Act or, as the case may be, such enactment, as may appear to it to be necessary or expedient for removing the difficulty:

Provided that no order shall be made under this section—

(a) in the case of any difficulty arising in giving effect to any provision of this Act, after the expiry of three years from the commencement of such provision;

(b) in the case of any difficulty arising in giving effect to the provisions of any enactment extended under this Act, after the expiry of three years from the extension of such enactment.

(2) Every order made under this section shall be laid, as soon as may be after it is made, before each House of Parliament.

STATEMENT OF OBJECTS AND REASONS

The Bill is a sequel to the latest Constitution Amendment Bill relating to the substitution of article 297 by a new article. According to new article 297, all lands, minerals and other things of value underlying the ocean within the territorial waters, or the continental shelf, or the exclusive economic zone, as well as all other resources of the exclusive economic zone, vest in the Union to be held for the purposes of the Union. The new article also provides that the limits of the territorial waters, the continental shelf, the exclusive economic zone and other maritime zones of India shall be such as may be specified, from time to time, by or under any law made by Parliament.

2. At present, India does not have a comprehensive legislation on the Law of the Sea. The limits of the territorial waters and the continental shelf are governed by the Proclamations issued by the President. As envisaged by new article 297, it is intended to provide for the limits of the territorial waters, the continental shelf, the exclusive economic zone and other maritime zones of India by a Parliamentary law. For safeguarding the interests of the nation, it is also necessary to provide for a general legal framework specifying the nature, scope and extent of India's rights, jurisdiction and control in relation to the various maritime zones, the maritime boundaries between India and other States whose coasts are opposite or adjacent to those of India, and for the exploration, exploitation and protection of the resources of our continental shelf and exclusive economic zone. Hence this Bill.

3. The maritime zones of India include the territorial waters, the contiguous zone, the continental shelf, the exclusive economic zone and the historic waters of India. The territorial waters and the continental shelf are traditional concepts in International Law and the national jurisdiction in these zones is well established. The concept of the exclusive economic zone which has been developed at the initiative of developing countries has gained acceptance of the international community of States. The concept of contiguous zone which is located within the exclusive economic zone and over which additional jurisdiction is claimed by coastal States has also been accepted by the international community of States. Provision has also been made in the Bill regarding the historic waters of India which are adjacent to its land territory and over which India has sovereignty. The limits of these waters, such as the waters in the Palk Bay and the Gulf of Manaar, will be specified by the Central Government by notification in the

Official Gazette. The limits of other maritime zones of India have been specified in the Bill itself. The Bill empowers the Central Government to alter, by notification in the Official Gazette, the limits of these maritime zones. It has been made clear that notifications for altering the limits as specified in the Bill shall not be issued unless both Houses of Parliament have passed resolutions approving the issue of such notifications.

4. It is proposed to undertake separate legislation in future as and when need arises for dealing in greater detail with the regulation, exploration and exploitation of particular resources or particular groups of resources of the continental shelf and the exclusive economic zone as well as with other matters in which India has jurisdiction in the maritime zones, and with regard to these matters the Bill makes only broad general provisions.

New Delhi; Y.B. Chavan
The 25th May, 1976

FINANCIAL MEMORANDUM

The Bill provides for the limits of India's maritime zones and for the nature, scope and extent of India's rights, jurisdiction and control in relation to the various maritime zones. The Bill also makes provisions for the regulation, exploration and exploitation of the resources of the continental shelf and the exclusive economic zone of India.

2. Sub-clause (4) of clause 5 of the Bill relating to the contiguous zone of India empowers the Central Government to exercise such powers and take such measures in or in relation to the contiguous zone as it may consider necessary with respect to security of India, and immigration, sanitation, customs and other fiscal matters.

3. Sub-clause (5) of clause 6 of the Bill relating to the continental shelf provides for the declaration of any area of the continental shelf and its superjacent waters to be a designated area and for the making of such provisions with respect to the exploration, exploitation and protection of the resources of the continental shelf within such designated area and other matters mentioned in the sub-clause, as may be deemed necessary by the Central Government. Sub-clause (6) of clause 7 of the Bill relating to the exclusive economic zone also makes similar provisions with regard to designation of areas in the exclusive economic zone and for the making of such provisions as the Central Government may deem necessary with respect to the exploitation, exploration and protection of such designated area and other matters mentioned in the sub-clause.

4. Clause 15 of the Bill provides for the making of rules, *inter alia,* with regard to the regulation and conduct of persons in any maritime zone of India, regulation of the exploration, exploitation, conservation and management of the resources of the continental shelf and the exclusive economic zone, the preservation and protection of the marine environment and the prevention and control of marine pollution, and the authorisation, regulation and control of the conduct of scientific research.

5. While the various measures which may be taken in pursuance of the aforementioned provisions of the Bill, when enacted and brought into operation, will involve expenditure, both of a recurring and nonrecurring nature, from the Consolidated Fund of India, at the present stage it is not possible to indicate with any degree of accuracy the quantum of such expenditure. A carefully planned programme will have to be evolved with regard to the various maritime zones for the exploration and exploitation of their resources, and the priorities with regard to different matters will have to be fixed. Bearing these programmes and priorities in mind, and having regard to the available finances, the expenditure to be incurred will have to be determined. Any expenditure whether of a recurring or non-recurring nature, which may have to be incurred, will be met from out of the grants is the different Ministries and after due appropriation made by Parliament by law. It may also be mentioned in this connection that the intention is

to undertake separate legislation in future for dealing in greater detail with the regulation, exploration and exploitation of particular resources or particular groups of resources of the continental shelf and exclusive economic zone, and the Bill, as stated in the Statement of Objects and Reasons, is intended to provide only the broad general legal framework.

MEMORANDUM REGARDING DELEGATED LEGISLATION

Sub-clause (5) of clause 5 of the Bill seeks to empower the Central Government to extend any enactment relating to the security of India, immigration, sanitation, customs and other fiscal matters for the time being in force in India or any part thereof to the contiguous zone. Sub-clause (6) of clause 6 of the Bill seeks to empower the Central Government to extend, by notification in the Official Gazette, any enactment for the time being in force in India or any part thereof to the continental shelf or any part thereof. Sub-clause (7) of clause 7 of the Bill makes a similar provision in respect of extension of enactments to the exclusive economic zone or any part thereof.

Sub-clause (5) of clause 6 of the Bill seeks to empower the Central Government to declare, by notification in the Official Gazette, any area of the continental shelf and the superjacent waters to be a designated area and to make such provisions as it may deem necessary in such notification with respect to the exploration, exploitation and protection of the resources of the continental shelf within such designated area, the safety and protection of artificial islands and other structures and devices in such designated area, the protection of marine environment of such designated area and customs and other fiscal matters in relation to such designated area. Sub-clause (6) of clause 7 of the Bill makes similar provisions in respect of the exclusive economic zone.

Clause 15 of the Bill empowers the Central Government to make rules of carrying out the purposes of this legislation. These relate, *inter alia,* to the regulation of the conduct of any person in the territorial waters, contiguous zone, continental shelf, exclusive economic zone or any other maritime zone, the exploration and exploitation, conservation and management of the resources of the continental shelf and of the exclusive economic zone, the construction, maintenance and operation of artificial islands, off-shore terminals. Installations and other structures and devices in the continental shelf and exclusive economic zone, preservation and protection of the marine environment and prevention and control of marine pollution, conduct of scientific research, fees for various purposes, etc. Sub-clause (3) of the clause provides that in making any rule, the Central Government may provide that a contravention thereof shall be punishable with imprisonment which may extend to three years, or with fine which may extend to any amount, or with both.

The nature, scope and extent of India's rights, jurisdiction and control in relation to the various maritime zones have been set out in the Bill itself. The rules and other provisions will be confined to specific measures for the regulation and conduct of persons in various zones, technical matters, matters of procedure and other matters of administrative detail. In the present stage of the scientific, technological and other developments, if is not practicable to visualise the various enactments which have to be extended to these zones and the specific measures which will have to be taken for the protection of the nation's interests in these zones and for the proper exploration and exploitation of the resources of the various zones to the best advantage of the nation. Having regard to the immense value of the resources of the zones, it is necessary to provide for effective sanctions against persons acting contrary to the national interests. Further, the rules and the notifications under clauses 6(5) and 7(6), when made or issued, will be laid before both Houses of Parliament. In the circumstances, the delegation of legislative power is of a normal character.

NOTIFICATIONS BY INDIA OF THE EXCLUSIVE ECONOMIC ZONE*

(15 January 1977)

India issued two Notifications today under the Maritime Zones Act, 1976 (The Territorial Waters, Continental Shelf, Exclusive Economic Zone and Other Maritime Zones Act, 1976). The first Notification brought into force its provisions concerning the contiguous zone of India and the exclusive economic zone of India, and the second specified the limits of historic waters of India in the Palk Strait, Palk Bay and the Gulf of Manaar.

2. It will be recalled that Parliament of India passed the Constitution (40th Amendment) Act, 1976 which was assented to by the President on May 27, 1976. By this Act, Article 297 of the Constitution was amended by including therein reference to the exclusive economic zone of India and vesting rights therein in the Union.

3. Pursuant to this Act, Parliament also enacted 'The Territorial Waters, Continental Shelf, Exclusive Economic Zone and Other Maritime Zones Act, 1976' on August 17, 1976, which was assented to by the President on August 25, 1976.

4. The Maritime Zones Act, 1976 is a comprehensive piece of legislation and makes provisions for a 12-mile territorial waters, contiguous zone, continental shelf, exclusive economic zone and historic waters of India. All its provisions except those concerning the contiguous zone of India and the exclusive economic zone of India came into force forthwith.

5. The provisions concerning the contiguous zone of India and the exclusive economic zone of India have been brought into force by the Central Government by a Gazette Notification published on January 15, 1977.

6. The contigous zone of India extends into the sea outside the territorial waters upto a distance of 24 nautical miles measured from the appropriate baseline from which the breadth of territorial waters is measured. In this area the Central Government will have powers to take measures with regard to (a) the security of India, and (b) immigration, sanitation, customs and other fiscal matters.

7. The exclusive economic zone of India extends into the sea outside the territorial waters upto a distance of 200 nautical miles measured from the appropriate baseline from which the breadth of territorial water is measured. In this zone, the Union has sovereign rights for exploring and exploiting its living and non-living resources as well as for other economic uses, and exclusive jurisdiction to authorise, conduct and control scientific research and take measures to preserve and protect the marine environment.

8. For immediate purposes, exclusive jurisdiction in the economic zone will have bearing on exploitation of fishery resources, petroleum and natural gas, minerals, chemicals and plants, the establishment of offshore terminals, and on other economic uses. No person, including a foreign Government, shall explore or exploit the resources of the zone without an express agreement with the Government of India or without obtaining a licence or letter of authority from it. The Government of India will also be able to make measures against smuggling etc. in the contiguous zone. The Maritime Zones Act contains penal clauses for violation of its provisions.

9. The action taken by the Government of India in this regard is in conformity with the consensus which has emerged at the United Nations Conference on the Law of the Sea during its deliberations since 1973. State practice conforming to the consensus and trends has also emerged in favour of the establishment of these zones. Thus, in addition to action already taken by some Latin American and African States, during the past year or so, Mexico, Norway, Canada, Iceland and EEC countries have established economic zones or fishery jurisdiction extending to 200 miles from the coast. Their legislation came into

* Source: Ministry of External Affairs.

force on January 1, 1977. The USSR has also taken measures in December 1976 to establish the exclusive fishery jurisdiction upto 200 miles forthwith. The United States enacted a law establishing a 200-mile fishery jurisdiction in April 1976, which will come into force on March 1, 1977. Some of India's neighbours, including Sri Lanka and Pakistan, have also established economic zones. It was thus necessary for India to take measures to protect its essential interests in the maritime zones around its coast forthwith.

10. In the case of countries with which India's coast is either opposite or adjacent and the maritime zones overlap, maritime boundary will be settled to demarcate the respective zones. Such boundary has already been settled by agreements with Sri Lanka, Maldives and Indonesia. With other countries, namely, Thailand, Burma, Bangladesh and Pakistan, negotiations will be undertaken.

11. The second Notification issued on January 15, 1977 relates to the historic waters of India in Palk Strait, Palk Bay and the Gulf of Manaar between India and Sri Lanka. These waters have been under the jurisdiction of India and Sri Lanka respectively from historical times. The waters of the Palk Bay between the Indian coast and the maritime boundary will be the internal waters of India. The waters of the Gulf of Manaar between the Indian coast and the maritime boundary have the same status as the territorial waters of India. The waters in the Gulf of Manaar will be bounded by a line joining Tiruchehendur on the Indian coast with a turning point on the boundary between the two countries. The limits of the historic waters in the Palk Strait and the Gulf of Manaar have been specified in the Notification.

12. The texts of the two Notifications read as follows:

I

> 'In excercise of the powers conferred by sub-section (2) of section 1 of the Territorial Waters, Continental Shelf, Exclusive Economic Zone and other Maritime Zones Act, 1976 (80 of 1976), the Central Government hereby appoints the 15th day of January, 1977, as the date on which sections 5 and 7 of the said Act shall come into force.'

Text of Sections 5 and 7 of the Maritime Zones Act reads as follows:

'5. (1) The contiguous zone of India (hereinafter referred to as the contiguous zone) is an area beyond and adjacent to the territorial waters and the limit of the contiguous zone is the line every point of which is at a distance of twenty-four nautical miles from the nearest point of the baseline referred to in sub-section (2) of section 3.

(2) Notwithstanding anything contained in sub-section (1), the Central Government may, whenever it considers necessary so to do having regard to International Law and State practice, alter, by notification in the Official Gazette, the limit of the contiguous zone.

(3) No notification shall be issued under sub-section (2) unless resolutions approving the issue of such notification are passed by both Houses of Parliament.

(4) The Central Government may exercise such powers and take such measures in or in relation to the contiguous zone as it may consider necessary with respect to:

(a) the security of India, and

(b) immigration, sanitation, customs and other fiscal matters.

(5) The Central Government may, by notification in the Official Gazette:

(a) extend with such restrictions and modifications as it thinks fit, any enactment, relating to any matter referred to in clause *(a)* or clause *(b)* of sub-section (4), for the time being in force in India or any part thereof, to the contiguous zone, and

(b) make such provisions at it may consider necessary in such notification for facilitating the enforcement of such enactment and any enactment so extended shall have effect as if the contiguous zone is a part of the territory of India.

7. (1) The exclusive economic zone of India (hereinafter referred to as the exclusive economic zone) is an area beyond and adjacent to the territorial waters, and the limit of such zone is two hundred nautical

miles from the baseline referred to in sub-section (2) of section 3.

(2) Notwithstanding anything contained in subsection (1), the Central Government may whenever it considers necessary so to do having regard to International Law and State practice, alter, by notification in the Official Gazette, the limit of the exclusive economic zone.

(3) No notification shall be issued under sub-section (2) unless resolutions approving the issue of such notification are passed by both Houses of Parliament.

(4) In the exclusive economic zone, the Union has:

(a) sovereign rights for the purpose of exploration, exploitation, conservation and management of the natural resources, both living and non-living as well as for producing energy from tides, winds and currents;

(b) exclusive rights and jurisdiction for the construction, maintenance or operation of artificial islands, off-shore terminals, installations and other structures and devices necessary for the exploration and exploitation of resources of the zone or for the convenience of shipping or for any other purpose;

(c) exclusive jurisdiction to authorise, regulate and control scientific research;

(d) exclusive jurisdiction to preserve and protect the marine environment and to prevent and control marine pollution; and

(e) such other rights as are recognised by International Law.

(5) No person (including a foreign Government) shall, except under and in accordance with the terms of any agreement with the Central Government or a licence or a letter of authority granted by the Central Government, exploit any resources of the exclusive economic zone or carry out and search or excavation or condut any research within the exclusive economic zone or drill therein or construct, maintain or operate any artificial island, off-shore terminal, installation or other structure or device therein for any purpose whatsoever:

Provided that nothing in this sub-section shall apply in relation to fishing by a citizen of India.

(6) The Central Government may, by notification in the Official Gazette,

(a) declare any area of the exclusive economic zone to be a designated area; and

(b) make such provisions as it may deem necessary with respect to,

(i) the exploration, exploitation and protection of the resources of such designated area; or

(ii) other activities for the economic exploitation and exploration of such designated area such as the production of energy from tides, winds and currents; or

(iii) the safety and protection of artificial islands, off-shore terminals, installations and other structures and devices in such designated area; or

(iv) the protection of marine environment of such designated area; or

(v) customs and other fiscal matters in relation to such designated area.

Explanation— A notification issued under this sub-section may provide for the regulation of entry into and passage through the designated area of foreign ships by the establishment of fairways, sealanes, traffic separation schemes or any other mode of ensuring freedom of navigation which is not prejudicial to the interests of India.

(7) The Central Government may, by notification in the Official Gazette,

(a) extend, with such restrictions and modifications as it thinks fit, any enactment for the time being in force in India or any part thereof to the exclusive economic zone or any part thereof; and

(b) make such provisions as it may consider necessary for facilitating the enforcement of such enactment,

and any enactment so extended shall have effect as if the exclusive economic zone or the part thereof to which it has been extended is a part of the territory of India.

(8) The provisions of sub-section (7) of section 6 shall apply in relation to the laying or maintenance of submarine cables or pipelines on the seabed of the exclusive economic zone as they apply in relation to the laying or maintenance of submarine cables or pipelines on the seabed of the continental shelf.

(9) In the exclusive economic zone and the air space over the zone, ships and aircraft of all States shall, subject to the exercise by India of its rights within the zone, enjoy freedom of navigation and overflight.'

THE TABLE

S. No.	*Description of the area of sea*	*Limits of historic waters of India*
I	*II*	*III*
1.	Palk Strait and Palk Bay	The area of sea bounded by: *(a)* the cost of the mainland of India, *(b)* the maritime boundary settled by the Agreement between India and Sri Lanka on the Boundary in Historic Waters between the two Countries and Related Matters, which came into force with effect from July 8, 1974, and *(c)* the arc of Great Circle between the following position defined by latitude and longitude in the Palk Strait: *(i)* 10 degrees 17.5 minutes North, 79 degrees 52.7 minutes East, *(ii)* 10 degrees 05.0 minutes North, 80 degrees 03.0 minutes East.
2.	Gulf of Manaar	The area of sea bounded by: *(a)* the coast of the mainland of *(b)* India, the maritime boundary settled by the Agreement between India and Sri Lanka on the Maritime Boundary between the two Countries in the Gulf of Manaar and the Bay of Bengal and Related Matters, which came into force with effect from May 10, 1976, and *(c)* the arc of Great Circle between the following positions defined by latitude and longitude: *(i)* 08 degrees 30.0 minutes North, 78 degrees 07.9 minutes East, *(ii)* 08 degrees 22.2 minutes North, 78 degrees 55.4 minutes East.

2. The historic waters of India in Palk Strait and Palk Bay area of sea are internal waters of India. The historic waters of India beyond the appropriate baseline referred to in section 3 (2) of the Act in the Gulf of Manaar area of sea have the same status as the territorial waters of India.'

II

'In exercise of the powers conferred by sub-section (1) of section 8 of the Territorial Waters, Continental Shelf, Exclusive Economic Zone and other Maritime Zones Act, 1976 (80 of 1976) (hereinafter referred to as the Act), the Central Government hereby notifies that the limits of the historic waters of India in each of the areas of sea specified in column II of the Table below are as specified in the corresponding entry in column III of the Table.

29. Indonesia

A. Declaration.
Entered into force: March 21, 1980.
Source: *United Nations LE 113 (3–3)*, June 9, 1980.

B. Act No. 5 of 1983 on the Indonesian Exclusive Economic Zone.
Source: Department of Information, Republic of Indonesia.

DECLARATION BY THE GOVERNMENT OF THE REPUBLIC OF INDONESIA CONCERNING THE EXCLUSIVE ECONOMIC ZONE OF INDONESIA

The Government of the Republic of Indonesia

Bearing in mind: that improving the nation's welfare by exploiting all available natural resources, both living and non-living, is the aim and purpose of the Indonesian Government and Nation.

Being aware: that in order to attain the above aim and purpose, the natural resources of the sea-bed and sub-soil and the superjacent waters have to be protected and managed in an appropriate, purposeful and rational manner.

Noting: that state practice indicates that the regime of an exclusive economic zone of 200 nautical miles has been accepted as part of the new international law of the sea.

Recognizing: the need for Indonesia to proclaim a Government Declaration concerning the Exclusive Economic Zone of Indonesia.

Declares as follows:

1. The Exclusive Economic Zone of Indonesia is the area beyond the Indonesian Territorial Sea as promulgated by virtue of Law No. 4 of 1960 concerning Indonesian Waters, the breadth of which extends to 200 nautical miles from the baselines from which the breadth of the Indonesian Territorial Sea is measured.

2. In the Exclusive Economic Zone, Indonesia has and exercises:

(a) sovereign rights for the purpose of exploring and exploiting, managing and conserving living and non-living natural resources of the sea-bed and sub-soil and the superjacent waters and sovereign rights with regard to other activities for the economic exploration and exploitation of the zone, such as the production of energy from the water, currents and winds;

(b) jurisdiction with regard to:

(1) the establishment and use of artificial islands, installations and structures.

(2) marine scientific research.

(3) the preservation of the marine environment.

(4) other rights based on international law.

3. The sovereign rights of Indonesia as referred to in paragraph 2 of this Government Declaration shall, with respect to the sea-bed and sub-soil, continue to be exercised in accordance with the provisions of the laws and regulations of Indonesia concerning Indonesian Waters and the Indonesian Continental Shelf, international agreements and international law.

4. In the Exclusive Economic Zone of Indonesia, the freedoms of navigation and overflight and of the laying of sub-marine cables and pipelines will continue to be recognized in accordance with the principles of the new international law of the sea.

5. Where the boundary line of the Exclusive Economic Zone of Indonesia poses a problem of delimitation with an adjacent or opposite State, the Indonesian Government is prepared, at an appropriate time, to enter into negotiations with the State concerned with a view to reach an agreement.

6. The above provisions will further be regulated by a law and regulations.

This Government Declaration will come into force on the date of its announcement.

Jakarta, 21 March 1980
President of the Republic of Indonesia

Soeharto

B. Act. No. 5 of 1983 on the Indonesian Exclusive Economic Zone
Source: Department of Information, Republic of Indonesia.

ACT No. 5 of 1983

ON
THE INDONESIAN EXCLUSIVE ECONOMIC ZONE

BY THE GRACE OF GOD
THE PRESIDENT OF THE REPUBLIC OF INDONESIA

Considering:

(a) that on March 21, 1980, the Announcement on the Indonesian Exclusive Economic Zone has been issued by the Government of the Republic of Indonesia;

(b) that improvement of the people's welfare by using all available natural resources, both living and non-living, is the goal and unanimous will of the Indonesian Government and people;

(c) that, in order to achieve said goal, the natural resources found on the seabed and in the subsoil thereof as well as in the water space above it, have to be protected and managed in proper, systematic and wise manner;

(d) that any marine scientific research activities in waters falling under the sovereignty and jurisdiction of Indonesia, have to be arranged and carried out for the benefit and in the interest of Indonesia;

(e) that the marine environment of the waters falling under the sovereignty and jurisdiction of the Republic of Indonesia, has to be protected and conserved;

(f) that all living and non-living natural resources, found in the Indonesian Exclusive Economic Zone, potentially and effectively, are assets and common property of the Indonesian Archipelagic Outlook;

(g) that both, the practice of states and the Convention of the Law of the Sea as produced by the Third United Nations Conference on the Law of the Sea, have indicated the recognition of the exclusive economic zone regime as wide as 200 (two hundred) nautical miles as part of the new international law of the sea;

(h) that, in relation to what is mentioned above, it is necessary to provide an act as the basic for the effectuation of the sovereign rights and other such rights, jurisdiction and duties of the Republic of Indonesia within the Indonesian Exclusive Economic Zone.

In view of:

1. Article 5, paragraph (1), Article 11, Article 20, paragraph (1), and Article 33, paragraph (3), of the 1945 Constitution;

2. Decree No. II/MPR/1983 of the People's Consultative Assembly of the Republic of Indonesia, on the Guidelines of State Policy;

3. Act No. 4 Prp*) of 1980, on the Indonesian Waters (State Gazette of 1960 No. 22, Supplementary State Gazette No. 1942;

4. Act No. 44 Prp of 1960, on Extraction of Oil and Natural Gas (State Gazette of 1960 No. 133, Supplementary State Gazette No. 2070;

5. Act No. 11 of 1967 on the Basic Rules of Mining (State Gazette of 1967 No. 22, Supplementary State Gazette No. 2831;

6. Act No. 1 of 1973 on the Indonesian Continental Shelf (State Gazette of 1973 No. 1 Supplementary State Gazette No. 2294;

7. Act No. 8 of 1981 on the Code of Criminal Procedure as in State Gazette of 1981 No. 76, Supplementary State Gazette No. 3209;

8. Act No. 4 of 1982 on the Basic Rules of Life Environmental Management (State Gazette of 1982 No. 12, Supplementary State Gazette No. 3215;

9. Act No. 20 of 1982 on the Basic Rules on Defence and Security of the Republic of Indonesia (State Gazette of 1982 No. 51, Supplementary State Gazette No. 3234.

With the consent of the House of People's Representatives of the Republic of Indonesia,

has decided:

to sanction: Act on the Indonesian Exclusive Economic Zone

Chapter I
General provision

Article 1

Meant in this act by:

(a) living natural resources are all species of animals and plants, including their divisions, found on the seabed and in the water area of the Indonesian Exclusive Economic Zone;
(b) non-living natural resources are natural substances being no living natural resources, found on the seabed and in the subsoil thereof as well as in the water area of the Indonesian Exclusive Economic Zone;
(c) scientific research is any activity in connection with the research on any maritime aspects on the water surface, in the water area, on the seabed and in the subsoil thereof the sea floor in the Indonesian Exclusive Economic Zone;

*) Prp is the abbreviation of Peraturan Pemerintah meaning Government Regulation.

(d) conservation of natural resources are all efforts aimed at protecting and preserving the natural resources in the Indonesian Exclusive Economic Zone;

(e) marine environmental protection and conservation is any effort aimed at preserving and maintaining the whole of the marine ecosystem within the Indonesian Exclusive Economic Zone.

Chapter II

Indonesia's Exclusive Economic Zone

Article 2

The Indonesian Exclusive Economic Zone is the outer strip bordering the Indonesian territorial sea as determined by the law applicable to the Indonesian waters, covering the seabed, the subsoil thereof and the water above it with an outermost limit of 200 (two hundred) sea miles, measured from the baseline of the Indonesian territorial sea.

Article 3

1. In the event that the Indonesian Exclusive Economic Zone is overlapping the exclusive economic zone of another state which coastline is opposite or adjacent to that of Indonesia, then the boundary line between the exclusive economic zone of Indonesia and that of the other state shall be established by agreement between the Republic of Indonesia and the state concerned.

2. So long as such agreement as meant in paragraph (1) does not exist, and no special conditions need to be considered, then the boundary line between the exclusive economic zone of Indonesia and that of the other state shall be the median line or line which is equidistant from the baselines of the Indonesian territorial sea or the outermost points of Indonesia and the baselines of the territorial sea or outermost points of the other state, except if an agreement has been reached with the said state on a provisional arrangement of the boundaries of the Indonesian Exclusive Economic Zone.

Chapter III

Sovereign rights, other rights, jurisdiction and duties

Article 4

1. Within the Indonesian Exclusive Economic Zone, the Republic of Indonesia shall have and exercise:

(a) its sovereign rights to conduct the exploration, exploitation, management and conservation of the living and non-living resources on the seabed and in the subsoil thereof as well as the water above it, including other activities for the purpose of economic exploration and exploitation of said zone, such as the generation of power by means of water, current and wind;

b) its jurisdiction in connection with:

(i) the construction and use of artificial islands, installations and other structures;

(ii) marine scientific research;

(iii) the protection and conservation of the marine environment;

(c) other rights and duties, based on the applicable Convention of the Law of the Sea.

2. As far as it concerns the seabed and the subsoil thereof, the sovereign rights and other rights, jurisdiction and duties of Indonesia as meant in paragraph (1), shall be exercised in accordance with the legislative provisions on the Indonesian Continental Shelf, agreements concluded between the Republic of Indonesia and neighbouring states and the rules of International law in force.

3. Within the Indonesian Exclusive Economic Zone, the freedom of international navigation and overflight as well as the freedom of laying submarine cables and pipelines, shall be respected in accordance with the principles of the international law of the sea.

Chapter IV

Activities within the Indonesian Exclusive Economic Zone

Article 5

1. Without prejudice to the provision in Article 4, paragraph (2), whoever conducting the exploration and/or exploitation of natural resources or any other activities for the purpose of the economic exploration or exploitation of said natural resources, such as generation of power by means of water, current or wind within the Indonesian Exclusive Economic Zone, may do so based on the permission of the Government of the Republic of Indonesia, or on an international agreement concluded with the Government of the Republic of Indonesia whereas such activity has to be carried out under the conditions of such permit or such international agreement.

2. Without prejudice to the provision in paragraph (1), any exploration and/or exploitation of the living natural resources, shall abide by the provisions on management and conservation as stipulated by the Government of the Republic of Indonesia.

3. Without prejudice to the provision in Article 4, paragraph (2), any exploration and/or exploitation of the living resources in a certain area within the Indonesian Exclusive Economic Zone, conducted by any person, a corporate body or government of a foreign state, may be permitted provided that the catch as allowed by the Government of the Republic of Indonesia of the species in question, is in excess of Indonesia's capacity to harvest the allowable catch.

Article 6

Whoever constructing and/or using any artificial island or installations or other structures within the Indonesian Exclusive Economic Zone, may do so based on the permission of the Government of the Republic of Indonesia, whereas such activities have to be carried out under the conditions of such permit.

Article 7

Whoever conducting any scientific research activity in the Indonesian Exclusive Economic Zone has to ensure that such activity shall obtain the prior consent of and be carried out under the conditions as determined by the Government of the Republic of Indonesia.

Article 8

1. Whoever conducting any activity within the Indonesian Exclusive Economic Zone, has the duty to take steps towards preventing, minimizing, controlling and surmounting the pollution of the environment.

2. Discharge of waste in the Indonesian Exclusive Economic Zone may be effected only after having obtained the permission of the Government of the Republic of Indonesia.

Chapter V

Indemnity

Article 9

Whoever conducting any activity in violation of the provisions of the statutory regulations of the Republic of Indonesia and international law in relation to artificial islands, installations or other structures within the Indonesian Exclusive Economic Zone and causing loss, shall be liable for such loss and, shall pay indemnity to the owner of such artificial islands, installations and/or other structures.

Article 10

Without prejudice to the provision in Article 7, whoever conducting any activity within the Indonesian Exclusive Economic Zone being in violation of the provisions of the statutory regulations of the Republic of Indonesia and the rules of international law, as applicable to the field of marine scientific research and causing loss, shall be held responsible for such loss and, shall pay indemnity to the Republic of Indonesia.

Article 11

1. Without prejudice to the provision in Article 8 and with due observance to a fixed maximum of indemnity, whoever causing the pollution of the marine environment and/or damage to the natural resources within the Indonesian Exclusive Economic Zone, shall be held fully responsible for such pollution or damage and, shall pay immediately a reasonable amount of rehabilitation costs for the marine environment and/or natural resource.

2. Exempted from the full responsibility as meant in paragraph (1), are those who can prove that such pollution of the marine environment and/or damage to the natural resources, was the result of:

(a) a natural calamity, being beyond one's power;
(b) a damage which wholly or partly was caused by an act or negligence of a third party.

3. The form, type and size of the loss resulting from the pollution of the marine environment and/or damage to the natural resources, shall be fixed on the basis of the outcome of an ecological investigation.

Article 12

The regulation pertaining to the limit of maximum indemnity, method of ecological investigation and claim for damages, as referred to in Article 11, shall be dealt with by statutory regulations as meant in Article 20.

Chapter VI

Law enforcement

Article 13

In the frame of exercising the sovereign rights and other rights, jurisdiction and duties, as meant in Article 4, paragraph (1), the competent law-enforcement apparatus of the Republic of Indonesia may take law-enforcement measures in accordance with Act No. 8 of 1981 on the Code of Criminal Procedure with the following exceptions:

(a) Any of a ship and/or persons, presumed of having committed an offence within the Indonesian Exclusive Economic Zone, shall include the detention of the ship until the handing over of such ship and/or persons at the port, where said case can be further prosecuted.
(b) The handing over of such ship and/or persons shall take place as soon as possible, not exceeding a period of 7 (seven) days, except in case of a force majeure.
(c) For the purpose of detention, the criminal act as referred to in Article 16 and Article 17, shall come under the category of criminal acts as meant in Article 21, paragraph (4), letter b, Act No. 8 of 1981, on the Code of Criminal Procedure.

Article 14

1. The law-enforcement apparatus in the field of investigation within the Indonesian Exclusive Economic Zone is a Navy Officer of the Indonesian Armed Forces, so assigned by the Commander-in-Chief of the Armed Forces of the Republic of Indonesia.

2. The plaintiff is the public prosecutor attached to the court of first instance as meant in paragraph (3).

3. The court of justice authorized to try offences of the provisions of this act, is the court of first instance which jurisdiction covers the port where the detention of such ship and/or persons as meant in Article 13, letter a, has taken place.

Article 15

1. Any request for the release of such ship and/or persons arrested on the ground of being accused of having committed violation of this act or any legislative provision issued on the basis of this act, may be filed at any time prior to the verdict of the competent court of first instance.

2. Any request for such release as meant in paragraph (1), may be complied with after the claimant and has handed over a reasonable amount of bail as fixed by the competent court of first instance.

Chapter VII
Penal provisions

Article 16

1. Whoever committing an act violation of the provisions in Article 5, paragraph (1), Article 6, Article 7, shall be punished by a fine to a maximum of Rp 225,000,000 (two hundred and twenty-five million rupiahs).

2. The judge in its verdict may decide up on the confiscation of the products of activity, the ship and/or the equipment used in committing of the criminal act as meant in paragraph (1).

3. Whoever deliberately commits an act causing damage to the life environment or the pollution of the life environment within the Indonesian Exclusive Economic Zone, shall be threatened with punishment in accordance with the legislative provisions applicable to the field of life environment.

Article 17

Whoever damaging or destroying the evidences used in committing a criminal act as meant in Article 16, paragraph (1), with the purpose to avoid the confiscation of said evidences during the investigation, shall be punished by a fine to a maximum of Rp 75,000,000 (seventy-five million rupiahs).

Article 18

The criminal act as meant in Article 16 and Article 17, shall be regarded as a crime.

Chapter VIII
Transitional provision

Article 19

Any provisions on the exploration and/or exploitation of the living resources, enacted before the promulgation of this act, shall remain in force until changes are made by virtue of legislative provisions issued on the basis of this act.

Chapter IX
Closing provisions

Article 20

1. Implementation of the provisions under this act shall be further arranged in other statutory regulations.

2. The Government Regulation arranging the implementation of the provisions of this act may stipulate a maximum fine of Rp 75,000,000 (seventy-five million rupiahs) against any violation of its provisions.

Article 21

This act shall come into force as from the date of its promulgation. In order that everybody may have knowledge of it, the promulgation of this act is hereby ordered through its Placing in the State Gazette of the Republic of Indonesia.

Done in Jakarta
On 18th October 1983

The president of the Republic of Indonesia

(signed)

Soeharto

Promulgated in Jakarta
On October 1983

Minister/state secretary of the Republic of Indonesia

(signed)

Soedharmono, L.L.M.

State Gazette of the Republic of Indonesia of 1983, No. 44.

ELUCIDATION
OF
ACT No. 5 of 1983

ON
INDONESIA's EXCLUSIVE ECONOMIC ZONE

I. General

The Government of the Republic of Indonesia has since long felt the great importance of the exclusive economic zone to support the realisation of the Archipelagic Outlook in the frame of improving the welfare of the Indonesian nation, by way of utilising all natural resources, both, living and non-living, found within its exclusive economic zone.

Based on what is mentioned above, and in order to safeguard the national interest, particularly in the matter of satisfying the need of the Indonesian people for animal protein and in regard to the utilisation of non-living resources, protection and conservation of the marine environment and marine scientific research, the Government of the Republic of Indonesia has issued the Government Announcement of March 21, 1980, on the Indonesian Exclusive Economic Zone.

International law on the exclusive economic zone has been developed by the international community through the Third Conference of the United Nations Organisation on the Law of the Sea and State Practice, aimed at protecting the interests of the coastal state against the danger of exhaustion of the natural resources adjacent to its coast by fishery activities on the basis of the regime of the high seas.

Besides, the exclusive economic zone also serve to protect the interests of coastal states in the field of the conservation of the marine environment and the conduct of marine scientific research in the framework of supporting the utilisation of natural resources within the exclusive economic zone.

The United Nations Organisation Convention on the Law of the Sea has provided the Republic of Indonesia in its capacity as a coastal state, with the sovereign right to explore and exploit the natural resources found within the exclusive economic zone and the jurisdiction relating to the exercise of such sovereign right.

On the other hand Indonesia has the duty to respect the right of other states in its exclusive economic zone, such as the freedom of navigation and overflight as well as the freedom of the laying of submarine cables and pipelines within the exclusive economic zone.

With special reference to the utilisation of the living resources found within the Indonesian Exclusive Economic Zone, any other state may, in accordance with the United Nations Organisation Convention on the Law of the Sea, take part in utilising the living resources, so long as Indonesia has not yet fully utilised the whole of these living resources.

Besides the announcing of above-mentioned principles and basic policies which are primarily directed towards the outside world, it was found necessary also that, said principles and basic policies, be laid down in an act so as to provide a solid basis for the exercise of the sovereign right, other rights, jurisdiction and duties within the exclusive economic zone, so that, in this way, legal security may be establised as well.

It was in this connection that the act on the Indonesian Exclusive Economic Zone was drawn up which stipulates the sovereign right, other rights, jurisdiction and duties of the Republic of Indonesia within its exclusive economic zone.

This act only provides the basic rules, while further implementation of the provisions of this act to be laid down in other statutory regulations.

II. Article by article

Article 1

Meant by the term 'living resources' in this act is the same as meant by term 'fishery resources' in the provisions of the statutory regulations on fishery.

Article 2

This article clarifies and confirms the geographical definition on the Indonesian Exclusive Economic Zone as contained in the Announcement of the Government of the Republic of Indonesia dated March 21, 1980, on the Indonesian Exclusive Economic Zone.

Article 3

Paragraph (1). Sufficiently clear.

Paragraph (2). This paragraph provides that the principles of equidistance is applied to determine the boundaries between the exclusive economic zone of Indonesia and a neighbouring state, except in case of special conditions necessitating consideration, so as not to prejudice the national interest.

Such special conditions, for example, may include the presence of an island belonging to another country, located at a distance less than 200 (two hundred) sea miles from the baseline from which the breadth of the Indonesian Exclusive Economic Zone is measured.

Article 4

Paragraph (1). Meant in this act by 'Indonesian sovereign right' is not the same as or cannot be equalised with the full sovereignty as owned and exercised by Indonesia over its territorial sea, inter-islands waters and inland waterways.

Based on what is mentioned above, so the sanctions imposed on the Indonesian Exclusive Economic

Zone differ from those imposed upon the waters falling under the sovereignty of the Republic of Indonesia.

Other rights, based on international law, include the right of the Republic of Indonesia to enforce the law upon and undertake a hot pursuit of any foreign ships committing a violation of the provision of Indonesia's statutory regulations on the exclusive economic zone.

Another duty, based on international law, is the duty of the Republic of Indonesia to respect the rights of other states, such as the freedom of navigation and overflight as well as the freedom for the laying of submarine cables and pipelines.

Paragraph (2). This paragraph stipulates that, as far as it concerns the living and non-living resources found on the seabed and in the subsoil thereof, within the boundaries of the Indonesian Exclusive Economic Zone, the Indonesian sovereign right shall be exercised and arranged on the basis of Indonesia's statutory regulations as applicable to the continental shelf regime, as well as international agreements on the continental shelf determining the boundaries between the continental shelves of Indonesia and neighbouring states whose coasts are opposite or adjacent to those of the Republic of Indonesia.

Paragraph (3). In accordance with the applicable principles of international law, such as those originating from the practice of states and laid down in the United Nations Organisation Convention on the Law of the Sea as adopted at the Third Conference of the United Nations Organisation on the Law of the Sea, within the Exclusive Economic Zone, any state, whether coastal or landlocked, shall enjoy the freedom of international navigation and overflight as well as the freedom for the laying of submarine cables and pipelines and using the sea pursuant to said freedoms, such as the operation of ships and aircrafts and the maintenance of submarine cables and pipelines.

Article 5

Paragraph (1). Any exploratory or exploitation activity of the natural resources or any other activity for the purpose of economic exploration and/or exploitation, such as the generation of power from water, current and wind, conducted within the Indonesian Exclusive Economic Zone by any Indonesian national or corporate body, shall be based on a permit granted by the Government of the Republic of Indonesia.

Activities as meant above conducted by a foreign state, foreigner or foreign corporate body, shall be based on an international agreement concluded between the Government of the Republic of Indonesia and the foreign state concerned.

The terms and conditions of such international treaty or agreement have to state the rights and duties to be observed by those conducting exploratory or exploitation activities within the said zone, such as the duty to pay levies to the Government of the Republic of Indonesia.

Paragraph (2). Living resources basically have the quality to recover, but not in the sense of being unlimited. Therefore, with the presence of such quality, the Government of the Republic of Indonesia, in the management and conservation of the living resources, has decided upon the degree of utilisation in the Indonesian Exclusive Economic Zone, in part or in whole.

Paragraph (3). In the frame of conserving the living resources, Indonesia has the duty to guarantee the maximum sustainable yield of the living resources within the Indonesian Exclusive Economic Zone.

With due observance to said maximum sustainable yield, Indonesia has also the duty to fix the maximum quantity of allowable catch of the living resources.

In the event that the Indonesian fishery industry is not yet fully capable of utilising said maximum quantity of allowable catch, then, the difference between the allowable catch and the Indonesian harvest capacity may be utilised by another state with the permission of the Government of the Republic of Indonesia on the basis of an international agreement.

Suppose the allowable catch is fixed at 1,000 (one thousand) tons, while Indonesia's harvest capacity has but reached as many as 600 (six hundred) tons, so, another state may participate in utilising the remainder of 400 (four hundred) tons, with the permission of the Government of the Republic of Indonesia on the basis of an international agreement.

The reference to Article 4, paragraph (2), is meant to clarify that sedentary species found on the seabed within the Exclusive Economic Zone, are subject to the continental shelf regime (Article 1, letter b, Act No. 1 of 1973, on the Indonesian Continental Shelf). Therefore, they are not subject to the provision under this paragraph.

Article 6

In accordance with Article 4, paragraph (1), the Republic of Indonesia has the exclusive right to develop, licence and arrange the development, operation and use of artificial islands, installations and other structures.

Besides, Indonesia has the exclusive jurisdiction over such artificial islands, installations and structures, including the jurisdiction relating to the implementation of legislative provisions in the field of customs, taxation, health, safety and immigration.

Although Indonesia has the exclusive jurisdiction over such artificial islands, installations and structures, nevertheless they do not have the status of islands in the sense of state territories, and therefore, do not have a territorial sea of their own, whereas their presence does not affect the boundaries of the Indonesian territorial sea, the Exclusive Economic Zone or Continental Shelf.

Article 7

Any marine scientific research within the Indonesian Exclusive Economic Zone, may only be carried out after the request for such research has been approved before-hand by the Government of the Republic of Indonesia.

In the event that in 4 (four) months following receipt of such request, the Government of the Republic of Indonesia fails to state:

(a) its objection against such request, or

(b) that the information provided by the applicant is not consistent with the reality or is incomplete, or

(c) that the applicant has not fulfilled his duty in the matter of an earlier research project,

then, the marine scientific research project may be implemented within 6 (six) months following receipt of a research application by the Government of the Republic of Indonesia.

Article 8

Paragraph (1). The authority to protect and conserve the natural resources within the Indonesian Exclusive Economic Zone is based internationally on the practice of states which has now also been included in the United Nations Organisation Convention on the Law of the Sea, whereas from the national point of view, its basis is to be found in Act No. 4 of 1982, on the Basic Provisions pertaining to Live Environmental Management.

Paragraph (2). Dumping in the sea may cause pollution of the marine environment, and for that reason it was deemed necessary to arrange the site, manner and frequency of dumping as well as the type, content and volume of the materials to be dumped under licence. Such dumping covers the dumping of rubbish and other materials which are to cause pollution of the marine environment. Ordinary disposal of refuse by ships during their voyage does not need a permit.

Article 9

Sufficiently clear.

Article 10

Sufficiently clear.

Article 11

Paragraph (1). The duty to bear strict liability and to pay indemnity for the rehabilitation of the marine environment and/or natural resources, is the consequence of the duty to maintain environmental harmony and equilibrium.

Therefore, such duty shall rest upon whomsoever committing an act, not committing an act or allowing the occurrence of the pollution of the marine environment and/or damage to the natural resource.

'Strict liability' implies the meaning that said liability takes effect as from the very moment that pollution of the marine environment and/or damage to the natural resource cannot be avoided, and, the producing of evidence in terms of procedure, is no longer necessary.

Paragraph (2). Sufficiently clear.

Paragraph (3). The form, type and size of loss caused by the pollution of the marine environment and/or damage to the natural resources, shall determine the amount of indemnity. Ecological investigation on the form, type and size of such loss, shall be conducted by a team comprising members representing the Government, the sufferers and the offenders. Such special team is meant to be set up for each case.

Article 12

Sufficiently clear.

Article 13

Any ship and/or persons being suspected of having committed a criminal act based on sufficient preliminary evidences at sea, particularly in case of a foreign ship and/or foreigners, further investigation may be conducted by way of arresting the ships and/or persons concerned.

Any ship and/or persons having the Indonesian nationality, can be given and ad hoc order to proceed to a port or base appointed by the investigator at sea, for further prosecution.

Above-mentioned arrest cannot always be made conform to the time limit of arrest, i.e. one day, as fixed in Act No. 8 of 1981, on the Code of Criminal Prosedure.

Therefore, for an arrest at sea, a reasonable period of time is needed so as to enable the law-enforcement apparatus at sea to escort such ship and/or persons to any port or base.

A period of time of seven days is considered to be the maximum time required to haul or tow such ship from the farthest point within the Indonesian Exclusive Economic Zone to any port or base.

The provision on detention for reasons of a criminal act according to this Act, has not yet been dealt with in Act No. 8 of 1981, whereas the detention of such criminal act is a means to enable further prosecution of the case.

In this connection, although the criminal threat that can be imposed is in the form of a fine, nevertheless, for its being qualified as a crime, such criminal act should come under the category of criminal acts as meant in Article 21, paragraph (4), letter b, Act No. 8 of 1981, on the Code of Criminal Procedure.

Article 14

Paragraph (1). Meant by the Navy Officer of the Indonesian Armed Forces who may be appointed as investigator, are for instance the ship's captain, Navy District Commander, Base Commander and Navy Station Commander. The appointment of a Navy Officer of the Indonesian Armed Forces as the investigating apparatus within the Indonesian Exclusive Economic Zone, is in conformity with the provision of Article 30, paragraph (20), Act No. 20 of 1982, on the Basic Provisions of Defence and Security of the Republic of Indonesia, and Article 17, Government Regulation No. 27 of 1983, concerning the Execution of Act No. 8 of 1981, on the Code of Criminal Procedure.

Paragraph (2). Sufficiently clear.

Paragraph (3). Sufficiently clear.

Article 15

Paragraph (1). The request for the release of a ship and/or person arrested for being suspected of having committed an offence, based on conventional practice, can be filled by the leg tion of the state of the foreign ship concerned, the owner or the captain or whomsoever having any work or business relation with the ship or person concerned, based on legal evidences.

Paragraph (2). The fixing of the amount of bail is based on the value of the ship, its equipment and proceeds of its activities increased by the maximum amount of fine.

Article 16

Paragraph (1). Sufficiently clear.

Paragraph (2). Sufficiently clear.

Paragraph (3). Sufficiently clear.

Article 17

Sufficiently clear.

Article 18

Sufficiently clear.

Article 19

Sufficiently clear.

Article 20

Sufficiently clear.

Article 21

Sufficiently clear.

SUPPLEMENTARY STATE GAZETTE OF THE REPUBLIC OF INDONESIA NO. 3260

30. Ivory Coast

Law No. 77-926.
Entered into force: November 17, 1977.
Source: *Journal Officiel of the Republic of Ivory Coast,* December 26, 1977, p. 2523 (Translated from French by the Department of State).

Law No. 77-926 of November 17, 1977 delimiting the maritime zones placed under the national jurisdiction of the Republic of Ivory Coast

The National Assembly has adopted, and
The President of the Republic hereby promulgates the following law:

Title I
The Territorial Sea

Article 1

The outer limit of the territorial sea of the Republic of Ivory Coast is established at a distance of 12 nautical miles from the lowest water mark.

As concerns gulfs, bays, roadsteads, estuaries, and in general all cases in which the coast is deeply indented, decrees shall determine the straight baselines from which that breadth is measured.

Title II
Two-Hundred-Nautical-Mile Zone placed under national jurisdiction

Article 2

For economic purposes, the Republic of Ivory Coast exercises jurisdiction over a maritime zone extending 200 nautical miles and called the exclusive economic zone.

The breadth of this zone, lying outside the territorial sea and adjacent to it, is measured from the baseline used to measure the territorial sea.

Article 3

Within the zone described in the preceding Article, the Republic of Ivory Coast exercises sovereign and exclusive rights as concerns:

1. The exploration, exploitation, conservation, and management of natural living and non-living resources of the sea-bed, its subsoil, and superjacent waters;
2. Other activities involving the use of the said zone for economic purposes, including the production of energy from the water, currents, and winds;
3. The construction, establishment, and use of artificial islands, installations, and similar devices used for the purposes provided for by this Article, including related regulations on customs, tax, health, safety, and immigration matters.

These rights shall be exercised in the terms and conditions laid down by Articles 4 and 5 hereof.

Article 4

The pertinent provisions of Law No. 70-489 of August 3, 1970 establishing the Oil Code shall apply to the zone delimited in Article 2 above.

Article 5

Articles 129 and 130 of Law No. 61-349 of November 9, 1961, establishing the Merchant Marine Code to restrict fishing in territorial waters to Ivoirian vessels and, subject to reciprocity, to vessels of other States of equivalent recognized law, shall be applicable to the zone delimited in Article 2 above.

Maritime fishing violations committed in such zone shall be punished, in accordance with the provisions of the aforesaid Law of November 9, 1961, specifically Articles 126-130 and 212-225. However, only the fines stipulated in the said Articles may be imposed.

Article 6

Throughout the zone delimited in Article 2 above, the Republic of Ivory Coast also reserves the right to take any measures and to undertake any action to prevent, reduce, or control pollution of the marine environment, irrespective of the source.

All scientific research activities conducted in the said zone shall be subject to the prior consent of the State, under the conditions established by decree.

Article 7

The sovereign rights exercised by the Republic of Ivory Coast in the zone delimited in Article 2 above shall not impede the exercise by all coastal or non-coastal States of the freedoms of navigation, overflight, and the laying of submarine cable and pipelines, or impede other uses of the sea related to navigation and communications which are recognized as legitimate by international law.

Title III
Miscellaneous Provisions

Article 8

With respect to adjoining coastal States, the territorial sea and zone referred to in Article 2 of this Law shall be delimited by agreement in conformity with equitable principles and using, if necessary the median line or the equidistance line, taking all pertinent factors into account.

Article 9

As necessary, decrees issued by the Council of Ministers shall specify the terms of application of this Law.

Article 10

All provisions contrary to this Law, particularly Decree No. 67-334 of August 1, 1967, are hereby rescinded.

Article 11

This Law shall be published in the *Journal Officiel* of the Republic of Ivory Coast and enforced as State law.

Done at Abidjan on November 17, 1977.

Félix Houphouet-Boigny

31. Kenya

Presidential Proclamation.
Entered into force: February 28, 1979.
Source: Ministry of Foreign Affaires Communication to the Secretary-General of the United Nations, March 5, 1979.

Proclamation by the president of the Republic of Kenya

Whereas the Law of Nations is in the process of development by the Third United Nations Conference on the Law of the Sea, to recognize the right of a coastal state to establish beyond and adjacent to its territorial sea an area commonly referred to as an Exclusive Economic Zone, and to exercise thereon sovereign rights for the purpose of exploring, exploiting, conserving and managing the natural resources whether renewable or non-renewable, of the water column, sea-bed and sub-soil.

And whereas, it is already recognized by the said Law of the Sea Conference that the extent of the area referred to as the Exclusive Economic Zone, aforesaid, shall not exceed two hundred nautical miles measured from the same base line as the territorial sea.

And whereas, it is necessary that a declaration be made establishing the extent of the said Exclusive Economic Zone of the Republic of Kenya.

Now therefore, I, Daniel Arap Moi, President and Commander-in-chief of the Armed Forces of the Republic of Kenya, do hereby declare and proclaim in accordance with the Constitution of the Republic of Kenya:—

1. That notwithstanding any rule of law or any practice which may hitherto have been observed in relation to Kenya or the waters beyond or adjacent to the territorial Sea of Kenya, the Exclusive Economic Zone of the Republic of Kenya extend across the sea to a distance of two hundred nautical miles measured from the appropriate base line from where the territorial sea is measured as indicated in the Map annexed to this Proclamation. Without prejudice to the foregoing, the Exclusive Economic Zone of Kenya shall:—

(a) in respect of its southern territorial waters boundary with the United Republic of Tanzania be an eastern latitude north of Pemba island to start at a point obtained by the northern intersection of two arcs one from the Kenya Light-house at Mpunguti ya Juu, and the other from Pemba island Light-house at Ras Kigomasha.

(b) in respect of its northern territorial waters boundary with Somali Republic be on eastern latitude South of Diua Damasciaca Island being latitude 1° 38° degrees South.

2. That this Proclamation shall not affect or be in derogation of the vested rights of the Republic of Kenya over the Continental Shelf as defined in the Continental Shelf Act 1973.

3. All states, shall subject to the applicable laws and regulations of Kenya, enjoy in the Exclusive Economic Zone the freedom of navigation and overflight and of the laying of sub-marine cables and pipelines and other internationally lawful recognized uses of the sea related to navigation and communication.

4. That the scope and regime of the Exclusive Economic Zone shall be as defined in the schedule attached to this Proclamation.

Signed and sealed with the Public Seal of the Republic of Kenya at Nairobi this 28th day ot February One Thousand Nine Hundred and Seventy-Nine.

Daniel Arap Moi
President of the Republic of Kenya

Schedule: the scope and regime of exclusive economic zone

1. In and throughout the zone Kenya exercises the following:—

(a) Sovereign rights for the purpose of exploring, exploiting, conserving and managing the natural resources, whether renewable or non-renewable of the water column, the sea-bed, and the sub-soil thereof.

(b) Sovereign rights with regard to other activities for the economic exploration and exploitation of the zone, such as the production of energy from the water currents, and winds.

(c) (i) Jurisdiction with respect to regulation control and preservation of marine environment including pollution control and abatement.

(ii) Exclusive jurisdiction with respect to authorization and control of scientific research.

(iii) Exclusive jurisdiction with respect to the establishment and use of artificial islands, installations, structures and other devises including customs, fiscal, health, public order and immigration regulations pertaining thereto.

(iv) Other rights and duties compatible with international conventions or protocols to which Kenya is or may become party.

2. Kenya may permit other States or Nationals of such states to fish in the zone on such terms and conditions and subject to compliance with such regulations as it may prescribe. In particular and without prejudice to the generality of the foregoing these may inter alia relate to the following:—

(a) Licensing of fishermen, fishing vessels and gear including payment of fees and other forms of remuneration.

(b) Conservation measures to preserve and manage the exploitation of fisheries resources including measures relating to and determining the species which may be caught and fixing quotas per vessel over a period of time or to the catch by nationals of any State during a specified period.

(c) Regulating seasons and areas of fishing, the types, sizes and amount of gear, and the numbers, sizes and types of fishing vessels that may be used in the zone.

(d) Fixing the age and size of fish and other species that may be caught.

(e) Specifying information required of fishing vessels, including catch and effort statistics and vessel position reports.

(f) Requiring under the authorization and control of Kenya, the conduct of specified fisheries research programmes and regulating the conduct of such research, including the sampling of catches, disposition of samples, and reporting of associated scientific data.

(g) The placing of Kenyan observers or trainees on board such vessels.

(h) The landing of all or any part of the catch by such vessels in the ports of Kenya.

(i) Terms and conditions relating to joint ventures or other co-operative arrangements.

(j) Requirements for training personnel and transfer of fisheries technology including enhancement of Kenya's capability of under taking fisheries research, management and development of the living resources of the zone.

(k) Measures for the enforcement of Law and regulations in accordance with this Proclamation.

32. Kiribati

Marine Zones (Declaration) Act 1983 (No. 7 of 1983)
Entered into force: May 16, 1983
Source: Government of Kiribati.

REPUBLIC OF KIRIBATI
(No. 7 of 1983)

I assent,

I.T. TABAI
Beretitenti
16th May 1983

AN ACT TO MAKE PROVISION IN RESPECT OF THE INTERNAL WATERS, THE ARCHIPELAGIC WATERS, THE TERRITORIAL SEA AND THE EXCLUSIVE ECONOMIC ZONE OF KIRIBATI.

Commencement:
16th May 1983

MADE by the Maneaba ni Maungatabu and assented to by the Beretitenti.

Short title:
PART I — PRELIMINARY

1. This Act may be cited as the Marine Zones (Declaration) Act 1983.

Interpretation

2. (1) In this Act, unless the context otherwise requires—

'the baseline of Kiribati' means the low-water line of the seaward side of the reef fronting the coast of any part of Kiribati or bounding any lagoon waters adjacent to any part of that coast, or where a reef is not present the low-water line of the coast itself;

'conservation and management' includes all rules, regulations, methods and measures that—

(a) are required to build, restore or maintain, or are useful in rebuilding, restoring or maintaining, any fishery resource or the marine environment; or

(b) are designed to ensure that—

(i) a supply of food and other products may be taken, and that recreational benefit may be obtained, on a continuing basis; and

(ii) irreversible or long-term ill-effects on fishery resources or the marine environment are avoided; and

(iii) there will be a multiplicity of options available with respect to future uses of those resources;

'fishery resource' means any fishery, stock of fish, species of fish or habitat of fish;

'low-tide elevation' means a naturally-formed area of land that is surrounded by and is above water at

mean low-water spring tides but is submerged at mean high-water spring tides;
'the low-water line', in relation to any area, means the line of low water at mean low-water spring tides as depicted on the largest scale nautical chart of the area held by the Minister responsible for marine affairs;
'the median line' means a line every point of which is equidistant from the nearest point of—

(a) the inner limits of the territorial sea of Kiribati; and

(b) the corresponding baseline of any other country;

'nautical mile' means an international nautical mile of 1,852 metres.

(2) For the purposes of this Act, permanent harbour works that form an integral part of a harbour system shall be treated as forming part of the coast.

Reference to rules of international law

3. Where in this Act it is provided that anything shall be done by the Republic of Kiribati or by the Cabinet or a Minister, or any law or order shall be made, in accordance with the rules of international law, the question, whether it was so done or made, is non-justiciable.

PART II – THE MARINE ZONES

Internal waters

4. (1) For the purposes of any law of Kiribati, the internal waters of Kiribati are all waters inland of the base-line of Kiribati, and where closing lines are drawn in accordance with subsection (2) the waters inland of those lines to the extent that they are outside the base-line of Kiribati.

(2) The Minister may, in accordance with the rules of international law, declare, by reference to physical features marked on official charts or to lists of geographical co-ordinates specifying the geodetic datums, the points between which closing lines are to be drawn for the purpose of determining the outer limits of the internal waters of Kiribati, in the case of the mouths of or entrances to lagoons.

Archipelagic waters

5. (1) For the purposes of any law of Kiribati, the archipelagic waters of Kiribati comprise all areas of sea contained within the baselines established under subsection (2).

(2) The Minister may, in accordance with the rules of international law, declare, by reference to physical features marked on official charts or to lists of geographical co-ordinates specifying the geodetic datums, the points between which straight base-lines are to be drawn for the purpose of determining the outer limits of the archipelagic waters of Kiribati and the inner limits of the territorial sea.

Territorial seas

6. (1) Subject to subsection (2), for the purposes of any law of Kiribati the territorial seas of Kiribati are those parts of the sea within 12 nautical miles from the outer limits of the internal waters of Kiribati.

(2) Where archipelagic baselines are drawn under Section 5 (2) the breadth of the territorial sea shall be measured from those baselines to the extent to which they are outside the outer limits of the internal waters of Kiribati.

The exclusive economic zone

7. (1) Subject to the succeeding provisions of this section, for the purposes of any law of Kiribati the exclusive economic zone of Kiribati comprises those parts of the sea having as their inner limits the outer limits of the territorial sea and as their outer limits a line drawn 200 nautical miles seaward from the outer limits of the inland waters of Kiribati.

(2) The Minister may, in accordance with the rules of international law declare, by reference to physical features marked on official charts or to lists of geographical co-ordinates specifying the geodetic datums, points between which straight baselines are to be drawn for determining the outer limits of the exclusive economic zone.

(3) Where baselines are drawn in accordance with subsection (2) the breadth of the exclusive economic zone shall be measured from those baselines.

(4) The Minister may, by order, for the purpose of implementing any international agreement or the award of any international body, or otherwise declare that the order limits of the exclusive economic zone of Kiribati extend to such line, being a line to the landward of the outer limits of the exclusive economic zone as defined in accordance with subsection (1) or subsection (3), as the case requires as is specified in the order.

(5) Where the median line is less than 200 nautical miles from the line which the breadth of the territorial sea is to be measured, the outer limits of the exclusive economic zone extend to the median line.

(6) All areas of seabed, and the subsoil under the seabed, of the exclusive economic zone shall be treated, for the purposes of any law of Kiribati, as part of the continental shelf of Kiribati.

Legal character of marine zones, etc.

8. (1) The sovereignty of the Republic of Kiribati extends beyond its land territory and internal waters over the territorial sea, and to the airspace over them and the seabed and subsoil under them.

(2) Within the exclusive economic zone the Republic of Kiribati has sovereign rights for the purpose of exploring and exploiting, conserving and managing the natural resources, whether living or non-living, of the seabed and the subsoil under the seabed, and the waters over the sea-bed.

(3) The sovereignty and sovereign rights of the Republic of Kiribati under this section shall be exercised in accordance with the rules of international law.

Rights of States in marine zones.

9. (1) Subject to the succeeding provisions of this section, ships and aircraft of all States have, in accordance with the rules of international law, the right of free passage through and over the territorial seas and archipelagic waters of Kiribati.

(2) The Minister may, in accordance with the rules of international law, by order designate sealanes and air routes suitable for the continuous and expeditious passage of foreign ships and aircraft, through and over the archipelagic waters and the adjacent territorial seas, and may also prescribe traffic separation schemes for the purpose of ensuring the safe passage of ships through narrow channels in such sealanes.

(3) In sealanes and air routes designated under subsection (2) ships and aircraft may, in accordance with rules of international law, enjoy the right of navigation and overflight in their normal modes, for the purpose of continuous, expeditious and unobstructed transit through and over the archipelagic waters and the adjacent territorial seas, from one part of the exclusive economic zone to another part of it.

(4) Until sealanes and air routes are prescribed under section (2) the rights of navigation and overflight referred to in subsection (3) may be exercised through and over all routes normally used for international navigation and overflight.

(5) The rights of navigation and overflight referred to in subsections (3) and (4) are subject to all laws of Kiribati made in accordance with the rules of international law.

(6) Subject to this and any other Act and to the rules of international law, all States and their nationals shall enjoy in the exclusive economic zone the high seas freedoms of navigation and overflight and of the laying of submarine cables and pipelines, and all other internationally lawful uses of the sea related to those freedoms, compatible with the rules of international law.

General regulations as to the exclusive economic zone.

10. Where no other provision is made in or under any other Act for the purpose, the Minister may make regulations, in accordance with the rules of international law, for all or an of the following purposes:—

(a) regulating the conduct of scientific research within the exclusive economic zone; and
(b) regulating the exploration and exploitation of the exclusive economic zone for the production of

energy from waters, currents and winds, and for other economic purposes; and

(c) regulating the construction, operation and use of artificial islands, installations and structures within the exclusive economic zone, including requirements of the establishment of safety zones around islands, installations and structures; and

(d) prescribing measures for the protection and preservation of the marine environment of the exclusive economic zone; and

(e) providing for such other matters as are necessary or expedient to give effect to the rights and obligations of the Republic of Kiribati in relation to the exclusive economic zone, or are necessary to give full effect to the provision of this Act.

Charts, publicity etc.

11. (1) The Minister shall cause all closing lines, baselines and other lines drawn for the purposes of this Act for determining the limits of the internal waters, the archipelagic waters, the territorial seas and the exclusive economic zone of Kiribati to be clearly indicated on charts of a scale or scales adequate for them to be readily determined, and shall give adequate publicity to Gazette and otherwise.

(2) A question, whether publicity given to any matter under subsection (2) is adequate, is non-justiciable.

(3) A copy of each chart referred to in subsection (1) shall be deposited with the Secretary-General of the United Nations and the Secretary-General of the South Pacific Commission.

Evidentiary provision

12. In any proceedings before a court or a person acting judicially, a certificate purporting to be signed by the Marine Superintendent stating that any, specific nautical chart or any area is a chart to which Section 11 applies that is held by the Minister is evidence of the matters stated in the certificate, and the chart is evidented of the matters set out in it.

This printed impression has been carefully examined by me with the Bill which was passed by the Maneaba ni Maungatabu on the 28th day of April 1983, and is found by me to be a true and correctly printed copy of the said Bill.

ATIERA TETOA
Clerk to the Maneaba
ni Maungatabu

I certify that the above Act was on the 28th day of April 1983 passed by the Maneabe ni Maungatabu on a certificate of urgency under Section 68 (3) (a) of the Constitution.

M. TANIERA
Speaker

Published by exhibition

(a) at the Public Office of the Beretitenti on 16th May 1983.

T. GREIG
for Secretary to the Cabinet

(b) at the Maneaba ni Maungatabu on 16th May 1983.

ATIERA TETOA
Clerk to the Maneaba
ni Maungatabu

THE MARINE ZONES (DECLARATION) ACT (1983)
EXPLANATORY MEMORANDUM

This Act provides for an extension of the territorial seas outer limit from the previous three miles to twelve.

The act also makes it clear that the archipelagic waters of Kiribati are as defined by baselines to be drawn under S.5(2). This will mean that where an archipelago is defined in a group of islands sovereignty will extend over the waters between the islands is such group. It is not possible to claim that the whole of Kiribati comprising several groups of islands is one archipelago.

The principal object of the Act is to declare a 200 mile exclusive economic zone the start point being the outer limit of the territorial seas. By declaring an archipelago the natural consequence is to create an extensive economic zone. Under S.11 of the Act, public charts have to be prepared indicating the extent of the zone and of internal waters, archipelagic waters and territorial seas.

The zone includes the seabed and subsoil and the Act gives the Republic sovereignty over the same, and the right to exploit any natural resources therein. The creation of the zone therefore gives wide rights to exploit resources, not merely fisheries.

R.L. DAVEY
Attorney General

LEGAL REPORT

I hereby certify may opinion that none of the provisions of the above Act conflict with the Constitution and that the Beretitenti may properly assent to the Act.

R.L. DAVEY
Attorney General

8 March 1983

33. Korea, North

Announcement.
Entered into force: August 1, 1977.
Sources: *The Pyongyang Times,* July 9, 1977, and the *Foreign Broadcasting Information Service,* July 1, 1977.

THE DEMOCRATIC PEOPLE'S REPUBLIC OF KOREA

THE REPORT ON THE DECREE OF JUNE 22, 1977, ON ESTABLISHING AN ECONOMIC SEA ZONE

The Pyongyang Times, July 9, 1977, and Foreign Broadcast Information Service, Vol. IV, North Korea, July 1, 1977, D2. The text of the Decree is not available, but the following report describes it in substantive terms.—Ed.

Pyongyang July 1 (KONA)—A decree of the Central People's Committee on the establishment of the economic sea zone of the Democratic People's Republic of Korea was adopted. On June 21, 1977, the Central People's Committee of the Democratic People's Republic of Korea adopted a decree on the establishment of the economic sea zone of the Democratic People's Republic of Korea to protect and conserve the Marine resources of our country and actively develop and exploit them.

According the the decree, the economic sea zone of the Democratic People's Republic of Korea is up to 200 miles from the starting line of the territorial water and to the half-line of the sea in those waters where the 200-mile economic sea zone cannot be established. The decree also stipulates that the Democratic People's Republic of Korea exercises her jurisdiction over the living and non-living resources in this sea zone (in the water, at and under the seabed).

The decree stipulates that without the prior consent of the organs concerned of the Democratic People's Republic of Korea foreigners, foreign ships and foreign planes are prohibited from catching fish, establishing structures, conducting prospection and development and other acts destructive to the economic activities of the DPRK and doing any acts harmful to the lives of the people and resources, including the pollution of the sea and the air, in the economic sea zone of the Democratic People's Republic of Korea.

The decree will go into force from August 1, 1977.

34. Madagascar

A. Ordinance No. 73-060
Entered into force: September 28, 1973
Source: *Journal Officiel,* September 28, 1973 (Translated from French by the Department of State).

B. Ordinance No. 85-013
Entered into force: September 16, 1985
Source: *Journal Officiel,* September 21, 1985, pp. 1916-1920. (Translated from French by the Department of State).

MALAGASY REPUBLIC

MINISTRY OF FOREIGN AFFAIRS
MINISTRY OF DEVELOPMENT
ORDINANCE No. 73-060

fixing the limits of the territorial sea and the continental shelf of the Malagasy Republic

Lieutenant-General Gabriel Ramanantsoa,
Chief of Government,

Considering the Constitutional Act of 7 November 1972;

Considering Ordinance No. 60-047 of 25 June 1960, as amended and supplemented by Ordinance No. 62-012 of 10 August 1962 and Act No. 66-00 of 5 July 1966 concerning the Maritime Code and in particular article 1-2-01;

Considering Act No. 70-016 of 15 July 1970 concerning the maritime regulation of installations and other facilities on the continental shelf;

Considering Decree No. 63-131 of 27 February 1963 fixing the limit of the territorial sea of the Malagasy Republic;

Considering Decision No. 63-CSI/D of 12 September 1973 of the Superior Council of Institutions;

Meeting in the Council of Ministers on 31 August 1973,

HEREBY ORDERS AS FOLLOWS:

Article 1

The territorial sea of the Malagasy Republic shall extend to a limit fixed at *fifty (50) nautical* miles from the baselines.

Article 2.

The 'continental shelf' of the Malagasy Republic (exclusive economic zone) shall extend to a limit fixed at one hundred (100) nautical miles beyond its territorial sea.

Nevertheless, in the absence of a special agreement, the Malagasy continental shelf shall not extend beyond a median line, every point of which is equidistant from the nearest points of the baselines of the Malagasy coast and of the coasts of States which are opposite thereto.

The term 'continental shelf' is used as referring to the sea-bed and subsoil of the submarine areas adjacent to the Malagasy coast but outside the area of the territorial sea of the Malagasy Republic.

Article 3

The baselines from which the breadth of the territorial sea is measured shall be fixed by decree.

Article 4

All provisions contrary to those of this Ordinance shall stand repealed, and in particular:

The second paragraph of article 1-2-01 of annex 2 of Act No. 66-00 of 5 July 1966 concerning the Maritime Code;

Article 1 of Decree No. 63-131 of 27 February 1963.

Article 5

The present Ordinance shall be published in the Official Gazette of the Republic.

It shall be given effect as an Act of State.

Promulgated at Tananarive, on 28 September 1973

Gabriel RAMANANTSOA

By authority of the Chief of Government,

Brigadier-General Gilles ANDRIAMAHAZO,
Minister of Development

Commander Didier RATSIRAKA,
Minister for Foreign Affairs

OFFICE OF THE PRESIDENT OF THE DEMOCRATIC REPUBLIC OF MADAGASCAR

Ordinance

Statement of the motives for the Ordinance regarding the determination of the breadth of the maritime zones (territorial sea, continental shelf, and exclusive economic zone) of the Democratic Republic of Madagascar.

During the past twenty years, the law of the sea has been a law formulated by a handful of affluent coastal States that, on the strength of their knowledge and power, monopolize the exploitation of maritime expanses.

The birth of many States which are all developing countries has caused the international community to review the law of the sea.

The most important result of the new law of the sea for world fishing is the universal agreement on the fact that coastal States must be able to declare jurisdiction over the fisheries.

This new convention, while confirming a definite right to internal maritime and territorial waters up to a limit of 12 miles, created an Exclusive Economic Zone (EEZ) 188 miles beyond the territorial sea, in which the coastal State exercises sovereign rights for the purpose of exploring and exploiting, conserving and managing, the natural resources, and jurisdiction over scientific research, pollution control, and the positioning of installations in the zone.

Madagascar, following the example of the other coastal countries, has the possibility of planning the development of fisheries by controlling the resources of the EEZ, which will permit more effective utilization of marine resources.

If the economic needs of the country dictate the obligation of maximizing the utilization of our marine resources (including fish products) for the dual purpose of reaching food self-sufficiency as soon as possible and improving our balance of payments for foreign trade, it would be our obligation to adopt the clauses of the new law of the sea, internationally recognized provisions on which various nations have based bilateral or multilateral agreements on the exploitation of the sea.

This leads the Malagasy State to:

1. Reduce to 12 nautical miles the breadth of our territorial sea (set at 50 miles in the past) but extend our exclusive economic zone to 200 miles (that is to say 188 miles plus 12 miles);

2. Extend its continental shelf well-beyond its geomorphological boundaries while remaining within the framework of the rules of the new law of the sea. (Ordinance No. 73-060 of September 28, 1973, in Article 12, confuses 'continental shelf' with 'exclusive economic zone' setting them at 100 nautical miles beyond the territorial sea of 50 miles);

3. Anticipate the exclusivity of mining the physicochemical components of the ocean, in addition to the actual resources, since they could become a source of energy in the near future.

4. Extend its sovereignty to internal maritime waters, the territorial sea, and the EEZ, for the purposes of exploring and exploiting, conserving and managing, the natural resources as well as all the activities carried out in those zones.

This is the purpose of this Ordinance.

Ordinance No. 85-013

establishing the boundaries of the maritime zones (territorial sea, continental shelf, and exclusive economic zone) of the Democratic Republic of Madagascar.

The President of the Democratic Republic of Madagascar, Considering the Constitution,

Considering Ordinance No. 60-047 of June 15, 1960, as amended and supplemented by Ordinance No. 62-042 of August 10, 1962, and Law No. 66-007 of July 7, 1966, establishing the Maritime Code,

Considering Law No. 70-016 of July 15, 1970 establishing maritime regulations on installations and other devices on the continental shelf,

Considering Ordinance No. 73-060 of September 28, 1973, establishing the boundaries of the territorial sea and the continental shelf of the Malagasy Republic, Considering decision No. 122-HCC/D of September 11, 1985 of the Constitutional High Court,

Meeting in Supreme Revolutionary Council,

Orders:

Article 1

The exclusive economic zone of the Democratic Republic of Madagascar extends beyond the territorial sea to a distance of 200 miles from the baselines used for calculating the breadth of the territorial sea.

In cases where there is not a distance of 400 miles between the baseline of the Democratic Republic of Madagascar and those of one or several bordering States, delimitation shall be by agreement with the State(s) concerned.

Article 2

The exclusive economic zone includes the subsoil, the seabed, and the superjacent waters within the boundaries defined in Article 1.

In this zone, the Democratic Republic of Madagascar exercises sovereign and exclusive rights over the exploitation of known natural resources of the natural resources to be discovered, as well as over the exploration or exploitation of other elements of the zone such as water, currents, and winds, and has jurisdiction over the manmade islands, scientific research, and pollution control.

Article 3

No exploration or exploitation of the zone defined in Article 1 shall be carried out by the nationals of third countries without authorization from the Government of the Democratic Republic of Madagascar.

Article 4

The territorial sea of the Democratic Republic of Madagascar, where the State exercises sovereignty, extends to a limit established 12 nautical miles from the baselines.

Article 5

The continental shelf of the Democratic Republic of Madagascar includes the seabed and subsoil beyond the territorial sea to a distance of 200 nautical miles from the baselines from which the breadth of the territorial sea is measured, or to a limit established by agreement with the bordering States, or up to 100 nautical miles from the 2,500 meter isobath.

Article 6

The baseline from which the breadth of the territorial sea is measured shall be established by decree.

Article 7

The internal maritime waters of the Democratic Republic of Madagascar in which the State exercises its sovereignty are included between the following boundaries:

— at sea, the straight baseline used to calculate the breadth of the territorial sea, as it is defined by Decree No. 63-131 of February 27, 1963;

— on land, the high-water line.

Article 8

In this Ordinance, the high-water line is understood to be the extreme limits of the sea, reached by the highest tides outside of those occuring during exceptional storms, along the coasts as well as in the bays, harbors, ports, and havens, and in the channels, small estuaries, salt marshes, lagoons, and ponds connected with the sea, and in the case of rivers, up to the transverse limit of the sea.

Article 9

At the mouth of a river, the limit of the sea is composed of the imaginary line which extends the coastline on either side of the mouth, with the exception of the rivers listed in the article below.

Article 10

The limit of the sea is set back upstream, to the first natural or artificial obstacle which prevents the passage of oceangoing ships, in some estuaries and rivers navigated by them. The following table indicates the limit for each of the rivers.

Article 11

In the rivers listed in Article [10], the limit of the sea along the rivers is the highest of the following lines:

(a) The line reached by the highest waters;

(b) The line reached by the highest recurrent and regular tides.

Article 12

The area of geometric pitches as established in Article 4 C-36 of Ordinance No. 60-099 of September 21, 1960, does not apply along the banks of the rivers listed in Article 4 or to the stretches of water considered in Article [illegible].

Article 13

All provisions contrary to those of this Ordinance are hereby abrogated, in particular those of Ordinance No. 73-060 of September 28, 1973, establishing the boundaries of the territorial sea and the continental shelf of the Malagasy Republic.

Article 14

This Ordinance shall be published in the *Journal officiel* [official gazette] of the Republic.

It shall be implemented as law of the State.

Promulgated at Antananarivo, September 16, 1985

by Didier Ratsiraka
President of the Democratic Republic of Madagascar

Countersigned by the members of the Supreme Revolutionary Council.

Rivers	Designation of Limits	Coordinate on Laborde Grid
Ambazoana	Ambatoharanana bridge	X = 644,200
	RIGN n° 11	Y = 1 393,500
	Ambanja bridge	X = 618,200
		Y = 1 376,000
Djangoa	Ambanja bridge road	X = 605,800
	Maromandia	Y = 1 365,400
Andranomalaza	Maromandia ferry	X = 578,000
	Maromandia road	Y = 1 318,500
	Befotaka ferry	X = 572,400
		Y = 1 283,500
Laloza	Antsohihy port	X = 566,200
		Y = 1 245,500
Mahajamba	Junction of Mah-Mah	X = 472,500
	Mahajamba-Mahajambakely rivers	Y = 1 163,400
Andranoboka	Village of Andranoboka	X = 448
		Y = 1 163
Estuaire de la	West de Marovoay	X = 418
Betsiboka		Y = 1 107
Namakia	Village of Namakia	X = 335,800
		Y = 1 130,200
Andimaka	Village of Andimaka	X = 322
		Y = 1 144
Mahavavy	Monkara bridge river	X = 341,500
	Mahavavy river	Y = 1 128,000
Andasibe-Mahombo	Village of Ankasakasa	X = 232,000
		Y = 1 080,000

Sambao	Junction of Sambao	X = 199,000
	Koja rivers	Y = 1 050,000
Manongoza	Besalampy bridge	X = 193,000
		Y = 1 037,800
		X = 170,000
Ranobe	Berevo on Ranobe village	Y = 985,000
Soaninana	Soatanana village	X = 189,000
		Y = 814,000
Tsiribihina	Belo on Tsiribihina	X = 202,000
		Y = 709,000
Antanambalana	Ambinanitelo village	X = 734
		Y = 1 170

35. Malaysia

Exclusive Economic Zone Bill 1984.
Entered into force: Not yet in force.
Source: Malaysian Ministry of Foreign Affairs.

ARRANGEMENT OF CLAUSES

Part I
Preliminary

Clause

Part II
Exclusive Economic Zone

Part III
Fisheries

Part IV
Protection and preservation of the marine environment

Part V
Marine scientific research

Clause

Part VI

Artificial islands, installations and structures

Part VII

Submarine cables and pipelines

Part VIII

Enforcement

Part IX

Offences, penalties, legal proceedings and compensations

Part X

Miscellaneous

An act pertaining to the exclusive economic zone and certain aspects of the continental shelf of Malaysia and to provide for the regulation of activities in the zone and on the continental shelf and for matters connected therewith.

Be it enacted by the Duli Yang Maha Mulia Seri Paduka Baginda Yang di-Pertuan Agong with the advice and consent of the Dewan Negara and Dewan Rakyat in Parliament assembled, and by the authority of the same, as follows:

Part I

Preliminary

Short title, application and commencement

1. (1) This Act may be cited as the Exclusive Economic Zone Act 1984 and shall apply to the exclusive economic zone and continental shelf of Malaysia.

Act 83

(2) The provisions of this Act pertaining to the continental shelf shall be in addition to, and not in derogation of, the provisions of the Continental Shelf Act 1966.

(3) In the event of any conflict or inconsistency between the provisions of this Act and of any applicable written law, the provisions of this Act shall supersede the conflicting or inconsistent provisions of that applicable written law and the latter shall be construed as so superseded.

(4) The provisions of any applicable written law which are not in conflict or inconsistent with the provisions of this Act shall otherwise continue to apply.

(5) This Act shall come into force on such date as the Yang di-Pertuan Agong may appoint by notification in the *Gazette* and the may appoint different dates for the coming into force of different provisions of this Act in different areas of the exclusive economic zone and continental shelf.

Interpretation

2. In this Act, unless the context otherwise requires—

'applicable written law' means any written law—

(a) provided to be applicable in respect of the exclusive economic zone, continental shelf or both, as the case may be, by an orde made under section 42 or otherwise specifically provided to be so applicable; or

(b) applicable in respect of the continental shelf under the provisions of the Continental Shelf Act 1966.

and includes the Continental Shelf Act 1966;

Act 210. Ord. 70/52. Act 41/67. Act 235. Act 77

'authorized officer' means any fishery officer as defined in section 2 of the Fisheries Act 1963, any port officer as defined in section 2 of the Merchant Shipping Ordinance 1952, any police officer not below the rank of sergeant as defined in section 2 of the Police Act 1967, any customs officer as defined in section 2 of the Customs Act 1967, any officer of the armed forces as defined in section 2 of the Armed Forces Act 1972, any public officer, irrespective of rank, in command of a vessel belonging to the Government or any other person or class of persons appointed to be an authorized officer or authorized officers under section 39;

'continental shelf' means the continental shelf of Malaysia as defined in section 2 of the Continental Shelf Act 1966;

Act 127

'Director-General' means the Director-General of Environmental Quality as defined in section 2 of the Environmental Quality Act 1974;

'dumping' means—

(a) any deliberate disposal of wastes or other matter from vessels, aircraft, piatforms or other man-made structures at sea; or

(b) any deliberate disposal of vessels, aircraft or other man-made structures at sea,

but 'dumping' does not include—

(i) the disposal of wastes or other matter incidental to, or derived from, the normal operations of vessels aircraft, platforms or other man-made structures at sea and their equipment, other than wasters or other matter transported by or to vessels, aircraft, platforms or other man-made structures at sea, operating for the purpose of disposal of such matter or derived from the treatment of such wastes or other matter on such vessels, aircraft, platforms or structures; or

(ii) placement of matter for a purpose other than the mere disposal thereof, provided that such placement is not contrary to the aims of this Act, any applicable written law or international law;

'exclusive economic zone' or 'zone' means the exclusive economic zone of Malaysia determined in accordance with section 3.

Act 2

'Government' means the Government of Malaysia and includes any Minister charged with responsibility by an order made under the Ministerial Functions Act 1969 for the matter in relation to which the reference to the Government is made under this Act, and any other Minister exercising temporarily the functions of such Minister;

'Malaysian fisheries waters' means all waters comprising the internal waters, the territorial sea and the exclusive economic zone of Malaysia in which Malaysia exercises sovereign and exclusive rights over fisheries;

'maritime casualty' means a collision of vessels, stranding or other incident of navigation, or other occurrence on board a vessel or external to it resulting in material damage or imminent threat of material damage to a vessel or cargo;

'master', in relation to a vessel, includes every person (except a pilot or port officer as defined in section 2 of the Merchant Shipping Ordinance 1952) having for the time being command or charge of the vessel, or lawfully acting as the master thereof;

'mixture containing oil' means—

(a) a mixture with an oil content of one hundred parts or more in one million parts of the mixture; or

(b) a mixture with such oil content as is prescribed by the Minister charged with responsibility for the environment by order in the *Gazette* to be a mixture containing oil for the purposes of this Act;

'oil' means—

(a) crude oil, diesel oil, fuel oil or lubricating oil; or

(b) any other description of oil which is prescribed by the Minister charged with responsibility for the environment by order in the *Gazette* to be oil for the purposes of this Act;

'owner', in relation to a vessel, means any person or body of persons, whether incorporated or not, by whom the vessel is owned and includes any charterer, subcharterer, lessee or sub-lessee of the vessel;

'pollutant' means any substance which, if introduced into the sea, is liable to create hazards to human health or to harm living resources in the sea or other marine life, or to damage amenities or interfere with other legitimate uses of the sea and, without limiting the generality of the foregoing, includes any substance that is prescribed by the Minister charged with responsibility for the environment by order in the *Gazette* to be a pollutant for the purposes of this Act;

'State' shall have the meaning assigned to that expression under international law;

P.U. (A) 307a/69

'territorial sea' means the territorial waters of Malaysia determined in accordance with the Emergency (Essential Powers) Ordinance, No. 7/1969;
'this Act' includes regulations and other subsidiary legislation made under this Act and anything done under this Act or under such regulations or other subsidiary legislation;
'vessel' includes every description of ship or floating or submarine craft or structure;
'waste' includes—

(a) any matter, whether liquid, solid, gaseous or radioactive, which is discharged, emitted, deposited or dumped in the marine environment in such volume, composition or manner as to cause an alteration of the environment; or
(b) any matter which is prescribed by the Minister charged with responsibility for the environment by order in the *Gazette* to be waste for the purposes of this Act.

Part II
Exclusive economic zone

The exclusive economic zone of Malaysia

3. (1) The exclusive economic zone of Malaysia, as proclaimed by the Yang di-Pertuan Agong *vide* P.U. (A) 115/80, is an area beyond and adjacent to the territorial sea of Malaysia and, subject to subsections (2) and (4), extends to a distance of two hundred nautical miles from the baselines from which the breadth of the territorial sea is measured.

(2) Where there is an agreement in force on the matter between Malaysia and a State with an opposite or adjacent coast, questions relating to the delimitation of the exclusive economic zone shall be determined in accordance with the provisions of that agreement.

(3) The Yang di-Pertuan Agong may cause the limits of the exclusive economic zone to be published in maps or charts from time to time.

(4) Where, having regard to international law, State practice or an agreement referred to in subsection (2), the Yang di-Pertuan Agong considers it necessary so to do, he may by order published in the *Gazette* alter the limits of the exclusive economic zone determined in accordance with subsection (1).

Sovereign rights in, and jurisdiction over, the exclusive economic zone

4. In the exclusive economic zone Malaysia has—

(a) sovereign rights for the purpose of exploring and exploiting, conserving and managing the natural resources, whether living or non-living, of the sea-bed and subsoil and the superjacent waters, and with regard to other activities for the economic exploitation and exploration of the zone, such as the production of energy from the water, currents and winds;
(b) jurisdiction with regard to—
  (i) the establishment and use of artificial islands, installations and structures;
  (ii) marine scientific research;
  (iii) the protection and preservation of the marine environment; and
(c) such other rights and duties as are provided for by international law.

Prohibition of activities in the exclusive economic zone or on the continental shelf except where authorized

5. Except where authorized in accordance with the provisions of this Act or any applicable written law, no person shall in the exclusive economic zone or on the continental shelf—

(a) explore or exploit any natural resources, whether living or non-living;
(b) carry out any search, excavation or drilling operations;
(c) conduct any marine scientific research; or
(d) construct or authorize and regulate the construction, operation and use of—
(i) any artificial island;
(ii) any installation or structure for any of the purposes provided for in section 4 or for any other economic purpose; or
(iii) any installation or structure which may interfere with the exercise of the rights of Malaysia in the zone or on the continental shelf.

Part III
Fisheries

Seas in the zone to be part of Malaysian fisheries waters

6. The seas comprised in the exclusive economic zone shall be part of Malaysian fisheries waters.

Minister responsible for fisheries in the zone

7. The Minister charged with responsibility for fisheries shall also be responsible for fisheries in the exclusive economic zone.

Written law relating to fisheries to be applicable in the zone and on the continental shelf

8. Except as otherwise provided in this Act, any written law relating to fisheries shall be applicable in the exclusive economic zone and on the continental shelf with such necessary modifications or exceptions as may be provided in an order made under section 42.

Part IV
Protection and preservation or the marine environment

Sovereign right of Malaysia to exploit her natural resources

9. Malaysia has the sovereign right to exploit her natural resources in the exclusive economic zone pursuant to her environmental policies and in accordance with her duty to protect and preserve the marine environment in the zone.

Offence in respect of the discharge or escape of certain substances

10. (1) If any oil, mixture containing oil or pollutant is discharged or escapes into the exclusive economic zone from any vessel, land-based source, installation, device or aircraft, from or through the atmosphere or by dumping—

(a) the owner or master of the vessel, if the discharge or escape is from a vessel;
(b) the owner or occupier of the place on land, if the discharge or escape is from land;
(c) the owner or person in charge of the installation or device, if the discharge or escape is from an installation or a device; or
(d) the owner or pilot of the aircraft, if the discharge or escape is from an aircraft,

shall each be guilty of an offence and shall be liable to a fine not exceeding one million ringgit.

(2) Where the act or omission of a person other than any of the persons mentioned in subsection (1) caused the discharge or escape mentioned in that subsection, then such other person shall also be guilty of an offence and shall be liable to a fine not exceeding one million ringgit.

(3) Subsection (2) shall not operate to absolve or relieve the persons mentioned in subsection (1) from liability for an offence under subsection (1).

(4) Notwithstanding the provisions of this section, dumping of wastes or other matter may be carried

out under a licence issued by the Director-General and subject to such conditions as he may impose.

Defence to a charge under section 10

11. Where a person is charged with an offence under section 10, it shall be a defence to prove that the discharge or escape of the substance mentioned in subsection (1) of that section was caused for the purpose of securing the safety of the vessel, the place on land, the installation, device or aircraft concerned, or for the purpose of saving life but a defence under this section shall not operate if the court is satisfied that the discharge or escape was not necessary for the alleged purpose or was not a reasonable step to take in the circumstances.

Requirement for discharge or escape of certain substances to be reported

12. (1) If any oil, mixture containing oil or pollutant is discharged or escapes into the exclusive economic zone from any vessel, land-based source, installation, device or aircraft, the owner or master of the vessel, the owner or occupier of the place on land, the owner or person in charge of the installation or device or the owner or pilot of the aircraft, as the case may be, shall immediately report the occurrence of such discharge or escape to the Director-General.

(2) Any person who fails to comply with this section shall be guilty of an offence and shall be liable to a fine not exceeding ten thousand ringgit.

Measures relating to a maritime casualty

13. (1) The Government may specify measures in relation to the exclusive economic zone which are necessary to protect Malaysia's coastline or any segment or element of the environment or related interests, including fishing, from pollution or threat of pollution following upon a maritime casualty or acts relating to such casualty, which may reasonably be expected to result in major harmful consequences.

(2) The measures referred to in subsection (1) shall be proportionate to the actual or threatened damage to the coastline or segment or element of the environment or related interests, including fishing.

Directions and action to remove, disperse, destroy or mitigate damage

14. (1) Where Malaysia's coastline or any segment or element of the environment or related interests, including fishing, in the exclusive economic zone is damaged or threatened to be damaged as a result of any discharge or escape of any substance mentioned in section 10, the Director-General may issue such directions as are, or take such action as is, necessary to remove, disperse, destroy or mitigate the damage or threat of damage.

(2) Any person who fails to comply with any direction given by the Director-General under subsection (1) shall be quilty of an offence and shall be liable to a fine not exceeding ten thousand ringgit.

(3) The owner and the master of the vessel, the owner and the occupier of the place on land, the owner and the person in charge of the installation or device, or the owner and the pilot of the aircraft, as the case may be, from which the substance mentioned in section 10 was discharged or escaped shall be liable jointly and severally for all costs and expenses incurred in carrying out all or any of the work required under subsection (1) to remove, disperse, destroy or mitigate the damage or threat of damage, and such costs and expenses shall be a first charge on any property or interest held by such person.

(4) Where the Act or omission of a person other than any of the persons mentioned in subsection (3) caused such discharge or escape, then such other person shall also be liable jointly and severally with the persons mentioned in that subsection for all costs and expenses incurred in carrying out all or any of the work required under subsection (1) to remove, disperse, destroy or mitigate the damage or threat of damage, and such costs and expenses shall be a first charge on any property or interest held by such other person.

Power to detain and sell vessel

15. (1) The Director-General may detain any vessel from which the oil, mixture containing oil or pollutant escaped or was discharged in the circumstances mentioned in subsection (1) of section 14.

(2) The Director-General may release any vessel detained under subsection (1) upon the owner depositing with the Government such sum of money or furnishing such security as, in the opinion of the Director-General, would be adequate to meet all costs and expenses incurred in carrying out the work required to remove, disperse, destroy or mitigate the damage or threat of damage caused by such escape or discharge.

(3) If any vessel which has been detained proceeds to sea without being released under subsection (2), the owner or master of the vessel or any other person who causes the vessel to proceed to sea shall be guilty of an offence and shall be liable to a fine not exceeding one million ringgit.

(4) Where the owner or master of such vessel or any other person found guilty of an offence under this section is unable to pay the fine or the costs and expenses incurred in carrying out the work required under subsection (1) of section 14, the court may, on the application of the Director-General, order the sale of such vessel and the application of the proceeds of the sale towards the payment of the fine and the costs and expenses incurred.

Part V

Marine scientific research

Government consent required for conduct of marine scientific research

16. (1) No marine scientific research may be conducted in the exclusive economic zone or on the continental shelf without the express consent of and subject to conditions imposed by the Government.

(2) Subject to section 17, the Government shall give its consent where the marine scientific research would be carried out by any State or competent international organization for peaceful purposes and to increase scientific knowledge of the marine environment.

Right to withold consent

17. The Government may withhold it consent to the conduct of a marine scientific research project by any State or competent international organization in the exclusive economic zone or on the continental shelf if it has reason to believe that the project—

(*a*) is of direct significance to the exploration and exploitation of natural resources, whether living or non-living;

(*b*) involves drilling into the continental shelf, the use of explosives or the introduction of pollutants into the marine environment;

(*c*) involves the construction, operation or use of artificial islands, installations or structures;

(*d*) contains information communicated pursuant to section 18 regarding the nature and objectives of the project which is inaccurate or if the researching State or competent international organization has outstanding obligations to Malaysia from a prior research project; or

(*e*) would interfere with activities undertaken by Malaysia in the exercise of its sovereign rights and jurisdiction provided for under this Act, any applicable written law or international law.

Duty to provide information

18. Any State or competent international organization which intends to undertake marine scientific research in the exclusive economic zone or on the continental shelf shall, not less than six months in advance of the expected starting date of the marine scientific research project, provide the Government with a full description of—

(*a*) the nature and objectives of the project;
(*b*) the method and means to be used, including name, tonnage, type and class of vessels and a description of scientific equipment;
(*c*) the precise geographical areas in which the project is to be conducted;
(*d*) the expected date of first appearance and final departure of the research vessels, or deployment of the equipment and its removal, as appropriate;
(*e*) the name of the sponsoring institution, its director, and the person in charge of the project; and
(*f*) the extent to which it is considered that Malaysia should be able to participate or to be represented in the project.

Duty to comply with certain conditions

19. (1) Every State or competent international organization undertaking marine scientific research in the exclusive economic zone or on the continental shelf shall comply with the following conditions:

(*a*) ensure the right of the Government, if it so desires, to participate or be represented in the marine scientific research project, especially on board research vessels and other craft or scientific research installations, when practicable, without payment of any remuneration to the scientists of Malaysia and without obligation to contribute towards the costs of the project;
(*b*) provide the Government with preliminary reports, as soon as practicable, and with the final results and conclusions after the completion of the research;
(*c*) undertake to provide access for the Government, at its request, to all data and samples derived from the project and likewise to furnish it with data which may be copied and samples which may be divided without detriment to their scientific value;
(*d*) if requested, provide the Government with an assessment of such data, samples and research results or provide assistance in their assessment or interpretation;
(*e*) ensure, unless otherwise specified by the Government, that the research results are made internationally available through appropriate national or international channels, as soon as practicable;
(*f*) inform the Government immediately of any major change in the research programme;
(*g*) unless otherwise agreed, remove the scientific research installations or equipment once the research is completed.

(2) This section is without prejudice to the conditions established by the Government for the exercise of its discretion to give or withhold consent pursuant to section 16 or 17, as the case may be, including requiring prior agreement for making internationally available the research results of a project of direct significance for the exploration and exploitation of natural resources.

Suspension or cessation of marine scientific research activities

20. (1) The Government may order the suspension of any marine scientific research activities in progress within the exclusive economic zone or on the continental shelf if—

(*a*) the research activities are not being conducted in accordance with the information provided under section 18 upon which the consent of the Government was based; or
(*b*) the State or competent international organization conducting the research activities fails to comply with the provisions of section 19.

(2) The Government may order the cessation of any marine scientific research activities—

(*a*) which in deviating from the information provided under section 18 have amounted to a major change in the research project or the research activities; or
(*b*) if any of the situations contemplated in subsection (1) are not rectified within a reasonable period of time, as determined by the Government.

(3) Following notification by the Government of the order of suspension or cessation, the State or competent international organization shall immediately terminate all or any of the marine scientific research activities that are the subject of such a notification.

(4) An order of suspension under subsection (1) may be lifted by the Government and the marine scientific research activities allowed to continue if the researching State or competent international organization complies with the conditions required under sections 18 and 19 within a reasonable period of time, as determined by the Government.

Part VI

Artificial islands, installations and structures

Prohibition of construction, operation or use of artificial island, etc. except with authorization

21. (1) No person shall construct, operate or use any artificial island, installation or structure in the exclusive economic zone or on the continental shelf except with the authorization of the Government and subject to such conditions as it may impose.

(2) The Government shall have exclusive jurisdiction over artificial islands, installations and structures in the zone and on the continental shelf, including jurisdiction with regard to customs, fiscal, health, safety and immigration laws.

(3) The Government may, where necessary, establish reasonable safety zones around such artificial islands, installations and structures in which it may take appropriate measures to ensure the safety both of navigation and of the artificial islands, installations and structures.

(4) The breadth of the safety zones shall be determined by the Government, taking into account applicable international standards. Due notice shall be given of the extent of the safety zones.

(5) All vessels must respect these safety zones and shall comply with any directions which the Government may give in accordance with generally accepted international standards regarding navigation in the vincinity of artificial islands, installations, structures and safety zones.

Part VII

Submarine cables and pipelines

Consent of Government neccessary for delineation of course for laying of sub-marine cables and pipelines

22. (1) No person shall lay submarine cables or pipelines in the exclusive economic zone or on the continental shelf without the consent of the Government as to the delineation of the course for the laying of such cables and pipelines.

(2) Without prejudice to subsection (1), the Government may impose such conditions as it may consider necessary for the laying or maintenance of such cables and pipelines in the exercise of its right to take reasonable measures for the exploration of the continental shelf, the exploitation of natural resources and the prevention, reduction and control of pollution from such cables or pipelines.

Duty of owner of submarine cable or pipeline

23. The owner of any submarine cable or pipeline which has fallen into disue or is beyond repair shall forthwith inform the Government thereof and shall, if so directed by the Government, remove such cable or pipeline within such period of time as the Government may direct.

Part VIII

Enforcement

Powers of authorized officer

24. (1)For the purpose of ensuring compliance with the provisions of this Act or any applicable written law, any authorized officer may, where he has reason to believe that an offence has been committed under this Act or such written law, without a warrant—

(a) stop, board and search any vessel within the exclusive economic zone and inspect any licence, permit, record, certificate or any other document required to be carried on board such vessel under this Act, such written law or any generally accepted international rules and standards, and make copies of the same;
(b) make such further enquiries and physical inspection of the vessel, its crew, equipment, gear, furniture, appurtenances stores and cargo as may be necessary to ascertain whether or not a suspected violation of the provisions of this Act or such written law has been committed;
(c) enter and search any place in which he has reason to believe that an offence under this Act or such written law is about to be or has been committed;
(d) arrest any person who he has reason to believe has committed any offence under this Act or such written law;
(e) detain any article which he has reason to believe has been used in the commission of any offence under this Act or such written law;
(f) detain any vessel, including its equipment, gear, furniture, appurtenances, stores and cargo, which he has reason to believe has been used in the commission of any offence or in relation to which any offence has been committed under this Act or such written law.

(2) A written acknowledgement shall be given for any article, vessel or thing detained under sub-section (1).

Hot pursuit

25. (1) Where any authorized officer has reason to believe that a foreign vessel has contravened any provision of this Act or any applicable written law, he may undertake the hot pursuit of such vessel with a view to stopping and arresting it and bringing it within the exclusive economic zone in accordance with international law.

(2) The powers conferred on an authorized officer under section 24 shall be exercisable pursuant to this section in respect of such vessel beyond the limits of the exclusive economic zone to the extent allowed by international law.

(3) Except as otherwise provided by any regional or bilateral agreement to which Malaysia is a party, the right of hot pursuit shall cease as soon as the vessel pursued enters the territorial sea or exclusive economic zone of its own State or any third State.

How person arrested to be dealt with

26. (1) An authorized officer making an arrest under this Act or any applicable written law shall without unnecessary delay produce the person arrested before a Magistrate.

(2) No authorized officer shall keep in custody a person arrested for a longer period than under all the circumstances of the case is reasonable.

F.M.S. Cap. 6

(3) Such period shall not in the absence or after the expiry of a special order of a Magistrate under section 117 of the Criminal Procedure Code exceed twenty-four hours, exclusive of the time necessary for the journey from the place of arrest to the Magistrate's Court.

How detained vessel to be dealt with

27. Any vessel detained under this Part and the crew thereof shall be taken to the nearest or most convenient port and dealt with an accordance with the provisions of this Act or any applicable written law.

Obstruction of authorized officer, etc.

28. Any person who—

(a) wilfully obstructs any authorized officer in the exercise of any of the powers conferred on him by this Act or any applicable written law;

(b) fails to comply with any lawful order or requirement under this Act or such written law; or

(c) fails to comply with any of the provisions of this Act or such written law for which no punishment is provided for failure to comply therewith,

shall be guilty of an offence.

Part IX

Offences, penalties, legal proceedings and compensations

General penalty

29. Any person who is guilty of an offence under this Act for which no punishment is provided shall be liable to a fine not exceeding one million ringgit.

Offences by companies, partnerships, etc.

30. Where any offence under this Act or any applicable written law has been committed by a company, partnership, firm or business, every director and every officer of that company directly connected with the activity resulting in the commission of the offence, every member of that partnership and every person concerned with the management of that firm or business shall each be guilty of that offence and shall be liable to the punishment provided in section 29.

Master liable for offence committed on his vessel

31. Where an offence under this Act or any applicable written law has been committed by any person on board a vessel, the master of such vessel shall also be guilty of that offence and shall be liable to the punishment provided in section 29.

Detention and forfeiture of vessel, etc.

32. (1) Any article, vessel or thing detained under the provisions of this Act or any applicable written law shall, unless otherwise provided under this Act, be held pending the outcome of any proceedings under this Act or such written law:

Provided, however, that an authorized officer or the court may release the article, vessel or thing so detained upon the furnishing of a bond or other security to the satisfaction of the authorized officer or the court by any person claiming ownership, or acting on behalf of the owner, of the article, vessel or thing to produce the same when required so to do.

(2) Where an article, vessel, or thing is detained under the provisions of this Act or any applicable written law, the authorized officer who detains the article, vessel or thing shall, as soon as may be, cause notice thereof to be given in writing to the owner; and where the owner cannot be found, a notice to that effect shall be published in the *Gazette* and, if the article, vessel or thing is foreign-owned, the authorized officer shall cause the diplomatic representative in Malaysia of the flag State of the vessel concerned or of the country of which the owner of the article or thing is a nationl to be informed of such fact through the Ministry responsible for foreign affairs.

(3) If the owner of the article, vessel or thing cannot be found in spite of all courses of action taken under subsection (2) and by reason of the owner not being found proceedings under this Act or any applicable written law cannot be instituted, the article, vessel or thing detained shall be held for a period of one month from the date of the last course of action taken under subsection (2) at the end of which period the article, vessel or thing shall be forfeited to the Government unless a claim is received in respect thereof

within the aforesaid period, in which event an enquiry shall be held by a court of competent jurisdiction to determine the validity of the claim and the article, vessel or thing shall be disposed of in such manner as the court may direct.

Power of court to order forfeiture

33. Where any person is found guilty of an offence under this Act or any applicable written law, the court shall, in addition to any other penalty that may be imposed, order that any article, vessel or thing which was the subject-matter of, or was used in the commission of, the offence be forfeited and that any licence or permit issued or consent given under this Act or such written law be suspended for such period of time as the court may think fit or be cancelled or withdrawn, as the case may be.

Disposal of article, vessel or thing ordered to be forfeited

34. Any article, vessel or thing ordered to be forfeited under section 33 shall be disposed of in such manner as the court may direct.

Court may order forfeiture in certain circumstances

35. Where it is proved to the satisfaction of a court that any article, vessel or thing detained under the provisions of this Act or any applicable written law was the subject-matter of, or was used in the commission of, an offence under this Act or such written law, the court may order the forfeiture of such article, vessel or thing notwithstanding that no person may have been found guilty of such offence.

Sessions Court and Court of Magistrate of First Class to have full jurisdiction and powers under Act or applicable written law

36. (1) Notwithstanding any written law to the contrary, any offence committed under this Act or any applicable written law shall be deemed to have been committed in Malaysia for the purpose of conferring jurisdiction on a court to try that offence, and a Sessions Court or a Court of a Magistrate of the First Class shall each have full jurisdiction and powers for all purposes under this Act or such written law.

(2) Subsection (1) shall not be construed a derogating in any way from the jurisdiction and powers of the High Court to try any offence under any written law.

(3) Any proceedings in respect of an offence under this Act or any applicable written law shall be brought before the Sessions Court or the Court of a Magistrate of the First Class which is nearest the place where the offence was committed, or which is located in the most convenient place for trial in the circumstances of the case as determined by the Public Prosecutor.

(4) This section shall be without prejudice to the provisions of the Criminal Procedure Code relating to the transfer of cases.

Presumption as to maps, plans or charts made by authority of Governments

37. For the purposes of this Act or any applicable written law, the court shall presume that maps, plans or charts purporting to be made by the authority of—

(a) the Federal Government;

(b) the Government of any State in Malaysia; or

(c) the Government of a State as defined in section 2 and approved by the Federal Government or the Government of any State in Malaysia for use,

were so made and are accurate.

Prosecution of offence

38. (1) A prosecution for an offence under this Act or any applicable written law shall not be instituted except by or with the consent of the Public Prosecutor:

Provided that a person who is to be charged with such an offence may be arrested, or a warrant for his arrest may be issued and executed, and any person so arrested may be remanded in custody or released on bail, notwithstanding that the consent of the Public Prosecutor to the institution of a prosecution for the offence has not been obtained, but the case shall not be further prosecuted until that consent has been obtained.

(2) When a person is brought before a court under this section before the Public Prosecutor has consented to the prosecution, the charge shall be read and explained to him but he shall not be called upon to plead thereto, and the provisions of the Criminal Procedure Code shall be modified accordingly.

Yang di-Pertuan Agong may appoint other persons to be authorized officers

39. Without prejudice to the definition of 'authorized officer' in section 2, the Yang di-Pertuan Agong may, by order in the *Gazette,* appoint such other person or class of persons as he may consider necessary to be an authorized officer or authorized officers for the purposes of this Act or any applicable written law.

Damage caused to any person or property or to environment in exclusive economic zone or on continental shelf

40. (1) Where, by reason of any act or omission in contravention of this Act or any applicable written law, damage is caused to any person or property in or on, or to any segment or element of the environment or related interests within, the exclusive economic zone or continental shelf, the owner and the master of the vessel, the owner and the occupier of the place on land, the owner and the person in charge of the installation or device, or the owner and the pilot of the aircraft, as the case may be, causing the damage, or the owner and the master of the vessel, the owner and the occupier of the place on land, the owner and the person in charge of the installation or device, or the owner and the pilot of the aircraft from which any oil, mixture containing oil or pollutant was discharged or escaped resulting in the damage, shall be liable jointly and severally for such damage unless otherwise provided under this Act or such written law.

(2) Where the act or omission of a person other than any of the persons mentioned in subsection (1) caused such damage, discharge or escape, then such other person shall also be liable jointly and severally with the persons mentioned in that subsection for such damage, unless otherwise provided under this Act or such written law.

(3) Without prejudice to the generality of subsections (1) and (2) such liability shall extend to the payment of compensation for any damage caused to a person, vessel, gear, facility of structure used in any activity, including fishing and related activities, connected with the exercise of the rights of the Government and Malaysian nationals, and of other persons where such rights are exercised with the consent of the Government, in the exclusive economic zone or on the continental shelf, and compensation shall also be paid for policing and surveillance activities and activities for the protection of the environment and shipping necessitated by the damage referred to in subsection (1).

(4) Any claim for compensation under this section may be brought before any High Court, Sessions Court or Court of a Magistrate of the First Class in Malaysia, as the case may be, according to the value or amount of the claim; and where a claim is so brought, the court concerned shall have full jurisdiction and powers to adjudicate thereon.

Part X
Miscellaneous

Power to make regulation

41. (1) The Yang di-Pertuan Agong may make regulations for carrying out the provisions of this Act.

(2) Without prejudice to the generality of subsection (1), such regulations may provide for any of the following matters:

(a) regulating the conduct of marine scientific research within the exclusive economic zone and on the continental shelf;

(b) prescribing measures for the protection and preservation of the marine environment of the exclusive economic zone, including conditions to be complied with by foreign vessels before entering any port or the internal waters of Malaysia or calling at any offshore terminal;

(c) regulating the construction, operation and use of artificial islands and of other installations and structures within the exclusive economic zone or on the continental shelf, including the establishment of safety zones around such islands, installations and structures;

(d) regulating the exploration and exploitation of the exclusive economic zone for the production of energy from the water, currents and winds and for other economic purposes;

(e) providing for such other matters as are necessary or expedient for giving full effect to Malaysia's rights in and jurisdiction over the exclusive economic zone and the continental shelf.

Written laws to be applicable in exclusive economic zone or on continental shelf or both by order

42. (1) The Yang di-Pertuan Agong may, by order in the *Gazette,* provide for any written law to be applicable in the exclusive economic zone, on the continental shelf or both.

(2) Any order made by the Yang di-Pertuan Agong under this section may provide for such written law to be applicable with such modifications or exceptions thereto as he considers necessary and where he so does, such written law shall be construed accordingly in its application in the exclusive economic zone, on the continental shelf or both.

(3) The modifications mentioned in subsection (2) may include amendments to such written law which the Yang di-Pertuan Agong may consider necessary—

(a) to make such written law effective in its application in the exclusive economic zone, on the continental shelf or both;

(b) to avoid any conflict or inconsistency between the provisions of such written law and this Act or any other applicable written law; or

(c) to bring the provisions of such written law into accord with the provisions of this Act or any other applicable written law.

(4)Any order made under this section shall be laid before the House of Representatives as soon as may be after it is made and if a motion is moved and carried by that House, within three months of the date on which the order is laid before it, disallowing the order, the order shall thereafter be void but, without prejudice to the validity of anything done under the order or to the making of any new order.

Explanatory statement

The purpose of this Bill is to make provision pertaining to the exclusive economic zone and to certain aspects of the continental shelf of Malaysia and to provide for the regulation of activities in the zone and on the continental shelf and for matters connected therewith.

2. Part 1 provides for preliminary matters. *Clause 1* deals with the citation, application and commencement of the proposed Act. *Sub-clause (1)* of *clause 1* specifies that the proposed Act shall apply to the exclusive economic zone and continental shelf of Malaysia. *Sub-clause (2)* seeks to make clear that the provisions of the proposed Act pertaining to the continental shelf are to be in addition to, and not in derogation of, the provisions of the Continental Shelf Act 1966. *Sub-clause (3)* provides that where there is any conflict or inconsistency between the provisions of the proposed Act and any applicable written law (as defined in *clause* 2), the provisions of the proposed Act are to supersede the conflicting or inconsistent provisions of the applicable written law and that the latter law shall be construed as so superseded. *Sub-clause (4)* stipulates that the provisions of any applicable written law which are not in conflict or inconsistent with the provisions of the proposed Act shall otherwise continue to apply. *Sub-clause (5)* provides the modality for bringing into force the proposed Act. *Clause 2* provides for the definition of various expressions.

3. Part II deals with the exclusive economic zone. *Sub-clause (1)* of *clause 3* stipulates that the exclusive economic zone of Malaysia is an area beyond and adjacent to the territorial sea of Malaysia and extends to a distance of two hundred nautical miles from the baselines from which the breadth of the territorial sea is measured. *Sub-clauses (2)* and *(4)*, however, provide for the limits of the zone to be altered in accordance with international law, State practice or an agreement in force on the matter between Malaysia and a State with an opposite or adjacent coast. *Clause 4* spells out the extent of the sovereign rights of Malaysia in, and jurisdiction over, the exclusive economic zone. As a corollary to this provision, *clause 5* prohibits the carrying out of certain activities in the zone or on the continental shelf unless otherwise authorized under the proposed Act or any applicable written law.

4. Part III relates to fisheries generally. *Clauses 6* and *7* provide that the seas comprised in the exclusive economic zone are to be part of Malaysian fisheries waters and that the Minister charged with responsibility for fisheries shall also be responsible for fisheries in the zone. *Clause 8* is intended to make any written law relating to fisheries to be applicable in the zone with such necessary modifications or exceptions as may be provided in an order made under *clause 42*.

5. Part IV seeks to make provision for the protection and preservation of the marine environment in the exclusive economic zone. *Clause 9* spells out the sovereign right of Malaysia to exploit her natural resources in the zone pursuant to her environmental policies and in accordance with her duty to protect and preserve the marine environment. *Clause 10* creates an offence in respect of the discharge or escape into the zone of certain substances. *Clause 11* deals with the defence which may be raised where a person is charged with committing an offence under *clause 10*. *Clause 12* makes it mandatory for certain persons to report to the Director-General of Environmental Quality the discharge or escape of certain substances into the zone. *Clause 13* enables the Government to specify measures to be taken in relation to the zone which are necessary to protect Malaysia's coastline or any segment or element of the environment or related interests from pollution or threat of pollution following a maritime casualty or acts relating to such casualty, which may reasonably be expected to result in major harmful consequences. *Clause 14* deals with the power of the Director-General of Environmental Quality to issue directives or take such action as is necessary to remove, disperse, destroy or mitigate the damage or threat of damage to any segment or element of the environment in the zone. *Clause 15* gives the Director-General certain powers of detention and sale.

6. Part V embodies provisions dealing with marine scientific research. *Clause 16* requires the express consent of the Government to be obtained for the conduct of marine scientific research in the exclusive economic zone or on the continental shelf. In giving its consent, the Government may impose such conditions as it may deem fit. The Government must give its consent where the marine scientific research is to be carried out by any State or competent international organization for peaceful purposes and to increase scientific knowledge of the marine environment. But by *clause 17*, the Government has the right to withhold its consent in the circumstances spelt out in that clause. *Clause 18* imposes a duty upon any State or competent international organisation which intends to undertake marine scientific research in the exclusive economic zone or on the continental shelf to provide certain information and *clause 19* requires every such State or competent international organization to comply with the conditions specified in that clause. *Clause 20* enables the Government to order the suspension or cessation of any marine scientific research activities in progress within the exclusive economic zone or on the continental shelf where the conditions specified in that clause are not fulfilled.

7. Part VI relates to artificial islands, installations and structures. *Clause 21* prohibits their construction, operation or use except with the authorization of the Government and subject to such conditions as it may impose. This clause also confers the Government with exclusive jurisdiction over artificial islands, installations and structures in the exclusive economic zone and on the continental shelf, including jurisdiction with regard to customs, fiscal, health, safety and immigration laws. The Government is further empowered to establish reasonable safety zones around these artificial islands, installations and structures and it may take appropriate measures to ensure the safety both of navigation and of the artificial islands, installations and structures. The breadth of the safety zones is to be determined by the Government and a duty is imposed upon all vessels to respect the safety zones and to comply with any appropriate directions which the Government may give.

8. Part VII sets out the provisions dealing with submarine cables and pipelines. *Clause 22* stipulates that no person shall lay submarine cables or pipelines in the exclusive economic zone or continental shelf without the consent of the Government as to the delineation of the course for the laying of such cables and pipelines. This clause also enables the Government to impose certain conditions which it may consider necessary. *Clause 23* imposes a duty upon the owner of any submarine cable or pipeline which has fallen into disuse or which is beyond repair to inform the Government of that fact and to remove such cable or pipeline if so directed.

9. Part VII sets out the provisions dealing with the enforcement of the proposed Act and any applicable written law. This Part deals with the powers of an authorized officer (*clause 24*), hot pursuit (*clause 25*), arrest (*clause 26*), the treatment of a vessel detained under this Part and its crew (*clause 27*) and the obstruction of an authorized officer in the exercise of his powers and related matters (*clause 28*).

10. Part IX deals with offences, penalties, legal proceedings and compensations. *Clause 29* provides a general penalty of a fine not exceeding one million ringgit for an offence under the proposed Act for which no punishment is specifically provided, *Clause 30* provides for offences committed by companies, partnerships, firms or businesses while *clause 31* makes the master of a vessel also guilty of an offence under the proposed Act or any applicable written law where such offence is committed by any person on board the vessel. *Clause 32* stipulates how an article, vessel or thing which is detained under the proposed Act or any applicable written law shall be dealt with. *Clause 33* empowers the court to order forfeiture of any article, vessel or thing and to suspend or cancel or withdraw any licence or permit issued or consent given under the proposed Act or any applicable written law. *Clause 34* provides that any article, vessel or thing ordered to be forfeited under *clause 33* shall be disposed of in such manner as the court may direct while *clause 35* enables the court to order forfeiture of any article, vessel or thing detained under the proposed Act or any applicable written law notwithstanding that no person may have been found guilty of an offence under the proposed Act or such written law. *Clause 36* provides for the trial of offences committed under the proposed Act or any applicable written law. Under *clause 37*, a presumption is to be made that maps, plans or charts purporting to be made by the authority of certain Governments were so made and are accurate. *Clause 38* deals with the prosecution of offences while *clause 39* empowers the Yang di-Pertuan Agong to widen the definition of 'authorized officer' in *clause 2* by order in the *Gazette* so as to include such other persons or class of persons in the category of authorized officers. *Clause 40* pertains to damage caused to any person or property or to any segment or element of the environment in the exclusive economic zone or on the continental shelf and it further spells out the persons who are to be held liable for such damage.

11. Part X contains miscellaneous provisions. *Clause 41* empowers the Yang di-Pertuan Agong to make regulations for carrying out the provisions of the proposed Act. By *clause 42*, the Yang di-Pertuan Agong may by order in the *Gazette* provide for any written law to be applicable in the exclusive economic zone or on the continental shelf or both. Such order may be subject to such modifications or exceptions as are considered necessary and may include amendments to such written law. The purpose of this provision is to extend the operation of certain written laws into the exclusive economic zone or to the continental shelf or both in order to make more effective the exercise of Malaysia's sovereign rights in, and jurisdiction over, the exclusive economic zone and continental shelf.

12. Other provisions of this Bill not specifically referred to are consequential or minor in nature or otherwise amplify the provisions adverted to.

Financial implications

This Bill will involve the Government in extra financial expenditure, the amount of which cannot at present be ascertained.

[PN. (U²) 1097]

36. Maldives

A. Law No. 30/76.
Entered into force: December 5, 1976.
Sources: Department of Information and Broadcasting, Male, Republic of Maldives, and *United Nations ST/LEG/SER. B/19,* p. 230.

B. Law No. 32/76
Entered into force: December 5, 1976
Sources: Deputy to the Head of the Department of External Affairs of the Republic of Maldives, January 16, 1977. Reprinted in *United Nations ST/LEG/SER. B/19,* pp. 134–135.

LAW NO. 30/76 of 27TH NOVEMBER 1976, RELATING TO THE EXCLUSIVE ECONOMIC ZONE OF THE REPUBLIC OF MALDIVES.

No. 30/76
5th December, 1976

1. The area, including the sea as well as the sea-bed and sub-soil thereof, situated within the line joining the points of which the co-ordinates are given below, shell constitute the Exclusive Economic Zone of the Republic of Maldives.

(1)	7° 57′ 27″ N	69° 35′ 45″ E
(2)	7° 57′ 27″ N	69° 11′ 48″ E
(3)	4° 02′ 20″ S	69° 11′ 48″ E
(4)	4° 02′ 20″ S	77° 05′ 42″ E
(5)	3° 27′ 15″ N	77° 05′ 42″ E
(6)	4° 47′ 04″ N	77° 01′ 40″ E
(7)	4° 52′ 15″ N	76° 56′ 48″ E
(8)	5° 05′ 35″ N	76° 43′ 15″ E
(9)	5° 13′ 56″ N	76° 36′ 48″ E
(10)	6° 28′ 14″ N	75° 41′ 34″ E
(11)	6° 33′ 21″ N	75° 38′ 31″ E
(12)	6° 51′ 06″ N	75° 25′ 46″ E
(13)	7° 15′ 27″ N	75° 16′ 19″ E
(14)	7° 24′ 00″ N	75° 12′ 06″ E
(15)	7° 25′ 19″ N	75° 11′ 18″ E
(16)	7° 51′ 30″ N	74° 56′ 09″ E
(17)	7° 48′ 30″ N	74° 29′ 45″ E
(18)	7° 41′ 50″ N	73° 38′ 34″ E
(19)	7° 39′ 02″ N	73° 19′ 38″ E
(20)	7° 40′ 52″ N	73° 03′ 23″ E
(21)	7° 42′ 19″ N	72° 49′ 30″ E
(22)	7° 42′ 54″ N	72° 42′ 26″ E
(23)	7° 49′ 05″ N	72° 03′ 45″ E

(24)	8° 05′ 38″ N	70° 15′ 08″ E
(25)	7° 57′ 27″ N	69° 35′ 45″ E

2. The Republic of Maldives shall have the sovereign rights and exclusive jurisdiction over its Economic Zone for the purpose of exploitation, conservation and management of the natural resources therein, both living and non-living, or for any other economic purpose. Thus the use and exploitation of the products or natural resources found in the said Zone for any economic purpose, or the conduct of scientific researches, or the construction, maintenance or operation of artificial structures and devices for any purpose within the said Zone shall not be executed by non-Maldivians without assent of the Government of the Republic of Maldives.

3. Any person or persons contravening the sovereign rights of the Republic of Maldives over its Economic Zone shall be liable to prosecution and conviction in accordance with Laws and Regulations of the Republic of Maldives.

B. Law No. 32/76

EIF: December 5, 1976

Sources: Deputy to the Head of the Department of External Affairs of the Republic of Maldives, January 16, 1977. Reprinted in *United Nations ST/LEG/SER. B/19,* pp. 134–135.

LAW NO. 32/76 of 5 DECEMBER 1976 RELATING TO THE NAVIGATION AND PASSAGE BY FOREIGN SHIPS AND AIRCRAFTS THROUGH THE AIRSPACE, TERRITORIAL WATERS AND THE ECONOMIC ZONE OF THE REPUBLIC OF MALDIVES*

1. Ships of all States shall enjoy the right of innocent passage through the territorial waters and other exclusive economic zone of the Republic of Maldives. Passage shall be considered innocent only if such passage is not prejudicial to the peace, good order and security of the Republic of Maldives.

However, no foreign warship shall enter the territorial sea of the Republic of Maldives, nor a foreign fishing vessel shall enter its economic zone without prior consent of the Government of the Republic of Maldives. While navigating in the territorial waters of Maldives foreign warships shall fly their national flag. Submarines shall navigate on the surface and show their flag.

2. No foreign aircraft shall enter or pass through the air space of the territory of the Republic of Maldives except in conformity with the international norms and in accordance with the laws and regulations in force in the Republic of Maldives. Foreign military aircraft shall not enter or pass through the air space of the territory of the Republic of Maldives without prior consent of the Government of the Republic of Maldives.

Salvage and rescue operations of foreign ships within the territorial waters of the Republic of Maldives shall be carried out in accordance with the regulations and practices in effect in the Republic of Maldives.

3. Any foreign ship which runs aground on an island, a reef or a sandbank within the territory of the Republic of Maldives, if abandoned, without notifying the incident to the Government of the Republic of Maldives, shall be property of the Government.

4. All ships shall bear responsibility for any damage caused within the territory or economic zone to any other party by the negligence or deliberate action of those ships.

* Text transmitted by the Deputy to the Head of the Department of External Affairs of the Republic of Maldives in a note dated 16 January 1977.

5. Any person or persons who act in contravention of the provisions of this law shall be guilty of an offence and shall upon conviction be penalized in accordance with the laws and regulations of the Republic of Maldives.

6. In this law unless the context otherwise requires—

'Ship' means any description of ship or vessel or boat or craft or any other description of vessel used in navigation on or below the waters.

'Warship' means a ship belonging to the armed forces of a State, or a ship which by reason of the equipment contained therein could be used for any warlike purpose.

'Military aircraft' means an aircraft belonging to the armed forces of a State or an aircraft which by reason of the equipment contained theirein could be used for any warlike purpose.

37. Mauritania

Law 78–043
Entered into force: February 28, 1978.
Source: Mauritanian Ministry of Foreign Affairs (Translated from French by the Department of State).

Islamic Republic **of Mauritania**

Law No. 78,043 of February 28, 1978 Establishing the Code of the Merchant Marine and Maritime Fisheries

Title I
Maritime Navigation

Chapter I
Definition of Maritime Navigation

Article 1

Maritime navigation is navigation at sea, in ports and roadsteads, and in the saline parts of rivers, streams, and canals, in principle up to the first permanent obstacle that impedes the passage of maritime vessels, or up to a limit established by the regulatory texts in force.

Navigation in fluvial waters, when it is accessory to navigation principally effected in maritime waters, shall be considered maritime navigation.

The limits of maritime and fluvial waters shall be established by decree.

Title V
Maritime Public Domain and Territorial Waters

Chapter I
Maritime Public Domain

Article 172

The maritime public domain is the part of the national public domain formed by the sea and the areas subject to the influence which it covers permanently or temporarily.

Article 173

The maritime public domain is constituted by a natural public domain and an artificial domain:

1. The natural public domain includes:
The seashore;
Saline ponds and internal waters; The territorial sea, its seabed, and subsoil,
Certain foreshores of the sea.

2. The following are incorporated in the maritime public domain by this law:
A 100 m strip of land along the shore;
Any land acquired along the sea by the State to satisfy needs of public interest.

3. The artificial public domain is constituted by:
Maritime port and their facilities;
Structures built outside ports limits (lighthouses, beacons, buoys, etc.);
Lands artifically subjected to the action of the sea.

Article 174

The terms and conditions of delimitation, as well as the competent enforcement authorities, shall be established, as needed, by decree.

Article 175

The maritime public domain shall be inalienable, indefeasible, and nondistrainable.

Article 176

Movement shall be unrestricted in the maritime public domain, subject to compliance with the police regulations in force.

Article 177

No concession may be granted in the maritime public domain for the setting up of any establishment whatsoever without prior approval of the Minister in charge of the Merchant Marine and the Minister in charge of Fisheries, of applicable.

Article 178

The general conditions in which the maritime public domain may be occupied or granted, the rules applicable to mining in the maritine public domain and to other forms of exploitation, as well as related law and order and police measures, shall be established by decree.

Chapter II

Territorial Waters of 'Territorial Sea'

Article 179

1. The Mauritanian territorial waters extend for a breadth of 70 nautical miles measured from the following baselines:

(a) A straight baseline joining Pointe Dunfort to Cap Barbas;
(b) A straight baseline running from Cap Blanc to Cap Timéris; and
(c) The low-water line everywhere else.

2. The maritime waters coastward from the baselines established above (gulfs, bays, roadsteads, estuaries) shall be part of the inland waters.

Article 180

The sovereignty of the Mauritanian State shall extend fully over the territorial waters (including the airspace, seabed, and subsoil). National laws and regulations shall be applicable there, subject to the provisions of international conventions or treaties and special agreements ratified by the Mauritanian State.

The principles of maritime international law relating to innocent passage or access to Mauritanian ports without discrimination of foreign vessels shall apply in Mauritanian territorial waters, provided that they do not disturb the peace, order, or security of the Mauritanian State.

Article 181

1. In territorial waters, the Mauritanian State may take any steps necessary to prevent any passage that is not innocent according to the definition given in general international maritime agreements.

A decree enacted on the report of the Minister in charge of the Merchant Marine shall establish the list of activities at sea not considered as innocent passage.

2. In territorial waters, submarines and other submersible vessels must navigate on surface and hoist their flag.

Article 182

The Mauritanian State may enact laws and regulations applicable to innocent passage in the following cases of need:

(a) Conservation of marine living resources;
(b) Prevention of violations of fishery regulations;
(c) Navigational safety and regulation of maritime traffic;
(d) Preservation of the environment and prevention and control of marine pollution;
(e) Protection of devices and navigational aids;
(f) Prevention of violations of customs, tax, immigration, or health regulations;
(g) Protection of cables and pipelines and of marine scientific research.

The maritime authorities may, as necessary, draw up special rules with which vessels must comply.

Article 183

The jurisdiction of the Mauritanian State shall not apply on board a foreign vessel proceeding in the territorial sea enroute from foreign ports.

Mauritanian penal jurisdiction may apply in this case only if:

The consequences of the violation extend beyond the vessel to Mauritanian territory or are apt to disrupt law and order in Mauritanian territorial waters;

The assistance of the Mauritanian authorities is requested by the captain of the vessel or by the diplomatic and consular agent of the flag State;

This action is required to control traffic internationally recognized as illicit (drugs, etc.).

However, the Mauritanian State may take any steps authorized by its law to have its penal or civilian jurisdiction applied to persons on board a foreign vessel proceeding in [Mauritanian] territorial waters enroute from Mauritanian ports and inland waters.

Chapter III

Exclusive Economic Zone

Article 184

A 200-nautical-mile exclusive fishery zone is hereby established which shall extend from the baselines used to measure the breadth of the territorial sea up to a maximum limit of 200 nautical miles seaward.

This 200-nautical-mile zone, known as the exclusive exonomic zone, shall include the 70 nautical miles of territorial sea and the 130-mile economic zone located beyond the territorial sea and adjacent to it.

Article 185

In the 130-mile exclusive economic zone the Mauritanian State shall:

1. Exercise its sovereign rights for the purpose of exploration, exploitation, conservation, and management of the natural living or mineral resources of the seabed, its subsoil, and superjacent waters, as well as concerning other activities related to exploration or exploitation of the zone for economic purposes, such as energy production from water or another source.

2. Excerise its jurisdiction as concerns:

(a) Explacement and use of artificial islands, platforms, and other installations or devices;
(b) Marine scientific research;
(c) Preservation of the marine environment.

The provisions of the present code on continental shelf and fishery regulations shall be applicable to the exclusive economic zone.

Article 186

1. In the 130-mile economic zone the rights and freedoms of States with respect to navigation, overflight, the laying of cables and pipelines, as provided for on the high seas, shall not be amended unless they adversely affect the provisions of Article 185 above and the security of the Mauritanian State.

2. For the exploitation and management of its economic zone, the Mauritanian State may take all pertinent steps to conclude with any State or enterprise special, partnership, concession, or joint stock agreements for the exploitation of the zone concerned.

Article 187

A decree shall establish the terms of application of the foregoing provisions.

Chapter IV

Continental Shelf

Article 188

The continental shelf includes the submarine areas which constitute the natural extension of the land area of the Islamic Republic of Mauritania, i.e. the seabed and subsoil of the aforesaid submarine areas which extend beyond the territorial sea up to the outer edge of the continental margin, or to a limit of 200 nautical miles from the baselines from which the breadth of the territorial sea is measured, when the outer edge of the continental shelf (or continental margin) does not extend to that distance.

Article 189

1. The Mauritanian State shall exercise exclusive and sovereign rights over the continental shelf with regard to the exploration and exploitation of the natural resources of the seabed and its subsoil, whether they be mineral resources or sedentary living organisms remaining constantly in physical contact with the seabed (shellfish, algae, crabs, etc.).

2. The rights of the Mauritanian State over the continental shelf are exclusive in the sense that no one may undertake activities to explore and exploit the continental shelf without the express consent of the Mauritanian State. Moreover, the Mauritanian State alone may authorize or regulate drillings on the continental shelf irrespective of the purposes. These rights shall be independent of any actual or fictious occupation as well as any express proclamation by the Mauritanian State.

Article 190

The legal regime governing superjacent waters, as concerns freedom of navigation and anchoring, and the overflight of the airspace above these waters, is not amended by the provisions of this Chapter.

However, the provisions concerning the territorial sea or the exclusive economic zone shall apply to the legal regime of such waters and the airspace.

The maritime authorities shall, as necessary, draw up the rules with which vessels must comply.

Article 191

A decree shall establish the conditions and procedures relating to the exploration and exploitation of the continental shelf, in particular the rules with the competent authorities shall determine for operations to be conducted there.

Title VI

Maritime Fishery

Chapter I

Definition of Maritime Fishery

Article 192

Maritime fisherv means the harvest by appropriate means, breeding, or conservation in maritime waters of any animal living completely or partially in the sea or in the maritime part of ponds, rivers, and canals.

Article 193

1. The excercise of maritime fishery shall be free for Mauritanian nationals under the fishery regulations in force.

For aliens it shall be subject to the advance authorization of the Mauritanian Government.

2. Fishery by use of either dynamite or any other explosive or similar device, or by chemical bait or substances apt to have a destructive effect on fauna or the marine environment is strictly prohibited in Mauritanian waters.

38. Mauritius

A. Maritime Zones Act 1977, Act No. 13 of 1977 (and Proclamation No. 7 of 1977).
Entered into force: August 1, 1977.
Source: *Government Printing,* July 1977 (4210/7/77–180) and August 1977 (6095/8/77–71).

B. Notice No. 199 of 1984.
Entered into force: December 27, 1984.
Source: *Legal Supplement to the Government Gazette of Mauritania* No. 119 of 24 December 1984, pp. 515–516.

Proclamation No. 7 of 1977

TO FIX THE DATE FOR THE COMING INTO OPERATION OF THE MARITIME ZONES ACT 1977

A.R.M. Osman
Governor-General

In the Name of Her Majesty ELIZABETH II, Queen of Mauritius and of Her other Realms and Territories, Head of the Commonwealth,

&c., &c., &c.

L.S.

Abdool Raman Mahomed Osman—*By His Excellency* Sir Abdool Raman Mahomed Osman, *Knight Grand Cross of the Most Distinguished Order of Saint Michael and Saint George, Commander of the Most Excellent Oràer of the British Empire, Governor-General and Commander-in-Chief of Mauritius,*

&c., &c., &c.

Whereas by section 16 of the Maritime Zones Act 1977 it is provided that the said Act shall come into operation on a day to be fixed by Proclamation;

Now, therefore, by virtue of the said provision, I do hereby proclaim that the said Act shall come into operation on the first day of August, one thousand nine hundred and seventy-seven.

Given at Government House, Le Réduit, this first day of August one thousand nine hundred and seventy-seven.

GOD SAVE THE QUEEN!

THE MARITIME ZONES ACT 1977

Act No. 13 of 1977

I assent,

3rd June 1977 A.R.M. Osman

Governor-General

Arrangement of Sections

An Act

To provide for certain matters relating to the territorial waters, the continental shelf, the exclusive economic zone and the historic waters of Mauritius

ENACTED by the Parliament of Mauritius, as follows—

Short title

1. This Act may be cited as the Maritime Zones Act 1977.

Interpretation

2. In this Act—
'baseline' means the baseline as determined in accordance with the straight baseline system;
'continental shelf' means the continental shelf of Mauritius;
'designated area' means an area declared as such under section 9;
'exclusive economic zone' means the exclusive economic zone of Mauritius;
'historic waters' means the historic waters of Mauritius and includes such places or areas, as may be designated by the Minister by notice published in the *Gazette*, rights over which are, or may become exercisable by the State of Mauritius;

'limit', in relation to the territorial waters, the continental shelf, the exclusive economic zone or the historic waters of Mauritius, means the limit of such waters, shelf, exclusive economic zone or historic waters with reference to the individual or composite group or groups of islands constituting the territory of Mauritius;
'resources' includes living and non-living resources as well as resources for the production of energy from tides, winds and currents;
'submarines' includes underwater vehicles however propelled;
'territorial waters' means the territorial waters of Mauritius.

Sovereignty over and limits of territorial waters

3. (1) The sovereignty of Mauritius extends and has always extended to the territorial waters and to the seabed and subsoil underlying, and the air space over, such waters.

(2) The limit of the territorial waters is the line every point of which is at a distance of twelve nautical miles from the nearest point of the baseline.

(3) Notwithstanding anything contained in subsection (2), where the Prime Minister considers it necessary so to do having regard to International Law and State practice, he may, subject to subsection (4), by Order published in the *Gazette,* amend the limit of the territorial waters.

(4) No Order shall be made under subsection (3) unless the draft of the Order has been approved by the Legislative Assembly.

Use of territorial waters by foreign ships

4. (1) Without prejudice to any other enactment in force, but subject to subsections (2), (3) and (4), all foreign ships (other than warships, including submarines) shall enjoy the right of innocent passage through the territorial waters.

(2) Foreign warships, including submarines, may enter or pass through the territorial waters after giving notice to the Permanent Secretary, Prime Minister's Office.

(3) Submarines shall, while passing through the territorial waters, navigate on the surface and show their flag.

(4) Where the Prime Minister is satisfied that it is necessary so to do—

(a) in the interest of public safety, public order, defence or security of Mauritius or any part thereof; or

(b) in pursuance of any treaty to which Mauritius is a party,

he may, by Order published in the *Gazette,* suspend, whether absolutely or subject to such exceptions and qualifications as may be specified in the Order, the entry of any class of foreign ships into such area of the territorial waters as may be specified in the Order.

Continental shelf

5. (1) The continental shelf comprises the seabed and subsoil of the submarine areas that extend beyond the limit of the territorial waters throughout the natural prolongation of the land territory of Mauritius–

(a) to the outer edge of the continental margin; or

(b) to a distance of two hundred nautical miles from the baseline where the outer edge of the continental shelf does not extend up to that distance.

(2) Mauritius has, and always had, full and exclusive sovereign rights in respect of the continental shelf.

Exclusive economic zone

6. (1) The exclusive economic zone is the area beyond and adjacent to the territorial waters and which extends to a distance of two hundred nautical miles from the baseline.

(2) Notwithstanding anything contained in subsection (1), where the Prime Minister considers it

necessary so to do having regard to International Law and State practice, he may, subject to subsection (3), by Order published in the *Gazette,* amend the limit of the exclusive economic zone as specified in subsection (1).

(3) No Order shall be made under subsection (2) unless the draft of the Order has been approved by the Legislative Assembly.

Rights over continental shelf and exclusive economic zone.

7. (1) Without prejudice to sections 3, 5 and 6, but subject to subsections (3) and (6) Mauritius has, in the continental shelf and the exclusive economic zone—

(a) sovereign rights for the purposes of exploration, exploitation, conservation and management of all resources;

(b) exclusive rights and jurisdiction for the construction, maintenance or operation of artificial islands, off-shore terminals, installations and other structures and devices necessary for the exploration and exploitation of resources or for the convenience of shipping or for any other purpose;

(c) exclusive jurisdiction to authorise, regulate and conduct scientific research;

(d) exclusive jurisdiction to preserve and protect the marine environment and to prevent and control marine pollution; and

(e) such other rights as are recognised by International Law or State practice.

(2) Except in accordance with the terms of any agreement entered into with Mauritius or of a licence granted by or under the authority of the Prime Minister, no person shall, in relation to the continental shelf or the exclusive economic zone—

(a) explore or exploit any resources;

(b) carry out any search, excavation or drilling operations;

(c) conduct and research;

(d) construct, maintain or operate any artificial island, off-shore terminal, installation or other structure or device.

(3) Subject to subsection (4) and to any measures that may be necessary for protecting the interest of Mauritius, foreign States may lay or maintain cables or pipelines on the continental shelf and the seabed of the exclusive economic zone.

(4) No cables or pipelines shall be laid on the continental shelf or on the seabed of the exclusive economic zone unless the authority of the Prime Minister has been obtained for the delineation of the course of the cables or pipelines.

(5) Nothing in subsection (2) shall apply in relation to fishing by a citizen of Mauritius or a body corporate registered in Mauritius and approved by the Minister of Fisheries.

(6) Ships and aircraft of all States shall, subject to the exercise by Mauritius of its sovereign rights over its continental shelf or within the exclusive economic zone, enjoy the following freedoms—

(a) freedom of navigation; and

(b) freedom of overflight.

Historic waters

8. (1) The Prime Minister may, by Order published in the *Gazette,* specify the limits of the historic waters.

(2) The sovereign rights of Mauritius extends, and has always extended, so the historic waters and to the seabed and subsoil underlying, and the air space over, the historic waters.

Designated areas of the continental shelf and exclusive economic zone.

9. The Prime Minister may, by Order published in the *Gazette*—

(a) declare any area of the continental shelf or the exclusive economic zone to be a designated area; and

(b) make such provisions as he considers necessary with respect to—

(i) the exploration, exploitation and protection of the resources within the designated area;

(ii) the safety and protection of artificial islands, off-shore terminals, installations and other structures and devices in the designated area;

(iii) the regulation and conduct of scientific research in the designated area;

(iv) the protection of the marine environment in the designated area;

(v) customs and other fiscal matters in relation to the designated area;

(vi) the regulation of entry into and passage of foreign ships through the designated area;

(vii) the establishment of fairways, sealanes, traffic separation schemes or any other mode of ensuring freedom of navigation which is not prejudicial to the interest of Mauritius.

Extension of enactments

10. The Prime Minister may, by Order published in the *Gazette*—

(a) extend with such restrictions and modifications as he thinks fit, any enactment in force to the continental shelf or the exclusive economic zone, or any part thereof, including any designated area;

(b) make such provisions as he considers necessary for facilitating the enforcement of that enactment.

Publication of charts

11. The Prime Minister may cause the baseline, the limits of the territorial waters, the continental shelf, the exclusive economic zone and the historic waters to be published in charts.

Offences

12. (1) Any person who contravenes any provision of this Act or any regulation or Order made under this Act, shall commit an offence and shall, on conviction, be liable to a fine not exceeding two hundred thousand rupees or to penal servitude not exceeding five years.

(2) Any person who commits an offence shall be tried in the Intermediate Court

Offences by agent and body corporate

13. (1) Where an offence is committed by—

(a) an agent, the person for whom the agent is acting;

(b) a body corporate, every person who, at the time of the commission of the offence, was concerned in the management of the body corporate or was purporting to act in a managerial capacity,

shall also commit the like offence, unless he proves that the offence was committed without his knowledge or consent and that he took all reasonable steps to prevent the commission of the offence.

(2) Notwithstanding subsection (1), where an offence has been committed by a body corporate and it is proved that the offence has been committed with the consent, whether express or implied, or the connivance of, or is attributable to any neglect on the part of the director, manager, secretary or other officer of the body corporate, such director, manager, secretary or other officer shall commit the like offence.

Application of Act

14. Where any provision of this Act or of any regulation or Order made under this Act is in conflict with the provision of any other enactment in force, such provision of this Act or of such regulation or Order shall prevail

Regulations

15. (1) The Prime Minister may make such regulations as he considers necessary for carrying out the purposes of this Act.

(2) In particular and without prejudice to the foregoing power, regulations made under subsection (1) may provide for all or any of the following matters—

(a) the regulation of the conduct of any person in the territorial waters, the continental shelf, the exclusive economic zone or the historic waters;

(b) the regulation of the exploration and exploitation, conservation and management of the resources of the continental shelf and the exclusive economic zone;

(c) the regulation of the construction, maintenance of artificial islands, off-shore terminals, installations and other structures and devices;

(d) the preservation and the protection of the marine environment and the prevention and control of marine pollution;

(e) the regulation and conduct of scientific research;

(f) the fees in relation to licences; and

(g) any matter incidental to any of the matters specified in paragraphs *(a)* to *(f)*.

Commencement

16. This Act shall come into operation on a day to be fixed by Proclamation.

Passed in the Legislative Assembly on the thirty-first day of May, one thousand nine hundred and seventy-seven.

GUY T. D'ESPAIGNET
Clerk of the Legislative Assembly.

B. Notice No. 199 of 1984.
Entered into force: December 27, 1984.
Source: *Legal Supplement to the Government Gazette of Mauritania* No. 119 of 24 December 1984, pp. 515–516.

Government Notice No. 199 of 1984.

REGULATIONS MADE BY THE PRIME MINISTER UNDER SECTION 15 OF THE MARITIME ZONES ACT 1977

1. These regulations may be cited as the Maritime Zones (Exclusive Economic Zones) Regulations 1984.

2. The exclusive economic zones falling within the jurisdiction of Mauritius extend and have always extended from the base lines of the territory of Mauritius within the coordinates specified in the First and Second Schedules.

3. These regulations are without prejudice to the continental shelf of Mauritius as defined in the Maritime Zones Act 1977.

Made at Port Louis by the Prime Minister on 27 December 1984.

FIRST SCHEDULE

(regulation 2)

Geographical Coordinates adopted to designate the limits of the exclusive economic zones for the Islands of Mauritius, Rodrigues, Cargados Caragos (St. Brandon), Agalega and Tromelin

Latitude (South)			*Longitude (East)*		
°	′	″	°	′	″
08	58	00	54	28	04
08	48	55	55	56	00
08	40	21	57	15	09
08	33	29	58	20	19
08	26	13	59	23	13
09	36	54	59	57	30
10	28	42	60	04	44
11	20	30	59	59	06
12	08	42	59	38	00
12	57	15	58	58	00
12	57	48	60	11	12
13	41	30	61	48	36
14	35	00	62	38	43
15	25	12	62	57	54
16	18	48	63	09	44
16	25	46	64	18	36
16	56	36	65	30	12
18	16	17	66	41	43
19	59	19	67	02	02
20	51	12	66	50	27
22	06	37	66	00	00
22	42	42	65	12	44
23	10	02	63	20	40
23	03	03	62	24	41
22	10	28	60	47	34
23	22	24	59	26	36
23	48	05	58	14	23
22	00	32	57	14	40
21	18	19	56	50	09
20	35	55	56	27	44
20	04	57	56	17	39
19	00	49	55	50	45
15	17	06	52	33	22
14	01	33	52	45	33
13	31	25	52	58	48
12	43	06	53	33	54
12	17	52	53	48	02
11	44	15	53	49	25
10	36	15	53	51	58
09	38	16	53	54	17

SECOND SCHEDULE

(regulation 2)

Geographical Coordinates adopted to designated the limits of the exclusive economic zones for Chagos Archipelago

Latitude (South)		*Longtitude (East)*	
°	′	°	′
01	37	71	48
01	37	73	07
02	04	74	23
02	58	75	20
04	03	75	55
05	15	76	06
06	28	75	54
07	45	75	58
08	53	75	38
09	54	74	55
10	39	73	40
10	53	72	18
10	34	70	55
09	52	69	52
08	43	69	04
07	26	68	46
06	20	68	15
05	08	68	08
03	55	68	24
02	37	69	13
01	52	70	21

39. Mexico

Amendment to Article 27 of the Constitution.
Entered into force: July 31, 1976.
Source: *United Nations ST/LEG/SER.B/19,* pp. 233–240.

DECREE OF 26 JANUARY 1976 ADDING A NEW PARAGRAPH 8 TO ARTICLE 27 OF THE CONSTITUTION OF THE UNITED MEXICAN STATES,[1] TO PROVIDE FOR EXCLUSIVE ECONOMIC ZONE BEYOND THE TERRITORIAL SEA

Sole article. The following paragraph shall be added after the seventh paragraph of article 27 of the Political Constitution of the United Mexican States:

'Article 27 . . .

'The Nation exercises in an exclusive economic zone beyond and adjacent to the territorial sea, sovereign rights and jurisdictions as determined by laws adopted by Congress. The exclusive economic zone shall extend to a distance of 200 nautical miles from the baseline from which the territorial sea is measured. In those cases in which such extension causes overlapping with the exclusive economic zones of other States, the delimitation of the zones will be determined, as appropriate, by agreement with those States.'

TRANSITIONAL PROVISION

Sole article. This Decree shall enter into force 120 days after its publication in the *Diario Oficial* of the Federation.

(c) ACT OF 10 FEBRUARY 1976[2] REGULATING THE PROVISIONS OF PARAGRAPH 8 OF ARTICLE 27 OF THE POLITICAL CONSTITUTION OF THE UNITED MEXICAN STATES CONCERNING THE EXCLUSIVE ECONOMIC ZONE[3]

Article 1

The Nation exercises in an exclusive economic zone beyond and adjacent to the territorial sea the sovereign rights and jurisdiction determined by this Act.

Article 2

The outer limits of the exclusive economic zone shall be a line the points of which shall all be at a distance of 200 nautical miles from the baseline from which the breadth of the territorial sea is measured. In those cases in which such extension causes overlapping with the exclusive economic zones of other States, the delimitation of the zones will be determined, as appropriate, by agreement with those States.

[1] *Diarrio Official* of 6 February 1976, p. 2. Spanish text provided by the Permanent Representative of Mexico to the United Nations in a note verbale of 21 June 1977. Translation by the Secretariat of the United Nations.

[2] *Diario Official* of 13 February 1976. Spanish text provided by the Permanent Representative of Mexico to the United Nations in a note verbale of 21 June 1977. Translation by the Secretariat of the United Nations.

[3] *Supra (b)*

Article 3

The islands which are part of the national territory, except those which cannot be kept inhabited or which do not have an economic life of their own, shall also have an exclusive economic zone the limits of which shall be fixed in accordance with the provisions of the preceding article.

Article 4

In the exclusive economic zone, the Nation has:

I. Sovereign rights for purposes of exploration and exploitation, conservation and management of the natural resources, both renewable and non-renewable, of the sea-bed, including the subsoil and the superjacent waters;

II. Exclusive rights and jurisdiction with respect to the establishment and utilization of artificial islands, installations and structures;

III. Exclusive jurisdiction with respect to other activities pertaining to the exploration and economic exploitation of the zone.

IV. Jurisdiction with respect to:

(a) The preservation of the marine environment, including pollution control and elimination.

(b) Scientific research.

Article 5

Foreign States shall enjoy in the exclusive economic zone freedoms with respect to navigation and overflight, the laying of submarine cables and pipelines, and other internationally lawful uses of the sea relating to navigation and communications.

Article 6

The Federal Executive Branch shall ensure through proper management and conservation measures that the living resources are not endangered by over-exploitation.

The Federal Executive shall determine the allowable catch of living resources in the exclusive economic zone.

Article 7

Without prejudice to the provisions of the preceding article, the Federal Executive shall promote the optimum utilization of the living resources of the exclusive economic zone.

Article 8

When the total allowable catch of a species is greater than the fishing and hunting capacity of Mexican vessels, the Federal Executive Branch shall allow foreign vessels access to the surplus of the allowable catch, in accordance with the national interest and under the conditions set forth in the Federal Fishery Promotion Act.

Article 9

The provisions of this Act do not modify the régime of the continental shelf.

First. In implementing this Act, the Federal Executive Branch shall, as necessary, observe those laws and regulations in force which are applicable to the subjects covered by article 4 of this Act, until such time as specific legal provisions are enacted for each subject.

Second. This Act shall enter into force simultaneously with the addition of paragraph 8 to article 27 of the Constitution, for the implementation of which this Act establishes regulations.

(d) DECREE OF 4 JUNE 1976 ESTABLISHING THE OUTER LIMIT OF THE EXCLUSIVE ECONOMIC ZONE OF MEXICO[1]

Luis Echeverria Alvarez, Constitutional President of the United Mexican States, exercising the powers bestowed upon me by section 1 of article 89 of the Constitution, and in keeping with the provisions of articles 2 and 3 of the Act establishing regulations for the implementation of the eighth paragraph of article 27 of the Constitution, concerning the Exclusive Economic Zone and

Considering

That the Act establishing regulations for the implementation of the eighth paragraph of article 27 of the Constitution, concerning the Exclusive Economic Zone, published in the *Diario Oficial* of 13 February 1976, states that the outer limit of that zone shall be a line the points of which shall all be at a distance of 200 nautical miles from the baseline from which the breadth of the territorial sea is measured and that in those cases in which such extension causes overlapping with the exclusive economic zones of other States, the delimitation of the zones will be determined, as appropriate, by agreement with those States.

That in accordance with article 18, section II, of the General Act on National Property, the breadth of the territorial sea is measured from the low-water line on the coasts and islands that are part of the national territory, but that it can also be measured, according to the provisions of the second paragraph of the aforementioned article, according to other criteria that are equally acceptable under international law.

That, for the above reason, it is necessary, in order for the Act establishing regulations for the implementation of the eighth paragraph of article 27 of the Constitution to have the desired effect, that navigators and the public in general have an exact knowledge of the outer limit of the Exclusive Economic Zone.

That this requirement can only be met by publishing such general rules as may be necessary to determine, by means of geographical coordinates, the outer limit of the Exclusive Economic Zone of Mexico, I have deemed it advisable to issue the following

DECREE ESTABLISHING THE OUTER LIMIT OF THE EXCLUSIVE ECONOMIC ZONE OF MEXICO

Article 1.

The outer limit of the Exclusive Economic Zone of Mexico is made up of a series of arcs joining the points the geographical co-ordinates of which are as follows:

Latitude			*Longitude*		
Degrees	*Minutes*	*Seconds*	*Degrees*	*Minutes*	*Seconds*
I. In the Pacific Ocean:					
32	35	22.11	117	27	49.43
32	35	21.	117	28	4.
32	35	32.	117	29	06.
32	37	37.	117	49	31.
32	17	22.	117	59	41.
32	01	52.	118	07	16.0

[1] *Diario Official* of 7 June 1976, pp. 3–6. Spanish text provided by the Permanent Representative of Mexico to the United Nations in a note verbale of 21 June 1977. Translation by the Secretariat of the United Nations.

Latitude			*Longitude*		
Degrees	*Minutes*	*Seconds*	*Degrees*	*Minutes*	*Seconds*
31	32	58.	118	19	46.
31	21	25.	118	25	10.
31	20	55.0	118	25	35.
31	07	58.0	118	36	18.
30	59	00.	118	45	02.
30	58	06.	119	34	12.
30	57	21.	120	04	19.
30	53	28.	120	22	12.
30	52	05.	120	28	24.
30	32	31.20	121	51	58.37
30	12	57.57	122	0	16.69
29	49	11.25	122	6	55.46
29	24	53.10	122	10	9.90
29	3	54.52	122	10	13.50
28	36	8.81	122	6	26.95
28	17	7.07	122	1	14.41
28	2	43.59	121	57	35.94
27	39	28.72	121	48	59.70
27	17	19.12	121	37	20.82
26	56	33.82	121	22	51.00
26	37	30.49	121	5	44.01
26	20	25.26	120	25	15.46
26	5	32.46	120	24	42.58
25	51	30.14	119	57	56.69
25	43	11.83	119	36	39.41
25	36	2.56	119	10	49.56
25	31	42.61	118	44	15.82
25	30	15.56	118	17	20.00
25	31	51.89	117	49	3.27
25	19	42.07	117	36	12.91
25	8	55.27	117	22	50.48
24	53	10.08	117	7	10.79
24	36	58.24	116	47	4.48
24	19	33.39	116	18	26.35
24	10	18.39	115	58	1.73
24	4	51.12	115	50	30.55
23	58	49.43	115	41	20.19
23	44	22.69	115	37	54.18
23	21	4.64	115	29	43.99
22	58	51.22	115	18	36.46
22	38	1.64	115	4	42.56
22	18	53.81	114	48	15.37
22	1	64.05	114	29	29.84
21	46	46.95	114	8	42.59
21	36	27.37	113	50	36.86
21	38	15.57	113	58	9.07
21	41	58.95	114	20	15.47
21	43	30.58	114	46	25.00
21	41	58.95	115	12	34.53
21	37	25.51	115	38	19.12
21	29	54.63	116	3	14.32
21	19	33.45	116	26	56.60

Latitude			Longitude		
Degrees	Minutes	Seconds	Degrees	Minutes	Seconds
21	6	31.80	116	49	3.85
20	51	1.98	117	9	15.71
20	33	18.54	117	27	13.91
20	13	38.02	117	42	42.58
19	52	18.65	117	55	28.44
19	29	40.04	118	5	20.93
19	6	2.86	118	12	12.33
18	41	48.51	118	15	57.78
18	17	18.78	118	16	35.25
17	58	12.50	118	14	53.39
17	40	26.03	118	11	47.35
17	20	8.74	118	6	6.48
17	0	31.92	117	58	16.66
16	38	46.91	117	46	33.19
16	18	33.10	117	32	13.03
16	0	8.02	117	15	29.30
15	43	47.58	116	56	37.02
15	29	45.88	116	35	52.81
15	18	14.95	116	13	34.74
15	9	24.68	115	50	2.08
15	3	22.62	115	25	35.00
15	0	13.94	115	0	34.37
15	0	13.94	114	31	45.63
15	2	53.84	114	9	27.60
15	4	43.83	113	59	7.74
15	10	4.68	113	38	12.72
15	18	54.95	113	11	39.98
15	30	25.87	112	52	21.84
15	40	44.82	112	36	37.60
15	39	13.50	112	23	32.69
15	31	55.44	112	4	24.57
15	25	29.14	111	40	1.48
15	21	55.56	111	15	1.82
15	21	17.74	110	49	46.84
15	23	36.22	110	24	37.99
15	28	49.03	109	59	56.64
15	36	51.71	109	36	3.84
15	47	37.40	109	13	19.99
16	0	56.87	108	52	4.67
16	16	38.70	108	32	36.32
16	34	29.38	108	15	12.06
16	54	13.54	108	0	7.40
17	17	34.21	107	46	36.57
17	4	30.82	107	34	39.55
16	47	52.62	107	15	57.94
16	37	5.11	107	0	58.31
16	28	2.78	106	48	19.82
16	15	26.58	106	26	33.64
16	6	25.72	106	6	1.88
15	57	5.00	105	56	44.62
15	41	3.56	105	37	35.35
15	27	22.70	105	16	36.67

Latitude			*Longitude*		
Degrees	*Minutes*	*Seconds*	*Degrees*	*Minutes*	*Seconds*
15	16	14.16	104	54	6.81
15	7	56.35	104	30	54.45
15	3	36.69	104	20	2.15
14	58	32.24	104	4	18.99
14	54	4.21	103	52	36.35
14	48	1.58	103	31	55.01
14	46	15.75	103	23	47.41
14	44	23.22	103	20	35.25
14	40	28.52	103	13	26.04
14	31	55.07	103	1	33.44
14	20	56.23	102	43	10.42
14	11	51.61	102	23	44.50
14	4	33.34	102	2	40.09
14	0	32.34	101	53	1.57
13	54	46.85	101	36	5.41
13	51	42.93	101	24	23.99
13	45	56.56	101	14	15.26
13	36	51.60	100	54	52.43
13	29	46.65	100	34	39.07
13	25	7.27	100	15	35.64
13	16	14.26	99	57	22.47
13	9	23.52	99	39	5.65
13	0	17.98	99	23	8.03
12	50	16.25	99	0	19.82
12	43	0.16	98	36	28.63
12	38	43.84	98	12	57.57
12	31	48.56	97	54	9.29
12	27	26.27	97	38	0.79
12	22	6.70	97	17	27.84
12	19	36.48	97	2	35.85
12	17	36.09	96	44	34.56
12	17	23.43	96	19	38.86
12	20	2.53	95	55	23.40
12	22	7.61	95	39	32.06
12	25	51.89	95	22	7.52
12	32	0.83	95	2	27.54
12	28	33.78	94	58	35.88
12	25	13.49	94	55	26.72
11	58	07.07	94	26	02.83
14	22	55.60	92	22	09.60
II. In the Gulf of Mexico and the Caribbean Sea:					
25	58	30.5	96	55	27.37
26	01	17.00	95	00	02.00
26	00	33.00	93	28	07.00
25	59	48.28	93	26	42.19
25	48	42.45	93	27	8.00
25	34	46.77	93	28	38.49
25	20	58.76	93	31	12.47
25	7	22.39	93	34	48.83
24	54	1.56	93	39	26.21
24	44	13.42	93	43	33.32

Latitude			*Longitude*		
Degrees	*Minutes*	*Seconds*	*Degrees*	*Minutes*	*Seconds*
24	40	12.09	93	45	26.32
24	47	8.55	93	36	12.94
24	55	20.24	93	23	46.83
25	2	42.20	93	10	43.43
25	9	12.13	92	57	6.70
25	14	48.00	92	43	0.81
25	19	28.05	92	28	30.10
25	23	10.81	92	13	39.10
25	25	55.10	91	58	32.46
25	27	40.07	91	43	14.91
25	28	4.18	91	37	18.11
25	33	15.47	91	27	5.36
25	39	18.77	91	13	10.50
25	42	13.05	91	5	24.89
25	42	45.	91	01	27.
25	46	39.	90	32	21.
25	46	52.00	90	29	41.00
25	46	49.0	90	28	30.0
25	46	41.0	90	24	36.0
25	43	40.	89	12	45.
25	41	56.52	88	23	5.54
25	37	25.05	88	11	13.42
25	31	8.29	87	57	28.07
25	23	58.96	87	44	13.20
25	15	59.30	87	31	34.83
25	7	11.79	87	19	36.76
25	0	6.39	87	11	6.80
24	56	35.25	87	7	13.67
24	56	36.86	87	4	10.00
24	56	34.98	87	0	19.71
24	56	29.35	86	56	29.50
24	56	28.83	86	56	16.69
23	30	31.50	86	24	14.70
23	26	54.30	86	22	33.80
22	45	32.80	86	06	55.00
22	18	55.80	86	00	35.20
21	41	31.50	85	52	43.40
21	36	00.10	85	51	18.20
21	35	20.90	85	51	9.30
20	49	36.40	85	32	23.10
20	17	46.70	85	7	24.25
20	04	37.10	84	57	56.30
19	39	16.60	84	42	46.50
19	32	25.80	84	38	30.66
19	14	50.04	84	59	51.64
19	8	16.39	85	7	30.07
18	23	32.25	85	26	24.32
18	9	43.80	85	31	56.68
18	0	12.92	85	48	43.53
17	47	5.41	86	8	48.53
17	49	59.80	86	28	45.30
17	55	24.41	87	26	5.26
18	3	31.32	87	39	22.00

Article 2

The Secretariat of the Navy shall publish the charts showing the outer limit of the Exclusive Economic Zone, plotted according to the co-ordinates set forth in the preceding article.

TRANSITIONAL PROVISIONS

First. This Decree shall enter into force on 31 July 1976.

Second. The Secretariat of the Navy and the Secretariat of Industry and Commerce shall take all necessary steps, within their respective spheres of competence, to enforce the provisions of the Act establishing regulations for the implementation of the eighth paragraph of article 27 of the Constitution as of the data on which this Decree enters into force.

40. Morocco

Decree No. 1-81-179.
Entered into force: April 8, 1981.
Source: *Bulletin Officiel No. 3575,* May 6, 1981. (Translated from French by the Department of State).

Decree No. 1-81-179 of 3 Jumada II 1401 (April 8, 1981) promulgating Law No. 1-81 establishing an exclusive economic zone extending 200 nautical miles off the Moroccan coasts.

(Great seal of His Majesty King Hassan II)

Know all men by these presents

This His Majesty,

Considering the Constitution, particularly Article 26 thereof,

Has resolved the following:

Article 1

Law No. 1-81 establishing an exclusive economic zone extending 200 nautical miles off the Moroccan coasts, passed by the Chamber of Representatives on 10 Safar 1401 (December 18, 1980), is hereby promulgated and reads as follows:

Law No. 1-81 establishing an exclusive economic zone extending 200 nautical miles off the Moroccan coast.

Article 1

A maritime zone designated an exclusive economic zone is hereby established beyond and adjacent to the territorial waters.

This zone shall extend a distance of 200 nautical miles calculated from the straight or normal baselines used to measure the breadth of the territorial sea.

Article 2

Within this zone the Moroccan State shall enjoy sovereign rights for purposes of exploration, exploitation, conservation, and management of the biological and non-biological natural resources of the sea-beds and subsoil, and their superjacent waters, and for other activities related to the exploration and exploitation of the zone for economic purposes, such as the production of energy from water, currents, and wind.

Article 3

The exercise of fishing rights within this zone shall be reserved exclusively for Moroccan-flag vessels or those operated by Moroccan natural or juristic persons in conformity with the terms and conditions and subject to the sanctions set forth in the decree concerning Law No. 1-73-255 of 27 Shawwal 1393 (November 23, 1973) regulating maritime fishery.

Article 4

Without prejudice to other rights recognized by international law, the Moroccan State shall have exclusive jurisdiction within this zone with respect to:

1. Emplacement and use of artificial islands, rigs, and devices;
2. Marine scientific research;
3. Protection of the marine environment.

Article 5

Any scientific or archeological research or exploration within the exclusive economic zone by a foreign state or by the nationals of a foreign state must be authorized in advance by the Moroccan government.

Article 6

1. The establishment of the exclusive economic zone shall not affect, beyond the outer limit of the territorial sea, freedom of navigation, overflight, the laying of undersea cables and pipelines, or other lawful international uses of the sea connected with these freedoms, such as the operation of vessels, aircraft, and undersea cables and pipelines;

2. Foreign states and their nationals exercising the freedoms referred to in paragraph 1 above must, in conformity with international law, consider the sovereign rights of the Moroccan State and respect its laws and regulations;

3. All foreign vessels exercising their freedom of navigation within this zone shall be prohibited from engaging in any fishing activities, including the stowage of fishing gear and devices, any research activities, or any acts of pollution or damage to the marine environment that may be detrimental to the resources of this zone or to the economic security of the Moroccan state.

Article 7

The Moroccan State shall exercise the necessary control over an area 24 nautical miles beyond and adjacent to the territorial sea, calculated from the straight or normal baselines used to measure the breadth of the territorial sea and designated the contiguous zone, in order to:

—Prevent violations of its customs, tax, health, and immigration laws within its territory or territorial sea;

—Sanction violations of these laws committed within its territory or territorial sea.

In order to prevent and sanction the violations referred to in paragraph 1 above, Article 25 of the Code of Customs and Indirect Taxes (under the Customs and Indirect Taxes Administration), ratified by Decree No. 1-77-339 of 25 Shawwal 1397 (October 9, 1977), is amended as follows:

'Article 25:

1. The customs area shall encompass a maritime zone and a land zone;

2. The maritime zone of the customs area shall correspond to the Moroccan territorial waters and the contiguous zone;

3. The land zone shall extend:' (remainder of text unchanged).

Article 8

The title of the Decree concerning Law No. 1-73-211 of 26 Muharram 1393 (March 2, 1973) is amended as follows:

'Decree concerning Law No. 1-73-211 of 26 Muharram 1393 (March 2, 1973) establishing the limit of the territorial waters.'

Articles 4, 5, and 6 of the aforementioned decree are hereby revoked.

Article 9

In the Decree concerning Law No. 1-73-255 of 27 Shawwal 1393 (November 23, 1973) regulating maritime fishing, the term 'exclusive economic zone' shall be substituted for the term 'exclusive fishing zone' in Articles 2, 36, and 37 et al.

Article 10

The provisions of Decree No. 1-58-227 of 4 Muharram 1378 (July 21, 1958) concerning a code on the prospection and mining of hydrocarbon deposits shall apply to the exploration and mining of the resources in the soil and subsoil of the exclusive economic zone.

Article 11

Without prejudice to geographic or geomorphic conditions under which, taking all relevant factors into consideration, delimitation must be carried out in accordance with the equitable principles established by international law under bilateral agreements between states, the outer limit of the exclusive economic zone shall not extend beyond a median line whose points are all equidistant from the closest points of the baselines of the Moroccan coasts and the coasts of foreign countries facing or bordering on the Moroccan coasts.

Article 12

The provisions of Article 3 of Decree No. 1-58-227 of 4 Muharram 1378 (July 21, 1958) concerning the code on prospecting and mining hydrocarbon deposits shall be supplemented by a paragraph 4 to read as follows:

'The provisions of paragraphs 2 and 3 above shall apply without prejudice to special geographic or geomorphic conditions under which, taking all relevant factors into consideration and in accordance with the equitable principles established by international law, the delimitation of sea areas shall be carried out under bilateral agreements between states.'

Article 13

The provisions of this law shall not obstruct the principles of international cooperation subscribed to by Morocco and implemented by agreements with other states, without prejudice to its sovereign rights and respecting its national interests.

In particular, in consideration of African solidarity, Morocco will uphold the principle of privileged cooperation concerning biological resources with landlocked neighboring countries under terms and conditions to be established by bilateral, regional, or subregional agreements.

Art. 2. This decree shall be published in the *Bulletin Officiel.*

Done at Marrakech, 3 Jumada II 1401 (April 8, 1981).

Maati Bouabid
Prime Minister

41. Mozambique

Decree Law No. 31/76.
Entered into force: August 19, 1976.
Source: Mozambique Ministry of Foreign Affairs (Translated from Portuguese by the U.S. Embassy, Maputo).

It has become imperative that the Peoples Republic of Mozambique should define its rights regarding the economic resources of the sea adjoining its coastline.

In doing so, therefore, the Peoples Republic of Mozambique, conscionus of its international responsibilities, and taking into account that the United Nations Conference on the Law of the Sea is presently meeting to draft an Agreement, has avoided taking a position on matters which may be considered controversial, or proceeding with excessive detailing of all aspects which it feels should be included in legislative consideration, thereby contributing to the creation of a favorable atmosphere for the establishment of an international understanding on matters pertaining to the law of the sea.

The Peoples Republic of Mozambique could not, however, avoid adopting, at this time a minimum of measures designed to safeguard the legitimate rights and interests of the Mozambican people, (thereby) defending its maritime areas from plunder and other abuses to which they have been subject.

Accordingly, in terms of the rulings of clause c) of Article 54 of the Constitution, the Council of Ministers hereby decrees:

Article 1

1. The extensions of the territorial sea of the Peoples Republic of Mozambique is 12 nautical miles from the base line.

2. The normal base line from which the extension of the territorial sea is measured is defined by the low-tide line along the coast as indicated in the maritime charts officially recognized for the purpose by the Peoples Republic of Mozambique.

3. The normal base line is supplemented by closing lines and straight base lines to be drawn by the Peoples Republic of Mozambique, in keeping with international law, between points along its coast line, which shall be defined in an Order to be jointly issued by the Ministers of Development and Economic Planning, and of Transportation and Communication.

Article 2

In the zone adjoining the territorial sea extending up to 200 nautical miles from the base line, the Peoples Republic of Mozambique has sovereign rights concerning prospecting, exploitation, conservation and management of the natural, biological and non-biological resources of the sea bed, of its subsoil, and of the overlying sea waters.

Article 3

1. Whenever there is no agreement to the contrary, and whenever there is found a superimposition of the boundaries established in the preceding articles with those established by States whose coasts are opposite those of the Peoples Republic of Mozambique, the boundaries established by the Peoples Republic of Mozambique shall not extend beyond the line equidistant from the points closest to the base lines from which the extension of the territorial sea and the exclusive economic zone of each of the two States is measured.

2. If the equidistant line referred to in the preceding article is situated within the limits of the territorial waters and the exclusive economic zone established by the States whose coast lines are opposite those of the Peoples Republic of Mozambique, the exclusive economic zone determined by the present legislation shall extend to that line.

Approved in the Council of Ministers.

Let it be published.

The President of the Republic, SAMORA MOISES MACHEL

42. New Zealand

Territorial Sea and Exclusive Economic Zone Act 1977.
Entered into force: April 1, 1978.
Source: *United Nations ST/LEG/SER.B/19,* pp. 65-85.

TERRITORIAL SEA AND EXCLUSIVE ECONOMIC ZONE ACT, 1977[1]

1. *Short title and commencement*—(1) This Act may be cited as the Territorial Sea and Exclusive Economic Zone Act 1977.

(2) Section 29 of this Act shall come into force on the passing of this Act.

(3) Except as provided in subsection (2) of this section, the provisions of this Act shall come into force on a date to be appointed by the Governor-General by Order in Council.

(4) For the purposes of subsection (3) of this section, one or more Orders in Council may be made

(a) Bringing different provisions of this Act into force on different dates; and

(b) Bringing provisions of this Act into force on different dates in respect of specified parts of New Zealand.

2. *Interpretation*—(1) In this Act, unless the context otherwise requires

'Bay' means an indentation of the coast such that its area is not less than that of the semi-circle whose diameter is a line drawn across the mouth of the indentation (for the purposes of which definition—

(a) The area of an indentation shall be taken to be the area bounded by low-water mark around the shore of the indentation and the straight line joining the low-water marks of its natural entrance points; and

(b) Where, because of the presence of islands, an indentation has more than one mouth, the length of the diameter of the semi-circle referred to shall be the sum of the lengths of the straight lines drawn across each of the mouths; and

(c) In calculating the area of an indentation, the area of any islands lying within it shall be treated as part of the area of the indentation):

'Exclusive economic zone' and 'zone' mean the exclusive economic zone of New Zealand described in section 9 of this Act;

'Fish' means every description of fish and shellfish and their young or fry or spawn, except sedentary species as described in paragraph (b) of the definition of the term 'natural resources' in section 2 of the Continental Shelf Act 1964;[1]

'Fishery' means one or more stocks of fish that can be treated as a unit for the purposes of conservation and management;

'Fishing' means—

(a) Taking any fish; or

(b) Engaging in any activity relating to the taking of any fish, including (*inter alia*) any activity involving the preparation, supply, storage, refrigeration, transportation, or processing of any fish; or

[1] Of 26 September 1977. Text provided by the Permanent Representative of New Zealand to the United Nations in a note verbale of 18 December 1978.

[1] Reproduced in ST/LEG/SER.B/15, p. 389.

(c) Engaging in any activity relating to the provision of any services to any fishing craft to enable or assist that craft to engage in fishing;

'Fishing craft' means any vessel, aircraft, hovercraft, submersible craft, or other craft, of whatever size, that is capable of being used for fishing;

'Foreign fishing craft' means any fishing craft that is not a New Zealand fishing craft;

'Highly migratory species' means species that, in the course of their life cycle, migrate over great distances of ocean;

'International agreement' means any bilateral or multilateral treaty, convention, or agreement, to which New Zealand is a party, and any understanding concluded by the Government of New Zealand and the government of any other country;

'Island' means a naturally formed area of land that is surrounded by and above water at mean high-water spring tides;

'Licence' means a licence issued under section 15 of this Act in respect of a foreign fishing craft; and 'licensed' has a corresponding meaning;

'Licensee' means the person to whom a licence is issued;

'Low-tide elevation' means a naturally formed area of land that is surrounded by and above water at mean low-water spring tides but is submerged at mean high-water spring tides;

'Master', in relation to a fishing craft, means the person for the time being having command or charge of the craft;

'Median line', as between New Zealand and any other country, means a line every point of which is equidistant from the nearest points of the baseline of the territorial sea of New Zealand and the corresponding baseline of that other country;

'Minister' means the Minister of Fisheries;

'Nautical mile' means the international nautical mile of 1,852 metres;

'New Zealand' (except for the purposes of Part II of this Act and section 29 of this Act) includes the Ross Dependency;

'New Zealand fisheries waters' has the same meaning as it has in section 2 (1) of the Fisheries Act 1908;

'New Zealand fishing craft' means a fishing craft—

(a) That is a New Zealand ship within the meaning of section 2 (1) of the Shipping and Seamen Act 1952; or

(b) That is an aircraft registered in New Zealand under the Civil Aviation Act 1964; or

(c) In which no person who is not a New Zealand citizen has any legal or equitable interest (except by way of security only for any advance made by him to the owner);

'New Zealand Government ship' has the same meaning as it has in section 2 (1) of the Shipping and Seamen Act 1952;

'Owner', in relation to a fishing craft, includes any body of persons, whether incorporated or not, by whom the craft is owned, and any charterer, sub-charterer, lessee, or sub-lessee of the craft;

'Prescribed' means prescribed by regulations made under this Act;

'Shellfish' includes every description of molluscs, crustaceans, and echinoderms found in New Zealand fisheries waters, and their young or spawn, but does not include oysters;

'Take' includes—

(a) To take, catch, kill, attract, or pursue by any means or device; and

(b) To attempt to do any act specified in paragraph (a) of this definition;

'Total allowable catch', with respect to the yield from any fishery, means the amount of fish that will produce from that fishery the maximum sustainable yield, as qualified by any relevant economic or environmental factors, fishing patterns, the interdependence of stocks of fish, and any generally recommended subregional, regional or global standards.

(2) For the purposes of this Act, permanent harbour works that form an integral part of a harbour system shall be treated as forming part of the coast.

Part I
The territorial sea of New Zealand

3. *The territorial sea*— The territorial sea of New Zealand comprises those areas of the sea having, as their inner limits, the baseline described in sections 5 and 6 of this Act and, as their outer limits, a line measured seaward from that baseline, every point of which line is distant 12 nautical miles from the nearest point of the baseline.

4. *Internal waters*— The internal waters of New Zealand include any areas of the sea that are on the landward side of the baseline of the territorial sea of New Zealand.

5. *Baseline of territorial sea*— (1) Except as otherwise provided in section 6 of this Act, the baseline from which the breadth of the territorial sea of New Zealand is measured shall be the low-water mark along the coast of New Zealand, including the coast of all islands.

(2) For the purposes of this section, a low-tide elevation that lies wholly or partly within the breadth of sea that would be territorial sea if all low-tide elevations were disregarded for the purpose of the measurement of the breadth of the territorial sea shall be treated as an island.

6. *Baseline of territorial sea adjacent to bay*— In the case of the sea adjacent to a bay, the baseline from which the breadth of the territorial sea is measured—

(a) Where the bay has only one mouth and the distance between the low-water marks of the natural entrance points of the bay does not exceed 24 nautical miles, shall be a straight line joining those low-water marks; and

(b) Where, because of the presence of islands, the bay has more than one mouth and the distances between the low-water marks of the natural entrance points of each mouth added together do not exceed 24 nautical miles, shall be a series of straight lines across each of the mouths so as to join those low-water marks; and

(c) Where neither paragraph (a) nor paragraph (b) of this section applies, shall be a straight line 24 nautical miles in length drawn from low-water mark to low-water mark within the bay in such a manner as to enclose the maximum area of water that is possible with a line of that length.

7. *Bed of territorial sea and internal waters vested in Crown*— Subject to the grant of any estate or interest therein (whether by or pursuant to the provisions of any enactment or otherwise, and whether made before or after the commencement of this Act), the sea-bed and subsoil of submarine areas bounded on the landward side by the low-water mark along the coast of New Zealand (including the coast of all islands) and on the seaward side by the outer limits of the territorial sea of New Zealand shall be deemed to be and always to have been vested in the Crown.

8. *Regulations in territorial sea*— Where no other provision is for the time being made by any other enactment for any such purposes, the Governor-General may from time to time, by Order in Council, make regulations for all or any of the following purposes:

(a) Regulating the conduct of scientific research within the territorial sea;

(b) Prescribing measures for the protection and preservation of the marine environment of the territorial sea;

(c) Regulating the construction, operation, and use of artificial islands (whether permanent or temporary), and other installations and structures in the territorial sea, including the establishment of safety zones around such islands, installations, and structures;

(d) Regulating the exploration and exploitation of the territorial sea for the production of energy from the water, currents, and winds, and for any other economic purposes;

(e) Providing for such other matters as are necessary or expedient for giving full effect to the sovereignty of New Zealand in relation to the territorial sea;

(f) Providing that a breach of any such regulations shall be a criminal offence, and imposing penalties by way of fine not exceeding $10,000 for any such offences;

(g) Providing for such other matters as are contemplated by or necessary for giving full effect to the provisions of this Part of this Act and for, its due administration.

Part II

The exclusive economic zone of New Zealand

9. *The exclusive economic zone*— (1) The exclusive economic zone of New Zealand comprises those areas of the sea, sea-bed, and subsoil that are beyond and adjacent to the territorial sea of New Zealand, having as their outer limits a line measured seaward from the baseline described in sections 5 and 6 of this Act, every point of which line is distant 200 nautical miles from the nearest point of the baseline.

(2) Notwithstanding subsection (1) of this section, where—

(a) Any part of the median line between New Zealand and any other country is less than 200 nautical miles from the nearest part of the baseline of the territorial sea of New Zealand; and

(b) No other outer limit of the exclusive economic zone is for the time being determined by an Order in Council made under subsection (3) or subsection (4) of this section—

that part of the median line shall be an outer limit of the zone.

(3) The Governor-General may from time to time, by Order in Council, declare that any specified provisions of this Part of this Act, and any other specified provisions in this Act relating to the exclusive economic zone, shall apply to the Ross Dependency, with such modifications and exceptions (if any) as he may specify in the order.

(4) For the purposes of implementing any international agreement, or the arbitral award of any international body, or the judgement of any international Court, or for any other purpose in accordance with international law, the Governor-General may from time to time, by Order in Council, declare that the exclusive economic zone shall not extend to any specified area of the sea, sea-bed, or subsoil, that would otherwise be included within the exclusive economic zone by virtue of this section.

10. *Seas in zone to be New Zealand fisheries waters*— (1) The seas comprised in the exclusive economic zone shall be part of New Zealand fisheries waters.

(2) The following enactments shall apply accordingly (subject to any provisions to the contrary in those enactments) within the exclusive economic zone:

(a) The Fisheries Act 1908 (except Part II of that Act);[1]

(b) The Whaling Industry Act 1935.[2]

11. *Calculation of total allowable catch*— The Minister shall from time to time determine, in respect of every fishery within the exclusive economic zone, the total allowable catch.

12. *Calculation of allowable catch by foreign fishing craft*— (1) The Minister shall from time to time determine, in respect of the total allowable catch for every fishery within the exclusive economic zone, the portion that New Zealand fishing craft have the capacity to harvest.

[1] Partially reproduced in ST/LEG/SER.B/6, p. 540; ST/LEG/SER.B/15, p. 649; and ST/LEG/SER.B/16, p. 309.

[2] Partially reproduced in ST/LEG/SER.B/6, p. 543.

(2) Where the Minister has determined, in respect of the total allowable catch for a fishery within the exclusive economic zone, the portion that New Zealand fishing craft have the capacity to harvest, the remaining portion shall constitute the allowable catch for that fishery for foreign fishing craft.

13. *Apportionment of allowable catch for foreign fishing craft*— (1) The Minister may from time to time apportion, among countries other than New Zealand, the allowable catch for foreign fishing craft in respect of any fishery within the exclusive economic zone, as determined under section 12 of this Act.

(2) In making an apportionment under subsection (1) of this section, the Minister may take into account (*inter alia*) the following considerations:

(*a*) Whether the fishing craft of countries to which the apportionment applies have engaged habitually in fishing within the exclusive economic zone;

(*b*) Whether such countries have co-operated with New Zealand in fisheries research and in the identification of fish stocks within the zone;

(*c*) Whether such countries have co-operated with New Zealand in the conservation and management of fisheries resources within the zone, and in the enforcement of New Zealand law relating to such resources;

(*d*) The terms of any relevant international agreement;

(*e*) Such other matters as the Minister, after consultation with the Minister of Foreign Affairs, determines to be relevant.

14. *Prohibition of operation of unauthorised foreign fishing craft in zone*— No foreign fishing craft shall be used for fishing within the exclusive economic zone except in accordance with a licence issued by the Minister under section 15 of this Act in respect of that fishing craft.

15. *Grant of licences*— (1) Subject to subsection (2) of this section, the Minister may grant and issue to the owner of any named foreign fishing craft a licence to fish within the exclusive economic zone.

(2) The Minister shall exercise the powers conferred on him by this section in such a manner as to ensure that—

(*a*) The catch that all foreign fishing craft licensed under this section are for the time being authorised to harvest from any fishery within the exclusive economic zone does not exceed the allowable catch for foreign fishing craft for that fishery as determined under section 12 of this Act; and

(*b*) The catch that all foreign fishing craft of a particular country licensed under this section are for the time being authorised to harvest from any fishery within the zone does not exceed the apportionment made under section 13 of this Act for that fishery in respect of that country.

(3) In granting a licence under this section, the Minister may attach to the licence conditions relating (*inter alia*) to all or any of the following matters;

(*a*) The areas within the exclusive economic zone in which fishing is authorised; and

(*b*) The seasons, times, and particular voyages during which fishing is authorised;

(*c*) The species, size, age, and quantities of fish that may be taken;

(*d*) The methods by which fish may be taken;

(*e*) The types, size, and amount of fishing gear that may be used or carried by a foreign fishing craft, and the modes of storage of that gear when not in use;

(*f*) The use, transfer, transhipment, landing, and processing of fish taken;

(*g*) Entry by the foreign fishing craft to New Zealand ports, whether for the inspection of its catch or for other purposes;

(*h*) The compensation payable to New Zealand citizens or to the Crown in the event of any loss or damage caused by the foreign fishing craft to other fishing craft, or their gear or catch, or to fish stocks, or to pipelines or cables, or to other New Zealand interests;

(i) Statistical and other information required to be given by the foreign fishing craft to the Ministry of Agriculture and Fisheries, including statistics relating to catch and effort and reports as to the positions of the craft;

(j) The conduct by the foreign fishing craft of specified programmes of fisheries research;

(k) The training of New Zealand personnel in the methods of fishing employed by the foreign fishing craft and the transfer to New Zealand of technology relating to fisheries;

(l) The display on board the foreign fishing craft of the licence issued in respect of it;

(m) The marking of the foreign fishing craft, and other means for its identification;

(n) Directions, instructions, and other requirements given or made by vessels or aircraft of the New Zealand Armed Forces or other New Zealand Government ships or aircraft to the foreign fishing craft that shall be complied with by the craft;

(o) The placing of New Zealand observes on the foreign fishing craft and the reimbursement to the Ministry of Agriculture and Fisheries by the licensee of the costs of doing so;

(p) The installation on the foreign fishing craft and maintenance in working order of a transponder or other equipment for the identification and location of the craft, and of adequate navigational equipment to enable its position to be fixed from the craft;

(q) The carriage on board the foreign fishing craft of specified nautical charts, nautical publications, and nautical instruments;

(r) Such other matters as the Minister considers necessary or expedient for the conservation or management of fisheries resources within the zone.

16. *Renewal of licences*— Subject to section 15 (2) of this Act, the Minister may from time to time renew any licence granted under section 15 of this Act.

17. *Variation of licenses*— (1) Subject to section 15 (2) of this Act, the Minister may from time to time, where he is satisfied that it is necessary or expedient for the proper regulation of fishing within the exclusive economic zone to do so, vary the terms and conditions of any licence or licences, or class or classes of licence, granted under section 15 of this Act.

(2) Notice of every variation of any licence under this section shall be given as soon as practicable to the licensee.

18. *Licensing fees*— There shall be payable by every licensee to the Crown in respect of the granting of a licence under section 15 of this Act, or the renewal of a licence under section 16 of this Act, such fee as may from time to time be prescribed.

19. *Licensing offences*— (1) Where any foreign fishing craft that is not licensed under section 15 of this Act is used for fishing in the exclusive economic zone, each of them, the owner, the master and every crew member of the craft, commits an offence against this Act.

(2) Where any foreign fishing craft that is not licensed under section 15 of this Act displays within New Zealand fisheries waters any marking or other means of identification that indicates that it is licensed under that section, each of them, the owner, the master and every crew member of the craft, commits an offence against this Act.

(3) Where any foreign fishing craft is used for fishing within the exclusive economic zone in contravention of any condition of a licence issued in respect of it under section 15 of this Act, each of them, the licensee, the master and every crew member of the craft, commits an offence against this Act.

(4) Every owner or master of a foreign fishing craft who commits an offence specified in subsection (1) or subsection (2) of this section is liable on summary conviction to a fine not exceeding $100,000.

(5) Every crew member of a foreign fishing craft who commits an offence specified in subsection (1) or

subsection (2) of this section is liable on summary conviction to a fine not exceeding $5,000.

(6) Every licensee or master of a foreign fishing craft who commits an offence specified in subsection (3) of this section is liable on summary conviction to a fine not exceeding $25,000.

(7) Every crew member of a foreign fishing craft who commits an offence specified in subsection (3) of this section is liable on summary conviction to a fine not exceeding $1,500.

(8) In this section, 'crew member' does not include a licensee, owner, or master of a foreign fishing craft, or any New Zealand personnel or New Zealand observer on the craft pursuant to a condition attached to a licence under section 15 (3) of this Act.

20. *Suspension and cancellation of licences*— (1) Where the Minister is satisfied that—

(a) Any foreign fishing craft in respect of which a licence has been granted under section 15 of this Act is being or has been used for fishing within the exclusive economic zone in contravention of any condition of the licence or of any New Zealand law that applies to fishing within the zone; or

(b) Any licensee, master, or crew member of a foreign fishing craft has been convicted of an offence against this Act, or against any regulations made under section 22 of this Act, or against any other New Zealand law relating to fishing within the zone; or

(c) Any licensee, master, or crew member of a foreign fishing craft has failed to pay to the Crown, within the time limit specified in section 26 (8) of this Act, the amount of any penalty imposed on him under that section by the Minister—

he may suspend the licence of the craft for such period as he shall specify, or cancel the licence.

(2) Where, the Minister, after consultation with the Minister of Foreign Affairs, determines that it is necessary or expedient for the proper regulation of fishing within the exclusive economic zone to do so, he may suspend any licence or licences or class or classes of licence for such period as he shall specify, or cancel any licence or licences or class or classes of licence.

(3) While a licence is suspended under this section, it shall have no effect.

21. *Review by Courts*— No exercise by the Minister of any power conferred on him by section 17 or section 20 (2) of this Act shall be liable to be challenged, reviewed, quashed, or called into question in any Court on the ground that the conditions for the exercise of the power by him had not arisen or had ceased.

22. *Fisheries regulations*— (1) The Governor-General may from time to time, by Order in Council, make regulations for all or any of the following purposes:

(a) Prescribing the manner of applying for licences under section 15 of this Act, and for the renewal of such licences under section 16 of this Act, and forms of applications;

(b) Prescribing the terms of duration of licences;

(c) Prescribing the forms of licences to be issued by the Minister;

(d) Prescribing the fees payable to the Crown for the issue of licences and for their renewal;

(e) Providing for the production of licences by licensees to specified New Zealand authorities when required to do so, and the inspection of licences by such authorities;

(f) Requiring applicants for licences, and licensees, to designate authorised agents in New Zealand in respect of foreign fishing craft;

(g) Providing for such other measures as are necessary or expedient to ensure that foreign fishing craft are used for fishing within the exclusive economic zone only in accordance with the terms and conditions of their licences;

(h) Prescribing conditions, not inconsistent with this Act, under which fishing may be undertaken within the zone by foreign fishing craft;

(i) Prescribing measures, not inconsistent with this Act, for the conservation and management of fisheries resources within the zone;

(j) Specifying particular types of high migratory species of fish, and regulating, in a manner not inconsistent with this Act, fishing for those species within the zone, and also, in the case of New Zealand fishing craft, beyond the zone;

(k) Providing that a breach of any such regulation shall be a criminal offence, and imposing penalties by way of fine not exceeding, in the case of a licensee, owner or master of a fishing craft, $ 10,000 for any such offences and, in the case of any other crew member, $ 1,000 for any such offences;

(l) Prescribing the form of bonds for the purposes of section 25 of this Act;

(m) Prescribing forms of notices and procedures to be followed for the purposes of section 26 of this Act;

(n) Providing, in respect of notices, summonses, and other documents to be served under this Act or in any civil or criminal proceedings under this Act, that specified methods of service (including service on the authorised agent of a foreign fishing craft or on the diplomatic or consular representative in respect of New Zealand of the country in which the craft is registered) shall be deemed to be service on any licensee, owner, master, or crew member of the craft, and providing that specified methods of proof of service shall be deemed to be sufficient proof of service.

(2) Regulations made under this section may make different provisions for different parts of the exclusive economic zone and for different species of fish.

(3) In prescribing fees in regulations made under this section, the Governor-General in Council may—

(a) Take into account (inter alia) the cost of implementing the provisions of this Act and of the Fisheries Act 1908[1] with respect to fishing by foreign fishing craft within the exclusive economic zone, including the cost of the conservation and management of fisheries resources, and of fisheries research, and of the administration and enforcement of such enactments; and

(b) Prescribe different fees for different classes of foreign fishing craft (whether by reference to size, catch, method of fishing, function, or otherwise).

23. *Fishing for research, experimental, and sporting purposes*— Notwithstanding section 14 or section 19 of this Act, a foreign fishing craft may be used for fishing within the exclusive economic zone for the purpose of fisheries research or of experimentation or sport, subject always to the prior consent in writing of the Minister to such activity and in accordance with such conditions (if any) as the Minister may impose in giving his consent.

24. *Apprehension of offenders*— (1) Any officer specified in subsection (16) of this section may at any time stop, board, inspect, and search any foreign fishing craft in New Zealand fisheries waters, and inspect any fish on board the craft; and where he has reasonable cause to believe that an offence against this Act, or against regulations made under section 22 of this Act, or against any other New Zealand law, relating to fishing within the exclusive economic zone, has been committed in respect of any foreign fishing craft he may—

(a) Seize and detain all fish on board the craft; and

(b) Apprehend any person whom he has reasonable cause to believe has committed any offence specified in this subsection; and

(c) If he has reasonable cause to believe that any such offence has been committed by the licensee, owner, or master of the craft, seize and detain the craft.

(2) Any officer specified in subsection (16) of this section may exercise the powers conferred on him by subsection (1) of this section with the aid of such assistants as he considers to be necessary for the purpose.

(3) Where any foreign fishing craft is detained under subsection (1) of this section, it shall be held in the custody of the Crown until—

[1] Partially reproduced in ST/LEG/SER.B/6, p. 540; ST/LEG/SER.B/15, p. 649; and ST/LEG/SER.B/16, p. 309.

(a) A decision is made not to lay any information or charge in respect of the alleged offence for which the craft was detained; or

(b) Where such an information or charge is laid, the security required by section 25 of this Act is given in respect of the craft.

(4) The decision whether or not to lay an information or charge in respect of an alleged offence for which a foreign fishing craft is detained under subsection (1) of this section shall be made as soon as reasonably practicable after the craft is detained.

(5) The release of a foreign fishing craft from detention shall not affect any subsequent forfeiture of the craft in respect of the conviction of any person for an offence.

(6) On the conviction of any licensee, owner, or master of a foreign fishing craft for any offence specified in subsection (1) of this section, the craft shall be forfeited to the Crown, and shall be disposed of in such manner as the Minister shall order, in addition to any fine that may be imposed by any Court on the convicted person.

(7) Where any fish is detained under subsection (1) of this section, it shall be held in the custody of the Crown (either on board the foreign fishing craft from which it was seized or in such other place as the Minister may direct) until—

(a) A decision is made not to lay any information or charge in respect of the alleged offence for which the fish was detained; or

(b) Where such an information or charge is laid, any security required by section 25 of this Act is given in respect of the fish.

(8) The release of any fish from detention shall not affect any subsequent forfeiture of the fish on the conviction of any person for an offence.

(9) The Crown shall not be liable to any person for any deterioration in the quality of any fish detained under subsection (1) of this section, whether such deterioration is caused by the negligence of the Crown or otherwise.

(10) On the conviction of any person for any offence specified in subsection (1) of this section in respect of any fish detained under that subsection, the fish shall be forfeited to the Crown and shall be disposed of in such manner as the Minister shall order, in addition to any fine that may be imposed by any Court on the convicted person.

(11) Where any officer specified in subsection (16) of this section apprehends any person under subsection (1) of this section, the officer shall cause the person to be taken as soon as reasonably practicable before a Court to be dealt with in accordance with law.

(12) Where any foreign fishing craft or fish is held in the custody of the Crown under this section, then on the conviction of any person for any offence specified in subsection (1) of this section in respect of the craft or fish, as the case may be, the costs of the Crown in holding it in custody under this section shall be a debt due to the Crown jointly and severally by each of them the licensee, the owner, and the master of the craft, and shall be recoverable accordingly by the Crown in any Court of competent jurisdiction.

(13) Without limiting any other manner of recovering any debt due to the Crown under subsection (12) of this section, on the conviction of the licensee, owner, or master of any foreign fishing craft for any offence referred to in that subsection, the Court by which he is convicted may make an order that he shall pay to the Crown any costs for which he is liable under that subsection.

(14) Subject to subsection (9) of this section, but notwithstanding any other provision in this section, where any foreign fishing craft or fish has been detained under subsection (1) of this section, then on the acquittal of every person who is charged with any offence for which the craft or fish, as the case may be, is subject to forfeiture under this section, the craft or fish, as the case may require, shall forthwith be released from the custody of the Crown.

(15) Any person who in any way prevents or hinders any officer specified in subsection (16) of this

section, or any assistant of the officer, in exercising the powers conferred by this section commits an offence against this Act, and is liable on summary conviction to a fine not exceeding $10,000.

(16) Subsection (1) of this section refers to any of the following officers:

(a) The officer in command of any vessel or aircraft of the New Zealand Armed Forces;

(b) Any Inspector of Sea Fishing appointed in accordance with section 4 of the Fisheries Act 1908;

(c) Any constable;

(d) The master of any New Zealand Government ship.

(17) In this section, 'foreign fishing craft' includes all equipment on board or used by the craft.

25. *Security for release of foreign fishing craft*— (1) Where any foreign fishing craft is detained under section 24 of this Act, and an information or charge is laid against the licensee, owner, or master of the craft in respect of the offence for which the craft has been detained, the licensee, owner, or master of the craft may at any time before the determination of the information or charge apply to the Court by which the information or charge will be determined for the release of the craft on the provision of security in accordance with this section.

(2) On hearing the application, the Court shall order the release of the foreign fishing craft on the execution by any suitable person or persons approved by the Court for the purpose, of a bond in favour of Her Majesty the Queen, in the prescribed form and conditioned in accordance with subsection (4) of this section, in an amount not less than the aggregate of the value of the craft, the costs that the Crown may recover under section 24 (12) of this Act if the defendant is convicted of the offence, and the maximum fine to which the defendant will be liable if he is convicted of the offence.

(3) Notwithstanding subsection (2) of this section, the Court may, where it is satisfied that are special circumstances to justify it in doing so, order that the bond shall be in a specified amount that is less than the amount required by that subsection.

(4) The condition of the bond shall be that if—

(a) The defendant is formed not guilty of the information or charge; or

(b) The defendant on being convicted of the information or charge pays in full within 14 days after he is convicted the amount of the fine imposed by the Court, and the amount of all costs due by him to the Crown under section 24 (12) of this Act, and the foreign fishing craft is within that time surrendered to the Crown for forfeiture—

then the bond shall be of no effect, but that otherwise the bond shall remain in full force and effect.

(5) The amount specified in the bond shall be recoverable in full, in any Court of competent jurisdiction, as a debt due to Her Majesty the Queen jointly and severally by the person or persons by whom the bond is given, unless the person or persons prove the due performance of the condition on which the bond is defeasible.

(6) In this section, 'foreign fishing craft' includes all equipment on board or used by the craft, and also includes all fish that has been seized from the craft under section 24 (1) of this Act and is detained on board the craft in the custody of the Crown under that section.

26. *Administrative penalties for minor fisheries offences*—

(1) Where the Minister has reasonable cause to believe that—

(a) An offence against this Act, or against regulations made under section 22 of this Act, or against any other New Zealand law, relating to fishing within the exclusive economic zone, may have been committed by any person in respect of any foreign fishing craft; and

(b) Having regard to all the circumstances relating to the alleged offence it is of a minor nature, and having regard to the previous conduct of the craft and of the person concerned in New Zealand fisheries waters, it would be appropriate to impose a penalty under this section—

he may cause a notice in writing in accordance with subsection (2) of this section, and otherwise in the prescribed form, to be served on that person.

(2) A notice under subsection (1) of this section shall specify—

(a) The date and nature of the offence;

(b) A summary of the facts on which the allegation that an offence has been committed is based (being a sufficient summary to fully and fairly inform the person of the allegation against him); and

(c) Any other matters (not being previous convictions) that the Minister considers relevant to the imposition of a penalty—

and shall be endorsed with a statement setting out the provisions of this section.

(3) Any person on whom a notice under subsection (1) of this section is served may, within 28 days after the notice is served on him, by a notice in writing in the prescribed form served on the Director-General of Agriculture and Fisheries require that any proceedings in respect of the alleged offence shall be dealt with before a Court, in which case the following provisions shall apply:

(a) No further proceedings shall be taken under this section by the Minister;

(b) Nothing in this section shall be construed to prevent the subsequent laying of any information or charge in respect of the alleged offence, or the conviction of the person of the offence by a Court, or the imposition of any penalty under any enactment or forfeiture under this Act on such a conviction.

(4) Any person on whom a notice under subsection (1) of this section is served, who does not require that any proceedings in respect of the alleged offence shall be dealt with before a Court, may by notice in writing served on the Director-General of Agriculture and Fisheries—

(a) Admit the offence; and

(b) In any case make submissions to the Minister as to the matters he wishes the Minister to take into account in imposing any penalty under this section.

(5) Where a person on whom a notice under subsection (1) of this section is served does not, within 28 days after the notice is served on him,—

(a) Require that any proceedings in respect of the alleged offence shall be dealt with before a Court; or

(b) Admit the offence—

he shall on the expiration of that period be deemed to have admitted the offence.

(6) Where under this section a person admits or is deemed to have admitted an offence, the Minister may, after taking into account any submissions made by that person under subsection (4) of this section, impose a monetary penalty on the person in respect of the offence, not exceeding one-third of the maximum monetary penalty to which the person would be liable if he were convicted of the offence by a Court.

(7) Where the Minister imposes a penalty on a person under this section in respect of an offence, the Minister shall cause a notice in writing in the prescribed form of the particulars of the penalty to be served on the person.

(8) A person on whom a penalty is imposed under this section shall pay the amount of the penalty to the Crown within 28 days after the notice of the penalty is served on him in accordance with subsection (7) of this section.

(9) Without prejudice to the requirements of subsection (8) of this section, or to section 20 (1) of this Act, a penalty that has been imposed under this section shall be recoverable by the Crown, from the person on whom it has been imposed, in the same manner as a fine is recoverable on summary conviction for any offence.

(10) Notwithstanding the provisions of sections 19, 22, 24, and 25 of this Act, or of any other enactment, where any offence has been admitted under this section, no information or charge may be laid in respect of

the offence against the person by whom it is admitted.

(11) Nothing in this section shall apply—

(a) In respect of any offence or alleged offence under subsection (1) or subsection (2) of section 19 of this Act; or

(b) In respect of any offence or alleged offence in respect of which any information or charge has been laid.

27. *General regulations in zone*— Where no other provision is for the time being made by any other enactment for any such purposes, the Governor-General may from time to time, by Order in Council, make regulations for all or any of the following purposes:

(a) Regulating the conduct of scientific research within the exclusive economic zone;

(b) Prescribing measures for the protection and preservation of the marine environment of the zone;

(c) Regulating the construction, operation, and use of artificial islands (whether permanent or temporary), and other installations and structures within the zone, including the establishment of safety zones around such islands, installations, and structures;

(d) Regulating the exploration and exploitation of the zone for the production of energy from the water, currents, and winds, and for any other economic purposes;

(e) Providing for such other matters as are necessary or expedient for giving full effect to the sovereign rights of New Zealand in relation to the zone;

(f) Providing that a breach of any such regulations shall be a criminal offence, and imposing penalties by way of fine not exceeding $10,000 for any such offences;

(g) Providing for such other matters as are contemplated by or necessary for giving full effect to the provisions of this Part of this Act (other than matters for which regulations may be made under section 22 of this Act) and for its due administration.

28. *General provisions as to offences in zone*— (1) Any offence against this Act, or against any regulations made under this Act, that is committed within the exclusive economic zone shall be deemed to have been committed in New Zealand.

(2) Where any licensee, owner, master, or crew member of a foreign fishing craft is charged with any offence specified in section 19 of this Act or in any regulations made under section 22 of this Act, in respect of any activity described in paragraph (b) or paragraph (c) of the definition of the term 'fishing' in section 2 (1) of this Act, it shall be a defence to the charge if the defendant proves that such activity related only to fish taken beyond the outer limits of the exclusive economic zone.

(3) Where any power of apprehension of any person, or of stopping, boarding, or searching any fishing craft, or of inspecting, seizing, or detaining any fishing craft or fish, is conferred on any person under this Part of this Act, that power may be exercised with or without a warrant.

Part III

Miscellaneous Provisions

29. *Interim and transitional measures*— (1) Pending the coming into force of Part II of this Act, the Governor-General may from time to time, by Order in Council, make regulations prescribing interim or transitional measures for the conservation and management of fisheries resources beyond the territorial sea of New Zealand but within 200 nautical miles of the baseline described in sections 5 and 6 of this Act, and for the limitation of fishing by foreign fishing craft in any areas to which those measures relate.

(2) Regulations made under this section may provide that a breach of any such regulations shall be a criminal offence, and may impose penalties by way of fine not exceeding $100,000 for any such offences, and may declare that any such offences shall be deemed to have been committed within New Zealand.

(3) Regulations made under this section may provide that the provisions of sections 24, 25, and 26 of this Act shall apply in respect of offences committed against such regulations.

30. *Modifications to give effect to international agreement*— The Governor-General may, from time to time, by Order in Council, limit any provision of this Act relating to the exclusive economic zone so far as it is necessary to do so to give full effect to any convention that is adopted by the Third United Nations Conference on the Law of the Sea.

31. *Official charts*— (1) For the purposes of this Act, in any proceedings in any Court the line of low water for any area depicted on the charts held in the Territorial Limits Chart Folio held by the Royal New Zealand Navy Hydrographic Office shall be sufficient evidence of the line of the low-water mark for that area.

(2) For the purposes of this Act, in any proceedings in any Court, a certificate purporting to be signed by an officer of the New Zealand Naval Forces authorized by the Secretary of Defence or the Deputy Secretary of Defence that any specified chart is a chart referred to in subsection (1) of this section shall be admissible as evidence of the matters stated in the certificate.

(3) Every person signing any such certificate shall, in the absence of proof to the contrary, be presumed to be duly authorised to sign it.

32. *Onus of proof in respect of offences*— In any criminal proceedings under this Act where a defendant is charged with having committed an offence specified in section 19 of this Act, or with having contravened any other provision in any regulations made under this Act under which a licence or permit, or the consent of any person is required for the doing of any act, the onus shall be on the defendant to prove that at the time to which the charge relates, the requisite licence, permit, or consent was duly held.

33. *Amendments, repeal, and savings*— (1) The enactments specified in the Schedule to this Act are hereby amended in the manner indicated in that Schedule.

(2) Unless in any case the context otherwise requires, every reference in any other enactment or in any regulation, rule, order, agreement, deed, instrument, application, notice, licence, or other document whatsoever, in force at the commencement of this section,—

(a) To the territorial sea of New Zealand as defined by section 3 of the Territorial Sea and Fishing Zone Act 1965,[1] or to the fishing zone of New Zealand established by section 8 of that Act, shall hereafter be read as a reference to the territorial sea of New Zealand as defined by section 3 of this Act:

(b) To the internal waters of New Zealand as defined by section 4 of that Act, shall hereafter be read as a reference to the internal waters of New Zealand as defined by section 4 of this Act.

(3) The Territorial Sea and Fishing Zone Act 1965 is hereby repealed.[1]

(4) Except as expressly provided by this Act, the provisions of this Act are in addition to and not in substitution for the provisions of every other enactment, and accordingly nothing in this Act shall limit or derogate from the provisions of any other enactment.

Schedule

Enactments Amended

Enactment Amended 1908, No. 65 — The Fisheries Act 1908 (Reprinted 1966, Vol. 3, p. 2321)[1]

By inserting after section 1, but before the heading 'Part I — Sea Fisheries', the following section:

[1] Reproduced in ST/LEG/SER.B/15, p. 102.

[1] Partially reproduced in ST/LEG/SER.B/6, p. 540; ST/LEG/SER.B/15, p. 649; and ST/LEG/SER.B/16, p. 309.

1A. *Application of Act to exclusive economic zone*— (1) Nothing in this Act shall be construed—

(a) To require the licensing or registration or obtaining of a permit or of any consent by a foreign fishing craft for the purpose of fishing within the exclusive economic zone of New Zealand; or

(b) To authorise the making of any regulations in derogation of the provisions of the Territorial Sea and Exclusive Economic Zone Act 1977, or of any regulations made under that Act, relating to fishing within the exclusive economic zone; or

(c) To authorise the boarding, search, seizure, taking of possession, detention, or forfeiture under this Act of any such foreign fishing craft, or of any equipment or fish on board the craft, or the arrest of any crew member of such craft, in respect of any offence relating to fishing within the exclusive economic zone; or

(d) To authorise the imposition of a term of imprisonment on any crew member of any such foreign fishing craft in respect of any such offence.

(2) Nothing in Part III of this Act or in section 12A of the Fisheries Amendment Act 1963 shall apply to fishing by foreign fishing craft within the exclusive economic zone.

(3) Where, but for the provisions of subsection (1) of this section, a person would be liable to suffer imprisonment for the commission of any-offence, he shall instead of such imprisonment be liable on summary conviction to a fine not exceeding in the case of any licensee, owner, or master of the foreign fishing craft $ 10,000, and not exceeding in the case of any other crew member of the foreign fishing craft $ 1,000.

(4) Any offence against this Act that is committed within the exclusive economic zone of New Zealand shall be deemed to have been committed in New Zealand.

(5) In this section, the terms 'exclusive economic zone', 'fish', 'fishing', and 'foreign fishing craft' have the meanings assigned to them by section 2 (1) of the Territorial Sea and Exclusive Economic Zone Act 1977.'

By omitting the definition of the term 'New Zealand fisheries waters' in section 2 (1) (as inserted by section 11 of the Territorial Sea and Fishing Zone Act 1965), and substituting the following definition; 'New Zealand fisheries waters' means—

(a) All waters in the exclusive economic zone of New Zealand (as described in section 9 of the Territorial Sea and Exclusive Economic Zone Act 1977);

(b) All waters of the territorial sea of New Zealand (as defined by section 3 of that Act);

(c) All internal waters of New Zealand (as defined by section 4 of that Act); and

(d) The waters of every lake, river and stream where fish indigenous to New Zealand are found'.

By repealing section 67 (1) (as inserted by section 11 of the Territorial Sea and Fishing Zone Act 1965).

1950, No. 34 — The Harbours Act 1950[1] (Reprinted 1966, Vol. 3, p. 2395)

By omitting from section 2 (2) (as inserted by section 11 of the Territorial Sea and Fishing Zone Act 1965) the words 'Fishing Zone Act 1965', and substituting the words 'Exclusive Economic Zone Act 1977'.

1961, No. 43 — The Crimes Act 1961[2]

By omitting from the definition of the term 'New Zealand' in section 2 (1) (as inserted by section 11 of the Territorial Sea and Fishing Zone Act 1965) the words 'and Fishing Zone Act 1965', and substituting the words 'and Exclusive Economic Zone Act 1977'.

[1] Section 2 (2) reproduced in ST/LEG/SER.B/15, p. 168.

[2] Section 2 (1) reproduced in ST/LEG/SER.B/15, p. 498.

1964, No. 28 — The Continental Shelf Act 1964[3]

By omitting from section 2 the definition of the term 'continental shelf', and substituting the following definition:

'Continental shelf' means the seabed and subsoil of those submarine areas that extend beyond the territorial limits of New Zealand, throughout the natural prolongation of the land territory of New Zealand, to the outer edge of the continental margin, or to a distance of 200 nautical miles from the baselines from which the breadth of the territorial sea is measured (as described in sections 5 and 6 of the Territorial Sea and Exclusive Economic Zone Act 1977) where the outer edge of the continental margin does not extend to that distance.'

By inserting in section 2, after the definition of the term 'continental shelf', the following definition:

'Mineral includes coal.'

By renumbering section 2 as subsection (1) of that section, and adding the following subsection:

(2) For the purposes of implementing any international agreement, or for any other purpose in accordance with international law, the Governor-General may from time to time, by Order in Council, delineate the actual boundaries of the continental shelf.'

1966, No. 5 — The Submarine Cables and Pipelines Protection Act 1966[1]

By omitting from the definition of the term 'low-water mark', in section 2, the words 'Fishing Zone Act 1965', and substituting the words 'Exclusive Economic Zone Act 1977'.

By omitting from section 7 (2) the words 'fishing zone of New Zealand', and substituting the words 'exclusive economic zone of New Zealand (as described in section 9 of the Territorial Sea and Exclusive Economic Zone Act 1977)'.

[3] Reproduced in ST/LEG/SER.B/15, p. 389.

43. New Zealand dependencies

A. Cook Islands
Act No. 16.
Entered into force: November 14, 1977
Source: *Government Printing,* Government of the Cook Islands-1977

1977 Territorial Sea and Exclusive Economic Zone No. 16

An Act to make provision with respect to the territorial sea of the Cook Islands; and to establish an exclusive economic zone of the Cook Islands adjacent to the territorial sea, and in the exercise of the sovereign rights of the Cook Islands to make provision for the exploration and exploitation and conservation and management, of the resources of the zone and for matters connected with those purposes

(14 November 1977)

ANALYSIS

PART II

BE IT ENACTED by the Legislative Assembly of the Cook Islands in Session assembled, and by the authority of the same, as follows—

1. *Short Title and commencement*

(1) This Act may be cited as the Territorial Sea and Exclusive Economic Zone Act 1977.

(2) Section 25 of this Act shall come into force on the passing of this Act.

(3) Except as provided in subsection (2) of this section, the provisions of this Act shall come into force on a date to be appointed by the High Commissioner by Order in Executive Council.

(4) For the purposes of subsection (3) of this section, one or more Orders in Executive Council may be made—

(a) Bringing different provisions of this Act into force on different dates; and
(b) Bringing provisions of this Act into force on different dates in respect of specified parts of the Cook Islands.

2. *Interpretation*

(1) In this Act, unless the context otherwise requires,—

'Cook Islands fishing craft' means any fishing vessel based in and operating from the Cook Islands:

'Exclusive economic zone' and 'zone' mean the exclusive economic zone of the Cook Islands described in section 8 of this Act:

'Fish' means every description of fish and shellfish and their young or fry or spawn, except sedentary species as described in paragraph (b) of the term 'natural resources' in section 2 of the Continental Shelf Act 1964 of the New Zealand Parliament as applied to the Cook Islands:

'Fishery' means one or more stocks of fish that can be treated as a unit for the purposes of conservation and management:

'Fishing' means—

(a) Taking any fish; or
(b) Engaging in any activity relating to the taking of any fish, including (inter alia) any activity involving the preparation, supply, storage, refrigeration, transportation, or processing of any fish:

'Fishing craft' means any vessel, aircraft, hovercraft, or other craft, or whatever size and however propelled, that is capable of being used for fishing:

'Foreign fishing craft' means any fishing craft that is not a Cook Islands fishing craft:

'Highly migratory species' means species that, in the course of their life cycle, migrate over great distances of ocean:

'International agreement' means any bilateral or multilateral treaty, convention, or agreement, to which

the Cook Islands is a party, and any understanding concluded by the Government of the Cook Islands and the government of any other country:
'Island' means a naturally formed area of land that is surrounded by and above water at mean high-water spring tides:
'Licence' means a licence issued under section 13 of this Act in respect of a foreign fishing craft; and 'licensed' has a corresponding meaning:
'License' means the person to whom a licence is issued:
'Low-water mark' has the meaning assigned to that expression by section 27 of this Act:
'Low-tide elevation' means a naturally formed area of land that is surrounded by and above water at mean low-water spring tides but is submerged at mean high-water spring tides:
'Master', in relation to a fishing craft, means the person for the time being having command or charge of the craft:
'Median line' as between the Cook Islands and any other country means a line every point of which is equidistant from the nearest points of the baseline of the territorial sea of the Cook Islands and the corresponding baseline of that other country:
'Minister' means the Minister responsible for Fisheries:
'Nautical mile' means the international nautical mile:
'Owner', in relation to a fishing craft, includes any body of persons, whether incorporated or not, by whom the craft is owned, and any charterer, sub-charterer, lessee, or sub-lessee of the craft:
'Prescribed' means prescribed by regulations made under this Act:
'Take' includes—

(a) To take, catch, kill, attract, or pursue by any means or device, and

(b) To attempt to do any act specified in paragraph (a) of this definition:

'Total allowable catch', with respect to the yield from any fishery, means the amount of fish that will produce from that fishery the maximum sustainable yield, as qualified by any relevant economic or environmental factors and taking into account fishing patterns, the interdependence of stocks of fish, and any generally recommended subregional, regional, or global standards.
(2) For the purposes of this Act, permanent harbour works that form an integral part of a harbour system shall be treated as forming part of the coast.

3. *The territorial sea*— The territorial sea of the Cook Islands comprises those areas of the sea having, as their inner limits, the baselines described in section 5 of this Act and, as their outer limits, a line measured seaward from that baseline, every point of which is distant 12 nautical miles from the nearest point of the baseline.

4. *Internal waters*— The internal waters of the Cook Islands include any areas of the sea that are on the landward side of the baseline of the territorial sea of the Cook Islands.

5. *Baseline of territorial sea*— The baseline from which the breadth of the territorial sea of the Cook Islands is measured shall be—

(a) In the case where there is a coral reef surrounding any island or any part of any island, the mean low water mark along the outer edge of the coral reef;

(b) In the case where the island or any part of the island is not surrounded by a coral reef the mean low water mark along the coast of the island;

(c) In the case of the sea adjacent to any harbour a straight line joining the low water marks of the natural entrance points of the harbour.

6. *Bed of territorial sea and internal waters vested in Crown*— Subject to the grant of any estate or interest therein (whether by or pursuant to the provisions of any enactment or otherwise, and whether made before or after the commencement of this Act), the seabed and subsoil of submarine areas bounded on the landward side by the low-water mark along the coast of of all islands of the Cook Islands and on the seaward side by the outer limits of the territorial sea of the Cook Islands shall be deemed to be and always to have been vested in the Crown.

7. *Regulations in territorial sea*— Where no other provision is for the time being made by any other enactment for any such purposes, the High Commissioner may from time to time, by Order in Executive Council make regulations not inconsistent with any other enactment for all or any of the following purposes:

(*a*) Regulating the conduct of scientific research within the territorial sea:

(*b*) Prescribing measures for the protection and preservation of the marine environment of the territorial sea:

(*c*) Regulating the construction, operation, and use of artificial islands (whether permanent or temporary), and other installations and structures in the territorial sea, including the establishment of safety zones around such islands, installations, and structures:

(*d*) Regulating the exploration and exploitation of the territorial sea for the production of energy from the water, current, and winds, and for any other economic purposes:

(*e*) Providing for such other matters as are necessary or expediens for giving full effect to the sovereignty exercised by the Cook Islands in relation to the territorial sea:

(*f*) Providing that a breach of any such regulations shall be a criminal offence, and imposing penalties by way of fine not exceeding $10,000 for any such offences:

(*g*) Providing for such other matters as are contemplated by or necessary for giving full effect to the provisions of this Part of this Act and for its due administration.

PART II
THE EXCLUSIVE ECONOMIC ZONE OF THE COOK ISLANDS

8. *The exclusive economic zone*— (1) The exclusive economic zone of the Cook Islands comprises those areas of the sea, seabed, and subsoil that are beyond and adjacent to the territorial sea of the Cook Islands, having as their outer limits a line measured seaward from the baseline described in section 5 of this Act, every point of which line is distant 200 nautical miles from the nearest point of the baseline.

(2) Notwithstanding subsection (1) of this section, where—

(*a*) Any part of the median line between the Cook Islands and any other country is less than 200 nautical miles from the nearest part of the baseline of the territorial sea of the Cook Islands; and

(*b*) No other outer limit of the exclusive economic zone is for the time being determined by an Order in Executive Council made under subsection (4) of this section—

that part of the median line shall be an outer limit of the zone.

(4) For the purposes of implementing any international agreement, or the arbitral award of any international body, or the judgment of any international Court, or for any other purpose in accordance with international law, the High Commissioner may from time to time, by Order in Executive Council, declare that the exclusive economic zone shall not extend to any specified area of the sea, seabed, or subsoil, that would otherwise be included with the exclusive economic zone by virtue of the section.

9. *Calculation of total allowable catch*— The Minister shall from time to time determine, in respect of every fishery within the exclusive economic zone, the total allowable catch.

10. *Calculation of allowable catch by foreign fishing craft*— (1) The Minister shall from time to time determine, in respect of the total allowable catch for every fishery within the exclusive economic zone, the portion that Cook Islands fishing craft have the capacity to harvest.

(2) Where the Minister has determined, in respect of the total allowable catch for a fishery within the exclusive economic zone, the portion that Cook Islands fishing craft have the capacity to harvest, the remaining portion shall constitute the allowable catch for that fishery for foreign fishing craft.

11. *Apportionment of allowable catch for foreign fishing craft*— (1) The Minister may from time to time apportion, among countries other than the Cook Islands, the allowable catch for foreign fishing craft in respect of any fishery within the exclusive economic zone, as determined under section 10 of this Act.

(2) In making an apportionment under subsection (1) of this section, the Minister may take into account (inter alia) the following considerations:

(a) Whether, the fishing craft of countries to which the apportionment applies have engaged habitually in fishing within the exclusive economic zone:

(b) Whether such countries have co-operated with the Cook Islands in fisheries research and in the identification of fish stocks within the zone:

(c) Whether such countries have co-operated with the Cook Islands in the conservation and management of fisheries resources within the zone, and in the enforcement of Cook Islands law relating to such resources:

(d) The terms of any relevant international agreement:

(e) Such other matters as the Minister, after consultation with the Premier, determines to be relevant.

12. *Prohibition of operation of unlicensed foreign fishing craft in zone*— No foreign fishing craft shall be used for fishing within the exclusive economic zone except in accordance with a licence issued by the Minister under section 13 of this Act in respect of that fishing craft.

13. *Grant of licences*— (1) Subject to subsection (2) of this section, the Minister may grant and issue to the owner of any named foreign fishing craft a licence to fish within the exclusive economic zone.

(2) The Minister shall exercise the powers conferred on him by this section in such a manner as to ensure that—

apportionment applies have engaged habitually in fishing within the

(a) The catch that all foreign fishing craft licensed under this section are for the time being authorised to harvest from any fishery within the exclusive economic zone does not exceed the allowable catch for foreign fishing craft for that fishery calculated under section 10 of this Act; and

(b) The catch that all foreign fishing craft of a particular country licensed under this section are for the time being authorised to harvest from any fishery within the zone does not exceed the apportionment made under section 11 of this Act for that fishery in respect of that country.

(3) In granting a licence under this section, the Minister may attach to the licence conditions relating (inter alia) to all or any of the following matters:

(a) The areas within the exclusive economic zone in which fishing is authorised; and

(b) The reasons, times, and particular voyages during which fishing is authorised:

(c) The species, size, age, and quantities of fish that may be taken:

(d) The methods by which fish may be taken:

(e) The types, size, and amount of fishing gear that may be used or carried by a foreign fishing craft, and the modes of storage of that gear when not in use:

(f) The use, transfer, transhipment, landing, and processing of fish taken:

(g) Entry by the foreign fishing craft to Cook Islands ports, whether for the inspection of its catch or for other purposes:

(h) The compensation payable to Cook Islanders residents of the Cook Islands or to the Cook

Islands Government in the event of any loss or damage caused by the foreign fishing craft to other fishing craft, or their gear or catch, or to fish stocks, or to other Cook Islands interests:

(i) Statistical and other information required to be given by the foreign fishing craft to the Ministery of Economic Services and Natural Resources, including statistics relating to catch and effort and reports as to the positions of the craft:

(j) The conduct by the foreign fishing craft of specified programmes of fisheries research:

(k) The training of Cook Islands personnel in the methods of fishing employed by the foreign fishing craft and the transfer to the Cook Islands of technology relating to fisheries:

(l) The display on board the foreign fishing craft of the licence issued in respect of it:

(m) The marking of the foreign fishing craft, and other means for its identification:

(n) Directions, instructions and other requirements given or made by Cook Islands Government ships or aircraft to the foreign fishing craft that shall be complied with by the craft:

(o) The placing of Cook Islands observers on the foreign fishing craft and the reimbursement to the Ministry of Economic Services and Natural Resources by the licensee of the costs of doing so:

(p) The installation on the foreign fishing craft and maintenance in working order of a transponder or other equipment for the fixing of its positions or its identification, and of adequate navigational equipment to enable it to fix its positions itself:

(q) The carriage on board the foreign fishing craft of specified nautical charts:

(r) Such other matters as the Minister considers necessary or expedient for the conservation or management of fisheries resources within the zone.

14. *Renewal of licences*— Subject to section 13 (2) of this Act, the Minister may from time to time renew any licence granted under section 13 of this Act.

15. *Variation of licences*— (1) The Minister may from time to time, where he is satisfied that it is necessary or expedient for the proper regulation of fishing within the exclusive economic zone to do so, vary the terms and conditions of any licence or licences, or class or classes of licence, granted under section 13 of this Act.

(2) Notice of every variation of any licence under this section shall be given as soon as practicable to the licensee.

16. *Licensing fees*— There shall be payable by every licensee to the Crown in respect of the granting of a licence under section 13 of this Act, or the renewal of a licence under section 14 of this Act, such fee as may from time to time be prescribed.

17. *Licensing offences*— (1) Where any foreign fishing craft that is not licensed under section 13 of this Act is used for fishing in contravention of section 12 of this Act, each of them the owner, the master, and every crew member of the craft commits an offence against this Act.

(2) Where any foreign fishing craft is used for fishing within the exclusive economic zone in contravention of any condition of a licence granted in respect of it under section 13 of this Act, each of them the licensee, the owner, the master, and every crew member of the craft commits an offence against this Act.

(3) Every owner or master of a foreign fishing craft who commits an offence specified in subsection (1) of this section is liable on conviction to a fine not exceeding × 100,000.

(4) Every crew member of a foreign fishing craft who commits an offence specified in subsection (1) of this section is liable on conviction to a fine not exceeding $5,000.

(5) Every licensee, owner, or master of a foreign fishing craft who commits an offence specified in subsection (2) of this section is liable on conviction to a fine not exceeding $25,000.

(6) Every crew member of a foreign fishing craft who commits an offence specified in subsection (2) of this section is liable on conviction to a fine not exceeding $1,500.

(7) In this section, 'crew member' does not include a licensee, owner, or master of a foreign fishing craft.

18. *Suspension and cancellation of licences*— (1) Where the Minister is satisfied that—

(a) Any foreign fishing craft in respect of which a licence has been granted under section 13 of this Act is being or has been used for fishing within the exclusive economic zone in contravention of any condition of the licence or of any Cook Islands law that applies to fishing within the zone; or

(b) Any licensee, owner, master, or crew member of a foreign fishing craft has been convicted of an offence against this Act, or against any regulations made under section 19 of this Act, or against any other Cook Islands law relating to fishing within the zone—

he may suspend the licence for such period as he shall specify, or cancel the licence.

(2) Where the Minister, after consultation with the Premier, determines that it is necessary or expedient for the proper regulation of fishing within the exclusive economic zone to do so, he may suspend any licence or licences for such period as he shall specify, or cancel any licence or licences.

(3) No determination, variation, suspension, concellation, or other action of the Minister under subsection (2) of this section shall be reviewable by any Court of Law.

(4) While a licence is suspended under this section, it shall have no effect.

19. *Fisheries regulations*— (1) The High Commissioner may from time to time, by Order in Executive Council, make regulations for all or any of the following purposes:

(a) Prescribing the manner of applying for licences under section 13 of this Act, and for the renewal of such licences under section 14 of this Act, and forms of applications:

(b) Prescribing the terms of duration of licences:

(c) Prescribing the forms of licences to be issued by the Minister:

(d) Prescribing the fees payable to the Cook Islands Government for the issue of licences and for their renewal:

(e) Providing for the production of licences by licensees to specified Cook Islands authorities when required to do so, and the inspection of licences by such authorities:

(f) Providing for such other measures as are necessary or expedient to ensure that foreign fishing craft are used for fishing within the exclusive economic zone only in accordance with the terms and conditions of their licences:

(g) Prescribing conditions, not inconsistent with this Act, under which fishing may be undertaken within the zone by foreign fishing craft:

(h) Prescribing measures, not inconsistent with this Act, for the conservation and management of fisheries resources within the zone:

(i) Specifying particular types of highly migratory species of fish, and regulating, in a manner not inconsistent with this Act, fishing for those species within the zone, and also, in the case of Cook Islands fishing craft, beyond the zone:

(j) Providing that a breach of any such regulation shall be a criminal offence, and imposing penalties by way of fine not exceeding in the case of allicensee, owner, or master of a fishing craft, $10,000 for any such offences and, in the case of any other crew members, $1,000 for any such offences:

(k) Prescribing the form of bonds for the purposes of section 22 of this Act.

(2) Regulations made under this section may make different provisions for different parts of the exclusive economic zone and for different species of fish.

(3) In prescribing fees in regulations made under this section, the High Commissioner in Executive Council may—

(a) Take into account (inter alia) the costs of implementing the provisions of this Act, including the cost of the conservation and management of fisheries resources, and of fisheries research, and of

the administration and enforcement of such enactments; and

(b) Prescribe different fees for different classes of foreign fishing craft (whether by reference to size, catch, method of fishing, function, or otherwise).

20. *Fishing for research, experimental, and sporting purposes*— Nothwithstanding section 12 of this Act, a foreign fishing craft may be used for fishing within the exclusive economic zone for the purpose of fisheries research, or of experimentation, or sport, subject always to the prior consent in writing of the Minister to such activity and in accordance with such conditions (if any) as the Minister may impose in giving his consent.

21. *Apprehension of offenders*— (1) Where any officer specified in subsection (11) of this section has reasonable cause to believe that an offence against this Act, or against regulations made under section 19 of this Act, or against any other Cook Islands law relating to fishing within the exclusive economic zone, has been committed in respect of any foreign fishing craft, he may—

(A) Stop, board, and

(b) Inspect, seize, and detain all fish on board the craft; and

(c) Apprehend any person who he has reason to believe has committed any offence specified in subsection (1) of this section; and

(d) Where he has reason to believe that any such offence has been committed by the licensee, owner or master of the draft, seize and detain the craft.

(2) Any officer specified in subsection (11) of his section may exercise the powers conferred on him by subsection (1) of this section with the aid of such assistants as he considers to be neccessary for the purpose.

(3) Where any foreign fishing craft is detained under subsection (1) of this section, it shall be held in the custody of the Crown until—

(a) A decision is made not to lay any information or charge in respect of the alleged offence for which the craft was detained; or

(b) Where such an information or charge is laid, the security required by section 22 of this Act is given in respect of the craft.

(4) The decision whether or not to lay an information or charge in respect of an alleged offence for which a foreign fishing craft is detained under subsection (1) of this section shall be made as soon as reasonably practicable after the craft is detained.

(5) The release of a foreign fishing craft from detection shall not affect any subsequent forfeiture of the craft in respect of the conviction of any person for an offence.

(6) On the conviction of any licensee, owner, or master of a foreign fishing craft for any offence specified in subsection (1) of this section, the craft shall be forfeited to the Crown, and shall be disposed of in such manner as the Minister shall order, in addition to any fine that may be imposed by any Court on the convicted person.

(7) Where any officer specified in subsection (11) of this section detains any fish under subsection (1) of this section, the fish shall be held in the custody of the Crown until a decision is made not to lay an information or charge in respect of the alleged offence for which it was detained, or where such an information or charge is laid, until the information or charge is determined.

(8) On the conviction of any person for any offencs specified in subsection (1) of this section in respect of any fish detained under that subsection, the fish shall be forfeited to the Crown and shall be disposed of in such manner as the Minister shall order, in addition to any fine that may be imposed by any Court on the convicted person.

(9) Where any officer specified in subsection (11) of this section apprehends any person under subsection (11) of this section, the officer shall cause the person to be taken as soon as reasonably

practicable before a Court to be dealt with in accordance with law.

(10) Any person who in any way prevents or hinders any officer specified in subsection (11) of this section, or any assistant of the officer, in exercising the powers conferred by this section commits an offence against this Act, and is liable on conviction to a fine not exceeding $10,000.

(11) Subsection (1) of this section refers to any of the following officers:

(a) Any members of the Police Force:

(b) Any officers and employees of the Ministry of Economic Services and Natural Resources;

(c) Any other person appointed for this purpose by the Minister.

(12) In this section, 'foreign fishing craft' includes all equipment on board the craft.

22. *Security for release of foreign fishing craft*— (1) Where any foreign fishing craft is detained under section 21 of this Act, and an information or charge is laid against the licensee, owner, or master of the craft in respect of the offence for which the craft has been detained, the licensee, owner, or master of the craft may at any time before the determination of the information or charge apply to the Court by which the information or charge will be determined for the release of the craft on the provision of security in accordance with this section.

(2) On hearing the application, the Court shall order release of the foreign fishing craft on the execution by any suitable person or persons approved by the Court for the purpose, of a bond in favour of Her Majesty the Queen, in the prescribed from and conditioned in accordance with subsection (4) of this section, in an amount not less than the aggregate of the value of the craft and the maximum fine to which the defendant will be liable if he is convicted of the offence.

(3) Notwithstanding subsection (2) of this section, the Court may, where it is satisfied that there are special circumstances to justify it in doing so, order that the bond shall be in a specified amount that is less than the amount required by that subsection.

(4) The condition of the bond shall be that if—

(a) The defendant is found not guilty of the information or charge; or

(b) The defendant on being convicted of the information or charge pays in full within 14 days after he is convicted the amount of the fine imposed by the Court and the foreign fishing craft is within that time surrendered to the Crown for forfeiture—

then the bond shall be of no effect, but that otherwise the bond shall remain in full force and effect.

(5) The amount specified in the bond shall be recoverable in full as a debt due to Her Majesty the Queen jointly and severally by the person or persons by whom the bond is given, unless the person or persons prove the due performance of the condition on which the bond is defeasible.

(6) In this section, 'foreign fishing craft' includes all equipment on board the craft.

23. *General regulations in zone*— (1) Where no other provision is for the time being made by any other enactment for any such purposes the High Commissioner may fromtime to time, by Order in Executive Council, make regulations not inconsistent with any other enactment for all or any of the following purposes:

(a) Regulation the conduct of scientific research within the exclusive economic zone:

(b) Prescribing measures for the protection and preservation of the marine environment of the zone:

(c) Regulating the construction, operation, and use of artificial islands (whether permanent or temporary), and of other installations and structures within the zone, including the establishment of safety zones around such islands, installations, and structures:

(d) Regulating the exploration and exploitation of the zone for the production of energy from the water, current, and winds, and for any other economic purposes:

(f) Providing that a breach of any such regulations shall be a criminal offence, and imposing penalties by way of fine not exceeding $10,000 for any such offences:

(g) Providing for such other matters as are contemplated by or necessary for giving full effect to the provisions of this Part of this Act (other than matters for which regulations may be made under section 19 of this Act) and for its due administration.

(2) Regulations made under this section may declare that the provision of any enactment (whether made before or after the passing of this Act) shall apply, with such modifications and exceptions (if any) as may be specified in the regulations,—

(a) Within the exclusive economic zone; or

(b) Within any specified part of the zone; or

(c) To acts and omissions within the zone—

and the provisions of that enactment (with such modifications and exceptions, if any) shall apply accordingly as if the zone or the specified part of the zone were within the territorial limits of the Cook Islands.

24. *Offences in zone deemed to be committed in the Cook Islands*— Anyoffence against this Act that is committed within the exclusive economic zone shall be deemed to have been committed in the Cook Islands.

PART III
MISCELLANEOUS PROVISIONS

25. *Interim and transitional measures*— Pending the coming into force of Part II of this Act, the High Commissioner may from time to time, by Order in Executive Council, prescribe interim or transitional measures for the conservation and management of fisheries resources beyond the territorial sea of the Cook Islands but within 200 nautical miles of the baseline described in section 5 of this Act, and for the limitation of fishing by foreign fishing craft in any areas to which those measures relate.

26. *Modifications to give effect to international agreement*— The High Commissioner may, from time to time, by Order in Executive Council, limit any provision of this Act relating to the exclusive economic zone so far as it is necessary to do so to give full effect to any convention that is adopted by the Third United Nations Conference on the Law of the Sea.

27. *Official charts*— (1) For the purposes of this Act, the low-water mark in any specified area shall be the line of low water at mean low-water spring tides as depicted on the largest scale New Zealand Government nautical chart for the time being of that area, or, where no such chart of that area exists, the largest scale British Admiralty chart for the time being of that area.

(2) In any proceedings in any Court, a certificate purporting to be signed by an officer of the New Zealand Naval Forces authorised by the Secretary of Defence of the New Zealand Government or a Deputy Secretary of Defence of that Government that—

(a) Any specified New Zealand Government nautical chart of any area is the largest scale New Zealand Government nautical chart for the time being of that area; or

(b) No New Zealand Government nautical chart for any area exists and that any specified British Admiralty chart of that area is the largest Scale British Admiralty chart for the time being of that area—

shall be admissible as evidence of the matters stated in the certificate. Every person signing any such certificate shall, in the absence of proof to the contrary, be presumed to be duly authorised to sign it.

28. *Onus of proof in respect of offences*— In any criminal proceedings under this Act where a defendant is charged with having contravened section 12 of this Act, or with having contravened any other provision in any regulations made under this Act under which a licence or permit, or the consent of any person is required for the doing of any act, the onus shall be on the defendant to prove that at the time to which the charge relates, he held the requisite licence, permit, or consent.

29. *Repeal and savings*— (1) The Fisheries Protection Act 1976 is hereby repealed.

(2) Except as expressly provided by this Act, the provisions of this Act are in addition to and not in substitution for the provision of every other enactment, and accordingly nothing in this Act shall limit or derogate from the provisions of any other enactment.

This Act is administered in the Ministry of Economic Services and Natural Resource.

BAROTONGA, COOK ISLANDS: Printed under the authority of the Cook Islands Government by T. KAPI, Government Printer—1977.

B. Niue

Act No. 38.
Entered into force: April 1, 1978
Source: *Government Printing,* New Zealand

NIUE ASSEMBLY

TERRITORIAL SEA AND EXCLUSIVE ECONOMIC ZONE ACT 1978
No. 38

ANALYSIS

AN ACT to make provision with respect to the territorial sea of Niue; and to establish an exclusive economic zone of Niue adjacent to the territorial sea, and in the exercise of the sovereign rights of Niue to make provision for the exploration and exploitation, and conservation and management, of the resources of the zone; and for matters connected with those purposes.

BE IT ENACTED by the Niue Assembly in Session assembled, and by the authority of the same, as follows:

1. *Short Title*— (1) This Act may be cited as the Territorial Sea and Exclusive Economic Zone Act 1978.

(2) This Act shall be deemed to have come into force on the 1st day of April 1978.

2. *Interpretation*— (1) In this Act, unless the context otherwise requires—

'*Cabinet*' means the Cabinet of Ministers of Niue established by article 2 of the Niue Constitution Act 1974:
'*Chief Officer of Police*' means the officer in charge of the police in Niue:
'*Court*' means any Court of competent jurisdiction:
'*Director of Agriculture*' means the officer in charge of the Department of Agriculture:
'*Exclusive economic zone*' and 'zone' means the exclusive economic zone of Niue described in section 10 of this Act:
Fish' means any marine animal; and includes molluscs, curstaceans, polyps and all other forms of maritime animal life:
'*Fishery*' means one or more stocks of fish that can be treated as a unit for the purposes of conservation and management:
'*Fishing*' means taking, hunting, pursuing, catching, killing or possessing any fish, and 'to fish' has the same meaning:
'*Fisheries officer*' means any fisheries officer employed in the Fisheries Division of the Department of Agriculture and includes the Director of Agriculture:
'*Foreign fishing vessel*' means any vessel of whatever size and however propelled which is used in fishing or for the processing or storage of fish for the purpose of sale and which is owned or controlled by a person or persons not ordinarily resident in Niue; but does not include any canoe or other vessel of any kind whatsoever used for the transport of fish or fish products as part of its general cargo:
'*Foreshore*' means all land lying between the highwater line at mean high-water spring tides and the low-water line at mean low-water spring tides:
'*High Court*' means the High Court of Niue:

'Highly migratory species' means species that, in the course of their life cycle, migrate over great distances of ocean:
'Licence' means a licence issued under section 13 of this Act in respect of a foreign fishing vessel:
'Licensee' means the person to whom a licence is issued:
'Low-water mark' has the meaning assigned thereto by section 8 of this Act:
'Master', in relation to a fishing vessel, means the person for the time being having command or charge of the vessel:
'Median line' as between Niue and any other country, means a line every point of which is equidistant from the nearest points of the baseline of the territorial sea of Niue and the corresponding baseline of that other country:
'Nautical mile' means the international nautical mile:
'Owner', in relation to a fishing vessel, includes any body of persons, whether incorporated or not, by whom the vessel is owned, and any charterer, sub-charterer, lessee or sub-lessee of the vessel:
'Police officer' means the Chief Officer of Police and includes any sergeant, corporal and constable acting with the authority of the Chief Officer of Police:
Prescribed' means prescribed by regulations made under this Act:
'Territorial sea' means that area of the sea defined in section 4 of this Act:
'Total allowable catch', with respect to the yield from any fishery, means the amount of fish that will produce from that fishery the maximum substainable yield, as qualified by any relevant economic or environmental factors, fishing patterns, the interdependence of stocks of fish, and andy generally recommended subregional, regional, or global standards.

(2) Subject to the provisions of subsection (1) of this section, expressions defined ina the Niue Act 1966 and the Niue Constitution Act 1974 have the meanings so defined.

3. *Administration*— The Administration of this Act shall be under the control and direction of Cabinet, which may delegate, either generally or particularly, all or any of the powers conferred on it under this Act.

PART I
TERRITORIAL SEA

4. *Territorial sea*— The territorial Sea of Niue comprises those areas of sea having, as their inner limits, the baseline described in section 6 of this Act and, as their outer limits, a line measured seaward from that baseline, every point of which is distant 12 nautical miles from the nearest point of the baseline.

5. *Internal waters*— The internal waters of Niue include any area of the sea that are on the landward side of the baseline of the territorial sea of Niue.

6. *Baseline of territorial sea*— The baseline from which the breadth of the territorial sea of Niue is measured shall be the low-water mark along the coast of Niue, or, where there is a coral reef along any part of the coast of Niue, the low-water mark along the outer edge of that coral reef.

7. *Foreshore, bed of internal waters, and territorial sea vested in Crown*— (1) The seabed and subsoil of the submarine areas of the internal waters of Niue shall be deemed to be and always to have been vested in the Crown.

(2) The foreshore of Niue and the seabed and subsoil of the territorial sea shall be deemed to be and always to have been vested in the Crown.

8. *Official Chart*— (1) For the purposes of this Act, the low-water mark in any specified area shall be the line of low water at mean low-water spring tides as depicted on the largest scale British Admiralty chart for the time being of that area.

(2) In any proceedings in any court, a certificate purporting to be signed by an officer of the New Zealand Naval Forces authorised by the Secretary of Defence or a Deputy Secretary of Defence, that any specified British Admiralty chart for the time being of that area shall be admissible as evidence of the matters stated in the certificate.

9. *Permanent Harbour works*— For the purposes of this Act, permanent harbour works which form an integral part of a harbour system shall be treated as forming part of the coast.

PART II
EXCLUSIVE ECONOMIC ZONE OF NIUE

10. *Exclusive economic zone*— (1) The exclusive economic zone of Niue comprises those areas of the sea, seabed, and subsoil that are beyond and adjacent to the territorial sea of Niue, having as their outer limits a line measured seaward from the baseline described in section 6 of this Act, every point of which line is distant 200 nautical miles from the nearest point of the baseline.

(2) Notwithstanding subsection (1) of this section where any part of the median line between Niue and any other country is less than 200 nautical miles from the nearest part of the baseline of the territorial sea of Niue that part of the median line shall be an outer limit of the zone.

11. *Total allowable catch*— The Cabinet shall from time to time determine, in respect of every fishery within the exclusive economic zone, the total allowable catch as follows:

(a) The portion that Niue fishing vessel have the capacity to harvest; and

(b) The remaining portion shall constitute the allowable catch for that fishery for foreign fishing vessels.

12. *No fishing by foreign fishing vessels*— No foreign fishing vessel shall be used in fishing within the exclusive economic zone of Niue except in accordance with a licence issued by the Cabinet under section 13 of this Act in respect of that fishing vessel.

13. *Grant of licences*— (1) Cabinet may grant and issue to the owner of any named foreign fishing vessel a licence to fish within the exclusive economic zone.

(2) In granting a licence under this section the Cabinet may attach to the licence such conditions as are provided for the regulations.

(3) The Cabinet shall exercise the powers conferred on it by this section in such manner as to ensure that the catch that all foreign fishing vessels licensed under this section are for the time being authorised to harvest from any fishery within the exclusive economic zone does not exceed the allowable catch for foreign fishing vessels for that fishery as determined under section 11 of this Act.

14. *Renewal of licences*— The Cabinet may from time to time renew any licence granted under section 13 of this Act.

15. *Variation of licences*— (1) Subject to section 15(2) of this Act the Cabinet may from time to time, where it is satisfied that it is necessary or expedient for the proper regulation of fishing within the exclusive economic zone to do so, vary the terms and conditions of any licence or licences, or class or classes of licence, granted under section 13 of this Act.

(2) Notice of every variation of any licence under this section shall be given as practical to the licensee.

16. Licensing fees— There shall be payable by every licensee to the Crown in respect of the granting of a licence under section 13 of this Act or the renewal of a licence under section 14 of this Act, such fee as may from time to time be prescribed.

17. *Offence and penalty*— (1) Where any foreign fishing vessel that is not licensed under section 13 of this Act is fishing or used in fishing in the exclusive economic zone:

(*a*) That vessel together with its tackle, engines, nets, gear, apparatus, cargo and stores and all fish taken or possessed shall be seized and forfeited to the Government of Niue and all things so forfeited shall be disposed of as Cabinet thinks fit; and

(*b*) The owner and the master of the vessel and every member of the crew each commits an offence, and is liable—

(i) In the case of an offence committed by the owner or master, to a fine not exceeding $100,000, or imprisonment for a term not exceeding 10 years, or both; or

(ii) In the case of an offence committed by any member of the crew to a fine not exceeding $15,000 or imprisonment for a term not exceeding 5 years, or both.

(2) Where any foreign fishing vessel is fishing or used in fishing within the exclusive economic zone in contravention of any condition of a licence issued in respect of it under section 13 of this Act:

(*a*) Every licensee or master of that foreign fishing vessel commits an offence and is liable to a fine not exceeding $25,000; and

(*b*) Every crew member of that foreign fishing vessel commits an offence and is liable to a fine not exceeding $5,000.

18. *Powers to apprehend offenders*— (1) Any Fisheries officer or Police officer shall have the power under this Part of this Act—

(*a*) The pursue, board, seize and take possession of any foreign fishing vessel (together with its tackle, engines, nets, gear, apparatus, cargo and stores) within the exclusive economic zone of Niue or from which he has reasonable cause to believe that an offence against this Part of this Act is being or has been committed; and

(*b*) At any time board any foreign fishing vessel within the exclusive economic zone of Niue and there search, seize and take possession of any fish in respect of which he has reasonable cause to believe that an offence against this Part of this Act has been committed; and

(*c*) To arrest with or without a warrant, any person (being the owner, or the master, or a crew member of a foreign fishing vessel) committing an offence or whom he has reasonable cause to believe has committed an offence against this Part of this Act.

(2) All persons if called upon to assist any Police officer or Fisheries officer in the execution of any power vested in him under this Part of this Act, are hereby authorized and required to render such assistance.

19. *Obstruction of Fisheries officer and Police Officer*—

Any Person who—

(*a*) Wilfully obstructs any Fisheries officer of Police officer in the exercise of any of his powers under this Part of this Act; or

(*b*) Fails to comply with any lawful requirement imposed or to answer any lawful enquiry made by any Fisheries officer or Police Officer under this part of this Act; or

(*c*) Being on board any vessel being pursued or about to be boarded by any Fisheries officer or Police officer throws over board or destroys any fish, fishing gear or any other thing whatsoever—

shall be guilty of an offence against this Part of this Act, and shall be liable to a fine not exceeding $1,000 or to imprisonment for a term not exceeding 2 years, or both and if the said offence takes place on board or alongside a fishing vessel, the master of the fishing vessel shall be guilty of a like offence and liable to a like penalty.

20. *Sale of seized fish*— Where no adequate facilities are available to preserve the fish taken or possessed in contravention of this Part of this Act, Cabinet shall take all necessary steps for the sale of such fish, at its reasonable market value, pending the determination of the Court proceedings in respect of the taking or possession such fish, and the net proceeds of such sale shall be paid to the Registrar of the High Court pending the making of a final order by the Court in respect of the forefeiture or otherwise of those proceeds.

21. *Discharge of seized fish on security*— Any fish taken under this part of this Act may be discharged by Cabinet upon receiving suitable and adequate security for the equivalent value of fish by way of bond, guarantee or other stipulations, conditional for payment of such equivalent value in the event that such amount shall be judged by the Court to be forfeited to the Government of Niue.

22. *Reward to informers and others*— Cabinet may direct the payment, and the Treasurer is hereby empowered to pay,—

(*a*) To any person, other than an officer mentioned in section 18 of this Act, who submits to any such officer original information concerning the commission of any offence against this Part of this Act, leading to any penalty or forfeiture incurred in respect of such offence; and

(*b*) To any person or the dependents of any person who renders assistance to any officer pursuant to subsection (2) of section 18 of this Act, and who in so doing, suffers personal injury or death;

a reward of not more than $5.000, and in no case exceeding one half of the amount of such penalty or forfeiture.

23. *Boarding of foreign fishing vessels prohibited*— Any person not being a Fisheries officer or Police officer who boards or attempts to board any foreign fishing vessel or who accepts fish from such foreign fishing vessel without any authority to do so shall be guilty of an offence and liable to a fine not exceeding $100.

24. *Fishing for research, experimental, and sporting purposes*— Notwithstanding section 12 or section 17 of this Act, of foreign fishing vessel may be used for fishing within the exclusive economic zone for the purpose of fisheries research or of experimentation or sport, subject always to the prior consent in writing of Cabinet to such activity and in accordance with such conditions (if any) as Cabinet may impose in giving its consent.

25. *Regulations*— Cabinet may from time to time make regulations for any purpose for which regulations are required or comtemplated by this Act or are necessary for giving full effect to the provisions of this Act.

26. *Repeal*— The Territorial Sea and Fishing Zone Act 1977 is hereby repealed.

I, SAM PATA EMANI TAGELAGI, Speaker of the Niue Assembly hereby certify the requirements of Article 34 of the Niue Constitution have been duly complied with.

SIGNED AND SEALED at the Assembly Chambers this 7th day of April 1975

(S.P.B. Tagelagi)
Speaker

COUNTERSIGNED in the presence of the Speaker

(T. Pihigia)
Clerk of the Assembly

This Act was passed by the Niue Assembly on 30th day of March 1978.

C. Tokelau

Tokelau Act 1977.
Entered into force: December 23, 1977
Source: *Government Printing,* Government of New Zealand–1978, No. 125

An Act to make provision with respect to the territorial sea of Tokelau, and for the establishment of an exclusive economic zone of Tokelau, and for matters connected with those purposes

[*23 December 1977*]

ANALYSIS

BE IT ENACTED by the General Assembly of New Zealand in Parliament assembled, and by the authority of the same, as follows:

1. *Short Title and commencement*— (1) This Act may be cited as the Tokelau (Territorial Sea and Exclusive Economic Zone) Act 1977, and shall be read together with and deemed part of the Tokelau Act 1948.

(2) This Act shall come into force on a date to be appointed by the Governor-General by Order in Council.

(3) For the purposes of subsection (2) of this section, one or more Orders in Council may be made—

(a) Bringing different provisions of this Act into force on different dates; and

(b) Bringing provisions of this Act into force on different dates in respect of specified parts of Tokelau.

2. *Interpretation*— In this Act, unless the context otherwise requires,—
'*Court*' means the High Court of Niue:
'*Exclusive economic zone*' and 'zone' mean the exclusive economic zone of Tokelau described in section 7 of this Act:
'*Fish*' means every kind of marine animal and its young, fry, eggs, or spawn; and includes shellfish, crustaceans, spronge, holothurian (bêche-de-mer), and turtle:
'*Fishing*' means—

(*a*) Taking any fish; or
(*b*) Engaging in any activity relating to the taking of any fish, including (inter alia) any activity involving the preparation, supply, storage, refrigeration, transportation, or processing of any fish; or
(*c*) Engaging in any activity relating to the provision of any services to any fishing craft to enable or assist that craft to engage in fishing:

'*Fishing craft*' means any vessel, aircraft, hovercraft, submersible craft, or other craft, of whatever size, that is capable of being used for fishing:
'*Foreshore*' means all land lying between the highwater line and the low-water line:
'*Foreign fishing craft*' means any fishing craft that is not a Tokelauan fishing craft:
'*Master*', in relation to a fishing craft, means the person for the time being having command or charge of the craft:
'*Median line*', as between Tokelau and any country, means a line every point of which is equidistant from the nearest points of the baseline of the territorial sea of Tokelau and the corresponding baseline of that country:
'*Nautical mile*' means the international nautical mile of 1852 metres:
'*Owner*', in relation to a fishing craft, includes any body of persons, whether incorporated or not, by whom the craft is owned, and any charterer, subcharterer, lessee, or sub-lessee of the craft:
'*Take*' includes—

(*a*) To take, catch, kill, attract, or pursue by any means or device; and
(*b*) To attempt to do any act specified in paragraph (a) of this definition:

'*Territorial sea*' means the territorial sea of Tokelau defined by section 3 of this Act:
'*Tokelauan fishing craft*' means a fishing craft in which no person who is not a Tokelauan has any legal or equitable interest (except by way of security only for any advance made by him to the owner).
Cf. 1976, No. 140, s. 2

The Territorial Sea of Tokelau

3. *The territorial sea*— The territorial sea of Tokelau comprises those areas of the sea having, as their inner limits, the baseline described in section 5 of this Act and, as their outer limits, a line measured seaward from that baseline, every point of which is distant 12 nautical miles from the nearest point of that baseline.
Cf. 1976, No. 140, ss. 4, 7

4. *Internal waters*— The internal waters of Tokelau include any areas of the sea that are on the landward side of the baseline of the territorial sea.
Cf. 1976, No. 140. s. 3

5. *Baseline of territorial sea*— The baseline from which the breadth of the territorial sea is measured shall be the low-water line along the seaward edge of the reef, except that where there is a break or passage through or over the reef, the baseline shall be a straight line joining the entrance points of that break or passage.

Cf. 1976, No. 140, s. 5

6. *Prohibition of foreign fishing in territorial sea*— (1) No foreign fishing craft shall be used for fishing within the territorial sea.

(2) Where any foreign fishing craft is used in contravention of subsection (1) of this section, each of them the owner, the master, and every crew member of the craft commits and offence against this Act and is liable on conviction—

(*a*) In the case of the owner or master, to a fine not exceeding $100,000; and

(*b*) In the case of any other crew member, to a fine not exceeding $5,000.

(3) The Court, on the conviction of any person of an offence under this section, may onder in addition to any penalty that it may impose—

(*a*) The immediate forfeiture in the Crown of the foreign fishing craft in respect of which the offence was committed and of any equipment on board or used by the craft, and of any fish on board the craft; or

(*b*) The detention for a specified period of the foreign fishing craft and of any such equipment and fish, and the forfeiture to the Crown of the craft, equipment, and fish if any fine or fines imposed in respect of the offence are not paid within that specified period.

Cf. 1976, No. 140, s. 8 (1), (2), (3), (4)

The Exclusive Economic Zone of Tokelau

7. *The exclusive economic zone*— (1) The exclusive economic zone of Tokelau comprises those areas of the sea, seabed, and subsoil that are beyond and adjacent to the territorial sea, having as their outer limits a fine measured seaward from the baseline described in section 5 of this Act, every point of which line is distant 200 nautical miles from the nearest point of the baseline.

(2) Notwithstanding subsection (1) of the section, where—

(*a*) Any part of the median line between Tokelau and any country is less than 200 nautical miles, from the nearest part of the baseline of the territorial sea of Tokelau; and

(*b*) No other outer limit of the exclusive economic zone is for the time being determined by an Order in Council made under subsection (3) of this section—

that part of the median line shall be an outer limit of the zone.

(3) For the purposes of implementing any international agreement, or the arbitral award of any international body, or the judgment of any international Court, or for any other purpose in accordance with international law,a the Governor-General may from time to time, by Order in Council, declare that the exclusive economic zone shall not extend to any specified area of the sea, seabed, or subsoil, that would otherwise be included within the zone by virtue of this section.

8. *Control of foreign fishing in zone*— (1) The Governor-General may from time to time, by Order in Council, make regulations for all or any of the following purposes:

(*a*) Providing for the determination of the total allowable catch for any species of fish (other than marine mammals' within the exclusive economic zone, the determination of the portion that Tokelauan fishing craft have the capacity to harvest, and the apportionment of any surplus otherwise than among Tokelauan craft:

(*b*) Prohibiting fishing within the zone by foreign fishing craft that are not licensed pursuant to regulations made under this section:

(*c*) Appointing or establishing a licensing authority for the purposes of regulations made under this section:

(d) Providing for the licensing of foreign fishing craft for the purposes of fishing in the zone:
(e) Providing separate licensing procedures for marine mammals:
(f) Prescribing conditions that shall be deemed to the implied in licences, and empowering the licensing authority to impose any other conditions in granting licences:
(g) Prescribing the fees payable to the Administrator of Tokelau for the issue of licences, and for their renewal:
(h) Providing for the suspension or cancellation of a licence—
(i) Where the licensing authority is satisfied that the foreign fishing craft in respect of which the licence has been granted has been used for fishing within the zone in contravention of any condition of the licence or of any law relating to fishing within the zone:
(ii) Where the licensee or master or any crew member of the foreign fishing craft in respect of which the licence has been granted has been convicted of any offence against this Act, or against any regulations made under this section, or against any other law relating to fishing within the zone:
(i) Providing for the suspension or cancellation of any licence of licences, or class or classes of licence, where the licensing authority, with the concurrence of the Minister of Foreign Affairs, is satisfied that it is necessary or expedient for the proper regulation of fishing in the zone to do so:
(j) Providing for such other measures as are necessary or expedient to ensure that foreign fishing craft are used for fishing within the zone only in accordance with the terms and conditions of their licences:
(k) Providing that a breach of any regulation made under this section shall be a criminal offence, and imposing penalties by way of fine for any such offences, not exceeding—
(i) In the case of the owner or master of an unlicensed foreign fishing craft, $100,000; and
(ii) In the case of any other crew member of an unlicensed foreign fishing craft, $5,000; and
(iii) In the case of the licensee or master of a licensed foreign fishing craft, $25,000; and
(iv) In the case of any other crew member of a licensed foreign fishing craft, $1,500:
(l) Providing that—
(i) On the conviction of any licensee, owner, or master of a foreign fishing craft for any offence against that Act, or against any regulations made under this section, or against any other law relating to fishing within the zone, the Court may, in addition to any penalty that it may impose, exercise in respect of the craft or any equipment on board or used by the craft any of the powers specified in section 6 (3) of this Act; and
(ii) On the conviction of any licensee, owner, master, or other crew member of a foreign fishing craft for any offence referred to in subparagraph (i) of this paragraph, the Court may, in addition to any penalty that it may impose, exercise in respect of any fish on board the craft any of the powers specified in section 6 (3) of this Act:
(m) Providing for the release of a foreign fishing craft, and any equipment on board or used by the craft, and any fish on board the craft, pending the determination of any proceedings which may result in the forfeiture of the craft or such equipment or fish, on the provision of adequate security for its surrender to the Crown in the event that it is ordered to be forfeited.

(2) No exercise by the licensing authority of any power conferred on him or it pursuant to any regulation made under subsection (l) (i) of this section, or concurrence by the Minister of Foreign Affairs in the exercise of the power by the licensing authority, shall be liable to be challenged, reviewed, quashed, or called into question in any Court of law on the ground that the conditions for the exercise of the power, or for that concurrence, had not arisen or had ceased.

9. *Offences in zone deemed to have been committed in Tokelau*— Any offence against this Act, or against any regulations made under this Act, that is committed within the exclusive economic zone shall be deemed to have been committed in Tokelau.

General Provisions

10. *Foreshore, bed, and subsoil vested in Crown*— The foreshore of Tokelau, and the seabed and subsoil of the submarine areas of its internals waters, territorial sea, and exclusive economic zone, shall be deemed to be and always to have been vested in the Crown.

Cf. 1976, No. 140, s. 6

11. *General regulations*— Where no other provision is for the time being made by any other enactment for any such purposes, the Governor-General may from time to time, by Order in Council, make regulations for all or any of the following purposes:

(a) Regulating the conduct of scientific research within the territorial sea and the exclusive economic zone:

(b) Prescribing measures for the protection and preservation of the marine environment of the territorial sea and the zone:

(c) Regulating the construction, operation, and use of artificial islands (whether permanent or temporary), and other installations and structures within the territorial sea or the exclusive economic zone, including the establishment of safety zones around such islands, installations, and structures:

(d) Regulating the exploration and exploitation of the territorial sea and the exclusive economic zone for the production of energy from the water, currents, and winds, and for any other economic purposes:

(e) Providing for the designation or appointment of authorised officers for the purposes of this Act:

(f) Providing for the conservation and management of fisheries resources within the territorial sea and the zone:

(g) Providing for such other matters as are necessary or expedient for giving full effect to sovereignty in respect of Tokelau in relation to the territorial sea, and to the sovereign rights of Tokelau in relation to the zone:

(h) Providing that a breach of any regulations made under this section shall be a criminal offence, and imposng penalties by way of fine not exceeding $ 10,000 for any such offences:

(i) Providing for such other matters as are contemplated by or necessary for giving full effect to the provisions of this Act and for its due administration.

12. *General provisions as to enforcement*— (1) Any constable or authorised officer may at any time (with or without a warrant) stop, board, inspect, and search any foreign fishing craft within the internal waters, territorial sea, or exclusive economic zone of Tokelau, and any equipment on board or used by the craft, and any fish on board the craft.

(2) Where any constable or authorised officer has reasonable cause to believe that any offence against this Act, or against any regulations made under this Act, or against any other law relating to fishing within the internal waters, territorial sea, or exclusive economic zone of Tokelau, has been committed in respect of any foreign fishing craft, he may (with or without a warrant)—

(a) Seize and detain all fish on board the craft; and

(b) Apprehend and detain any person whom he has reasonable cause to believe has committed any such offence; and

(c) If he has reasonable cause to believe that any such offence has been committed by the licensee, owner, or master of the craft, seize and detain the craft, and any equipment on board or used by the craft—

to be dealt with in accordance with law.

(3) Any constable or authorised officer may exercise the powers conferred on him by subsections (1) and (2) of this section with the aid of such assistants as he considers to be necessary for the purpose.

(4) Where any foreign fishing craft, equipment, or fish is ordered to be forfeited to the Crown pursuant to this Act or to any regulations made under this Act, that craft, equipment, or fish shall be deemed to be forfeited accordingly, and shall be disposed of in such manner as the Administrator of Tokelau thinks fit.

Cf. 1976, No. 140, s. 8 (5)

13. *Onus of proof in respect of offences*— In any criminal proceedings under this Act, where a defendant is charged with having committed an offence against any provision in regulations made under this Act under which a licence is required for the doing of any act, the onus shall be on the defendant to prove that, at the time to which the charge relates, the requisite licence was duly held.

14. *Repeal*— The Tokelau (Territorial Sea and Fishing Zone) Act 1976 is hereby repealed.

Cf. 1976, No. 140, s. 9.

This Act is administered in the Ministry of Foreign Affairs.

WELLINGTON, NEW ZEALAND: Printed under the authority of the New Zealand Government, by E.C. KEATING, Government Printer, 1978

44. Nigeria

Decree No. 28
Entered into force: October 5, 1978.
Source: Nigerian Ministry of Information, Printing Division, Lagos.

EXCLUSIVE ECONOMIC ZONE DECREE 1978

[2nd October 1978] Commencement

THE FEDERAL MILITARY GOVERNMENT hereby decrees as follows:

Delimitation of Exclusive Economic Zone of Nigeria

1. (1) Subject to the other provisions of this Decree, there is hereby denominated a zone to be known as the Exclusive Economic Zone of Nigeria (hereinafter referred to as the 'Exclusive Zone') which shall be an area extending from the external limits of the territorial waters of Nigeria up to a distance of two hundred nautical miles from the baselines from which the breadth of the territorial waters of Nigeria is measured.

(2) Notwithstanding subsection (1) above but subject to the provisions of any treaty or other written agreement between Nigeria and any neighbouring littoral State, the delimitation of the Exclusive Zone between Nigeria and any such State shall be the median or equidistance line.

(3) For the purposes of this section, 'the median or equidistance line' means the line every point of which is equidistant from the nearest points of the baselines from which the breadth of the territorial waters of Nigeria and the State concerned are measured.

Exploitation, etc. of Exclusive Zone. 1967 No. 5., 1969 No. 51., 1971 No. 30

2. (1)Without prejudice to the Territorial Waters Decree 1967, the Petroleum Decree 1969 or the Sea Fisheries Decree 1971, sovereign and exclusive rights with respect to the exploration and exploitation of the natural resources of the sea bed, subsoil and superjacent waters of the Exclusive Zone shall vest in the Federal Republic of Nigeria and such rights shall be exercisable by the Federal Military Government or by such Federal Commissioner or agency as that Government may from time to time designate in that behalf either generally or in any special case.

(2) Subsection (1) of this section shall be subject to the provisions of any treaty to which Nigeria is a party with respect to the exploitation of the living resources of the Exclusive Zone.

Power to errect installations, etc. and offences in relation thereto

3. (1) For the purpose of exploring and exploiting, conserving and managing the natural resources and other activities for the economic exploration and exploitation of the Exclusive Zone, the appropriate authority may establish, or permit the establishment, operation and use by any other person subject to such conditions as may be prescribed, in designated areas–

(a) artificial islands;

(b) installations and structures.

(2) The appropriate authority may, for the purpose of protecting any installation in a designated area by order published in the *Gazette,* prohibit ships, subject to any exceptions provided in the order, from entering without its consent such part of that area as may be specified in such order.

(3) If any ship enters any part of a designated area in contravention of an order made under this section, its owner or master shall be liable on conviction to a fine of N 5,000 or imprisonment for 12 months or to both unless he proves that the prohibition imposed by the order was not, and would not on reasonable inquiry have become, known to the master.

(4) In this section, 'designated area' means any area of the Exclusive Zone so designated by the appropriate authority for the purposes of subsection (1) above.

Applicability of criminal and civil laws, etc.

4. (1) Any act or omission which–

(a) takes place on, under or above an installation in a designated area or any waters within 200 metres of such an installation; and

(b) would, if taking place in any part of Nigeria, constitute an offence under the enactment in force in that part,

shall be treated for the purposes of that law as taking place in Nigeria.

(2) Offences under subsection (1) above shall be triable by the Federal Revenue Court whether or not such offence would, if actually committed in Nigeria, be triable under the applicable enactment by a court other than the Federal Revenue Court.

(3) The prosecution of any offence under this Decree shall be at the instance of the Attorney-General of the Federation.

(4) In this section, 'enactment' means any Act, Decree, Law, Edict relating to criminal or civil law (including torts) and any subsidiary instrument made thereunder including rules of court and, in matters other than criminal matters, rules of law applicable to or adopted in any part of Nigeria.

Offences by bodies corporate

5. (1) Where a body corporate is guilty of an offence under this Decree and the offence is proved to have been committed with the consent or connivance of, or to be attributable to any neglect on the part of, any director, manager, secretary, or other similar officer of the body corporate or of any person who was purporting to act in any such capacity he, as well as the body corporate, shall be guilty of the offence and shall be liable to be proceeded against and punished accordingly.

(2) For the purposes of this section, 'director' in relation to a body corporate established for the purpose of carrying on under national ownership any industry or part of an industry or undertaking being a body corporate whose affairs are managed by its members, means a member of that body corporate.

Interpretation

6. In this Decree, unless the context otherwise requires–

'the appropriate authority' means the Federal Military Government or any other person or authority designated in that behalf by the Federal Military Government by virtue of section 2 of this Decree;

'designated area' has the meaning assigned thereto by section 3 (4) of this Decree;

'the Exclusive Zone' means the Exclusive Economic Zone of Nigeria as delimited by section 1 of this Decree;

1967 No. 5

'territorial waters of Nigeria' has the meaning assigned thereto by the Territorial Waters Decree 1967.

Citation

7. This Decree may be cited as the Exclusive Economic Zone Decree 1978.

MADE at Lagos this 2nd day of October 1978.

Lt-General O. Obasanjo,
Head of the Federal Military Government,
Commander-in-Chief of the Armed Forces,
Federal Republic of Nigeria

Explanatory Note

(This note does not form part of the above Decree but is intended to explain its purport)

The Decree delimits the Exclusive Economic Zone of Nigeria, being an area extending up to 200 nautical miles seawards from the coasts of Nigeria. Within this Zone, and subject to universally recognised rights of other states (including land-locked States), Nigeria would exercise certain sovereign rights especially in relation to the conservation or exploitation of the natural resources (minerals, living species, etc.) of the seabed, its subsoil and superjacent waters and the right to regulate by law the establishment of artificial structures and installations and marine scientific research, amongst other things.

Published by Authority of the Federal Military Government of Nigeria and Printed by the Ministry of Information, Printing Division, Lagos.

45. Norway

A. Act No. 91, and B. Royal Decree of December 17, 1976.
Entered into force: January 1, 1977.
Source: *United Nations ST/LEG/SER.B/19*, pp. 241-243.

(A) ACT NO. 91 OF 17 DECEMBER 1976 RELATING TO THE ECONOMIC ZONE OF NORWAY[1]

Paragraph 1

An economic zone shall be established in the seas adjacent to the coast of the Kingdom of Norway. The King shall determine the date for the establishment of the economic zone and the waters to which it shall apply.

The outer limit of the economic zone shall be drawn at a distance of 200 nautical miles (1 nautical mile = 1,852 metres) from the applicable baselines, but not beyond the median line in relation to other States.

The establishment of the economic zone shall not entail changes in the provisions regarding the territorial sea of Norway.

Paragraph 2

The establishment of the economic zone shall not affect the right of navigation through or overflight over the waters in question, or the right to lay submarine cables and pipelines.

The establishment of the economic zone shall not affect the contents of, or the field of application of, the Act of 21 June 1963 No. 12[2] relating to the exploration for and exploitation of submarine natural resources, or of regulations issued pursuant thereto.

Paragraph 3

Persons who are not Norwegian nationals, or placed on an equal footing with Norwegian nationals under the Act of 17 June 1966 No. 19 relating to Norway's fishery limit and prohibition against fishing etc. by aliens inside the fishery limit, may not engage in fishing or hunting within the Norwegian economic zone. The provisions of the said Act shall apply correspondingly in the economic zone.

The provisions in the first paragraph shall apply unless otherwise provided in regulations issued pursuant to paragraphs 4 or 6 of this Act.

Paragraph 4

The King may issue regulations on fishing and hunting in the economic zone, including regulations concerning:

(a) Total allowable catch and maximum catch effort, with regard to over-all fisheries as well as with regard to individual species and specific areas.

(b) Access for fishermen from other States to fish allotted shares of the allowable catch, and the terms and conditions for such fishing.

(c) Measures for assuring the rational and proper conduct of fishing activities, including provisions as to the number and size of vessels, use of gear, restrictions of gear, close periods, trawler-free zones and other area restrictions.

[1] Entered into force on 17 December 1976 pursuant to paragraph 9. English text provided by the Permanent Representative of Norway to the United Nations in a note verbale of 27 December 1976.

[2] Reproduced in ST/LEG/SER.B/15, p. 393.

(d) Other measures for the protection, conservation and reproduction of stocks of fish, shellfish and other living resources.

Paragraph 5

Prior to the implementation of the Norwegian economic zone, the King may, for areas referred to in paragraph 1, lay down interim provisions for the protection of fish stocks, for the limitation of foreign fishing and for the rational and proper conduct of fishing activities.

Paragraph 6

For the area of the economic zone between 12 and 200 nautical miles from the baselines, the King may, when necessary by reason of agreements with other States or where special considerations so require, make exceptions to the provisions of paragraphs 3, 4 and 5 or from regulations issued pursuant to these provisions. For areas where the Act of 17 June 1966 No. 19 relating to Norway's fishery limit and prohibition against fishing etc. by aliens inside the fishery limit has not been put into effect, such exceptions may also be applied to areas inside 12 nautical miles.

Paragraph 7

Subject to the rules of international law, the King may issue specific regulations in respect of the zone, including regulations concerning:

(a) The protection of the environment.
(b) Scientific research.
(c) Permanent or temporary artificial islands, installations, including artificial port facilities, and other structures.
(d) Cables and pipelines.
(e) The exploration and exploitation of the economic zone for other economic purposes, including the production of energy.

Paragraph 8

Anyone wilfully or negligently violating the provisions of this Act or regulations issued pursuant thereto, or aiding and abetting therein, shall be punished by fines. Attempted violations shall be similarly punished.

In the event of any violation of the provisions of this Act, or of regulations issued pursuant thereto, the vessel which has been used in such violation, together with the equipment, catch and gear on board, may be seized, irrespective of ownership. In lieu of the property, its value may be confiscated, in whole or in part, from the offender or from the person on whose behalf he has acted, or from the owner himself. It may be decided that any mortgage or other title or lien in the property seized shall be forfeited in whole or in part. The provisions of paragraph 37 C of the penal code shall apply correspondingly.

For an interim period, or pursuant to agreement with another State, the King may limit, in whole or in part, the application of the first and second paragraphs.

(B) ROYAL DECREE OF 17 DECEMBER 1976 RELATING TO THE ESTABLISHMENT OF THE ECONOMIC ZONE OF NORWAY[1]

(1) Pursuant to the Act of 17 December 1976 relating to the economic zone of Norway, the economic zone shall be established in the waters off the Norwegian mainland with effect from 1 January 1977. The outer limit for the economic zone shall be at a distance of 200 nautical miles (1 nautical mile = 1,852 metres) from and parallel to the established baselines. Where the economic zone is adjacent to the area of

[1] English text provided by the Permanent Representative of Norway to the United Nations in a note verbale of 27 December 1976.

jurisdiction of another State, the limit shall be drawn according to agreement.

(2) Pursuant to the Act of 17 December 1976 relating to the economic zone of Norway, paragraph 4, subparagraph B, from 1 January 1977 and until further notice, access to fishing and hunting in Norway's economic zone, beyond a distance of 12 nautical miles from the established baselines and on the terms deriving from items (3) and (4) below, shall be accorded to fishermen from States which have entered into an agreement with Norway concerning such access to fishing and hunting, or which are engaged in negotiations with Norway with a view to arriving at such an agreement.

(3) Pursuant to paragraph 4 in the said Act, the Ministry of Fisheries shall be empowered to issue regulations on fishing and hunting in the economic zone, comprising provisions in respect of quotas and other catch limitations, including area limitations, for such foreign fishing operations as may take place according to item (2) above. The Ministry of Fisheries shall likewise be empowered, pursuant to paragraph 6 in the Act, to issue regulations on exceptions to provisions in paragraph 3 of the said Act, first paragraph, second sentence.

(4) With effect from 1 January 1977, foreign vessels engaged in fishing or hunting in Norway's economic zone, in accordance with the provisions in items (2) and (3) above, shall notify the Directorate of Fisheries in Bergen as to when such fishing is commenced and discontinued, and shall submit weekly reports on the amount of catch harvested of each separate species of fish and on the catch areas. In cases where quotas for the year 1977 have not yet been determined, the volume of catch taken shall be regarded as an advance to be deducted from such quotas as may be allocated at a later date.

(5) The provisions laid down above do not affect the provisions in the royal decree of 31 January 1975 on the introduction of certain no-trawling zones, cf. the Act on no-trawling zones of 17 January 1975.

46. Oman

Royal Decree No. 15/81.
Entered into force: February 20, 1981.
Source: Ministry of Foreign Affairs (Unofficial translation from Arabic by Ministry of Foreign Affairs).

SULTAN'S DECREE

In respect of territorial Waters, Continental shelf and exclusive economic Zone

We QABOOS BIN SAID, Sultan of Oman

Having reviewed the Sultan's Decree No. 26/75 in respect of forming the State's Administrative System and its amendments,

and the Sultan's Decree issued on 20-7-1972 in respect of territorial waters, continental shelf and fishing zone and its amendments in accordance with the Sultan's Decree No. 44/77 dated 15/6/1977

and in observance of public interest.

We have decreed as follows

Article 1. Territorial waters

The Sultanate of Oman shall have full soverignty over its territorial waters, the airspace above them and the seabed within their limits in accordance with the Sultanate's rules and in conformity with the principle of surface traffic for foreign ships and aircraft through and over international straits.

Article 2

The territorial waters of the Sultanate shall extend for twelve nautical miles (22224 metres) in the outshore direction and shall be determined in the light of the following measurements and rules;

(a) The outer boundary of the territorial waters shall be the line passing all points that are twelve nautical miles from the base-line.
(b) Unless excepted by this decree, the normal baseline by which territorial waters are determined shall begin at the end of the shores of the mainland, islands or rocks.
(c) The Government of the Sultanate of Oman shall issue a declaration determining the procedure of using the straight base-lines delineating the base-lines on any part of the Omani coast, the water-blocking lines among inlets and fiords and the waters between the islands and the coast line. Any line having such a quality shall be considered as a base-line.

The Government of the Sultanate of Oman shall amend or rescind this item should there be any need to do so.

Article 3. Internal waters

The Sultanate of Oman's internal waters shall comprise all the waters on the side facing the coast beginning from the base-line of territorial waters. Internal waters shall be subject to Omani legislature applied on ports, jetties and fiords.

Article 4. Exclusive economic zone

The Sultanate of Oman shall have all sovereignty of the exclusive economic zone for the purposes of exploring and developing its aquatic and other wealth.

Article 5

The exclusive economic zone shall extend for two hundred nautical miles and shall begin at the same base-lines from which territorial waters shall be measured.

Article 6. Continental shelf

The Sultanate of Oman shall have full sovereignty over its continental shelf for the purposes of exploring its natural wealth.

Article 7

The Government of the Sultanate of Oman shall issue a declaration determining the stretch of its continental shelf.

Article 8. General rules

Should there be coasts of other States facing or adjacent to the Sultanate's coast, the outer limits of territorial waters, exclusive economic zone and continental shelf shall be determined by means of the median line which divides the area comprising the local waters of both States into two equal parts when measured from the nearest base-line points.

Article 9

The exact limits of the Sultanate's territorial waters, exclusive economic zone and continental shelf shall be determined by the Government of the Sultanate of Oman on hydrographic charts and drawings and in geodetic data.

Article 10

The rules of the Sultan's decree dated 20/7/1972 in respect of territorial waters, continental shelf and fishing zone shall be abolished together with the rules of the Sultan's decree No. 44/77 dated 15-6-1977 and any other rules contradicting this decree.

Article 11

This decree shall be published in the Gazette and shall take effect as from the date of its publication.

10 February 1981

Qaboos Bin Said
Sultan of Oman

47. Pakistan

Territorial Waters and Maritime Zones Act, 1976.
Entered into force: December 31, 1976.
Source: Ministry of Foreign Affairs.

BILL

to provide for the declaration of the territorial waters and maritime zones of Pakistan

WHEREAS it is expedient to provide for the declaration of the territorial waters and maritime zones of Pakistan and for matters connected therewith:

It is hereby enacted as follows:—

1. Short title and commencement

(1) This Act may be called the Territorial Waters and Maritime Zones Act, 1976.

(2) It shall come into force at once.

2. Territorial waters

(1) The sovereignty of Pakistan extends and has always extended to the territorial waters of Pakistan, hereinafter referred to as the territorial waters, as well as to the air space over, and the bed and sub-soil of such waters.

(2) The limit of the territorial waters is twelve nautical miles beyond the land territory and internal waters of Pakistan measured from the baseline.

(3) The baseline from which such limit shall be measured and the waters on the landward side of which shall form part of the internal waters of Pakistan shall be specified by the Federal Government by notification in the official Gazette.

(4) Where a single island, rock or a composite group thereof constituting a part of the territory of Pakistan is situated off the main coast, the baseline referred to in sub-section (3) shall be drawn along the outer seaward limits of such island, rock or composite group.

3. Use of territorial waters by foreign ships

(1) Without prejudice to the provisions of any other law for the time being in force and subject to the provisions of sub-section (2) and sub-section (3), all foreign ships shall enjoy the right of innocent passage through the territorial waters.

Explanation.— For the purposes of this section, passage is innocent so long as it is not prejudicial to the peace, good order or security of Pakistan.

(2) Foreign warships, including submarines and other under water vehicles and Foreign Military Aircraft may enter or pass through the territorial waters and the air space over such waters with the prior permission of the Federal Government.

Provided that submarines and other under water vehicles shall navigate on the surface and show their flag while passing through such waters.

(3) Foreign super tankers, nuclear powered ships and ships carrying nuclear or other inherently dangerous or noxious substances or materials may enter or pass through the territorial waters after giving prior notice to the Federal Government.

(4) The Federal Government may, if satisfied that it is necessary so to do in the interest of the peace,

good order or security of Pakistan or any part thereof, suspend, by notification in the official Gazette, subject to such exceptions and qualifications, if any, as may be specified in the notification, the entry of all or any class of foreign ships into such area of the territorial waters as may be specified in the notification.

4. Contiguous Zone

(1) The Contiguous Zone of Pakistan, hereinafter referred to as the Contiguous Zone, is an area adjacent to and beyond the territorial waters and extending seawards to a line twenty-four nautical miles measured from the baseline declared under sub-section (3) of section 2.

(2) The Federal Government may exercise such powers and take such measures in or in respect of the Contiguous Zone as it may consider necessary to prevent and punish the contravention of, and an attempt to contravene, any law in force in Pakistan relating to—

(a) the security of Pakistan;
(b) immigration and sanitation; and
(c) customs and other fiscal matters.

(3) The Federal Government may, by notification in the official Gazette,—

(a) extend to the Contiguous Zone any law relating to any matter referred to in clause (a) or clause (b) or clause (c) of sub-section (2), for the time being in force in Pakistan or any part thereof, with such modifications, if any, as may be specified in the notification; and
(b) make such provisions as it may consider necessary for facilitating the enforcement of such law and any law so extended shall have effect as if the Contiguous Zone formed part of the territory of Pakistan.

5. Continental Shelf

(1) The Continental Shelf of Pakistan, hereinafter referred to as the Continental Shelf, shall comprise the seabed and sub-soil of the submarine areas that extend beyond the limit of the territorial waters of Pakistan throughout the natural prolongation of the land territory of Pakistan to the outer edge of the continental margin or, where the outer edge of the continental margin does not extend up to a distance of two hundred nautical miles from the baseline declared under sub-section (3) of section 2, up to that distance.

(2) Pakistan has, and always had, full and exclusive sovereign rights in respect of its Continental Shelf, including

(a) exclusive sovereign rights for the purpose of exploration, development exploitation, conservation and management of all resources, both living and non-living;
(b) exclusive rights and jurisdiction to authorize, regulate and control scientific research;
(c) exclusive rights and jurisdiction for the construction, maintenance or operation of artificial islands, off-shore terminals, installations and other structures and devices necessary for the exploration and exploitation of the resources of the Continental Shelf, for the convenience of shipping or for any other purpose; and
(d) exclusive jurisdiction to preserve and protect the marine environment and to prevent and control marine pollution.

(3) No person, including a foreign Government, shall, except under, and in accordance with the terms of, any agreement with the Federal Government of a licence or letter of authority granted by the Federal Government, explore the Continental Shelf or exploit its resources or carry out any search or excavation or conduct any research within the Continental Shelf or drill therein or construct, maintain or operate therein for any purpose whatsoever any artificial islands, off-shore terminal, installation or other structure or device.

(4) The Federal Government may, by notification in the official Gazette,—

(a) declare any area of the Continental Shelf and its superjacent waters to be a designated area; and

(*b*) make such provisions as it may deem necessary with respect to all or any of the following matters, namely:—

(i) the exploration, development, exploitation and protection of the resources of the Continental Shelf within such designated area;

(ii) the safety and protection of artificial islands, off-shore terminals, installations and other structures and devices in such designated area;

(iii) the protection of marine environment of such designated area;

(iv) customs and other fiscal matters in relation to such designated area; and

(v) the regulation of entry into and passage through the designated area of foreign ships by the establishment of fairways, sealanes, traffic separation schemes or any other mode of ensuring freedom of navigation which is not prejudicial to the interests of Pakistan.

(5) The Federal Government may, by notification in the official Gazette,—

(*a*) extend to the whole or any part of the Continental Shelf any law for the time being in force in Pakistan or any part thereof, with such modifications, if any, as may be specified in the notification; and

(*b*) make such provisions as it may consider necessary for facilitating the enforcement of such law;

and any law so extended shall have effect as if the Continental Shelf or, as the case may be, the part thereof to which it has been extended formed part of the territory of Pakistan.

(6) Subject to any measures that may be necessary for protecting the interests of Pakistan, and without prejudice to the provisions of sub-section (2), the Federal Government may not impede the laying or maintenance of submarine cables or pipelines on the seabed of the Continental Shelf by foreign States:

Provided that the consent of the Federal Government shall be necessary for the delineation of the course for the laying of such cables or pipelines.

6. Exclusive Economic Zone

(1) The Exclusive Economic Zone of Pakistan, hereinafter referred to as the Exclusive Economic Zone, is an area beyond and adjacent to the territorial waters the limit of which is two hundred nautical miles from the baseline declared under sub-section (3) of section 2.

(2) In the Exclusive Economic Zone, its bed and sub-soil and the superjacent waters, Pakistan has—

(*a*) exclusive sovereign rights for the purpose of exploration, development, exploitation, conservation and management of all resources, both living and non-living, as well as for producing energy from tides, winds, currents and the sun.

(*b*) exclusive rights and jurisdiction for the construction, maintenance or operation of artificial islands, off-shore terminals, installations and other structures and devices necessary for the exploration and exploitation of the resources of the Zone or for the convenience of shipping or for any other purpose;

(*c*) exclusive rights and jurisdiction to authorize, regulate and control scientific research;

(*d*) exclusive jurisdiction to preserve and protect the marine environment and to prevent and control marine pollution; and

(*e*) such other rights as are recognized by international law.

(3) No person, including a foreign Government, shall, except under, and in accordance with the terms of any agreement with the Federal Government or a licence or letter of authority granted by the Federal Government, explore or exploit any resources of the Exclusive Economic Zone or carry out any search or excavation or conduct any research within the Exclusive Economic Zone or drill therein or construct, maintain or operate therein for any purpose whatsoever any artificial island, off-shore terminal, installation or other structure or device:

Provided that fishing in the Exclusive Economic Zone shall be regulated by the provisions of the

Exclusive Fishery Zone (Regulation of Fishing) Act, 1975 (XXII of 1975).

(4) The Federal Government may, by notification in the official Gazette,—

(a) declare any area of the Exclusive Economic Zone to be a designated area; and

(b) make such provisions as it may deem necessary with respect to all or any of the following matters, namely:—

(i) the exploration, development, exploitation and protection of the resources of such designated area;

(ii) other activities for the economic exploitation and exploration of such designated area, such as the production of energy from tides, winds, currents and the sun;

(iii) the safety and protection of artificial islands, off-shore terminals, installations and other structures and devices in such designated area;

(iv) the protection of marine environment of such designated area;

(v) customs and other fiscal matters in relation to such designated area; and

(vi) the regulation of entry into and passage through the designated area of foreign ships by the establishment of fairways, sealanes, traffic separation schemes or any other mode of ensuring freedom of navigation which is not prejudicial to the interest of Pakistan.

(5) The Federal Government may, by notification in the official Gazette,—

(a) extend to the whole or any part of the Exclusive Economic Zone any law for the time being in force in Pakistan or any part thereof subject to such modifications as may be specified in the notification; and

(b) make such provisions as it may consider necessary for facilitating the enforcement of such law, and any law so extended shall have effect as if the Exclusive Economic Zone or, as the case may be, the part thereof to which it has been extended formed part of the territory of Pakistan.

(6) The provisions of sub-section (6) of section 5 shall apply in relation to the laying or maintenance of submarine cables or pipelines on the seabed of the Exclusive Economic Zone as they apply in relation to the laying or maintenance of submarine cables or pipelines on the seabed of the Continental Shelf.

(7) In the Exclusive Economic Zone and the air space over the Zone, ships and aircraft of all States shall, subject to the exercise by Pakistan of its rights within the Zone, enjoy freedom of navigation and overflight.

7. Historic waters

(1) The Federal Government may, by notification in the official Gazette, specify the limits of such waters adjacent to its land territory as are the historic waters of Pakistan.

(2) The sovereignty of Pakistan extends, and has always extended, to the historic waters of Pakistan and to the seabed and subsoil underlying, and the air space over, such waters.

8. Maritime boundaries between Pakistan and States having coasts opposite or adjacent to those of Pakistan

(1) Notwithstanding anything contained in any other provision of this Act,—

(a) the delimitation of the territorial waters between Pakistan and any other state whose coast is opposite or adjacent to that of Pakistan shall be determined by agreement between Pakistan and such state and pending such agreement and unless any other provisional arrangements are agreed to between them, the boundary with regard to the territorial waters between Pakistan and such state shall not extend beyond the line every point of which is equidistant from the baseline from which the breadth of the territorial waters of Pakistan and of such state is measured; and

(b) the delimitation of the Contiguous Zone, the Continental Shelf, the Exclusive Economic Zone and other maritime zones between Pakistan and any other state whose coast is opposite or adjacent to that of Pakistan shall be effected by agreement in accordance with equitable

principles and taking account of all the relevant circumstances, and pending such agreement or a settlement Pakistan and such state shall make provisional arrangements taking into account the said principles for delimitation of the Contiguous Zone, the Continental Shelf, the Exclusive Economic Zone and other maritime zones.

(2) Every agreement referred to in clauses (a) and (b) of sub-section (1) shall, as soon as may be after it is entered into, be published in the official Gazette.

9. Publication of charts

The Federal Government may cause the baseline referred to in sub-section (3) of section 2, the limits of the Territorial Waters, the Contiguous Zone, the Continental Shelf and the Exclusive Economic Zone and the maritime boundaries as settled by agreements referred to in section 8 to be published in charts.

10. Offences

Whoever contravenes any provision of this Act or of any rule of notification made or issued thereunder shall, without prejudice to any other action which may be taken against such person under any other provision of this or of any other law, be punishable with imprisonment for a term which may extend to three years, or with fine, or with both.

11. Offences by companies

(1) Where an offence punishable under section 10 has been committed by a company, every person who, at the time the offence was committed, was in charge of, and was responsible to the company for, the conduct of the business of the company, as well as the company, shall be deemed to be guilty of the offence and shall be liable to be proceeded against and punished accordingly:

Provided that nothing contained in this sub-section shall render any such person liable to any punishment provided in this Act if he proves that the offence was committed without his knowledge or that he exercised all due diligence to prevent the commission of such offence.

(2) Notwithstanding anything contained in sub-section (1), where an offence punishable under section 10 has been committed by a company and it is proved that the offence has been committed with the consent or connivance of, or is attributable to any neglect on the part of, any director, manager, secretary or other officer of the company, such director, manager, secretary or other officer shall also be deemed to be guilty of that offence and shall be liable to be proceeded against and punished accordingly.

Explanation.— For the purpose of this section,—

(a) 'company' means any body corporate and includes a firm or other association of individuals; and

(b) 'director', in relation to a firm, means a partner in the firm.

12. Place of trial

Any person committing an offence punishable under section 10 or under any of the laws extended under this Act may be tried for the offence in such place or places as the Federal Government may, by general or special order published in the official Gazette, direct in this behalf.

13. Previous sanction of the Federal Government for prosecution

No prosecution shall be instituted against any person in respect of any offence punishable under section 10 or under any of the laws extended under this Act without the previous sanction of the Federal Government or such officer or authority as may be authorised by that Government by order in writing in this behalf.

14. Power to make rules

(1) The Federal Government may, by notification in the official Gazette, make rules for carrying out the purposes of this Act:

(2) In particular and without prejudice to the generality of the foregoing power, such rules may provide

for all or any of the following matters, namely:—

(a) regulation of the conduct of any person in the Territorial Waters, the Contiguous Zone, the Continental Shelf, the Exclusive Economic Zone or any other maritime zone of Pakistan;

(b) regulation of the exploration, development, exploitation, conservation and management of the resources of the Continental Shelf;

(c) regulation of the exploration, development, exploitation, conservation and management of the resources of the Exclusive Economic Zone;

(d) regulation of the construction, maintenance and operation of artificial islands, off-shore terminals, installations and other structures and devices referred to in section 5 and section 6;

(e) preservation and protection of the marine environment and prevention and control of marine pollution;

(f) authorisation, regulation and control of the conduct of scientific research;

(g) fees in relation to licences and letters of authority referred to in sub-section (3) of section 5 and sub-section (3) of section 6 or for any other purpose; or

(h) any matter incidental to any of the matters specified in clauses (a) to (g).

48. Papua New Guinea

Offshore Seas Proclamation, 1978 referencing the National Seas Act, Act No. 7 of 1977
Entered into force: March 31, 1978
Source: *Papua New Guinea National Gazette, No. G24,* March 30, 1978

NOTICE OF COMMENCEMENT

1. Tore Lokoloko, G.C.M.G. Governor-General, by virtue of the powers conferred by the undermentioned Act and all other powers me enabling, acting with, and in accordance with, the advice of the Minister for Foreign Affairs and Trade, hereby advise that the said Act shall come into operation on and from 31st March, 1978.

No. 7 of 1977—*National Seas Act* 1977.

Dated this 17th day of March, 1978.

TORE LOKOLOKO,
Governor-General.

THE INDEPENDENT STATE OF PAPUA NEW GUINEA

National Seas Act 1977

OFFSHORE SEAS PROCLAMATION 1978,

Being a Proclamation—

(a) to delimit the offshore seas of the State; and

(b) to provide that certain waters do not form part of the territorial sea of the state,

and for other purposes,

MADE by the Head of State, acting with, and in accordance with, the advice of the National Executive Council under the *National Seas Act* 1977.

1. Outer limit of offshore seas

The line consecutively described in Schedules 1, 2 and 3 is the line for the purposes of Section 6 of the *National Seas Act* 1977 and, subject to Sections 3(2) and 4 of this Proclamation, the offshore seas of the State shall be deemed to comprise all the waters outside the baselines and within the line so described.

2. Line described in schedules 1 and 3

(1) That part of the line described in Schedules 1 and 3 is drawn—

(a) to give effect to agreements with other states where agreement on the line has been reached; and

(b) without prejudice to the ultimate location of appropriate boundary lines, to adopt an interim boundary in areas where no agreement with other states has been reached; and

(c) to adopt limits of 200 miles from the baselines where no boundary lines with other states may appropriately be drawn.

(2) Subject to Subsection (3), the description contained in Schedules 1 and 3 is based on the nautical charts BA3250, BA3832, BA3830, BA214, BA3419, BA208 and BA2759a in respect of the areas covered by those charts.

(3) The points described in the Schedules as Points 30 to 42 inclusive, and the descriptions of those parts of the line commencing at Point 30 and ending at Point 38 and commencing at Point 39 and ending at Point 42 respectively, have been based on the current World Aeronautical Charts of the area in which those points and parts of the line are located.

3. Temporary limit

(1) In this section 'Secondary Area' means the area of sea bounded by the temporary line described in Schedule 2 and a more southerly line between Points 38 and 39 provisionally agreed upon between the State and Australia to be proclaimed after an opportunity for further consultation between the two governments on outstanding matters of substance concerning the nature and manner of exercise of jurisdiction in that area so as to safeguard the interests of all affected parties.

(2) For the purposes of this Proclamation, so much of the waters of the sea as are within three miles of the land of the islands specified in Schedule 5 that would not, but for this section, fall within the Secondary Area shall be deemed to be within the Secondary Area.

(3) Nothing in Subsection (2) shall be construed as indicating that the State abandons its seabed resources jurisdiction associated with the islands specified in Schedule 5, but that subsection shall be read as indicating only that the State intends to suspend temporarily the exercise of such jurisdiction over and in respect of so much of the area of those waters as lies north of the temporary line described in Schedule 2 pending the outcome of further negotiations between the State and Australia.

4. Certain waters not included in offshore seas

The offshore seas of the State shall not be deemed to include the waters described in Schedule 4.

5. Certain waters not included in territorial sea

For the purposes of Section 2 of the *National Seas Act* 1977, so much of the waters of the sea in the area described in Schedule 6 as are contained between the baselines and the 12 mile outer-limit line that are more than three miles seaward from the nearest point on the baselines do not form parts of the territorial sea.

SECS 1 AND 2. SCHEDULE 1

Part of proclaimed line

Commencing at the point of the intersection of the meridian 141° east longitude with the mean low water line on the northern coast of the island of New Guinea (Point 1) thence along straight lines successively linking that point and the following points:—

Point 2: the intersection of the parallel 2° 08′ 30″ south latitude with the meridian 141° 01′ 30″ east longitude.

Point 3: the intersection of the parallel 1° 04′ 00″ south latitude with the meridian 141° 23′ 42″ east longitude.

Point 4: the intersection of the parallel 0° 55′ 54″ south latitude with the meridian 141° 20′ 30″ east longitude.

Point 5: the intersection of the parallel 0° 47′ 00″ north latitude with the meridian 140° 49′ 00″ east longitude,

thence along a straight line towards the intersection of the parallel 2° 41′ 00″ north latitude with the meridian 140° 46′ 00″ east longitude to the most northerly point on that line (Point 6) that is 200 miles from the nearest point on a baseline, thence in a generally easterly direction along a line every point on which is 200 miles from the nearest point on a baseline to the first point (Point 7) on that line that is 200 miles from a base point in the Caroline Islands (hereinafter called 'the Micronesian base point') which base point shall be deemed to be the intersection of the parallel 1° 02′ 00″ north latitude with the meridian 154° 46′ 00″ east longitude; thence in a generally easterly direction along a median line between the nearest points on the baselines and the Micronesian base point to the next point on that median line (Point 8) that is 200 miles from the nearest point on a baseline; thence in a generally easterly and southerly direction along a line every point on which is 200 miles from the nearest points on the baselines to the first point on that line (Point 9) that is 200 miles from the nearest point of land in the Solomon Islands; thence in a generally westerly direction along a median line between the nearest points on the baselines and the nearest points of land in the Solomon Islands to the point on that median line (Point 10) that is 20 miles in a generally south easterly direction from the nearest point on a baseline of Nukumanu Atoll; thence along the geodesics successively linking Point 10 and the following points:—

Point 11: the intersection of the parallel 4° 48′ 30″ south latitude with the meridian 158° 46′ 30″ east longitude.

Point 12: the intersection of the parallel 4° 45′ 00″ south latitude with the meridian 158° 26′ 00″ east longitude.

Point 13: the intersection of the parallel 4° 47′ 00″ south latitude with the meridian 158° 09′ 00″ east longitude.

Point 14: the intersection of the parallel 5° 04′ 30″ south latitude with the meridian 158° 07′ 00″ east longitude.

Point 15: the intersection of the parallel 5° 37′ 00″ south latitude with the meridian 157° 59′ 00″ east longitude.

Point 16: the intersection of the parallel 5° 52′ 00″ south latitude with the meridian 157° 56′ 00″ east longitude.

Point 17: the intersection of the parallel 5° 05′ 00″ south latitude with the meridian 157° 20′ 00AI east longitude.

Point 18: the intersection of the parallel 5° 40′ 00″ south latitude with the meridian 156° 30′ 00″ east longitude.

Point 19: the intersection of the parallel 5° 54′ 00″ south latitude with the meridian 156° 26′ 00″ east longitude.

Point 20: the intersection of the parallel 6° 19′ 00″ south latitude with the meridian 156° 16′ 30″ east longitude;

thence along the geodesic to Point 21 that is the first point 12 miles seaward and equidistant from the nearest point on the baseline of OTUA Island and the nearest point of land in the Solomon Islands; thence along a line passing to the south of Bougainville Island being a median line between the nearest points on the baselines and the nearest points of land in the Solomon Islands, to a point to that line (Point 22) 12 miles in a generally south easterly direction from the nearest point on the baseline of KABUKEA Island; thence along the geodesics successively linking Point 22 and the following points:—

Point 23: the intersection of the parallel 7° 15′ 00″ south latitude with the meridian 155° 13′ 30″ east longitude.

Point 24: the intersection of the parallel 7° 29′ 00″ south latitude with the meridian 154° 52′ 00″ east longitude.

Point 25: the intersection of the parallel 9° 20′ 00″ south latitude with the meridian 155° 31′ 00″ east longitude.

Point 26: the intersection of the parallel 10° 41′ 00″ south latitude with the meridian 156° 40′ 00″ east longitude.

Point 27: the intersection of the parallel 11° 14′ 00″ south latitude with the meridian 157° 05′ 00″ east longitude.

Point 28: the intersection of the parallel 12° 52′ 00″ south latitude with the meridian 157° 25′ 00″ east longitude.

Point 29: the intersection of the parallel 13° 43′ 00″ south latitude with the meridian 157° 07′ 30″ east longitude.
Point 30: the intersection of the parallel 14° 05′ 00″ south latitude with the meridian 156° 40′ 00″ east longitude.
Point 31: the intersection of the parallel 14° 45′ 00″ south latitude with the meridian 154° 15′ 00″ east longitude.
Point 32: the intersection of the parallel 14° 38′ 00″ south latitude with the meridian 152° 07′ 00″ east longitude.
Point 33: the intersection of the parallel 13° 15′ 00″ south latitude with the meridian 148° 10′ 00″ east longitude.
Point 34: the intersection of the parallel 13° 10′ 00″ south latitude with the meridian 148° 03′ 00″ east longitude.
Point 35: the intersection of the parallel 12° 35′ 00″ south latitude with the meridian 147° 05′ 00″ east longitude.
Point 36: the intersection of the parallel 12° 20′ 00″ south latitude with the meridian 146° 30′ 00″ east longitude.
Point 37: the intersection of the parallel 9° 51′ 00″ south latitude with the meridian 144° 44′ 00″ east longitude.
Point 38: the intersection of the parallel 9° 30′ 00″ south latitude with the meridian 144° 15′ 00″ east longitude.

SEC. 1 SCHEDULE 2

Temporary line

Commencing at Point 38 described in Schedule 1 and proceeding in a northerly direction along the meridian 144° 15′ 00″ east longitude to the intersection of that meridian with a composite line being the line every point of which is on—

(a) the seaward limit of the declared offshore area under the *Petroleum (Submerged Lands) Act* 1975 as at 16th September 1975; or

(b) the seaward limit of the declared fishing zone described in Section 2 of the *Fisheries Act* 1974, as in force on 16th September 1975, as if the baseline within the meaning of the *National Seas Act* 1977 were the baseline referred to in that section,

whichever limit is, on any meridian of longitude, the more southern; thence in a generally westerly direction along that composite line to its intersection with the meridian 141° 20′ 00″ east longitude; and thence along that meridian of longitude south to Point 39 being the intersection of that meridian with the parallel 10° 10′ 30″ south latitude.

SEC. 1. SCHEDULE 3

Part of proclaimed line

Commencing at Point 39 described in Schedule 2 and thence along the geodesics successively linking that point and the following points:—

Point 40: the intersection of the parallel 10° 59′ 00″ south latitude with the meridian 140° 00′ 00″ east longitude.
Point 41: the intersection of the parallel 11° 09′ 00″ south latitude with the meridian 139° 23′ 00″ east longitude.
Point 42: the intersection of the parallel 10° 50′ 00″ south latitude with the meridian 139° 12′ 00″ east longitude;

thence along straight lines successively linking Point 42 and the following points:—

Point 43: the intersection of the parallel 10° 24′ 00″ south latitude with the meridian 139° 46′00″ east longitude.

Point 44: the intersection of the parallel 9° 52′ 00″ south latitude with the meridian 140° 29′ 00″ east longitude.

Point 45: the intersection of the parallel 9° 24′ 30″ south latitude with the meridian 140° 49′ 30″ east longitude.

Point 46: the intersection of the parallel 9° 23′ 00″ south latitude with the meridian 140° 52′ 00″ east longitude;

and thence along a straight line between Point 46 and a point described as 'point B3' in Articles 3 and 4 of the Agreement set forth in the Schedule to the *Indonesian Border Agreement Act* 1973, to the point where that line crosses the southern coast of the island of New Guinea, or if that line does not cross that coast, to that point B3 and thence by a straight line between that point and the position of the marker described as 'MM14' in Article 1 of that Agreement to the point where that line first crosses the coast or enters the internal waters of the State, as the case may be.

SEC. 4. SCHEDULE 4

Waters not included in offshore seas

1. The waters of the sea contained in the area bounded by a line every point on which is three miles seaward from the nearest points on the coast of the islands of SAIBAI (including for this purpose, KAUAMAG) and DAUAN, except where such a line is less than three miles from any other land, where the line shall be a median line between those islands and that other land.

2. The waters of the sea contained in the area bounded by a line every point on which is three miles seaward from the nearest point on the coast of BOIGU Island (including for this purpose, AUBUSI and MOIMI), except where such a line is less than three miles from any other land, where the line shall be a median line between that island and that other land.

SEC. 3(2). SCHEDULE 5

Islands

1. Deliverance Island.
2. Black Rocks.
3. Bramble Cay.
4. Anchor Cay.
5. East Cay.

SEC. 5. SCHEDULE 6

Area for purposes of section 5

The area bounded by a line commencing at the intersection of the parallel 9° 21′ 30″ south latitude with the meridian 142° 33′ 15″ east longitude; thence along the geodesic to the intersection of the parallel 9° 08′ 15″ south latitude with the meridian 143° 52′ 00″ east longitude; thence south along that meridian of longitude to the parallel 9° 40′ 00″ south latitude; thence west along that parallel of latitude to the meridian 142° 03′ 30″ east longitude; thence north along that meridian of longitude to its point of intersection with the southern coastline of the island of New Guinea at mean low water springs; thence in a generally easterly direction along the coastline to its intersection with the meridian 142° 33′ 15″ east longitude; and thence south along that meridian to the point of commencement.

Dated this 28th day of March, 1978.

TORE LOKO
Governor-General

49. Philippines

Presidential Decree No. 1599
Entered into force: July 11, 1979
Source: *Official Gazette,* April 30, 1979

ESTABLISHING AN EXCLUSIVE ECONOMIC ZONE AND FOR OTHER PURPOSES

Whereas, an exclusive economic zone extending to a distance of two hundred nautical miles from the baselines from which the territorial sea is measured is vital to the economic survival and development of the Republic of the Philippines.

Whereas, such a zone is now a recognized principle of international law;

Now, therefore, I, FERDINAND E. MARCOS, President of the Philippines, by virtue of the powers vested in me by the Constitution, do hereby decree and order:

Section 1

There is hereby established a zone to be known as the exclusive economic zone of the Philippines. The exclusive economic zone shall extend to a distance of two hundred nautical miles beyond and from the baselines from which the territorial sea is measured: Provided, That, where the outer limits of the zone as thus determined overlap the exclusive economic zone of an adjacent or neighboring state, the common boundaries shall be determined by agreement with the state concerned or in accordance with pertinent generally recognized principles of international law on delimitation.

Section 2

Without prejudice to the rights of the Republic of the Philippines over its territorial sea and continental shelf, it shall have and exercise in the exclusive economic zone established herein the following:

(a) Sovereign rights for the purpose of exploration and exploitation, conservation and management of the natural resources, whether living or non-living, both renewable and non-renewable, of the sea-bed, including the subsoil and the superjacent waters, and with regard to other activities for the economic exploitation and exploration of the resources of the zone, such as the production of energy from the water, currents and winds;

(b) Exclusive rights and jurisdiction with respect to the establishment and utilization of artificial islands, off-shore terminals, installations and structures, the preservation of the marine environment, including the prevention and control of pollution, and scientific research;

(c) Such other rights as are recognized by international law or state practice.

Section 3

Except in accordance with the terms of any agreement entered into with the Republic of the Philippines or of any license granted by it or under authority by the Republic of the Philippines, no person shall, in relation to the exclusive economic zone:

(a) explore or exploit any resources;

(b) carry out any search, excavation or drilling operations;

(c) conduct any research;

(d) construct, maintain or operate any artificial island, off-shore terminal, installation or other structure or device; or

(*e*) perform any act or engage in any activity which is contrary to, or in derogation of, the sovereign rights and jurisdiction herein provided

Nothing herein shall be deemed a prohibition on a citizen of the Philippines, whether natural or juridical, against the performance of any of the foregoing acts, if allowed under existing laws.

Section 4

Other states shall enjoy in the exclusive economic zone freedoms with respect to navigation and overflight, the laying of submarine cables and pipelines, and other internationally lawful uses of the sea relating to navigation and communications.

Section 5

(a) The President may authorize the appropriate government office/agency to make and promulgate such rules and regulations which may be deemed proper and necessary for carrying out the purposes of this decree.

(b) Any person who shall violate any provision of this decree or of any rule or regulation promulgated hereunder and approved by the President shall be subject to a fine which shall not be less than two thousand pesos (₱2,000.00) nor be more than one hundred thousand pesos (₱100,000.00) or imprisonment ranging from six (6) months to ten (10) years, or both such fine and imprisonment, in the discretion of the court. Vessels and other equipment or articles used in connection therewith shall be subject to seizure and forfeiture.

Section 6

This Decree shall take effect thirty (30) days after publication in the Official Gazette.

DONE in the City of Manila, this 11th day of June, in the year of Our Lord, nineteen hundred and seventy eight.

50. Portugal

A. Law No. 33/77.
Entered into force: May 28, 1977.
Sources: *Diario da Republica,* May 28, 1977, pp. 1241-1243, and *United Nations ST/LEG/SER.B/19,* pp. 93-95 (Translated from Portuguese by the Permanent Representative of Portugal to the United Nations).

B. Decree Law No. 119/78.
Entered into force: June 1, 1978.
Source: *Diario da Republica,* June 1, 1978, pp. 984-988.

A. ACT NO. 33/77 OF 28 MAY 1977

Article 1. Portuguese territorial sea

1. The breadth of the Portuguese territorial sea is 12 nautical miles.

2. The outer limits of the Portuguese territorial sea are those established by Portuguese law, in accordance with international law.

Article 2. Exclusive economic zone

1. An exclusive economic zone is hereby established, the outer limit of which is a line where each point is at a distance of 200 nautical miles from the point closet to the baseline from which the breadth of the Portuguese territorial sea is measured.

2. Pending the entry into force of the agreements with States whose coasts are opposite or adjacent to those of Portugal, the limits of the zone referred to in paragraph 1 shall not extend beyond the median line, every point of which is equidistant from the nearest point on the baselines from which the breadth of the territorial sea of each State is measured.

3. The provisions of the preceding paragraphs shall not affect the legal status of the Portuguese territorial sea.

Article 3. International law

Establishment of the exclusive economic zone shall take into account the rules of international law, namely those concerning passage and overflight.

Article 4. Conservation and management of living resources

1. In the zone referred to in article 2, the Portuguese State holds exclusive jurisdiction with regard to conservation and management of living resources.

2. Without prejudice to the exceptions provided for in the present act, foreign vessels are not permitted to fish in the exclusive economic zone.

3. For the purposes of the present act, it is understood that 'fishing' means the search for, the catch, the harvesting or the utilization of any living resources in that sea, but also the exercise of activities defined as 'preparatory to fishing', in accordance with paragraph 2 of article 2 of Decree Law No. 47947, of 18 September 1967, and the practice of acts adversely affecting to the execution of such activities by Portuguese citizens or by others with similar legal status for the purposes of fishing, defined as 'acts adversely affecting to the exercise of fishing', in accordance with paragraph 3 of article 2 of the decree-law referred to above.

Article 5. Regulation of fishing in the exclusive economic zone

The Government shall enact and enforce regulation of fishing in the exclusive economic zone, including *inter alia*:

(*a*) The total allowable catch and the maximum sustainable yield for the fisheries as a whole, as well as for each individual species or population and for each part of any specific area;
(*b*) The terms and conditions of fishing of the catch quota allowed to aliens, allocated by country;
(*c*) The rational and appropriate practice of fishing activities, including the number and size of fishing vessels, use of equipment and fishing gear and their limitation, when required, closed seasons and areas;
(*d*) Protection, conservation and restoration of the living resources of the exclusive economic zone.

Article 6. International co-operation

Portugal shall co-operate with the competent subregional, regional or global international organizations, in matters of conservations of the living resources of the sea.

Article 7. Special regulations for the exclusive economic zone

Pursuant to the applicable rules of international law of the sea, the Government may establish special regulations for the exclusive economic zone, namely with regard to:

(*a*) protection of the environment;
(*b*) scientific research;
(*c*) artificial installations, permanent or temporary;
(*d*) submarine pipelines and cables;
(*e*) survey and exploitation, for economic purposes, including energy production, or living and non-living natural resources of the sea-bed, subsoil thereof and superjacent waters.

Article 8. Penalties

1. The Government shall submit to the Assembly of the Republic proposals for legislation establishing civil responsibility and penalties incurred by individual and collective persons, nationals and aliens, who violate the provisions of the present act and its regulations.

2. The legislation referred to in the previous paragraph shall include, depending on the gravity of the infractions, *inter alia,* measures for cancelling fishing authorization, arrest of vessels and of their equipment, nets, gear and catch, and their seizure by the State, as well as fines and imprisonment.

3. Pending the entry into force of the legislation referred to in preceding paragraphs, the penalties established in Decree-Law No. 49947 of 18 September 1967, in regard to 'fishing waters under jurisdiction', shall be applied to the zone defined in article 2 of the present law; provisions of paragraphs 2 and 3 of article 5 of the same decree-law shall be applied to infractions committed by foreign vessels in the Portuguese territorial sea.

Article 9. Living resources of the continental shelf

The present act does not affect the sovereign rights of the Portuguese State over sedentary species on its continental shelf.

Article 10. Review of the present act

The present act, as well as the additional provisions of the juridical status of maritime space under national sovereignty or jurisdiction shall be reviewed in the light of the achievements of the Third United Nations Conference on the Law of the Sea and other developments with implications for the future law of the sea.

Article 11. Conformity with special laws in effect

1. Articles III and V of Law No. 2130 of 22 August 1966, are hereby revoked.

2. Paragraphs 2, 3 and 4 of article 10 of Decree-Law No. 47771, of 29 June 1967, are hereby revoked, and the phrase '. . . and on the coasts of the provinces of Guiné, Angola and Moçambique' is hereby deleted from the body of that same article.

Article 12. Fishing by foreign vessels

During an interim period, not exceeding 12 months, the Government may permit fishing by foreign vessels in the exclusive economic zone, without complete fulfilment of the conditions established by this act.

B. Decree Law No. 119/78.
Entered into force: June 1, 1978.
Source: *Diario da Republica,* June 1, 1978, pp. 984-988.

LAW DELIMITING EXCLUSIVE ECONOMIC ZONE PUBLISHED

Lisbon DIARIO DA REPUBLICA (Series I, Number 125) in Portuguese 1 Jun 78, pp. 984-988

[Decree Law No. 119/78 of the Council of Ministers, issued 1 Jun 78]

Whereas Law No. 33/77 of 28 May created an exclusive economic zone for which it is the government's responsibility to draw up legislation and make it respected there, which insures, among other things the protection, conservation and reclamation of all living resources;

Whereas Article 2 of that law determines the outer boundary of that zone, whose creation, in terms of the same law, will take into account the standards of international law, which require the publication of an official map which shows that boundary line or the suitable description in a legal document of the geographic coordinates of the points which mark it;

Whereas although, in what was mentioned regarding international law, the boundaries of the zone, as they are indicated in the present document and the respective map, are without prejudice to negotiations and agreements to be concluded with adjoining countries.

Using the authority conferred by Article 5 of Law No. 33/77 of 28 May, the government, having heard the chief of the Navy General Staff decrees the following in the terms of item b) of No. 1 of Article 201 of the Constitution:

Article 1

For the purpose of the present document there is understood by:

(a) 'Exclusive economic zone', the zone created in the terms of Article 2 of Law No. 33/77 of 28 May, in which the Portuguese state, in accordance with international law, in addition to exercising jurisdiction, namely over the creation and utilization of artificial islands and other installations and structures, which are also artificial, over scientific maritime investigation and over the protection of the marine environment, has sovereign rights:

(i) For purposes of prospecting and exploring, conserving and managing natural resources, living or not, of the sea bottom and its subsoil and the superjacent waters;

(ii) Over all other activities which have as their purpose the study or economic exploitation of the zone, such as production of power on the basis of water, currents and winds;

(b) 'Base lines', normal base lines, and direct base lines, on the basis of which the width of the Portuguese territorial sea is measured, are accordingly defined in Law No. 2130 of 22 August 1966, and Decree Law No. 47, 771 of 27 June 1967, with the modifications introduced by Article 11 of Law No. 33/77 of 28 May;

(c) 'Outside line' at a distance of a specified number of miles, the geometric location of the points on the sea whose distance to the closest points of the base lines is at a specified distance, a location which is obtained by determining the envelopment over the sea of the arcs of the circumference of the radius equal to that distance, centered on the base lines.

(d) 'Outer boundary of the exclusive economic zone', the perimiter formed by the line or outer lines at 200 miles and by the line or lines which delimit that area, from waters under the exclusive jurisdiction of adjacent states;

(e) 'Lower boundary of the exclusive economic zone', the line or lines which make up the outer limit of the Portuguese territorial sea, or that is, the line or outer lines at 12 miles;

(f) 'Median line' or 'median' between territories of two countries, the geometric location of the points over the sea which meet at an equal distance from the closest points of the base lines of those two territories;

(g) 'Triple point' between territories of three countries, the point of intersection of the median lines between the adjustments two by two of these three territories;

(h) 'Mile', the nautical mile of 1,852 meters.

Article 2

1. The exclusive economic zone is divided into three subregions, designated respectively as:
Subregion I — Continental subregion;
Subregion II — Madeira subregion;
Subregion III — Azores subregion.

2. It is the responsibility of the secretary of state for fisheries to subdivide these subregions, by decreasing order of size and importance, into divisions, subdivisions, sections and subsections, according to suitability for fishing.

3. The subdivision process provided for in the previous number does not prevent organs of sovereignty establishing for other purposes and through the respective competent authorities, with suitable designations, other forms of subdivision of subregions.

Article 3

1. The outer limit of the continental subregion (subregion I) is determined by:

(a) From point 1 to point 1A — the median line between Portugal and Spain;

(b) From point 1A to point 5 — the outer line at 200 miles;

(c) From point 5 to point 12 — the median line between Portugal and Morocco, to the triple point between Portugal, Morocco and Spain;

(d) From point 12 to point 13 — the median line between Portugal and Spain;

(e) From point 13 to point N — the outer limit of Spain's territorial sea.

2. The designation and geographic coordinates of the centers of the outer line indicated in item (b) of the previous number are indicated in attachment 1.

3. Attachment 1A gives the geographic coordinates of points, indicated by letters, located on the boundary line of the Portuguese and Spanish territorial seas and of numbered points located on the outer limit of subregion 1, so as to make this limit more real in practice.

Article 4

1. The outer limit of the Madeira (subregion 2) is determined by:

(a) From point 14 to 17 — the outer line at 200 miles;

(b) From point 17 to 26 — the median line between Madeira and the Canary Islands, to the triple point between Madeira, the Canary Islands and Morocco;

(c) From point 26 to 14 — the median line between Madeira and Morocco.

2. The designation and geographic coordinates of the centers of the outer line indicated in item (a) of the previous number are indicated in attachment II.

3. Attachment II — A gives the geographic coordinates of the numbered points located on the outer limit of subregion 2, so as to make it more real in practice.

Article 5

The outer limit of the Azores subregion (subregion 3) is indicated by the outer line at 200 miles.

2. The designation and geographic coordinates of the centers of the outer line mentioned in the previous number are indicated in attachment III.

3. Attachment III-A gives the geographic coordinates of the numbered points indicated on the outer limit of subregion 3, so as to make it more real in practice.

Article 6

1. The outer limit of the exclusive economic zone and the delimitation of the Portuguese and Spanish territorial seas, without prejudice to any agreement to be concluded, are indicated in map No. 1001-E of the Hydrographic Institute, reproduced in attachment IV.

2. As an aid to navigators, the Hydrographic Institute may publish the geographic coordinates of additional numbered points indicated on the outer limit of any of the subregions, so as to give additional assistance to navigators in determining the position of that limit. It is the responsibility of the institute itself to publish and circulate new maps on which these additional points appear.

Article 7

Determining the outer limit of the exclusive economic zone does not affect at all the legal status of the continental shelf, as it is defined in legal provisions in force, in areas of the sea bottom not subjacent to the territorial sea, bounded by the perpendicular of the above mentioned outer limit, nor the legal status of any adjacent area which may be established in accordance with international maritime law.

Seen and approved in the Council of Ministers — Mario Soares

Promulgated on 10 May 1978

Let it be published

The president of the republic, Antonio Ramalho Eanes

Attachment I.

Exclusive economic zone. Continental subregion (subregion 1). List of coordinates of centers of circumferences.

Centers	Geographic coordinates		Number of map IH and scale
	Latitude	Longitude	
Montedor Promontory (most westerly point)	41° 45′ 08″ N.	08° 52′ 51″ W.	1/150 000 (1)
Farilhoes — Forcadas (most westerly point)	39° 28′ 14″ N.	09° 33′ 26″ W.	1/40 000 (11)
Roca Cape — Pedra das Gaivotas (most westerly point)	38° 46′ 31″ N.	09° 30′ 01″ W.	1/25 000 (72)
Raso Cape (most westerly point)	38° 42′ 29″ N.	09° 29′ 08″ W.	1/25 000 (72)
Cape St. Vincent — Pedra do Gigante	37° 01′ 14″ N.	08° 59′ 46″ W.	1/20 000 (86)

Attachment I-A.

Territorial sea. Exclusive economic zone. Continental subregion (subregion 1). List of coordinates of reference points of boundaries.

Points	Geographic coordinates		Definition
	Latitude	Longitude	
A	41° 51′ 57″ N.	08° 52′ 21″ W.	Point of boundary line of territorial sea.
B	41° 51′ 57″ N.	09° 08′ 25″ W.	Same
1	41° 50′ 15″ N.	09° 08′ 20″ W.	Intersection of the outer line at 12 miles with the median between Portugal and Spain.
1A	41° 28′ N.	13° 18′ W.	Intersection of the median between Portugal and Spain with the outer line at 200 miles, that is the arc of the circumference of 200 miles of radius with the center in the most westerly point of Montedor Promontory.
1B	41° 09′ N.	13° 16′ W.	Intersection of arcs of the circumference of 200 miles of radius with centers in the most westerly point of Montedor Promontory and in the most westerly point of Forcadas (Farilhoc).
2	38° 43′ N.	13° 46′ W.	Intersection of arcs of circumference of 200 miles of radius with centers in the most westerly point of Forcadas (Farilhoes) and in Pedra das Gaviotas (most westerly point of Roca Cape).
3	38° 10′ N.	13° 42′ W.	Intersection of arcs of circumference of 200 miles of radius with centers in Pedra das Gaviotas (most westerly point to Cape Roca) and in the most westerly point of Cape Raso.
4	37° 00′ N.	13° 09′ W.	Intersection of arcs of circumference of 200 miles of radius with centers in the most westerly point of Cape Raso and Pedra do Gigante (Cape St. Vincent).
5	34° 57′ N.	12° 17′ W.	Intersection of the outer line at 200 miles, that is of the arc of the circumference of 200 miles of radius with the center in Pedra do Gigante (Cape St. Vincent), with the median between Portugal and Morocco.
6	34° 55′ N.	11° 40′ W.	Point of the median between Portugal and Morocco.
7	35° 01′ N.	10° 30′ W.	Same
8	35° 07′ N.	09° 13′ W.	Same
9	35° 11′ N.	08° 53′ W.	Same
10	35° 19′ N.	08° 21′ W.	Same
11	35° 26′ N.	08° 05′ W.	Same
12	35° 46′ N.	07° 32′ W.	Triple point between Portugal, Morocco and Spain.
13	36° 58′ 10″ N.	07° 19′ 30″ W.	Intersection of the median between Portugal and Spain, with the outer line at 12 miles.
N	36° 57′ 55″ N.	07° 23′ 48″ W.	Point of the boundary line of the territorial sea.
N	37° 09′ 55″ N.	07° 23′ 48″ W.	Same

Attachment II.
Exclusive economic zone. Madeira subregion (subregion II). List of coordinates of centers of circumferences.

Centers	Geographic coordinates		Number of map IH and scale
	Latitude	Longitude	
Madeira — Tristao Point	32° 51′ 59″ N.	17° 11′ 27″ W.	1/80 000 (102)
Madeira — Pargo Point	32° 48′ 40″ N.	17° 15′ 43″ W.	1/80 000 (102)
Porto Santo — Fora Island	33° 07′ 27″ N.	16° 16′ 53″ W.	1/50 000(103)

Attachment II-A.
Exclusive economic zone. Madeira subregion (subregion II). List of coordinates of reference points on the outer boundary.

Points	Geographic coordinates		Definition
	Latitude	Longitude	
14	34° 22′ N.	12° 37′ W.	Intersection of the outer line at 200 miles, that is of the arc of the circumference of 200 miles of radius with the center in Fora Island (Porto Santo), with the median between Madeira and Morocco.
15	36° 04′ N.	18° 03′ W.	Intersections of the arcs of the transferences of 200 miles of radius with centers in Fora Island (Porto Santo) and in Tristao Point (island of Madeira).
16	35° 11′ N.	20° 00′ W.	Intersection of the arcs of circumference of 200 miles of radius, with centers in Tristao Point (island of Madeira) and Pargo Point (island of Madeira).
17	31° 14′ N.	20° 46′ W.	Intersection of outer line at 200 miles, that is of the arc of circumference of 200 miles of radius with the center at Pargo Point (island of Madeira) with the median between Madeira and the Canary Islands.
18	30° 53′ N.	18° 12′ W.	Point of the median between Madeira and the Canary Islands.
19	29° 24′ N.	16° 53′ W.	Same
20	29° 21′ N.	16° 32′ W.	Same
21	29° 15′ N.	15° 07′ W.	Same
22	29° 26′ N.	14° 57′ W.	Same
23	29° 48′ N.	14° 41′ W.	Same
24	31° 44′ N.	13° 52′ W.	Same
25	32° 10′ N.	13° 15′ W.	Same
26	32° 17′ N.	13° 03′ W.	Triple point between Madeira, the Canary Islands and Morocco.
27	33° 02′ N.	12° 48′ W.	Point of median between Madeira and Morocco.
28	33° 16′ N.	12° 44′ W.	Same

Attachment III.
Exclusive economic zone. Azores subregion (subregion 3). List of coordinates of centers of circumferences.

Centers	Geographic coordinates		Number of map IH and scale
	Latitude	Longitude	
Santa Maria — Fora Island (Cabeca de Fora Point)	36° 56′ 22″ N.	25° 10′ 30″ W.	1/50 000 (110)
Santa Maria — Malbusca Point	36° 55′ 40″ N.	25° 04′ 03″ W.	1/50 000 (110)
Santa Maria — Goncalo Velho	36° 55′ 40″ N.	25° 00′ 50″ W.	1/50 000 (110)
S. Miguel — Arnel Point	37° 49′ 24″ N.	25° 08′ 09″ W.	1/100 000 (111)
S. Miguel — Ribeira Point	37° 50′ 57″ N.	25° 08′ 58″ W.	1/100 000 (111)
Terceira — Hospital Point	38° 47′ 26″ N.	27° 06′ 08″ W.	1/100 000 (112)
Graciosa — Barro Vermelho Island	39° 05′ 59″ N.	28° 01′ 39″ W.	1/50 000 (113)
Corvo — Marco Point	39° 43′ 30″ N.	31° 06′ 12″ W.	1/100 000 (115)
Flores — Monchique Island	39° 29′ 36″ N.	31° 16′ 18″ W.	1/100 000 (115)
Flores — Ilheus Point	39° 22′ 27″ N.	31° 15′ 00″ W.	1/100 000 (115)
Faial — Castelo Branco Point	38° 31′ 21″ N.	28° 45′ 15″ W.	1/125 000 (114)
Pico — St. Matthew Point	38° 25′ 15″ N.	28° 26′ 44″ W.	1/125 00 (114)
Pico — Queimada Point	38° 22′ 54″ N.	28° 14′ 24″ W.	1/125 000 (114)

Attachment III-A.
Exclusive economic zone. Azores subregion (subregion 3). List of coordinates of reference points on the outer boundary.

Points	Geographic coordinates		Definition
	Latitude	Longitude	
29	40° 58′ N.	23° 55′ W.	Intersection of arcs of circumference of 200 miles of radius with centers at Ribeira Point (St. Michael) and at Hospital Point (Terceira).
30	41° 55′ N.	25° 48′ W.	Same with centers at Hospital Point (Terceira) and Barro Vermelho Island (Graciosa).
31	42° 20′ N.	28° 30′ W.	Same with centers at Barro Vermelho Island (Graciosa) and Marco Point (Corvo).
32	41° 01′ N.	35° 06′ W.	Same with centers at Marco Point (Corvo) and Monchique Island (Flores).
33	38° 44′ N.	35° 28′ W.	Same with centers at Monchique Island (Flores) and Ilheu Point (Flores).
34	35° 58′ N.	31° 43′ W.	Same with centers on Ilheu Point (Flores) and Castelo Branco Point (Faial).
35	35° 18′ N.	30° 09′ W.	Same with centers in Castelo Branco Point (Faial) and St. Matthew Point (Pico).
36	35° 05′ N.	29° 22′ W.	Same with centers in St. Matthews Point (Pico) and Quemada Point (Pico).
37	34° 59′ N.	28° 34′ W.	Same with centers in Queimada Point (Pico) and Cabeca de Fora Point of Vila Island (Santa Maria).
38	33° 33′ N.	25° 33′ W.	Same with centers in Cabeca de Fora Point of Vila Island (Santa Maria) or in Malbusca Point (Santa Maria).
39	33° 32′ N.	24° 50′ W.	Same with centers in Malbusca Point (Santa Maria) and in Goncalo Velho Lighthouse (Santa Maria).
40	37° 35′ N.	20° 37′ W.	Same with centers at Goncalo Velho Lighthouse (Santa Maria) and at Arnel Point (St. Michael).
41	39° 09′ N.	21° 18′ W.	Same with centers at Arnel Point (St. Michael) and Ribeira Point (St. Michael).

51. Qatar

Ministry of Foreign Affairs Declaration
Entered into force: June 2, 1974
Source: United Nations. *Law of the Sea Bulletin No. 2,* December 1983, p. 71. (Translated from Arabic by the United Nations Secretariat).

DECLARATION BY THE MINISTRY OF FOREIGN AFFAIRS OF 2 JUNE 1974

I. The State of Qatar shall have exclusive and absolute sovereign rights over natural and marine resources and fisheries in the areas contiguous to the territorial sea off the coasts of the State and its islands, without prejudice to the freedom of international sea and air navigation, in accordance with the established principles of international law.

The outer limits of these areas shall be in accordance with bilateral agreements which have been, or shall be, concluded. In the absence of any particular agreement, the outer limits of the continental prolongation of the State of Qatar, or the median line in which every point is equidistant from the baseline from which the territorial sea of the State of Qatar and of other States concerned is measured, shall be regarded as the determining factor in accordance with the principles of international law.

II. Within the territorial area specified in the preceding section, the State of Qatar shall have exclusive rights in regard to exploration, prospecting, exploitation, development, fishing and the establishment of installations and zones for the security, control and protection of all marine and natural resources on, under or above the sea-bed.

52. Saint Christopher and Nevis

Maritime Areas Act
Entered into force: August 1984.
Source: *Foreign Broadcasting Information Service,* August 31, 1984

PARLIAMENT ESTABLISHES 200-MILE ECONOMIC ZONE

FL311832 Bridgetown CANA in English 1727 GMT 31 Aug 84

Basseterre, Aug 31, CANA— The St Kitts and Nevis Parliament has passed a bill providing for a exclusive 200-mile economic zone.

At yesterday's first parliamentary sitting since general elections in June, the Maritime Areas Act (1984) was introduced by Attorney General Tapley Seaton and passed with the opposition Labour Party absent from the sitting.

Labour parliamentarian Joseph France, one of two elected to the 11-seat legislature, declined to explain the oppositions' non-attendance.

The Maritime Areas Act provides for an extension of the country's territorial sea from 3 nautical miles to 12 miles, a contiguous zone of 24 miles, a continental shelf, and an exclusive economic zone.

Exploitation of the country's natural maritime resources without government permission would lead to fine of up to 100,000 dollars (one E.C. dollar , 37 cents U.S.).

The bill also officially recognises the presence of countries which are in close proximity to St Kitts-Nevis and provides for unmolested passage of commercial and non-hostile military shipping.

Agriculture Minister Hugh Heyliger introduced the Fisheries Act (1984), which relates to the management and development of a fisheries plan and seeks the appointment of a fisheries advisory committee within the Ministry of Agriculture.

Other bills sought the requirement of visas for foreigners, other than those from the Commonwealth and the United States, visiting the country and provision of additional registrars of companies.

53. Saint Lucia

Maritime Areas Act, 1984
Entered into force: July 18, 1984.
Source: Ministry of Foreign Affairs.

Maritime Areas Act

SAINT LUCIA

No. 6 of 1984

ARRANGEMENT OF SECTIONS

PART I
Preliminary

Sections

PART II
Maritime Areas of Saint Lucia

PART III
Rights in respect of Maritime Areas of Saint Lucia

PART IV

Innocent passage and transit passage

PART V

Charts and geographical co-ordinates

PART VI

Jurisdiction of courts and other legal matters

PART VII

Regulations, saving and amendments

[L.S.]

I Assent,

Allen Lewis,
Governor-General

18th July, 1984

SAINT LUCIA

No. 6 of 1984

An Act to make provision with respect to the territorial sea and the continental shelf of Saint Lucia; to establish a contiguous zone and an exclusive economic zone adjacent to and beyond the territorial sea; and for related purposes.

[18th July, 1984.]

Be it enacted by the Queen's Most Excellent Majesty, by and with the advise and consent of the Parliament of Saint Lucia, and by the authority of the same, as follows:—

PART I
Preliminary

Short title and commencement

1. (1) This Act may be cited as the Maritime Areas Act, 1984.

(2) This Act shall come into operation upon such date as the Minister may, by notice published in the *Gazette,* appoint.

Definitions

2. In this Act, unless the context otherwise requires—

'baseline of the territorial sea' means the baseline from which the breadth of the territorial sea is measured as described in section 4;

'contiguous zone' means the contiguous zone of Saint Lucia as described in section 6;

'continental shelf' means the continental shelf of Saint Lucia as described in section 7 and, to the extent that section 9 applies, as delimited pursuant to section 9;

'exclusive economic zone' means the exclusive economic zone of Saint Lucia as described in section 8 and, to the extent that section 9 applies, as delimited pursuant to section 9;

'foreign vessel' means a vessel that—

(a) is registered in a foreign State;

(b) belongs to an authority or instrumentality of a foreign State; or

(c) is held by any person on behalf of, or for the benefit of, a foreign State;

'foreign State' means a State other than Saint Lucia;

'internal waters' means the internal waters of Saint Lucia as described in section 5;

'maritime areas of Saint Lucia' means the internal waters, the territorial sea, the contiguous zone, the continental shelf and the exclusive economic zone;

'master', in relation to vessel means the person for the time being having command or charge of the vessel;

'Minister' means the Minister of Foreign Affairs;

'nautical mile' means the international nautical mile of 1852 metres;
'resources' includes living and non-living resources;
'territorial sea' means the territorial sea of Saint Lucia as described in section 3;
'the Regulations' means regulations made under this Act.

PART II

Maritime areas of Saint Lucia

Territorial sea

3. (1) Subject to subsection (2), the territorial sea of Saint Lucia comprises those areas of the sea having, as their inner limits, the baseline of the territorial sea and, as their outer limits, a line measured seaward from that baseline, every point of which is 12 nautical miles distant from the nearest point of that baseline.

(2) Wherever the equidistance line between Saint Lucia and an adjacent State is less than 12 nautical miles from the nearest point of the baseline of the territorial sea, the delimitation of the territorial sea shall, if possible, be effected by agreement between Saint Lucia and the adjacent State; but to the extent that no such agreement is effected, that equidistance line shall constitute the outer limits of the territorial sea.

(3) In this section, 'equidistance line', as between Saint Lucia and an adjacent State, means a line every point of which is equidistant from the nearest point of the baseline of the territorial sea and the corresponding baseline of the adjacent State.

Baseline of territorial sea

4. (1) Except as otherwise provided in this section, the baseline from which the breadth of the territorial sea is measured shall be the low-water mark along the coast of Saint Lucia, including the coast of all islands.

(2) In the case of the sea adjacent to a bay, the baseline from which the breadth of the territorial sea is measured—

(a) where the bay has only one mouth, shall be a straight line joining the low-water marks of the natural entrance points; and

(b) where, because of the presence of islands, the bay has more than one mouth, shall be a series of straight lines across each of the mouths so as to join those low-water marks.

(3) For the purpose of delimiting the territorial sea, the outermost permanent harbour works which form an integral part of any harbour system shall be treated as forming part of the coast, but for that purpose offshore installations and artificial islands shall not be considered as permanent harbour works.

(4) The Minister may, whenever he considers it necessary to do so having regard to international law and practice, by Order published in the *Gazette,* direct that, to the extent set out, the baseline from which the breadth of the territorial sea is measured shall be as prescribed in, or determined by or in accordance with, the Order.

(5) In this section, 'bay' means an indentation of the coast such that its area is not less than that of the semi-circle whose diameter is a line drawn across the mouth of the indentation.

(6) For the purpose of the definition of 'bay' in subsection (5)—

(a) the area of an indentation shall be taken to be the area bounded by the low-water mark around the shore of the indentation and the straight line joining the low-water marks of its natural entrance points;

(b) where, because of the presence of islands, an indentation has more than one mouth, the length of the diameter of the semi-circle referred to shall be the sum of the lengths of the straight lines drawn across each of the mouths; and

(*c*) in calculating the area of an indentation, the area of any islands lying within it shall be treated as part of the area of the indentation.

Internal waters

5. The internal waters to Saint Lucia comprise any areas of the sea that are on the landward side of the baseline of the territorial sea.

Contiguous zone

6. (1) Subject of subsection (2), the contiguous zone of Saint Lucia comprises those areas of the sea that are beyond and adjacent to the territorial sea having, as their outer limits, a line, measured seaward from the baseline of the territorial sea, every point of which is 24 nautical miles distant from the nearest point of that baseline.

(2) The contiguous zone shall not extend into any part of the territorial sea of a foreign State and, where appropriate, the operation of subsection (1) shall be modified to the extent necessary to meet the requirement of this subsection.

Continental Shelf

7. (1) Subject to subsection (2) and section 9, the continental shelf of Saint Lucia comprises those areas of the seabed and subsoil of the submarine areas that are beyond and adjacent to the territorial sea throughout the natural prolongation of the land territory of Saint Lucia to the outer edge of the continental margin, or to a distance of 200 nautical miles from the nearest point of the baseline of the territorial sea when the outer edge of the continental margin does not extend up to that distance.

(2) For the purposes of subsection (1), wherever the continental margin extends beyond 200 nautical miles from the nearest point of the baseline of the territorial sea, the outer limits of the continential shelf shall be established with all due regard to the requirements and limitations of international law relevant to the establishment and delineation of the continental shelf beyond that distance.

(3) For the purposes of this section, the continental margin comprises the submerged prolongation of the land mass of Saint Lucia consisting of the seabed and subsoil of the shelf, the slope and the rise, but does not include the deep ocean floor with its oceanic ridges or the subsoil thereof.

Exclusive economic zone

8. Subject to section 9, the exclusive economic zone of Saint Lucia comprises those areas of the sea that are beyond and adjacent to the territorial sea having, as their outer limits, a line, measured seaward from the baseline of the territorial sea, every point of which is 200 nautical miles distant from the nearest point of that baseline.

Delimitation of continental shelf or exclusive economic zone in certain cases

9. (1) Wherever the equidistance line between Saint Lucia and an adjacent State is less than 200 nautical miles from the nearest point of the baseline of the territorial sea—

(*a*) the delimitation of the continential shelf shall be effected by agreement between Saint Lucia and the adjacent State on the basis of international law in order to achieve an equitable settlement; and

(*b*) the delimitation of the exclusive economic zone shall be effected between Saint Lucia and the adjacent State on the basis of international law in order to achieve and equitable settlement.

(2) Where, in any case, an agreement of the kind referred to in paragraph (*a*) or (*b*) of subsection (1) cannot be reached, Saint Lucia shall have recourse to the procedures provided by international law for the settlement of any dispute.

(3) Pending the delimitation of—

(*a*) the continental shelf pursuant to subsection (1) (*a*) or (2); or *(b)* the exclusive economic zone pursuant to subsection (1) (*b*) or (2),

the equidistance line between Saint Lucia and the adjacent State shall constitute the outer limits of the continental shelf or, as the case may be, the exclusive economic zone, unless Saint Lucia and the adjacent State make other provisional arrangements with respect to those limits.

(4) For the purpose of implementing any agreement under subsection (1), any settlement pursuant to subsection (2) or any provisional arrangements under subsection (3), the Minister may, from time to time, by Order published in the *Gazette,* declare that the continental shelf or the exclusive economic zone shall not extend to any specified area of the sea, seabed or subsoil that would otherwise be included therein by virtue of section 7 or, as the case may be, section 8, and the Order, while it remains in force, shall, subject to section 30, have effect according to its tenor, notwithstanding anything in this Act.

(5) In this section, 'equidistance line', as between Saint Lucia and an adjacent State, means a line every point of which is equidistant from the nearest point of the baseline of the territorial sea and the corresponding baseline of the adjacent State.

PART III

Rights in respect of maritime areas of Saint Lucia

Sovereignty in respect of territorial sea

10. The sovereignty in respect of—

(a) the territorial sea;

(b) the airspace over, and the seabed under, that sea; and

(c) the subsoil of that seabed,

is, and shall be deemed always to have been, vested in Saint Lucia, and subject to international law, is exercisable by Saint Lucia.

Rights in respect of contiguous zone

11. Saint Lucia has and may exercise in respect of the contiguous zone such rights as may be necessary to prevent, or punish, the infringement, within Saint Lucia (including the territorial sea), of any enactment providing controls or prohibitions for or with respect to customs, excise, immigration or sanitation.

Rights in respect of exclusive economic zone and continental shelf

12. (1) Saint Lucia has and may exercise in respect of the exclusive economic zone

(a) sovereign rights

(i) for the purpose of the exploration for, and the exploitation, conservation and management of, resources of the waters superjacent to the seabed and of the seabed and subsoil; and

(ii) for the production of energy from the waters, currents and winds;

(b) jurisdiction with regard to

(i) the establishment and use of artificial islands, installations and structures;

(ii) marine scientific research; and

(iii) the protection and preservation of the marine environment;

(c) the exclusive right to construct and to authorise and regulate the construction, operation and use of

(i) artificial islands;

(ii) installations and structures for the purposes provided for under paragraph *(a)* or any other economic purposes;

(iii) installations and structures which may interfere with the exercise by Saint Lucia of rights in respect of the exclusive economic zone; and *(d)* the exclusive right to regulate, authorise and conduct marine scientific research.

(2) Saint Lucia has and may exercise in respect of the continental shelf

(a) sovereign rights for the purpose of the exploration for, and the exploitation, conservation and management of, natural resources;

(b) the exclusive right to construct and to authorise and regulate the construction, operation and use of

(i) artificial islands;

(ii) installations and structures for the purposes provided for under paragraph *(a)* or any other economic purposes;

(iii) installations and structures which may interfere with the exercise by Saint Lucia of rights in respect of the continental shelf; and

(c) the exclusive right to regulate, authorise and conduct marine scientific research.

(3) In the exercise of jurisdiction and rights under subsection (1) in respect of the exclusive economic zone, Saint Lucia shall have due regard to the rights and duties of foreign States and shall act in a manner compatible with international law.

(4) In the exercise of

(a) rights under subsection (1) *(a)* (i) in respect of the seabed and subsoil of the exclusive economic zone; or

(b) rights under subsection (2) *(a)* in respect of the continental shelf,

Saint Lucia shall not infringe or unjustifiably interfere with rights of navigation or other rights and freedom of foreign States, under international law.

(5) The sovereign rights conferred by this section in respect of the continental shelf shall be deemed always to have been vested in Saint Lucia.

(6) In subsection (2) *(a)*, 'natural resources' means mineral and other non-living resources of the seabed and subsoil together with living organisms belonging to sedentary species, that is to say, organisms which, at the harvestable stage, either are immobile on or under the seabed or are unable to move except in constant physical contact with the seabed or subsoil.

Rights to lay cables and pipelines

13. (1) Subject to subsection (2), every foreign State may exercise, in accordance with international law, the right to lay cables and pipelines on the continental shelf or in the exclusive economic zone.

(2) The right, under subsection (1), to lay cables or pipelines

(a) shall not be exercised on any occasion unless there has first been obtained any consent required by or under the Regulations or any enactment in relation to the delineation of the course of the cables or pipelines to be laid on that occasion;

(b) shall be exercised in conformity with the provisions of the Regulations, and any enactment, for or with respect to the prevention, reduction and control of pollution from pipelines; and

(c) is subject to the exercise of rights or jurisdiction pursuant to section 12 for or with respect to the control or prevention of the laying of cables or pipelines in connection with the exploration for or exploitation of, resources, or the use of artificial islands, installations or structures.

Prohibited activities

14. (1) No person shall

(a) within the limits of the continental shelf

(i) explore for or exploit the natural resources, as defined in section 12 (6);

(ii) conduct any marine scientific research; or

(iii) construct, operate or use any artificial island, or any installation or structure for the purpose of the exercise of any right referred to in section 12 (2) *(b)* (ii), or which may interfere with the exercise of rights referred to in section 12 (2) *(b)* (iii);

(b) within the limits of the exclusive economic zone

(i) explore for or exploit the resources;

(ii) produce energy from the waters, currents or winds;

(iii) conduct any marine scientific research; or

(iv) construct, operate or use any artificial island, or any installation or structure for the purpose of the exercise of any right or purposes referred to in section 12 (1) *(c)* (ii), or which may interfere with the exercise of rights referred to in section 12 (1) *(c)* (iii); or

(c) within the limits of the territorial sea engage in any of the activities referred to in paragraph *(b)*,

except when authorised by, under or pursuant to this Act or any other enactment, or in any other lawful manner, to engage in the activity, and in accordance with the authorisation.

(2) Any person who contravenes subsection (1) is guilty of an offence and liable on conviction to a fine of twenty thousand dollars.

(3) Where the owner or master of a vessel which is detained pursuant to section 23 (1) *(c)* is convicted of an offence against this section, the court may, in addition to any other penalty imposed, order that the vessel, including any equipment on board the vessel used in the commission of the offence, shall be forfeited to the Crown, and in that event the vessel and any such equipment shall be disposed of in such manner as the Minister shall order.

PART IV

Innocent Passage and Transit Passage

Interpretation

15. (1) In this Part, unless the context otherwise requires

'competent authority', in relation to any provision in this Part, means the Minister, and any person, or person belonging to any class or description of persons, designated pursuant to subsection (2) for the purposes of that provision;

'designated strait' means any strait for the time being designated under subsection (3);

'proscribed activity' means

(a) any threat or use of force against the sovereignty, territorial integrity or political independence of Saint Lucia, or acts in any other manner in violation of the principles of international law embodied in the Charter of the United Nations;

(b) any exercise or practice with weapons of any kind;

(c) any act aimed at collecting information to the prejudice of the defence or security of Saint Lucia;

(d) any act of propaganda aimed at affecting the defence or security of Saint Lucia;

(e) the launching, landing or taking on board of any aircraft or military device;

(f) the loading or unloading of any person, commodity or currency contrary to the customs, fiscal, immigration or sanitary laws;

(g) any wilful act of pollution calculated or likely to cause damage or harm to Saint Lucia, its resources or its marine environment;

(h) any fishing activities;

(i) the carrying out of research or survey activities;

(j) any act aimed at interfering with any systems of communication or any other facilities or installations of Saint Lucia; or

(k) such other activity as may be prescribed.

(2) The Minister may, by notice published in the *Gazette,* designate any person, or class or description of persons, for the purposes of any provision of this Part; and the Minister may, in like manner, revoke any such designation.

(3) Where the Minister is satisfied that any strait between Saint Lucia and an adjacent State is being used for international navigation between

(a) one part of the high seas or an exclusive economic zone; and

(b) another part of the high seas or an exclusive economic zone,

he shall, by Order published in the *Gazette,* designate that strait, as delimited in the Order; and the Minister, if he ceases to be so satisfied, may, in like manner, revoke the designation of a strait.

Innocent passage

16. (1) Every foreign vessel may, subject to and in accordance with this section and international law, exercise the right under international law of innocent passage, that is to say, the right of passage by navigating through the territorial sea for the purpose of

(a) traversing the territorial sea without entering internal waters or calling at a roadstead or port facility outside internal waters; or

(b) proceeding to or from internal waters or a call at any such roadstead or port facility, where the passage is innocent.

(2) The passage of a foreign vessel–

(a) is innocent so long as it is not prejudicial to the peace, good order or security of Saint Lucia; and

(b) is deemed to be prejudicial to the peace, good order or security of Saint Lucia if the vessel, in the territorial sea, engages in any proscribed activity.

(3) In exercising the right of innocent passage, a vessel shall comply with

(a) generally accepted international regulations, procedures and practices for safety at sea which have effect in the territorial sea, or any part thereof; and

(b) the provisions of the Regulations, and any enactment, order or direction, which have effect in the territorial sea, or any part thereof, for or with respect to–

(i) the safety of navigation and the regulation of maritime traffic, including the use of sea lanes and the operation of traffic separation schemes;

(ii) the protection of navigational aids and facilities, and other facilities or installations;

(iii) the protection of cables and pipelines;

(iv) the conservation of resources;

(v) fishing and fisheries;

(vi) the preservation of the environment and the prevention, reduction and control of pollution;

(vii) marine scientific research and hydrographic surveys; and

(viii)controls or prohibitions in relation to customs, excise, immigration or sanitation.

(4) The Minister may, where he is satisfied that it is essential to do so for the protection of the security of Saint Lucia, including weapons exercises, by Order published in the *Gazette,* suspend, for such period as is specified in the Order, the right of innocent passage through the territorial sea, or through any part of the territorial sea identified in the Order.

(5) An Order made under subsection (4) shall not operate to suspend the right of transit passage of a designated strait.

Transit passage

17. (1) Every foreign vessel or aircraft may, subject to and in accordance with this section and international law, exercise in relation to a designated strait the right under international law of transit passage, that is to say the right of freedom of navigation and overflight solely for the purpose of continuous and expeditious transit of a designated strait between

(a) one part of the high seas or an exclusive economic zone; and

(b) another part of the high seas or another part of an exclusive economic zone.

(2) For the purposes of subsection (1), a vessel or aircraft that engages in a designated strait in any

proscribed activity shall be deemed to engage in an activity which is not an exercise of the right of transit passage.

(3) In exercising the right of transit passage of a designated strait a vessel shall comply with

(a) generally accepted international regulations, procedures and practices for safety at sea, or for the prevention, reduction and control of pollution from vessels, which have effect in the strait; and

(b) the provisions of the Regulations, and any enactment, order or direction, which have effect in the strait, for or with respect to

(i) the safety of navigation and the regulation of marine traffic, including the use of sea lanes and the operation of traffic separation schemes;

(ii) fishing vessels, and the prevention of fishing including the stowage of fishing gear; and

(iii) customs, excise, immigration or sanitation controls in relation to the loading or unloading of any commodity, currency or person.

(4) In exercising the right of transit passage of a designated strait, an aircraft

(a) shall observe the Rules of the Air established by the International Civil Aviation Organisation as they apply to civil aircraft, and a state aircraft shall normally comply with such safety measures and shall at all times operate with due regard for the safety of navigation;

(b) shall at all times monitor the radio frequency assigned by the appropriate internationally designated air traffic control authority or the appropriate international distress radio frequency.

Engaging in proscribed activities prohibited

18. (1) No foreign vessel, shall, while in the territorial sea, without the permission of a competent authority given to the master of the vessel, engage in any proscribed activity.

(2) Where a foreign vessel, in contravention of subsection (1), engages in any proscribed activity, the master of the vessel and any other person on board the vessel participating in that activity are each guilty of an offence and liable on conviction to a fine of twenty thousand dollars.

(3) No prosecution for an offence against this section

(a) shall be brought against a person who is entitled to State or other immunity recognised by law; or

(b) shall be commenced without the consent in writing of the Attorney-General.

(4) Where the master of a foreign vessel which is detained pursuant to section (23) (2) *(d)*, is convicted of an offence against this section, the court may, in addition to any other penalty imposed, order that the vessel shall be forfeited to the Crown, and in that event the vessel shall be disposed of in such manner as the Minister shall order.

(5) This section has effect notwithstanding that the area of the territorial sea, in which a vessel engages in any proscribed activity, is within a designated strait.

PART V

Charts and Geographical Co-ordinates

Charts of maritime areas

19. The Minister shall cause to be prepared such charts or lists of geographical co-ordinates as he thinks fit showing all or any of the following matters, namely

(a) the maritime areas of Saint Lucia or any part thereof;

(b) the baseline of the territorial sea;

(c) the outer limits of the continental shelf or the exclusive economic zone; or

(d) sea lanes or traffic separation schemes.

Evidence of charts

20. A document, purporting to be certified by the Minister to be a true copy of a chart or list of geographical co-ordinates prepared pursuant to section 19, shall be received in any proceedings as evidence of any matter shown in the document, but without prejudice to the right to adduce evidence in rebuttal.

Publicity with respect to charts

21. The Minister shall cause

(a) due publicity to be given to charts or lists of geographical co-ordinates prepared pursuant to section 19; and

(b) a copy of each such chart list to be deposited with the Secretary-General of the United Nations.

PART VI

Jurisdiction of Courts and other Legal Matters

Jurisdiction

22. (1) The jurisdiction and powers of the courts of Saint Lucia extend to the maritime areas of Saint Lucia for the purpose of

(a) this Act; and

(b) any enactment which applies or is applied pursuant to section 28 to maritime areas of Saint Lucia, or any part thereof.

(2) For the purposes of the exercise of any jurisdiction and powers pursuant to subsection (1), a court is a court of competent jurisdiction

(a) for the purpose of any criminal proceedings, if it would have cognisance of the offence concerned if it had been committed within the limits of its ordinary criminal jurisdiction; and

(b) for the purpose of any proceedings, other than criminal proceedings, if it would have jurisdiction if the act, omission or other matter giving rise to the proceedings had occurred or arisen within the limits of its ordinary jurisdiction.

(3) The Minister, after consultation with the Attorney-General may make rules for carrying out or giving effect to this section.

(4) The jurisdiction and powers conferred by this section are in addition to and not in derogation of any other jurisdiction or powers exercisable by a court of Saint Lucia.

Apprehension of certain offenders

23. (1) Subject to this section, where an authorised person has reasonable cause to believe and believes that an offence has been committed against section 14, he may exercise all or any of the following powers, namely

(a) within the maritime areas of Saint Lucia, stop, board, inspect and search any vessel, or enter, inspect and search any installation, which he has reasonable cause to believe is being used for or in connection with the commission of the offence;

(b) arrest, with or without a warrant, any person on board the vessel, or on the installation, referred to in paragraph *(a)*, or found elsewhere in Saint Lucia, whom he has reasonable cause to believe has committed an offence against that section;

(c) detain the vessel, referred to in paragraph *(a)*, if he has reasonable cause to believe that an offence against that section has been committed by the owner or master of the vessel; and

(d) enter, inspect and search any installation whose establishment, construction, operation or use would constitute the offence against that section and arrest, with or without a warrant, any person on the installation, or found elsewhere in Saint Lucia, whom he has reasonable cause to believe has committed the offence.

(2) Subject to this section, where an authorised person has reasonable cause to believe and believes that an offence has been committed against section 18, he may, within the territorial sea, exercise all or any of the following powers, namely

(a) stop, board, inspect and search the foreign vessel which, in contravention of that section, engages in any proscribed activity;

(b) arrest, with or without a warrant, the master of the vessel;

(c) arrest, with or without a warrant, any other person on board the vessel whom he has reasonable cause to believe has committed an offence against that section; and

(d) detain the vessel.

(3) An authorised person may exercise any of the powers conferred on him by subsection (1) or (2) with the aid of such assistants as he considers necessary for the purpose.

(4) Where a vessel is detained pursuant to subsection (1) *(c)* or subsection (2) *(d),* it shall be held in the custody of the Crown until

(a) a decision is made not to bring a prosecution in respect of the alleged offence in relation to which the vessel was detained; or

(b) where a decision is made to bring such a prosecution, the security required under subsection (6) is given in respect of the vessel.

(5) The decision whether or not to bring a prosecution in respect of an alleged offence in relation to which a vessel is detained shall be made with all due expedition.

(6) The security required in respect of any vessel for the purposes of subsection (4) shall be in such form and reasonable amount, and shall be given by such person, as the Minister may order.

(7) The release of a vessel from detention shall not affect any subsequent forfeiture of the vessel, pursuant to section 14 (3) or 18 (4).

(8) The power under subsection (1) or (2) shall not be exercised in relation to a vessel that is, or in relation to a person who is, entitled to State or other immunity recognised by law.

(9) The powers and rights under this section are in addition to and not in derogation of any other powers and rights which Saint Lucia may have under international law or otherwise.

(10) In the exercise under this section of the power of enforcement against a foreign vessel, an authorised person shall not endanger the safety of navigation or otherwise create any hazard to a vessel, or bring it to an unsafe port or anchorage, or expose the marine environment to an unreasonable risk.

(11) In this section

'authorised person' means a person, or a person belonging to a class or description of persons, designated for the purposes of this section by the Minister by Order made under this subsection and published in the *Gazette*; 'owner', in relation to any vessel, includes any body of persons, whether incorporated or not, by whom the vessel is owned, and any charterer or sub-charterer of the vessel.

Arrest on board foreign vessel in territorial sea

24. (1) Subject to this section, where an offence is committed on board a foreign vessel (being a merchant ship or a government ship operated for commercial purposes) during its passage through the territorial sea, a prescribed power may be exercised, in relation to the offence, on board the vessel during that passage, only if

(a) the consequences of the offence extend to Saint Lucia;

(b) the offence is of a kind likely to disturb the peace of Saint Lucia or the good order of the territorial sea;

(c) the assistance of the Government or any public officer has been requested by the master of the foreign vessel or by a diplomatic agent or consular officer of the relevant foreign State; or

(d) it is necessary to exercise a prescribed power for the purpose of suppressing any illicit traffic in

narcotic drugs or psychotropic substances.

(2) The limitations in subsection (1) shall not apply in any case where a foreign vessel is passing through the territorial sea after leaving internal waters.

(3) Subject to this section, where a foreign vessel, proceeding from a port outside Saint Lucia, is passing through the territorial sea without having entered internal waters, a prescribed power may be exercised, in relation to any offence committed before the ship entered the territorial sea, on board the ship during that passage only if

(a) there are clear grounds for believing that the vessel has, in the exclusive economic zone, committed a violation of

(i) applicable international rules and standards for the prevention, reduction and control of pollution from vessels; or

(ii) any provision of the Regulations or any enactment conforming to and giving effect to any such rules and standards; and

(b) there

(i) are clear grounds for believing that that violation has resulted in a substantial discharge causing or threatening significant pollution of the marine environment; or

(ii) is clear objective evidence that that violation has resulted in a discharge causing major damage or the threat of major damage to the coastline of Saint Lucia, or to any resources of its territorial sea or exclusive economic zone.

(4) Nothing in this section shall affect the exercise of any power under section 23.

(5) The decision to exercise, and the exercise of, a prescribed power in circumstances of the kind referred to in subsection (1) or (3) shall be made or, as the case may be, carried out, with due regard to the interests of navigation.

(6) The prescribed power referred to in subsection (8) *(a)* shall not be exercised in relation to a vessel unless the vessel has refused, when lawfully required to do so, to give information regarding its identity and port of registry, its last and next port of call and other relevant information required to establish whether a violation of the kind referred to in subsection (3) *(a)* has occurred.

(7) The prescribed power referred to in subsection (8) *(b)* shall not be exercised in relation to a vessel whenever appropriate procedures, which bind Saint Lucia, have been established, either through the competent international organisation or as otherwise agreed, whereby compliance with requirements for landing or other appropriate financial security has been assured in relation to the vessel.

(8) For the purposes of this section, 'prescribed power' means the power lawfully to arrest any person or to conduct an investigation into any alleged offence, and

(a) for the purposes of subsection (3) *(b)* (i), includes a power to undertake a physical inspection of a vessel for matters relating to a violation of the kind referred to in subsection (3) *(a)*; and

(b) for the purposes of subsection (3) *(b)* (ii), includes a power to detain a vessel.

Certificate of Attorney-General

25. Where, in any criminal proceedings, a question arises whether or not an act or omission occured within the limits of internal waters, the territorial sea, the contiguous zone, the continental shelf or the exclusive economic zone, a certificate, purporting to be signed by the Attorney-General, to the effect that the act or omission did or did not so occur shall be received as evidence of that fact, but without prejudice to the right to adduce evidence in rebuttal.

Civil jurisdiction

26. (1) All questions and disputes of a civil nature concerning or arising out of acts or omissions which occur within the limits of the continental shelf or the exclusive economic zone in connection with

(a) the exploration for or exploitation of resources;

(b) the conduct of any research or survey activities;

(c) the establishment, construction, operation or use of any artificial islands, installation or structure;

(d) the laying of cables or pipelines; or

(e) the production of energy from the waters, currents or winds,

may be dealt with by a court of competent jurisdiction.

(2) Subsection (1) shall not affect the validity of any agreement to submit a dispute to arbitration by any person outside Saint Lucia.

(3) The jurisdiction conferred by this section is in addition to and not in derogation of any other jurisdiction exercisable by a court in Saint Lucia.

Civil jurisdiction in relation to foreign vessels in territorial sea

27. (1) No foreign vessel passing through the territorial sea shall be stopped or diverted for the purpose only of the exercise of any civil jurisdiction in relation to a person on board the vessel.

(2) Subject to subsection (3), no person shall arrest or levy execution against a foreign vessel passing through the territorial sea for the purpose of any civil proceedings, except where the proceedings are in respect of obligations or liabilities assumed or incurred in relation to the vessel in the course or for the purpose of its voyage through the territorial sea.

(3) Subsection (2), in so far as it prohibits the arrest of, or levying of execution against a foreign vessel, shall not apply in the case of a foreign vessel which is lying in or passing through the territorial sea after leaving internal waters.

Application of enactments to maritime area

28. (1) The minister may, by regulations made under section 29, extend to the maritime areas of Saint Lucia, or any part thereof, the application of any enactment, subject to

(a) the limitations (if any); and

(b) modifications (if any) to facilitate the application or enforcement of the enactment,

as may be prescribed in the regulations, and the enactment shall apply accordingly.

(2) The power under subsection (1) includes a power to extend the application of an enactment to any artificial island, installation or structure for the purpose of the exercise of any rights or jurisdiction under section 12.

PART VII

Regulations, Saving and Amendments

Regulations

29. (1) The Minister may make regulations for carrying out or giving effect to this Act.

(2) Regulations may be made with respect to the territorial sea for all or any of the following purposes, namely

(a) regulating the conduct of scientific research within the territorial sea;

(b) prescribing measures for the protection and preservation of the marine environment of the territorial sea;

(c) regulating, for the purposes of section 12, the construction, operation, and use of artificial islands (whether permanent or temporary), and other installations and structures in the territorial sea, including the establishment of safety zones around such islands, installations, and structures;

(d) regulating the exploration and exploitation of the territorial sea for the production of energy from the water, currents, and winds, and for any other economic purposes;

(e) providing for such other matters as are necessary or expedient for giving full effect to the

sovereignty of Saint Lucia in relation to the territorial sea; and

(f) providing for such other matters as are contemplated by or necessary for giving full effect to the provisions of Part II, III, or IV.

(3) Regulations may be made with respect to the continental shelf or the exclusive economic zone, or both, for all or any of the following purposes, namely

(a) regulating the conduct of scientific research within the continental shelf or the exclusive economic zone;

(b) prescribing measures for the protection and preservation of the marine environment of that shelf or zone;

(c) regulating, for the purposes of section 12, the construction, operation, and use of artificial islands (whether permanent or temporary), and other installations and structures within that shelf or zone, including the establishment of safety zones around, but not exceeding 500 metres distance from, such islands, installations, and structures;

(d) regulating the exploration and exploitation of that shelf or zone for economic purposes;

(e) providing for such other matters as are necessary or expedient for giving full effect to the sovereign rights and jurisdiction of Saint Lucia in relation to that shelf or zone; and

(f) providing for such other matters as are contemplated by or necessary for giving full effect to the provisions of Part II, III, or IV.

(4) Regulations may be made with respect to the exclusive economic zone for the exploration and exploitation of that zone for the production of energy from the water, currents and winds.

(5) Regulations may be made with respect to the investigation and institution of proceedings in respect of any discharge from a vessel outside the maritime areas of Saint Lucia in violation of applicable international rules and standards established through the competent international organisation or general diplomatic conference.

(6) The regulations may provide that a breach of any of the regulations shall be a criminal offence, and may provide for the imposition of a penalty not exceeding twenty thousand dollars for any such offence.

(7) The power under this section to make regulations may be exercised

(a) either in relation to all of the cases to which the power extends, or in relation to all those cases subject to specified exceptions, or in relation to any specified cases or class or description of cases; and

(b) so as to make, with respect to the cases in relation to which it is exercised

(i) the same provision for all those cases, or different provision for different cases or classes or description of cases, or different provisions with respect to the same case or clases or description of cases for different purposes of this Act; or

(ii) any such provision either unconditionally or subject to any specified condition.

Saving of Agreement

30. (1) In this section, 'the Agreement' means the Agreement between the Government of Saint Lucia and the Government of the French Republic done in Paris on the 4th day of March, 1981.

(2) Nothing in this Act affects the operation of the Agreement and, while it remains in force, the Agreement shall have effect according to its tenor for the purpose of the delimitation of any of the maritime areas of Saint Lucia affected by its provisions.

(3) A document purporting to be certified by the Minister to be a true copy of the Agreement is admissible in any proceedings as evidence of the contents of the Agreement.

Amendments

31. The enactments referred to in Column 2 of the Schedule are amended to the extent shown in Column 1 of the Schedule.

SCHEDULE

(Section 31)

Amendments

Criminal Code Chapter 250

Amend section 1242 in subsection (1) by substituting 'the territorial sea' for 'three miles of the shore of this Island'.

Amend section 1273 in subsection (1) by substituting 'the territorial sea' for 'three miles of any part thereof'.

Wireless Telegraphy Ordinance Chapter 146

Amend section 4 in subsection (1)

(a) by substituting in paragraph (a) 'territorial sea' for 'territorial waters of the Colony',
(b) by substituting in paragraph (b) 'territorial sea' for 'territorial waters thereof'.

Amend section 15 by substituting the 'territorial sea' for 'territorial waters of the Colony'.

Oil in Navigable Waters Ordinance

Amend section 2 by deleting subsection (3) and substituting the following subsection:

Chapter 91

(3) The waters to which this Ordinance applies are the waters of the territorial sea and the waters of harbours in the State.

Power Craft Ordinance, 1964. No. 4 of 1964

Amend Ordinance by substituting 'territorial sea' for 'territorial waters of this Island' wherever it occurs.

Amend section 3 by substituting 'that sea' for 'those waters'.

Amend/section 4 in subsection (1) by substituting 'that sea' for 'such waters' wherever it occurs.

Customs Act, 1967. (No. 25 of 1967)

Repeal the interpretation of 'waters of the Island' in section 2 and substitute the following interpretation.

'waters of the Island' means 'the inland waters and the territorial sea'.

Interpretation Act, 1968. (No. 18 of 1968)

Amend section 41 by inserting the following definitions in the appropriate place:

'contiguous zone' means the contiguous zone of Saint Lucia as defined in section 2 of the Maritime Areas Act, 1984;

'continental shelf' means the continental shelf of Saint Lucia as defined in section 2 of the Maritime Areas Act, 1984;

'exclusive economic zone' means the exclusive economic zone of Saint Lucia as defined in section 2 of the Maritime Areas Act, 1984;

'internal waters' means the internal waters of Saint Lucia as defined in section 2 of the Maritime Areas Act, 1984;

'territorial sea' means the territorial sea of Saint Lucia as defined in section 2 of the Maritime Areas Act, 1984;

Amend the definition of 'The Island' in section 41 by substituting 'territorial sea' for 'territorial waters adjacent thereto'.

Passed in the House of Assembly this 15th day of June, 1984.

W. St. Clair-Daniel
Speaker.

Passed in the Senate this 26th day of June, 1984.

E. Henry Giraudy,
President.

54. Saint Vincent and the Grenadines

Maritime Areas Act, 1983, (Act No. 15)
Entered into force: June 8, 1983.
Source: *The Government Printer,* at the Government Printing Office, Kingstown, St. Vincent and the Grenadines.

ACT No 15 of 1983

I Assent,

Sydney D. Gun-Munro,
Governor-General
8th June, 1983

An act to declare the Maritime areas and for matters incidental thereto and connected therewith.

On Proclamation

Be it enacted by the Queen's Most Excellent Majesty, by and with the advice and consent of the House of Assembly of Saint Vincent and the Grenadines and by the authority of the same as follows:—

1. This Act may be cited as the Maritime Areas Act, 1983 and shall come into operation on such date as the Governor General may, by Proclamation, specify.
2. In this Act, unless the context otherwise requires—

'Archipelagic sea lanes passage' means the exercise of the rights of navigation and over flight in accordance with the international law in the normal mode solely for the purpose of continuous expeditious and unobstructed transit between one part of the high seas or an exclusive economic zone and another part of the High Seas or an economic zone.
'Competent Authority' means the Minister or any person designated by him as the Competent Authority for the purposes of this Act.
'Innocent passage' means sea or air passage through the waters of Saint Vincent and the Grenadines which is not prejudicial to peace, good order or security.
'Minister' means the Minister for Foreign Affairs.
'Warship' means a ship belonging to the armed forces of a state bearing the external marks distinguishing such ships, of its nationality, under the command of an officer duly commissioned by the Government of the state and whose name appears in the appropriate service list or its equivalent and manned by a crew which is under regular armed forces discipline.
'Waters of Saint Vincent and the Grenadines' means the internal waters, archipelagic waters and territorial sea of Saint Vincent and the Grenadines.

3. The internal waters of Saint Vincent and the Granadines comprises the waters from the landward side of the archipelagic closing lines to the low water mark of all the island areas of Saint Vincent and the Grenadines.

4. The archipelagic waters of Saint Vincent and the Grenadines comprise the waters from the landward side of the archipelagic baselines to the archipelagic closing lines.

5. The territorial sea of Saint Vincent and the Grenadines comprise the waters from its archipelagic baseline seaward to a limit of 12 nautical miles.

6. The contiguous zone of Saint Vincent and the Granadines comprises the waters contiguous to its territorial sea from its archipelagic baselines seaward to a limit of 24 nautical miles.

7. The exclusive economic zone of Saint Vincent and the Grenadines comprises the waters; seabed and subsoil, contiguous to its territorial sea from its archipelagic baselines seaward to a limit of 200 nautical miles.

8. The continental shelf of Saint Vincent and the Grenadines comprises the seabed, subsoil and the submarine areas contiguous to its territorial sea from its archipelagic baselines seaward to a limit of 200 nautical miles.

9. The waters of Saint Vincent and the Grenadines including the airspace above and the bed and subsoil thereof form part of the territory of Saint Vincent and the Grenadines.

10. (1) Subject to subsections (2) and (4) and section 14, a foreign ship is entitled to enjoy the right of innocent passage through the waters of Saint Vincent and the Grenadines.

(2) A Foreign war ship shall not navigate in the waters of Saint Vincent and the Grenadines without the prior permission of the Competent Authority obtained by the State to which the war ship belongs.

(3) The Minister may by notification in the Gazette, make regulations relating to the innocent passage of foreign vessels through the waters of Saint Vincent and the Grenadines in respect of any or all of the following—

(a) The safety of navigation and the regulation of maritime traffic;
(b) the protection of navigational aids and facilities and other facilities or installations;
(c) the protection of cables and pipelines
(d) the conservation of the living resources of the sea;
(e) the prevention of infringement of the laws and regulations of Saint Vincent and the Granadines governing marine living resources;
(f) the prevention of the environment of Saint Vincent and the Grenadines and the prevention, reduction and control of pollution thereof;
(g) marine scientific research and hydrographic surveys; and
(h) the prevention of infringment of the customs, fiscal, immigration or sanitary laws and regulations of Saint Vincent and the Grenadines.

(4) The Minister may, by order published in the Gazette, suspend temporarily in specified areas of the waters of Saint Vincent and the Grenadines the innocent passage of Foreign ships if, such suspension is essential for the protection or the security of Saint Vincent and the Grenadines.

11. (1) The passage of a foreign ship is prejudicial to the peace, good order or security of Saint Vincent and the Grenadines where, without the prior permission of the Competent Authority obtained by the state to which the ship belongs or the captain or the person in charge of the ship, the ship while in the waters of Saint Vincent and the Grenadines engages in any of the following activities:—

(a) any threat or use of force against the sovereignity, territorial integrity or political independence of Saint Vincent and the Grenadines, or acts in any other manner in violation of the principles of international law embodied in the Charter of the United Nations;
(b) any exercise or practice with weapons of any kind;
(c) any act aimed at collecting information relating to the defence or security, economic condition or social condition of Saint Vincent and the Grenadines.
(d) any act by way of propaganda or otherwise aimed at affecting the defence or security of Saint Vincent and the Grenadines;

(e) the launching, landing or taking on board of any aircraft;
(f) the launching, landing or taking on board of devices;
(g) the taking on board or off-loading of any person, fiscal, immigration or sanitary laws or regulations of Saint Vincent and the Granadines.
(h) any act of pollution calculated to or likely to cause damage or harm to Saint Vincent and the Grenadines, its resources or its marine environment;
(i) any fishing activities;
(j) the carrying out of research or survey activities;
(k) any act aimed at interfering with any systems of communication or any other facilities or installation of Saint Vincent and the Grenadines;
(l) such other activity as may be prescribed.

(2) The passage of a foreign warship in the waters of Saint Vincent and the Grenadines is prejudicial to the peace, good order or security of Saint Vincent where the warship navigates such waters without the permission requirèd in subsection (2) of section 10.

12. (1) The Minister may, by order published in the Gazette, dosignate sea lanes and air routes thereabove suitable for the continuous and expeditious passage of foreign ships and aircraft through or over the archipelagic waters and the adjacent territorial sea;

(2) All ships and aircraft enjoy the right of archipelagic sea lanes passage in such sea lanes and air routes;

(3) All ships and aircraft shall not navigate closer to the coasts of Saint Vincent and the Grenadines than ten percent of the distance between the nearest points on islands and the axis lines of the sea lanes.

(4) The Minister may, by notification in the Gazette, establish traffic separation schemes for the safe passage of ships through narrow channels in such sea lanes and modify and substitute them from time to time.

13. (1) Every ship in passage shall respect applicable sea lanes and traffic separation schemes established in accordance with this Act.

(2) Every ship or aircraft exercising the right of archipelagic sea lanes passage shall—
(a) proceed without delay through the sea lanes;
(b) refrain from any threat or use force against the sovereignity, territorial integrity or political independence of states bordering straits, and shall not act in any manner in violation of the principles of international law embodied in the Charter of the United nations; and
(c) refrain from any activities other than those incidental to their normal modes or continuous and expeditious passage unless rendered necessary by force majeure or by distress:

(3) Ships in distress shall—
(a) comply with generally accepted international regulations, procedures and practices for safety at sea, including the International Regulations for preventing collision at Sea; and
(b) comply with generally accepted international regulations, procedures and practices for the prevention, reduction and control of pollution from ships.

(4) Aircraft in passage shall—
(a) observe the rules of the Air established by the International Civil Aviation Organisation as they apply to civil aircraft and every state aircraft shall normally comply with such safety measure and shall at all times operate with due regard for the safety of navigation;
(b) at all times monitor the radio frequency assigned, by the appropriate internationally designated air traffic control authority or the appropriate international distress radio frequency.

(5) During its passage through archipelagic sea lanes, a foreign ship, including maritime scientific research and hydrograph survey ship, may not carry out any research or survey activities without prior authorisation of the Minister.

14. (1) The Minister may, by notification in the Gazette, make regulations relating to archipelagic sea lanes passage in respect of any or all of the following:

(a) the safety of navigation and the regulation of maritime traffic;

(b) the prevention; reduction and control of pollution, by giving effect to applicable international regulations regarding the discharge of oil, oily wastes and other various and polluting substances;

(c) with respect to fishing vessels, the prevention of fishing including the storage of fishing gear;

(d) the embarking or loading or disembarking or unloading of any person, commodity, or currency in contravention of the customs, fiscal, immigration or sanitary laws and regulations of Saint Vincent and the Grenadines.

(2) Every Foreign ship exercising the right of archipelagic sea lanes passage shall comply with all the laws and regulations applicable to it.

(3) The flag state of a ship or aircraft entitled to sovereign immunity which acts in a manner contrary to any law or regulation shall bear international responsibility for any lesser damage which results to Saint Vincent and the Grenadines.

(4) The Minister may levy charges upon foreign ships passing through the waters of Saint Vincent and the Grenadines for specific services rendered to them.

15. In designating or substituting sea lanes or prescribing or substituting traffic separation scheme, the Minister shall refer proposals to the International Maritime Organisation, or its successors, with a view to their adoption.

16. The Minister shall publish charts and lists of coordinates of:

(a) The low water mark of all the islanders of Saint Vincent and the Grenadines;

(b) the archipelagic closing lines of Saint Vincent and the Grenadines;

(c) the archipelagic baselines of Saint Vincent and the Grenadines;

(d) the outer limits of the territorial sea of Saint Vincent and the Grenadines;

(e) the outer limits of the continuous zone of Saint Vincent and the Grenadines;

(f) the outer limits of the exclusive economic zone of Saint Vincent and the Grenadines;

(g) the outer limits of the continental shelf of Saint Vincent and the Grenadines;

(h) the axis of any archipelagic sea lanes of Saint Vincent and the Grenadines;

(i) any traffic separation scheme in the waters of Saint Vincent and the Grenadines;

and give due publicity to the charts and lists and deposit a copy of each chart or list with the Secretary General of the United Nations.

17. (1) Where the rights of Saint Vincent and the Grenadines in relation to:

(a) the territorial sea,

(b) the contiguous zone,

(c) the exclusive economic zone, or

(d) the continental shelf,

overlap with the territorial sea, the contiguous zone, the exclusive economic zone, or the continental shelf of an adjacent state, until such time as a delimitation agreement is reached the seaward limits of the affected offshore areas of Saint Vincent and the Grenadines shall extend to the equidistance line between the archipelagic baselines of Saint Vincent and the Grenadines and the territorial sea baselines of the other state.

(2) The temporary offshore boundaries created by subsection (1) shall in no way be interpreted as prejudicing any claims which Saint Vincent and the Grenadines may in the future advance pursuant to the conclusion of maritime boundary delimination with neighbouring states.

18. (1) The criminal jurisdiction of Saint Vincent and the Grenadines shall not be exercised on board a foreign ship passing through the territortal sea or archipelagic waters of Saint Vincent and the Grenadines nor shall any investigation in connection with any crime committed, save only in cases where—

(a) the consequences of the crime extend to Saint Vincent and the Grenadines; or

(b) the crime is of a kind to disturb the peace of Saint Vincent and the Grenadines or the good order of the territorial seas;

(c) the assistance of the local authorities has been requested by the ship or by a diplomatic agent or consular officer of the flag state; or

(d) such measures are necessary for the suppression of illicit traffic in narcotic drugs or psychotropic substance.

(2) The Minister may by, notification in the Gazette, make regulations with regard to the customs, fiscal, health, safety and immigration matters over artificial islands, installations and structures in the exclusive economic zone or on the continental shelf of Saint Vincent and the Grenadines beyond the territorial sea.

19. The Minister may, by notification in the Gazette, make regulations relating to the exercise of control in the contiguous zone:

(a) to prevent infringement of the customs, fiscal, immigration or sanitary regulations in force on the territory or territorial sea of Saint Vincent and the Grenadines; and

(b) to punish breach of the said regulations committed within the territory or territorial sea of Saint Vincent and the Grenadines.

20. The Minister may, by notification in the Gazette, make regulations regarding the exercises of control in the exclusive economic zone with regards to:

(a) the exploration and exploitation, conservation and management of living and non-living resources of the seabed and subsoil and the superjacent waters;

(b) other activities for the economic exploitation of the zone;

(c) the establishment and use of artificial islands, installations and structures;

(d) marine scientific research;

(e) the protection and preservation of the marine environment; and

(f) any other functional area of jurisdiction which may be accorded to coastal states by international law.

21. The Minister may, by notification in the Gazette make regulations relating to the exercise of control on the continental shelf with regards to:

(a) the exploration and exploitation of the living and non-living resources;

(b) the establishment and use of artificial islands, installations and structures: and

(c) the prevention, reduction and control of marine pollution arising from or in connection with seabed activities.

22. The Minister may, where necessary establish reasonable safety zones around such artificial islands, installations and structures to ensure the safety both of navigation and of the artificial islands, installations and structures in the exclusive economic zone or on the continental shelf of Saint Vincent and the Grenadines.

23. (1) Every law in existence at the commencement of this Act shall be construed with such modifications, adaptations, qualifications and exceptions as may be necessary to bring it into conforminity with the provisions made by or under this Act and the same shall prevail in every case where there is any conflict between any of the provisions and any such existing law.

(2) The expression 'Modification, adaptions, qualifications and exceptions' shall include the automatic extension, as far as the law applicable to other parts of Saint Vincent and the Grenadines to the whole of the area within the territorial extent set out in section 9.

(3) Without prejudice to the generality of subsection (1), the Governor-General may, by order made at any time before the expiration of five years from the commencement of the Act, make such alterations to any law in existence as is referred to in subsection (1) as may appear to him to be necessary to bring the provisions of the law in accordance with the provisions of subsection (1).

Passed in the House of Assembly this 19th day of May, 1983.

55. Sao Tome and Principe

Decree Law No. 15/78.
Entered into force: June 16, 1978.
Source: *Diario da Republica,* June 16, 1978 (Translated from Portuguese by the Department of State).

Considering the need to safeguard the legitimate rights and fundamental interests of the nation with respect to the living and non-living resources of the maritime space of the Democratic Republic of Sao Tome and Principe;

Considering the importance for the national economy of fisheries and the development of the living and nonliving natural resources of the seabed, subsoil, and the superjacent waters adjoining the territorial sea delimited by law;

Taking into account the evolution of international maritime law, particularly the work of the United Nations Conference on the Law of the Sea;

In view of the need to establish an exclusive economic zone beyond the territorial sea and adjacent thereto in which the State of Sao Tome and Principe will have sovereign rights and exclusive jurisdiction over all the living and nonliving natural resources found therein,

In exercise of the powers conferred by Article 26 (1) of the Constitution, the Government of the Democratic Republic of Sao Tome and Principe decrees and I promulgate the following:

Article 1

The State of the Democratic Republic of Sao Tome and Principe hereby establishes an exclusive economic zone adjacent to its territorial sea extending 200 nautical miles from the baseline from which the breadth of the territorial sea is measured.

Article 2

The outer line of this exclusive economic zone is delimited by geographic coordinates.

Article 3

The State of Sao Tome and Principe will respect the equal rights of the neighboring States to their respective economic zones and declares its willingness to conduct bilateral negotiations on any conflict of rights which may arise from the application of these principles.

Article 4

In the exclusive economic zone established by this decree-law, the Democratic Republic of Sao Tome and Principe will exercise the following rights:

1. Sovereign rights for purposes of research, exploitation, conservation, and management of the living and nonliving natural resources of the seabeds including the subsoil and the superjacent waters.
2. Exclusive rights and jurisdiction with respect to the establishment and utilization of artificial islands, installations, and structures.
3. Exclusive jurisdiction over other activities related to economic research and development of the zone, including the use of marine currents and such others as may become feasible through technical and scientific development.

4. Jurisdiction with respect to:
   (a) Preservation of the marine environment, especially the control and elimination of pollution,
   (b) Scientific research.

Article 5

Foreign States shall enjoy within the exclusive economic zone the freedoms of navigation, overflight, and laying of pipelines and submarine cables as well as other internationally lawful uses of the sea related to navigation and communications.

1. The laying of pipelines and submarine cables shall be subject to agreement with the State of Sao Tome and Principe.

Article 6

In order to promote optimum utilization of the living resources in the exclusive economic zone, the State of the Democratic Republic of Sao Tome and Principe may, through bilateral agreements, grant access to other States for the rational harvesting of the surplus of the allowable catch.

Article 7

All pertinent legal provisions contrary to this decree-law are hereby revoked.

Article 8

This decree-law shall enter into effect immediately.

Article 9

Examined and approved in the Council of Ministers on May 18, 1978.

[Names and titles of cabinet Ministers]

Promulgated on June 13, 1978

To be published.

Manuel Pinto da Costa,
President of the Republic

56. Seychelles

A. Maritime Zones Act, 1977 (Act No. 15).
Entered into force: August 1, 1977.
Source: *Supplement to Official Gazette,* December 26, 1978, pp. 419-420.

B. Exclusive Economic Zone (No. 2) Order, 1978.
Source: *United Nations ST/LEG/SER.B/19,* pp. 250.

A. The Maritime Zones Act, 1977
Arrangement of sections

Section

1. Citation and commencement.
2. Interpretation.
3. Sovereignty over and limits of territorial waters.
4. Use of territorial waters by foreign ships.
5. Continental shelf.
6. Exclusive economic zone.
7. Rights over continental shelf and exclusive economic zone.
8. Historic waters.
9. Designated areas of the continental shelf and the exclusive economic zone.
10. Extension of enactments.
11. Publication of charts.
12. Offences.
13. Offences by agent and body corporate.
14. Application of Act.
15. Regulations.

SEYCHELLES
Act No. 15 of 1977

I Assent,

James R. Mancham,
President.

20 May, 1977

An Act to provide for certain matters relating to the territorial waters, the continental shelf, the exclusive economic zone and the historic waters of Seychelles.

Enacted by the Parliament of Seychelles.

Citation and commencement

1. This Act may be cited as the Maritime Zones Act, 1977 and shall come into operation on such date as the President may, by order, appoint.

Interpretation

2. In this Act

'baseline' means the baseline as determined in accordance with the straight baseline system;

'continental shelf' means the continental shelf of Seychelles;

'designated area' means an area declared as such under section 9;

'exclusive economic zone' means the exclusive economic zone of Seychelles;

'historic waters' means the historic waters of Seychelles;

'limit', in relation to the territorial waters, the continental shelf, the exclusive economic zone or the historic waters of Seychelles, means the limit of such waters, shelf, exclusive economic zone or historic waters with reference to the individual or composite group or groups of islands constituting the territory of Seychelles;

'resources' includes living and non-living resources as well as resources for the production of energy from tides, winds and currents;

'submarines' includes underwater vehicles however propelled;

'territorial waters' means the territorial waters of Seychelles.

Sovereignty over and limits of territorial waters

3. (1) The sovereignty of Seychelles extends and has always extended to the territorial waters of Seychelles and to the seabed and subsoil underlying, and the air space over, such waters.

(2) The limit of the territorial waters is the line every point of which is at a distance of twelve nautical miles from the nearest point of the baseline.

(3) Notwithstanding anything contained in subsection (2), where the President considers it necessary so to do having regard to International Law and State practice, he may, subject to subsection (4), by Order published in the *Gazette,* amend the limit of the territorial waters.

Territorial waters by foreign ships

4. (1) Without prejudice to any other enactment in force but subject to subsection (2), (3) and (4), all foreign ships (other than warships, including submarines) shall enjoy the right of innocent passage through the territorial waters.

(2) Foreign warships, including submarines, may enter or pass through the territorial waters after giving notice to the President's Office.

(3) Submarines shall, while passing through the territorial waters, navigate on the surface and show their flag.

(4) Where the President is satisfied that it is necessary so to do—

(a) in the interest of public safety, public order, defence or security of Seychelles or any part thereof; or

(b) in pursuance of any treaty to which Seychelles is a party,

he may, by Order published in the *Gazette,* suspend, whether absolutely or subject to such exceptions and qualifications as may be specified in the Order, the entry of any class of foreign ships into such area of the territorial waters as may be specified in the Order.

Continental shelf

5. (1) The continental shelf comprises the seabed and subsoil of the submarine areas that extend beyond the limit of the territorial waters throughout the natural prolongation of the land territory of Seychelles—

(a) to the outer edge of the continental margin; or

(b) to a distance of two hundred nautical miles from the baseline where the outer edge of the continental shelf does not extend up to that distance.

(2) Seychelles has, and always had, full and exclusive sovereign rights in respect of the continental shelf.

Exclusive economic zone

6. (1) The exclusive economic zone is the area beyond and adjacent to the territorial waters and which extends to a distance of two hundred nautical miles from the baseline.

(2) Notwithstanding anything contained in subsection (1), where the President considers it necessary so to do having regard to International Law and State practice, he may, subject to subsection (3), by Order published in the *Gazette,* amend the limit of the exclusive economic zone as specified in subsection (1).

Rights over continental shelf and exclusive economic zone

7. (1) Without prejudice to sections 3, 5 and 6, but subject to subsection (3) and (6) Seychelles has, in the continental shelf and the exclusive economic zone—

(a) sovereign rights for the purposes of exploration, exploitation, conservation and management of all resources;

(b) exclusive rights and jurisdiction for the constructions, maintenance or operation of artificial islands, off-shore terminals, installations and other structures and devices necessary for the exploration and exploitation of resources or for the convenience of shipping or for any other purpose;

(c) exclusive jurisdiction to authorise, regulate and conduct scientific research;

(d) exclusive jurisdiction to preserve and protect the marine environment and to prevent and control marine pollution; and

(e) such other rights as are recognised by International Law or State practice.

(2) Except in accordance with the terms of any agreement entered into with Seychelles or of licence granted by or under the authority of the President, no person shall, in relation to the continental shelf or the exclusive economic zone—

(a) explore or exploit any resources;

(b) carry out any search, excavation or drilling operations;

(c) conduct any research;

(d) construct, maintain or operate any artificial island, off-shore terminal installation or other structure or device.

(3) Subject to subsection *(d)* and to any measures that may be necessary for protecting the interest of Seychelles, foreign States may lay or maintain cables or pipelines on the continental shelf and the seabed of the exclusive economic zone.

(4) No cables or pipelines shall be laid on the continental shelf or on the seabed of the exclusive economic zone unless the authority of the President has been obtained for the delineation of the course of the cables or pipelines.

(5) Nothing in subsection (2) shall apply in relation to fishing by a citizen of Seychelles or a body corporate registered in Seychelles and approved by the Minister of Fisheries.

(6) Ships and aircraft of all States shall, subject to the exercise by Seychelles of its sovereign rights over its continental shelf or within the exclusive economic zone enjoy the following freedoms—

(a) freedom of navigation; and

(b) freedom of overflight.

Historic waters

8. (1) The President may, by Order published in the *Gazette,* specify the limits of the historic waters.

(2) The sovereign rights of Seychelles extends, and has always extended, to the historic waters and to the seabed and subsoil underlying, and the air space over, the historic waters.

Designated areas of the continental shelf and the exclusive economic zone

9. The President may, by Order published in the *Gazette—*

(*a*) declare any area of the continental shelf or the exclusive economic zone to be a designated area; and

(*b*) make such provisions as he considers necessary with respect to—

(i) the exploration, exploitation and protection of the resources within the designated area;

(ii) the safety and protection of artificial islands, off-shore terminals, installations and other structures and devices in the designated area;

(iii) the regulation and conduct of scientific research in the designated area;

(iv) the protection of the marine environment in the designated area;

(v) customs and other fiscal matters in relation to the designated area;

(vi) the regulation of entry into and passage of foreign ships through the designated area;

(vii) the establishment of fairways, sealanes, traffic separation schemes or any mode of ensuring freedom of navigation which is not prejudicial to the interest of Seychelles.

Extension of enactments

10. The President may, by Order published in the *Gazette*—

(*a*) extend with such restrictions and modifications as he thinks fit, any enactment in force to the continental shelf or the exclusive economic zone, or any part thereof, including any designated area;

(*b*) make such provisions as he considers necessary for facilitating the enforcement of that enactment.

Publication of charts

11. The President may cause the baseline, the limits of the territorial waters, the continental shelf, the exclusive economic zone and the historic waters to be published in charts.

Offences

12. (1) Any person who contravenes any provisions of this Act or any regulation or Order made under this Act, shall commit an offence and shall, on conviction, be liable to a fine not exceeding two hundred thousand rupees or to imprisonment for a term not exceeding five years.

(2) Any person who commits an offence shall be tried in the Supreme Court.

Offences by agent and body corporate

13. (1) Where an offence is committed by—

(*a*) an agent, the person for whom the agent is acting;

(*b*) a body corporate, every person who, at the time of the commission of the offence, was concerned in the management of the body corporate or was purporting to act in a managerial capacity,

shall also commit the like offence, unless he proves that the offence was committed without his knowledge or consent and that he took all reasonable steps to prevent the commission of the offence.

(2) Notwithstanding subsection (1), where an offence has been committed by a body corporate and it is proved that the offence has been committed with the consent, whether express or implied, or the connivance of, or is attributable to any neglect on the part of the director, manager, secretary, or other officer of the body corporate, such director, manager, secretary or other officer shall commit the like offence.

Application of Act

14. Where any provision of this Act or of any regulation or Order made under this Act is in conflict with the provision of any other enactment in force, such provision of this Act or of such regulation or Order shall prevail.

Regulations

15. (1) The President may make such regulations as he considers necessary for carrying out the purposes of this Act.

(2) In particular and without prejudice to the foregoing power, regulations made under subsection (1) may provide for all or any of the following matters—

(a) the regulation of the conduct of any person in the territorial waters, the continental shelf, the exclusive economic zone or the historical waters;

(b) the regulation of the exploration and exploitation, conservation and management of the resources of the continental shelf and the exclusive economic zone;

(c) the regulation of the construction, maintenance of artificial islands, off-shore terminals, installations and other structures and devices;

(d) the preservation and the protection of the marine environment and the prevention and control of marine pollution;

(e) the regulation and conduct of scientific research;

(f) the fees in relation to licences; and

(g) any matter incidental to any of the matters specified in paragraphs *(a)* to *(f)*.

I certify that this is a correct copy of the Bill which was passed by the National Assembly on the 27th day of April, 1977.

J. Renaud,
Clerk of the National Assembly.

S. I. No. 125 of 1978.

B. MARITIME ZONES ACT, 1977
(No. 15 of 1977)

Exclusive Economic Zone (No. 2) Order, 1978.

In exercise of the powers conferred by section 6 (2) of the Maritime Zone Act, 1977, the President, considering it necessary so to do having regard to international law and state practice, hereby makes the following Order—

Citation

1. This Order may be cited as the Exclusive Economic Zone (No. 2) Order, 1978.

Limit of exclusive economic zone

2. The limit of the exclusive zone is delineated by the boundary of Area A as shown on Chart No. ML/ADN/52 filed in the office of the Chief Surveyor and more fully described in the Schedule.

Revocation of S. I. No. 23 of 1978

3. The Exclusive Economic Zone Order, 1978, is hereby revoked.

SCHEDULE

Description of the limit of the Exclusive Economic Zone

The boundary from point I through points 2, 3, 4, 5, 6, 7, 8, 9, 10, 11, 12 to 13 is formed by the locus of a point 200 nautical miles from the nearest land mass of the Republic of Seychelles.

From point 13 through points 14, 15, 16, 17 to point 18, the boundary is the medium line equidistant between the Republic of Seychelles and the Territory of Mauritius.

The boundary than follows the locus of a point 200 nautical miles from the nearest landmass of the Republic of Seychelles to point 19.

From point 19 through points 20, 21, 22, 23, 24, 25, 26, 27, 28 to 29 the boundaries is formed by the median line equidistant between the Republic of Seychelles and the Malagasy Republic, Isles Glorieuses (France), Mayotte Island, Iles Comores and Mafia Island (Tanzania).

The geographical coordinates of the points referred to above are listed below.

Points	Latitude South of Equator	Longitude East of Greenwich
1	07° 46′	43° 15′
2	06° 04′	46° 41′
3	06° 19′	47° 49′
4	06° 30′	48° 40′
5	05° 41′	49° 57′
6	04° 32′	50° 04′
7	01° 38′	52° 36′
8	00° 29′	56° 03′
9	02° 39′	58° 48′
10	04° 01′	59° 15′
11	05° 34′	59° 09′
12	07° 10′	59° 30′
13	08° 27′	59° 22′
14	08° 33′	58° 23′
15	08° 45′	56° 25′
16	08° 56′	54° 30′
17	09° 39′	53° 53′
18	12° 17′	53° 49′
19	12° 47′	53° 14′
20	11° 31′	50° 29′
21	11° 05′	50° 12′
22	10° 17′	49° 26′
23	11° 01′	48° 30′
24	10° 47′	47° 33′
25	10° 37′	46° 56′
26	11° 12′	45° 47′
27	10° 55′	45° 31′
28	10° 27′	44° 51′
29	08° 05′	43° 10′

Made this 7th day of December, 1978.

F.A. Rene,
President

57. Solomon Islands

Delimitation of Marine Waters Act, Act No. 32.
Entered into force: August 14, 1979.
Source: Communication of the Office of Prime Minister to the Secretary-General of the United Nations, September 1, 1979.

Assented to in Her Majesty's name and on Her Majesty's behalf this 21st day of December 1978.

B. DEVESI
Governor-General

AN ACT

of Parliament to make provisions for the demarcation of the marine waters appertaining to Solomon Islands to declare the rights of Solomon Islands in relation thereto and for matters connected therewith and incidental thereto

Date of Commencement

Enacted by the National Parliament of Solomon Islands.

Citation and commencement

1. This Act may be cited as the Delimitation of Marine Waters Act, 1978, and shall come into force on such date as the Minister may by notice appoint:

Provided that the Minister may specify different dates for the coming into force of different sections of this Act.

Interpretation

2. (1) In this Act, unless the context otherwise requires

'archipelago' means a group of islands, including parts of islands, inter-connecting waters and other natural features which are so closely inter-related that such islands, waters and other natural features form an intrinsic geographical entity, and which has been declared by the Minister by Order published in the Gazette to be an archipelago;

'archipelagic baselines' means the baselines drawn under the provisions of subsection (2) of section 4;

'island' means a naturally formed area of land which is surrounded by and above water at mean high-water spring tides;

'low-water line' means the line of low water at mean low-water spring tides as depicted on the largest scale nautical chart of the area produced by any authority and for the time being held and used by the Minister responsible for marine affairs;

'median line' means a line every point of which is equidistant from the nearest points of the baselines from which the breadth of the territorial seas of Solomon Islands and of any opposite or adjacent State of territory are measured;

'mile' means the international nautical mile;

'Minister' means the Minister responsible for Foreign Affairs;

'territorial seas' means the territorial seas of Solomon Islands as defined in section 5.

(2) For the purposes of this Act, permanent harbour works that form an integral part of a harbour system shall be treated as forming part of the coast.

Internal waters

3. (1) Except where closing lines are drawn under the provisions of subsection (2), all waters on the landward side of the baselines of the territorial seas of Solomon Islands are the internal waters of Solomon Islands.

(2) When making an order under the provisions of section 4, the Minister may also declare, by reference to physical features marked on official charts or to lists of geographical co-ordinates specifying the geodetic datum, the points between which closing lines are to be drawn for the purpose of determining the outer limits of the internal waters of any archipelago in Solomon Islands.

(3) Where closing lines are drawn under the provisions of subsection (2) the internal waters of any archipelago in Solomon Islands shall include all waters on the landward side of those closing lines.

Archipelagic waters

4. (1) The archipelagic waters of each archipelago in Solomon Islands shall comprise all areas of sea contained within the baselines established under the provisions of this section.

(2) The Minister in accordance with the rules of international law may by order published in the Gazette, by reference to physical features marked on official charts or to lists of geographical co-ordinates specifying the geodetic datum, the points between which straight baselines are to be drawn for the purpose of determining the outermost limits of the archipelagic waters of any archipelago in Solomon Islands and the innermost limits of the territorial sea of any archipelago in Solomon Islands.

Territorial waters

5. (1) The territorial seas of Solomon Islands comprise all areas of sea having as their innermost limits the baselines established under the provisions of this section and as their outermost limits a line measured seaward from those baselines every point of which is at a distance of twelve miles from the nearest point of the baselines:

Provided that where the median line between Solomon Islands and the sovereign State of Papua New Guinea is less than twelve miles from the baselines from which the breadth of the territorial seas of Solomon Islands and Papua New Guinea are respectively measured, the outermost limits of the territorial waters of Solomon Islands shall be those declared by the Minister by order published in the Gazette.

(2) Where archipelagic baselines are drawn under the provisions of section 4, those baselines shall be the baselines from which the breadth of the territorial sea of any archipelago in Solomon Islands shall be measured.

(3) In all other cases the baselines from which the breadth of the territorial sea is measured is the low-water line along the coast of each island except that in the case of islands situated on atolls or islands having fringing reefs the baseline is the seaward low-water line of the reef.

Exclusive economic zone

6. (1) Subject to the following provisions of this section, the exclusive economic zone of Solomon Islands comprise all areas of sea having, as their innermost limits the outermost limits of the territorial seas, and, as their outermost limits, a line drawn seaward from the baselines every point of which is at a distance of 200 miles from the nearest point of the appropriate baselines.

(2) The Minister may by order published in the Gazette, for the purpose of implementing any international agreement or the award of any international body, or otherwise, declare that the outer limits of the exclusive economic zone of Solomon Islands extend to such line, any point of which may be at a distance of less than 200 miles from the nearest point of the appropriate baseline, as may be specified in such order.

(3) Where the median line is less than 200 miles from the nearest baselines, and no other line is for the time being specified under the provisions of subsection (2), the outerlimits of the exclusive economic zone of Solomon Islands extend to the median line.

Continental Shelf Act, 1970 to apply. No. 4 of 1970

7. All areas of seabed and the subsoil thereof contained within the exclusive economic zone of Solomon Islands are deemed to form part of the continental shelf of Solomon Islands for the purposes of the Continental Shelf Act, 1970, and to be subject to the provisions of that Act as if they were areas designated under the provisions of subsection (3) of section 3 of that Act.

Charts and publicity

8. (1) The Minister shall cause all closing lines, baselines and other lines drawn under the provisions of this Act for the purpose of determining the limits of the internal waters, territorial seas and exclusive economic zone of Solomon Islands to be clearly indicated on charts of a scale or scales adequate for them to be readily determined and shall give due publicity to such charts by notice in the Gazette and shall cause a copy of each such chart to be deposited with the Secretary General of the United Nations.

(2) In any proceedings in any court, a certificate purporting to be signed by the Chief Marine Officer that any specified nautical chart of any area is the nautical chart of that area most suited for the purposes of determining the limits of the internal waters territorial seas or exclusive economic zone of Solomon Islands, as the case may be, and is for the time being held by the Minister responsible for Marine affairs shall be admissible in evidence of the matters stated in the certificate.

Legal character of marine waters

9. (1) The sovereignty of Solomon Islands extends beyond its land territory and internal waters over its archipelagic waters and territorial seas and to the airspace thereover as well as to the seabed and subsoil thereunder.

(2) Within the exclusive economic zone Solomon Islands has sovereign rights for the purpose of exploring and exploiting, conserving and managing the natural resources, whether living or non-living of the seabed and subsoil and the superjacent waters.

(3) The exercise by Solomon Islands of its sovereignty and sovereign rights under the provisions of this section is subject to the customary rules of international law.

Rights of passage

10. (1) Subject to the provisions of subsections (2), (3), (4) and (5), ships and aircraft of all States shall, in accordance with the rules of international law, have the right of innocent passage through and over the territorial seas and archipelagic waters.

(2) The Minister may, in accordance with the rules of international law, by order published in the Gazette designate sealanes and air routes, suitable for the continuous and expeditious passage of foreign ships and aircraft, through and over the archipelagic waters and the adjacent territorial seas, and may also prescribe traffic separation schemes for the purpose of ensuring the safe passage of ships through narrow channels in such sealanes.

(3) In such sealanes and air routes all ships and aircraft may, in accordance with the rules of international law, enjoy the right of navigation and overflight, in their normal modes, for the purpose of continuous, expeditious and unobstructed transit through and over the archipelagic waters and the adjacent territorial seas, from one part of the exclusive economic zone to another part of the exclusive economic zone.

(4) Until such time as sealanes or air routes are designated under the provisions of subsection (2) the rights of navigation and overflight referred to in subsection (3) may be exercised through and over all routes normally used for international navigation and overflight.

(5) The rights of navigation and overflight referred to in subsection (3) are subject to all laws of Solomon Islands made in accordance with the rules of international law.

(6) Subject to the provisions of this Act and of any other written law made in accordance with the relevant rules of international law all States and their nationals shall enjoy, in the exclusive economic zone, the high seas freedoms of navigation and overflight and of the laying of submarine cables and pipelines, and all other internationally lawful uses of the sea related to those freedoms, compatible with the rules of international law.

Regulations

11. Where no other provision is for the time being made in any other written law for any such purpose, the Minister may make regulations, in accordance with the rules of international law, for all or any of the following purposes:

(a) regulating the conduct of scientific research within the exclusive economic zone;

(b) regulating the exploration and exploitation of the exclusive economic zone for the production of energy from the waters, currents and winds, and for other economic uses;

(c) regulating the construction, operation and use of artificial islands, installations and structures within the exclusive economic zone, including, but not confined to, the establishment of safety zones around islands, installations and structures;

(d) prescribing measures for the protection and preservation of the marine environment of the exclusive economic zone; and

(e) providing for such other matters as are necessary or expedient to give effect to Solomon Islands rights and obligations in relation to the exclusive economic zone or are necessary to give full effect to the provisions of this Act.

Passed by the National Parliament this fourteenth day of December one thousand nine hundred and seventy eight.

This printed impression has been carefully compared by me with the Bill passed by the National Parliament and found by me to be a true and correct copy of the said Bill.

L.O. Poznanski
Clerk to the National Parliament

58. Soviet Union

Decree of the Presidium of the Supreme Soviet of the USSR on the Economic Zone of the USSR—28 February 1984.
Entered into force: March 1, 1984.
Source: *United Nations Law of the Sea Bulletin No. 4,* February 1985, pp. 31–40.

The Presidium of the Supreme Soviet of the USSR has adopted a Decree on the Economic Zone of the USSR. For the conservation and optimum utilization of living and other resources and the protection of other economic interests of the USSR in maritime areas adjacent to the coast of the USSR, taking into consideration the relevant provisions of the United Nations Convention on the Law of the Sea designed to establish a uniform régime of economic zones, and with the aim of promoting the implementation of those provisions, the Decree states that there shall be established in the maritime areas beyond and adjacent to the territorial waters (territorial sea) of the USSR, including areas surrounding islands belonging to the USSR, an economic zone of the USSR, the outer limit of which shall be situated at a distance of 200 nautical miles, measured from the same baselines as the territorial waters (territorial sea) of the USSR.

It is established that in its economic zone the USSR shall exercise sovereign rights for the purpose of exploring and exploiting, conserving and managing the natural resources, whether living or non-living, situated on the sea-bed, in its subsoil and in the superjacent waters; the USSR shall exercise sovereign rights with regard to other activities for the economic exploration and exploitation of the zone, have jurisdiction with regard to the establishment and use of artificial islands, installations and structures, marine scientific research and the protection and preservation of the marine environment, and have other rights provided for in the Decree, in other legislative instruments of the USSR and in the generally recognized norms of international law.

In the economic zone of the USSR, all States, whether coastal or land-locked, shall enjoy, subject to the provisions of the Decree and other relevant legislative instruments of the USSR, as well as the generally recognized norms of international law, the freedoms of navigation and overflight and of the laying of submarine cables and pipelines, and other internationally lawful uses of the sea related to those freedoms.

The USSR shall have the exclusive right to construct, permit and regulate the establishment, operation and utilization in the economic zone of the USSR of any artificial, as well as any kind of installations and structures intended for conducting scientific research in its economic zone, for the exploration and exploitation of its natural resources and for other economic purposes.

It is provided that persons guilty of illegal exploration or exploitation of the natural resources of the economic zone of the USSR, of polluting the marine environment as a result of the illegal discharge in the economic zone of the USSR of substances harmful to human health or to the living resources of the sea, or as a direct consequence of drilling or other activities for the exploration or exploitation of mineral resources of the sea-bed in the economic zone of the USSR, persons guilty of conducting marine scientific research in the economic zone of the USSR without the consent of the competent Soviet authorities, persons guilty of establishing artificial islands, constructing installations and structures in the economic zone of the USSR and establishing safety zones around them without the required permission, and likewise persons guilty of violating other provisions of the Decree, shall bear administrative liability, unless those violations by their nature entail criminal liability in accordance with the current legislation of the USSR.

The Decree of the Presidium of the Supreme Soviet of the USSR on the economic zone of the USSR shall enter into force on 1 March 1984.

The full text of the Decree is published in the Gazette of the Supreme Soviet of the USSR.

'Izvestia', 29 February 1984

Decree of the Presidium of the Supreme Soviet of the USSR on the Economic Zone of the USSR, 28 February, 1984

For the conservation and optimum utilization of living and other resources and the protection of other economic interests of the USSR in maritime areas adjacent to the coast of the USSR, taking into consideration the relevant provisions of the United Nations Convention on the Law of the Sea designed to establish a uniform régime of economic zones, and with the aim of promoting the implementation of those provisions, the Presidium of the Supreme Soviet of the USSR determines:

1. In maritime areas beyond and adjacent to the territorial waters (territorial sea) of the USSR, including areas surrounding islands belonging to the USSR, there shall be established an economic zone of the USSR, the outer limit of which shall be situated at a distance of 200 nautical miles measured from the same baselines as the territorial waters (territorial sea) of the USSR.

The delimitation of the economic zone between the USSR and States with coasts opposite or adjacent to the coast of the USSR shall be effected, taking into account the legislation of the USSR, by agreement on the basis of international law, in order to achieve an equitable solution.

2. In its economic zone, provided for in article 1 of this Decree, the USSR shall have:

(a) sovereign rights for the purpose of exploring and exploiting, conserving and managing the natural resources, whether living or non-living, situated on the sea-bed, in its subsoil and in the superjacent waters;

(b) sovereign rights with regard to other activities for the economic exploration and exploitation of the zone;

(c) jurisdiction with regard to:

(i) the establishment and use of artificial islands, installations and structures;

(ii) marine scientific research; and

(iii) the protection and preservation of the marine environment;

(d) other rights provided for in this Decree, in other relevant legislative instruments of the USSR and in the generally recognized norms of international law.

The rights and jurisdiction set out in this article with respect to the sea-bed of the economic zone and its subsoil shall be exercised in accordance with the legislation of the USSR concerning the continental shelf of the USSR.

3. The USSR shall exercise the rights stemming from its primary interest in and responsibility for anadromous stocks of fish which originate in its rivers.

The competent Soviet authorities shall ensure the conservation of such anadromous stocks by the adoption of appropriate measures and by the establishment of rules regulating their fishing, including the establishment of total allowable catches, both in its economic zone and beyond the limits of the zone.

The USSR shall ensure compliance with the measures and rules pertaining to anadromous stocks beyond the limits of its economic zone on the basis of treaties between the USSR and other interested States.

Fishing by other States of anadromous stocks originating in the rivers of the USSR, beyond the outer limits of the economic zone of the USSR, shall be conducted on the basis of treaties between the USSR and other interested States concerning the terms and conditions of such fishing, giving due regard to the conservation requirements and the needs of the USSR in respect of such stocks.

The terms and conditions of the utilization and conservation of anadromous stocks originating in the rivers of the USSR shall be determined by the Council of Ministers of the USSR.

4. In the economic zone of the USSR, all States, whether coastal or land-locked, shall enjoy, subject to the provisions of this Decree and other relevant legislative instruments of the USSR, as well as the generally recognized norms of international law, the freedoms of navigation and overflight and of the laying of submarine cables and pipelines, and other internationally lawful uses of the sea related to those freedoms.

5. The USSR shall ensure the optimum utilization of fish and other living resources in its economic zone through proper conservation and management measures, taking into account the best scientific evidence and, where appropriate, in co-operation with the competent international organizations.

To this end, for instance, the competent Soviet authorities shall determine annually the total allowable catch of every species of fish and other living resources and the portion of this catch to which access may be granted to foreign States, and shall take measures to ensure rational conduct of fishing, conservation and reproduction of living resources as well as their protection, including inspection, detention and arrest of ships.

The terms and conditions of the utilization and protection of fish and other living resources of the economic zone of the USSR shall be determined by the Council of Ministers of the USSR.

6. The harvesting of fish and other living resources, as well as research, exploration and other operations connected with such harvesting, hereinafter referred to as 'fishing', may be performed by foreign juridical or natural persons in the economic zone of the USSR only on the basis of international treaties or other agreements between the USSR and the foreign States concerned.

Foreign juridical or natural persons engaging in fishing in the economic zone of the USSR in accordance with the first paragraph of this article shall comply with the measures for the conservation of living resources and the other provisions and conditions established by this Decree, by other relevant legislative instruments of the USSR and by the rules adopted on the basis thereof.

7. In the economic zone of the USSR, the USSR shall have the exclusive right to construct and to authorize and regulate the construction, operation and use of any artificial islands and any kind of installations and structures for the purpose of conducting scientific research in its economic zone, as well as for the exploration and exploitation of its natural resources and for other economic purposes. This right shall also cover the construction, operation and use of installations and structures which may interfere with the exercise of the rights of the USSR in the economic zone.

The USSR shall have exclusive jurisdiction over such artificial islands, installations and structures, including jurisdiction with regard to customs, fiscal, health, safety and immigration laws and regulations.

Around such artificial islands, installations and structures, safety zones shall be established wherever necessary, which shall not exceed a distance of 500 metres around them, measured from each point of their outer edge, except as authorized by generally accepted international standards or as recommended by the competent international organization. The competent Soviet authorities shall determine in these zones the appropriate measures to ensure the safety both of navigation and of the artificial islands, installations and structures.

Soviet organizations, foreign States and their juridical or natural persons responsible for the maintenance and operation of the above mentioned artificial islands, installations and structures shall provide for the maintenance in good working order or permanent means for giving warning of their presence. Any installations, structures and equipment which are abandoned or disused shall be removed as soon as possible and to such an extent as to create no obstacle to navigation and fishing and no danger of polluting the marine environment.

The construction of artificial islands, the erection of installations and structures, the establishment of safety zones around them, as well as the complete or partial liquidation of these installations and structures, shall be announced in 'Notices to Mariners'.

8. Marine scientific research in the economic zone of the USSR shall be carried out in accordance with the legislation of the USSR and in accordance with the international treaties concluded by the USSR.

Marine scientific research in the economic zone of the USSR may be carried out by foreign States and competent international organizations only with the consent of the competent Soviet authorities. In normal circumstances, the competent Soviet authorities shall grant their consent for marine scientific research by foreign States in the economic zone of the USSR on condition that this research is carried out exclusively for peaceful purposes and in order to increase scientific knowledge of the marine environment for the benefit of all mankind.

Such consent may be withheld if the marine scientific research:

- *(a)* is of direct significance for the exploration and exploitation of the natural resources of the economic zone of the USSR, whether living or non-living;
- *(b)* involves drilling into the sea-bed of the economic zone, the use of explosives or the introduction of harmful substances into the marine environment;
- *(c)* involves the construction, operation or use of artificial islands, installations and structures.

Foreign States and competent international organizations which intend to undertake marine scientific research in the economic zone of the USSR shall, not less than six months in advance of the expected starting date of the research, provide the competent Soviet authorities with complete information about the planned research.

If the information provided in accordance with the fourth paragraph of this article is inaccurate, or if the foreign State and the competent international organization carrying out the research have outstanding obligations towards the USSR stemming from previous marine scientific research, the competent Soviet authorities may withhold consent for such research.

9. Foreign States and competent international organizations shall be obliged, while carrying out marine scientific research in the economic zone of the USSR:

- *(a)* to ensure the right of Soviet representatives to participate in the marine scientific research, especially on board research vessels and other craft or scientific research installations;
- *(b)* to provide the competent Soviet authorities, at their request, with preliminary reports, as soon as practicable, and with the final results and conclusions after the completion of the research;
- *(c)* to provide access for the competent Soviet authorities, at their request, to all data and samples derived from the marine scientific research and likewise to furnish them with data which may be copied and samples which may be divided without detriment to their scientific value;
- *(d)* if requested, to provide the competent Soviet authorities with an assessment of such data, samples and research results;
- *(e)* not to obstruct activity carried out in exercise of the sovereign rights and jurisdiction envisaged in articles 2 and 3 of this Decree;
- *(f)* to inform the competent Soviet authorities immediately of any major change in the research programme;
- *(g)* unless otherwise agreed, to remove as quickly as possible the scientific research installations or equipment once the research is completed.

10. Marine scientific research in the economic zone of the USSR which is not being conducted in accordance with the information communicated under article 8 of this Decree, or which violates the provisions of article 9 of this Decree, may be suspended by the competent Soviet authorities. Resumption of the research shall be permitted only after the elimination of the violations committed and the receipt of guarantees that such violations will not occur in future.

Marine scientific research in the economic zone of the USSR conducted without the consent of the competent Soviet authorities, or with a deviation from the information communicated under article 8 of this Decree which amounts to a major change in the original research project, shall be liable to immediate termination.

11. The terms and conditions for the carrying out of marine scientific research, for the construction of artificial islands, for the erection, maintenance, operation, protection and removal of installations, structures and safety zones around them, as well as for the issue of permits for the execution of all the aforementioned work in the economic zone of the USSR, shall be established by the Council of Ministers of the USSR.

12. The prevention, reduction and control of pollution of the marine environment arising out of or connected with activity in the economic zone of the USSR shall be effected in accordance with the legislation of the USSR, as well as with international treaties concluded by the USSR.

13. With regard to particular clearly defined areas of the economic zone of the USSR, where the establishment of special mandatory measures for the prevention of pollution from vessels is required for technical reasons in relation to their oceanographical and ecological conditions, as well as their utilization or the protection of their resources and the particular character of their traffic, such measures, including those relating to navigational practice, may be established by the Council of Ministers of the USSR in areas determined by it. The limits of such special areas shall be published in 'Notices to Mariners'.

14. The competent Soviet authorities may, in the manner determined by the legislation of the USSR, establish regulations for the prevention, reduction and control of pollution of the marine environment, and also for the safety of navigation, and enforce such regulations in ice-covered areas possessing special natural characteristics, where pollution of the marine environment could cause major harm to or irreversible disturbance of the ecological balance.

15. Where there are clear grounds for believing that a vessel navigating in the territorial waters (territorial sea) of the USSR or in the economic zone of the USSR has, in that zone, committed a violation of the legislation mentioned in articles 12 to 14 of this Decree or of applicable international rules for the prevention, reduction and control of pollution of the marine environment from vessels, the competent Soviet authorities may:

- *(a)* require the vessel to give the information necessary to establish whether a violation has occurred;
- *(b)* undertake an inspection of the vessel in connection with the violation, if it has resulted in a substantial discharge of polluting substances causing or threatening significant pollution of the marine environment and if, at the same time, the vessel has refused to give the necessary information or the information is at variance with the evident factual situation.

Where there is clear objective evidence that a vessel navigating in the territorial waters (territorial sea) of the USSR or in the economic zone of the USSR has, in that zone, committed a violation of the laws and regulations mentioned in the first paragraph of this article through a discharge of polluting substances causing major damage or threat of major damage to the coastline of the USSR, to interests relating to that coastline or to any resources of the territorial waters (territorial sea) of the USSR or of the economic zone of the USSR, proceedings may be instituted in respect of this violation, including detention of the vessel in accordance with the laws of the USSR.

When a foreign vessel enters a Soviet port, the competent Soviet authorities may institute proceedings in respect of any violation of the laws or regulations mentioned in the first paragraph of this article committed by the vessel in the economic zone of the USSR.

The procedure for the exercise by the competent Soviet authorities of the rights provided for in this article shall be determined by the Council of Ministers of the USSR.

16. Dumping within the limits of the economic zone of the USSR of wastes or other materials and objects shall be carried out only with the permission and under the control of the competent Soviet authorities. The terms and conditions for dumping and for the issue of such permits shall be determined by the Council of Ministers of the USSR.

17. If a collision of vessels, the stranding of a vessel or other maritime casualty occurring in the economic zone of the USSR or beyond its outer limits, or acts relating to such a casualty may result in major harmful consequences for the coastline of the USSR and related interests, including fishing, the competent Soviet authorities shall be entitled, pursuant to international law, to take the necessary measures proportionate to the actual or threatened damage, with the aim of preventing pollution or threat of pollution.

18. Where there is good reason to believe that a foreign ship has violated the provisions of this Decree or of other relevant legislative instruments of the USSR, and when it attempts to flee, the right to pursue the offender with a view to making an arrest and subsequently establishing liability shall be exercised in the manner established by the competent Soviet authorities. Such pursuit shall commence when the offending ship or one of its boats is within the limits of the economic zone of the USSR, after a signal to stop has been given, and shall cease as soon as the ship pursued enters the territorial waters (territorial sea) of its own country or of any third State.

19. Persons guilty of:

(a) illegal exploration or exploitation of the natural resources of the economic zone of the USSR;

(b) illegal removal, for the purpose of dumping within the limits of the economic zone of the USSR, from vessels and other floating devices, from aircraft or from artificial islands constructed in the sea, from installations and structures of substances harmful to human health or to the living resources of the sea, or of other wastes, materials and objects which may harm or obstruct lawful forms of utilization of the sea;

(c) pollution of the marine environment resulting from the illegal discharge in the economic zone of the USSR from vessels and other floating devices, from aircraft or from artificial islands constructed in the sea, from installations and structures of substances harmful to human health or to the living resources of the sea, of compounds containing such substances in amounts exceeding established norms, or of other wastes, materials and objects which may harm recreational zones or prevent other lawful forms of utilization of the sea;

(d) pollution of the marine environment directly resulting from drilling or other types of work for the exploration or exploitation in the economic zone of the USSR of the mineral resources of the sea-bed;

(e) other violations of regulations pertaining to the prevention, reduction and control of pollution of the marine environment in the economic zone of the USSR;

(f) the conduct in the economic zone of the USSR of marine scientific research without the consent of the competent Soviet authorities;

(g) the creation of artificial islands, the construction of installations and structures in the economic zone of the USSR, as well as the establishment of safety zones around them, without the required permission;

(*h*) failure to provide installations and other structures in the economic zone of the USSR with permanent means for giving warning of their presence, violation of regulations concerning the maintenance of those means in good working order and of regulations concerning the removal of installations and structures, the operation of which has finally ceased, as well as violations of other provisions of this Decree as connected with the performance of obligations stemming from international treaties concluded by the USSR,

shall be liable to measures of administrative punishment consisting of a fine of up to 10,000 roubles imposed at the place where the violation was discovered.

If the said violations have caused substantial damage or other major consequences, or if they have been repeated, those guilty shall be liable to a fine of up to 100,000 roubles, imposed by the regional (urban) people's court. In cases of violations provided for in subparagraphs 1, 6 and 7 of the first paragraph of this article, the court may order, as an additional administrative penalty, the confiscation of the vessel, installations, fishing implements, equipment, instruments and other objects which were used by the offender, as well as of everything illegally harvested.

In cases of arrest or detention of foreign vessels, the competent Soviet authorities shall promptly notify the flag State of the action taken and of any penalties subsequently imposed. Detained vessels and their crews shall be promptly released upon the posting of reasonable bond or other security.

20. Persons guilty of violations covered by article 19 of this Decree shall bear administrative liability, unless such violations by their nature entail criminal liability in accordance with the current legislation of the USSR.

21. The adoption of the administrative measures provided for in this Decree shall not absolve offenders from compensating for damage caused by them to living and other resources of the economic zone of the USSR, in accordance with the existing legislation of the USSR.

22. The procedure for the protection of the economic zone of the USSR shall be established by the Council of Ministers of the USSR.

23. This Decree shall enter into force on 1 March 1984.

24. The following are suspended:

Decree dated 10 December 1976 of the Presidium of the Supreme Soviet of the USSR 'On Provisional Measures to Conserve Living Resources and Regulate Fishing in the Sea Areas Adjacent to the Coast of the USSR' (Gazette of the Supreme Soviet of the USSR, 1976, No. 50, page 728; 1982, No. 15, page 238); Resolution dated 22 March 1977 of the Presidium of the Supreme Soviet of the USSR on the procedure for the implementation of article 7 of the Decree of the Presidium of the Supreme Soviet of the USSR 'On Provisional Measures to Conserve Living Resources and Regulate Fishing in the Sea Areas Adjacent to the Coast of the USSR' (Gazette of the Supreme Soviet of the USSR, 1977, No. 13, page 217).

25. The Council of Ministers of the USSR shall bring the decisions of the Government of the USSR into line with this Decree.

59. Spain

Law No. 15/1978.
Entered int force: February 20, 1978.
Source: *United Nations ST/LEG/SER.B/19,* pp. 250-252.

LAW 15/1978 OF 20 FEBRUARY ON THE ECONOMIC ZONE

In accordance with the law enacted by the *Cortes,* I hereby promulgate the following:

Article 1

1. In a belt of sea to be called the exclusive economic zone, which shall extend from the outer limit of the Spanish territorial sea for a distance of 200 nautical miles from the base lines used to measure the breadth of the territorial sea, the Spanish State shall have sovereign rights for the purposes of exploring and exploiting the natural resources of the sea-bed, subsoil thereof and its superjacent waters.

In the case of archipelagos, the outer limit of the economic zone shall be measured from straight base lines joining the outermost points of the islands and islets forming the archipelagos, so that the resulting perimeter conforms to the general configuration of each archipelago.

2. In accordance with the provisions of the preceding paragraph, the rights of the Spanish State shall include:

(a) The exclusive right to the natural resources of the Zone;
(b) The authority to enact regulations concerning the preservation of, exploration for and exploitation of such resources with a view to the protection of the marine environment;
(c) Exclusive jurisdiction to enforce all relevant measures;
(d) Such other rights as may be determined by the Government in accordance with international law.

Article 2

1. Except as provided in international treaties with States whose coasts are opposite or adjacent to Spanish coasts, the outer limit of the economic zone shall be the median or equidistant line.

2. For the purposes of this article, 'median or equidistant line' shall mean the line every point of which is equidistant from the nearest points on the base lines drawn in accordance with international law from which the breadth of the territorial sea of each State is measured.

In the case of archipelagos, the median or equidistant line shall be determined on the basis of the archipelagic perimeter drawn in accordance with article 1, paragraph 1.

Article 3

1. Fishing in the economic zone shall be reserved for Spanish nationals and, subject to agreements between the Governments concerned, to nationals of those countries whose fishing vessels have habitually fished in the zone.

2. Foreign fishermen not covered by the preceding paragraph may not fish in the economic zone, except as provided in international treaties to which Spain is a party.

Article 4

The provisions of Law No. 93/1962 of 24 December setting forth penalties for fishing violations committed by foreign vessels shall be applicable in the economic zone.

Article 5

1. The establishment of an economic zone shall not affect the freedom of navigation, the freedom of overflight and the freedom to lay submarine cables.

2. In the exercise of the freedom of navigation, foreign fishing vessels must comply with Spanish laws designed to prevent such vessels from fishing in the economic zone, including the laws concerning the carrying of fishing tackle.

FINAL PROVISIONS

1. The application of the provisions of this law shall be limited to the Atlantic coasts of Spain, both of the mainland and the islands, including the coasts on the Cantabrián Sea; the Government shall have the right to extend these provisions to other coasts of Spain.

2. Law No. 93/1962 of 24 December setting forth penalties for fishing violations committed by foreign vessels, Law No. 20/1967 of 8 April on the extension of the reserved fishing belt and any other laws which are contrary to the provisions of this Law shall be amended as may be necessary for the application of this Law.

3. The Government and the competent official bodies shall adopt the necessary measures for the application of this Law.

DONE in Madrid on 20 February 1978.

Juan Carlos

President of the *Cortes,*
Antonio Hernandez Gil

60. Sri Lanka

A. Maritime Zones Law No. 22 of 1976, and B. Presidential Proclamation.
Entered into force: January 15, 1977.
Source: *United Nations ST/LEG/SER.B/19,* pp. 120-126.

A. MARITIME ZONES LAW NO. 22 OF 1976[1]

2. (1) The President of the Republic of Sri Lanka may, by Proclamation published in the *Gazette,* declare the limits of the sea beyond the land territory and internal waters of Sri Lanka which shall be the territorial sea of Sri Lanka, specifying in such Proclamation the base lines from which such limits shall be measured. The waters on the landward side of such base-lines shall form part of the internal waters of Sri Lanka.

(2) Where an island or rock, or a group of islands and rocks, or a group of islands or a group of rocks, constituting part of the territory of Sri Lanka is situated seaward from the main coast or base-line, the territorial sea shall extend to the limits declared by the Proclamation under subsection (1) measured from the low-water mark of ordinary spring tides along the seaward edge of such island or rock, or group of islands and rocks, or group of islands or group of rocks.

(3) The sovereignty of the Republic extends to the territorial sea and to the air space over the territorial sea as well as to its bed and sub-soil.

3. (1) Ships of all States shall enjoy the right of innocent passage through the territorial sea. Passage is innocent only so long as such passage is not prejudicial to the peace, good order or security of the Republic:

Provided that no foreign warship shall enter or pass through the territorial sea except with the prior consent of, and subject to such conditions as may be specified by, the Minister.

(2) No foreign aircraft shall enter or pass through the air space above the territorial sea, except in accordance with the written laws in force in Sri Lanka:

Provided that no foreign military aircraft shall enter or pass through the air space above the territorial sea except with the prior consent of, and subject to such conditions as may be specified by, the Minister.

(3) A foreign ship or foreign aircraft which acts in contravention of the provisions of this section is liable to confiscation.

(4) The Minister may, by Order published in the *Gazette,* suspend, in a specified area or areas of the territorial sea the right of innocent passage of any ship, if, in his opinion, such suspension is necessary in order to safeguard the peace, good order or security of the Republic.

4. (1) The President may, by Proclamation published in the *Gazette,* declare the limits of a zone contiguous to the territorial sea and extending seawards from the outer limits of the territorial sea which shall be the contiguous zone of Sri Lanka.

[1] Of 1 September 1976. Text transmitted by the Permanent Representative of Sri Lanka to the United Nations in a note verbale dated 26 May 1977.

(2) Where there is a reasonable apprehension of the contravention of any written laws of Sri Lanka in relation to

(a) the security of the Republic;
(b) immigration, health and sanitation; or
(c) customs and other revenue matters,

the relevant Minister shall take such measures as may be necessary in respect of the contiguous zone in order to secure the enforcement of, or to prevent the contravention of, such laws.

5. (1) The President may, by Proclamation published in the *Gazette,* declare any zone of the sea adjacent to the territorial sea, as well as the sea-bed and sub-soil thereof, to be the exclusive economic zone of Sri Lanka. The limits of such zone shall be specified in the Proclamation.

(2) All the natural resources, both living and non-living, within the exclusive economic zone, on and under the sea-bed and in the sub-soil and on the water surface and within the water column shall vest in the Republic.

(3) In the exclusive economic zone the Republic has—

(a) sovereign rights for the purpose of exploration, exploitation, conservation and management of the natural resources, both living and non-living, as well as for the production of energy from tides, winds and currents, and for other economic uses;
(b) exclusive rights and jurisdiction to authorize, regulate and control scientific research;
(c) exclusive rights and jurisdiction for the construction, maintenance or operation of artificial islands, off-shore terminals, installations and other structures and devices necessary for the exploration and exploitation of the resources of the zone, for the convenience of shipping or for any other purpose; and
(d) other rights recognized by international law.

6. (1) The continental shelf of Sri Lanka shall comprise

(a) the sea-bed and sub-soil of the submarine areas that extend beyond the territorial sea of Sri Lanka throughout the natural prolongation of the land territory of Sri Lanka to the outer edge of the continental margin or to a distance of two hundred nautical miles from the base line from which the territorial sea is measured where the outer edge of the continental margin does not extend up to that distance; and
(b) the sea-bed and sub-soil of the analogous submarine areas adjacent to the coast of any island or rock, or group of islands and rocks, or group of islands or group of rocks, constituting part of the territory of Sri Lanka.

(2) All the natural resources, both living and non-living, on and under the sea-bed and in the sub-soil of the continental shelf shall vest in the Republic.

(3) In respect of the continental shelf the Republic has

(a) sovereign rights for the purpose of exploration, exploitation, conservation and management of the natural resources, both living and non-living;
(b) exclusive rights and jurisdiction to authorize, regulate and control scientific research;
(c) exclusive rights and jurisdiction for the construction, maintenance or operation of artificial islands, off-shore terminals, installations and other structures and devices necessary for the exploration and exploitation of the resources of the continental shelf, for the convenience of shipping or for any other purpose; and
(d) other rights recognized by international law.

7. (1) The President may, by Proclamation published in the *Gazette,* declare any zone of the sea adjacent to the territorial sea, and of the sea-bed and sub-soil thereof, to be the pollution prevention zone of Sri Lanka. The limits of such zone shall be specified in the Proclamation.

(2) The relevant Minister shall take such steps as may be necessary to control and prevent the pollution of, and to preserve the ecological balance within, such zone.

8. Notwithstanding the provisions of this Law or any other written law

(a) the boundary between Sri Lanka and India in the waters from Palk Strait to Adam's Bridge shall be the arcs of Great Circles between the following positions in the sequence given hereunder defined by latitude and longitude:

Position 1 : 10° 05′ North, 80° 03′ East
Position 2 : 09° 57′ North, 79° 35′ East
Position 3 : 09° 40.15′ North, 79° 22.60′ East
Position 4 : 09° 21.80′ North, 79° 30.70′ East
Position 5 : 09° 13′ North, 79° 32′ East
Position 6 : 09° 06′ North, 79° 32′ East;

(b) the boundary between Sri Lanka and India in the Gulf of Mannar shall be the arcs of Great Circles between the following positions in the sequence given hereunder defined by latitude and longitude:

Position 1m : 09° 06.0′ North, 79° 32.0′ East
Position 2m : 09° 00.0′ North, 79° 31.3′ East
Position 3m : 08° 53.8′ North, 79° 29.3′ East
Position 4m : 08° 40.0′ North, 79° 18.2′ East
Position 5m : 08° 37.2′ North, 79° 13.0′ East
Position 6m : 08° 31.2′ North, 79° 04.7′ East
Position 7m : 08° 22.2′ North, 78° 55.4′ East
Position 8m : 08° 12.2′ North, 78° 53.7′ East
Position 9m : 07° 35.3′ North, 78° 45.7′ East
Position 10m : 07° 21.0′ North, 78° 38.8′ East
Position 11m : 06° 30.8′ North, 78° 12.2′ East
Position 12m : 05° 53.9′ North, 77° 50.7′ East
Position 13m : 05° 00.0′ North, 77° 10.6′ East;

(c) the boundary between Sri Lanka and India in the Bay of Bengal shall be the arcs of Great Circles between the following positions in the sequence given hereunder defined by latitude and longitude:

Position 1b : 10° 05.0′ North, 80° 03.0′ East
Position 1ba : 10° 05.8′ North, 80° 05.0′ East
Position 1bb : 10° 08.4′ North, 80° 09.5′ East
Position 2b : 10° 33.0′ North, 80° 46.0′ East
Position 3b : 10° 41.7′ North, 81° 02.5′ East
Position 4b : 11° 02.7′ North, 81° 56.0′ East
Position 5b : 11° 16.0′ North, 82° 24.4′ East
Position 6b : 11° 26.6′ North, 83° 22.0′ East.

9. (1) The President may by Proclamation published in the *Gazette* declare the limits of the historic waters of Sri Lanka.

(2) The Republic of Sri Lanka shall exercise sovereignty, exclusive jurisdiction and control in and over the historic waters, as well as in and over the islands and the continental shelf and the sea-bed and sub-soil thereof within such historic waters.

10. As soon as may be convenient after the coming into operation of this Law, and thereafter whenever necessary, the Minister may require the Surveyor-General to publish or cause to be published a map indicating the low-water mark of ordinary spring tides; the base-lines for measurement of the territorial sea, and the outer limits of the territorial sea and other maritime zones and jurisdiction of Sri Lanka declared in accordance with the provisions of this Law.

11. Notwithstanding anything to the contrary in any other written law, every reference in any written law to the expressions 'territorial waters', 'territorial sea', 'coastal waters', 'contiguous zone', 'exclusive economic zone', 'continental shelf' or 'pollution prevention zone' shall be read and construed subject to and in accordance with the provisions of this Law.

12. In order to give effect to the principles and provisions of this Law, all written laws in force in Sri Lanka shall be read and construed as though the applicability of such laws, wherever relevant, extends to the limits of the contiguous zone, the exclusive economic zone, the continental shelf, or the pollution prevention zone, as the case may be.

13. (1) The Minister may make regulations for the purpose of giving effect to the provisions of this Law.

(2) Every regulation made by the Minister shall be published in the *Gazette* and shall come into operation on the date of such publication or upon such later date as may be specified in the regulation.

(3) Every regulation made by the Minister shall, as soon as convenient after its publication in the *Gazette,* be brought before the National State Assembly for approval. Every regulation which is not so approved shall be deemed to be rescinded as from the date of such disapproval, but without prejudice to anything previously done thereunder.

14. In any proceedings before any court in Sri Lanka, if a question arises as to whether any act or omission has been done or omitted to be done within or without the territorial sea of Sri Lanka, or in any other zone or jurisdiction declared under this Law, a certificate of the Minister signed by him shall be *prima facie* proof of the place where such act or omission was done or omitted to be done.

15. In this Law, unless the context otherwise requires–

'foreign aircraft' shall have the same meaning as in the Navigation Act'

'militairy aircraft' means an aircraft which, by reason of the equipment contained therein, could be used for any warlike purpose;

'ship' means any description of ship or vessel or boat, or any other description of vessel used in navigation on or below the waters and not exclusively propelled by oars, paddles or poles, and includes all equipment, apparel and appurtenances (excluding supplies for maintenance) which are necessary for navigation and conduct of the business of the ship; and

'warship' means a ship which, by reason of the equipment contained therein, could be used for any warlike purpose.

B. PROCLAMATION BY THE PRESIDENT OF THE REPUBLIC OF SRI LANKA OF 15 JANUARY 1977[1] IN PURSUANCE OF MARITIME ZONES LAW NO. 22 OF 1976

Whereas the National State Assembly has enacted the Maritime Zones Law, No. 22 of 1976, which provides for the declaration of the territorial sea and other maritime zones of Sri Lanka and all other matters connected therewith or incidental thereto:

And whereas it has become necessary to declare in accordance with the provisions of the said Maritime Zones Law the extents, respectively, of the territorial sea, the contiguous zone, the exclusive economic zone, the pollution prevention zone and the historic waters:

Now therefore, I, William Gopallawa, President of the Republic of Sri Lanka, do by this Proclamation declare, in pursuance of the powers vested in me by sections 2, 4, 5, 7 and 9 respectively of the Maritime Zones Law, No. 22 of 1976[1]–

(1) that the territorial sea of Sri Lanka shall, notwithstanding anything in any prior proclamation declaring the territorial sea of Sri Lanka, and except as provided in paragraph 7 (iii) hereof, extend to the sea to a distance of 12 nautical miles measured from the baselines described in paragraph (2);

(2) that the breadth of the territorial sea shall be measured from the low water mark of ordinary spring tides along the coast of the mainland and along the seaward edge of islands:

Provided that for the purpose of determining the baselines for delimiting the territorial sea:

(i) a low tide elevation which lies wholly or partly within the breadth of sea which would be territorial sea if all low tide elevations were disregarded for the purpose of the measurement of the breadth thereof shall be treated as islands,

(ii) permanent installations further out to sea which form an integral part of a port system shall be considered as part of the coast of the mainland,

(iii) the method of straight baselines may be employed in drawing the baselines where there are deep bays and inlets in the coast or where there is a fringe of islands immediately adjacent to the coast, provided that such baselines shall not depart appreciably from the general direction of the coast and the areas of the sea lying landward from these lines shall be sufficiently closely linked to the land domain to be subject to the régime of internal waters;

Provided further that baseline from which the breadth of the territorial sea shall be measured in the sea north of Point Pedro shall be the arc of Great Circle between the following positions defined by latitude and longitude in the Palk Strait–

(i) 09° 49′ 8″ North, 80° 15′ 2″ East,

(ii) 10° 05′ 0″ North, 80° 03′ 0″ East;

(3) that the contiguous zone of Sri Lanka shall extend 24 nautical miles seaward from the baselines from which the territorial sea is measured;

(4) that the exclusive economic zone of Sri Lanka shall extend to the sea to a distance of 200 nautical miles from the baselines from which the territorial sea is measured;

(5) that the pollution prevention zone shall extend to the sea to a distance of 200 nautical miles from the baselines from which the territorial sea is measured;

(6) that notwithstanding anything in paragraphs (4) and (5), the exclusive economic zone and the pollution prevention zone of Sri Lanka in the Gulf of Mannar and the Bay of Bengal shall extend to the sea up to the maritime boundary between Sri Lanka and India as defined in section 8 of the Maritime Zones Law No. 22 of 1976[1];

[1] The Gazette Extraordinary of the Republic of Sri Lanka No. 248/1 of 15 January 1977. Text provided by the Permanent Representative of Sri Lanka to the United Nations in a note verbale of 26 March 1977.

(7) (i) that the historic waters of Sri Lanka shall comprise the areas of sea in the Palk Strait, Palk Bay and the Gulf of Mannar bounded by:

(a) the coast of the mainland of Sri Lanka;

(b) the maritime boundary between Sri Lanka and India as defined in Section 8 of the Maritime Zones Law, No. 22 of 1976;

(c) the arc of Great Circle between the following positions defined by latitude and longitude in the Gulf of Mannar:

(i) 08° 15′ 0″ North, 79° 44′ 0″ East,

(ii) 08° 22′ 2″ North, 78° 55′ 4″ East; and

(d) the arc of Great Circle between the following positions defined by latitude and longitude in the Palk Strait:

(i) 09° 49′ 8″ North, 80° 15′ 2″ East,

(ii) 10° 05′ 0″ North, 80° 03′ 0″ East;

(ii) the historic waters in the Palk Bay and Palk Strait shall form part of the internal waters of Sri Lanka;

(iii) the historic waters in the Gulf of Mannar shall form part of the territorial sea of Sri Lanka.

61. Suriname

Law Concerning the Extension of the Territorial Sea and the Establishment of a Contiguous Economic Zone, 1978, Law No. 26.
Entered into force: June 11, 1978.
Source: *United Nations ST/LEG/SER.B/19,* pp. 127-130.

Article 1

1. The sovereignty of the Republic of Suriname extends beyond the land territory and the internal waters to:

(a) A belt of sea adjacent to its coast and described as the territorial sea;
(b) The air space above the territorial sea and
(c) The sea-bed and the subsoil of the territorial sea.

The Republic of Suriname exercises this sovereignty with due observance of the rules of international law.

Article 2

The outer limit of the territorial sea is determined by a line, each point of which is situated at a distance of 12 nautical miles from the nearest point on the line of the low-water mark along the shore, the so-called baseline.

Article 3

The belt of sea adjacent to and extending from the outer limit of the territorial sea of the Republic of Suriname to a distance of 200 nautical miles, measured from the line of the low-water mark as defined in article 2 of this law, is considered the economic zone.

Article 4

1. In the economic zone the Republic of Suriname has sovereign rights concerning the exploration, exploitation, conservation and management of natural resources, living as well as non-living, on the sea-bed and in the subsoil and the superjacent waters.

2. Without prejudice to the above it can be decreed that the provisions of this law and the instructions based thereon shall also apply to:

(a) To erect and use artificial islands, installations and similar structures;
(b) To protect the sea environment; this includes taking measures against pollution;
(c) To conduct scientific research and experiments;
(d) To extract energy from water currents and winds;
(e) To engage in other activities aimed at the economic exploration and exploitation of this zone.

Article 5

In the economic zone described above, all nations, with due observance of the international law, enjoy:

(a) Freedom of navigation;
(b) Freedom of overflight;
(c) Freedom to lay submarine cables and pipelines;
(d) Freedom to exercise internationally recognized rights in connection with navigation and communication.

Article 6

1. No one is allowed, without a license previously issued by government decree, to engage in activities in the economic zone which constitute an infringement of the rights stated in Article 4.

2. General conditions which a license holder will have to meet may be laid down by Government decree. Moreover, when a license is granted, special conditions may be made in it or obligations attached to it.

3. A license may be revoked at all times on account of activities which violate one or more conditions or obligations under which it was granted and, furthermore, at the exclusive discretion of the appropriate authority, on the ground of reasons which derive from the public interest or if the national interest may so require. A similar decision will mention the grounds on which it is based. In special cases this may be omitted.

Article 7

1. Intentional violation of the provisions stated in or resulting from this law will be punishable with a prison term of maximum six years and a fine of maximum five hundred thousand guilders.

2. In the case of a prison sentence, the judge may impose a fine as well.

Article 8

1. Non-intentional violation of the provisions stated in or resulting from this law will be punishable with a jail term of maximum one year or a fine of maximum one hundred thousand guilders.

2. In the case of a jail sentence the judge may impose a fine as well.

Article 9

A person who does not fulfill one or more conditions attached to the license, as stated in Article 6, or who does not do so on time or in full, or a person who acts in violation of such conditions, will be punished with a fine of maximum one hundred thousand guilders.

Article 10

The acts made punishable in Article 7 will be considered as criminal offences and those made punishable in Articles 8 and 9 as misdemeanors.

Article 11

The objects used to commit offenses as described in Articles 7, 8 and 9, as well as goods obtained from the offense, may be confiscated.

Article 12

1. If the offender is unknown or has died before the start of the prosecution, the confiscation may be decided upon by judicial decree, at the request of the public prosecutor.

2. The decree will be made public by the Registrar in the *Advertentieblad* of the Republic of Suriname and/or in one or more newspapers to be chosen by the judge.

3. The decree will take effect, except if a party concerned files a petition with the Registrar within two months after publication and if it appears in the course of further investigation that no offence was committed regarding the matter in question.

4. During fourteen days the Attorney General has the right to appeal decrees issued in accordance with paragraph 1, to the Court. The same applies to decrees issued on account of paragraph 3, resulting from a petition.

Article 13

If one of the acts made punishable in Articles 7, 8 and 9 is committed by or through a group or corporation, criminal prosecution will be instituted and the sentence pronounced against the one who ordered the perpetration of the act or who was the actual leader of the unlawful activity or neglect.

Article 14

1. The public prosecutor has the authority, in the case of acts made punishable by Articles 7, 8 and 9, to lay down conditions the voluntary fulfilment of which will cancel the right to prosecution.

2. The legal provisions which apply in this matter to misdemeanors, will be applicable in a similar fashion to criminal offenses as described in Article 7.

Article 15

1. With the investigation of acts made punishable by this law are charged, besides persons assigned by Article 8 of the Penal Code, persons belonging to the armed forces of Suriname and/or other persons, especially assigned by the Minister of Justice and Police.

2. The investigators are at all times authorized to confiscate, or claim for confiscation, all objects which may lead to the discovery of the truth or of which the confiscation or destruction, total or partial, may be ordered.

Article 16

1. If the goods confiscated on the ground of Article 15 contain perishables, the Attorney General may grant permission for the sale of these goods or merchandise.

2. The sale will be conducted in public by the investigators, and according to local custom.

3. Proceeds from the sale of goods or merchandise mentioned above may be confiscated.

62. Thailand

Royal Proclamation.
Entered into force: February 23, 1981.
Source: Unknown.

By Royal Command of His Majesty the King, it is hereby proclaimed that:

For the purpose of exercising the sovereign rights of the Kingdom of Thailand with regard to the exploitation and conservation of the natural resources, whether living or non-living, of the sea,

It is deemed appropriate to establish the exclusive economic zone of the Kingdom of Thailand as follows:—

1. The exclusive economic zone of the Kingdom of Thailand is an area beyond and adjacent to the territorial sea whose breadth extends to two hundred nautical miles measured from the baselines used for measuring the breadth of the territorial sea.

2. In the exclusive economic zone, the Kingdom of Thailand has:

(a) sovereign rights for the purpose of exploring and exploiting, conserving and managing the natural resources, whether living or non-living, of the sea-bed and subsoil and the superjacent waters, and with regard to other activities for the economic exploration and exploitation of the zone, such as the production of energy from the water, currents and winds;

(b) jurisdiction with regard to:

(i) the establishment and use of artificial islands, installations and structures;

(ii) marine scientific research;

(iii) the preservation of the marine environment.

(c) other rights as may exist under international law.

3. In the exclusive economic zone, the freedoms of navigation and overflight and of the laying of submarine cables and pipelines shall be governed by international law.

4. In any case where the exclusive economic zone of the Kingdom of Thailand is adjacent or opposite to the exclusive economic zone of another coastal State, the Government of the Kingdom of Thailand is prepared to enter into negotiations with the coastal State concerned with a view to delimiting their respective exclusive economic zones.

Proclaimed on the 23rd day of February, B.E. 2524, being the thirty sixth year of the present Reign.

Countersigned by;

General Prem Tinsulanonda,
Prime Minister.

63. Togo

Ordinance No. 24.
Entered into force: August 16, 1977.
Source: Office of the President, Togo.

ORDINANCE NO. 24

Concerning the delimitation of territorial waters and creation of a protected maritime economic zone

The President of the Republic

Considering Ordinance No. 1 dated 14 January 1967;

Considering Ordinance No. 15 dated 14 April 1967;

The Council of Ministers orders:

Article 1

Territorial waters are fixed at a distance of 30 nautical miles counting from the lowest water mark at low tide.

Article 2

A protected economic maritime zone is created of 200 nautical miles from the baseline which establishes the territorial sea.

Article 3

In this zone the state reserves to itself the exploration and exploitation of biological and non-biological natural resources. The extent of its jurisdiction includes the entirety of economic resources situated on the surface of the water, in the ocean and in the sub-soil.

Article 4

In the spirit of intra-African solidarity, the Togolese State engages itself to allow neighboring states in the hinterland to participate in the exploration of biological resources in the context of bilateral and regional agreements.

Article 5

The present Ordinance will be published in the Official Journal of the republic of Togo.

Lome, 16 August 1977

Signed: General of the army
G. Eyadema

64. Tonga

Territorial Sea and the Exclusive Economic Zone Act, Act No. 30, 1978.
Entered into force: June 25, 1979.
Source: Unknown.

I assent,

TAUEA'AHAU TUPOU IV

25th June, 1979

An Act to make provision with respect to the territorial sea of Tonga; and to establish an exclusive economic zone of Tonga adjacent to the territorial sea, and in the exercise of the sovereign rights of Tonga to make provision for the exploration and exploitation, and conservation and management, of the resources of the zone and for matters connected with those purposes.

[23rd October, 1978]

BE IT ENACTED by the King and the Legislative Assembly of Tonga in the Legislature of the Kingdom as follows:

Short Title and commencement

1. (1) This Act may be cited as The Territorial Sea and Exclusive Economic Zone Act, 1978.

(2) This Act shall come into force on a date to be appointed by the King in Privy Council.

Interpretation

2. (1) In this Act, unless the context otherwise requires,—

'Bay' means an indentation of the coast such that its area is not less than that of the semi-circle whose diameter is a line drawn across the mouth of the indentation (for the purposes of which definition—

(a) The area of an indentation shall be taken to be the area bounded by low-water mark around the shore of the identation and the straight line joining the low-water marks of its natural entrance points; and

(b) Where, because of the presence of islands, an indentation has more than one mouth, the length of the diameter of the semicircle referred to shall be the sum of the lengths of the straight lines drawn across each of the mouths; and

(c) In calculating the area of an indentation, the area of any islands lying within it shall be treated as part of the area of the indentation):

'Exclusive economic zone' and 'zone' mean the exclusive economic zone of Tonga described in Section 9 of this Act;

'Fish' means every description of fish and shellfish and their young or fry or spawn, and includes sedentary species of fish, mammals, and all other forms of marine life;

'Fishery' means one or more stocks of fish that can be treated as a unit for the purposes of conservation and management;

'Fishing' means—

(*a*) Taking any fish; or
(*b*) Engaging in any activity relating to the taking of any fish, including (inter alia) any activity involving the preparation, supply, storage, refrigeration, transportation, or processing of any fish; or
(*c*) Engaging in any activity relating to the provision of any services to any fishing craft to enable or assist that craft to engage in fishing:

'Fishing craft' means any vessel, aircraft, hovercraft, submersible craft, or other craft, or whatever size, that is capable of being used for fishing;
'Foreign fishing craft' means any fishing craft that is not a Tongan fishing craft;
'Highly migratory species' means species that, in the course of their life cycle, migrate over great distances of ocean;
'International agreement' means any bilateral or multilateral treaty, convention, or agreement, to which Tonga is a party, and any understanding concluded by the Government of Tonga and the government of any other country;
'Island' means a naturally formed area of land that is surrounded by and above water at mean high-water spring tides;
'Licence' means a licence issued under Section 15 of this Act in respect of a foreign fishing craft; and 'licensed' has a corresponding meaning;
'Licensee' means the person to whom a licence is issued;
'Low-tide elevation' means a naturally formed area of land that is surrounded by and above water at mean low-water spring tides but is submerged at mean high-water spring tides;
'Master', in relation to a fishing craft, means the person for the time being having command or charge of the craft;
'Median line' as between Tonga and any other country, means a line every point of which is equidistant from the nearest points of the baseline of the territorial sea of Tonga and the corresponding baseline of that other country;
'Minister' means the Minister responsible for Fisheries;
'Nautical mile' means the international nautical mile of 1852 metres;
'Tongan fishing craft' means a fishing craft—

(*a*) That is registered in Tonga under the Shipping Act 1972; or
(*b*) That is an aircraft registered in Tonga under the Civil Aviation Act 1973; or
(*c*) In which no person who is not a Tongan citizen has any legal or equitable interest (except by way of security only for any advance made by him to the owner);

'Tonga Government ship' means a ship that is owned by Government;
'Owner' in relation to a fishing craft, includes any body of persons, whether incorporated or not, by whom the craft is owned, and any charterer, sub-charterer, lessee, or sub-lessee of the craft;
'Prescribed' means prescribed by regulations made under this Act;
'Shellfish' includes every description of molluscs, crustaceans, and echinoderms and their young or spawn;
'Take' includes—

(*a*) To take, catch, kill, attract, or pursue by any means or device; and
(*b*) To attempt to do any act specified in paragraph (a) of this definition;

'Total allowable catch', with respect to the yield from any fishery means the amount of fish that will produce from that fishery the maximum sustainable yield, as qualified by any relevant economic or environmental factors, fishing patterns, the inter-dependence of stocks of fish, and any generally recommended subregional, regional or global standards.
(2) For the purposes of this Act, permanent harbour works that form an integral part of a harbour system

shall be treated as forming part of the coast.

Part I

The territorial sea of Tonga

3. The territorial sea of Tonga comprises those areas of the sea having, as their inner limits, the baseline described in Sections 5 and 6 of this Act and, as their outer limits, a line measured seaward from that baseline, every point of which line is distant 12 nautical miles from the nearest point of the baseline.

Internal waters

4. The internal waters of Tonga include any areas of the sea that are on the landward side of the baseline of the territorial sea of Tonga.

Baselines of territorial sea

5. (1) Except as otherwise provided in Section 6 of this Act, the baseline from which the breadth of the territorial sea of Tonga is measured shall be—

(a) In the case of islands situated on atolls or of islands having fringing reefs, the low water mark along the seaward edge of the reef;

(b) In the case of islands not situated on atolls or of islands not having fringing reefs, the low water mark along the coast of those islands.

(2) For the purposes of this section, a low-tide elevation that lies wholly or partly within the breadth of sea that would be territorial sea if all low-tide elevations were disregarded for the purpose of the measurement of the breadth of the territorial sea shall be treated as an island.

Baseline of territorial sea adjacent to bay

6. In the case of the sea adjacent to a bay, the baseline from which the breadth of the territorial sea is measured—

(a) Where the bay has only one mouth and the distance between the low-water marks of the natural entrance points of the bay does not exceed 24 nautical miles, shall be a straight line joining those low-water marks; and

(b) Where, because of the presence of islands, the bay has more than one mouth and the distances between the low-water marks of the natural entrance points of each mouth added together do not exceed 24 nautical miles, shall be a series of straight lines across each of the mouths so as to join those low-water marks; and

(c) Where neither paragraph (a) nor paragraph (b) of this section applies, shall be a straight line 24 nautical miles in length drawn from low-water mark to low-water mark within the bay in such a manner as to enclose the maximum area of water that is possible with a line of that length.

Bed of territorial sea and internal waters vested in Crown

7. Subject to the grant of any estate or interest therein (whether by or pursuant to the provisions of any enactment or otherwise, and whether made before or after the commencement of this Act) the seabed and subsoil of submarine areas bounded on the landward side by the low-water mark along the coast of all islands of Tonga and on the seaward side by the outer limits of the territorial sea of Tonga shall be deemed to be and always to have been vested in the Crown.

Regulations for Territorial Sea

8. The King in Council may from time to time, by Order in Council, make regulations for all or any of the following purposes:

(a) Regulating the conduct of scientific research within the territorial sea;

(b) Prescribing measures for the protection and preservation of the marine environment of the territorial sea;

(*c*) Regulating the construction, operation, and use of artificial islands (whether permanent or temporary), and other installations and structures in the territorial sea, including the establishment of safety zones around such islands, installations, and structures;

(*d*) Regulating the exploration and exploitation of the territorial sea for the production of energy from the water, currents, and winds, and for any other economic purposes;

(*e*) Providing for such other matters as are necessary or expedient for giving full effect to the sovereignty of Tonga in relation to the territorial sea;

(*f*) Providing that a breach of any such regulations shall be a criminal offence, and imposing penalties by way of fine not exceeding $ 10,000 for any such offences;

(*g*) Providing for such other matters as are contemplated by or necessary for giving full effect to the provisions of this Part of this Act and for its due administration.

Part II

The exclusive economic zone of Tonga

The exclusive economic zone

9. (1) The exclusive economic zone of Tonga comprises those areas of the sea, seabed, and subsoil that are beyond and adjacent to the territorial sea of Tonga, having as their outer limits a line measured seaward from the baseline described in Sections 5 and 6 of this Act, every point of which line is distant 200 nautical miles from the nearest point of the baseline.

(2) Notwithstanding subsection (1) of this section, where—

(*a*) Any part of the median line between Tonga and any other country is less than 200 nautical miles from the nearest part of the baseline of the territorial sea of Tonga; and

(*b*) No other outer limit of the exclusive economic zone is for the time being determined by agreement with a neighbouring country or by an Order-in-Council made under subsection (3) of this section that part of the median line shall be an outer limit of the zone.

(3) For the purposes of implementing any international agreement, or the arbitral award of any international body, or the judgment of any international Court, or for any other purpose in accordance with international law, the King may from time to time, by Order-in-Council, declare that the exclusive economic zone shall not extend to any specified area of the sea, seabed, or subsoil, that would otherwise be included within the exclusive economic zone by virtue of this section.

Calculation of total allowable catch

10. The Minister shall from time to time determine, in respect of every fishery within the exclusive economic zone, the total allowable catch.

Calculation of allowable catch by foreign fishing craft

11. (1) The Minister shall from time to time determine, in respect of the total allowable catch for every fishery within the exclusive economic zone, the portion that Tongan fishing craft have the capacity to harvest.

(2) Where the Minister has determined, in respect of the total allowable catch for a fishery within the exclusive economic zone, the portion that Tongan fishing craft have the capacity to harvest, the remaining portion shall constitute the allowable catch for that fishery for foreign fishing craft.

Apportionment of allowable catch for foreign fishing craft

12. (1) The Minister may from time to time apportion, among countries other than Tonga, the allowable catch for foreign fishing craft in respect of any fishery within the exclusive economic zone, as determined under Section 11 of this Act.

(2) In making an apportionment under subsection (1) of this section, the Minister may take into account

(inter alia) the following consideration:

(a) Whether the fishing craft of countries to which the apportionment applies have engaged habitually in fishing within the exclusive economic zone;

(b) Whether such countries have co-operated with Tonga in fisheries research and in the identification of fish stocks within the zone;

(c) Whether such countries have co-operated with Tonga in the conservation and management of fisheries resources within the zone, and in the enforcement of Tongan law relating to such resources;

(d) The terms of any relevant international agreement;

(e) Such other matters as the Minister, after consultation with the Minister of Foreign Affairs, determines to be relevant.

Prohibition of operation of unauthorised foreign fishing craft in zone

13. No foreign fishing craft shall be used for fishing within the exclusive economic zone except in accordance with a licence issued by the Minister under Section 14 of this Act in respect of that fishing craft.

Grant of licences

14. (1) Subject to subsection (2) of this section, the Minister may grant and issue to the owner of any named foreign fishing craft a licence to fish within the exclusive economic zone.

(2) The Minister shall exercise the powers conferred on him by this section in such a manner as to ensure that—

(a) The catch that all foreign fishing craft licensed under this section are for the time being authorised to harvest from any fishery within the exclusive economic zone does not exceed the allowable catch for foreign fishing craft for that fishery as determined under Section 11 of this Act; and

(b) The catch that all foreign fishing craft of a particular country licensed under this section are for the time being authorised to harvest from any fishery within the zone does not exceed the apportionment made under Section 12 of this Act for that fishery in respect of that country.

(3) In granting a licence under this section, the Minister may attach to the licence conditions relating (inter alia) to all or any of the following matters:

(a) The areas within the exclusive economic zone in which fishing is authorised; and

(b) The seasons, times, and particular voyages during which fishing is authorised;

(c) The species, size, age, and quantities of fish that may be taken;

(d) The methods by which fish may be taken;

(e) The types, size, and amount of fishing gear that may be used or carried by a foreign fishing craft, and the modes of storage of that gear when not in use;

(f) The use, transfer, transhipment, landing, and processing of fish taken;

(g) Entry by the foreign fishing craft to Tongan ports, whether for the inspection of its catch, or for other purposes;

(h) The compensation payable to Tongan citizens or to the Crown in the event of any loss or damage caused by the foreign fishing craft to other fishing craft, or their gear or catch or to fish stocks, or to pipelines or cables, or to other Tongan interests;

(i) Statistical and other information required to be given by the foreign fishing craft to the Ministry of Agriculture Forest and Fisheries, including statistics relating to catch and effort and reports as to the positions of the craft;

(j) The conduct by the foreign fishing craft of specified programmes of fisheries research;

(k) The training of Tongan personnel in the methods of fishing employed by the foreign fishing craft and the transfer to Tonga of technology relating to fisheries;

(l) The display on board the foreign fishing craft of the licence issued in respect of it;
(m) The marking of the foreign fishing craft, and other means for its identification;
(n) Directions, instructions, and other requirements given or made by vessels or aircraft of Tonga. Government ships or aircraft or by any officer authorised under Section 23 of this Act to the foreign fishing craft that shall be complied with by the craft;
(o) The placing of Tongan observers on the foreign fishing craft and the reimbursement to the Ministry of Agriculture Forest and Fisheries by the licensee of the costs of doing so;
(p) The installation on the foreign fishing craft and maintenance in working order of a transponder or other equipment for the identification and location of the craft, and of adequate navigational equipment to enable its position to be fixed from the craft;
(q) The carriage on board the foreign fishing craft of specified nautical charts, nautical publications, and nautical instruments;
(r) Such other matters as the Minister considers necessary or expedient for the conservation or management of fisheries resources within the zone.

Renewal of licences

15. Subject to Section 14 (2) of this Act, the Minister may from time to time renew any licence granted under Section 14 of this Act.

Variation of licences

16. (1) Subject to Section 14 (2) of this Act, the Minister may from time to time, where he is satisfied that it is necessary or expedient for the proper regulation of fishing within the exclusive economic zone to do so, vary the terms and conditions of any licence or licences, or class or classes of licence, granted under Section 14 of this Act.

(2) Notice of every variation of any licence under this sections shall be given as soon as practicable to the licensee.

Licensing fees

17. There shall be payable by every licensee to the Crown in respect of the granting of a licence under Section 14 of this Act, or the renewal of licence under Section 15 of this Act, such fee as may from time to time be prescribed.

Licensing Offences

18. (1) Where any foreign fishing craft that is not licenced under Section 14 of this Act is used for fishing in the exclusive economic zone, each of them the owner, the master, and every crew member of the craft commits an offence against this Act.

(2) Where any foreign fishing craft that is not licensed under Section 14 of this Act displays within the exclusive economic zone any marking or other means of identification that indicates that it is licensed under that section, each of them, the owner, the master, and every member of the craft commits an offence against this Act.

(3) Where any foreign fishing craft is used for fishing within the exclusive economic zone in contravention of any condition of a licence issued in respect of it under Section 14 of this Act, each of them the licensee, the master, and every crew member of the craft commits an offence against this Act.

(4) Every owner or master of a foreign fishing craft who commits an offence specified in subsection (1) or subsection (2) of this section is liable on conviction to a fine not exceeding $ 100,000.

(5) Every crew member of a foreign fishing craft who commits an offence specified in subsection (1) or subsection (2) of this section is liable on conviction to a fine not exceeding $ 5,000.

(6) Every licensee or master of a foreign fishing craft who commits an offence specified in subsection (3) of this section is liable on conviction to a fine not exceeding $ 25,000.

(7) Every crew member of a foreign fishing craft who commits an offence specified in subsection (3) of this section is liable on conviction to a fine not exceeding $1,500.

(8) In this section, 'crew member' does not include a licensee, owner, or master of a foreign fishing craft, or any Tongan personnel or observer on the craft pursuant to a condition attached to a licence under Section 14 (3) of this Act.

Suspenson and cancellation of licences

19. (1) Where the Minister is satisfied that—

(a) Any foreign fishing craft in respect of which a licence has been granted under Section 14 of this Act is being or has been used for fishing within the exclusive economic zone in contravention of any condition of the licence or of any law of Tonga that applies to fishing within the zone; or

(b) Any licensee, master, or crew member of a foreign fishing craft has been convicted of an offence against this Act, or against any regulations made under Section 21 of this Act, or against any other law of Tonga relating to fishing within the zone; or

(c) Any licensee, master, or crew member of a foreign fishing craft has failed to pay to the Crown, within the time limit specified in Section 25 (8) of this Act, the amount of any penalty imposed on him under that section by the Minister – he may suspend the licence of the craft for such period as he shall specify, or cancel the licence.

(2) Where the Minister, after consultation with the Minister of Foreign Affairs, determines that it is necessary or expedient for the proper regulation of fishing within the exclusive economic zone to do so, he may suspend any licence or licences or class or classes of licence for such period as he shall specify, or cancel any licence or licences or class or classes of licence.

(3) While a licence is suspended under this section, it shall have no effect.

Review by Courts

20. No exercise by the Minister of any power conferred on him by Section 16 or Section 19 (2) of this Act shall be liable to be challenged, reviewed, quashed, or called in question in any Court on the ground that the conditions for the exercise of the power by him had not arisen or had ceased.

Fisheries regulations

21. (1) The King may from time to time, by Order-in-Council, make regulations for all or any of the following purposes:

(a) Prescribing the manner of applying for licences under Section 14 of this Act, and for the renewal of such licences under Section 15 of this Act, and forms of applications;

(b) Prescribing the terms of duration of licences;

(c) Prescribing the forms of licences to be issued by the Minister;

(d) Prescribing the fees payable to the Crown for the issue of licences and for their renewal;

(e) Providing for the production of licences by licensees to specified Tongan authorities when required to do so, and the inspection of licences by such authorities;

(f) Requiring applicants for licences, and licensees, to designate authorised agents in Tonga in respect of foreign fishing craft;

(g) Providing for such other measures as are necessary or expedient to ensure that foreign fishing craft are used for fishing within the exclusive economic zone only in accordance with the terms and conditions of their licences;

(h) Prescribing conditions, not inconsistent with this Act, under which fishing may be undertaken within the zone by foreign fishing craft;

(i) Prescribing measures, not inconsistent with this Act, for the conservation and management of fisheries resources within the zone;

(j) Specifying particular types of highly migratory species of fish, and regulating, in a manner not inconsistent with this Act, fishing for those species within the zone, and also, in the case of Tongan fishing craft, beyond the zone;

(k) Providing that a breach of any such regulation shall be a criminal offence, and imposing penalties by way of fine not exceeding, in the case of a licensee, owner, or master of a fishing craft, $ 10,000 for any such offences and, in the case of any other crew member, $ 1,000 for any such offences;

(l) Prescribing the form of bonds for the purposes of Section 24 of this Act;

(m) Prescribing forms of notices and procedures to be followed for the purposes of Section 25 of this Act;

(n) Providing, in respect of notice, summonses, and other documents to be served under this Act or in any civil or criminal proceedings under this Act, that specified methods of service (including service on the authorised agent of a foreign fishing craft or on the diplomatic or consular representative in respect of Tonga of the country in which the craft is registered) shall be deemed to be service on any licensee, owner, master, or crew member of the craft, and providing that specified methods of proof of service shall be deemed to be sufficient proof of service.

(2) Regulations made under this section may make different provisions for different parts of the exclusive economic zone and for different species of fish.

(3) In prescribing fees in regulations made under this section, the King in Council may—

(a) Take into account (inter alia) the cost of implementing the provisions of this Act, including the cost of the conservation and management of fisheries resources, and of fisheries research, and of the administration and enforcement of such enactments; and

(b) Prescribe different fees for different classes of foreign fishing craft (whether by reference to size, catch, method of fishing, function, or otherwise).

Fishing for research, experimental, and sporting purpose

22. Notwithstanding Section 13 or Section 18 of this Act, a foreign fishing craft may be used for fishing within the exclusive economic zone for the purpose of fisheries research or of experimentation or sport, subject always to the prior consent in writing of the Minister to such activity and in accordance with such conditions (if any) as the Minister may impose in giving his consent.

Apprehension of offenders

23. (1) Any officer specified in subsection (16) of this Section may at any time stop, board, inspect, and search any foreign fishing craft in the territorial sea and exclusive economic zone, and inspect any fish on board the craft; and where he has reasonable cause to believe that an offence against this Act, or against regulations made under Section 21 of this Act, or against any other law of Tonga, relating to fishing within the exclusive economic zone, has been committed in respect of any foreign fishing craft he may—

(a) Seize and detain all fish on board the craft; and

(b) Apprehend any person whom he has reasonable cause to believe has committed any offence specified in this subsection; and

(c) If he has resonable cause to believe that any such offence has been committed by the licensee, owner, or master of the craft, seize and detain the craft.

(2) Any officer specified in subsection (16) of this section may exercise the powers conferred on him by subsection (1) of this section with the aid of such assistants as he considers to be necessary for the purpose.

(3) Where any foreign fishing craft is detained under subsection (1) of this section, it shall be held in the custody of the Crown until—

(a) A decision is made not to lay any information or charge in respect of the alleged offence for which the craft was detained; or

(b) Where such an information or charge is laid, the security required by Section 24 of this Act is

given in respect of the craft.

(4) The decision whether or not to lay an information or charge in respect of an alleged offence for which a foreign fishing craft in detained under subsection (1) of this section shall be made as soon as reasonably practicable after the craft is detained.

(5) The release of a foreign fishing craft from detention shall not affect any subsequent forfeiture of the craft in respect of the conviction of any person for an offence.

(6) On the conviction of any licensee, owner, or master of a foreign fishing craft for any offence specified in subsection (1) of this section, the craft shall be forfeited to the Crown, and shall be disposed of in such manner as the Minister shall order, in addition to any fine that may be imposed by any Court on the convicted person.

(7) Where any fish is detained under subsection (1) of this section, it shall be held in the custody of the Crown (either on board the foreign fishing craft from which it was seized or in such other place as the Minister may direct) until—

(a) A decision is made not to lay any information or charge in respect of the alleged offence for which the fish was detained; or

(b) Where such an information or charge is laid, any security required by Section 24 of this Act is given in respect of the fish.

(8) The release of any fish from detention shall not affect any subsequent forfeiture of the fish on the conviction of any person for an offence.

(9) The Crown shall not be liable to any person for any deterioration in the quality of any fish detained under subsection (1) of this section, whether such deterioration is caused by the negligence of the Crown or otherwise.

(10) On the conviction of any person for any offence specified in subsection (1) of this section in respect of any fish detained under that subsection, the fish shall be forfeited to the Crown and shall be disposed of in such manner as the Minister shall order, in addition to any fine that may be imposed by any Court on the convicted person.

The officer shall cause the person to be taken as soon as reasonably section apprehends any person under subsection (1) of this section

(11) Where any officer specified in subsection (16) of this practiable before a Court to be dealt with in accordance with law.

(12) Where any foreign fishing craft or fish is held in the custody of the Crown under this section, then on the conviction of any person for any offence specified in subsection (1) of this section in respect of the craft or fish, as the case may be, the costs of the Crown in holding it in custody under this section shall be a debt due to the Crown jointly and severally by each of them the licensee, the owner, and the master of the craft, and shall be recoverable accordingly by the Crown in any Court of competent jurisdiction.

(13) Without limiting any other manner of recovering any debt due to the Crown under subsection (12) of this section, on the conviction of the licensee, owner, or master of any foreign fishing craft for any offence referred to in that subsection, the Court by which he is convicted may make an order that he shall pay to the Crown any costs for which he is liable under that subsections.

(14) Subject to subsection (9) of this section, but notwithstanding any other provision in this section, where any foreign fishing craft or fish has been detained under subsection (1) of this section, then on the acquittal of every person who is charged with any offence for which the craft or fish, as the case may be, is subject to forfeiture under this section, the craft or fish, as the case may require, shall forthwith be released from the custody of the Crown.

(15) Any person who in any way prevents or hinders any officer specified in subsection (16) of this section, or any assistant of the officer, in exercising the powers conferred by this section commits an offence against this Act, and is liable on conviction to a fine not exceding $10,000.

(16) Subsection (1) of this section refers to any of the following officers:

(a) members of the Police Force;

(b) commissioned officers of the Tonga Defence Services;

(c) persons in command or charge of any vessel or aircraft operated by or on behalf of the Tonga Defence Services of the Government;

(d) any other person appointed for this purpose by the Minister.

Security for release of foreign fishing craft

24. (1) Where any foreign fishing craft is detained under Section 23 of this Act, and an information or charge is laid against the licensee, owner, or master of the craft in respect of the offence for which the craft has been detained, the licensee, owner, or master of the craft may at any time before the determination of the information or charge apply to the Court by which the information or charge will be determined for the release of the craft on the provision of security in accordance with this section.

(2) On hearing the application, the Court shall order the release of the foreign fishing craft on the execution by any suitable person or persons approved by the Court for the purpose, of a bond in favour of the Government, in the prescribed form and conditioned in accordance with sub-section (4) of this section, in an amount not less than the aggregate of the value of the craft, the costs that the Crown may recover under Section 23 (12) of this Act if the defendant is convicted of the offence, and the maximum fine to which the defendant will be liable if he is convicted of the offence.

(3) Notwithstanding subsection (2) of this section, the Court may, where it is satisfied that there are special circumstances to justify it in doing so, order that the bond shall be in a specified amount that is less than the amount required by that subsection.

(4) The condition of the bond shall be that if—

(a) The defendant is found not guilty of the information or charge; or

(b) The defendant on being convicted of the information or charge pays in full within 14 days after he is convicted the amount of the fine imposed by the Court, and the amount of all costs due by him to the Crown under section 23 (12) of this Act, and the foreign fishing craft is within that time surrendered to the Crown for forfeiture

then the bond shall be of no effect, but that otherwise the bond shall remain in fall force and effect.

(5) The amount specified in the bond shall be recoverable in full in any Court of competent jurisdiction, as a debt due to the Government jointly and severally by the person or persons by whom the bond is given, unless the person or persons prove the due performance of the condition on which the bond is defeasible.

(6) In this section, 'foreign fishing craft' includes all equipment on board or used by the craft, and also includes all fish that has been seized from the craft under Section 23 (1) of this Act and is detained on board the craft in the custody of the Crown under that section.

Administrative penalties for minor fisheries offences

25. (1) Where the Minister has reasonable cause to believe that–

(a) An offence against this Act, or against regulations made under Section 21 of this Act, or against any other law of Tonga relating to fishing within the exclusive economic zone, may have been committed by any person in respect of any foreign fishing craft; and

(b) Having regard to all the circumstances relating to the alleged offence it is of a minor nature, and having regard to the previous conduct of the craft and of the person concerned in the exclusive economic zone, it would be appropriate to impose a penalty under this section

he may cause a notice in writing in accordance with subsection (2) of this section, and otherwise in the prescribed form, to be served on that person.

(2) A notice under subsection (1) of this section shall specify—

(a) The date and nature of the offence;

(*b*) A summary of the facts on which the allegation that an offence has been commited is based (being a sufficient summary to fully and fairly inform the person of the allegation against him); and

(*c*) Any other matters (not being previous convictions) that the Minister considers relevant to the imposition of a penalty—

and shall be endorsed with a statement setting out the provisions of this section.

(3) Any person on whom a notice under subsection (1) of this section is served may, within 28 days after the notice is served on him, by a notice in writing in the prescribed form served on the Minister require that any proceedings in respect of the alleged offences shall be dealt with before a Court, in which case the following provisions shall apply:

(*a*) No further proceedings shall be taken under this section by the Minister;

(*b*) Nothing in this section shall be construed to prevent the subsequent laying of any information or charge in respect of the alleged offence, or the conviction of the person of the offence by a Court, or the imposition of any penalty under any enactment or forfeiture under this Act on such a conviction.

(4) Any person on whom a notice under subsection (1) of this section is served, who does not require that any proceedings in respect of the alleged offence shall be dealt with before a Court, may by notice in writing served on the Minister—

(*a*) Admit the offence; and

(*b*) In any case make submissions to the Minister as to the matters he wishes the Minister to take into account in imposing any penalty under this section.

(5) Where a person on whom a notice under subsection (1) of this section is served does not, within 28 days after the notice is served on him,—

(*a*) Require that any proceedings in respect of the alleged offence shall be dealt with before a Court; or

(*b*) Admit the offence—

he shall on the expiration of that period be deemed to have admitted the offence.

(6) Where under this section a person admits or is deemed to have admitted an offence, the Minister may, after taking into account any submissions made by that person under subsection (4) of this section, impose a monetary penalty on the person in respect of the offence, not exceeding one-third of the maximum monetary penalty to which the person would be liable if he were convicted of the offence by a Court.

(7) Where the Minister imposes a penalty on a person under this section in respect of an offence, the Minister shall cause a notice in writing in the prescribed form of the particulars of the penalty to be served on the person.

(8) A person on whom a penalty is imposed under this section shall pay the amount of the penalty to the Crown within 28 days after the notice of the penalty is served on him in accordance with subsection (7) of this section.

(9) Without prejudice to the requirements of subsection (8) of this section, or to Section 19 (1) of this Act, a penalty that has been imposed under this section shall be recoverable by the Crown, from the person on whom it has been imposed, in the same manner as a fine is recoverable on conviction for any offence.

(10) Notwithstanding the provisions of Sections 18, 21, 23 and 24 of this Act, or of any other enactment, where any offence has been admitted under this section, no information or charge may be laid in respect of the offence against the person by whom it is admitted.

(11) Nothing in this section shall apply—

(*a*) In respect of any offence or alleged offence under subsection (1) or subsection (2) of Section 18 of this Act; or (*b*) In respect of any offence or alleged offence in respect of which any information or charge has been laid.

General regulations in zone

26. The King may from time to time, by Order-in-Council, make regulations for all or any of the following purposes:

(*a*) Regulating the conduct of scientific research within the exclusive economic zone;

(*b*) prescribing measures for the protection and preservation of the marine environment of the zone;

(*c*) regulating the constructions, operation, and use of artificial islands (whether permanent or temporary), and other installation and structures within the zone, including the establishment of safety zones around such islands, installation, and structures;

(*d*) regulating the exploration and exploitation of the zone for the production of energy from the water, currents, and winds, and for any other economic purposes;

(*e*) providing for such other matters as are necessary or expedient for giving full effect to the sovereign rights of Tonga in relation to the zone;

(*f*) providing that a breach of any such regulations shall be a criminal offence, and imposing penalties by way of fine not exceeding $10,000 for any such offences;

(*g*) providing for such other matters as are contemplated by or necessary for giving full effect to the provisions of this Part of this Act (other than matters for which regulations may be made under Section 21 of this Act) and for its due administration.

General provisions as to offences in zone

27. (1) Any offence against this Act, or against any regulations made under this Act, that is committed within the exclusive economic zone shall be deemed to have been committed in Tonga.

(2) Where any licensee, owner, master, or crew member of a foreign fishing craft is charged with any offence specified in Section 18 of this Act, or in any regulations made under Section 21 of this Act, in respect of any activity described in paragraph (b) or paragraph (c) of the definition of the term 'fishing' in Section 2 (1) of this Act, it shall be a defence to the charge if the defendant proves that such activity related only to fish taken beyond the outer limits of the exclusive economic zone.

(3) Where any power of apprehension of any person, or of stopping, boarding, or searching any fishing craft, or of inspecting, seizing, or detaining any fishing craft or fish, is conferred on any person under this Part of this Act, that power may be exercised with or without a warrant.

Part III

Miscellaneous provisions

Modifications to give effect to international agreement

28. The King may, from time to time by Order-in-Council, limit any provision of this Act relating to the exclusive economic zone so far as it is necessary to do so to give full effect to any convention that is adopted by the Third United Nations Conference on the Law of the Sea.

Official charts

29. (1) For the purposes of this Act, the low-water mark in any specified area shall be the line of low-water at mean low-water spring tides as depicted on the largest scale British Admiralty chart for the time being of that area.

(2) In any proceedings in any Court, a certificate purporting to be signed by the Harbour Master that any specified British Admiralty chart of that area is the largest scale British Admiralty chart for the time being available of that area shall be admissible as evidence of that matter.

Onus of proof in respect of offences

30. In any criminal proceedings under this Act where a defendant is charged with having committed an offence specified in Section 18 of this Act, or with having contravened any other provision in any regulations made under this Act under which a licence or permit, or the consent of any person is required for the doing of any act, the onus shall be on the defendant to prove that at the time to which the charge relates, the requisite licence, permit, or consent was duly held.

Amendment repeal, and savings

31. (1) The enactments specified in the Schedule to this Act are hereby amended in the manner indicated in that Schedule.

(2) The Fisheries Protection Act 1973 is hereby repealed.

(3) Except as expressly provided by this Act, the provisions of this Act are in addition to and not in substitution for the provisions of every other enactment, and accordingly nothing in this Act shall limit or derogate from the provisions of any other enactment.

Schedule

Enactments Amended

Enactment Amended	Amendment
The Interpretation Act (1903–1972) Cap. 1	By repealing Section 33
The Minerals (Temporary Provisions) Act 1949–1968	By omitting from Section 2 the definition of the term 'land' and substituting the following definition: 'land' includes all submerged lands lying within the internal waters, territorial sea and exclusive economic zone as described in the Territorial Sea and Exclusive Economic Zone Act 1978.
The Petroleum Mining Act 1969	By omitting from Section 2 the definition of the term 'off-shore land' and substituting the following definition: 'off-shore land' means all submerged lands lying within the internal waters, territorial sea, and exclusive economic zone as described in the Territorial Sea and Exclusive Economic Zone Act 1978.
The Petroleum (Income Tax) Act 1969	By inserting in Section 3 (1) in the definition of the word 'Tonga' immediately after the words 'continental shelf' appearing in the last line, the words 'or exclusive economic zone'.

Passed in the Legislative Assembly this 23rd day of October, 1978.

65. Trinidad and Tobago

Ministry of Foreign Affairs Notice No. 500 of 1983.
Entered into force: May 27, 1983.
Source: Ministry of External Affairs of the Republic of Trinidad and Tobago Note 500, May 27, 1983.

The Ministry of External Affairs of the Republic of Trinidad and Tobago presents its compliments to the Diplomatic Missions accredited to Trinidad and Tobago and has the honour to enclose for their information the following texts of recent statements made by the Honourable Minister of External Affairs of Trinidad and Tobago, Senator Basil A. Ince

(i) Statement proclaiming a 200-mile Exclusive Economic Zone for the Republic of Trinidad and Tobago and establishing the Republic of Trinidad and Tobago as an archipelagic State;

(ii) Statement on the occasion of the Dinner held in honour of Dr. Jose Alberto Zambrano Velasco;

(iii) Address delivered to the Board Meeting of the West Indies Jaycees at Gaspar Grande

and the joint communique issued by the Governments of the Republic of Trinidad and Tobago and the Republic of Venezuela on the occasion of the recent visit to Trinidad and Tobago by His Excellency the Minister of External Relations of the Republic of Venezuela, Dr. Jose Alberto Zambrano Velasco.

The Ministry of External Affairs of the Republic of Trinidad and Tobago avails itself of this opportunity to renew to the Diplomatic Missions accredited to Trinidad and Tobago the assurances of its highest consideration.

Port-of-Spain. May 27, 1983.

Statement by the Honourable Minister of External Affairs proclaiming a 200-mile Exclusive Economic Zone for the Republic of Trinidad and Tobago and establishing the Republic of Trinidad and Tobago as an archipelagic State:

Mr Speaker, Honourable Members,

With the approval of Cabinet, I wish to make the following statements:

The Government of Trinidad and Tobago, in pursuance of its desire to protect its marine environment and to optimize benefits from the exploration and exploitation of both the living and non-living resources of its ocean space, has decided to proclaim a 200-mile Exclusive Economic Zone and to declare the Republic of Trinidad and Tobago, with its twenty-three islands, an archipelagic State.

Government's decision to proclaim a 200-mile Exclusive Economic Zone and to declare Trinidad and Tobago an archipelagic state comes shortly after the signing ceremony for the new United Nations Convention on the Law of the Sea which was held in Montego Bay, Jamaica on 10th December, 1982.

Trinidad and Tobago is one of 123 states which signed the Convention in Montego Bay. The adoption of the new Convention on the Law of the Sea marked the culmination of more than ten years of painstaking negotiation and is the finest example of international cooperation. There exist only few similar international legal instruments of comparative comprehensiveness which lay down rules and principles governing the conduct of states in international relations.

Mr Speaker, the Convention on the Law of the Sea has three hundred and twenty (320) articles and nine (9) Annexes. It lays down principles and codifies rules governing the entire spectrum of issues pertaining to the sea and its use by man; rules relating to the sovereignty of coastal States over marine areas and the delimitation of such areas; the establishment of an Exclusive Economic Zone up to a breadth of 200 miles beyond a State's territorial sea; the implementation by States like Trinidad and Tobago of the archipelagic principle in the drawing of baselines. (It provides rules governing international navigation, be it passage through a State's territorial sea, through international Straits or on the high seas;) it provides for the conservation and management of the living resources of the high seas. It codifies the concept of the common heritage of mankind under which all the mineral resources of the seas and of the sea-bed beyond the limits of national jurisdiction are to be exploited for the benefit of all mankind and not only for the benefit of the few who have the financial resources and technological capability to mine the resources of the deep sea-bed. It establishes an International Authority (with an Assembly, a Council, an Enterprise and Technical Commissions) through which States Parties to the Convention shall organise and control activities in the 'Area beyond the limits of national jurisdiction'.

These, Mr Speaker, are but a few of the areas for which the Convention lays down in its myriad provisions, specific rules and guidelines for application by Parties to it.

It is in accordance with this Convention that the Government of Trinidad and Tobago has decided to declare Trinidad and Tobago an archipelagic State and establish a 200-mile Exclusive Economic Zone. Government has also been mindful of the precedents laid down by ninety (90) States including neighbouring States such as Barbados, Brazil, Colombia, Grenada, Guyana, Suriname and Venezuela which have made declarations establishing Exclusive Economic Zones. Trinidad and Tobago did not take action before because it was awaiting the adoption of the Convention, which has now enshrined the principles of the 200-mile Exclusive Economic Zone and the archipelagic State.

The declaration of an Exclusive Economic Zone for Trinidad and Tobago will enable the country to exercise sovereign rights over all resources, living and non-living, within the zone; the right to establish artificial islands, installations and structures, and to exercise exclusive jurisdiction over them, including jurisdiction with regard to customs, fiscal, health, safety and immigration laws and regulations. Trinidad and Tobago will also have in the Zones jurisdiction over marine scientific research and with respect to the protection and preservation of the marine environment in the zone, particularly against marine pollution.

Similarly, the establishment of Trinidad and Tobago as an archipelagic state allows certain tangible and important benefits to accrue to Trinidad and Tobago. Such benefits include sovereignty over an area of sea referred to as archipelagic waters, sovereignty over the airspace above these waters as well as their bed, sub-soil and the resources contained therein.

The Exclusive Economic Zone of the Republic of Trinidad and Tobago is a zone contiguous to the territorial sea extending to a distance of 200 nautical miles from the baselines from which the breadth of the territorial sea is measured. In cases where the distances between Trinidad and Tobago and neighbouring states are less then 400 nautical miles, the boundary of the Exclusive Economic Zone shall be determined by agreement between the Republic of Trinidad and Tobago and opposite or adjacent states concerned on the basis of International law in order to achieve an equitable solution.

Within the Exclusive Economic Zone, the Republic of Trinidad and Tobago has:

(a) sovereign rights for the purpose of exploring, exploiting, conserving and managing the natural resources, both living and non-living of the sea-bed and sub-soil and the superjacent waters and with regard to other activities for the economic exploration and exploitation of the zone such as the production of energy from the water currents and winds;

(b) jurisdiction with regard to 'the' establishment and use of artificial islands, and installations and structures having economic purposes and used for the protection and preservation of the marine environment.

The Republic of Trinidad and Tobago will exercise these sovereign rights and jurisdiction in accordance with the rules of international law.

Without prejudice to the sovereign rights and jurisdiction of the Republic of Trinidad and Tobago, the Exclusive Economic Zone remains an area beyond the territorial sea of the Republic of Trinidad and Tobago in which all states shall enjoy the high seas freedoms of navigation, overflight, laying of submarine cables and pipelines and other legitimate uses of the sea.

Trinidad and Tobago satisfies all the criteria laid down in the Convention for an archipelagic state. An archipelagic state means, according to the Convention, a State constituted wholly by one or more archipelagos and may include other islands.

The archipelagic state of the Republic of Trinidad and Tobago comprines a group of twenty-three (23) islands and inter-connecting waters which are so closely related that such islands and waters form an intrinsic geographical, economic and political entity.

An archipelagic state may draw straight baselines joining the outermost points of the outermost islands and drying reefs of the archipelago provided that within such baselines are included the main islands and an area in which the ratio of the area of the water to the area of the land including atolls, is between 1 to 1 and 9 to 1. It is from such baselines that Trinidad and Tobago measures both its territorial sea, its Exclusive Economic Zone and its continental shelf.

The sovereignty of the Republic of Trinidad and Tobago extends to its archipelagic waters, to the air space over the archipelagic waters, as well as to their bed and sub-soil and the resources contained therein.

Without prejudice to the sovereignty of the Republic of Trinidad and Tobago all existing agreements, traditional fishing rights and other legitimate activities of the immediately adjacent neighbouring states in certain areas falling within the archipelagic waters shall be respected.

In order to secure these benefits, steps to give legislative effect to this declaration have already been initiated.

66. Tuvalu

Marine Zones (Declaration) Ordinance 1983.
Entered into force: January 1, 1984.
Source: Ministry of Foreign Affairs.

ARRANGEMENT OF SECTIONS

A BILL FOR AN ORDINANCE

To make provision in respect of the internal waters, the archipelagic waters, the territorial sea, the exclusive economic zone and the contiguous zone of Tuvalu.

Commencement:

Enacted by the Parliament of Tuvalu:

Short title and commencement

1. This Ordinance may be cited as the Marine Zones (Declaration) Ordinance 1983, and shall come into operation on such date as the Minister may, by notice, appoint.

Interpretation

2. (1) In this Ordinance, unless the context otherwise requires—

'the base-line of Tuvalu' means the low-water line of the seaward side of the reef fringing the coast of any part of Tuvalu or bounding any lagoon waters adjacent to any part of that coast, or where a reef is not present the low-water line of the coast itself;

'conservation and management' includes all rules, regulations, methods and measures that—

(a) are required to build, restore or maintain, or are useful in building, restoring or maintaining, any fishery resource or the marine environment; or

(b) are designed to ensure that—

(i) a supply of food and other products may be taken, and recreational benefites may be obtained, on a continuing basis; and

(ii) irreversible or long-term ill-effects on fishery resources or the marine environment are avoided; and

(iii) there will be a multiplicity of options available with respect to uses of those resources;

'fishery resource' means any fishery, stock of fish, species of fish or habitat of fish;

'low-tide elevation' means a naturally-formed area of land that is surrounded by and is above water at mean low-water spring tides but is submerged at mean high-water spring tides;

'the low-water line', in relation to any area, means the line of low water at mean low-water spring tides as depicted on the largest-scale nautical chart of the area held by the Minister;

'the median line' means a line every point of which is equidistant from the nearest points on—

(a) the base-lines from which the territorial sea of Tuvalu is measured; and

(b) the corresponding base-lines of any other country;

'nautical mile' means an international nautical mile of 1,852 metres.

(2) For the purposes of this Ordinance, permanent harbour works that form an integral part of a harbour system shall be regarded as forming part of the coast, but this subsection does not apply to off-shore installations or artificial islands.

References to rules of international law

3. Where in this Ordinance it is provided that anything shall be done, or any law or order shall be made, in accordance with the rules of international law, the question, whether it was so done or made, is nonjusticiable.

Application of this Ordinance

4. The provisions of this Ordinance shall be read subject to the provisions of any treaty or other international obligation which is ratified or finally accepted by or on behalf of Tuvalu.

Internal waters

5. (1) For the purposes of any law of Tuvalu, the internal waters of Tuvalu are—

(a) all waters on the landward side of the base-lines from which the breadth of the territorial sea is measured; and

(b) where closing lines are drawn in accordance with Subsection (2) — the waters inland of these lines to the extent that they are outside those base-lines.

(2) The Minister may, in accordance with the rules of international law, declare, by reference to—

(a) physical features marked on official charts; or

(b) lists of geographical co-ordinates, specifying the geodetic datums, the points between which closing lines are to de drawn for the purpose of determining the outer limits of the internal waters of Tuvalu in the case of the mouths of or entrances to lagoons.

Archipelagic waters

6. (1) For the purposes of any law of Tuvalu, the archipelagic waters (if any) of Tuvalu comprise all areas of sea contained within the base-lines established under Subsection (2).

(2) The Minister may, in accordance with the rules of international law, declare, by reference to—

(a) physical features marked on official charts; or

(b) lists of geographical co-ordinates, specifying the geodetic datums,

the points between which straight base-lines are to be drawn for the purpose of determining—

(c) the outer limits of the *archipelagic* waters of Tuvalu; and

(d) the inner limits of the territorial sea.

The territorial sea

7. (1) Subject to Subsection (2), for the purposes of any law of Tuvalu the territorial sea of Tuvalu is those parts of the sea within 12 nautical miles from the base-line of Tuvalu.

(2) Where archipelagic base-lines are drawn under Section 6 (2), the breadth of the territorial sea shall be measured from those base-lines to the extent to which they are outside the outer limits of the internal waters of Tuvalu.

The exclusive economic zone

8. (1) Subject to the succeeding provisions of this section, for the purposes of any law of Tuvalu the exclusive economic zone of Tuvalu comprises those parts of the sea having—

(a) as their inner limits — the outer limits of the territorial sea; and

(b) as their outer limits — line drawn 200 nautical miles seaward from the base-lines from which the breadth of the territorial sea is measured.

(2) The Minister may, in accordance with the rules of international law, declare, by reference to—

(a) physical features marked on official charts; or

(b) lists of geographical co-ordinates, specifying the geodetic datums,

the points between which straight base-lines are to be drawn for determining the outer limits of the exclusive economic zone.

(3) Where base-lines are drawn in accordance with Subsection (2), the breadth of the exclusive economic zone shall be measured from those base-lines.

(4) The Minister may, by order, for the purpose of implementing any international agreement or the award of any international body, or otherwise, declare that the outer limits of the exclusive economic zone of Tuvalu are such as are specified in the order.

(5) Where the median line is less than 200 nautical miles from the line from which the breadth of the territorial sea is to be measured, the outer limits of the exclusive economic zone extend only to the median line.

The contiguous zone

9. For the purposes of any law of Tuvalu, the contiguous zone of Tuvalu is those parts of the sea within 24 nautical miles from the base-lines from which the breadth of the territorial sea is measured.

Legal character of marine zones, etc.

10. (1) The sovereignty of Tuvalu extends beyond its land territory and internal waters, and its archipelagic waters (if any), over its territorial sea, and to the airspace over them and the seabed and subsoil under them, and the resources contained in them.

(2) Within the exclusive economic zone, Tuvalu has sovereign rights—

(a) for the purposes of exploring and of exploiting, conserving and managing the natural resources, whether living or non-living, of—

(i) the sea-bed; and

(ii) the subsoil under the sea-bed; and
(iii) the waters over the sea-bed; and

(b) with regard to other activities for the economic exploitation and exploration of the zone, such as the production of energy from the waters, currents and winds.

(3) Within the exclusive economic zone Tuvalu has such other rights as are conferred or recognised by international law.

(4) Within the contiguous zone, Tuvalu has all rights necessary—

(a) to prevent intringement of its customs, fiscal, immigration and sanitary laws and regulations within the territory, the territorial sea or the archipelagic waters (if any) of Tuvalu; and

(b) to punish any such infringement,

and all relevant laws of Tuvalu extend to the contiguous zone accordingly.

(5) The sovereignty and rights of Tuvalu under this section shall be exercised in accordance with the rules of international law.

Rights of other States in marine zones, etc.

11. (1) Subject to the succeeding provisions of this section, ships and aircraft of all States have, in accordance with the rules of international law, the right of free passage through and over the territorial sea and the archipelagic waters (if any) of Tuvalu.

(2) The Minister, may, by order—

(a) designate, in accordance with the rules of international law, sealanes and air routes suitable for the continuous and expeditious passage of foreign ships and aircraft through and over the archipelagic waters and the adjacent territorial sea; and

(b) prescribe traffic separation schemes for the purpose of ensuring the safe passage of ships through narrow channels in any such sealanes.

(3) In sealanes and air routes designated under Subsection (2) all ships and aircraft may, in accordance with the rules of international law, enjoy the right of navigation and overflight, in their normal modes, for the purpose of continuous, expeditious and unobstructed transit through and over the archipelagic waters and the adjacent territorial sea, from one part of the exclusive economic zone to another part of it.

(4) Until sealanes and air routes are designated under Subsection (2), the rights of navigation and overflight referred to in Subsection (3) may be exercised through and over all routes normally used for international navigation and overflight.

(5) The rights of navigation and overflight referred to in Subsections (3) and (4) are subject to all laws of Tuvalu made in accordance with the rules of international law.

(6) Subject to this and any other Ordinance and to the rules of international law, all States and their nationals shall enjoy in the exclusive economic zone the high seas freedoms of navigation and overflight and of the laying of submarine cables and pipelines, and all other internationally lawful uses of the sea related to those freedoms, compatible with the rules of international law.

General regulations as to the exclusive economic zone

12. Where no other provision is made by or under any other Ordinance for the purpose, the Minister may make regulations, which shall be in accordance with the rules of international law, for all or any of the following purposes;—

(a) regulating the conduct of scientific research within the exclusive economic zone; and

(b) regulating the exploration and exploitation of the exclusive economic zone for the production of energy from waters, currents and winds, and for other economic purposes; and

(c) regulating the construction, operation and use of artificial islands, installations and structures within the exclusive economic zone, including requirements for the establishment of safety zones around any such island, installation or structure; and

(d) prescribing measures for the protection and preservation of the marine environment of the exclusive economic zone; and

(e) providing for such other matters as arc necessary or expedient to give effect to the rights and obligations of Tuvalu in relation to the exclusive economic zone, or as are necessary to give full effect to the provisions of this Ordinance.

Courts, publicity, etc.

13. (1) The Minister shall cause all closing lines, base-lines and other lines drawn for the purposes of this Ordinance, for determining the limits of the internal waters, the archipelagic waters (if any), the territorial sea, the exclusive economic zone and the contiguous zone of Tuvalu, to be clearly indicated on charts of a scale or scales adequate for them to be readily determined, and shall give adequate publicity to them.

(2) A question, whether adequate publicity has been given under Subsection (1) to any matter, is non-justiciable.

(3) A copy of each chart referred to in Subsection (1) shall be deposited with the Secretary-General of the United Nations and the Secretary-General of the South Pacific Commission.

Evidentiary provisions

14. In any proceedings before a court or person acting judicially, a certificate purporting to be signed by the Minister stating that any specific nautical chart of any area is a chart to which Section 13 applies that is held by the Minister is evidence of the matters stated in the certificate, and the chart is evidence of the matters set out in it.

MARINE ZONES (DECLARATION) BILL 1983
EXPLANATORY MEMORANDUM

The purpose of this Bill is to clarify the jurisdiction of the Government of Tuvalu over the waters surrounding Tuvalu. It closely follows Parts I and II of the Marine Spaces Act (Cap 158A) of Fiji, and (except for Section 9), is almost identical with the Marine Zones (Declaration) Act 1983 (No. 7 of 1983) of Kiribati.

The Bill provides for—

(a) the internal waters (that is, the waters inland of the territorial sea); and

(b) the territorial sea, the breadth of which is to be 12 nautical miles, and over which the Government has complete jurisdiction (at present the territorial sea is 3 miles wide, but the UN Convention on the Law of the Sea and modern international practice accepts 12 miles); and

(c) a contiguous zone, in which infringements of customs, fiscal, immigration and sanitary laws within Tuvalu or the territorial sea can be prevented and punished (this is a new development, allowed for by the Convention on the Law of the Sea); and

(d) the exclusive economic zone of 200 miles, over which the Government has sovereign rights of exploitation, etc., and for which it may make general regulations (effectively, the EEZ will replace the exclusive fishery zone).

In addition, it provides for the possibility of the future declaration of 'archipelagic waters', if it is later decided to declare such waters. Again, the Convention on the Law of the Sea and modern international practice allows of this in appropriate case.

It should be noted that the Bill declares that the rules of international law will be followed, but because of doubts as to just what are those rules in particular cases that declaration is not made legally binding —

there is, of course, great controversy over just what is the international law of the sea.

The Bill also provides that it is to be read subject to any treaty or other international obligation ratified of finally accepted by Tuvalu.

C.J. Lynch,
Arttorney-General.

67. United Arab Emirates

Declaration of Ministry of Foreign Affairs.
Entered into force: August 25, 1980.
Source: *United Nations LE 113 (3-3),* March 18, 1981.

In the Name of God, the Merciful, the Compassionate

Declaration by the Ministry of Foreign Affairs of the United Arab Emirates concerning the exclusive economic zone and its delimitation

On the basis of the principles jointly affirmed by States in connexion with economic zones in marine waters adjacent to their coasts;

As an expression of developments in the rules of international law governing the rights of coastal States in those zones; and

Believing it to be necessary for the United Arab Emirates to protect its vital interests by affirming its sovereignty over all the natural resources in the economic zone, adjacent to its coasts irrespective of whether the existence of such resources is established in the superjacent waters, on the sea-bed or below the sea-bed;

The Government of the United Arab Emirates declares the following:

1. The United Arab Emirates possesses an exclusive economic zone adjacent to its main coasts and to the coasts of its islands in the Gulf and in the Sea of Oman.

2. The economic zone of the United Arab Emirates shall be measured from the baselines from which the territorial sea of the main coasts of the United Arab Emirates and of the coasts of its islands are measured.

3. The outer limit of the economic zone of the United Arab Emirates shall be determined in accordance with the provisions of the agreements concluded by the Emirates members of the Union in connexion with their continental shelf. If the Emirates members of the Union have not concluded such agreements, the outer limit of the economic zone of the United Arab Emirates shall extend to the median line every point of which is equidistant from the nearest points of the baseline.

4. The United Arab Emirates shall exercise full sovereign rights over the natural resources located within its exclusive economic zone for the purpose of the exploration, exploitation, management, development and conservation of such resources. The United Arab Emirates shall also possess full rights of jurisdiction within the said economic zone for the purpose of exercising supervision over scientific research conducted therein and taking the requisite measures for the protection of the marine environment and for the construction of the structures, installations and artificial islands needed for the purposes of the fishing zone.

5. Foreign vessels shall not be allowed to fish in the economic zone of the United Arab Emirates unless they are duly licensed by the competent authorities. Such license shall include, in particular, details regarding the compensation due in return for the license, the species for which fishing is permitted, the fishing methods to be used, the area covered by the license and the permitted quota of catch.

Under no circumstances shall a license be issued except in respect of surplus living resources in the fishing zone of the United Arab Emirates.

6. The rights exercised by the United Arab Emirates over the economic zone shall not prejudice international navigation rights exercised by States in general in accordance with the rules of international law.

7. This declaration shall not affect the status quo between Emirates members of the Union in regard to their respective territorial waters.

8. The Ministry of Agriculture and Fisheries, in collaboration with the ministries concerned, shall prepare official charts delimiting the economic zone in accordance with the provisions of this declaration. The said ministry, in collaboration with the ministries concerned, shall take the necessary action for the publication and dissemination of those charts.

68. United States

Presidential Proclamation No. 5030.
Entered into force: March 10, 1983.
Source: The White House, Office of the Press Secretary, March 10, 1983.

EXCLUSIVE ECONOMIC ZONE OF THE UNITED STATES OF AMERICA

by the President of the United States of America

A PROCLAMATION

Whereas the Government of the United States of America desires to facilitate the wise development and use of the oceans consistent with international law;

Whereas international law recognizes that, in a zone beyond its territory and adjacent to its territorial sea, known as the Exclusive Economic Zone, a coastal State may assert certain sovereign rights over natural resources and related jurisdiction; and

Whereas the establishment of an Exclusive Economic Zone by the United States will advance the development of ocean resources and promote the protection of the marine environment, while not affecting other lawful uses of the zone, including the freedoms of navigation and overflight, by other States;

Now, therefore, I, Ronald Reagan, by the authority vested in me as President by the Constitution and laws of the United States of America, do hereby proclaim the sovereign rights and jurisdiction of the United States of America and confirm also the rights and freedoms of all States within an Exclusive Economic Zone, as described herein.

The Exclusive Economic Zone of the United States is a zone contiguous to the territorial sea, including zones contiguous to the territorial sea of the United States, the Commonwealth of Puerto Rico, the Commonwealth of the Northern Mariana Islands (to the extent consistent with the Covenant and the United Nations Trusteeship Agreement), and United States overseas territories and possessions. The Exclusive Economic Zone extends to a distance 200 nautical miles from the baseline from which the breadth of the territorial sea is measured. In cases where the maritime boundary with a neighboring State remains to be determined, the boundary of the Exclusive Economic Zone shall be determined by the United States and other State concerned in accordance with equitable principles.

Within the Exclusive Economic Zone, the United States has, to the extent permitted by international law, (a) sovereign rights for the purpose of exploring, exploiting, conserving and managing natural resources, both living and non-living, of the seabed and subsoil and the superjacent waters and with regard to other activities for the economic exploitation and exploration of the zone, such as the production of energy from the water, currents and winds; and (b) jurisdiction with regard to the establishment and use of artificial islands, and installations and structures having economic purposes, and the protection and preservation of the marine environment.

This Proclamation does not change existing United States policies concerning the continental shelf, marine mammals and fisheries including highly migratory species of tuna which are not subject to United States jurisdiction and require international agreements for effective management.

The United States will exercise these sovereign rights and jurisdiction in accordance with the rules of international law.

Without prejudice to the sovereign rights and jurisdiction of the United States, the Exclusive Economic Zone remains an area beyond the territory and territorial sea of the United States in which all States enjoy the high seas freedoms of navigation, overflight, the laying of submarine cables and pipelines, and other internationally lawful uses of the sea.

In witness whereof, I have hereunto set my hand this tenth day of March, in the year of our Lord nineteen hundred and eighty-three, and of the Independence of the United States of America the two hundred and seventh.

Ronald Reagan

THE WHITE HOUSE

Office of the Press Secretary

March 10, 1983

STATEMENT BY THE PRESIDENT

The United States has long been a leader in developing customary and conventional law of the sea. Our objectives have consistently been to provide a legal order that will, among other things, facilitate peaceful, international uses of the oceans and provide for equitable and effective management and conservation of marine resources. The United States also recognizes that all nations have an interest in these issues.

Last July I announced that the United States will not sign the United Nations Law of the Sea Convention that was opened for signature on December 10. We have taken this step because several major problems in the Convention's deep seabed mining provisions are contrary to the interests and principles of industrialized nations and would not help attain the aspirations of developing countries.

The United States does not stand alone in those concerns. Some important allies and friends have not signed the Convention. Even some signatory States have raised concerns about these problems.

However, the Convention also contains provisions with respect to traditional uses of the oceans which generally confirm existing maritime law and practice and fairly balance the interests of all States.

Today I am announcing three decisions to promote and protect the oceans interests of the United States in a manner consistent with those fair and balanced results in the Convention and international law.

First, the United States is prepared to accept and act in accordance with the balance of interests relating to traditional uses of the oceans – such as navigation and overflight. In this respect, the United States will recognize the rights of other States in the waters off their coasts, as reflected in the Convention, so long as the rights and

Second, the United States will exercise and assert its navigation and overflight rights and freedoms on a worldwide basis in a manner that is consistent with the balance of interests reflected in the Convention. The United States will not, however, acquiesce in unilateral acts of other States designed to restrict the rights and freedoms of the international community in navigation and overflight and other related high seas uses.

Third, I am proclaiming today an Exclusive Economic Zone in which the United States will exercise sovereign rights in living and non-living resources within 200 nautical miles of its coast. This will provide

United States jurisdiction for mineral resources out to 200 nautical miles that are not on the continental shelf. Recently discovered deposits there could be an important future source of strategic minerals.

Within this Zone all nations will continue to enjoy the high seas rights and freedoms that are not resource-related, including the freedoms of navigation and overflight. My proclamation does not change existing United States policies concerning the continental shelf, marine mammals and fishrights including highly migratory species of tuna which are in subject to United States jurisdiction. The United States will continue efforts to achieve international agreements for the effective management of these species. The Proclamation also reinforces this government's policy of promoting the United States fishing industry.

While international law provides for a right of jurisdiction over marine scientific research within such a zone, the Proclamation does not assert this right. I have reacted not to do so because of the United States interest in encouraging marine scientific research and avoiding any necessary burdens. The United States will nevertheless recognize the right of other coastal States to exercise jurisdiction over marine scientific research within 200 nautical miles of their coasts, if that jurisdiction is exercised reasonably in a manner consistent with international law.

The Exclusive Economic Zone established today will also enable the United States to take limited additional steps to protect the marine environment. In this connection, the United States will continue to work through the International Maritime Organization and other appropriate international Organizations to develop uniform international measures for the protection of the marine environment while imposing no unreasonable burdens on commercial shipping.

The policy decisions I am announcing today will not affect the application of existing United States law concerning the high seas or existing authorities of any United States government agency.

In addition to the above policy steps, the United States will continue to work with other countries to develop a regime, free of unnecessary political and economic restraints, for mining deep seabed minerals beyond national jurisdiction. Deep seabed mining remains a lawful exercise of the freedom of the high seas open to all nations. The United States will continue to allow its firms to explore for and, when the market permits, exploit these resources.

The Administration looks forward to working with the Congress on legislation to implement these new policies.

69. Vanuatu

Maritime Zones Act No. 23 of 1981.
Entered into force: October 6, 1982.
Source: Note No. 01/FA/83 from the Vanuatu Ministry of Foreign Affairs to the Secretary-General of the United Nations.

REPUBLIC OF VANUATU

Arrangement of Sections

SCHEDULE

Archipelagic Baseline

THE MARITIME ZONES ART NO. 23 OF 1981

Assent: 15.12.1981
Commencement: See Section 16

To provide for the delimitation of the maritime zones of the Republic, and other matters incidental thereto.

Be it enacted by the President and Parliament as followe:

PART 1 — INTERPRETATION

Interpretation

1. In this Act, unless the context otherwise requires—

'bay' means an indentation of the coast with an area of not less then that of the semi-circle the diameter of which is a line drawn across the mouth of the indentation;

'island' means a naturally formed area of land, surrounded by water, which is above water at high tide;

'low waterline' means the relevant low-water datum line shown on the latest relevant British Admiralty Charts or where there is no such datum the lowest astronomical tide line. In any case where there is doubt as to which is the latest relevant British Admiralty Chart for the purposes of this definition the Minister may establish which is such chart by declaration published in the Gazette;

'nautical mile' means an international nautical mile of 1852 metres.

PART 2 — INTERNAL WATERS

Internal waters

2. The internal waters of Vanuatu comprise all waters that are contained within the baselines from which the breadth of the territorial sea is measured or for areas enclosed by straight archipelagic baselines, all waters that are contained within the innermost limits of the archipelagic waters.

PART 3 — ARCHIPELAGIC WATERS AND TERRITORIAL SEA

Sovereignty of Vanuatu

3. The sovereignty of Vanuatu extends beyond the land and internal waters of its islands to the archipelagic waters and territorial sea and to the airspace thereover as well as to the seabed and subsoil thereunder.

Archipelagic waters

4. (1) The archipelagic waters comprise waters other than internal waters contained within the archipelagic baseline as delimited in the schedule.

(2) The innermost limits of the archipelagic waters shall be—

(a) the low-water line; or

(b) in the case of the sea adjacent to a bay—

(i) where the bay has only one mouth and the distance between the low-water lines of the natural entrance points of the bay does not exceed 24 nautical miles, along a closing line joining those low-water lines;

(ii) where because of the presence of islands the bay has more than one mouth and the distance between the low-water lines of the natural entrance points of each mouth added together, do not exceed 24 nautical miles along a series of closing lines across each of the mouths so as to join those low-water lines;

(iii) where neither paragraph (a) nor paragraph (b) applies, along a closing line 24 nautical miles in length drawn from low-water line to low-water line within the bay in such a manner as to enclose the maximum area of water that is possible with a line of that length; and

(c) in the case of the mouth or each mouth of a river which flows into the sea, a closing line across the river mouth between points on the low-water line of its banks.

Territorial Sea

5. (1) The territorial sea comprises all areas of sea having as their innermost limits the baselines described in sub-section (2) and as their outermost limits, a line measured seaward from those baselines, every point of which is 12 nautical miles from the nearest point of the appropriate baseline.

(2) The baselines from which the territorial sea is measured shall be the archipelagic baseline and the low-water line of the coast of Matthew Island and Hunter Island.

Rights of Passage

6. (1) Subject to the provisions of this Act, all foreign ships may enjoy the right of innocent passage through the archipelagic waters and territorial sea.

(2) The Minister may, after consultation with the Minister responsible for transport and communications, by order published in the Gazette designate sea lanes and air routes, suitable for the continuous and expeditious passage of foreign ships and aircraft through or over the archipelagic waters and territorial sea and may also prescribe traffic separation schemes for the purpose of ensuring the safe passage of ships through narrow channels in such sealanes.

PART 4 — CONTIGUOUS ZONE

Contiguous Zone

7. (1) The contiguous zone is an area beyond and adjacent to the territorial sea having as its outermost limits a line measured seaward from the baselines from which the territorial sea is measured, every point of which is 24 nautical miles from the nearest point of the appropriate baseline.

(2) Vanuatu may exercise such powers and take such measures in relation to the contiguous zone as may be necessary in order to prevent or punish infringements of its customs, fiscal immigration and sanitary laws.

PART 5 — THE CONTINENTAL SHELF AND EXCLUSIVE ECONOMIC ZONE

Continental Shelf

8. The continental shelf comprises the seabed and subsoil of the submarine area that extend beyond the limits of the territorial waters throughout the natural prolongation of the land territory of Vanuatu—

(a) to the outer edge of the continental margin; or

(b) to a distance of 200 nautical miles from the baseline from which the territorial sea is measured where the outer edge of the continental shelf does not extend up to that distance.

Exclusive Economic Zone

9. (1) The exclusive economic zone comprises these areas of the sea, seabed, and sub-soil that are beyond and adjacent to the territorial sea having as their outermost limits a line measured seaward from the baselines from which the territorial sea is measured every point of which line is 200 nautical miles from the nearest point of the appropriate baseline.

(2) For the purposes of implementing any international agreement or otherwise, the Minister may by order published in the Gazette declare that the exclusive economic zone shall not extend to any specified area of the sea, seabed, or sub-soil, that would otherwise be included within the exclusive economic zone by virtue of this section.

Vanuatu rights over continental shelf and exclusive economic zone

10. Without prejudice to Sections 3, 7, and 8 Vanuatu has in the continental shelf and exclusive economic zone—

(a) sovereign rights for the purposes of exploration, exploitation, conservation and management of all resources;

(b) exclusive rights and jurisdiction for the construction, maintenance or operation of artificial islands, off-shore terminals, installations and other structures and devices necessary for the exploration and exploitation of resources or for the convenience of shipping or for any other purpose;

(c) exclusive jurisdiction to authorise, regulate and conduct scientific research;

(d) exclusive jurisdiction to preserve and protect the marine environment and to prevent and control marine pollution; and

(e) such other rights as are recognized by International Law or State practice.

PART 5 — MISCELLANEOUS

Restricted activities

Except in accordance with an agreement entered into with the Government of Vanuatu or under the authority of a license granted by the responsible Minister in person shall in relation to the continental shelf or exclusive economic zone:—

(a) explore or exploit any resources;

(b) carry out any search, excavation or drilling operations;

(c) conduct any research;

(d) construct, maintain or operate any artificial island, off-shore terminal, installation or other structure or device.

Offences and Penalties

12. (1) Any contravention of this Act, or of any order made hereunder, occurring within the archipelagic waters, territorial sea or exclusive economic zone shall be deemed to have occurred in Vanuatu.

(2) Where a contravention of this Act is triable in a Magistrate's Court it may be tried by any Senior Magistrate.

(3) Any person who contravenes this Act or any order made hereunder shall be liable on conviction to a fine not exceeding 1,000,000 VT or to imprisonment for 5 years or both such fine and imprisonment.

Orders

13. Where no other provision is for the time being made by any other law for any such purposes, the Minister may by order—

(a) amend the Schedule;

(b) provide for the protection and preservation of the marine environment of the continental shelf archipelagic waters, the territorial sea and the exclusive economic zone;

(c) regulate the conduct of foreign ships and aircraft in relation to the rights of navigation and overflight provided for in sections 6 and 15;

(d) regulate the conduct of scientific research within the archipelagic waters, the territorial sea and the exclusive economic zone;

(e) regulate the construction, operation, and use of artificial islands (whether permanent or temporary), and other installations and structures in the archipelagic waters, and the territorial sea and the exclusive economic zone and establish safety zones around such islands, installations, and structures;

(f) regulate the exploration and exploitation of the archipelagic waters, the territorial sea and the exclusive economic zone for the production of energy from the water, currents, and winds, and for any other economic purposes;

(g) provide for such other matters as may be required for giving full effect to the sovereignty of Vanuatu in relation to the archipelagic waters, the territorial sea and the exclusive economic zone;

(h) provide otherwise for the better carrying out of the provisions of this Act and for its due administration.

PART 7 — TRANSITIONAL AND COMMENCEMENT

Extension of laws to continental shelf and exclusive economic zone

14. The President may, on the advice of the Prime Minister, by order published in the Gazette—

(a) extend with such restrictions and modifications as may be included in such order any law of Vanuatu to the continental shelf, the exclusive economic zone or any part of them;

(b) make provision for enforcing such law.

Interim provision for sea lanes and air routes

15. Until such time as sea lanes or air routes are designated under the provisions of section 6 (2) or any other law, rights of navigation and overflight may, subject to the provisions of this Act or any other law, be exercised through and over the routes normally used for international ???.

Commencement

16. This Act shall come into force on such day as the Minister may appoint by Order published in the Gazette and the Minister may appoint different days for different provisions and any reference in any provision to the commencement of this Act shall be construed as a reference to the day appointed under this section for the coming into force of that provision.

SCHEDULE (Section 4)

Archipelagic Baseline

An archipelagic baseline commences at the outermost point of the low-water line on the Reef off Hiu Island co-ordinate 13° 0, 18″ South 166° 32′ 13″.8 East, British Admiralty Chart No. 1575 and, except where the contrary intention appears, following the geodesic lines successively linking the outermost points on the low-water lines of the land areas specified below:

Point	Land Areas	Co-ordinates		British Admiralty Chart Number*
		South	East	
1.	Vat Ganai Island	13° 15′ 10″.8	167° 38′ 10″.5	1575
2.	Vetvai Point on Motlav Island	13° 38′ 46″.8	167° 42′ 25″.5	1575
3.	Islet off Merelava Island	14° 26′ 22″.9	168° 04′ 10″.2	1575
4.	Treerock Point on Pentecost Island	15° 55′ 38″.4	168° 16′ 32″.5	1575
5.	Tongaraki Island	17° 00′ 38″.4	168° 38′ 27″	1576
6.	Maniaro Point on Efate Island	17° 41′ 42″	168° 35′ 10″	1576
7.	Goat Islet off Erremanga	18° 42′ 09″.6	169° 17′ 43″.5	1576
8.	Reef off Futuna Island	19° 30′ 42″	170° 13′ 44″.3	1576
9.	Masi Point on Futuna Island	19° 32′ 37″.7	170° 13′ 34″.7	1576
10.	Reef on Anoityum Island	20° 11′ 45″.6	169° 53′ 42″	1576
	and thence along the low-water line to point 11			
11.	Flat Rock off Anoityum Island	20° 15′ 30″	169° 50′ 42″.9	1576
12.	Reef off Aneityum Island	20° 15′ 58″.2	169° 46′ 25″.9	1576
13.	Imlae on Tanna Island	19° 34′ 51″.6	169° 16′ 42″.6	1576
	and thence along the low-water line to point 14			
14.	West Point Tanna Islands	19° 27′ 09″	169° 12′ 39″	1576
15.	Ountovin Point on Erremango Island	18° 52′ 51″	168° 59′ 03″.6	1576
16.	Tukutuku Point on Efate Island	17° 43′ 09″.6	168° 09′ 02″.4	1576
17.	Tomman Island	16° 35′ 37″.5	167° 27′ 17″.4	1575
18.	Reef off Santo	15° 39′ 24″.6	166° 45′ 58″.8	1575
19.	Remarkable Point on Santo Island	15° 24′ 04″.5	166° 38′ 27″	1575
20.	Reef off Santo Island	14° 51′ 06″	166° 32′ 00″.6	1576
21.	On NW Coast of Santo	14° 44′ 51″.6	166° 32′ 42″.6	1575
22.	Thomeuf Point on Hiu Island	13° 10′ 21″	166° 31′ 58″.5	1575
23.	On Reef off Hiu Island	13° 04′ 18″	166° 32′ 13″.8	1575

* The Editions of charts referred to in the fifth column are 1575 7th September 1979, 1576 24th November 1978.

70. Venezuela

Act Establishing an Exclusive Economic Zone Along the Coasts of the Mainland and Islands of the Republic of Venezuela.
Entered into force: July 26, 1978.
Sources: *Gaceta Oficiel Extraordinaire No. 2.291,* July 26, 1978, and *United Nations ST/LEG/SER.B/19,* pp. 261-264 (Translated from Spanish by the Secretariat of the United Nations).

ACT ESTABLISHING AN EXCLUSIVE ECONOMIC ZONE ALONG THE COASTS OF THE MAINLAND AND ISLANDS OF THE REPUBLIC OF VENEZUELA, 1978[1]

Article 1. Establishment of an exclusive economic zone

An exclusive economic zone is hereby established beyond and adjacent to the territorial sea, all along the coasts of the mainland and islands of the Republic of Venezuela, which zone shall be subject to the régimen established by this Act.

Article 2. Breadth of the exclusive economic zone

The outer limit of the exclusive economic zone shall be a line every point of which is a distance of two hundred (200) nautical miles from the baseline used to measure the breadth of the territorial sea.

Where this provision results in overlapping with the exclusive economic zones of other States, the zones shall be delimited, as necessary, by agreement between the States concerned.

Article 3. Rights of the Republic in the exclusive economic zone

1. In the exclusive economic zone established by this Act, the Republic has:

(a) Sovereign rights for the purpose of exploring and exploiting, conserving and managing the natural resources, whether living or non-living, of the sea-bed and subsoil and the superjacent waters, and with regard to other activities for the economic exploitation and exploration of the zone, such as the production of energy from the water, currents and wind.

(b) Jurisdiction as provided for in the relevant provisions of this Act and its regulations with regard to:

(i) The establishment and use of artificial islands, installations and structures;

(ii) Marine scientific research;

(iii) The preservation of the marine environment.

2. The rights set out in this article with respect to the sea-bed and subsoil shall be exercised in accordance with provisions relating to the continental shelf.

Article 4. Rights of other States in the exclusive economic zone

In the exclusive economic zone of the Republic, other States, whether coastal or land-locked, shall enjoy, subject to the relevant provisions of the present Act, the freedoms of navigation and overflight and of the laying of submarine cables and pipelines, and other internationally lawful uses of the sea associated with navigation and communication.

[1] Approved by the Congress of Venezuela on 26 July 1978 and published in the *Gaceta Oficial Extraordinaria,* No. 2.291 of the same date. Information communicated by the Permanent Mission of Venezuela to the United Nations. Spanish text provided by the Permanent Representative of Venezuela to the United Nations in a letter of 20 September 1978. Translation by the Secretariat of the United Nations.

Article 5. Conservation of the living resources

1. The National Executive shall periodically determine the allowable catch of the living resources in the exclusive economic zone of the Republic.

2. The National Executive, taking into account the available scientific evidence, shall ensure through proper conservation and management measures that the maintenance of the living resources in the exclusive economic zone is not endangered by over-exploitation. As appropriate, the Republic shall co-operate to that end with relevant subregional, regional and global organizations.

3. Such measures shall also be designed to maintain or restore populations of harvested species at levels which can produce the maximum sustainable yield in the light of relevant environment and economic factors.

Article 6. Utilization of the living resources

1. The Republic shall promote the optimum use of the living resources of the exclusive economic zone without prejudice to article 5 of this Act.

2. The National Executive shall periodically determine the capacity of the Republic to harvest the living resources of the exclusive economic zone. Where the National Executive determines that the Republic does not have the capacity to harvest the entire allowable catch, it shall, through agreements and other arrangements and pursuant to the terms, conditions and requirements laid down in the regulations giving effect to this Act, give other States access to the surplus of the allowable catch.

Article 7. Co-ordination with other States in respect of measures for the conservation of the living resources

1. The Republic shall seek, either directly or through appropriate subregional or regional organizations, to agree upon the measures necessary to co-ordinate and ensure the conservation and development of the same stock or stocks of associated species occurring within the exclusive economic zone of the Republic and the exclusive economic zones of neighbouring States.

2. Where the same stock or stocks of associated species occur both within the exclusive economic zone of the Republic and in an area beyond and adjacent to the zone but not within the exclusive economic zone of any other State, the Republic shall seek, either directly or through appropriate subregional or regional organizations, to agree with States whose nationals harvest these species upon the measures necessary for their conservation.

Article 8. Artificial islands, installations and structures in the exclusive economic zone

1. In the exclusive economic zone, the Republic shall have the exclusive right to construct and to authorize and regulate the construction, operation and use of:

(a) Artificial islands;

(b) Installations and structures for the purposes provided for in article 3 of this Act and other economic purposes;

(c) Installations and structures which may interfere with the exercise of the rights of the Republic in the zone.

2. The Republic shall have exclusive jurisdiction over such artificial islands, installations and structures, including jurisdiction with regard to customs, fiscal, health, safety and immigration regulations.

3. For the purpose of ensuring the safety of navigation, due notice must be given of the construction of such artificial islands, installations and structures, and permanent means for giving warning of their presence must be maintained. Any installations and structures which are abandoned or disused must be entirely removed.

4. The Republic may, where necessary, establish reasonable safety zones around such artificial islands, installations and structures in which it may take appropriate measures to ensure the safety both of navigation and of the artificial islands, installations and structures.

5. The breadth of the safety zones shall be determined by the National Executive, taking into account applicable international standards. Such zones shall be designed to ensure that they are reasonably related to the nature and function of the artificial islands, installations and structures and shall not exceed a distance of five hundred (500) metres, measured from each point of their outer edge, except as authorized by generally accepted international standards or as recommended by the appropriate international organizations.

6. All ships must respect these safety zones and shall comply with generally accepted international standards regarding navigation in the vicinity of artificial islands, installations, structures and safety zones. Due notice shall be given of the extent of safety zones.

7. Artificial islands, installations and structures and the safety zones around them may not be established where interference may be caused to the use of recognized sea lanes essential to international navigation.

8. Artificial islands, installations and structures have no territorial sea of their own and their presence does not affect the delimitation of the territorial sea, the exclusive economic zone or the continental shelf.

Article 9. Scientific research

1. Marine scientific research activities in the exclusive economic zone shall be conducted with the prior consent of the Republic.

2. The Republic will not withhold its consent to the conduct of a marine scientific research project unless that project:

(a) Is directly related to the exploration and exploitation of living and non-living natural resources;

(b) Involves drilling, the use of explosives or the introduction of harmful substances into the marine environment;

(c) Involves the construction, operation or use of artificial islands, installations and devices as referred to in article 15 of this Act;

(d) Unjustifiably interferes with activities undertaken by the Republic in accordance with its jurisdiction and as provided in this Act.

71. Vietnam

Statement.
Entered into force: May 12, 1977.
Source: *Foreign Broadcasting Information Service,* May 20, 1977.

ENGLISH TEXT OF SRV STATEMENT ON ECONOMIC ZONE

OW201549Y Hanoi VNA in English 1442 GMT 20 May 77 OW

[Text] Hanoi VNA May 20 — The Government of the Socialist Republic of Vietnam has issued a statement on the territorial sea, the contiguous zone, the exclusive economic zone, and the continental shelf of Vietnam.

The statement which is dated May 12, 1977, and has been approved by the Standing Committee of the SRV National Assembly, reads in full as follows:

The Government of the Socialist Republic of Vietnam,

After approval by the Standing Committee of the National Assembly of the Socialist Republic of Vietnam,

Declares that it has defined the territorial sea, the contiguous zone, the exclusive economic zone and the continental shelf of the Socialist Republic of Vietnam as follows:

1. The territorial sea of the Socialist Republic of Vietnam has a breadth of 12 nautical miles measured from a baseline which links the furthest seaward points of the coast and the outermost points of Vietnamese offshore islands, and which is the low-water line along the coast.

The waters on the landward side of the baseline constitute internal waters of the Socialist Republic of Vietnam.

The Socialist Republic of Vietnam exercises full and complete sovereignty over its territorial sea as well as the superjacent air space and the bed and subsoil of the territorial sea.

2. The contiguous zone on the Socialist Republic of Vietnam is a 12-nautical-mile maritime zone adjacent to and beyond the Vietnamese territorial sea, with which it forms a zone of 24 nautical miles from the baseline used to measure the breadth of the territorial sea.

The Government of the Socialist Republic of Vietnam exercises the necessary control in its contiguous zone in order to see to its security and custom and fiscal interests and to ensure respect for its sanitary, emigration and immigration regulations within the Vietnamese territory or territorial sea.

3. The exclusive economic zone of the Socialist Republic of Vietnam is adjacent to the Vietnamese territorial sea and forms with it a 200-nautical-mile zone from the baseline used to measure the breadth of Vietnam's territorial sea.

The Socialist Republic of Vietnam has sovereign rights for the purpose of exploring, exploiting, conserving and managing all natural resources, whether living or non-living, of the waters, the bed and subsoil of the exclusive economic zone of Vietnam; it has exclusive rights and jurisdiction with regard to the establishment and use of installations and structures, artificial islands; exclusive jurisdiction with regard to other activities for the economic exploration and exploitation of the exclusive economic zone;

exclusive jurisdiction with regard to scientific research in the exclusive economic zone of Vietnam; the Socialist Republic of Vietnam has jurisdiction with regard to the preservation of the marine environment, and activities for pollution control and abatement in the exclusive economic zone of Vietnam.

4. The continental shelf of the Socialist Republic of Vietnam comprises the seabed and subsoil of the submarine areas that extend beyond the Vietnamese territorial sea throughout the natural prolongation of the Vietnamese land territory to the outer edge of the continental margin, or to a distance of 200 nautical miles from the baseline used to measure the breadth of the Vietnamese territorial sea where the outer edge of the continental margin does not extend up to that distance.

The Socialist Republic of Vietnam exercise sovereign rights over the Vietnamese continental shelf in the exploration, exploitation, preservation and management of all natural resources consisting of mineral and other non-living resources, together with living organisms belonging to sedentary species thereon.

5. The islands and archipelagos, forming an integral part of the Vietnamese territory and beyond the Vietnamese territorial sea mentioned in Paragraph 1, have their own territorial sea, contiguous zones, exclusive economic zones and continental shelves, determined in accordance with the provisions of Paragraphs 1, 2, 3 and 4 of this statement.

6. Proceeding from the principles of this statement, specific questions relating to the territorial sea, the contiguous zone, the exclusive economic zone, and the continental shelf of the Socialist Republic of Vietnam will be dealt with in detail in further regulations, in accordance with the principle of defending the sovereignty and interests of the Socialist Republic of Vietnam, and in keeping with international law and practices.

7. The Government of the Socialist Republic of Vietnam will settle with the countries concerned, through negotiations on the basis of mutual respect for independence and sovereignty, in accordance with international law and practices, the matters relating to the maritime zones and the continental shelf of each country.

72. Western Samoa

A. Exclusive Economic Zone Act 1977
Source: *The Government of Western Samoa Printer,* 1980.

B. Diplomatic Note to the United States, October 10, 1980.
Entered into force: December 1, 1980
Source: Western Samoan Ministry of Foreign Affairs.

AN ACT to establish an exclusive economic zone of Western Samoa adjacent to the territorial sea, and in the excercise of the sovereign rights of Western Samoa to make provision for the exploration and exploitation, and conservation and management, of the resources of the zone; and for matters connected with these purposes.

[25 August 1977]

Analysis

BE IT ENACTED by the Legislative Assembly of Western Samoa in Parliament assembled as follows:—

Short title and commencement

1. (1) This Act may be cited as the Exclusive Economic Zone Act 1977.

(2) This Act shall come into force on a date to be appointed by the Head of State, acting on the advice of Cabinet, by Order.

Interpretation

2. In this Act, unless the context otherwise requires,

'Constable' includes any member of the Western Samoa Police:

'Exclusive economic zone' and 'zone' means the exclusive economic zone of Western Samoa described in section 3 of this Act:

'Fish' means every description of fish and shellfish and their young or fry or spawn and includes sedentary species of fish, mammals, and all other forms of marine life:

'Fishing' means

(a) Taking any fish; or

(b) Engaging in any activity relating to the taking of any fish, including (inter alia) any activity involving the preparation, supply, storage, refrigeration, transportation, or processing of any fish:

'Fishing craft' means any vessel, air-craft, hovercraft, or other craft, of whatever size and however propelled, that is capable of being used for fishing:

'Foreign fishing craft' means any fishing craft that is not a Western Samoan fishing craft:

'Highly migratory species' means species that, in the course of their life cycle, migrate over great distances of ocean:

'International agreement' means any bilateral or multilateral treaty, convention, or agreement, to which Western Samoa is a party, and any understanding concluded by the Government of Western Samoa and the government of any other country:

'Licence' means a licence issued under section 5 of this Act in respect of a foreign fishing craft; and 'licensed' has a corresponding meaning:

'Licensee' means the person to whom a licence is issued:

'Master', in relation to a fishing craft, means the person for the time being having command or charge of the craft:

'Median line' as between Western Samoa and any other country, means a line every point of which is equidistant from the nearest points of the baseline of the territorial sea of Western Samoa and the corresponding baseline of that other country:

'Minister' means the Minister for the time being responsible for Fisheries:

'Nautical mile' means the international nautical mile:

'Owner', in relation to a fishing craft, includes any body of persons, whether incorporated or not, by whom the craft is owned, any charterer, sub-charterer, lessee, or sublessee of the craft:

'Prescribed' means prescribed by regulations made under this Act:

'Take' includes

(a) To take, catch, kill, attract, or pursue by any means or device; and

(b) To attempt to do any act specified in paragraph (a) of this definition:

'Western Samoa fishing craft' means a fishing craft

(a) That is registered in Western Samoa under the Shipping Act 1972; or

(b) That is an air-craft registered in Western Samoa under the Civil Aviation Act 1963; or

(c) In which no person who is not a Western Samoa citizen has any legal or equitable interest (except by way of security only for any advance made by him to the owner).

The exclusive economic zone

3. (1) The exclusive economic zone of Western Samoa comprises those areas of the sea, sea bed, and subsoil that are beyond and adjacent to the territorial sea of Western Samoa, having as their outer limits a line measured seaward from the baseline described in sections 5 and 6 of the Territorial Sea Act 1971, every point of which line is distant 200 nautical miles from the nearest point of the baseline.

(2) Notwithstanding subsection (1) of this section, where

(a) Any part of the median line between Western Samoa and any other country is less than 200 nautical miles from the nearest part of the baseline of the territorial sea of Western Samoa; and

(b) No other outer limit of the exclusive economic zone is for the time being determined by Order made under subsection (3) of this section

that part of the median line shall be an outer limit of the zone.

(3) For the purposes of implementing any international agreement, or the arbitral award of any international body, or the judgment of any international Court, or for any other purpose in accordance with international law, the Head of State acting on the advice of Cabinet may from time to time, by Order, declare that the exclusive economic zone shall not extend to any specified area of the sea, sea bed, or subsoil, that would otherwise be included within the exclusive economic zone by virtue of this section.

Prohibition of operation of unlicensed foreign fishing craft in zone

4. No foreign fishing craft shall be used for fishing within the exclusive economic zone except in accordance with a licence issued by the Minister under section 5 of this Act in respect of that fishing craft.

Grant of licences

5. (1) The Minister may grant and issue to the owner of any named foreign fishing craft a licence to fish within the exclusive economic zone.

(2) In granting a licence under this section, the Minister may attach to the licence conditions relating (inter alia) to all or any of the following matters

(a) The areas within the exclusive economic zone in which fishing is authorised:

(b) The seasons, times, and particular voyages during which fishing is authorised:

(c) The species, size, age, and quantities of fish that may be taken:

(d) The methods by which fish may be taken:

(e) The types, size, and amount of fishing gear that may be used or carried by a foreign fishing craft and the modes of storage of that gear when not in use:

(f) The use, transfer, transhipment, landing, and processing of fish taken:

(g) Entry by the foreign fishing craft to Western Samoan ports whether for the inspection of its catch or for other purposes:

(h) The compensation payable to Western Samoa citizens or to the Western Samoa Government in the event of any loss or damage caused by the foreign fishing craft to other fishing craft, or their gear or catch, or to fish stocks, or to other Western Samoan interests:

(i) Statistical and other information required to be given by the foreign fishing craft to the Department of Agriculture, Forests and Fisheries, including statistics relating to catch and effort and reports as to the positions of the craft:

(j) The conduct by the foreign fishing craft of specified programmes of fisheries research:

(k) The training of Western Samoan personnel in the methods of fishing employed by the foreign craft and the transfer to Western Samoa of technology relating to fisheries:

(l) The display on board the foreign fishing craft of the licence issued in respect of it:

(m) The marking of the foreign fishing craft, and other means for its identification:

(n) Directions, instructions, and other requirements given or made by Western Samoa Government ships or air-craft or by any officer authorised under section 13 of this Act to the foreign fishing

craft that shall be complied with by the craft:

(o) The placing of Western Samoan observers on the foreign fishing craft and the reimbursement to the Department of Agriculture, Forests and Fisheries by the licensee of the costs of doing so:

(p) The installation on the foreign fishing craft and maintenance in working order of a transponder or other equipment for the fixing of its positions or its indentification, and of adequate navigational equipment to enable it to fix its positions itself:

(q) The carriage on board the foreign fishing craft of specified nautical charts:

(r) Such other matters as the Minister considers necessary or expedient for the conservation or management of fisheries resources within the zone.

Renewal of licences

6. The Minister may from time to time renew any licence granted under section 5 of this Act.

Variation of licenses

7. (1) The Minister may time to time, where he is satisfied that it is necessary or expedient for the proper regulation of fishing within the exclusive economic zone to do so, vary the terms and conditions of any licence or licences, or class or classes of licence, granted under section 5 of this Act.

(2) Notice of every variation of any licence under this section shall be given as soon as practicable to the licencee.

Licensing fees

8. There shall be payable by every licensee to the Government in respect of the granting of a licence under section 5 of this Act, or the renewal of a licence under section 6 of this Act, such fee as may from time to time be prescribed.

Licensing offences

9. (1) Where any foreign fishing craft that is not licensed under section 5 of this Act is used for fishing in contravention of section 4 of this Act, each of them the owner, the master, and every crew member of the craft commits an offence against this Act.

(2) Where any foreign fishing craft is used for fishing within the exclusive economic zone in contravention of any condition of a licence granted in respect of it under section 5 of this Act, each of them the licensee, the owner, the master, and every crew member if the craft commits an offence against this Act.

(3) Every owner or master of a foreign fishing craft who commits an offence specified in subsection (1) of this section is liable on conviction to a fine not exceeding $100,000.

(4) Every crew member of a foreign fishing craft who commits an offence specified in subsection (1) of this section is liable on conviction to a fine not exceeding $5,000.

(5) Every licensee, owner, or master of a foreign fishing craft who commits an offence specified in subsection (2) of this section is liable in conviction to a fine not exceeding $25,000.

(6) Every crew member of a foreign fishing craft who commits an offence specified in subsection (2) of this section is liable on conviction to a fine not exceeding $1,500.

(7) In this section, 'crew member' does not include a licensee, owner, or master of a foreign fishing craft.

Suspension and cancellation of licences

10. (1) Where the Minister is satisfied that

(a) Any foreign fishing craft in respect of which a licence has been granted under section 5 of this Act is being or has been used for fishing within the exclusive economic zone in contravention of any condition of the licence or of any Western Samoan law that applies to fishing within the zone; or

(b) Any licensee, owner, master, or crew member of a foreign fishing craft has been convicted of an

offence against this Act, or against any regulation made under section 11 of this Act, or against any other Western Samoan law relating to fishing within the zone he may suspend the licence for such period as he shall specify, or cancel the licence.

(2) Where the Minister, after consultation with the Minister of Foreign Affairs, determines that it is necesary or expedient for the proper regulation of fishing within the exclusive economic zone to do so, he may suspend any licence or licences for such period as he shall specify, or cancel any licence or licences.

(3) No determination, variation, suspension, cancellation, or other action of the Minister under subsection (2) of this section shall be reviewable by any Court of law.

(4) While a licence is suspended under this section, it shall have no effect.

Fisheries regulations

11. (1) The head of State, acting on the advice of Cabinet, may from time to time make regulations for all or any of the following purposes:

(a) Prescribing the manner of applying for licences under section 5 of this Act and for the renewal of such licences under section 6 of this Act, and forms of applications;

(b) Prescribing the terms of duration of licences;

(c) Prescribing the forms of licences to be issued by the Minister;

(d) Prescribing the fees payable to the Western Samoan Government for the issue of licences and for their renewal;

(e) Providing for the production of licences by licensees to specified Western Samoan authorities when required to do so, and the inspection of licenses by such authorities;

(f) Providing for such other measures as are necessary or expedient to ensure that foreign fishing craft are used for fishing within the exclusive economic zone only in accordance with the terms and conditions of their licences;

(g) Prescribing conditions, not inconsistent with this Act, under which fishing may be undertaken within the zone by foreign fishing craft;

(h) Prescribing measures not inconsistent with this Act, for the conservation and management of fisheries resources within the zone;

(i) Specifying particular types of highly migratory species of fish, and regulating, in a manner not inconsistant with this Act, fishing for those species within the zone, and also, in the case of Western Samoan fishing craft, beyond the zone;

(j) Providing that a breach of any such regulation shall be a criminal offence, and imposing penalties by way of fine not exceeding, in the case of a licensee, owner, or master of a fishing craft, $10,000 for any such offence and, in the case of any other crew member, $1,000 for any such offence;

(k) Prescribing the form of bonds for the purposes of section 14 of this Act.

(2) Regulations made under this section may make different provisions for different parts of the exclusive economic zone and for different species of fish.

(3) In prescribing fees in regulations made under this section, the Head of State acting on the advice of Cabinet may

(a) Take into account (inter alia) the cost of implementing the provisions of this Act and of the Agriculture, Forests and Fisheries Ordinance 1959 with respect to fishing by foreign fishing craft within the exclusive economic zone, including the cost of the conservation and management of fisheries resources, and of fisheries research, and of the administration and enforcement of such enactments; and

(b) Prescribe different fees for different classes of foreign fishing craft (whether by reference to size, catch, method of fishing, function, or otherwise).

Fishing for research, experimental, and sporting purposes

12. Nothwithstanding section 4 of this Act, a foreign fishing craft may be used for fishing within the exclusive economic zone for the purpose of fisheries research or of experimentation or sport, subject always to the prior consent in writing of the Minister to such activity and in accordance with such conditions (if any) as the Minister may impose in giving his consent.

Apprehension of offenders

13. (1) Where any officer specified in subsection (11) of this section has reasonable cause to believe that an offence against this Act, or against regulations made under section 11 of this Act, or against any other Western Samoa law relating to fishing within the exclusive economic zone, has been committed in respect of any foreign fishing craft, he may

(a) Stop, board, and search the craft; and

(b) Inspect, seize, and detain all fish on board the craft; and

(c) Apprehend any person who he has reason to believe has committed any offence referred to in subsection (1) of this section; and

(d) Where he has reason to believe that any such offence has been committed by the licensee, owner, or master of the craft, seize and detain the craft.

(2) Any officer specified in subsection (11) of this section may exercise the powers conferred on him by subsection (1) of this section with the aid of such assistants as he considers to be necessary for the purpose.

(3) Where any foreign fishing craft is detained under subsection (1) of this section, it shall be held in the custody of the Government of Western Samoa until

(a) A decision is made not to lay any information or charge in respect of the alleged offence for which the craft was detained; or

(b) Where such an information or charge is laid, the security required by section 14 of this Act is given in respect of the craft.

(4) The decision whether or not to lay an information or charge in respect of an alleged offence for which a foreign fishing craft is detained under subsection (1) of this section shall be made as soon as reasonably practicable after the craft is detained.

(5) The release of a foreign fishing craft from detention shall not affect any subsequent forfeiture of the craft in respect of the conviction of any person for an offence.

(6) On the conviction of any licensee, owner, or master of a foreign fishing craft for any offence referred to in subsection (1) of this section, the craft shall be forfeited to the Government and shall be disposed of in such manner as the Minister shall order, in addition to any fine that may be imposed by any Court on the convicted person.

(7) Where any officer specified in subsection (11) of this section detains any fish under subsection (1) of this section, the fish shall be held in the custody of the Government until a decision is made not to lay an information or charge in respect of the alleged offence for which it was detained, or where such an information or charge is laid, until the information or charge is determined.

(8) On the conviction of any person for any offence referred to in subsection (1) of this section in respect of any fish detained under that subsection, the fish shall be forfeited to the Government and shall be disposed of in such manner as the Minister shall order, in addition to any fine that may be imposed by any Court on the convicted person.

(9) Where any officer specified in subsection (11) of this section apprehends any person under subsection (1) of this section, the officer shall cause the person to be taken as soon as reasonably practicable before a Court to be dealt with in accordance with law.

(10) Any person who in any way prevents or hinders any officer specified in subsection (11) of this section, or any assistant of the officer, in exercising the powers conferred by this section commits an

offence against this Act, and is liable on conviction to a fine not exceeding $10,000.

(11) Subsection (1) of this section refers to

(a) Any constable; or

(b) Any person authorised in writing under the hand of the Minister, to enforce the provisions of this Act.

(12) In this section, 'foreign fishing craft' includes all equipment on board the craft.

Security for release of foreign fishing craft

14. (1) Where any foreign fishing craft is detained under section 13 of this Act, and an information or charge is laid against the licensee, owner, or master of the craft in respect of the offence for which the craft has been detained, the licensee, owner, or master of the craft may at any time before the determination of the information or charge apply to the Court by which the information or charge will be determined for the release of the craft on the provision of security in accordance with this section.

(2) On hearing the application, the Court shall order the release of the foreign fishing craft on the execution by any suitable person or persons approved by the Court for the purpose of a bond in favour of the Government, in the prescribed form and conditioned in accordance with subsection (4) of this section, in an amount not less than the aggregate of the value of the craft and the maximum fine to which the defendant will be liable if he is convicted of the offence.

(3) Nothwithstanding subsection (2) of this section, the Court may, where it is satisfied that there are special circumstances to justify it in doing so, order that the bond shall be in a specified amount that is less that the amount required by that subsection.

(4) The condition of the bond shall be that if

(a) The defendant is found not guilty of the information or charge; or

(b) The defendant on being convicted of the information or charge pays in full within 14 days after he is conconvicted the amount of the fine imposed by the Court and the foreign fishing craft is within that time surrendered to the Government for forfeiture—

then the bond shall be of no effect, but that otherwise the bond shall remain in full force and effect.

(5) The amount specified in the bond shall be recoverable in full as a debt due to the Government jointly and severally by the person or persons by whom the bond is given, unless the person or persons prove the due performance of the condition on which the bond is defeasible.

(6) In this section, 'foreign fishing craft' includes all equipment on board the craft.

General regulations in zone

15. (1) Where no other provision is for the time being made by any other enactment for any such purposes, the Head of State, acting on the advice of Cabinet, may from time to time, make regulations not inconsistent with any other enactment for all or any of the following purposes

(a) Regulating the conduct of scientific research within the exclusive economic zone;

(b) Prescribing measures for the protection and preservation of the marine environment of the zone;

(c) Regulating the construction, operation, and use of artifical islands (whether permanent or temporary), and of other installations and structures within the zone, including the establishment of safety zones around such islands, installations, and structures;

(d) Regulating the exploration and exploitation of the zone for the production of energy from the water, currents, and winds, and for any other economic purposes;

(c) Providing for such other matters as are necessary or expedient for giving full effect to the sovereign rights of Western Samoa in relation to the zone;

(f) Providing that a breach of any such regulations shall be a criminal offence, and imposing penalties by way of fine not exceeding $10,000 for any such offence;

(g) Providing for such other matters as are contemplated by or necessary for giving full effect to the

provisions of this Act (other than matters for which regulations may be made under section 11 of this Act) and for its due administration.

(2) Regulations made under this section may declare that the provisions of any enactment (whether made or after the passing of this Act) shall apply, with such modifications and exceptions (if any) as may be specified in the regulations

(a) Within the exclusive economic zone; or

(b) Within any specified part of the zone; or

(c) To acts and omissions within the zone

and the provisions of that enactment (with such modifications and exceptions, (if any) shall apply accordingly as if the zone or the specified part of the zone were within the territorial limits of Western Samoa.

Offences in zone deemed to be committed in the Western Samoa

16. Any offence against this Act that is committed within the exclusive economic zone shall be deemed to have been committed in Western Samoa.

Jurisdiction of Court

17. Notwithstanding any provision in any enactment the Supreme Court shall have exclusive jurisdiction over any case or controversy arising under the provisions of this Act.

Modifications to give effect to international agreement

18. The Head of State, acting on the advice of Cabinet may, from time to time, limit any provision of this Act relating to the exclusive economic zone so far as it is necessary to do so to give full effect to any convention that is adopted by the Third United Nations Conference on the Law of the Sea.

Onus of proof in respect of offences

19. In any criminal proceedings under this Act where a defendant is charged with having contravened section 4 of this Act, or with having contravened any other provision in any regulations made under this Act under which a licence or permit, or the consent of any person is required for the doing of any act, the onus shall be on the defendant to prove that at the time to which the charge relates, he held the requisite licence, permit, or consent.

Amendments and savings

20. (1) The enactments specified in the Schedule to this Act are hereby amended in the manner indicated in that Schedule.

(2) Except as expressly provided by this Act, the provisions of this Act are in addition to and not in substitution of the provisions of every other enactment, and accordingly nothing in this Act shall limit or derogate from the provisions of any other enactment.

SCHEDULE

Enactments Amended

Section 20

Enactments Amended	Amendment
1959. No. 6 — Agriculture, Forests and Fisheries Ordinance 1959	(1) By inserting after section 2, the following section:— '2A. *Application of Ordinance to exclusive economic zone* — Nothing in this Act shall be construed to authorise the making of any regulations in derogation of the provisions of the Exclusive Economic Zone Act 1977, or of any regulations made under that Act, relating to fishing'. (2) By inserting in paragraph (c) of section 4 after the word 'thereof' the words 'or in the exclusive economic zone of Western Samoa (as defined in the Exclusive Economic Zone Act 1977)'
1961, No. 13 — Crimes Ordinance 1961	By adding to the definition of the term 'Western Samoa' (as amended by section 10 of the 'Territorial Sea Act 1971) the words 'and the exclusive economic zone' of Western Samoa (as defined in the Exclusive Zone Act 1977)'
1972, No. 2 — Fisheries Protection Act 1972	(1) By inserting in the definition of 'Western Samoan waters' in section 2, after the word 'fishing' the words 'excluding the waters of the exclusive economic zone of Western Samoa (as defined in the Exclusive Economic Zone Act 1977)' (2) By inserting after section 2, the following section '2A. *Application of Act to exclusive economic zone* — Nothing in this Act shall be construed— *(a)* To permit the Minister to grant exemptions to a foreign fishing vessel for the purpose of fishing within the exclusive economic zone of Western Samoa; or *(b)* To authorise the making of any regulations in derogation of the provisions of the Exclusive Economic Zone Act 1977, or of any regulations made under that Act, relating to fishing; or *(c)* To authorise the boarding, search, taking of possession, detention, or forfeiture under this Act of any foreign fishing vessel, or of any tackle, engines, nets, gear, apparatus, cargo and stores or fish on board the vessel, or the arrest of any crew member of such vessel, in respect of any offence relating to fishing in the exclusive economic zone'.
1972, No. 18 — Shipping Act 1972	(1) By inserting in subsection (3) of section 29 after the words 'Western Samoa' the words 'or into the waters of the exclusive economic zone of Western Samoa as defined in the Exclusive Economic Zone Act 1977)' (2) By inserting in subsection (24) of section 37 after 'Western Samoa' the words 'or in the exclusive economic zone of Western Samoa (as defined in the Exclusive Economic Zone Act 1977)'

B. Diplomatic Note to the United States, October 10, 1980.
Entered into force: December 1, 1980.
Source: Western Samoan Ministry of Foreign Affairs.

The High Commission of Western Samoa presents its compliments to the Embassy of the United States of America and under instructions from its home office, has the honour to advise the Embassy that the Western Samoa exclusive economic zone will be brought into force on 1 December, 1980.

As the Western Samoa exclusive economic zone will meet the 200 mile zone deriving from America Samoa, the Western Samoan government wishes to give prior notice to the government of the United States of the intended implementation of the zone. The Western Samoan government intends that the provisional delimitation boundary between Western Samoa and American Samoa be calculated on the basis of the median line rule. The median line should be taken to mean a line every point of which is equidistant from the nearest points of the baseline from which the breadth of the territorial sea of each state is measured.

The Western Samoa government considers that the provisional delimitation boundary will not prejudice future delimitation negotiations for a permanent boundary between the American Samoa and Western Samoa zones.

The Western Samoa exclusive economic zone will be closed to all foreign fishing vessels, except those vessels which have been licensed to fish within the zone. This requirement will be strictly enforced by the Western Samoan authorities. The penalties for violations of the exclusive economic zone act 1977 are severe and include the forfeiture of any vessel found to not comply with Western Samoa's requirements.

The Western Samoan government proposed to negotiate an agreement with the government of the United States under which the government of the United States recognises Western Samoa's full sovereign rights under customary international law for the exploration and exploitation, and conservation and management of the resources of the exclusive economic zone. In accordance with the consensus achieved at the third United Nations Conference on the Law of the Sea, the government of the United States should also recognise the right of Western Samoa, were there is no regional organisation to do so, to conserve and manage the highly migratory species within the exclusive economic zone.

The government of Western Samoa shall be grateful to receive an indication from the government of the United States as to the acceptability of the above proposal.

73. Yemen (Aden)

The Territorial Sea, the Exclusive Economic Zone, the Continental Shelf, and other Maritime Zones Law of 1977, Act No. 45 of 1977.
Entered into force: January 15, 1978.
Source: *United Nations ST/LEG/SER.B/19,* pp. 21-26.

ACT NO. 45 OF 1977 CONCERNING THE TERRITORIAL SEA, EXCLUSIVE ECONOMIC ZONE, CONTINENTAL SHELF AND OTHER MARINE AREAS

In the name of the people,

The Chairman of the Presidential Council,

Having examined articles 3, 16, 91 and 92 of the Constitution; Act No. 8 of 1970 concerning the territorial waters and continental shelf of the Republic, as amended by Act No. 2 of 1972; Act No. 15 of 1972 concerning mines and quarries; Act No. 25 of 1976 on organizing the Oil and Minerales Authority; Act No. 18 of 1970; and Act No. 28 of 1977;

Pursuant to the representation by the Chairman of the Council of Ministers as approved by the Council;

Following the concurrence of the Presidential Council;

Issues the following Act;

Section I
Title and definitions

Article 1

This act shall be known as 'The Act of 1977 concerning the territorial sea, exclusive economic zone, continental shelf and other marine areas'.

Article 2

For the purpose of the present Act, the following words and terms shall, except where otherwise indicated, have the meanings assigned to them below:

Republic

The People's Democratic Republic of Yemen;

Prime Minister

The Chairman of the Council of Ministers of the People's Democratic Republic of Yemen

Coast

The continental and island coastlines of the People's Democratic Republic of Yemen facing the Gulf of Aden, the Bab El Mandab Strait, the Red Sea, the Arabian Sea and the Indian Ocean in accordance with the maps officially recognized by the Republic;

Island

A naturally formed area of land, surrounded on all sides by water, which is above the water level at high tide;

Internal waters

The waters on the side of base-lines from which the territorial sea is measured extending towards both the continental and the island land territory of the Republic;

Continental shelf

The sea-bed and subsoil thereof extending beyond the territorial sea throughout the natural prolongation of the Republic's land territory to the outer limit of the continental margin, or to a distance of 200 nautical miles from the baselines from which the breadth of the territorial sea is measured where the outer edge of the continental margin does not extend to that distance;

Contiguous zone

An expanse of water beyond the territorial sea of the Republic and adjacent to it as defined in article 11 of the present Act;

Bay

Any indentation or inlet or fjord or creek in the coastline or land protrusion in the sea;

Low tide elevation

A naturally-formed area of land which is surrounded by and above water at low tide but submerged at high tide;

Pollution of the marine environment

The introduction by man, directly or indirectly, of substances or energy into the marine environment resulting in such deleterious effects as harm to living resources, hazards to human health, hindrance to marine activities, including fishing and other legitimate uses of the sea, impairment of quality for use of sea water and reduction of amenities;

Nautical mile

One thousand eight hundred and fifty-two (1,852) metres.

Section II

The territorial sea and contiguous zone

Article 3

The territorial sea, its bed and subsoil thereof as well as the air space above it are subject to the sovereignty of the Republic.

Article 4

The territorial sea extends beyond the internal waters to a distance of 12 nautical miles seaward, measured from the straight baseline or from the low-water line along the coast as marked on large-scale charts officially recognized by the Republic.

Article 5

The baselines from which the territorial sea of the Republic is measured shall be as follows:

- *(a)* Where the coast is wholly open to the sea: lines drawn from the low-water mark along the coast;
- *(b)* In the case of islands situated on atolls or of islands having fringing reefs: lines drawn seaward from the low water line of the reef;
- *(c)* In the case of a bay facing the sea: lines drawn from one end of the land at the entrance of the bay to the other;
- *(d)* In the case of a port or harbour: lines drawn along the seaward side of the outermost harbour installations or roadsteads and lines also drawn between the tips of these installations;

(e) Where there is a low-tide elevation at a distance not exceeding 12 nautical miles from the coast: lines drawn from the low-water line on such elevations;

(f) In localities where the coastline is deeply indented, curved or cut into, or if there is a fringe of islands along the continental coast: straight baselines joining appropriate points.

Article 6

(a) Foreign ships shall enjoy the right of innocent passage through the territorial sea of the Republic. Such passage is innocent so long as it is not prejudicial to the security, integrity and independence of the Republic.

(b) Passage of a foreign ship or submarine or underwater vehicle shall not be deemed innocent if in the territorial sea it engages in any of the following activities:

1. Any threat or use of force against the sovereignty, territorial integrity or independence of the State;
2. Any exercise or practice of any kind;
3. Any act aimed at collecting information to the prejudice of the defence or security of the Republic;
4. The launching, landing or taking on board of any aircraft or military device;
5. The embarkig or disembarking of any currency, person or commodity contrary to the immigration, security, customs, fiscal or sanitary laws and regulations in forec;
6. Any act of wilful and serious pollution prejudicial to human health, living resources or the marine environment;
7. Any act of exploration, exploitation, or drilling for renewable or non-renewable natural resources;
8. Any survey or research activities;
9. Any act aimed at interfering with any systems of communication or any other facilities, installations or equipment;
10. Any activity which is not related to passage or is designed as to hamper international navigation.

Article 7

(a) The entry of foreign warships, including submarines and other underwater vehicles into and their passage through the territorial sea shall be subject to prior authorization from the competent authorities in the Republic;

(b) Submarines and other underwater vehicles are required to navigate on the surface and to show their flag while passing through the territorial sea.

Article 8

Foreign nuclear-powered ships or ships carrying nuclear substances or any other radio-active substances or materials shall give the competent authorities in the Republic prior notification of their entry into and passage through the territorial sea.

Article 9

The competent authorities shall have the right to take all necessary measures in the territorial sea to prevent passage which is not innocent as well as to suspend the admission of all or some foreign ships to specified areas of the territorial sea should the public interest so require, provided that such areas shall be specified in a prior notification.

Article 10

Foreign ships exercising the right of innocent passage in the territorial sea shall comply with the laws and regulations in effect in the Republic, as well as with the rules of international law and, in particular, such laws and regulations relating to transport and navigation.

Article 11

The outer limit of the contiguous zone shall be the line every point of which is at a distance of 24 nautical miles from the nearest point of the baseline referred to in article 4 above.

Article 12

The authorities of the Republic have the right to impose, in the contiguous zone, the control necessary to:

(a) Prevent any infringement of its security, customs, sanitary and fiscal laws and regulations within its territory or territorial sea;

(b) Punish infringement of the above laws and regulations whether committed within its territory or within its territorial sea.

Section III

The exclusive economic zone

Article 13

The Republic shall have an exclusive economic zone breadth of which extends 200 nautical miles from the baseline used to measure the territorial sea referred to in article 4 of this Act.

Article 14

In the exclusive economic zone, including its sea-bed and subsoil and the superjacent water column, the Republic has:

(a) Exclusive sovereign rights for the purpose of conserving, exploring, exploiting and managing its renewable and non-renewable natural resources, including the production of energy from the waters, currents and winds;

(b) Exclusive rights and jurisdiction with regard to the construction, repair, operation and use of artificial islands, installations, facilities and other structures necessary for the exploration and exploitation of the exclusive economic zone of the Republic;

(c) Exclusive jurisdiction over the marine environment with regard to its preservation and protection and to the prevention control and abatement of marine pollution, as well as to the authorization, regulation and control of scientific research;

(d) Other rights recognized in international law.

Article 15

Without prejudice to the rights pertaining to it, the Republic guarantees the freedom of navigation, overflight and laying of submarine cables and pipelines in its exclusive economic zone.

Section IV

The continental shelf

Article 16

The authorities of the Republic may, to the exclusion of others, in the continental shelf:

(a) Explore, exploit, manage and conserve its natural reseurces;

(b) Construct, maintain, operate and use artificial islands, installations, facilities and other structures necessary for the exploration and exploitation of the continental shelf of the Republic;

(c) Regulate, authorize and control scientific resourch;

(d) Preserve and protect the marine environment and control and abate marine pollution.

Section V
Marine boundaries

Article 17

(a) The demarcation of marine boundaries between the Republic and any State with adjacent or opposite coasts shall be effected, with regard to the territorial sea, the contiguous zone, the exclusive economic zone and the continental shelf, by agreement with that State;
(b) Pending agreement on the demarcation of the marine boundaries, the limits of the territorial sea, the contiguous zone, the exclusive economic zone and the continental shelf between the Republic and any State with coasts adjacent or opposite to it, the coast of the Republic shall not be extended to more than the median or equidistance line every point of which is equal in distance from the nearest points on the baselines from which the breadth of the territorial seas of both the Republic and the other State is measured.

Section VI
The island territory

Article 18

Each of the islands of the Republic shall have a territorial sea, contiguous zone, exclusive economic zone and continental shelf of its own, and all provisions of this Act shall be applicable to it.

Section VII
General provisions

Article 19

In exercising its sovereign rights and jurisdiction over the territorial sea, the exclusive economic zone and the continental shelf, the Republic shall have the right to take all necessary measures aimed at ensuring the implementation of its laws and regulations.

Article 20

Any foreign person, natural or juridical, shall be banned from exploring and exploiting the renewable and non-renowable natural resources of the territorial sea, exclusive economic zone and continental shelf of the Republic, from conducting any prospecting, drilling or search operations, undertaking any scientific research or prospecting drilling, construction or maintenance of any kind of artificial islands, stations (marine installations), devices or structures, or from conducting any operational or maintenance work for any purpose, unless he has entered into a special agreement with the Republic for this purpose or obtained a special permit from its competent authorities.

Article 21

Without prejudice to any more severe penalty laid down in any other law, any person violating the provisions of this Act or the rules and regulations issued under it shall be subject to a penalty of not more than three years imprisonment or a fine of not more than 10,000 dinars. However, the court may also order confiscation.

Article 22

Any person causing any pollution detrimental to human health or to the living resources of the marine environment in the internal waters, territorial sea or the exclusive economic zone of the Republic shall be punished with a prison sentence of not more than one year or with a fine of not more than 5,000 dinars.

Should such pollution result in serious harm, the penalty shall be a prison sentence of not more than three years or a fine not exceeding 10,000 dinars.

Article 23

The Prime Minister shall issue the decisions and regulations implementing and interpreting this Act.

Article 24

For the purposes of the present Act, any text which conflicts with its regulations, capacially Act No. 8 of 1970 and Act No. 2 of 1972, shall be rescinded.

Article 25

This Act shall enter into force on 15 January 1978.

Article 26

The Act shall be published in the *Official Gazette.*

Salem Rubayie Ali
Chairman of the Presidential Council

DONE at the Presidential Palace, this eigth day of Muharram 1398 A.H., corresponding to the seventeenth day of December 1977 A.D.

Index

(T1) refers to Table 1, (T2) to Table 2, etc.; A1 refers to Annex 1 (Chapter 1), pp. 13–16; A2 refers to Annex 2 (Chapter 1), pp. 17–23 (as this annex is listed chronologically an extra indication is provided by the year(s) in parentheses).